A BITCH
IS A BITCH
IS A BITCH

A BITCH IS A BITCH IS A BITCH

DORAMAE BROOKSHIRE

Library of Congress Control Number: 2020923866
ISBN: Hardcover   978-1-6641-4445-3
                Softcover   978-1-6641-4443-9
                eBook   978-1-6641-4444-6

Print information available on the last page.

Rev. date: 12/15/2020

To order additional copies of this book, contact:
Xlibris
844-714-8691
www.Xlibris.com
Orders@Xlibris.com
818775

CONTENTS

AUTHOR'S NOTE

THIS BOOK IS a memoir, and is taken from my personal experiences. All names of the people in the book, with a few exceptions of my family members, have been changed to protect their privacy.

In 1999, I was charged with Medicaid Fraud while practicing dentistry in South Georgia. During the entire process, I was given no chance to explain myself to the police, the GBI, the board of dentistry, or investigators of any kind. No questions were ever asked. I was not informed of the Grand Jury proceeding. I had no idea I was charged with anything until two GBI officers and a local deputy came bursting unannounced into our farmhouse one winter's evening. The hunt had begun. This is my story.

There may be times when we are powerless to prevent injustice,
but there must never be a time when we fail to protest.

Elie Wiesel

To oppressed people everywhere, especially the children.

To women who are abused emotionally, physically, verbally, and spiritually.

To those who exist day to day in poverty and hopelessness.

To women who enter male-dominated professions and are made to feel inferior.

To women who suffer the gender wage gap. (Women in America in 2018 earn seventy-four cents for every dollar earned by a male worker for the same job.)

To women who end up in jail for petty crimes and taking the fall for their men and to the children they leave back home who receive substandard health and dental care, while judges' and politicians' children receive top-notch health care.

To the downtrodden, the forgotten, the persecuted, the exploited, the disheartened, the tyrannized, the tormented, and the wronged *everywhere.*

PROLOGUE

I PRACTICED DENTISTRY IN a small town in the South in the 1980s and 1990s. The climate back then was extremely volatile to female dentists. The town was a "good ole boy" locale, and the seven male dentists who already occupied the town were fiercely protective of their already claimed territory. Times have really changed (thank god), but back when I attended dental school in the early 1980s, female dentists were a real rarity, and I went through pretty much a living hell trying to measure up to the male students. My graduating class of fifty included ten females, the largest percentage of females in a graduating class in history up until then. The ten female students were told repeatedly by the dental school professors that we had most likely chosen the wrong profession, that dentistry was a male-dominated profession for a reason, and that we, as females, should have chosen something different. (Were we *sure* we didn't want to be *dental hygienists* instead?) My nine other female colleagues and I were ostracized and singled out as inferior the entire four years of dental school, but that was nothing compared with what I faced from my fellow dentists (all male) in the heart of small-town Dixie.

I began to accept children on Medicaid as patients when I realized that the other dentists in town were refusing to accept Medicaid patients because Medicaid reimburses the dentist pennies on the dollar. According to them, it just wasn't worth their time. But the need for dental services for young patients on Medicaid in the South in the 1980s was horrendous. I could not allow these young victims of dental neglect to sit by and suffer from lack of proper care, so I became "the dentist who takes Medicaid kids." As a result of simple numbers and tremendous need, I also became extremely busy in my practice. This was not to say that I was raking in the dough as several of my fellow dentists were. (Remember, Medicaid pays pennies on the dollar.) But I was filling a niche that truly needed filling, and I felt good that I was helping the young patients with nursing bottle caries get out of pain and also helping their parents become educated on proper dental hygiene. I had been raised at home to truly care about others and to use any talents that I may have to reach out and do just that.

All that the male dentists in town perceived was my constantly full parking lot, and all they heard was much talk around town about how caring the new woman dentist was. The green-eyed monster reared its ugly head, and male politics ensued. Soon the male dentists in town were playing politics with their good buddies on the state dental board, and my practice was being closely scrutinized. Medicaid in the 1980s had very ambiguously written guidelines, and they could be interpreted just about any way the official interpreter wished.

There was an annual dental association meeting at the local country club. Of course, I was not invited, but I found out about it and decided to go anyway. After all, I was a local dentist and a paid member of the dental association, and there was probably information involving the local dental community that I needed to know. When I showed up to the meeting, all hell broke loose. I was shunned like an Amish girl who had come home drunk. The other dentists actually turned their backs on me and ignored me the entire evening.

Finally, I had had enough. I walked up to Dr. Boris Biget and said, "I guess that I am never going to be acknowledged as a capable dentist in this town because I am a woman."

He lifted his quite inebriated head from the table where he was sitting and replied in slurred speech, "Now that's just not true. *A bitch is a bitch is a bitch.*"

THE CAPTURE

T HERE THEY WERE. Four stocky Southern deputies were approaching me, handcuffs in tow. In a group effort, they slapped the cold iron rings around my shaking wrists and led me out of the courtroom, no apologies to the stunned jury or to my horror-struck family. I wondered why it took four male lawmen to escort me out the door. Wouldn't one have done just as nicely?

As soon as we were outside, only one of the four deputies remained as my chaperone to jail. The other three just kind of scattered like sheep fleeing from hungry wolves. The one who remained was a short, little stout guy with a clean face, a closely cut blond crew cut, and a tight, well-starched, and crisply ironed uniform. A revolver hung neatly at his hip. I wondered if this perfectly groomed arm of the law felt that he might find the need to shoot me on the way to jail. But he honestly did mind his manners; he was the perfect Southern gentleman.

This was nothing like my nightmarish experience back in February 1997, when the state bureau of investigation surrounded my home, forcefully handcuffed me against their unmarked car in my own driveway, and threw me in a squad car on my way to the county jail. They did not care that I cracked my head against the hard metal of the car on my way into the back seat. They cared even less that my handcuffs were so tight that they were cutting off my circulation. Looking back, I realized that their sole purpose on that frigid February night was simply to intimidate me into submission.

This guy was different though. As we approached one of the hundreds of squad cars in the enormous parking lot, he attempted to make some small talk. "We'll get there as soon as possible, OK?"

I nodded, unable to speak.

We made it to the car that we apparently were going to use. He stopped and unlocked the driver's door and then the back door on the passenger's side. He motioned for me to follow him to the back door. "Now watch your haid on the way in, ma'am," he said softly in a perfect Southern accent, and he reached down gently to help me in as he protected my head. He loosely fastened my seat belt.

"You OK now, ma'am?" he inquired.

"Yeah, thanks," I mumbled. That would be the last words we would ever speak to each other. He got himself situated in the front seat, fastened his seat belt, and started the car.

As soon as we left the county courthouse parking lot, I noticed that we were driving through that same quaint, yuppie little neighborhood that Bob and I had driven through on our way to the courthouse seven days previously. I gazed out my window, still in a trancelike stupor. Rows and rows of identical little shops in English-Tudor-style passed by. They reminded me of pictures I had seen of old English villages. I began to read the names of the various shops. "Ye Olde Candle Shoppe," I read. "Flowers by Daphne, the Drapery Boutique, Parfumes de Francais, Tiffany's Fine Gold Bijouterie, Madeline's Mocha Manor: Gourmet Coffees and Espresso."

The names of the yuppie ville specialty shops zipped by my dazzled eyes. Saturday afternoon shoppers clutched their precious packages encased in pricey wrappings with silver and gold trimmings. Even their shopping bags looked expensive, sporting fancy decorations of grand magnolias and blooming honeysuckle. The shoppers were bedecked in all the latest fashions, the ladies stepping carefully in their stilettos so as to keep their balance and still appear sophisticated. Their hairstyles were all the trendiest new cuts and were immaculately maintained. Their makeup was expertly painted on their china doll faces with just enough thickness to conceal any signs of aging. Their hair was perfectly coiffed, their teeth were flawlessly white and perfectly straight, and their ivory skin was unwrinkled. Their svelte bodies strutted past one another down the brick sidewalk on the boulevard, noses in the air. An occasional social gathering could be seen when a couple of the shoppers stopped to gossip, but for the most part, the participants were much too involved with themselves to give anyone else a second thought.

The patrol car continued down the streets of the city on its way to the jail. Five minutes after passing through the English Tudor village,

I looked out my back seat window and noticed that we were in quite a different type of neighborhood now. I began to read the names of the storefronts. "Bobby Ray's Butcher Shop" was scrawled in black marker across a rotting piece of wood. It hung in front of a clouded glass door on a dirty, littered sidewalk. "Kim's Laundry" was written in English and also in meticulous tiny Chinese symbols. Billows of thick steam poured out from the broken Laundromat window. "GIRLS! GIRLS! GIRLS!" one worn neon sign declared. "Showgirls from Vegas every night—No cover charge—Rated XXXX—We bare all!"

The store next door had uneven blue letters painted on the storefront window that read, "Blue's Magazines, Books, and Videos—Find everything you need here!" The grimy window had a display of seedy books and magazines revealing women's naked bodies posed in every position imaginable. Big Al's Liquor was a little dark bar leading to a narrow, garbage-filled pitch-black alley. There were run-down local bars and ratty strip joints on every corner.

The Saturday afternoon crowd was very different in this neck of the woods. Young Black men sat apathetically on broken tenement steps. They stared into space as if they had lost all hope of ever amounting to anything. Older men staggered down the filthy, trash-lined streets, their minds taken away years ago from alcoholism. Their nearly empty liquor bottles dangled from their crooked fingers. Several had decided to give up the fight and had passed out in the tiny doorways of the area businesses. Teenage mothers hurried down the cracked sidewalks, toting their unhappy offspring, who appeared to be born yearly. If you looked closely, you could see gatherings of young African American males behind giant dumpsters in the alleys, secretly exchanging rolled paper bills for little square packages.

I had lived in the South for twenty years now, but this type of contrast between geographically close neighborhoods still blew my mind. In the North, where I grew up, the affluent citizens resided on one side of town and the poverty-stricken residents on the opposite side, as many miles apart as physically possible. But in the South, anything could occur. I had seen countless tar paper shacks next to million-dollar plantations; in my hometown, folks in dilapidated shanties resided right next to mansions of great wealth. I thought of how this town was just one of many metropolitan suburbs and knew then that the rules of mixing the well-to-do with the down-and-out applied likewise in large Southern cities.

As I was still gathering my thoughts on the subject, the car began to slow down and turned into an endless parking lot. I looked up and saw the Coward County Jail (CCJ) looming in front of me. I had just been arrested for my current charge of Medicaid fraud and thrown into a holding cell three months earlier here, but the gigantic building seemed somewhat unfamiliar to me. It looked like a ten-story Cyclops, only instead of having one giant eye, it had three thousand tiny winking eyes, and they were all squinting at me, beckoning, *Come inside, Dr. Brookshire. Come into the bowels of hell, and you will never be the same.* Then I realized that the three thousand tiny winking eyes were, in reality, windows, the nature of which I had never seen before. They were closely spaced yet so narrow, such tiny slits of glass, that I wondered how any human being could begin to see out of them. Suddenly, the purpose for their shape and size became apparent to me. They were designed purposely to have these dimensions so none of the prisoners could escape through their cell windows.

About that time, the deputy's car pulled up to a tall gate, and a voice boomed through an intercom. "State your business."

The soft-spoken deputy declared, "I have a prisoner to admit here." The long chain-link fence rolled open, and we pulled into what looked like a basement garage. The car came to a halt, and he climbed out of the door. He walked around the car, opened my door, took me gently by the arm, and helped me out of the back seat. He led me silently across the cement floor, through a heavy door, and then up to a uniformed officer waiting behind an elevated desk. He carefully removed my handcuffs.

"What she bein' booked for?" the cold, unconcerned guard asked.

"Medicaid fraud," the deputy replied.

"OK den," the indifferent guard mumbled, and she glared at me.

Then the short, little deputy was gone, and it was just me and the apathetic prison guard. I gave her a good look. She was tall and thin with a headful of synthetic woven braids and huge dangling earrings. She was slowly writing something on a pink piece of paper and was having a hard time because her inch-long fake fingernails were getting in the way. Every few seconds, she glanced up to give me a piercing look. But when she started to talk, things weren't quite as scary as I had imagined. "Let see . . . one black pair of pants, one black jacket, one white shirt, one pair of . . . what you call them kinda shoe?"

"I guess they're called open-toed high heels," I answered, choking on my own words.

"Well, I just gonna call them black shoes," she announced and wrote that down.

As the guard compiled a list of my clothing, it suddenly struck me that I was wearing almost the exact same outfit that I had worn when I was first arrested in the same jail three months earlier. I wondered how in the world I had let that happen and vowed to get rid of my "bad luck outfit" as soon as I could.

While I was still thinking of clothes and outfits, a second guard appeared. She was very small in frame and sported the same hair and fingernails as the first guard. "Empty your pockets and stand against this wall!" she commanded in a loud voice.

I did as I was told. I glanced over my shoulder. She was having a struggle trying to pull a pair of surgical gloves over her long fingernails. She finally succeeded, although I was pretty sure that she perforated the gloves at the fingertips with her sharp nails.

"Spread-eagle against the wall, I told you!" she screamed.

I instantly assumed the position that I had seen on TV on all the cop shows. Then the ninety-pound ball of fire ran at me from behind and proceeded to frisk me with all the force of an army sergeant, running her sharp fingers up and down my torso, between my legs, and under my breasts. "She clean," she finally announced to no one in particular. With that, she exited the room, leaving me spread eagle against the wall, not knowing what was coming next.

In a few minutes, a third guard arrived, walking lethargically into the frisking room. She had a stocky build, and her uniform was so tight across her belly that there were large gaps between the buttons. "Come with me," she said.

I followed her down a long hallway and into a square room with many different colors of material draped against a tall wall. I looked down. Different lengths of tape were on the floor.

Suddenly, a fourth guard appeared, holding a dark camera. "Let see," she said out loud to herself. "You pretty light, so I think I'll use the black background." And she motioned for me to stand in front of the black portion of the wall.

"Place your feets on the red line," she commanded, and before I could get totally situated, she snapped my picture, blinding me for a second or two.

"Now turn to the left," she said, and the blinding light went off again.

"Turn to the right," she instructed before another bright flash.

"That's all," she said, and she walked away, clutching her camera.

The portly guard with the gaping buttons had watched as I got my mug shots taken, and now she was motioning for me to follow her again. This time, she dropped me off at a tiny room with a single plastic chair and what looked to be assorted medical supplies. A large woman in scrubs sporting surgical gloves appeared in the tiny doorway. "Get on the scale," she said softly.

I obediently stepped on the scales. She slowly moved the set of weights across the top of the scales and adjusted them until the bar balanced. Then she stretched a measuring tape to the top of my head and measured my height. She turned toward her little desk and methodically wrote the numbers down.

"Now sit down," she said, pointing to the single plastic chair.

I sat, wondering what would come next.

"Put your arm on the desk," she mumbled.

I hesitantly obeyed. I found myself wishing that these state employees would be more verbal with me and at least try to explain what was going to happen to me next. My stomach was tied in knots; my mouth was dry as cotton. I looked at the nurse. She was built like a refrigerator with a head. Ripples of fat hung from her arms. Her legs rubbed together when she walked. She had three chins. She breathed heavily as though it was a big chore for her to inflate and deflate her immense chest. I thought of how she evidently did not take her career choice as a nurse very seriously to have allowed herself to have gotten in such awful shape.

While I was still hanging on to that thought, she roughly tied a strip of rubber around my upper arm. Before I had time to gather my thoughts, she jabbed me hard with a long needle and began to draw blood. I felt faint, and the room began to spin. But she wasn't done yet. In the next few seconds, once the needle was pulled out of my arm and a Band-Aid positioned, she came at me with a second needle, aiming for my other arm.

"What is *this* for?" I asked her, thinking that she might stay there all evening, jabbing me in alternate arms if I didn't at least ask.

"TB test," she replied. "Everyone gots to have it." And with that, the second needle was lunged into my other arm.

Next came her attempt at taking a medical history. "You got anything wrong with you?" she asked.

"Like what?" I inquired, quite confused.

"Don't get smart with me! Like asthma, diabetes, heart problems, AIDS, hepatitis, anything like that."

"No," I answered. I thought back to my dental practice and how thorough and professional my staff and I were when it came to taking our patients' health histories. It usually took me quite a while to obtain an extensive health history on each and every patient who walked through my door. My patient health history forms contained one full page of conditions and diseases that I asked them in detail about, one by one. It inquired about extended family health history, hospitalizations, recent illnesses, medications being taken, allergic reactions, and special patient concerns.

I couldn't begin to comprehend how the state could even consider taking such an incomplete and sketchy health history from a person who was going to spend countless hours locked up away from any kind of medical care. What if I was on some sort of necessary, even lifesaving, medication? What if I had some rare but potentially deadly disease that was not included in her short list of five diseases? What if

I was highly allergic to some foods or substances in the jail? I could go on forever with what-ifs. The whole point was that I was in total shock over the state employees' apathetic overall approach to human safety and well-being.

As I was still comparing my dental practice with the state's medical practices, the listless nurse passively took my blood pressure and pulse, stuck a Band-Aid over my TB test, and told the waiting guard, "I done." With that, she disappeared around the corner.

I followed the next guard down another long hall, where she told me to sit in a bright orange plastic chair. Tables and tables of computers sat in front of me. "Now sit right there," she muttered, and she turned the corner and left.

Hmmmm, I thought, *this isn't half bad. At least I'm having to go through so much red tape that maybe I'll never have to go to a cell.* And I began to observe the guards around me out of pure boredom.

The Coward County Booking Department, or whatever it was called, was the largest string of rooms I had ever seen. The guards' desks went on for what seemed to be miles and miles. There had to be at least twenty or thirty guards just in the room I was in, and they were all engaged in their own special activities. A small group of female guards gathered around a large black boom box on one of the desks. Rap music exploded loudly from the box, and the guards danced wildly around the desk, giggling boisterously and bumping their generous behinds together. Seven or eight male guards gathered around a second desk, arguing loudly about last night's game. Two guards were comparing their lottery tickets in the corner. One female guard sitting at a desk near me was shouting into a phone. It wasn't long before I noticed several more guards engaged in personal conversations on the state phones.

My eyes continued to scan the room, not believing what I had seen so far. Most of the guards were sitting lethargically at their desks, faces staring straight ahead. None of them appeared to be working. A couple had given up the fight of boredom and had given in to sleep. Their heads had dropped down to their desktops, drool oozing out of the corners of their mouths.

Three large male guards were occupying their time by quietly harassing what appeared to be an older male inmate. The inmate was a slightly built light-skinned Black man who had begun to gray around the temples. He wore an orange jumpsuit and was permanently stooped over, pushing a large mop. "Jamal, you better push that mop faster, boy," they teased, "'cuz when you done with that, we have something you need to do over here."

The biggest guard spat calmly on the floor in front of the prisoner. "Hey, you missed a spot," he badgered, pointing to the spit. The elderly inmate obediently mopped up the sputum. One of the guards finally tired of tormenting the poor inmate and relocated Jamal and his mop to a safer zone, away from his two heckling buddies.

I began to mentally summarize what I had observed while sitting in the room. *Let's see, dancing to rap music, making personal calls on state phones, comparing lottery tickets, harassing the inmates, and best of all sleeping on the job.* I recalled reading a newspaper article recently about how much the state's prison system was costing the taxpayers. The article stated that thousands of prison guards were needed to keep the jails going. These guards were paid full benefits and adorned with vacation packages, medical coverage, the whole nine yards. I thought of how my own family had not had the luxury of benefits since I had lost my career that I had trained years and years to be able to do. If any of my family became ill, we would just have to suffer or die. Then another thought went through my mind.

Just a couple of hours ago, I had been forced to plead guilty to *one* count of Medicaid fraud. It amounted to admitting I took about $40. I wondered just exactly how many seconds of time it would take to pay all the foolish state employees in this room at the Coward County Jail to eat up that $40.

While I was still wondering about the answer to that question, I noticed two female guards arguing over something. They were standing by a desk close to me. "It's *your* turn! I *know* it is! I fingerprinted the last one!" one of the guards argued.

"Wuh, you *wrong* there," retorted the smaller guard, "'cuz I did that stinky Mexican girl that jist come in!"

"I ain't doin' this one. I need a break," said the first guard.

The second guard took a deep breath and mumbled under her breath, "You is such a baby, girl. I'll do this one then." She began to pull on a pair of surgical gloves and headed toward me. Just then, it struck me. They had been arguing over who was going to fingerprint me. She walked up to one of the computers and motioned for me to come over to where she was. I obeyed.

"Sit down," she said curtly, pointing to the chair in front of the computer.

I wondered what she was going to do. I had never been near computers when they had booked me before.

"Stick yer hands under here," she said lethargically, pointing to a small area under the computer screen.

I hesitantly placed my two hands in the position she had told me to, wondering what might become of them.

"Now hold still," she commanded, and she pressed a series of buttons.

Suddenly, images began to appear on the computer screen in front of me. They were giant pictures of my own fingerprints. The guard played around with the focus contraption, and when she tired of that, she ordered, "Now don't move." Then she pushed something that froze the current image of my fingerprints. After that, she pushed a couple of buttons to make the gigantic fingerprints spew forth from a printer. Copies in hand, she seemed to be satisfied. I wondered why in the world, the other time I had endured the ordeal of fingerprinting, they could not have taken them this easy way, instead of smearing messy black ink all over my fingers and then leaving me to clean it all up.

But the guard didn't seem to be quite done. She made sure my face was positioned squarely in front of the computer screen. Soon I could see an image of my face on the screen right in front of me. It too was larger than life. "Now hold still," she commanded once again, and she pushed a series of buttons like before. Several more papers came out of a different printer, located across the room this time.

"Now stay there!" she barked as if I were a dog she was trying to train.

Quite a while later, she reappeared, holding something in her hand. "Hold out your hand," she said.

I conceded, sticking out my right hand.

"No, not *that* one, the *other* one," she said with disgust.

I offered my left hand, and she snapped something bulky and plastic around my wrist. I glanced down at what this might be. It turned out to be a stiff plastic identification bracelet. It was at least two inches wide and had a miniature mug shot of me, my social security number, my height, my weight, my eye color, my hair color, and the county in which I resided. It had wide blue stripes and a series of letters and numbers that I didn't recognize. *This is kinda like having a very uncomfortable driver's license strapped around my wrist*, I thought.

The irritated guard finished off by roughly snapping a wide metal clip into place around the plastic bracelet. She cut off the excess strip of plastic.

Oh my god, I thought. *Am I going to have to wear this horrible bulky thing the whole time I am here? How am I ever going to wash my left arm without moisture getting up under this contraption and causing a rash? How am I going to keep this huge metal clip from rubbing me raw?*

But I didn't have much time to react to my new plastic addition. The hefty guard was once again motioning me to follow her. I thought how all these guards could use a good lesson in communication skills.

Down another long hall we went, and when she came to one of the holding cells in the same section as the one I had been in last February, she pulled out her keys, opened the door, and told me to go in. I dutifully did as I was told. A loud click of the heavy door, and I was locked in the dark holding cell. The guard turned and listlessly walked back down the hall.

WAITING FOR THE OTHER
SHOE TO DROP

T HE CELL WAS so dark that I had to give my eyes time to adjust. I cautiously took inventory of my new surroundings. I scanned the tiny holding cell. There was a stainless steel toilet with no seat, a stainless steel sink that was so little that I doubted if I could get both my hands under the faucet at once, and two short stainless steel benches.

I noticed that a young Black girl had already claimed one of the benches and was sitting, patiently waiting. She was in street clothes, like me, but had no makeup, no earrings, and no nail polish. Her coarse dark hair was unstyled. Her fingernails were cut short. She had no body piercings and no tattoos. She wore simple, everyday clothing. She smelled and looked very clean compared with my ten-minute cellmate back in February. Her facial expression looked as if she was very used to waiting and had resigned herself to the fact that she would do what she had to do. She had a certain peace about her.

Suddenly, it all hit me like a ton of bricks. The trial, the cold, calculating judge, the prosecution team, the Amazon woman, my precious eighty-year-old mother, my brother's face upon realizing that he could do nothing to save me, my heartbroken husband, and my precious kids—how in the world was I going to explain this to *them*? I collapsed onto the bench, put my face into my hands, and began to sob uncontrollably.

After what seemed to be an eternity of tears, I slumped down onto the bench and attempted to lie down, but the hard, cold bench was much too short to allow me to be in a reclining position. By this time, my emotions had totally taken over, and I knew that if I didn't lie down, I was probably going to pass out; so I curled up into a fetal position, turned my back to my cellmate, and continued to weep into my hands.

"Hey, lady, what's a matter with you?" the girl asked quietly. "Come on now, it can't be *that* bad. Why you jist a-cryin' and a-cryin' over there?"

I totally ignored her. I had made a solemn pact with myself not to speak to any of the devils in this horribly horrendous place, and quite frankly, her compassionate, calm nature had me feeling very uncomfortable after hours of being treated like I had.

She made a second attempt. "Don't cry now, honey. You is makin' me sad. Tell me what's on your mind, and you'll feel better, OK?"

But I just continued to cry silently, my entire face buried deep in my hands.

She evidently resigned herself to the fact that I wasn't going to talk no matter what, so she decided to take a different approach. "OK then, since you ain't talkin', let me tell you about what I is in for. Maybe then your case won't seem so bad to you. About a year ago, I was goin' to a party with three of my friends in the car my daddy had jist gave me. We was ridin' high, jist rappin' along with the radio and smokin' some locoweed, when all of a sudden, I hit a big ole puddle or somethin', and that's the last thing I remember. I think I was goin' too fast. When I woke up in the hospital, they all tells me that my best friend is dead, and the two girls that was in the back seat was hurt real bad. They say that I hit a tree, and my new car was smashed like a tin can. Before I can even believes all this, two policemans come and arrest me in my hospital bed and charge me with drivin' too fast for conditions, DUI with marijuana, and vehicular manslaughter. And that's what *I* is in for."

She waited to see if her story might bring me around, but it had no effect on me, except for the fact that I stopped bawling as loudly. She continued on, probably thinking that, since I hushed crying, maybe she at least had my attention now. "So my best friend, she gone. But my daddy, he goes and gets me the best lawyer around. His name be Johnny Ray Mims, and he wins every case he go after. He's something else. Really, he is! Well, he come to see me in the hospital, and he say we gonna work it so I got to do very little time, and that is jist what he done too! He say that everybody have to do time in county jail before they can go to the boot camp but me. He done something to get me right into that boot camp without no jail time. I wake up one morning and get dressed, and off I go right to that boot camp. *No jail!* And I only has to be there for two months too."

She paused and sized me up again. "So I don't know *what* you done, but I would recommend gettin' this here lawyer 'cuz he can git you off anything. You should see where that man live, in a fancy big ole house that's in the very best neighborhood. He drive a Ferrari too, a bright red one, so you can see him comin'."

She paused. My back was still turned to her, but I could feel her stare right through me. "Turn over here and have a look at this. Come on now, I's got somethin' important to shows you."

I slowly rolled over and stopped crying long enough to see what she wanted to show me out of pure curiosity, if nothing else. She was sitting up on the metal bench directly across from me. She began to lean over and pull up her pant leg. I could see a large leg brace of some sort. She unbuckled the brace, and to my total dismay, she pulled the brace and a large cumbersome athletic shoe off, all in one piece, only the shoe was not empty. It was acting as a holding device for a prosthetic left foot. I gasped and looked down at the place where her left foot was supposed to be, but there was no foot, just an ankle and a rounded stump. My heart skipped a beat.

"See what happened when I hits the tree? I cut my foot clean off, and the doctors, they couldn't fix it 'cuz they couldn't find it quick enough to sew it back on, so here I is, seventeen years old, an' I only gots one foot for the rest of my life. See it? Come on over here and have a good look at it. It won't bite you. It's only a foot in a shoe."

I meandered slowly off my bench and cautiously toward the fake foot. I had never witnessed anything like this before in my entire life.

"You can pick it up. Go on, it's OK."

I never did pick it up, but I could see it closely enough to satisfy my curiosity. The blue and white tennis shoe looked like any athletic shoe I had ever seen, and it matched her right shoe perfectly. The artificial foot had a sock on it to match her right sock. A large shiny metal brace fit up under the sole of the left shoe and was designed to fit on her left knee somehow. I tried really hard to find something to say, but I just could not muster up any words to express my shock and horror and pity.

"So you sees, lady, I's only seventeen years old, and I gots only one foot, and I'm charged with killin' my best friend in the world. So, lady, I don't know what you done, but it can't be no worser than this."

I stopped sniffing and seriously began to think. *Maybe she does have a point. She is only seventeen, and her whole life is already in shambles. At least I had a wonderful childhood. My problems came later in life. I couldn't imagine having to deal with being accused of killing my best friend during my vulnerable teenage years.* Besides, I halfway admired her quiet, compassionate nature, no flashy fake anything. She was all out in the open, just an honest, down to earth, calm-natured human being.

Amazingly, something began to happen to me. I breathed a heavy sigh, and a wave of serenity swept over me. Suddenly, I found myself wanting to talk to this stranger, wanting to share my story with her. But when I opened my mouth to speak, I shocked even myself by the words that came out. "Well, I'm kinda like you, only I'm charged with involuntary manslaughter of a child," I spurted out.

What was happening to me here? I was not even telling her about what I was really in for, Medicaid fraud. I was beginning to share my deepest, darkest, most intimate secret with a perfect stranger—and a jail inmate at that. What was making me bare my soul to this reject of society with just one foot? But it seemed I was unable to stop.

I continued on, "You see, I'm a dentist, or I *was* until they took my license. Four and a half years ago, a little girl died tragically in my dental chair. The state dental board, who was supposed to be there for my help and support, turned their backs on me and seized my dental license without even asking me one single question. The state bureau of investigation moved in, did what they called an investigation, and threatened my office staff with jail if they didn't 'cooperate' and tell the 'truth' about the evil Dr. Brookshire. Then the bureau turned it over to the district attorney, and he immediately charged me with involuntary manslaughter. So here I sit, almost five years later, and my attorney can't get the DA to even answer his phone or return calls, let alone go on with a trial. So that's my story." I leaned back against the dirty cell wall with my hands folded decisively across my chest.

I could not believe what I had just said. I wondered where all this had even come from. I didn't have to tell this outsider anything about me, let alone bare my innermost feelings to her. I should have just answered, "I'm in for Medicaid fraud, and I didn't do it." But then I realized something—something very wonderful. For some unknown reason, all of a sudden, I felt better, much, much better. I tried to analyze the situation, but before I could do it, she began to speak again.

"Hey, where your office be at?" she inquired.

"In a place called Goat Valley, Georgia," I replied.

"Oh, I remembers readin' about *you* in the newspaper, only you is supposed to look like a nasty big monster with red eyes or somethin', not like no *normal* lady."

I smiled. Her dialect tickled me. "Well, here I am," I replied.

"And I ain't no nasty big monster neither," I added, trying to sound a little like her.

"Wuh, ah'll be! I jist met a real-life celebrity." She pointed out. Then she stuck out her hand. "My name's Angelica. What's yours?"

"Doramae," I answered. "Good to meet you, Angelica." And I shook her hand.

Then before I knew it, we were conversing like old friends. She told me about her family and how they had come to visit her every visitation and how they were waiting for her to return home. She told me about her brother and how he was going to pick her up in his new car on the day she was released, how the family of her best friend had forgiven her, and how she had found Jesus. She told me about how she was going to go to school and make something of herself and start over again. At one point in the conversation, she asked me, "Where you goin' after this jail? I means, where they sendin' you off to?" When I answered that I was going to someplace called Nutter Women's Detention Center or something, I thought she was going to have a fit.

"Oh my goodness, child, you goin' right where I's been for a month now. I is only here at this jailhouse for two days 'cuz I gots a court date here. You gonna jist love it there, girl. It be sooooo nice there. It so clean, and the food is so good, and the beds is so soft and big—why, they so big I think they is a double bed or somethin'."

I opened my mouth to reply. I thought she was done, but she was just getting started.

"And the guards there, well, they a little bit mean at first, but they jist bein' that way so's all the girls can learn to control theyselves. And they really do cares about if you get in trouble again 'cuz they don't wants you to or nothin'. And they give you three smoke breaks a day. That be so nice and all. I didn't even smoke before I went in, but now I does. It jist be so very nice to stand outside and puff and puff on that cigarette."

I couldn't help but interject my opinion at this point. "Wait a minute. Let me get this straight. You say you didn't smoke until a month ago when you went to Nutter? Why in the world would you start a bad habit like that under terrible circumstances anyhow?"

"Oh, it ain't gonna hurt nothin'," she said calmly. "Ah'll jist quit when I gets home."

Just when I was taking a deep breath to explain how harmful cigarette smoking was and how difficult it was to quit, I heard a key turn in the door lock. It startled me, and I lost my train of thought. A chunky jail guard was pushing a metal cart. She took something off the cart and handed it to Angelica. Then she handed the same three items to me. As soon as she did, she locked the cell door back and was gone without a word.

I examined the items. It was food of some sort. I opened the plastic wrap and discovered two stale pieces of bread with some kind of awful-looking lunch meat between them. I decided to smell the meat but soon was very sorry that I did. The meat was warm and had started to turn greenish around the edges. It smelled rancid. I loosely wrapped the sandwich back up and laid it on the bench beside me. I told myself that maybe whatever the other two items were, they might be worth eating. But it turned out I was wrong. One of the things was a small carton of some kind of cheap imitation juice; the other item was a generic brand of cookie wrapped in cellophane. I opened the carton of juice and took a whiff. It smelled like Kool-Aid that had been left outside the refrigerator for too long. I reasoned that the cookie had to be all right, but when I squeezed it gently, it was so hard and stale that I decided maybe I wasn't that hungry after all. I laid the cookie and the carton of juice on the bench beside the spoiled sandwich.

Angelica immediately eyed the food. "Ain't ya gonna eat that?" she asked.

"I don't think so," I said. "I'm not too hungry right now."

Her eyes lit up. "Can I have it then?" she asked with excitement.

"Sure," I replied, gently handing over the awful excuse for a dinner.

She gobbled both of the sandwiches greedily and washed them down with the two cartons of cheap juice. Then she tore into both cookies like she was starved to death. "That was sooo good!" she exclaimed, taking her first breath in seconds.

After our interesting dinner, we talked for a while, but soon I found myself beginning to get depressed once again. I curled up and lay back down on the hard metal bench, and my mind began to poison me with terrifying thoughts. *What if all the food here is like that and I get food poisoning and die before anyone can help me? What if the outright filthiness of these cells gives me some awful disease and I suffer for months before any one of these guards finds me? What if the other inmates can sense how scared I am and they stab me with a pen or something sharp? What if my bed is full of fleas and cockroaches? What if I never see the light of day or breathe fresh air again?*

And those were not even the truly painful what-ifs, which were much too agonizing to even think about. No, I could not even bear to go into those what-ifs. But sometimes our minds take us places we don't want to go, and that was what was happening here. Try as I might, I just couldn't stop the flood of the unbearable what-ifs. *What if my husband gets tired of waiting for me and has an affair and falls in love with another woman? What if my children don't love me anymore and become ashamed of me because of what the papers say? What if they begin to deny even knowing me, like Peter did to Jesus? What if my family crumbles apart like that dry, stale cookie and we can't ever fix it? What if all my friends turn their backs on me because they believe that I'm a thief? What if people that I know look at me like I am a criminal and I am ostracized every time I go into Goat Valley to buy groceries? What if I lose my job and we can't pay the bills and we lose our house and we have to live on the street?*

The last one didn't bother me hardly as bad as the family ones did. I believed that I could survive any physical hardship before I could even begin to survive losing everyone whom I loved. Feelings of despair and despondency swept over me. My spirit was agonized; it was in excruciating torment. I was exhausted—physically, mentally, and emotionally. I wondered what time it was. It seemed like midnight.

Just then, Angelica jumped up from the bench and limped over to the cell door. She peeked out the tiny window. "They comin'! They comin'!" she screamed excitedly.

"Who's coming?" I asked softly.

"Wuh, they fixin' to take us upstairs now," she said.

"Upstairs *where*?" I asked nervously.

"You silly girl, upstairs to our cells. You don't wanna sleep on this little hard ole bench in this here holdin' cell all night, does ya? Now let me see what's the numbers on your band," she said, grabbing hold of my left wrist. She read them out loud. "SPN no. X08115/4SE303."

Suddenly, she began to jump up and down, her heavy left foot permanently grounded. "We's in the same pod!" she yelled. "Look!" And she held her band up for my inspection. "We both got 4 SE!"

Just as I was getting ready to ask her what a pod was, the heavy cell door clicked open. The same tall lean guard who had written down a list of my clothing earlier stood in our doorway. "Come on, follow me," she slurred together.

We both followed her to a large warehouse full of orange suits and dirty mattresses. She asked Angelica what size she was. She replied that she was about a three-dot bottom and a four-dot top. The guard plopped an orange top and an orange bottom in her hands.

Then she turned to me and asked me what size I was.

I replied that I was about a size 14 or maybe a 16.

"No, girl, not your skreet size," she said impatiently, "your *jail* size."

I looked at her blankly.

"You're sure a *stupid* one, ain't ya? You be about a six dot." And she threw an orange top and an orange bottom at me. "Now go put it on in there," she said, pointing to a small wooden door. "And be quick about it. I ain't got all night."

I cautiously went into the door, not knowing what to expect. But to my surprise, it was a little fairly clean restroom with a porcelain toilet and sink. I took my time and used the toilet and then the sink, ecstatic to be able to use clean, familiar facilities. I changed into my six-dot jail suit, but it was far too large, hanging on me like a big orange circus tent. Looking into the mirror, I could now see why the suits were called by a certain number of dots. There were six large black dots going down the side of the left pant leg. I couldn't see the dots on the top though. Curiosity struck me. I had to find those dots, so I quickly removed my orange top and began to examine it. It didn't take me long to find them. The six dots on the top traveled across the back, spreading across the shoulder blades like a plague of huge black bugs. I reflected on what an interesting concept the Georgia prison system had put in place. Sizing prison clothes with golf-ball-sized black dots was pretty creative, I speculated.

My daydream over, I reminded myself that the guard had seemed to be in an awful hurry, so I put my six-dot top back on and stole another quick glance in the mirror. Staring back at me was one pathetic creature. She was haggard and worn. Worry lines spread across her forehead. Her color was pasty; dark circles hung from underneath her expressionless eyes. Her lips were pale, her cheeks colorless. The bright orange color of the huge top that hung off her shoulders unmistakably identified her as a prisoner. *This isn't even me*, I thought as I dragged myself out of the bathroom door.

"Where you been, girl?" asked the irritated guard, and she grabbed my street clothes and stuffed them into a brown paper sack.

"I think it's too big," I said softly, pulling on the excess material to stress my point.

"You can change the size the next time you git one. I ain't got time for this," she grumbled.

I looked across the room, and there was Angelica, all dressed in orange, as excited as ever. "Come try on your shower shoes," she said, pointing to the floor.

I looked down, and there were three pairs of dirty plastic shoes in a pile on the floor. I asked Angelica if we got any socks, not wanting to put former prisoners' shoes on my bare feet.

"No, you gots to *buy* them," she replied.

The impatient guard jumped in. "Jist put a pair of shoes on, girl! This ain't no Holiday Inn!"

I quickly tried on all three pairs of shower shoes, but they were all way too large. I looked to see if the guard might try to help by taking a couple of pairs that were closer to my size off the nearby shelves that contained pairs and pairs of dirty shoes. But she was not moving a muscle to help. I grabbed the least offensive pair of shoes and walked over to her barefoot.

"Jesus Christ, put the damn shoes on your feets! You retarded or somethin', girl?"

I slipped the size 10 shoes on carefully, thinking that if I did it gently, maybe they wouldn't touch my feet so much.

She reached up on the shelves and began to pull things down, acting like it was straining her to no end. She started throwing large bulky items on the floor, displaying much disgust while doing so. Two filthy, worn mattresses plopped onto the dingy floor, raising a puff of dust. Likewise, two stained, grimy blankets dropped to the floor. Next came two torn sheets that I think were supposed to be white. All the bedding was worn paper thin and appeared to have not seen a washing machine in ages. The last items she retrieved were two discolored towels and two raggedy old washcloths. The storage room smelled of mildew and sweat. I knew deep in my gut that I was not going to be able to sleep on one of those mattresses or dry my face with one of those towels.

"Don't jist stand there and look at that stuff!" the guard screamed. "Pick it up!"

Angelica went into action. She rapidly scouted out the cleanest and least worn of all the items and grabbed them up. I dejectedly took the leftovers. I made a mental note to always act quickly from now on in this place. The angry guard shoved a small plastic bag into each of our left hands and then started to walk down the hall.

"Come on, follow her," Angelica told me.

I was halfway glad to have Angelica there to tell me what to do, seeing that the guards never explained anything. We went down a long hall, dragging our bulky mattresses, bedding, and towels. The only way to carry them seemed to be to sling them over our shoulders and let them drag behind us. The mattresses were limp and bulky; they had no body to them whatsoever. Dirty cotton stuffing was erupting from holes in their surface material, and we were leaving little clumps of rotten bedding behind us down the hall. I don't know why, but the story of Hansel and Gretel came to mind probably because I wanted so desperately to be able to trace my way back out of this hellhole someday soon.

After what seemed to be the longest hall I had ever gone down, we came on a big silver elevator. The guard stopped and pushed the up button. *Good*, I thought, *we aren't going to have to climb stairs with these things.* Soon the elevator dinged, and the doors flew open.

"Get on!" the guard ordered.

We obeyed, dragging our bedding along inside. I stood still, facing the elevator door, waiting for it to close.

"Turn and face the back wall!" the tired guard hollered.

Angelica and I turned around and faced the back of the elevator. I felt like a naughty child who had been placed in the corner for punishment. We rode up what seemed to be several floors, and I remembered how many stories this place appeared to have from the parking lot. I would later learn that the Coward County Jail had three thousand inmates, give or take a few.

When we got off the elevator, we began to follow the guard around a curved hallway. The lights were dim, but I could see definite signs of life, even at that late hour. It seemed like several different rooms full of girls in orange were arranged in an almost circular pattern around a tall tower with tinted black glass. After my eyes adjusted to the darkness in the hallway, I could begin to see forms inside the tall black tower. Then I realized that the lurking observation tower was full of uniformed guards who were staring at all the girls as if they were observing wild animals in glass cages.

We finally stopped at one of the huge metal doors, and the guard turned toward the other guards high up in the tower and pointed to the door. I noticed that the girls in orange who were in the glass cage behind the door were ceasing whatever they were doing and coming to the window to stare at Angelica and me. A resounding click made me jump as the massive metal door unlocked. They must be able to control that lock from the guard tower, I deduced.

The guard opened the door, and Angelica and I stepped into the huge glass cage full of girls in orange. I stretched and looked back over my lumpy mattress to see if the guard was coming into the glass room to tell us where to go, but she had disappeared down the hall. We were on our own. Big beads of sweat broke out on my forehead. I started to breathe heavily. A group of fifteen or twenty rough-looking inmates were surrounding us, sizing us up with their piercing, penetrating stares.

Angelica glanced at the number on my wristband once again and pointed me toward cell 303. I broke loose from the circle of inmates and started across the large room to my cell. I saw one of the inmates in the corner of the big room, standing off by herself. I saw her eyeball me. She didn't have the same deep, expressionless stare as the rest of them. I thought I might have even caught a glimmer of hope and maybe a little dose of mischievousness. Her curious dark eyes followed me all the way into my assigned cell.

WELCOME TO THE JUNGLE

CELL NUMBER 303 was a daunting damp dark cave that frightened me to the depths of my soul. Once inside, the first thing I noticed was an emaciated, frail, sickly human being. She was curled into a fetal position on the lower bunk, moaning silently. She appeared to have a fever and seemed to be having delusions along with it. Upon closer observation, I noticed she was pretty in her own way. She was thin and fragile with pecan-colored skin, straightened, coarse black hair, and vacant pea-green eyes.

I attempted to talk to her but to no avail. "Are you hurting? Can I help you with anything?" I asked.

She didn't acknowledge my presence but just kept moaning and holding her stomach, doubled over in apparent, excruciating pain.

Just then, two other inmates appeared in our doorway. "Serena, honey," the bigger one said, "pleeeease try to eat jist one little cracker for me, OK, sugar? We's all worried for you and your little baby inside. You ain't ate a bite for days. Do it for your little baby, OK?"

But Serena, if that was her name, was not about to eat anything at that moment. She behaved as if she were all alone in her own little world of hunger and pain and hopelessness.

The tall lanky one took her turn pleading with Serena. She decided to go the route of attempting to be humorous. "Now you know that it ain't doin' that little, bitty baby in your belly no good to go without no chitlins and corn bread, girl. Now you better open that big ugly mouth of yours and eat this before I have to stuff this here cracker down your throat myself, and you know I will 'cuz I is the queen of slam and dunk. I'll slam you ass on the floor and then dunk this here cracker down your throat."

Everyone else standing there found the inmate's last comment pretty funny as revealed by their faces. But Serena was having no part of it.

In fact, I was rather impressed with her ability to block out everything and everyone around her.

Suddenly, the compassion of the two cellmates hit a roadblock. It was as if they had a definite limit on the extent of their humanitarian acts. "All right then, Miss Stubborn Asshole, have it your way! We was jist tryin' to help you, but I guess you is jist too high and mighty for the like of us, ole common peoples. Jist go right ahead and get sick and make that poor little baby sick too. When you get sick all over them nice clean white sheets you layin' on, see if we help you then!"

She paused, probably waiting for any kind of reaction from Serena. None came. "We had to *buy* these soda crackers anyhow, you dumbass," she added, and they both huffed out.

I couldn't remember too many details of that first night in that frightening cell, but the feelings deep inside would never leave me if I lived to be one hundred. I climbed up into the cold, rusty, hard top bunk. I fought back tears as I climbed. I bit through my bottom lip and dug holes into my trembling palm to keep from showing any emotion to these creatures of the night. And then as soon as I was sure that no one could see or hear me, I collapsed onto the worn, thin, cracked mattress full of mildew. I pulled the threadbare, filthy old cover over my trembling head. I positioned my frightened, shocked body into a tight sideways curl and allowed all the feelings to burst forth—loneliness, fright, shame, hopelessness, disbelief, months and months of grief, and worry.

And finally, the tears came. I couldn't stop them; they just flowed and flowed—tears for my children; tears for my loving husband; tears for my heroic mother and my brother, who tried so hard to save me, and my attorney, who seemed genuinely shocked and truly sorry; tears for my career that I loved and my way of life that would never be the same; tears for the girls who were stuck in this hellhole and for Serena's baby; tears for what this whole thing would do to my family and for the fucked-up condition that the whole world had put itself in. I never realized how many tears one human being had inside them.

I didn't know exactly what time it was that day when I finally decided to crawl out from underneath my protective cover, but it was already definitely light outside, the sun rays dancing across my bed and creating an unusual elongated wispy pattern. I had never seen a pattern anything like it. As I tried to figure out why the sun rays were shaped like an unforgiving long whip, I suddenly noticed that the one tiny window in our cell was positioned above my upper bunk and couldn't have been more than four inches high and two feet in width. *What a stupid-looking window*, I thought. *Why did they even bother to put one in here if that is all the bigger it is going to be? Oh, how stupid of me! I get it. This is all a part of their plan to subtly drive us all insane. They're trying to give us the message that we are all such scum, such pieces of pure garbage, that we don't deserve any better. We don't deserve to be a part of the world. But here, you scumbags! Eat your hearts out! We'll give you just enough of the world through this tiny, little slit, this puny smeared piece of glass, that you just might lose your ever-loving minds simply trying to squint hard enough to see if there is still a world out there at all!*

I decided at that very moment that I might never look out of that dirty, splotched, narrow fissure again. *Why, this worthless piece of filthy glass is of no use to me at all*, I thought. I couldn't have been more wrong.

I snuck one last peek out the tiny window slit, thinking it might be my last. I noticed three people walking outside slowly toward the jail. They were all walking abreast, almost as if this was some type of planned demonstration march. The two fortyish men on the outside were wearing expressions of disbelief but seemed to be reacting to the emotion in very different manners. The worldly taller man was strolling with an air of confidence, although there was a definite sadness to his stroll. The shorter stockier man appeared to be in shock, trudging along out of pure necessity. In between the two men walked an elderly lady, not more than five foot three tall. She seemed to be in good shape for her age and did a pretty good job of keeping up with the two men. Her walk was one of determination, springing forth from years and years of hardship and personal experiences, of heartbreak and jubilation. The tall balding man seemed to be talking to the older woman, and his talk seemed to center on convincing her of something—something of great importance. His hand gestures were constant, his overall manner assertive. The lady was attentive to his argument, obediently nodding her small round head in agreement every so often.

What a strange, unlikely trio, I thought, still peering out of the tiny window crack, two guys in their forties hanging out with a sweet little senior citizen lady on the bad side of town early on a Sunday morning—and walking toward a *jail* at that.

As the three interesting characters got closer to my window slit, I began to notice more detail. They all appeared to be clad quite well—the tall guy in a starched plaid shirt and well-ironed khaki pants and the lady in a cheerful, conservative yet neat and clean flowered dress. The quiet man who was in shock seemed as if he had made a definite attempt to dress well that morning but had not quite made it. His long-sleeved gray shirt was slightly wrinkled, and one corner of it had come untucked from his crumpled stone-colored trousers. His wore loosely tied, well-worn tennis shoes with stains around the soles. Then for the first time, I noticed that when he walked, he almost sauntered, leaning so far to the left and right with alternating steps that sometimes I thought he might topple over. His lower legs were slightly bowed; his toes were turned in toward each other, which—when combined with his melancholy body language—made quite an unusual sight. Yet something deep inside me told me that this character was quite familiar to me—the walk, the clothes, the staunch body. *I know this guy*, I thought. *And I think I might know his two companions too.*

I blinked my aching eyes repeatedly to try to get a better look. Then I remembered that in my shock and frightened grief the previous night, I had forgotten to remove my contacts. This neglect on my part had left my eyes dry, aching, and scratchy. My vision was blurred and foggy as a result. I tried, but I could only see fuzzy outlines of the three people.

As they got closer to my tiny glass aperture, though, something struck a chord in me. I suddenly knew beyond a shadow of a doubt just *who* these folks were, and my sudden realization brought tears to my throbbing eyes. This improbable trio consisted of my concerned brother, my blessed mother, and my devoted husband, and they were walking toward the jail to visit *me*—sinful, undeserving, less than human *me*.

My heart started to pound in my chest; I became short of breath, and my head spun in dizzy rapture. *I'm not alone in this shame,* I thought. *My family is here for me. They have come to see me, to check on me, to see if I'm still alive.*

I wanted to jump down from my nasty bunk and shout out to the world, *I've got visitors! People who care about me! And they're coming to see me on my very first day in the throngs of hell! Hallelujah! Maybe I'm saved—saved from doing myself in, saved from living in purgatory surrounded by a roomful of Satans, saved from the bottomless pit, from the world of the damned!*

But try as I might, all I could do at that point was to climb slowly and carefully down from my hard metal bunk and try to get the attention of the sickly girl asleep on the bottom bunk. "Hey, you," I began, "wake up. My family is coming to visit me. I've been watching them from the window. They should be inside the jail by now. What is the procedure for visitors? *Please* tell me. Is there something I have to do to be able to see them?"

The skinny pale girl continued to sleep, not moving a muscle.

I decided to risk shaking her. She might awaken and stab me with a makeshift knife or strangle me with newly found strength, but the gamble was worth it, I concluded. I reached over and gave her bony, fragile shoulders a firm shake. "Wake up. I gotta know how they handle visitors around here," I said frantically.

She uncurled from the fetal position, stretched, and let out the eeriest groan I had ever heard. It made my blood curdle and the tiny hairs on the back of my neck stand up in pure fright. I instinctively took a step backward. And then something happened that would be ingrained in my memory forever.

The emaciated, hollow-cheeked, pasty-skinned girl opened her pea-green eyes and looked at me. Her fearsome glare cut right through me. Her catlike eyes became tiny slits. Her broad nose flared. Her thin colorless lips pursed with spite. Her sharp, piercing, penetrating look was that of pure hatred. "Figure it out yourself, White girl!" She spat out at me. And with that, she turned her bony back on me and drifted back to sleep.

At that one moment, I didn't think I was dealing with anything human. *I'm standing face-to-face with Satan himself,* I thought, and my heart stopped dead in its tracks. My entire body shuddered, and I didn't know what to do next. I wanted to escape from the creature of darkness, the she-devil of doom, but I knew that the two of us were locked in that stuffy, dingy, grimy pen possibly forever. So I did the only thing I knew to do.

I took a seat on the cold, hard, dirty floor, square in the corner. I shivered uncontrollably as my shaking arms pulled my knees against my thumping chest. Then I began to rock back and forth, staring straight ahead. *I'll never survive this,* I told myself.

About that time, I heard a muffled voice mumbling through what appeared to be some kind of speaker inside the big glass room. "Dorahmay Bahrooshy, you got visitor," the voice said.

What in the world was that? I wondered.

Maybe I already flipped out, and I'm hearing things, I thought.

The strange voice in the speaker mumbled again, this time louder but no more understandable. "*Doerahmay Bahrooshy, I said* you got visitor! Git out here—now!"

A second later, I heard an unfamiliar noise that in the coming weeks would become all too familiar to me. It was a loud, echoing click, a short, sharp sound like that of a heavy key turning in a giant lock. It caused a resounding boom, and the mystery noise seemed to be coming from the massive door to our cell.

Oh my god! I thought to myself. *Someone has just opened our cell door, and I think I am supposed to go out.* I cautiously rose to my feet, unlocking my human cannonball position on the floor. I moved mechanically toward the door, shuffling my heavy feet. I wondered if the deadweight door would even budge when I touched it. To my surprise, the cell door not only budged but it also quite easily swung open when I nudged it slightly.

I took a step forward and found myself in that same emotionless, frigid huge room through which I came in the previous night. I stood there motionless, unable to move my feet, my heart pounding, not knowing what to do next. The air around me was like ice. I was finding it hard to breathe.

Once out into the room with the high ceilings and the gritty tile floors, I could hear the voice much better. "Come on, girl! What the matter with you? I done told you that you got visitor. Don't you wanna go see them or *what*? I ain't got time for this shit, girl!" Her slurred, muttering voice sounded quite irritated through the booming speakers surrounding the humongous room.

Suddenly, it struck me. I knew what the voice on the speaker was talking about. I was supposed to somehow get to my visitors, but I didn't know how. Where was I to go? How was I to get there? No one was helping me here. What could I possibly do? I opened my mouth and an unfamiliar, frightened tiny voice came out. "Ma'am, what do I do?" I asked, trembling uncontrollably.

The foreign voice shot back at me, louder and much more irritated than before. "You dumb shit, you goes your ass back to your cell, and you git your damn shower shoes on and then bring your dumb ass back out here, and you come through this here door an' go your stupid ass to see your visitor. And that's what you does!"

My mind was reeling. I couldn't believe what the unseen guard had just said to me. I did, however, get this much out of the voice over the loudspeaker. Number one, I'd better go as fast as I could back to the cell and get my shower shoes on. Number two, if I had any hope whatsoever of seeing my three visitors, I'd better move *quickly* toward the door to the hall. A subtler number three hung in the air—I better never, and I mean *never*, ask these guards another question unless it was a matter of life and death.

I nearly tripped over my own feet running back to the cell to get my shower shoes on. I made a quick mental note that these oversize plastic shoes must have a very large importance around this place and that I should try my very best to keep them on my feet at all times. Before I knew it, there I was, standing at the intimidating door to the outside world of the hall—the hall that only last night had brought me into this hellish nightmare. And then there it was again—that click, that reverberating boom of a giant lock being opened, only this time it was the door to the hall that was being unlocked for me.

I ventured carefully out of the door and into the world of the hall. I glanced toward the tall tinted glass of the intimidating guard station that loomed over me, like an enormous black panther ready to pounce on me and consume me in one unforgiving large bite. I slowly turned toward the three-story-tall structure and ashamedly held out my hands, palms up, in a gesture of "what do I do next?"

I could barely see the guards through the darkness of the tinted glass. One guard, a lady who looked extremely bored and irritated, pointed toward a set of winding steps with a bright red guardrail. I looked back at her, not quite understanding. This time, she stared at me as if I needed to be horsewhipped, and she wagged her long sharp finger at me. Then she pointed once again to the steps. I wasn't sure if I was doing it right, but I began to climb the winding steps hesitantly.

At the top of the steps was another door, which I heard click loudly upon my arrival. I opened the door and went in. I found myself standing on a narrow landing. Along my side stood a row of several windows with round hard metal stools in front of them. Each window appeared to have a black phone on either side.

I slowly started to walk down the narrow passageway when I suddenly noticed three people sitting closely together at one of the windows near the end. It took a moment for it to register. These three people were my husband, Bob; my brother Dave; and my sweet mama. Their concerned faces couldn't have been more welcome in my world at that time if they had been three angels sent straight from heaven. I was so utterly overjoyed to see something familiar that I wanted to jump out of my skin. My husband was holding the black phone. He motioned for me to pick up the phone on my side of the window. I was moving in slow motion, mechanically obeying his request. I wanted to tell him how wonderful it was to see him. I wanted to tell him not to worry, that I was all right, that we would make it through this just fine. But when I picked up that phone and looked into his sad, worried eyes, a dam broke loose deep inside me. I placed my shaking hands over my eyes, threw down the phone, and began to weep uncontrollably.

Bob sat opposite from me—the thick, bulletproof glass wall between us—for several minutes. I couldn't really see what he was doing because my entire face was buried deeply in my hands. I had lost every bit of the control of my emotions; my spirit was crushed, my heart broken beyond repair.

Suddenly, I heard a strange sound. It made me stop sobbing for a second to check it out. It was like the strange, rhythmic sound of hail beating on the windows during a sudden summer storm. I peeked out from between my fingers, and I could see my brother tapping persistently on the glass that separated us. As soon as he saw me look, he began pointing to the phone that I had thrown down and then holding his phone to his ear. He repeated this gesture several times. It was quite obvious what he wanted me to do. His uncharacteristically patient eyes said, *Please pick up the phone.* I couldn't bear to disappoint my brother, who had done so very much for me during the trial; and besides, I knew him well enough to know that his stubbornness would outlast mine any day of the week. He would persevere and beat on that window until the cows came home. I looked at him with stinging red eyes.

"Tough night, huh?" he asked with more compassion in his voice than I had ever heard.

"Uh-huh," I replied, unable to say much more.

"Well, did you eat fifty hard-boiled eggs on a bet like Paul Newman in *Cool Hand Luke*?" He had decided to try humor, not knowing what else to do. "No, I know. You're hiding a parrot under your bunk, and during downtimes, you train it to peck escape holes through the wall, right? You're the Bird Woman of Coward County!"

I had no reaction to his double attempt at trying to make me laugh. I sat there on that cold, hard stool, totally stoic, not even cracking a smile.

He quickly realized that the humorous route was not the one to take at the moment, and he switched plans. The total lack of expression and the distant, vacant stare must have scared him, and he decided to try the army sergeant approach. "Now look at me, Doramae, and listen closely. Any human being who can make it through four years of dental

DORAMAE BROOKSHIRE

school and the pure torture that they call the dental boards can make it through a couple of months of this standing on their head."

Seeing that he was so upset now, I made up my mind to respond. "I know. I can do this," I said.

Happy to have gotten a response from me, he continued, "That trial was something else, huh? Did you see that fool, Dr. DeVout? I would never have believed anyone if they had tried to tell me that he did some of the things he did in a courtroom. You just had to be there and witness it firsthand. Remember when he got down on his knees, groping around the floor for one specific X-ray in a pile of spilled X-rays up to his ankles? The whole time he was yelling, 'It's here somewhere! I know I can find it!' What a buffoon!"

Dave continued on, relaying stories from the trial until he almost had me smiling. But before long, he said, "Doramae, I'm gonna let Bob talk to you. Our time will be up soon, and both Bob and Mom want a turn."

He began to put the phone down, and I surprised even myself by going into a sudden panic.

"Dave!" I screamed. "Don't go yet! I need to ask you something! I just wanted to say, please write me every day while I'm in this awful place, *please*! I really need you to do this!" I was in a frantic state of near panic. Some sixth sense was telling me that he was the rock of the family, the logical, strong, sensible one who kept things on an even keel in times of trouble.

"You know I will. I promise," he said with concern and sympathy. Then he handed the phone to Bob.

Bob had been pacing back and forth nervously behind Dave and Mom ever since I had broken down and burst into tears. He was acting like this whole ordeal was so painful that he was not going to be able to take it. Now that it was his turn to talk to me, though, he was determined to be as optimistic as humanly possible. "Hi, cutie. Love the outfit," he teased. "You look good in orange."

I looked down at the immense orange top and pants. The top was falling off my shoulders; the bottoms were sagging around my ankles and dragging the ground around my fashionable size 10 shower shoes.

I looked like some kind of circus freak. My worried face broke into a wide grin. I didn't know how, but my husband of nearly thirty years had always possessed the ability to make me happy in times of trouble.

"Are you doing all right in there? Nobody's hurting you, are they?" He had suddenly switched from Mr. Optimistic to worried husband.

"I'm fine. Everything's OK," I lied. I didn't want him to worry any more than he was going to anyway.

Once satisfied that I was under no physical danger or terrible emotional duress, he switched back to his old self and became positive once again. "Honey, I've already checked it out. I can come see you three times a week for ninety minutes each time. I'm gonna come every single minute I can. I promise. I'm not leaving Atlanta. I'm gonna go today and find a cheap motel or some place to stay that's real close to the jail so I can be close by. Don't worry, I won't leave you."

"No, Bob," I said. "Please go home so you can be near the kids. They need you right now. They're probably hurting and confused. Even though they're pretty well grown, they need one of their parents now."

He decided to make light of that situation. "Now don't worry about the kids. They are doing pretty well with this. I've talked to all three of them, and they seem to be doing fine. They understand what happened with the judge and all. I promise I'll stay in close contact with them."

I could see that he was bound and determined to stay close by me while I was in jail, and I had learned over the years that there was no use in trying to change his mind over such matters. I weakly nodded in agreement, and once he was satisfied that I had accepted the fact that he was not going home, he changed the subject once more.

"I'm gonna spend all my time looking into places we can move to. I think Alaska sounds good, don't you? Or maybe we should go back to Indiana. What about Washington State? We really liked it there when we went a couple of years ago, remember?" Then he added, "We just gotta get out of this shithole of a state. It's gotta be one of the most corrupt states there is. The amount of raw power and corruption in this good-ole-boy place is absolutely unbelievable. I wouldn't have believed it if I hadn't witnessed it with my own eyes. And the judges, who are supposed to be the most moral of all, are by far the most corrupt."

I looked into his face. It was turning bright red with anger. On top of that, I could detect a great deal of fear in his eyes. I made up my mind to change the subject and quickly. "There's this one girl whom I met that just came from Nutter, and she really liked it. She said it was much better than this."

This subject seemed to please him. "First chance I get, I'm gonna go check that place out so I can tell you all about it," he said.

Our fears, hurts, and anger having been addressed, we began to talk like two old friends. We laughed about Dr. DeVout, the dentist turned clown. We dreamed of exotic faraway places to live. We reminisced about funny things our three kids had done and said over the years. We talked about great adventures we had had, silly jobs we had worked, colorful characters we had met. Before long, the guard in the tower was signaling that our time was almost up, so I had to tell my best friend goodbye to give Mom a turn.

Mom picked up the phone with all the dignity of a queen and humbleness of a saint. "I am *so* proud of you, honey," she began. "You now join the company of some of the greatest people on the earth. Paul in the Bible, Gandhi, Nelson Mandela, Martin Luther King—they all served time in jail for standing up for their beliefs. And you have done the same thing. Because you wouldn't give up and plead like they wanted you to, because you stood your ground for your principles, because you weren't willing to tell a lie and say you did something that you did not, *this* is why you are serving time, but this is also what makes you unique—a true warrior for all the right things. You remind me of your daddy."

I was flabbergasted. I couldn't believe what I had just heard. Had I just been compared to Paul? Gandhi? Mandela? King? I most certainly didn't feel worthy to be compared to any of these great names. Then I began to think. Could it be? Could it be possible that instead of the miserable failure and the idiotic screwup that I felt like, I was instead some sort of courageous hero? Was I really like my daddy, the most precious man I had ever known, who had suffered a tragic death of drowning while vacationing in Florida with the family? The unforgiving gulf riptides had stolen his life away from us all at the tender age of forty-eight. I had been a vulnerable teen when Daddy had been taken away by the tide. It was a tragedy that I had never gotten over and probably never would. Mom's suggestion that I was a courageous warrior instead of a fuckup and her ability to see a ray of sunshine when everyone else saw clouds brought tears to my eyes once again. Memories of my beloved daddy rushed in, and great, big crocodile tears welled up in my aching eyes and began to roll down my cheeks and land in a pool on my enormous orange top.

"That's OK, sweetheart, go right ahead and cry. It's good for you. Don't worry, it's all very natural for you to do this. It'll get some of those emotions out onto the surface. Then you'll feel better." She must have been able to detect my embarrassment at my total inability to control my flood of tears because then she said, "Don't feel embarrassed. Go right ahead and cry. I'll wait."

And I did just that. I sat there and cried and cried until I felt like I had felt the night before, like I had been drained of all the liquids in my body. When I was done crying, Mom and I chitchatted about some things that were of no great importance. She reassured me that she and Dave were spending one more night in Atlanta, and they would be back to see me the next day before they left to go back to Indiana. She told me once more how much she loved me and how very proud she was of me.

Just then, the black phones cut off abruptly, and we were unable to say another word. I waved goodbye to all three of my angelic visitors, my saviors of the morning, and I threw them all kisses for good measure. Then they disappeared through a large metal door, and I was once again all alone.

I sat there on that hard metal stool, letting the whole visit sink in for a moment. Truth be known, the real reason why I remained for a while on that stool was so that I didn't have to return to the absolutely insane world of the giant glass cage with the little cages around its perimeter. I didn't get to daydream for long though. Soon the intimidating voice of the guard in the tall black tower filled the visitation room. "Girl! What be the matter with you? You gonna jist sit there all day? Get your sorry ass up and get back to your pod, giiirl!"

I didn't know exactly how I did it, but I might have just retraced my steps back to the number 4SE pod. I stood at the huge steel door, waiting for something to happen so I could get back into the glass cage, not that I really wanted to. Suddenly, the Big Click occurred, and I found myself back in the world of the damned. The booming voice over the loudspeaker commanded me to get back to my own cell, and I stood outside of cell number 303, waiting for the Big Click again. It was only a matter of seconds before it happened, and I found myself back in the little filthy, cramped cell with Serena, the sleeping psycho girl.

YEW GONNA EAT DAT?

"**G**IRL, YOU BETTER put on your shoes if you're gonna get in dat nasty-ass shower before you catch da fungus on yer feets," she called out the cell door. It was one of the first things I ever heard her say. I was shocked and a little confused that she should display any kind of caring at all.

I slipped the size 10 plastic flip-flops onto my size 8 feet, grabbed my tiny plastic bag of issued toiletries, and headed toward the door. As almost an afterthought, I decided to take inventory of the articles of personal hygiene lying limply in the bag. I quickly dumped the contents of the bag onto the hard metal desk in the cell. *Let's see*, I said softly to myself. *We've got one teeny-weeny bar of soap.* I picked it up to put it to my nose and smelled it.

"Ugh!" I said out loud. "This stuff *stinks*."

I noticed Serena snicker into the wall she was facing on her bed.

I continued my inventory. "And one black plastic comb." I wondered how in the world I would ever get that comb to go through the tangled mess that my curly, frizzy hair ended up in once washed. I suddenly found myself in awe of hairbrushes. I continued. "What is this contraption?" I wondered out loud. I was holding an off-white item about two inches in length with a cheap plastic handle and two crooked rows of bristles along its end.

"Dat's your toofbrush, girl." Serena laughed. "It's what ya use to brush your teef. Dat's all you gets in here."

I rolled the miniature toothbrush around in my hand. *How in the world does this thing even work?* I wondered. Try as I might, I couldn't imagine attempting to use a two-inch toothbrush. My thoughts on the matter continued. *How am I supposed to hold on to the handle? By the time I reach my back teeth, all my fingers will be stuffed in my mouth just to serve as an extension of the handle. And these bristles! Why, they aren't even the same length or density. The rows aren't even lined up, for Christ's sake. I've never seen anything like this in my life.*

Suddenly, an almost comical thought rushed through my confused mind. *I wonder if the American Dental Association [ADA] knows about toothbrushes like this being issued in jails and prisons.* Then almost as suddenly as the comical thought rushed into my mind, it disappeared upon my realization that the ADA was not actually any friend of mine.

But there was still one more mystery toiletry item for me to investigate before my first shower in jail. It appeared to be an itsy-bitsy tube of something. I picked it up and read the tiny black lettering on its front. "Dr. Isaac Smith's toothpaste," it read. I turned the miniature tube over and read, "Ingredients: zirconium silicate, propylene glycol, methyl cellulose, formaldehyde, flavorings."

Oh, this is just great, I thought. *This shit contains a harsh abrasive, a bitter humectant, a cheap binder, a preservative that's also used to fixate dead bodies, and lord knows what kind of flavorings.* The tiny tube contained all the cheap ingredients of a toothpaste, but the one most important ingredient was missing. Never mind it contained no surface active detergent to lower the surface tension, penetrate and loosen surface deposits, and emulsify the debris removed from the tooth surface—it was missing any form of fluoride.

I suddenly became nauseous, beginning to relive one of my most pronounced fears of recent years. My dental practice had been very active in the area of full-mouth extractions and denture placements due to its location in the rural Deep South. For nearly seven years, I had been having a recurring nightmare of which my husband only knew. In the nightmare, I was calmly sitting beside a patient in my office, performing a minor dental procedure when, suddenly, out of the blue, my *own* teeth began to loosen spontaneously and fall out of my mouth onto the hard tile floor. It reminded me of the beautiful dancing leaves on a magnificent tree one autumn day when, suddenly, the harsh north wind began to blow, and they all came showering down in an unplanned frenzy, dropping to the ground with a vengeance, only these were not colorful fall leaves; these were my own sacred teeth that were exploding from my mouth and dropping onto the cold tile floor before

I could do anything about it. The horrible noise of thirty-two teeth spewing forth out of my mouth and onto the rock-hard floor reminded me of when my boys were little, and they would intentionally pour a box full of their marbles onto our bathroom floor just for the thrill of hearing them hit the floor.

Anyway, in the dream, as soon as I realized what was happening to my own teeth, I swallowed all my pride and professional mannerisms and began to freak out in front of my patient. A cold sweat broke out on my forehead, and I dropped immediately to my knees and onto the stone-cold floor. Without giving it a second thought, I began frantically stuffing my fallen teeth back into my bleeding sockets, only I just can't seem to ever get the right teeth back into the right sockets. It was usually at this point in the dream that I awakened, my heart pounding and my nightshirt wringing wet with sweat.

After recalling my resurfacing bad dream and coming to the realistic deduction that I was never going to part with my natural teeth gracefully, I began to recall some of my dental school buddies who were now making their living working as dentists at various county jails and prisons. These pathetic creatures spent their miserable days drilling the rotten, neglected teeth of the thrown-away people of our society, and like the inmates they treated, these dentists had become hardened and apathetic over the years. Their spirits of compassion had been sucked dry; these pathetic docs seemed to view their shabby incarcerated patients as if they were nothing more than large chunks of dead meat. There was no respect for patient wishes and even less concern over choosing the appropriate dental treatment for each case. Instead, it was a cut-and-dried routine of two or three choices once the inmate's tooth went bad—yank it, drill it, or stuff it full of nasty, cheap temporary medication till the jailbird could one day miraculously spring free from captivity and get herself to a "real" dentist. Until then, the affected tooth was on its way to rapid deterioration and certain doom. Why, if an inmate stayed on the inside long enough, she was destined to be totally toothless within a matter of years.

The dreaded repeating dream along with my realization that dentists in correctional institutions were totally indifferent to everything and everyone around them combined to make me downright paranoid when it came to the subject of my teeth while in jail. From the very first day of my residence on the "inside," I became a total nut about my own oral hygiene. Mention just about any other topic of personal hygiene—showering, hair washing, face cleaning—and I was within normal boundaries. But venture into the realm of *oral* hygiene, and I totally lost it. I became 100 percent irrational—a certified mental case, a true oral hygiene psychopath.

From that first morning until the morning that I walked out of the women's detention center (WDC) eighty-two days later, I fixated on maintaining absolutely perfect oral hygiene round the clock. I scrubbed my pearly whites with that stubby toothbrush every time the notion struck me—morning, noon, and night. I squirted a big glob of that inferior tooth concoction onto that poor excuse of a toothbrush, and I commenced to scrubbing, brushing, scouring, scraping until most normal south Georgia folks would worry about rubbing the enamel completely off. Before long, the cheap uneven bristles were absolutely splayed, fanning out to such an extent that, looking back, I knew that I was probably brushing my teeth more with my fingers near the end of that particular toothbrush's life than with anything else. But for some bizarre unknown reason, this daily ritual of rigid oral hygiene seemed to help keep me sane during this time. I guess it gave me some kind of feeling of control over my own life in a place where one had lost all control over every aspect of living.

Anyhow, there I stood, staring vacantly down at the four cheesy items of personal hygiene spilled out on the gray stainless steel desk. How was I ever to make this two-inch-long toothbrush, inferior toothpaste, brittle black comb, and bar of soap that offended my nostrils suffice for my full repertoire of needed shower toiletries? Where was the shampoo? The face cream? The Q-tips? Where was the deodorant? The nail clippers? The hairbrush? And where was the mouthwash? But most importantly, where was the dental floss? I was totally certain that, without this important item, my teeth would surely rot in their interproximal spaces, the areas that a toothbrush could never reach, most especially *that* toothbrush.

Glancing over my shoulder and seeing that Serena had returned to full sleep and certainly was not about to help me, I just shook my head, gathered the items back up, and stuffed them in the little plastic bag. I grabbed my *one* worn white bath towel and my *one* thin washcloth that had been issued to me the previous night and headed for the cell door. I had no idea of exactly when the door would click open, but I did know that I was in bad need of a shower and some air other than the stale, heavy air that hung in that cell. Peeking through the small glass window on the cell door, the large open room with the round metal tables and stools, TV, and plastic TV chairs looked pretty good to me. I decided that until someone told me differently, I would dub this room the Big Room because it was so big compared with our tiny cramped cell. *I think the showers might be out in that room*, I thought.

Just then, I heard a noise that sent chills up my spine. It was that click, that clank, that startling, earsplitting reverberation of a heavy-duty lock on a two-ton door being unlocked, only this time the sound was magnified ten times over. It sounded like ten or twenty of such locks had been unlocked in unison. The noise was almost deafening. My eyes cut over to Serena to see if this racket was normal. It apparently was because she didn't move a muscle but went right on snoozing.

Oh boy, I thought, *the cell door just unlocked, and now I can take my shower.* And I rushed to the door so I could be the first one to grab a shower. But the cell door would not budge. Try as I might, it just stayed locked, tight as a drum. As I was still attempting to open that heavy door with my brute strength alone, I noticed something peculiar going on in the Big Room. Girls in orange suits and plastic shower shoes were pouring out of their cells and into the large room—tall girls, short girls, skinny girls, fat girls, girls with long hair and short hair, girls with white skin, black skin, and every color in between. Some were holding the generic white towels and washcloths, some were carrying decks of cards, most were toting plain brown grocery bags.

"What in the world is going on here?" I said to myself. "Why do *they* get to go to the Big Room with the fresh air and showers and I'm still stuck in *here*?" I decided that this must be some sort of mistake, and maybe our cell door was jammed or something. I hesitated for a moment but pretty quickly decided that this matter was serious enough to awaken Serena.

"Serena, Serena, wake up," I said. "All the other girls are out in that big room, and our door won't open. It must be stuck or something. What do I do?"

It took her a good minute to respond at all. She finally groaned that bloodcurdling moan, turned over in the bed with much effort, and whispered, "Giiirl, it time for *dair* rotation. What da *matter* with you, giiirl? You retarded or somethin'? Dey don't let us all out at da same time. We real *convicks* down here. We gotta take turns. We be out at eight forty-five." With that, she grunted, turned toward the cinder block wall, and drifted back off to sleep.

Now I was in a sure enough dilemma. What was a "rotation," and why did those girls get to be out in the Big Room while I was stuck in this musty cell with Scary Serena?

The next thirty minutes were spent feeling sorry for myself. Since there was no movable furniture inside our cell, it was impossible for me to observe through the door window while sitting down. So I stood at the window for what seemed to be an eternity, watching the girls' every move. I counted about nineteen of them when they stood still enough for me to count. They appeared to be engaging in several different activities in the Big Room. Some were sitting in the tacky plastic chairs, watching the TV that was mounted high on the wall, so high that they all had to strain their necks having to look up too far. The chairs—I counted ten of them—sat in two perfectly straight rows, the arms of each touching the adjacent ones. I wondered if they were connected and bolted to the floor, like the desk, bunk bed, and stool in our cell.

My eyes wandered. Other girls were sitting on the hard stainless steel stools, playing cards. They seemed to be the livelier ones, and they often got quite upset with one another, jumping suddenly up out of the stools to point a wagging finger in their opponent's face and curse loud obscenities when the card game was not going their way. I made a quick mental note. *Learn these faces. The card players are the ones to avoid.*

A few of the girls in the Big Room looked like they were keeping to themselves. They scattered around the room, sitting quietly at the different round tables. Some were reading, others were writing, still others were doing nothing at all but staring straight ahead, probably just relieved to get out of their cramped cells. I made a second mental note. *Try to get to know these loners. They are probably the good ones.*

My eyes continued to scan the Big Room. The third most popular activity, after card playing and TV watching, seemed to be messing with one another's hair. All throughout the room sat the victims—those girls who decided, for one reason or another, that it was time for a new do. Over them stood their make-believe hairdressers, twisting, curling, crimping, braiding, weaving, and frantically brushing and combing. They performed any procedure on the victims' hair that did not require heat, hair blowers, or curling irons. The most popular procedure appeared to be some sort of weird weaving of different-sized, long prefabricated black braids into the victims' existing hair. Down on the floor by the hairdressers' feet lay inches of fuzzy, synthetic, leftover black balls of material from these prefab, improvised dreadlocks. The balls of material blew around the pretend beauticians' feet like miniature tumbleweeds out West, scattering in the desert. Some of the hairdressers stood barefoot, and the puffs of black material stuck to their toes, making their feet look like the paws of some peculiar animal.

I zeroed in on the victims. They sat patiently for long periods, voluntarily enduring endless tugging, pulling, teasing, and twisting of their scalps and hair. When the torture was finally over, they stood in small groups, admiring one another's new dos, asking endlessly, "How does it look?" Apparently, no one was allowed to have a mirror. I wondered where they got the brushes.

After thirty minutes or so of this human observation, my aching feet began to get tired, and I decided to sit down and wait for my turn to go into the Big Room. So I sank down into the corner by the door and sat on the hard floor, pulling my legs toward my chest. After a while, I began to think. *Maybe I'm not the only one left locked up in my cell. Maybe some of the other girls are still locked up too. Let me see, Serena called it a rotation. That's it. Maybe we all take turns at going into the Big Room. Maybe it's kinda like having shifts.* But I decided to stay sitting close to the door in case I had this rotation thing figured out all wrong.

I must have fallen asleep sitting up in that corner because, the next thing I knew, I was awakened by that now familiar sound of several cell doors locking or unlocking—I couldn't tell which. Then I heard a muffled voice that seemed to be coming out of the walls of the Big Room. "Get back to your cells *now*! Y'all know better'n dat! Girl, you can go back, or Ah'll call and get help, and we'll *put* you back in dere and *mace* you too! Don't be lookin' at me like dat! Ah'll put your ass in lockdown, giiirrl!"

It didn't take me long to figure out that the mumbling voice was the same voice that, earlier this morning, told me, "Come on out the cell, girl. You got visitor."

I do not like that voice that comes through the walls of the Big Room or my cell, I told myself. *I will steer very clear of* it.

Before I knew it, the nineteen girls in the Big Room were no longer there. They had scattered and disappeared as suddenly as they had appeared. Where they went I did not know, but once I heard that heavy click again, I figured that they were probably back in their cells locked away. I tried to guess how long they had been out in the Big Room, but I really had no idea because I had fallen asleep. I began to look around the cell for any clocks, watches, timepieces, anything that would tell me the time. But I was unsuccessful. Maybe the Big Room had a clock. Yes, I was certain that it *had* to. They couldn't expect us to go day after day not knowing what time it was.

I glimpsed over at Serena. She was still asleep, dead to the world. Just as I was frantically thinking of what I could do in the cell to keep my sanity, the Big Click happened once again. This time, I would not allow myself to get excited and expect that the Big Click meant that *my* cell door had been unlocked. I very calmly walked over to the menacing door, reasoning that if I didn't rush like before, maybe the chances of the door being unlocked would be greater. I gave the door a tiny push with two fingers, and like a small miracle, it opened.

I nearly sprinted back across the cell and snatched up the plastic bag with the four shower items, my towel, and my washcloth. I almost tripped over my own feet getting out of the door fast enough to try to grab a shower in the Big Room. But as I emerged into the Big Room, I noticed that not a single soul was near the showers, the TV, or even the card-playing and hair-fixing tables. Then I realized that *everyone* in the Big Room—all the girls—were lined up in a straight, single-file row coming down a steep set of stairs near the back of the Big Room. I took a few steps backward to size up the situation more thoroughly. I had not noticed this stairway last night when I first arrived, nor had I noticed it in my Big Room observations this morning. It was an intimidating stairway with thick metal handrails leading to someplace high near the Big Room's ceiling.

My eyes followed the hard tile stairs upward and stopped with sudden astonishment upon the realization that they led to an entire row of cells that were upstairs. I told myself that this made the whole situation twice as hopeless because now there were *twice* as many girls in this horrible place as I had originally thought. *Oh well,* I thought, *I'd better stop gaping and snatch a shower.*

But before I could open the shower door to go in, a tall gangly pale-skinned girl caught my elbow. She had to have been at least six feet tall. Her crumpled orange suit hung on her bony frame. Her greasy, unkempt brown hair had been pulled back in a rubber band, but half of it had since decided to escape and stick out from her small head in all directions. Her rough skin had the deep pitted scars of a bad case of past acne. Her fingernails were cracked and dirty. When she spoke, a deep Southern accent emerged. "Hooneey, yew can't be a-goin' in that there shower raht now. It's a time fer lunch, sugar. Can't yew see that we-ins is all lahned up, a-waitin'? Now git in lahn, er yew'll git us awl in trouble."

I reluctantly placed my bag of four shower items and my towel and washcloth on one of the round stainless steel tables and slowly sauntered toward the steps to get in line. But the tall girl spoke once again.

"Honey chile, yew can't put yer stuff an' awl raht there on that there table at we is fixin' ta eat on. Now git it awl up an' tote it back to yer room raht now a-fore the pohleece lock yer door back. Yew'll be in shore 'nuff trouble then."

I snatched up the shower stuff and headed back toward the cell, concerned that, for some unknown reason, I may be getting the other girls "in trouble." Before I threw the articles down on the desk in the cell's corner, I cast a side glance toward Serena. She was still very much asleep on the bunk, curled once again into that fetal position with her face pressed toward the cinder block wall. I briefly considered awakening her for lunch, but my recollections of her foul moods that morning stopped me from doing it. I remembered that she had not eaten supper the night before, according to the inmates who were trying to get her to eat crackers upon my arrival, nor had she gotten up to eat breakfast. I knew that because several of the girls had attempted to get me up early this morning, and I refused, pulling my dirty covers back over my head. I noticed how very thin and frail her form was lying there on the bunk.

She doesn't seem to like to eat much anyway, I rationalized. *It would probably just be a waste of time to wake her up for lunch.* With that, I threw the towel and bag down on the stainless steel desk and ran out the door.

"Come on! Git in lahn, sugar! Hurry up now, honey! We's awl a-waitin' fer yew!" the gangly girl with the bad skin yelled. She was motioning to me with her long skinny arms. "Yew kin be the ferst one in lahn today seein' that yew is the newest one here and awl." She pointed to the place of honor. It was on the floor, right below the first step. I took my position, without even bothering to look at how many girls were lined up behind me. The tall Southern girl smiled at me and nodded. I noticed that her two front teeth and several others were missing, and the remaining teeth were all broken and stained. Some of them were yellow, others gray, and still others black with advanced dental decay. Her lower front teeth were elongated and moved in and out of her mouth as she breathed. Her gums were not healthy, firm, and pink but rather were inflamed, spongy, and red. Her breath reeked of advanced periodontal disease.

My stomach became queasy, and my head spun with dizziness. Brief images of patients' mouths that I had treated in my south Georgia dental practice flashed before my eyes. I began to think that maybe I had better skip lunch before I got sick.

Just then, the huge door to the Big Room clicked open, and in came two female guards dressed in tight navy blue uniforms. They were struggling to push a large cart with two shelves. The top shelf appeared to hold several brown paper sacks; the bottom shelf held a tall plastic jug full of red liquid. They had just gotten in the door good when two of the girls in orange ran over to the cart yelling, "My turn! My turn!" The two dirty girls snatched the plastic jug off of the cart, each one taking hold of a side handle, and raced over to a cinder block ledge on the far side of the Big Room. I couldn't help but notice that the ledge on which the two girls placed the jug served as the top of the wall for the one toilet in the Big Room. I made a mental note not to drink whatever was in that jug.

As my eyes were still fixated on the jug, the younger of the two girls unscrewed the lid and announced, "This shit needs to be stirred." With that, she thrust her grimy arm up to her elbow into the red liquid and began to rotate her arm round and round, wiggling her stained fingers with the dingy, cracked fingernails.

As I was still gawking with total disbelief at what was happening before my eyes, one of the guards began to bark orders at me. She was short and slightly built. Her black eyes were swollen and half closed as if she had just woken up. The expression on her dark face was that of half hatred and half pure boredom. "Girl, come on den! Get dat bag! You holdin' up everybody! You gonna eat, or you gonna stand dere? Get out da line den! Ain't nobody got time for dis!"

My heart began to race inside me. I wasn't quite sure of what I was supposed to do, but I quickly began to put two and two together. It was lunchtime, I was the first in line, there were fifty or so brown paper bags on a cart in front of me, and a guard was getting increasingly angry at me. I didn't know if what I was about to do was going to be correct, but obviously, I had to do *something*—and fast. So I sheepishly stepped forward and timidly held my shaking hand out to the pissed-off guard. *God, I hope I'm doing the right thing*, I thought. As soon as I held my hand out, the short, little guard thrust one of the brown bags into my hands with so much force that it stung my fingers. I looked around. I wasn't sure what to do next.

"Get out da way den, *giiirl*, and keep the line movin'. What's *wrong* witch you? Why you lookin' dat way? Go sit down and get out da way now!" the puny guard screamed.

All the other girls in line behind me howled with laughter. She had said to go sit down, so I figured I'd take my chances and sit at one of the round stainless steel tables with the round hard stools that were bolted to the floor. The girls were still laughing, so I decided to sit at the table right outside my cell door, far in the corner, with my back to them.

I cautiously opened the paper sack and peeked inside. There wasn't much in it, so I decided to gently dump it onto the table. Out tumbled two wrapped articles. One looked like a sandwich of some sort, and the other I recognized as a very inexpensive brand of cookie. I slowly started to unwrap the sandwich. The doughy white bread was stale and had begun to mold around the crust. I picked up the top piece of bread to see what kind of sandwich it was. But even when I was staring right at it, I wasn't quite sure *what* that stuff inside the bread was. It appeared to be some sort of meat, *maybe*. I picked it up to examine it further. It was thin and rubbery and had been pressed into a perfect square. The color was indecisive—not red, not pink, not even gray. It was close to a pinkish green beige with various-colored specks throughout. I decided to smell it, but even before I got it all the way to my nose, the outright stench of it started to turn my stomach.

The tables were beginning to fill up with girls in orange now. A large girl with bulging dark eyes and a huge mouth with thick lips plopped down beside me. "Hey, White girl, yew gonna eat dat? Girl, I'm gonna take your samwitch, and ain't nuttin' you gonna do." With that, she snatched up my entire sandwich and stuffed it in her gigantic mouth. "Hey, Snow, I jis' got yer samwitch." She proceeded to throw her big head back and laugh and laugh, big chunks of half-eaten sandwich flying in all directions. Her long black braids that had been woven into her own existing hair hung halfway down her back.

She continued to harass me, "Hey, girl, why you ain't got no Kool-Aid? You don' want nuttin' ta drink? Go get cha some. Ah'll watch chur cookie."

I wasn't sure in what direction this encounter was headed, but I didn't really want to know. I was pretty sure that, in another thirty seconds, she would have had my cookie too. But just then, the Big Click occurred once again; and all the girls grabbed their remaining lunches, bags and all, and their Styrofoam cups of red Kool-Aid and scurried into their cells. In a matter of seconds, the Big Click happened again, and we were locked back in our cells.

Serena was still lying lifeless on her bunk. She was in the same position; she had not moved a muscle. I placed what remained of my lunch on the desk in the corner and almost immediately began to feel sorry for myself. Let's see, I had not eaten the sandwich and cookie last night in the holding cell, I had voluntarily skipped breakfast this morning, and now all I had for lunch was a cheap cookie—no sandwich, nothing to drink, just one measly little cookie.

I suddenly remembered having read a recent newspaper article about how much a prisoner cost the taxpayers of Georgia. The article said that one prisoner cost close to $20,000 a year to feed and house. I looked around my cell. It was probably six feet by ten feet, all cinder block painted white. The furnishings consisted of a rickety metal bunk bed with one-inch raggedy bedrolls for the mattresses; a stainless steel desk and stool, both bolted to the floor; a stainless steel toilet with no seat; and a tiny metal sink that only trickled water, if any water came out at all. Then I looked down at my "lunch." Even if the big Black girl had not stolen my sandwich, this was not much of a lunch. Where was the piece of fruit? The milk? The whole-grain bread?

My thought process continued. *If each inmate costs the state of Georgia $20,000 a year, then where in the world is that money being spent?* All of a sudden, I remembered a second newspaper article. It stated that one of the wardens in the Atlanta area had recently been charged with pocketing monies meant to feed the inmates in his jail. He had evidently had the cooks change the jail menus to cut out any fruits or vegetables, dairy products, or whole grains and had substituted all white bread and starches. He was furthermore accused of not giving the inmates large enough portions of any kind of food. I decided then and there that this county jail was the one; this was where the evil warden had stolen the food money. And by the looks of things, he was still up to his same old trick.

JAILHOUSE ROCK: SHOWER TIME

I CHOKED DOWN THE dry, stale cookie over the miniature sink, cupping my hand under the little faucet and sipping water from my palm carefully. It was a slow go since the faucet had no handles but rather had two round buttons, one for hot and one for cold. To make the water come out, the buttons had to be pushed, after which a spurt of water would spew forth for about five seconds before the button had to be pushed again. I wondered how in the world I was going to wash my face or brush my teeth before bed every night.

My teeth! In all my distractions, I had forgotten about them. I quickly grabbed the stubby toothbrush, squeezed out a ribbon of cheap toothpaste, and commenced to scrub up and down for a good while. The familiarity of toothbrushing seemed to comfort me.

Just then, the Big Click happened. I wondered what was going on. I decided to try our door. To my great surprise, it opened. This time, I simply strolled over to the desk; retrieved my plastic bag, towel, and washcloth; and calmly exited the cell into the Big Room. I headed toward the showers. There were two showers, smack dab in the middle of the Big Room, where every inmate and all the guards outside in the tower could easily see them. They had little doors on them that reminded me of the tiny swinging doors on Western saloons in the movies. By the time I got out of my cell, both showers were full.

I pretended to be doing something different but continued to observe the strange phenomenon of the showers. Both girls could be seen from their shoulders up and from their legs down. The tiny swinging doors hid their torsos only. Every move was easily observed, from shampooing hair to washing under their arms. My heart sank. I had been waiting all this time to take a shower, and now I didn't know if I was going to be able to do this. I did not want to be on public display for every inmate and guard to see while I was doing some of my most private things. What was I going to do?

While thinking about what a horrible dilemma I was in, the actions of the two girls in the showers began to catch my eye. They had apparently learned to take full advantage of being on public display and had decided to flaunt the occasion. The younger of the two was singing at the top of her lungs and dancing so rapidly that I wondered how in the world she was able to keep her balance on the wet shower floor. She was a slightly built girl with light brown skin and delicate features. But her behavior was anything but delicate. She belted out her song like one of the Supremes on crack cocaine. "Bad girls! Bad girls! We's nothin' but a bunch o' bad girls! Bad girls, baby! Betta watch ya back when we's around!"

She especially seemed to be pleased when it was time for the chorus to come around. Every time she came to the chorus, she would step forward in the shower, stand still for a moment, and open the swinging door on the word *girls*. So it went something like this: "Bad girls!" Open the door and let the world see me naked. "Bad girls!" Do it again and so on. It seemed to really please her that the chorus was made up of essentially the two words, *bad girls*, which meant that she got to open the door and expose herself to the world quite often.

At first, I guess I gawked at her out of pure disbelief. She had an unbelievably huge Afro for such a petite person. And throughout her erotic song, she kept the Afro sudsed up with so much white shampoo that it looked like a snow-covered mountain on top of her tiny head. Her black eyes were unproportionately large also. Every time she belted out the incriminating word, *girls*, her ebony eyes bulged out of her little face as if they were going to pop out of their sockets. Her entire body was soaped up to the hilt, even the soles of her feet. She looked like a patient I once saw walking down the street at the school of dental education. Upon asking one of the med students what was wrong with this patient, he replied that she had a rare pigment-related disease that caused her to have large white blotches throughout her naturally black skin. I can't remember the name of the disease.

Anyhow, between choruses, she would spin around wildly, throwing her long skinny arms in the air and moving her feet so rapidly that I wondered what kept her from slipping and falling down. *She must have unbelievably excellent balance*, I reasoned. As soon as I got through that thought, it was time once again for the chorus, and I guess she decided to become more erotic this time. On this particular chorus, she decided to not only open the door every time the word *girls* rolled around but also add a distinct pelvic thrust along with it. This added feature was just a little too much for me, so I turned my head away and stopped gawking.

I guess this added feature of the dance was a little too much for some of the other girls also. They began to make wisecracks. "Jaaasmine, girl, you is 'bout ta make me vomick lookin' at chew. You know nobody watchin' you act da fool, giiirrl! You need to stop your madness and get out dat shower and let somebody else get in!"

But this remark didn't seem to faze Miss Jasmine. She continued her pornographic dance, swinging her hips harder than ever and belting out her naughty song louder than before.

About that time, I noticed that the girl taking a shower beside her was exhibiting strange behavior herself. I felt like I had seen this girl before. She was someone whom no one could miss, even in a crowd. She had to have been over six feet tall, and she wore large glasses with cheap rims that looked like the chrome on a bicycle. She had not bothered to take them off for her shower. Her face was butt ugly, so ugly that I jumped back a little when I first saw it. She had not one single feminine feature about her; I even wondered briefly if the guards might have mistakenly put a man in with us.

This was what she was doing in the shower. She would hold her homely large face up to the showerhead, glasses and all, tilting her head back as far as possible. Then she would begin to turn the cold water off and the hot water up until, as far as I could tell, there was nothing running out of the showerhead but purely scalding hot water. The steam arising from the piping hot water clouded her cheap glasses to where she couldn't see a thing. Burning hot water poured up her nostrils and pelted down her naked back, but she didn't move a muscle. She just stood there, all seventy-two-plus inches of her, solid as a rock, the most stoic human being I had ever seen. It was as if she was playing a sick little game with herself, one of self-torture and mental challenge, as if she was saying to herself, *Let's see just how long I can stand to be here and let this red-hot water burn me to my very core.* I wondered why the cheap chrome on the rims of her glasses didn't melt from the extreme temperatures. I felt certain that if her skin wasn't jet black, it would have been bright red with second-degree burns by now.

Just as I was turning my head away, not able to endure the torturous scene any longer, she took a large gulp of the boiling hot water and then began to gargle large mouthfuls, making a downright eerie sound as she did so. But that was not the end of it. About the time I thought that this scene could not get any more bizarre, it most certainly did. After her first few gargles, she began to add some strange-sounding words as she continued to gargle. In a couple of stanzas, I could begin to recognize her creepy song. She was singing "Burn, Baby, Burn" in a scary voice so low and scratchy that I knew it was lower than any man's voice I had ever heard. It was one of the strangest scenes I had ever witnessed. She would stand stoically under the scalding hot water, taking large mouthfuls of it, and then half-gargle and half-sing, "Buuurn, babyyy, *buuuurn!*"

After a few minutes of this eerie gargling chorus, strange sounds started to erupt deep down in her throat. It sounded as if there was something alive down there. Then suddenly, she made one all-encompassing huge loud throat noise as if she were trying to clear all her head sinuses and hock up a single gigantic loogie. Before I knew it, the throat noise was over, and a humongous glob of thick greenish phlegm spewed forth out of her ugly mouth like an infant's projectile vomit. She spit it forcefully against the shower floor. This seemed to really please her, and so she began to spit anything that she could muster up. She spat against the shower walls, the shower door, the shower ceiling, and even on her on feet. This one she seemed particularly delighted with. It was as if she was playing a game with herself—a game of just how grotesque she could be, almost of just how *manly* she could be.

I looked at her face again. Her glasses were still completely steamed up. Her little slitty eyes were squeezed tightly shut. Her short coarse hair was pulled tightly back into a rubber band, the ponytail not even one inch long. She had slicked her hair back with so much oil that it had managed to repel all the water that had hit it from the shower. The little stubby ponytail was standing straight out as if it had become frightened of her recent behavior. Her mouth was small and tightly drawn up; her teeth were crooked and rotten. Her large nostrils flared from all the excitement.

She eventually tired of her self-torturous burning, gargling, spitting game and finally turned the shower off. Then she emerged from the shower door in all her glory. I tried very hard to take my eyes off her and not gawk, but I absolutely could not help but stare at what was before me. She was huge, towering over all of us like a mountain. She had broad shoulders and large muscular arms with no hips or behind. Her chest was flat as a board, her thighs rippled with heavy, thick muscles. When she walked, she swaggered with manly big steps. I knew she had more testosterone than most of the men I had ever met. I would be ashamed to tell you this, but as she stood there outside the shower, naked to the world, my eyes checked her briefly for the presence of a penis.

Just as soon as she emerged from the shower, the other girls began to harass her. "Bicycle, get your big stupid ass out dat shower, nigger, an' let someone else get in dere, skeezer! You usin' all da water up!"

I drew in my breath, waiting to see how this machine full of male hormones might react. It certainly wasn't very long until I found out. "I ain't goin' *nowhere*! Git out my damn face! *'Scuse* me! You better move, or Ah'll *kick* ya ta sleep! Now play wid it, and Ah'll break yer ass sumtin' proper! *Ho*, dis ain't what choo want! Ah'll putt dees jumper cables on yer ass! Mudderfuckers, cum' git yerselfs sum! I don't give a *fuck*! Ah'll git out da shower when I git damn ready! Ain't nobody gonna fuck wid me! Play wid it if y'all wants to! Y'all can shut up, ya stupid mudderfuckin' bitches 'fore I come ovah dere an' putt da beat down on y'all's black asses!"

She was holding up her huge fists, thrashing them wildly through the air. Because her glasses were still fully steamed up, she seemed unable to get her bearings. "Y'all mudderfuckin' *hos* lucky I can't see y'all 'cuz I'd break y'all asses off sum'in' propa!"

She paused for a moment but then continued as if she couldn't quite get a hold of her temper. *"Ah'm* da captain o' dis ship. Ah don't give a *fuck* what y'all say! Ah kin stay in da showah as long as I git ready. So ya betta find sumtin' safe to do 'fore Ah fuck y'all up, and dat liddle sissy-ass nigger ya got ober dere, he ain't gonna know ya when Ah gits through witch yuh!"

That little speech was more than enough to convince me. I backed away and sat down quietly at the nearest vacant table, cowering in the corner. I noticed that most of the other girls were also backing down and going off in their separate directions. Then I saw a very remarkable thing.

A petite inmate, no more than five feet tall, seemed to be the only one who was not backing down from the masculine bully. "Bicycle, you big dumb color-blind stupid-ass nigger! I ain't never scared of you!" the tiny Black inmate said almost matter-of-factly.

She continued, "You big gorilla-lookin' bitch, I ain't scared of you. I'm fixin' to get in the shower *with* you. Let's shake, baby!"

I noticed right off that she wasn't like any of the others. First, she actually had some diction when she spoke. She appeared to have to make a real effort to bring herself "down" enough to speak proper prison Ebonics. Second, she seemed to truly possess a little self-confidence. I could even see evidence of that by the way she carried herself. She walked with an air of assurance, her shoulders held squarely, and her head held high. She positioned herself closely enough to the monster that they were eyeball to eyeball, and she didn't flinch a muscle.

The story of David and Goliath suddenly came to my mind. I thought of how the most admirable quality of all was her great courage. How anyone on the face of the earth could have stood up to that enormous subhuman creature at that very moment had me stumped. The fact that the tiny inmate was not even up to the giant's shoulders and probably weighed less than half what the Amazon did made me admire her even more. I literally held my breath, waiting to see what was going to happen to the brave pint-size hero. I was truly afraid that I might be witness to a murder in the next few seconds.

But that was not what happened at all. The towering monster they called Bicycle began to mumble to herself under her breath, "Manda, git yer ugly crackah-lovin' ass out my face. Yew ain't no better 'an da rest o' us! Yew ain't nuttin' but an ass kisser for dem crackahs. Git out my face 'fore Ah break yer ass down!" She was pulling on the same orange uniform that she had on before she took her shower, not even bothering to dry off first. Her large glasses were totally defogged now, and I could see her eyes well for the first time. They were like tiny black marbles hidden deeply in little slashes in her face. They reminded me of rattlesnake eyes, dead and expressionless; and no matter where you stood in the room, they were always looking at you.

Then I noticed the funniest thing. The monster was not looking at the minute girl she had called Manda. Instead, while she was mumbling, she was looking down at the ground. I started to think of my grandpa's veterinary office and of some of the animal behavior that I had observed there over the years. This confrontation between Bicycle and Manda reminded me of a Great Dane backing down from a Chihuahua. Manda had succeeded in breaking Bicycle down. David had tamed Goliath.

My attention suddenly turned from the frightening ogress to the remarkable heroine, and I decided to follow her actions for a while. As soon as Bicycle had exited the shower area, Manda slowly picked up her brown paper bag and sauntered over to that same shower. I wondered what was in the grocery bag. I soon found out. She leisurely reached into the bag and gently pulled out each and every item, methodically placing them in a row on top of the cement block wall that ran waist high in front of the shower. The showers both had a small tiled area, maybe three feet by three feet with a short block wall in front of it, but no walls on either side. This area was in front of the shower door. I never really knew what the purpose of that area was; I never used it myself. The original purpose was probably for this area to act as a place in which to dress and undress and maybe to dry off. But I never fully understood why, if the purpose of the area was to gain a little privacy, the wall was not built shoulder high and on all three sides.

The other girls, however, had created different, more original purposes for the small tiled area in front of the showers. Jasmine, for example, used the area for a striptease stage, erotically removing her garments piece by piece and sensually throwing them over the block wall. Bicycle used the area as a challenging space, loudly daring anyone around to "come try an' beat mah mudderfuckin' ass" both before and after her showers. Manda, on the other hand, had her own agenda for the tiled area in front of the shower. It was simply an area of usefulness, serving as both a place to arrange her shower paraphernalia and also a place of preshower socialization.

I watched as she displayed her full repertoire of shower accessories on the top of the wall. I was astonished to find that she owned a brush, a comb, assorted hair clips, rubber bands, barrettes, three bottles of different kinds of shampoo, two bottles of conditioner, a jar of hair oil, two different kinds of soap, four kinds of deodorant, a bottle of body lotion, a tube of hand lotion, a jar of Vaseline, a small bag of nail files, a disposable razor, three tubes of toothpaste, and five stubby toothbrushes. She carefully and methodically arranged her precious wares, placing them in a precise order as if she was a proud peddler displaying her merchandise for all to see.

When all her shower gear was acceptably in line, she began the socialization portion of her agenda. She slowly removed her orange suit top and the white T-shirt underneath and slipped out of her orange pants. Then she stood there in her bra and panties and started to converse with another short Black woman. "Ethel, I don't know why dey keep bringin' all dese stupid young-ass crackheads up in here. Dey think dey know everything. Dey just ain't like dey use ta be. Whatcha think?"

But Ethel was evidently a woman of few words. She stood near the shower, gazing at Manda like she was her hero, hanging on to every word. When Manda was done talking, Ethel looked down and softly said, "I guess you is raht, Manda. We saw bedda convicks in da ole days 'cuz dis ain't nuttin' but a buncha mess rollin' up in here."

The two friends conversed for several minutes mostly about their past history at the Coward County Jail. They seemed to go back a long ways, and this particular jail seemed to be their common ground. They gossiped about this girl and that girl until I began to wonder how many times each of these two women had been in jail and how often different girls came and went. Finally, Manda decided that she had had enough socialization and dismissed Ethel from the conversation. She unhurriedly finished undressing and cautiously stepped into the shower.

As soon as the shower was turned on, she began to sing at the top of her lungs. "Don't worry, be happy now!" she sang in her best reggae imitation. She made up her own revised lyrics as she went along. "The police say your bed ain't made. They might have to beat ya, spade! Don't worry, be happy!"

I noticed that even though her choice of songs was light and funny, she had quite an impressive singing voice. I also noticed that her way of speaking was very familiar to me. I couldn't place the accent, but I was quite sure that she did not originate from south Georgia. Her silly original lyrics continued, "When you're worried, your face will frown. Then the police will act the clown. Don't worry, be happy now!"

Between choruses, she leaped out from the shower and performed various procedures on her hair. She shampooed, conditioned, oiled, and rubber-banded. She combed through unbraided hair and braided those that were supposed to be. She removed some of the synthetic braids and placed others in. And every time she emerged from the shower, she was stark naked. I made a mental note that all the girls I had observed so far in these showers had displayed no modesty whatsoever.

When she was finally done with her shower, she stood in the tiled area for the longest time, just getting dressed like a snail and gathering up her belongings with great consideration. Oftentimes, she would look up to see if the others were watching her collect her great wealth of toiletries, almost as if she was an animal establishing her territory. In the meantime, the shower beside her became available. Jasmine had apparently tired of her striptease act, especially since the spotlight had been taken off her and put on Bicycle and Manda.

I grabbed up my measly plastic bag of four items and headed toward the vacant shower, wondering if some masculine inmate would knock me down and steal it away from me. But everyone seemed to be preoccupied at the moment. If they weren't playing cards or watching TV, they were talking on the phone or playing hairdresser and victim. I was just glad that I was getting the shower that Bicycle had not spat in. I decided to take my soap, comb, and washcloth inside the shower with me. I slung the white towel over the shower door. I wondered how I was going to wash my hair with soap; I had never had to do that before.

Just as I was beginning to take off my orange top, there was a knock on the shower door. I froze in my tracks, absolutely terrified. I thought, *This is it. This is when they beat me up and sexually molest me.* I started to panic. A second knock occurred. I sheepishly opened the shower door, fully expecting to see an angry gang of convicts. But instead, there stood one teeny, tiny inmate, humbly holding out her hand.

It was Manda, and she was holding a large bar of *real* soap, a small bottle of shampoo, and a stick of deodorant. "Thought you could use these for your shower," she said. "They sure don't give you much when you first come in, and it'll be next Thursday before you can order anything from commissary."

I was so taken aback by the first act of kindness since I had been admitted that I really didn't know what to do or think. I slowly reached out to accept the shower items and quietly said, "Thanks so much." I looked at Manda's face. For a second, it looked like she was full of true compassion for me; but suddenly, it became more hardened.

"Don't worry about it 'cuz we gotta look out for one another up in here. I always try to look after the new ones," she said. "Oh, by the way, I'm Amanda." Then she was gone.

I went back into the shower with my new wealth of toiletries. As I was cautiously taking off my orange suit, I began to notice something. The shower was good sized; it probably could have accommodated three showerheads and three inmates at a time. I sighed at that thought, so glad that no one in administration had entertained that notion. The only thing that could have been worse than climbing into that frightful shower alone would have been having to climb into it with some awful creature like Bicycle or Jasmine. I think I would have chosen to go months without showering at all. I suddenly found myself thanking God for the simple blessing of being able to shower alone.

That issue having been resolved in my head, I zeroed in more on examining the shower itself. It was constructed entirely of ceramic tiles, which were originally white in color, I think. The floor sloped down on

DORAMAE BROOKSHIRE

all sides and led to something I could barely see in the center. I blinked, trying to clear out the film that covered them from not having cleaned my contacts the night before. When I could finally see clearly, I could not believe my eyes. The thing that I could not make out before was a large metal drain, and the reason that I could not see it was that it was stopped up with so much nasty junk that it made my stomach turn.

Big wads of black hair, both genuine and fake, were stuck in the drain. But that was not all. Gobs of chewing gum and tiny sharp pieces of soap had lodged into the holes of the shower drain. Wrappers of all kinds—from soap and shampoo and gum and rubber bands—were scattered all over the floor. Tiny empty shampoo bottles and their caps were thrown down at random when they became empty. A collection of one-inch discarded toothbrushes and used rubber bands were slung into the corners. A pair of soaked, stained panties joined the toothbrushes. Chunks of wringing wet toilet paper clung up and down the shower walls and covered the shower floor. Sizable globs of toothpaste abounded, being found everywhere possible. A thick film of dirty oil covered the entire shower, along with an all-encompassing massive coat of soap scum. And to top it all off, a slimy greenish mass—an enormous chunk of unknown material—was looking up at me from the very center of the hidden drain.

My head started to spin; my stomach became so nauseous that I wondered for a minute if my own vomit was soon going to join the huge conglomeration of the other shower garbage. I found myself saying a second silent prayer, this time thanking God for the shower shoes on my feet. I hastily stripped off my orange suit while inside the shower, slung it over the saloon-type shower door, opened my new bar of soap, and began to shower, trying to avoid all the filthy trash that was in my way. I showered with haste and precision, feeling the entire time like several pairs of eyes were on me. I shampooed my hair and rinsed it as rapidly as possible; I wasted no time. I did not sing, play games with the hot water, primp with my hair, exhibit my half-naked body, or make a social event out of my shower. I simply soaped up and rinsed off as efficiently as humanly possible. I must admit, the soothing warm water felt wonderful as it pelted against my cold, clammy skin. And one positive thing could be said for this shower; the water pressure was fantastic. The main aspect of my first shower in jail that I enjoyed, I guess, was the familiarity of something that I had done daily at home. But because of the lack of privacy and the overall foul atmosphere of the shower itself, I hurried through my first jailhouse shower.

I went to apply some of the deodorant that Amanda had brought me when I noticed that it had been used several times before. I had noticed the same thing about the shampoo, but this was different. The shampoo was in a small plastic bottle, but the deodorant was a solid stick. It had been against Lord-knows-who's underarm or underarms. I had to make my decision quickly; I was standing in the shower half naked with the water off, and I was very afraid that one of the manly girls like Bicycle would yank the saloon door open. Should I apply the used deodorant and take a chance of the previous user or users being disease-free, or should I just go several days without deodorant? Amanda had said that it would be next Thursday before I could order anything from "commissary." I wondered what that meant. I made a note to ask her if I got the chance.

I decided to use the deodorant but to try to remove the top layer if possible. I took my wet washcloth and rubbed it several times over the stick of deodorant until I was satisfied that the previously used layers were no longer there. Then I applied the deodorant, dried off, got dressed as quickly as possible, gathered up my stuff, and exited the nasty shower as fast as I could. On my way out, I wondered just how long it had been since that shower had seen any kind of cleaning solution.

DORAMAE BROOKSHIRE

THE APPLE DUMPLING GANG

I HAD NOT BEEN out of the shower two minutes before I noticed the tall lanky mountain girl sitting at one of the round steel tables with three other women. The thing that struck me the most about that particular table was that all the ladies sitting there were White, which stuck out like a sore thumb. I had had time enough by then to look around at the majority of faces in that pod, and quite frankly, I was surprised to see that there were only six of us who were White. Yes, I didn't know about the other pods yet, but 4SE at Coward County Jail was definitely ruled by Black faces.

As I was checking out the all-White table, the hillbilly girl began to motion for me to come over. I didn't really want to, but I didn't know what else to do. "Sugar, git yerself over here a-raht now!" she shouted. "Ah's Erline, an' Ah wants y'all ta meet mah fren's."

I walked slowly over, not knowing what to expect next. She motioned for me to sit down. I did.

"This here's Big Charlotte," she said, pointing to a heavyset older woman who was clutching a Bible in one hand and her playing cards in the other. "Why, she's a regaler Mudder Tuh-*re*-sa."

Seconds after her introduction, the portly woman with long gray hair jumped up off the stool and began to thunderously recite various Bible verses. "'Blessed are they that mourn: for they shall be comforted. Blessed are the meek: for they shall inherit the earth' (Matthew 5:4–5)." The large woman with the sagging jowls looked at me sympathetically and then sat back down and peeked at her cards.

OK then, I thought. *So she has my present mindset figured out pretty well. I have been rather subdued today in my actions, and I am unquestionably mournful in spirit.*

The tall skinny Southern girl continued her introductions. "An' this here is Moleface. She's a-done helt up more banks in this here state than yew'll ever know. She's a-goin' away fer a *looong* tahm." She said it as if she was really proud of the lady.

I took a good look at the bank robber named Moleface. She was so short that I wondered if some kind of illness had stunted her growth as a child. And the fact that she was bent over permanently like the Hunchback of Notre Dame didn't help her height problem any. I didn't have to wonder long where her nickname came from. When I began to examine her face, it revealed two very tiny scrunched-up eyes that didn't appear to be able to see well, a long pointed, sharp nose, and a little pink tongue whose tip protruded out from her tightly pursed lips. Her two arms appeared to be too short and hung out horizontally from her shoulders as if they had been adapted for digging. She was built like a compact square as wide as she was tall. Her entire body was covered with a fine dark velvety blanket of hair, and to make matters worse, four large moles were scattered over her face and neck. *As if she needed any more excuse to be called Moleface*, I thought.

Upon her introduction, she did not do much of anything but stared at me to size me up. I noticed that she was by no means a young woman but was probably even older than Big Charlotte, who was close to sixty herself. I would have never guessed that so many little old grandmas could be locked away in jail.

"See dat there cell over dere? That's mine. Got it to myself. They won't let nobody be in wit' me. Don't go near it if you knows what's good fer ya." She spat the words out like a Chicago gangster. She seemed to be a woman of very few words. I decided never to so much as touch her cell door.

Big Charlotte must have read my dismay. "'Lay not up for yourselves treasures upon earth, where moth and rust does corrupt, and where thieves break through and steal; but lay up for yourselves treasures in heaven, where neither moth nor rust does corrupt, and where thieves do not break through and steal!'" she screamed with great emotion, glaring at Moleface the whole time.

Moleface looked back at her with a blank, bored expression and then rolled her beady eyes at me and squinted. "Like I said, don't go near my cell. I gots some t'ings in deir you don' need tah be messin' wit'." She stared down at her cards. "Are we gonna get on with this card game or what, Ellie Mae Clampett?" she demanded of Erline.

"Jis' a dawgawn minit, Moleface. Don't be a-gittin' in sich a downraht hurry er nuttin'. We ain't a-goin' nowheres anyhows, huh? Ah ain't tol' the new gerl about Pearl er nuttin' yet."

With that, she turned toward the one person whom I had not been introduced to yet and proudly announced, "An' this here is Pearl. We sumtimes call her Little Orphan Annie. She wuz a reeal weepin' willow when she ferst cummed in. She's the youngist un' in exceptin' fer Jasmine an' awl. They bofe of 'em went an' kilt some poor liddle ole buddy, 'ceptin' Ah *think* Pearl wuz only a-watchin' whawl her boyfren' done it an' awl."

The girl they called Pearl retorted almost immediately, "Erline, you so fuckin' stupid! I didn't fuckin' go and kill no-damn-body. My fuckin' boyfriend, Jack, *had* to fuckin' stick that knife into that fuckin' nigger in his garage, or else, he woulda fuckin' bin dead hisself right this minute. Goddamn drug dealers don't mess aroun', girl. *You* oughta fuckin' know *that*, you stupid drug-dealin' fucker!"

I sucked my breath in, fully expecting a terrible fight to break out in my presence, but the girl named Erline didn't seem to be fazed in the least. It almost seemed as if the table full of White women were used to Pearl's cursing overreactions and had trained themselves to put up with them because she was so young and restless.

Big Charlotte only had a half reaction this time and mumbled under her breath while staring down at her cards, "'Do not take the Lord thy God's name in vain.'"

Having set Erline straight in her mind, Pearl's attention turned toward me. "Glad to meetcha," she said, sticking her hand out to shake mine. "My name's Pearl, an' if you get any fuckin' thing in the mail or from the fuckin' store here or anything, I'd like it if you'd goddamn give me some of it, OK? I'm only seventeen fuckin' years old, an' the ladies kinda take care o' me like they was my fuckin' mamas or somethin' like that. Git my drift, lady?"

I recognized Pearl almost immediately as the girl who had stirred the Kool-Aid at lunch with her whole arm. She fidgeted on her stool and swung her right foot the entire time she was talking. Her nervous little eyes darted back and forth across the big glass room, constantly checking out what the others were doing. Her shoulders twitched, and her head seemed to engage in rhythmic little jerks whenever she spoke. She apparently found the need to put her cards down quite often to enable her to rub both hands rapidly against her thighs. She often stopped and scratched every part of her as if a million bugs were crawling up her skin. It actually made me quite exhausted just to watch her unceasing display of human hyperactivity. But being a mother myself for so many years, I recognized almost immediately that poor little Pearl was actually frightened to death of her whole situation. Sure, she might have been playing the tough-guy, I-can-cuss-more-than-you-can game on the exterior, but the truth was that she was terrified as a baby rabbit on the inside.

"Hi, Pearl. My name's Doramae, and I'll be more than happy to share anything I get in the mail or buy from the store with you," I said as calmly as possible.

With that, she stopped all her nervous fidgeting, grinned really big, and declared, "Well, what er we fuckin' waitin' for? Let's play some fuckin' cards!"

Erline started to gather up all the cards that the ladies now held and shuffle them. Then she dealt them out, two for each lady. She even gave me two. "Oh, I don't really want to play cards," I said, knowing that the last game of cards I had played was probably old maid or crazy eights with my children when they were little. Bob and I just were not card players.

"Now c'mon, honey, y'all gotta do sumthin' 'round this here awful place ta keep from a-goin' crazy as a loon. We-ins is jist a-playin' twenty-one. It's reel eazy."

"I just don't play many cards. I'm not too familiar with that game," I said.

"Did y'all fuckin' hear *that*? She doesn't fuckin' even know how to fuckin' play goddamn twenty-one!" screamed Pearl. "What a fuckin' loser!"

At that, Big Charlotte jumped up and professed, "'Judge not, lest ye be judged' (Matthew 7:1)."

Moleface threw me a sharp, piercing, penetrating look with her shifty little eyes as if to say, *I don't trust anyone who can't play poker.*

But good old Erline stood fast. "Now don't yew worry yer purdy liddle haid over this here card game. Ain't no big deal. It's eazy as pie. It's lahk this a-here. Ah's the dealer, an Ah gives y'all these here cards. Whatch'all tries ta do is ta git near as y'all kin ta twenty-one without goin' over er nuthin', aw raht?"

I didn't know exactly what to do. Pearl thought I was retarded because I couldn't play twenty-one, Moleface had apparently lost all trust in me, and Big Charlotte was overconcerned with everyone's salvation, but Erline, the hillbilly, still believed in me. So for Erline's sake, I decided to try a hand. I picked up my cards. I had an eight of clubs and a six of diamonds. *That adds up to fourteen*, I thought. *That's pretty low, actually. Let's see, if I take another card and I get anything from an ace to a seven, I'll be safe. I probably better go for it.*

Erline uncovered her hand. The dealer had a jack and a five—fifteen. *I can easily beat that*, I thought.

All around me, ladies were hollering, "Hit me!" And Erline was giving them another card. I decided to get into the act.

"Hit me!" I screamed, and Erline gave me another card.

Just then Pearl started jumping up and down and yelping like a wild dog. "I fuckin' did it on the fuckin' first hand! I fuckin' got fuckin' twenty-one! See! A fuckin' queen, a fuckin' four, and a goddamn lucky seven!"

"May the Lord descend upon you in the form of a snow-white dove and calm your restless spirit, child," proclaimed Big Charlotte quietly.

Moleface picked up her third card, looked at it and then at Pearl, and disgustedly threw all three cards on the table. "I'm out," she muttered. "And can't somebodies shut her sorry-ass mouth up?"

"Whadja get? Whadja get? Turn it over. We ain't got all day, lady." Pearl was jabbering excitedly at me.

I reluctantly turned over my third card to reveal a nine of spades.

"Goddamn, you are one stupid motherfucker, lady. That adds up to twenty-three, or can't ya fuckin' add, ya dumb fuck? That's fuckin' what we *tol'* your sorry fuckin' ass *not* to do, dumbass, to go *over* twenty-one! Lady, you can't play cards worth a fuck!"

"I ain't playin' no more if *she* plays," declared Moleface, no expression whatsoever on her drawn-up little face.

"'Thou shalt love the Lord thy God with all thy heart, and with all thy soul, and with all thy mind. And thou shalt love thy neighbor as thyself' (Matthew 22:37–39)," Big Charlotte burst forth, pointing her chubby finger at Pearl and then at Moleface.

Moleface shot Big Charlotte the fish eye and then began to push her stubby arms against the table as if she was going to stand up and hit her.

All this over a stupid card game, I thought, and I wasn't quite sure what to do at this point. But at that very second, the Big Click happened, and the girls in the Big Room started to gather up their stuff and head back toward their cells.

Saved by the click, I thought, chuckling inwardly at my private joke, and I grabbed my shower stuff and headed back toward cell 303. I certainly didn't want the scary voice through the wall screaming at me to "get back to yo' cells *now*!"

It didn't take long for the Big Click to lock us all back in our cells, and I found myself alone with Scary Serena once again. She was still asleep, lying in the same position that I had left her in hours ago. I speculated how in the world *anybody* could sleep as much as she did. *Maybe she's in some kind of light semicoma*, I thought, but with my medical training, I knew better. I began to put two and two together. *Let's see. What does this all add up to? Excessive lethargy, extreme emaciation, tremors, pallor, loss of appetite, nausea, and exaggerated mood swings.*

"Oh my god!" I gasped out loud. *She's withdrawing from a powerful drug, probably crack cocaine, and she's in her early months of pregnancy.* I knew the first trimester was the most critical for the fetus. This pathetic realization almost immediately sent me into a state of deep depression. For the next God only knows how long, I lay on my miserable bunk and thought nothing but pessimistic thoughts.

This world is so fucked up, I thought, borrowing Pearl's favorite word. That helpless tiny, little baby inside Serena never asked for his mother to be strung out on drugs as he was developing all his vital organs. I knew that this baby would be born puny and unhealthy, more than likely prematurely, shaking violently because he was addicted to the same drug as his mother. I knew all this because I had researched babies that were born to drug-addicted mothers, discovering that infants born to mothers who smoked crack cocaine were very often premature, had low birth weights and low Apgar scores, and oftentimes were born with various respiratory difficulties. My deep depression stemming from my realization about Serena's baby sent me into a state of total despondency.

I'm never going to get out of this hideous place, I thought. *The truth is that, once you're in here, nobody ever gets out. I'll be stuck in the bowels of hell, the bottomless pit, the depths of purgatory forever and ever. Nobody will be able to get me out, not even the best attorney in all the world, and I'll rot in here, growing old and gray. And nobody will try to help me out of my excruciating misery, no matter how hard I beg and beg for them to end my agonizing, tormented life. The guards will just yawn, and the inmates will just laugh. And my family will eventually forget me and will find another woman to take my place as their wife and mother.*

My present state of mind dared me to curse God for this cruel, heartless reality that angelic little unborn babies could be born addicted. But just as I was tempted to curse God, Jesus, and all that I had ever been taught about the Holy Spirit, Big Charlotte's corpulent face flashed before me. "'Thou shalt love the Lord thy God with all thy heart, and with all thy soul, and with all thy mind. This is the first and the greatest commandment,'" her voice said. And I hung my head in shame, knowing it wasn't God's fault that innocent tiny babes are born addicted to their mothers' drugs. With that comforting thought, that God was not to blame, I felt a wave of pure, indescribable peace descend over my whole stressed-out, exhausted body, and I fell into a serene deep slumber.

It didn't seem like I got much time to nap before the Big Click happened once again. *I wonder what it is now*, I thought. *Gee, they never let you rest around here.*

Right then, Serena rolled over, let out that same eerie groan, sat up slowly on her bunk, rubbed her eyes, and announced, "Guess I better go try ta eat some o' this slop." She sluggishly slipped her plastic shower shoes on, stood up with great effort, and shuffled toward the door.

I couldn't believe it was time for dinner already. I wondered what time it was. I peered out the tiny slit of a window. It didn't appear to be that late in the day. Having absolutely no access to any clocks or watches felt really weird. Was I to remain in this world of the unknown time forever? I was to find out later that we ate dinner every day at four o'clock.

I too slipped on my shower shoes and headed out into the Big Room. This time, I made sure that I wasn't the first in line. By the time I got near the line, I could see that the girls in my pod didn't mess around when it came time for dinner. Most of the long line was already formed when I got there, winding up the steep stairway. I quickly took a place near the end of the line. No sooner had I done that than two sour-tempered guards in tight uniforms once again came into the Big Room, pushing the same cart as they did at lunch, only this time it was full of cafeteria-type faded yellow trays all stacked, one on top of the other.

I thought, *Oh boy, we're about to get our first decent meal today. Dinner is probably the really nice meal of the day.* I couldn't have been more wrong. I watched as the same thing went on with the large jug of Kool-Aid.

Pearl and a short Asian girl ran out of line. Each grabbed a handle of the jug and ran with it over to the wall above the toilet. Pearl once again announced, "This shit needs to be stirred." And she thrust her entire arm into the purple Kool-Aid and stirred vigorously.

"Hot damn! We got grape tonight!" Pearl declared.

One of the grumpy guards looked at us and shouted, "Y'all betta gits your sorry asses in a skrate line, or y'all ain't gettin' no suppa tahnites. Y'all hears me?"

Everyone in line reluctantly straightened the line up but seemed in no big hurry to do so.

"OK den, come get y'all's suppa, an' I don't wants ta hear no talkin'!"

Every girl took her turn dutifully holding out her hand while one of the guards slapped a scratched-up yellow tray into it and repeatedly commanded, "Keep da line movin'. I ain't got awl day!"

By the time I got my tray, most of the tables had been filled. I looked around the room. Erline, Big Charlotte, Moleface, Pearl, and the Asian girl were at one table. Bicycle, Jasmine, a short masculine-looking girl, and the monstrous girl who had stolen my sandwich at lunch were at another table. Serena sat by herself in the darkest corner, situated sideways on the stool with her legs crossed. She was staring at the food on her tray as if it were going to jump up and bite her. She had the strangest look on her face, something between puzzlement and boredom. It was almost as if she was wondering what she was supposed to do with the food. At the same time, she glared defiantly at the other girls, daring them to come anywhere near her. It was apparently working; everyone was avoiding her table like the plague.

I continued to scan the room while I walked slowly. At another table sat a well-mannered quiet redheaded lady whom I had never seen before. She sat with four other calm, silent ladies. All appeared to be very well mannered. I wished that there had been a place open at that table. I only had a couple of choices, and I had to make one quickly. I could sit with Crazy Serena or with a table full of unknown hooligans who were throwing their peas at one another every time the guards turned their heads or with Amanda and her timid short friend Ethel. I quickly chose Amanda and her friend and sat down with them at the corner table outside cell 101, which belonged to Moleface.

For the first time, I looked down at my tray. The substances staring up at me almost turned my stomach. There was a large glob of some kind of mushy material with perfect tiny squares of dark brown matter scattered throughout, two pieces of doughy white bread, no more than a teaspoonful of canned peas, and a cheap cellophane-wrapped cookie.

Amanda began to talk. "Hey, new girl, how's it goin'? Ain't much of a meal, is it? Oh well, you'll get used to it. In case you're wonderin' what that junk is, it's supposed to be noodles with some kinda meat, only they overcook the noodles by about four hours until they're pure mush. Then like it couldn't get no worse, they throw in little chunks of mystery meat to make sure we all get good and sick."

I picked up my beat-up spork and attacked the spoonful of peas. I was so happy to see a vegetable that I didn't know what to do. Then only because I had not eaten breakfast and the large girl had stolen my lunch, I began to eat the overcooked noodle concoction with much caution. I had never tasted anything like that before. The noodles were so terribly overcooked that they were about the consistency of oatmeal. The tiny pieces of "mystery meat" tasted like no other meat I had ever eaten.

Amanda was busy talking Ethel out of her dinner, only it didn't take much convincing. She would stick her dirty finger into everything on Ethel's tray and ask, "Hey, you gonna eat *that*? Well, what about *that*?"

Ethel shook her head to every question Amanda asked, allowing her to take huge scoopfuls of the horrible food from her tray and place it sloppily onto Amanda's tray. No sooner would the food get onto Amanda's tray than she would gobble it up ravenously. Amanda ate Ethel's two pieces of white bread, her spoonful of peas, and her entire glob of mushy noodles. At the same time, she was eating her own portion and eyeballing my food. I decided that, since I had not eaten hardly anything that day, I'd better eat whatever this revolting substance was for the sake of my health, if for no other reason; and I began to eat it, swallowing it quickly before I could get a chance to taste it.

"See, it ain't so bad after all," Amanda said. "You *sure* ya wanna eat *all* that stuff? I'll eat some of it if you don't want it all." And she started to push her spoon toward my tray.

I could see that sitting with aggressive Amanda was going to be very challenging. I told her quite emphatically that I wanted all my noodles but that she could have a piece of my white bread. That seemed to satisfy her, and I watched her stuff the whole piece of bread in her mouth and finish off Ethel's and her cookies in record time. I was utterly amazed at how much food a tiny, little, petite thing like her could take in. It was like she was a human eating machine or something. I knew that if I sat with her again, I would probably have no chance of eating any of my meals in peace. I understood now why nobody but Ethel would sit with her. I made a mental note not to sit with Amanda again.

When we finally got done shoveling our food in—me to keep it away from Amanda and Amanda so she could scout around for more—we ended up having a little time to talk. Naturally, Amanda talked first. "You know that cellmate o' yours is slap-ass crazy. Won't nobody go near her. They's afraid she's been cursed er somethin'. She won't get up outa bed. She won't eat. She only gets up for supper, and then she just stares at her food like it alive er somethin'. She absolutely refuses to take a shower, an' she *stink* like the devil. I tell you, there somethin' *wrong* with that girl. Won't nobody else be in a cell with her. All her cellmates done asked to be moved. You better be careful, locked up with *that* crazy lady."

I tried to act tough. "Oh, I'm not afraid of *her* one bit. There's nothing wrong with her. She's probably just depressed. Besides, it's kinda nice having the cell so quiet and all."

Amanda hung on to my every word. Then she rolled her eyes and said, "Have it your way then. I just hope she doesn't get up in the middle of the night and stick her homemade shiv through your thumpin' gizzard, like the guy who dressed up like his mama in *Psycho*." And she began to draw back her hand and thrust a make-believe knife into my chest, the whole time screeching "eeee, eeee, eeee" like the eerie music in the movie.

Just as her recreation of the twisted son at the Bates Motel was beginning to unnerve me a bit, the Big Click occurred, and we all scurried to the front of the Big Room to return our ragged yellow trays so we could go back to our cells before the guards began to threaten. Once back in my cell, locked up with Scary Serena, I wasn't quite sure how to spend my first evening in jail. There was nothing to read, no TV, very little window to look out of, and no one to converse with. Out of sheer boredom, I crawled up on my bunk and closed my eyes. As I drifted off to sleep, I wondered how in the world I was going to be able to endure this living hell for the usual six to eight weeks it took until I would go to Nutter.

DAVID AND GOLIATH

THE BIG CLICK interrupted my sleep again. I wearily climbed down from my bunk and trudged over to the door to check it out. I pushed against our door; it was locked tight. I peered out the window; a group of girls was beginning another rotation. The usual was going on—TV watching, shower taking, hair fixing, and card playing. I was not about to stand at our door for hours, observing this phenomenon again. I had seen enough to get a general picture of what went on. The only difference I could see between morning rotation and evening rotation was that the natives seemed to be much more restless at night.

One group of girls was fighting over what TV show to watch, two girls were loudly arguing over who reached the shower first, and the victims were being much more demanding of the hairdressers. Even the card players were displaying a lot more body language, jumping up off the stools every now and then to shake an angry fist or loudly declare a victory. I wondered if it was a good idea to go out into the jungle of the night people. In northern Indiana, where I grew up, the Amish folks had a popular saying when one of their own went into town or left their community for a while. It went, "Be careful out there among those English." Gazing out that cell window, I knew exactly why that saying had come to mind.

I meandered back over to the bed, totally exhausted from the immense trauma of my first day in jail. It didn't seem like I had been asleep very long before the Big Click went off again and then again and then a third time. I wondered if maybe the Big Click had a malfunction. I shuffled over to our door and gave it a little nudge. It was open. Serena was dead to the world. I decided to leave well enough alone. I put on my shower shoes and reluctantly slipped out the door, not really knowing if I had made the right decision to go out among the English.

The noise was worse than I had imagined, but there was no turning back. Once the decision was made to go out into the Big Room, you had only one little minute to change your mind because, after that, the guards locked your cell back, and the door remained locked until rotation was over. I heard my cell door click, and I knew that I now must endure whatever was to happen in the night world of the Big Room. I looked around, and I certainly didn't like what I saw, but what I heard was much more disturbing. The incessant, nonstop uproar, the brawling, the screaming, the loud cursing, the pure animalistic pandemonium of the terrifying Big Room at night made me afraid that I might be driven totally mad by the end of my first day. At first, I tried to ignore it—the noise, I mean. I was so stir crazy from being locked up in a cage like an animal that I began to do something that shocked even me. I felt this need bubbling up inside me like a giant geyser about to erupt. It was the need to move, to breathe hard, to stretch every muscle in my frightened body to its very limit. So I did the only thing I could. It was my only choice.

I kicked off my oversize shower shoes, and I began to *walk*. And I walked, and I walked frantically, pacing the round filthy Big Room floor like a caged tiger hoping to escape someday. As I paced, I hugged the grimy walls of the immense cold room so I could avoid contact with any of these subhuman creatures and be outside their circle of insane chaos and fury. I kept entirely to myself, refusing to speak to, interact with, or even acknowledge their very presence in the room. Instead, it was eyes straight ahead, feet on the floor, arms swinging frantically, my heart pounding like it would explode from my heaving chest at any moment. I was totally and completely aloof, detached, withdrawn, lost in my own little world. I was to do these insane "laps," as I called them, for the next ten days every time rotation rolled around.

At first, I did them in my bare feet. After two days, they began to crack and bleed from the trash, grit, and filthy dirt on the Big Room floor. I believed that no human being had ever attempted to clean this floor. But I never felt the sharp, grimy, jagged pieces of dirt, foil gum wrappers, pencil leads, pieces of half-eaten hard candy, chewed-up gum, or metal pieces from pens firmly embedding themselves in the bleeding soles of my feet. No, I never did because I was so caught up in my own world—a world far distant to the reality of this nightmarish turmoil, this perpetual bad dream that would not go away.

It seemed like it was the middle of the night when I was suddenly awakened by the light in our cell coming on, followed by the Big Click, which was followed closely by Amanda pushing our door open and announcing, "Breakfast, new girl, get up!"

I rubbed my eyes and looked out the skinny window. It was pitch dark outside.

"My name's Doramae, and what time is it anyhow?" I mumbled.

"Oh about four o'clock, I guess, Mean Moanin' Mae-Mae," she returned with a twinkle in her eye. "C'mon, we gotta get out there before all the other girls get the coffee."

"Do we *have* to go to breakfast?" I asked.

"Hell no, but ya wanna starve to death, girl? Around here, ya eat when they tell ya to, and ya eat every chance ya get."

I grudgingly dragged myself out of bed and followed Amanda. I wondered why she had taken it on herself to take me under her wing. We got near the front of the line. In fact, the other girls stepped aside and let Amanda get in the front. I still found myself amazed at the amount of power this little dynamo commanded from the rest of the group.

The same chain of events occurred. Two very ill-tempered guards came in, and then Pearl and the little Asian girl got the jug off the cart and put it on the wall behind the toilet. This time, the jug was full of something dark black, and Pearl did not attempt to thrust her arm into it and stir. I figured it was probably coffee. The breakfasts were on the same beat-up trays that used to be yellow. I wondered just how many decades that jail had used those same dilapidated trays, and judging by the general filthiness of the entire jail, I wondered too just how thoroughly they were ever washed.

The guards thrust a tray and a warm carton of milk into each of our hands, and then Amanda motioned for me to follow her. I knew that she was probably planning to cunningly steal all my food, but I didn't know what else to do. I was afraid of most of the other girls, and she seemed to be a guardian angel of sorts. We sat at the same table, right outside Moleface's cell. I figured that Amanda probably did that on purpose to establish her territory since no other girl dared to go so close to the forbidden cell.

I glimpsed down at my tray. It actually looked better than supper had. It looked like a scoop of scrambled eggs, a huge portion of grits, a little chunk of Spam-like meat, and the usual two pieces of doughy white bread. This time, the tray contained a small packet of grape jelly and two packets of sugar. It might have looked better, but when I began to taste it, the whole breakfast turned my stomach. The eggs were ice cold and watery with large hunks of yellow powder throughout them. *These are* powdered *eggs, and they didn't even mix the powder up good,* I thought. I picked up the meatlike substance and took a nibble, but the stench alone made me nauseous, so I threw it back down. I started to spread the jelly on one of the pieces of white bread, until I noticed both of them were moldy around the crust. I opened my milk and took a sip. It was warm and sour. I checked the expiration date on the carton; it had expired five days ago.

By this time, Amanda had made a trip to the jug and brought us both back a plastic cup full of coffee. I picked the coffee up and swirled it around; it was black as tar and thick as molasses. I took a sip. It was the most awful coffee I had ever tasted, but at least it was a little bit warm. *At least one thing around here is the right temperature,* I thought.

Amanda was watching my every move. She had already shoveled in most of her own food and swallowed it whole. *Maybe that's the best way to eat this mess,* I thought.

"Ain't cha gonna eat chur eggs?" she asked. "And what about chur mystery meat? You don't like that *lovely* cuisine that our cooks have so lovingly created for us?" She let out a huge belly laugh.

"You'll get used to it. You gotta, or you'll starve. May I, dahling?" she asked, pointing to my eggs and mystery meat. "You don't want your bread neither?"

I shook my head.

"This shit makes the best egg sandwiches," she declared. Then she piled all my eggs onto the two pieces of bread, stuck the mystery meat on top, squeezed the rest of my grape jelly over the entire creation, and stuffed it in her little mouth. It was all gone in about three bites.

As she chewed with her mouth wide open, she took a sudden notion to educate me about the mystery meat. "This shit here's made outa pig peckers, guts, brains, tongues, snouts, ears, tails, and ground-up hooves. Shit, any part that *normal* folks would throw to the dogs, we get the out-and-out privilege of being served as a culinary delight at the fuckin' Coward County Concentration Camp."

I was still in shock over how unbelievably fast she could swallow anything. I was also in shock over her command of the English language. No one else around here was anywhere near this verbally expressive, nor was their vocabulary as extensive.

"From now on, you better save your packages of sugar and jelly if you know what's good for ya. Just stick them in your shirt pocket, like this, and sneak 'um back into the cell. They come in handy later, OK?" I couldn't believe that she was giving me little pointers to help me survive this living hell. She was the first person who had cared one bit at all, except for Angelica. Something told me, though, that Amanda had a personal agenda in her attempt to appear caring. She wanted to trick me out of my food each and every meal.

I tested the temperature of the grits, the one and only food item remaining on my tray. They were semiwarm, so I mixed one of the packets of sugar into them, placed the second packet of sugar in my pocket, and ate the grits quickly, alternating bites with gulping the horrible coffee for the sole purpose of getting something warm into my stomach.

I felt Amanda's eyes on me as I was forcing my repulsive breakfast down. She seemed to be eyeballing my oversize orange top that had fallen off my shoulders earlier. "We get new suits every Friday morning. Make sure ya ask for a four- or five-dot one this time. You're downright *pitiful* in that thing. And somethin' else, we fill out orders for commissary every Thursday for stuff we get the next Monday. Come to me, an' I'll help ya fill out yer order. But make sure somebody puts some money into yer account right now, or it'll be too late to show on the books for next week, OK?"

"What's commissary?" I asked.

"Honey chile, you got *a lot* to learn about bein' a jailbird." She laughed. "Commissary is the store here at the jail. The assholes here don't allow you to bring anything in with ya, an' they don't allow anybody to send ya anything. That way, yer forced ta buy everything ya need from their store, and the jail makes all kinds of money 'cuz they overcharge like the devil for every damn thing. Get it?"

"So I have to buy everything from their store here?"

"You got it, baby. You get yer necessities. They get yer family's money."

"What kinds of things do they have that I can buy?"

"Well, you name it, they got it and at double the price it would go for on the outside, sista—shampoo, *real* soap and toothpaste, hairbrushes, nail files, deodorant, lotion, paper to write home on, stamps, envelopes, pens, pencils, an' all kinds o' clothes—white T-shirts, panties, bras, socks, tennis shoes. But the best stuff on commissary list is the *food*. They got all kinds o' good junk—chips, candy, cookies, peanut butter, sweet rolls. *Shit*! Some o' the girls around here *live* on their commissary if they got someone who loves 'em enough to keep puttin' plenty o' spendin' loot in their account."

"So let me get this straight. I have to get my husband to put some money in my account *today* so I can order all that stuff this coming Thursday, but I don't get any of it till a week from Monday?"

"Honey, I don't care if Santa Claus puts money in yer account. Just get some-damn-body ta do it."

"How much ya reckon I need?" I asked, trying to talk more like her.

"Hey, ya don't get it yet, do ya? You musta led a very sheltered life or some such shit. However much ya can con yer old man outa, that's how damn much ya put in. This is the beauty of the whole thing. There ain't no damn limit, so it's always a good fuckin' idea ta have him put in a whole shit potful the first week while he still feels sorry fer ya and shit. Ya know what I mean, before he starts gettin' fed up with the whole fuckin' situation and shit—ya know, before he stops comin' ta see ya an' all that holy shit. Oh yeah, an' one more thing, it's always a *damn* good idea ta get all the money outa him ya can before he finds his sneaky-ass little self a cute little ho on the side to keep his ass company while yer in an' all." She threw back her little head and let out a cackle like an amused witchwoman.

My heart sank, and my empty stomach churned. I had not even included that fear in all my pessimistic possibilities. The prospect of my beloved husband giving up on me and running into the arms of another woman was more than I could bear. I could barely squeeze out the words "How much do you think I need if I want to buy some clothes, toiletries, and writing stuff?"

"Girl, you just ain't gonna give up, are ya? OK, have him put one hundred fifty damn dollars in for ya. That oughta be a good start anyhow."

Just then, the Big Click took place, and the weary girls straggled off to their awaiting cells. "Don't forget ta let me help ya fill out that form now, Mean Mae-Mae!" she called after me, and somehow I knew that she was going to sneak in a few items that she wanted on my order.

Seeing that it was probably only about four thirty in the morning, I returned promptly to my upper bunk and had no trouble at all going back to sleep. But I had an entire dreamathon of very disturbing nightmares full of caged wild animals and straying husbands, so I awoke with a start, my heart racing. I was lying on my stomach. I raised my head just in time to see the most gorgeous sight outside the tiny slit of a window. The morning sun was a giant bright, flaming orange ball, and it was rising behind Rock Mountain. "Oh my god!" I gasped, halfway out loud. "I can see Rock Mountain perfectly from my cell window."

Now Rock Mountain is a beautifully rounded huge mound of pure stone rising out of nowhere. It is located a few miles north of Atlanta, and it has always remained a local sort of mystery. One man was so thoroughly intrigued by the enigma that he devoted most of his life to carving larger-than-life replicas of the Confederate leaders on one side of the mountain. Bob and I had taken our kids to visit Rock Mountain several times when they were little; we had even climbed up the side of it. I never in a million years would have guessed that, one day, I would be looking at it from a jail cell window.

I continued to watch that first sunrise. I cannot put into words how radiantly that crimson ball shone, how gloriously it lit up the mountain, how brilliantly the early morning heavens exploded with color. My eyes remained glued to that little dirty window, from the time a tiny sliver of orange peeked from behind the mountain until the full circle of splendorous colors shone down from the very peak.

Then it suddenly hit me. It was no coincidence that my cell window was a perfect picture frame for Rock Mountain, nor was it a coincidence that I had awakened that first morning just in time to privately witness this amazing phenomenon. No, it was no coincidence; this was nothing short of a miracle. The sunrise that I had just observed was God's handwriting; it was his way of communicating with me. He was telling me that all would be well, that I was never alone in this, that he was with me every step of the way. Tears came to my eyes, and I said a silent prayer. I vowed to never miss a single sunrise while I was stuck in that den of iniquity.

I felt the sudden urge to hug someone or something. I most certainly was not about to hug Serena, and I couldn't hug my pillow because I didn't have one, so I reached around my whole mattress and gave it a good big bear hug. While I was doing this, I felt something up underneath my mattress. I pulled it out to discover a small religion-based magazine entitled *Guideposts*. I recognized it as a publication of the Baptist Church. I began to thumb through it; it was full of stories that people had written about miracles that had occurred in their lives. I wondered if I should write in about what had just happened to me— once I got paper and a pen, that is. I read the little magazine twice cover to cover because I was just that thrilled to have *anything* to read.

But my eyes were really bothering me that second morning. I had not pulled my contacts out yet because I had no place to put them at night. The guards had refused to let Mom or Bob bring me my contact solution or case. I wasn't sure what to do, but I knew that if I left them in too many more nights without taking them out or at least cleaning them, I would get a terrible eye infection.

While I was still contemplating what to do, I heard the Big Click, so I decided to get down off the bunk and try our door. It was open.

I quickly made my bed, grabbed my shower stuff, and went out the door. I told myself that I had to somehow figure out when it was time for my rotation.

Big Charlotte was sitting at a table across the room, and she motioned for me to come over. "Praise the Lord," she declared. "And what a glorious day his hands have created today!" She didn't know how very true that was for me that particular day.

"You'll have to excuse me this morning. I can hardly see anything 'cuz I wear contacts, and these people won't let my family bring me my contact solution, my case, or another pair of contacts. I can't take them out 'cuz I'm totally blind without them."

"And from out of the darkness, he shall lead you, and he shall show you the Way. Sweet child, I know the solution to your problem, for I wear contacts myself. The good Lord has brought you here to me today. They offer contact solution on the commissary list, but that don't do you no good until a week from Monday, so listen up. At lunchtime today, take you two plastic cups instead of one and then sneak them back into your room. At supper tonight, you should get a couple of packets of salt on your tray. Put 'em in your pocket and take them into your room. Then before you go to bed tonight, add one packet of salt to a couple of inches of water in each cup, mark one R for right and one L for left, pull those suckers out, and store them overnight in homemade salt water. And don't forget to say your prayers before you lay your sweet little head down to sleep."

All of a sudden, one of the guards' voices boomed over the loudspeaker. "Doramae Buhrockshir, you got visit."

This time, I knew what that meant. I jumped up from the table and started toward the door.

"'This is the day that the Lord hath made. Let us rejoice and be glad in it!'" she called after me.

When I got to the glass room for visitation, I could see Mom, Bob, and Dave on the other side of the thick glass. This time, I didn't cry though. I talked and talked like there was no tomorrow. I told Mom how it would be eight more days before I could get any clean underwear or socks, how the meals were all starches and no fruits or vegetables, and how I was going to make homemade contact solution. I told Dave what the mystery meat was made of, how there were no books to read anywhere, and all about the bizarre card game I was a part of yesterday. I told Bob how much I loved him and missed him and asked him to please put $150 in my account today. I didn't tell anyone about the rapturous sunrise over Rock Mountain that I had witnessed. That would remain my secret—for a while anyhow.

Before I knew it, their ninety minutes was up, and Dave and Mom were waving goodbye and throwing kisses because they were on their way back to Indiana as soon as they left. I got up to return to my cell, downtrodden because I knew it would be the last time that I would see my mom and Dave for quite a while.

As I was dragging myself toward the door, a guard's voice boomed. "Go sit back down. You gots somebody else."

I did as I was told and returned to my seat.

After a few seconds, in walked Jack and Jan. Jack took the stool first. "You OK?" he asked. He looked like he had had a rough night. His hair was tousled, his shirt was crumpled, and big black circles were under his bloodshot eyes. He was so pale that he looked like he was going to be sick. As soon as I smiled and reassured him that I was OK, he began to talk nonstop about the trial, especially the jurors.

"The jurors could not believe it when Judge Grudge called them back in and told them that you pleaded guilty. They were in pure shock. I've never seen anything like it. They hung around, talking to me. They even helped me carry all my stuff down to my car. Jan and I tried to get some feedback on what they were thinking, how it would have gone if we had been given a chance. You know what? We would have either won an acquittal, or at the very worst, we would have had a hung jury. Remember the little Black guy in the front row? He was a huge fan of ours. He was 100 percent convinced of your innocence. And the blond lady who owned the restaurant, she was totally supportive of us too. And do you remember the young guy who said he might be prejudiced at jury selection because he had so many friends who worked in dental offices? Well, he followed me all around, asking questions and conveying supportive statements that his friends had told him about the case. Hell, he was so into it all that I almost had to ask him to leave in the parking lot when I was ready to go. You had a lot of fans on the jury. Yep, we would have won had we chosen to go on, but the choice the judge gave us almost forced us to quit. In thirty-three years of practice, I've never seen anything that reprehensible. That is, without a doubt, the most unethical behavior from a judge, the best example of judicial misconduct I have ever seen."

His characteristically boyish face suddenly looked drawn and old, and his eyes looked tired and no longer full of fight. He turned his attention back toward me. "They treatin' you OK in there? Just do everything they say, and we'll be working every day on this end to get you out of here and into Nutter as soon as we can, OK? You were a real trouper in that courtroom. I know it was hard on you, but you came through. I love you, lady. Hang in there."

With that, he held his large hand up to the glass, and I held mine up on the other side to meet his. He dropped his big head down, shaking it, and it looked for a second like he was going to cry.

Jan came over to his phone briefly and announced, "We're on our way back to Tanaha. If you need anything, give us a call." Then with a wave of both their hands, they were gone.

I got up to go back to the cell. I was glad Jack had come to see me. It made me feel like he was more than just my lawyer.

By the time I got back to my cell, my rotation was over. Soon it was time for lunch. It was the exactly the same as the day before, only this time Amanda got my mystery meat sandwich instead of the big fat girl. I figured it was worth Amanda stealing most of my food to be able to pump her for information during meals. After all, she was the only one around there who would talk to me about such things. I started right in. "What do they call this big room anyhow?" I asked.

"Girl, if yer goin' to survive around here, you'd better learn the lingo quick. This big glass cage where the monkeys misbehave, our only taste of freedom—it's called the dayroom. Don't ask me why. Half the time when we're out there, it's *night*. And I guess you noticed we take turns comin' out. It's called rotation."

"Yeah, how does that work exactly?" I asked.

"This really *is* yer first time in jail, ain't it? Well, the first rotation is at nine o'clock or so, and it lasts till lunch around eleven. The second one is around one o'clock, and it lasts till about three. Now every other day, we alternate with which one we get. Then we always get a second one every night. The first is at seven. The second's at nine. Then it's night night at eleven."

"How do they figure out who takes the turns?" I asked.

"You ain't noticed how they do that yet, girl? It's real simple. The downstairs cells are always on rotation together, and the upstairs cells are together, only we don't like to call them cells. That's too depressing. We call them 'our little houses.'" Then she added, "Yep, you'd better get used to this here dayroom. It's the only time you get to move around. They're supposed to let us get fresh air every day, but the guards are too damn lazy to take us down to the rec room."

I was really interested in this. "Tell me about the rec room," I inquired.

"Girl, you just *full* of curiosity, ain't ya? If I keep answering these jail questions, I'm gonna need more sustenance to keep me goin'. I'll answer that one for yer cookie."

Even though it was the only thing on my plate I was going to eat, I really wanted to know about the chance to get fresh air, so I reached over and gave her my cellophane-wrapped cookie.

"Well, it's like this. The rec room is a big room just down the hall. It's got concrete floors, two basketball goals, and a really high ceiling."

"But what about the fresh air?" I whined.

"Jeez, I was getting to that. The top half of the outside wall has fence and shit all over it, but that's what it is. It's open to the outside world, girl. It's no big deal. It's not like we can get out or nothin'. All that fence and shit's really kinda depressin' anyhow. It reminds us of how *unfree* we really are." She paused. "Don't worry about it. Like I said, the guards don't never drag their sorry asses over to take us there anyhow, even though state regulations say we're supposed to get fresh air every day."

I was about to ask her how they could get away with that, but just then, the Big Click happened, and everyone dispersed back to their "little houses."

At one o'clock rotation that day, I decided to get my exercise while I waited for a shower. I looked around. Erline, Pearl, Big Charlotte, and Moleface were playing cards. Bicycle, the fat girl who stole my cookie, a little, short Black girl who looked just like a twelve-year-old boy, and Jasmine were watching a soap opera on TV, and several others were playing hairdresser and victim. I decided to play a game with myself.

I would set a number of laps to accomplish every rotation, and I would increase them a little every day. I told myself that first priority while I was locked away like an animal was to keep myself healthy. No one else around there certainly cared if I lived or died, and something told me that no help would be there for me if I got sick. So I kicked off my shower shoes and, once again, began to walk rapidly around the dayroom, picking up the pace as I went. I tried really hard to avoid bothering anyone, but that was a little difficult because the tables were close to the perimeter of the room, the cell doors were right at the perimeter, and the backs of the two showers were close to where I had to walk. But the two places that I began to get the dirtiest looks as I paced around the room were at the telephones and around the TV.

The three phones were against the back wall, and they were, by far, the most popular feature of the dayroom. At the beginning of every rotation, girls literally *ran* to grab a phone, and they would talk the entire rotation as long as the poor fool on the other end would pay the exorbitant collect-call prices. I learned later that the prices charged to the party on the other end of a county jail phone in the state of Georgia were about four times the rates for the general public. And there was no getting around it if one was in jail. The one and only way to call *anyone* on the outside was to call them collect, and then the unbelievably steep prices of the county jail kicked in. It was as if the jails in this state had their own little monopoly on setting phone prices.

After I learned this, I tried really hard not to call anyone while I was in jail. Why put such an unnecessary expense on my loved ones? Besides, I wasn't about to fight these girls for their precious phones.

Probably the worst fights I saw while incarcerated were fights over whose turn it was to use the phone. Anyhow, while I was doing my laps, it was always really congested around the phones; oftentimes there were even long lines waiting to use them. I had to be really careful not to bump into anyone.

The second place where it was a little tricky while doing laps was coming around the corner where the back of the TV was. See, the TV was kinda large, and it was mounted up from the ceiling so that all ten of the girls who sat in the chairs could see it except the person who mounted it put it at a really stupid height because the bottom of it was only about five feet off the floor, making it really easy for someone who was five feet six to bump into. To make matters worse, it was close enough to the wall that it was nearly impossible to squeeze between it and the wall. So every time I came around that corner, I had to time it so that I could duck under the TV.

Now it was near the end of my hundred laps, and I was getting really tired. I came close to bumping into a girl at the phones who was not paying attention and walked right out in front of me. For the last fifty laps, every time I ducked under the TV, Bicycle said, "Dat White lady really be gettin' on mah mudderfuckin' nerves," each time a little louder.

Then it happened on lap number 98. I couldn't help it; I was just so exhausted, and I knew I only had two laps to go. I got a little careless when I rounded that corner, and instead of ducking under the TV with the great coordination I had exhibited in the last 97 laps, I ran right smack dab into the back of that sucker. I stopped for a second. The TV had cut off. My head felt like it was splitting open. I held my breath, waiting to see what would happen. The four girls who were watching TV sat for a second or two, dumbfounded. Then Bicycle jumped up and started shaking her fist at me. I decided I had better get out of there—and fast. I began walking, doing my laps faster than ever.

"You see wha' da *fuck* ya did, honky! It was jis' gettin' to da good part, and yer mudderfuckin' White ass go an' fuckin' hit da mudderfuckin' TV! Wha' da fuck wrong wit' ya anyhows? Ya ass all da tahm walkin' an' walkin' like ya some mudderfuckin' retard or somet'in'. Hey! Cracka!

Don' chew walk away from me when I's mudderfuckin' talkin' to ya! Ah'll beat ya mudderfuckin' ass!"

She was shaking her fist violently and had puffed up her whole manly body like a Florida blowfish. She was alternating between trying to fix the back of the TV and taking giant masculine steps toward me. I continued to walk my laps and was now halfway across the dayroom from her, my heart pumping wildly. I was trying to figure out what I was going to do when it came time in a few seconds for me to pass by the TV again.

This is it, I thought. *I'm going to get killed by Bicycle my second day in jail, and the guards won't even bother to lift a finger to come and see about it.*

Just as I rounded the corner near the table where my new friends were playing cards, Pearl threw a whole plastic cup full of ice-cold water in my face as she was pretending to concentrate on her cards. I tried my best to look as if it didn't bother me and to continue walking, in short to act as if nothing had just happened. But the water was so very cold and the whole idea of someone just throwing a cupful of water directly in my face on purpose was so foreign that I know I gasped audibly and probably also gave Pearl the exact facial expression she wanted. "Oh god! Lady, I'm so fuckin' sorry. My fuckin' hand slipped on this fuckin' slippery-ass cup," Pearl stated.

Moleface, Erline, and Big Charlotte all looked down at their cards and began to snicker. "Way ta go, liddle Pearl. Dat lady makes me fuckin' crazy." Moleface chuckled.

Suddenly, Big Charlotte had a change of heart. She jumped up off her stool and held her chubby hand in the air. "And the wicked in his pride doth persecute the poor. His mouth is full of cursing and deceit and fraud. Under his tongue is mischief and vanity!' (Psalm 10:2, 7)." She divided her glares between Bicycle and Pearl, but neither was paying her any attention at all.

I held my head up high. I knew all eyes were on me, watching to see how I would react. I knew I had to keep walking to show all the girls in rotation how tough I was, or I would be labeled the Little Wimp of SE303 forever. I didn't dare reach up and wipe the water from my face.

Instead, I allowed it to drip down off my face and onto my neck and trickle down the front of my orange suit. I could feel my chest getting wet and my heart pounding like a drum. I didn't know what to do next. There was no place to escape. It was the middle of a rotation, and all the cell doors were locked tight.

I suddenly found myself wishing that I had stayed behind with Scary Serena. At least then I probably wouldn't be facing murder at the moment, I reasoned. My basic instincts kicked in. I knew that if it really came down to a physical altercation, I would lose miserably and within a short period. I was twice as old as Bicycle and half as strong.

I rounded the corner that passed by the TV. Bicycle, Jasmine, the fat girl who stole my lunch, and the little boyish girl were all gathered around the back of the TV, turning knobs and tugging at wires. Bicycle was watching me from the corner of her wicked left eye. I drew in a deep breath and closed my eyes, waiting for the inevitable to come next. *She'll probably knock me out cold with the first blow, and I won't even feel a thing until I wake up in the hospital, that is, if anyone around here bothers to take me to the hospital,* I thought.

As I approached her, I sucked in my breath and closed my eyes. I didn't especially want to see my own murder. Then suddenly, from out of nowhere, Amanda appeared. "This stupid motherfuckin' screen go blank on ya again?" She motioned for Bicycle to come around to the front of the TV. "The piece of shit did that to me the other day. Wanna see how to fix it? It's around here at one of the knobs in the front."

Bicycle glared at her as if she only halfway believed her story. But her curiosity was high enough; plus, she was missing her soap opera, so she reluctantly dragged herself to the front of the TV. The other three girls moved around to the front with her as if they were playing follow the leader. Amanda had managed to get all four of the girls out of my way just in the nick of time. I was able to swish right past the back of the TV, with them barely noticing me.

I passed by the TV just in time to see Amanda reach behind it and wiggle a wire that subsequently made it come back on. But the funny thing was this—she never took her right hand off the knob on the front of the TV, capturing her audience's total attention the whole time she fixed it with her left hand from behind. "There," she announced. "That damn knob must have a loose connection or somethin'."

The four girls sat back down in front of the TV and quickly became mesmerized by their silly drama. Amanda looked across the room and winked at me. I decided to skip my one hundredth lap and sat down at the table farthest away from Bicycle and her crew. I picked a table that was not too close to Pearl either. This place was just too foreign to me. I began to have serious doubts about whether I would ever be able to survive.

Just as I was having one tremendous pity party for myself, I happened to realize that I had picked a table that was right outside the two showers. As I was looking down at the floor, I noticed something quite peculiar. It was a long silver brace with a tennis shoe and a prosthetic foot in it, and it was standing straight up all by itself outside one of the showers. *Angelica!* I thought. *Oh my god! That poor thing has to take her foot off to take a shower.* I tried my best to picture poor Angelica, seventeen years old, balancing on one foot to take a shower for the rest of her life. And I was suddenly ashamed of myself and my petty fears.

After my close call with Bicycle, I soon learned to avoid any situation whatsoever that involved drawing attention to myself. I started to make a different pattern with my laps, avoiding the area of the TV altogether. I quickly began to acquire animalistic instincts, able to detect any kind of trouble that might result from any moves I made or things I said. In short, I was forced to become somewhat like all of them, sleeping with one eye open and never letting down my guard.

VISITS FROM HOME

T HE DAYS BEGAN to pass, and one miserable day ran into another. I decided to keep a journal, only I had to borrow some notebook paper and a pencil from Amanda to do so. In my journal entry dated May 21, 1999, I wrote:

> Day after lonely day goes by in this rathole, and it is always the same routine. I almost have it memorized. Get up at four thirty in the morning to *try* to swallow some of the most god-awful food on this planet. This is followed by being locked back in our tiny cramped cells until it is time for our "rotation." Now rotation means that one-half of us are allowed to come out of our nasty little cells and venture forth into what is called the dayroom. The dayroom is round with glass swooping all around it so the outside guards in the tower can watch us twenty-four hours a day. Its ceiling is high, with metal rafters going every which way, like a giant bird's nest. Every little noise seems to be magnified a million times because of this mammoth boom box of a room. The trick to the whole thing is this: when the guards open your cell door for rotation, you have exactly one minute to decide if you are coming out or staying in. Actually, the choice is between that of slowly going insane from being caged day after lonely day and being driven totally mad by the incessant, nonstop uproar, the brawling, screaming, pure animalistic pandemonium of the terrifying dayroom.

The only thing that saved my sanity was visitation. Bless my family and friends. I would owe them for the rest of my life. They all apparently got together and made up some kind of schedule or something where they took turns coming to visit me. There was only one day the entire twenty-two days I was incarcerated at the Coward County Jail that I did not have at least one visitor. The rules said that Bob could come see me three times a week for 30 minutes each session or two times a week for 90 minutes each session. Of course, since one of these visitation times added up to 90 minutes a week and the other choice added up to 180 minutes a week, this was a no-brainer.

At first, we were a little concerned that we were only going to be able to see each other twice a week, but the whole place was so utterly disorganized that he ended up sneaking in to see me about three to four times a week. One day near the beginning, he came in visibly laughing to himself. When I asked him what was so funny, he said that he had just asked the guard who was signing him in if he would have 90 minutes' visitation that day, and she replied, "Oh, no, you don't get no 90 minute. You jist gets an hour and a half is all."

After a while, all that mattered were the few precious moments every day that a visitor came to bring me news of the outside world, of my precious world before it got so turned upside down. Near the beginning of my stay in hell, lots of friends came to see me. I could usually tell by the look on their faces that the main reason they had come was to see if I had indeed kept my sanity. And another thing that really got to me was this—every single female friend who came to visit me was crying when I first sat down to talk to her, *every single one*. I did not know quite how to interpret this, coming from a world inside that dared never show female emotion or weakness. Were my friends feeling that sorry for me? Were they scared for my safety? Did they feel that they could never face me again and they were crying for the end of a friendship? Or did they, like me, realize the outrageous injustice, the horrible wrong that had been done to me?

Early one Sunday morning, Paula showed up for visitation. When I first walked in, I was absolutely taken aback that she somehow managed to break away from her unbearable situation at home. I wondered who was watching her three young children. I took my stool in front of her and picked up the phone. Upon seeing me in my orange suit, she burst out sobbing. She was crying so uncontrollably that I thought it best for me to speak first and try to calm her. "Hey, Paula, what the hell ya doin' here so early on a Sunday? And where are the kids? How'd ya find this place?"

She stopped bawling long enough to answer some of my questions. "I just had to come see you to see if you're OK." She sniffled. "The kids are fine. I left them asleep in a hotel with Chucky. I had to come to a dental seminar in Atlanta this weekend. I told Chucky that I had to go pick up some diapers for Rachel at Walmart. I can't stay long, or he'll catch me."

I took a good long look at her. Her eyes were red and puffy as if she had been crying for a very long time. She had attempted once again to cover two bruises on her face, one under her left eye and one on the opposite cheekbone, with layers of makeup. She was visibly nervous; her eyes darted around the place as if she expected someone to grab her at any moment. Little beads of sweat were forming on her forehead. Her hands were shaking uncontrollably. A sudden thought went through my mind. *Some folks are in jail literally for a few months. Others are in jail figuratively for a lifetime.*

I knew right away that I had to put Paula's mind at ease about my situation and, more importantly, that I had to act once again as her anchor in the storm. Yes, here I was, sitting in my jailhouse orange, shower shoes hanging off my feet, and I had to calm *her* down. I started with humor because that almost always worked on her. "The accommodations around here are great. The beds have big plush mattresses, they let you sleep till noon, and the food is superb. Besides, these guys really know what color looks good on a gal," I said with a grin, tugging on my huge orange top. "And they have personal tailors so they get your clothing and shoe sizes just right." I held up my foot and shook it at her through the window.

My plan had worked. She was beaming from ear to ear, and a look of pure relief spread momentarily across her frightened face. "Oh god, Dora, I thought I would come up here, and you would be stark raving mad by now or something," she confessed. "I just had to see that you were all right for myself. How the hell can you sit there and act just like your old self? Aren't you afraid to be here?"

She didn't know the half of it. I wanted to tell her about Bicycle and how I almost got my life snuffed out over a TV. I wanted to tell her about how the girls took showers and the card game and the Kool-Aid, about Pearl and her nonstop cursing, about Big Charlotte and her nonstop Bible quoting, about Scary Serena, and about the mighty little hero who saved me from Goliath. I wanted to tell her that I was locked up with murderers and bank robbers and thieves. But instead, I just grinned like a Cheshire cat and said, "Nah, it's just kinda like goin' to the circus."

As soon as she saw that all was as well as could be expected at Coward County Jail, she announced that she had better go because she was now going to have to really go buy diapers to legitimize her absence. I sat there on the other side of the glass wall and watched her calm, happy face turn back into that of a terrified, confused, lost soul, and I wept silently inside for all the injustices of the world.

Another time, late into our evening rotation, Kristy Cooke showed up. She, like Paula, was crying when I sat down at the window. My first thought was how out of character it was for Kristy to be crying; she was always such a tough guy on the outside. She was holding a newspaper article, waving it in the air. As soon as she got a hold of herself, she said, "I thought you might like to hear about the outside news. Here's an article about what happened at Heritage High School yesterday, right here in Atlanta."

"What happened?" I asked, expecting the worst.

"A sixteen-year-old kid opened fire with two guns on his fellow classmates," she replied. "No one was killed, but several were hurt and some pretty badly."

I couldn't believe what I had just heard. This school shooting in Atlanta was almost one month to the day after the horrible, tragic school shooting at Columbine High School in Colorado. That school massacre had left twelve students tragically murdered. What kind of insanity was going on in the world today? This was just what I needed to hear while I was locked up with thugs who all felt as at home with a sawed-off shotgun as with a cup of coffee. On the other hand, the "authorities" might very well discover that these teenaged school shooters were sons of mothers who were in jail for petty crimes.

"Oh, that's *awful*!" I exclaimed. "I hope they will all be OK. Why are all these kids shooting people at their schools lately?"

She didn't answer my question but instead changed the subject. "Why, why, *why* did you plead guilty, Doramae? What were you thinking?" she demanded.

My shocked voice came out like a timid mouse. "Haven't you talked to Bob? Didn't he explain what the judge did to us?" I asked her.

"Well, yeah, but you could have *still* gone on with the trial. You would have won. After all, you were innocent."

I had nothing more to say to her. I found myself at a total loss of words. There was no way to explain what went on that day in the courtroom. The shock of what we were being asked to decide, the rushed decision, the shame, the grief, the ripping out of five people's hearts, and the ultimate disappointment, that of realizing forever the true unjustness and crookedness of the American system through and through.

Knowing that Dr. DeVout had also been an integral part of her own recent courtroom incident and having remembered that she told me in her own words that he had "lied his ass off" during that, I decided to shift gears on her. "Hey, Kristy, I wish you could have seen what Jack did to Dr. DeVout. He caught him showing the jury the wrong tooth, and he turned him into a babbling idiot. I wish you could have been there. It was really something to see. At one point, he had dropped about a hundred X-rays on the floor, and he was crawling on his hands and knees, mumbling to himself, 'It's here somewhere. I'll find it.' Another time, he told the jury, 'Why am I trying to tell y'all anything to do with dentistry? You're only the jury.' I'm not kiddin' you. It was like a circus, and Dr. DeVout was Bozo the Clown. You know what? This was almost worth coming to jail for, to be able to see these buffoons exposed for what they really are."

I thought that would satisfy her or maybe even get her started on a different subject. But instead, she just shook her head and looked at the ground. "Unbelievable," she muttered. "Totally and truly unbelievable. Somebody has got to get the guts to stop this." She seemed to be in a permanent funk.

I got the definite feeling that I had been her last hope in this whole twisted mess, and now even I had let her down by her way of thinking.

The state dental board had made a practice of closely scrutinizing female dentists' practices, and Kristy had been no exception. The good-old-boy system in the state of Georgia had shown up unannounced one day in her office, messed with her, and charged her with bullshit allegations; and when she didn't cower down to the boys, they had dragged her to court and put her through a living hell that they would never dare put a male dentist through.

"A guy I've known for years who recently turned into a preacher will probably come by to see you. I told him about you," she said with no emotion whatsoever. "I'd better go. Did I tell you I'm pregnant again? The doctor doesn't want me to overexert myself since I've had the seven miscarriages."

"That's super!" I exclaimed. "Take really good care of yourself this time, and I know everything will turn out just fine. I'll keep you in my thoughts and prayers. Is Ryan excited?"

For the first time, her disappointed face lit up. "Oh yes, we're both absolutely elated about this baby. I can feel it. This one's going to be the one. We're finally going to get our baby." With that, she threw me a kiss and waved goodbye. "I'll be up to see you later on my first day off, OK? Take care of yourself."

I watched her walk away. She never came back to see me. I never heard from her again. Months later, I learned somehow that she had lost this baby too and that the doctors had told her to quit trying.

Still another visitation I could distinctly remember was when my good friend Liz came to see me on a Thursday night. She looked as if she was going to burst into tears as soon as she saw me in my jailhouse orange. A couple of jokes from me and a few stories later, she looked relieved, and she was able to speak. "Sorry, I'm so late, but Jeremiah called me and was going to ride up here with me. I waited and waited, but he never showed. I tried to call, but no one answered."

My heart sank. I would have loved to see my son. I hadn't really been around him for what seemed like a very long time. I had pretty much ignored him the weeks that I had been preparing for the trial, and then he had not shown up for a single day at the trial. I knew how very sensitive he was deep inside, even though what he presented to the world was a very tough-guy exterior. The mother in me began to worry, but putting Liz's mind at ease was my immediate task at hand. "I'm sorry he did that to you, but you know Jeremiah. He probably just had a change of heart. He never showed for the trial. I think he just can't take all this."

She must have sensed my worry because she quickly got a hold of herself and changed the subject quite intentionally. "Look what I brought you," she said, putting a clipped newspaper article against the window that separated us. "They're sticking up for you. *Finally*, somebody is showing guts enough to stand by you."

I struggled to read the headlines. They read, "Jailed Literacy Director to Retain Job." I squinted really hard so I could read the rest of the article. "A local woman who was the director of the Literacy Volunteers of America [LVA] in Goat Valley was sentenced to three months at the woman's detention center in Nutter after pleading guilty for Medicaid fraud. The charges stem from the years 1993 to 1995, when she had a private dental practice here in town. She was indicted in 1997 for Medicaid fraud and theft by taking. Several members of her literacy board gathered recently in her defense. Faye Bowen, a longtime board member, stated, 'Doramae has worked very hard and has really turned this program around. As far as we are all concerned, she has her job back as soon as she gets out.' Harriette Rowe added, 'We are all behind Doramae and are praying for her. We want her to come back to her job with LVA.'"

I was so touched that someone during this whole horrible nightmare was still on my side and still believed in me. I read on, though, and the article became more like my earlier articles in our lovely *Goat Valley Gazette*. "Dr. Brookshire had served a three-month suspension for quality of care back in 1991–1992. She was also indicted for involuntary manslaughter after a three-year-old patient died in her dental office in January 1995. These charges are still pending. She is currently being held in the Coward County Jail, awaiting transfer to the women's detention center in Nutter."

"That's a pretty nice article" was all I could get out.

"What do you mean 'pretty nice'?" asked Liz. "Why, it's *fantastic*! Believe me, coming from a journalist, this is great. They could have turned this into a nightmare for you. You know that, don't you?"

"Yeah, I guess they could have," I replied, still remembering the way the media had absolutely slaughtered me for weeks back in 1995. But I didn't tell Liz that, out of the whole article I had just read, I didn't remember the positive comments about me or the fact that they were holding my job or even the accomplishments mentioned. No, what I remembered was the subtle reference to the case of my little patient, the one event in my life that would crush my soul forever.

If visitation was the main thing that helped me maintain my sanity while I was locked up, mail call was a close second. It took me a couple of days to figure this one out. At first, I noticed that the girls on the one o'clock rotation would begin to gather in large numbers by the little window slot that the jail nurse would pass medications through every night and every morning. The medication window was just big enough to slip a few pills through—pills to make insomniacs sleep, schizophrenics less paranoid, bipolar depressives less depressed, violent personalities less violent, the high strung less anxious, the kleptomaniacs and pyromaniacs less impulsive, and the suicide prone less suicidal. I watched this pill-slipping slot with great interest for the first several days. But soon I learned that this miniature window slot had a second more important function.

I strained my eyes from my cell window the first few days to see what this great midday gathering of girls was around the window slot. I could tell it wasn't medication time because no one was excitedly throwing their heads back, drinking out of tiny plastic cups, and later throwing these cups down on the floor to crush them with their heavy feet. It wasn't until I had the one o'clock rotation one day that I could get close enough to the window slot to figure out what was going on. It was quite a strange phenomenon really. It would start precisely at one o'clock every day, even though the arrival of the peculiar little man and his treasures never occurred at any particular time. About half the girls in the dayroom would start to mosey on over to the window with Pearl absolutely always at the front. She would always say the exact same thing, starting at exactly one o'clock. "Where the fuck is that fuckin' mailman? He's so fuckin' stupid I'll bet he fuckin' forgot how ta fuckin' git here! Jesus Christ, everyone knows he can't even fuckin' read!"

This particular day, I decided to stay near the window slot to observe firsthand what was going on. I wasn't disappointed. After a while, the strangest-looking little Black man dressed in a uniform somewhat resembling a U.S. postal worker's and pushing a gigantic steel cart rounded the corner in the hallway and stopped at our window slot. He randomly picked up a fistful of mail and held several letters at a time up to the window. We could barely hear his muffled voice through the thick glass. "Who dis one for?" He seemed to be directly addressing Pearl.

"That's for fuckin' Erline," she said disappointingly.

Erline jumped up and down and clapped her skinny hands. She grabbed the letter and quickly read the envelope. "Wah, Aw'll be! Mah sweet liddle ole granny down in Missussippee has done gone an' wrote me a letter."

"An' who dis one for?" the pretend postman asked Pearl.

"Oh lord, that one's for fuckin' Big Charlotte. It's probably a fuckin' Bible or maybe a fuckin' letter from fuckin' Billy Graham or somethin'."

"Watch your mouf, young lady, or Ah'll call da pohleese," the bizarre little mailman threatened Pearl.

"All right, all right, but don't cha have nothin' f-f-f-for me today?" Pearl asked, trying her best to abandon her favorite adjective.

"No, you knows I neber have nutin' for you, giirrl," he stated matter-of-factly.

I stood back and observed the funny little mailman with all my might. He was no taller than four feet ten and was probably in his mid- to late forties. He tried his best to help his height issue along by donning a huge pair of black boots with heels that added at least three inches to his scrawny frame. He was very slightly built, almost puny, and I noticed that he compensated for this by puffing out his tiny chest and strutting, somewhat like Det. Stanley Snipe.

But the thing that caught my eye the most about the mailman was a characteristic that I had seen daily for almost two years now. It was this—he showed every single sign of being illiterate. He hesitated as he slowly held each letter up to the light. "Ah can't eben read dis here awful writin's," he complained. "Ain't dis a capital *C*?" He looked straight at Pearl.

"Yeah, that's for Caroline," she answered. "She lives upstairs."

He fidgeted more with the mail, allowing every little thing in the hallway to distract him. He went on to make more excuses for his incompetence. "My eyes is gettin' bad. Ah gots ta go to da eye doctor soon. Ah can't eben see dese here ledders. Hell, girl, Ah's way too busy ta read awl dese names. Can't cha help me out a liddle?"

Pearl seemed to know instinctively what was wrong with the strange little mailman, and she played along, buying his excuses of poor eyesight, undecipherable penmanship, and being overbusy. She began to read each and every name on the envelopes for him as he methodically held each letter up to the glass. He handed her the letters one by one through the tiny slot and allowed her to get them to their rightful owners. I thought I heard him heave a sigh of relief as Pearl took over, hollering for each inmate to "come get her fuckin' mail." As time went on, I began to notice that Pearl never seemed to get any mail herself. But she was always right there at the window every single mail call, helping her buddy, the jail mailman, to read the names on the letters.

At first, no mail came for me. I wasn't quite sure what to think. Sometimes late at night, when I lay on my top bunk, unable to sleep and all freaked out over being locked in a room with a psycho girl who could crack at any moment, I began to imagine reasons why nobody was writing to me. I told myself that all my friends and family thought I was a hideous creature, a horrible thief with no conscience who snatched money from the government that was intended to help the poor and the destitute, the handicapped and the elderly. I reasoned that, because I had pled guilty, everyone must now think that I had to be, indeed, guilty. My vivid imagination went on to deduce that, furthermore, most everyone in my life had now forgotten me, written me off as some two-bit criminal who would never be able to bounce back and would probably go stark raving mad anyhow. Yes, those lonely endless nights full of insomnia played some unworldly tricks on my weary mind.

It really wasn't too long before I received my first four letters. They were postmarked six days earlier than the day I finally received them. The postmarks read May 15, which meant that these four people had actually sat down, written a letter, and mailed it on the same day that I had gone to jail. At the time, I didn't think much of it because I had already been caged for almost a week; but later on as I began to have time to be more reflective, it amazed me that four people in my life would think enough of me to make a special effort to get a piece of mail off the same day that they had heard the bad news. The first four pieces of mail included a butterfly card from my niece Kim, declaring me to be her favorite aunt of all times and informing me that she cried for hours when her mother told her what had happened to me.

An encouraging long letter from my wonderful mother showed up in the first bunch of mail, along with a spiritually uplifting letter from my sister Chris. In Chris's letter were tiny cardboard cutouts, each with a different Bible verse or exalting phrase printed on it. "Father, give me the wisdom you have promised to those who seek you," one little piece of white cardboard declared.

"'Call upon me in the day of trouble: I will deliver thee, and thou shalt glorify me' (Psalm 50:15)," another stated. I found this one to totally pertain to my situation.

Some of Chris's Bible cards were quite helpful; others tended to pour salt into an already open wound, such as the one that avowed, "Oh, Lord, help me understand the reasons for your chastening."

The most unusual piece of mail I received in that first group of letters was a card from my brother Dave's attorney, Sam. The card had a beautiful wintry scene on it, and the inside asserted that I had definitely done the right thing by going to trial and that I was certainly to be commended for my courageousness and honor. As I read Sam's card, I couldn't help but glance down at my baggy orange jumpsuit that hung off my shoulders, my lack of undergarments, and my raggedy, worn-out shower shoes that were two inches too long. *Funny*, I said to myself. *I sure don't feel too courageous or honorable.*

If I was amazed at the four pieces of mail on May 21, I guess you would say I was totally flabbergasted on the next mail call when

I received seventeen pieces of mail. Judging by the reaction of the other inmates and the peculiar little mailman, I was not alone in my astonishment. "You get more fuckin' mail than I ever fuckin' saw in all my fuckin' life, lady," Pearl observed. "You gonna share any of that fuckin' mail with any of us?" The illiterate little mailman didn't waste any words. "You gits too much mail for one peoples," he stated matter-of-factly, looking directly at me as if to size me up.

The other girls had mixed reactions to my sudden barrage of mail. Some, like Erline and Big Charlotte, shared in my excitement and seemed to look on my whole mail situation as a special showering of written messages from a higher source beyond our control. Others, like Pearl and Amanda, mainly wanted to share in my newfound wealth, longing for a pretty card or two to hang on their own cell walls or to copy with their crayons and pencils to give them something to do. Still others, like Bicycle and Moleface, chose to distinctly ignore my newly acquired status of "mail girl," receiver of the most mail in the history of Coward County Jail.

But the one that bothered me the most was my own cellmate, Serena. Day after day, I would return to our cell after mail call and try my best to read letter after letter to Serena, hoping to both entertain her and break her depressive state with news from my friends and family. But try as I might, she never showed any reaction to my endless readings, nor did she acknowledge that I was even there at all. I guess the only good my oral readings did was to help me keep my own sanity and maintain my ties to the outside world.

MISSIVES TO WARD OFF MADNESS

O N THE DAY that I received my record seventeen pieces of mail, I had already been in jail for nine days. Most of the other girls didn't know what to think of me, and after that mail call, they were confused sure enough. A small group of them followed me to the table in the back corner, where I chose to plunk down and take my time reading through my precious stash of communications from the outside world as if I was enjoying a bottle of fine wine. I decided to begin by taking a short inventory of sources by glimpsing over return addresses. I discovered that the collection included two pieces from my brother Dave; two pieces from Bob; two pieces from my daughter, Sarah; two pieces from Chris; two pieces from Paula; and one letter each from my mom, my sister Annamae, my brother Phil, and three different friends from work.

On the bottom of the pile was a small envelope containing a letter from my eldest son, Rocky, who was living in Bellingham, Washington. My heart skipped a beat when I saw this one. I hadn't heard from him in ages. I decided to save this one for last.

I started to rip open one of Dave's first. It was written on Holiday Inn stationery and was dated May 17, 1999. It read:

Dora—

Greetings from beautiful Lexington, Kentucky. We have decided to stay overnight here, and I just got off the phone with Sam. I imagine he will drop you a note soon.

We left the jail and had lunch at Steak 'n' Shake and then headed out for home. Fortunately, we just missed the rush hour at Knoxville—got through the north end just at about 5:03 p.m.

Bob asked me if you had done anything like trained a cockroach under your bed to do backflips or anything, and it occurred to me on the drive today that if you had, you could not be the Birdman of Alcatraz but rather the Cockroach Woman of Coward County Jail. Think about it. Nice ring, huh?

Hang in there. We all miss you and love you and will see you sooner than you know.

Write you again soon.

Love,
Dave, Linda, and Jacob

Since this letter made me grin from ear to ear, I decided to read the second one from Dave. This one was dated May 18 and contained a rather hilarious birthday card along with a note written on yellow paper. The letter read:

Dora—

I thought I'd use this lovely legal pad to write you since we became so accustomed to communicating this way!

Mom and I had a pretty uneventful drive home although we had to have the obligatory breakfast at the Waffle House. I got the no. 1 waffle, sausage, two eggs, toast, and grits special. I tried to trade my meat for grits to the lady in the adjacent booth, but it was a no go. . . .

. . . All our thoughts and prayers are with you. Hang in there, and we will see you soon.

Love,
Dave & Linda & Jacob

P.S. "I know what you are trying to do here, and I won't let you!" Quotable quote no. 14-aa-b2a3

The girls were quickly losing interest in Dave's letters. They were failing to see the humor in training cockroaches to do backflips or attempting to swap breakfast items at Waffle House. So I decided to open some of the envelopes that obviously contained birthday cards. My forty-fifth birthday had come and gone two days previously with no celebration whatsoever, with the exception of a free birthday portrait drawn by Amanda in crayons on a manila envelope and then glued to a piece of cardboard with toothpaste.

A card from Paula had a happy little bear on the front. It said, "During this difficult time, remember this . . . You are loved!" And she wrote:

> Hey Dora,
>
> You pick the most stupid ways to avoid going to the gym at 7:00 a.m.! I hope you are fine. I promise I am trying to get there to see you soon. You have a happy birthday and know that I love you. Next year, you will have all this behind you. We will have the biggest most fat-filled, calorie-packed birthday cake ever. Please take care of yourself. I'm always thinking of you.
>
> I love you,
> Paula

The girls seemed to like this much better than Dave's letters. They began to argue loudly over who was to get the card for their cell. I chose to ignore them and go on to another card. The second card from Paula had an outdoor scene on it with trees, flowers, a rainbow, and fish swimming in a little stream. It was very popular with the girls. Its message was more serious than the previous card. It read:

> God bless you on your birthday and always. Today I was thinking of all the wonderful things God created—and you came to mind! Happy birthday.
>
> Dora, I love you,
> Paula

Then I opened the card from my daughter, Sarah. On the front was a cartoon character dressed in suspenders, a striped shirt, and a tie. It declared, "This is Larry, 'the Birthday Lawyer'!"

Inside, it said, "He's plea-bargained your age down to 29 years and 16 hours of community service!"

At the bottom, Sarah had written:

> I hope you have a very unique birthday this year. I felt this card was appropriate!
>
> > Love you,
> > Sarah

I decided to open the big purple envelope from my mother next. Inside was the cutest little birthday card shaped like Tweety Bird. She had handwritten a note inside:

Dear Dora,

> I know this birthday will not be too much fun for you. Just keep your faith strong and know we are all praying for you, and you will be home soon. Maybe some of your new friends can sing "Happy Birthday" for you.
>
> > All my love,
> > Mom

My immediate reaction to her note was total disbelief concerning her comment on "your new friends." What did she think this hellhole was like? That we all just sat around and chitchatted over cups of tea, forming friendships that would last a lifetime? She was really naive enough to picture me making *friends* with these creatures of darkness. But before I could finish my outrageous daydream about Bicycle and her stoolies singing "Happy Birthday" to me, Pearl began to jump up and down and scream excitedly at the top of her lungs, "I want this fuckin' card, lady! Oh please, please, pleeease let me have the Tweety

Bird card! It's sooo fuckin' *cute*! Don't give it to nobody else. I wanna hang it on my wall. I'll take such good care of it, just like it was my own. Pleeease, lady!"

I had been watching her with great interest. I especially noticed two things about her at that moment. One was how her blue eyes sparkled with anticipation, like a young child on Christmas Eve awaiting Santa Claus. And the other was how very hard she was trying to control herself and to actually make a good impression on me. She really wanted that Tweety Bird card. And in the end, I gladly handed over the card because she was only seventeen years old and never got any mail herself and because she helped the little illiterate mailman read the envelopes every day but mostly because she had shown true self-control with her request for the card by using her favorite adjective only two times in seven whole sentences. In fact, that was the least number of times I would ever hear her use that dreaded word. I handed her the card without a word myself.

She looked at me as if I was just teasing her. I nodded and continued to hold it out to her. Her young eyes met mine; she sized me up for a minute. "Lady, you're the fuckin' nicest one here. I really fuckin' mean that. This is the best fuckin' card in the whole fuckin' world."

Oh well, I thought, *there goes my main reason for rewarding her with Mom's card.*

She left my table and immediately began making her rounds in the dayroom, showing everyone she could her new treasure. Upon seeing the Tweety Bird card, several more inmates gathered around my table to try their luck on confiscating a wall decoration or two for their cell walls. Now I had an audience for sure.

I couldn't wait any longer. I had to open up one of the letters from my husband. I chose the large yellow envelope. Inside was another birthday card. On the front, it said:

To My Wife

> Do I [picture of a red heart] you
> More than the [picture of the sun],
> The [picture of the moon],

And the [picture of four stars]?
When I opened it up, it read:
Bet your cute, little [picture of a lady's butt]!
Happy birthday!
He had written:

I love you & will see you soon!

Love,
Bobby Ray

My new audience howled with laughter. "You bet yer cuuute liddle ole behind," Erline said.

"Ya dumb shit, that there card means cute little *ass*!" Moleface spat out. "*Ass*, not behind, ya damn hillbilly," she added under her breath.

"Ladies! Ladies! Ass, behind, butt, rump, bottom, posterior, derriere, crapper, haunches, gluteal region, backside, can, cheeks, tail, heinie, rear end, fanny, tush, arse—any of these will do. It's just a picture," Amanda conceded, cool as a cucumber. That seemed to shut them up as far as the exact meaning of the pictorial in the card. Amanda always had a way of doing that.

Bicycle was sitting at an adjacent table, pretending to play cards. "Don' ya mudderfuckahs git it? The crackah's ole man be fuckin' horny for a mudderfuckin' piece of ass. Dat's why I's don't mudderfuckin' mess wid no goddamn mudderfuckin' mens. Goddamn mudderfuckin' horny-ass bastards!" And she turned to Jazzy and gave her a kiss on her cheek while slowly feeling her left breast. She rolled her eyes toward us to catch our reaction. I felt my stomach churn but just looked down at my stack of mail.

I decided it was definitely time to bury Bob's birthday card deep within the pile and go on to another. I mentally instructed myself to never share any of his mail with the girls ever again. I quickly chose the letter from my sister who was in dental school, feeling that it would surely be "safe" to read aloud. But I soon found out that this too was a total misjudgment. At the very top of the paper, even before the date, in big block letters was written:

To: people keeping my sis hostage:

No fair if u read this letter cause my mom told me you'd only X-ray it for files & stuff!

I quickly glanced down the page and midway, I saw big block letters again, this time declaring:

You were robbed!
You were screwed!
You lived up to the standards of truth and honor while the prosecution lied!

I made a split-second decision to fold the letter back up and return it quickly to its envelope. These criminals certainly didn't need to hear my sister's bitter remarks about my trial. And I just plain wasn't up to being asked a hundred and one stupid, sarcastic questions about my case.

I swiftly tore into the envelope of my other sister's letter, deciding to try my luck with reading it aloud to my captive audience of felons, convicts, and crooks. Being the strongly devout person that she was, her opening didn't surprise me one bit. The chosen stationery was lined at the top with pretty little violets, and its heading read: "You make our world a better place to be."

Her letter read:

My dear strong survivor sister (child of God)—

I love u! I just got off the phone with Mom. She told me about how you barely have anything to wear and no toiletries. Hang in there!

I am going to start sending you *The Upper Room* pages because I feel they would be helpful. The other day one was about not being alone in your misery—there are others out there too. Anyway, it will give you a thought for the day.

You are "my hero." Probably the bravest person I know. And guts—well, woman, you have *guts*! I truly admire you.

Tomorrow is our kindergarten rodeo. We will have a calf roping, barrel racing, Western clothes relay, gold dig, oil spill relay, steer roping, bucking bronco, calf scramble, hot dog roast, and a cowboy serenade. This should be fun! I am having to peel my class off the ceiling on a regular basis!

Scott and Kim have finals starting Monday, and then Kim and Steph start summer classes on June 7.

Well, pray for my children's brains and for me to survive the upcoming last week of school.

Saturday is the senior banquet at church. Steph is doing the decorations. Kim and Scott are in the skit that roasts the seniors. They are doing a spoof on Jerry Springer. Sunday is Kim's piano recital. Pray for her as she never has time to practice.

OK, sweetie, I love you. I'll write tomorrow. Here is our address and phone number. Call-collect anytime.

Oh, I talked to Jeremiah almost an hour last night. He wanted to know trial details. He loves you and is like the rest of us—finding this whole thing hard to swallow. He said the Joneses called.

I ask God to cradle you in his secure hands nightly. I love you.

God bless you,
Chris

P.S. I'll call Sarah soon to check on her.

Big Charlotte was the first, this time, to comment. "What a wonderful Christian sister you have. 'For whosoever shall do the will of God, the same is my brother, and my sister, and my mother' (Mark 3:35)."

"I don' know 'bout all *dat* shit," broke in Coco. "But I can sure dig dat part about da chil'ins actin' like they was on *Da Jerry Springer Show*. That be *my* fav'rit' show."

"What's a-goin' on anyways? Is yer sister a teacher fer the kindergarten younguns ober dare in Texas er somet'in's like at dare?" interrupted

Erline. "'Cuz if'in she is, dat dare's 'bout the most wunderfulles' t'ing a liddle ole body kin do wifin dare life an' awl."

But before I had time to answer Erline and tell her that, yes, my sister was the greatest, most dedicated kindergarten teacher in the entire state of Texas, Jazzy—Bicycle's lesbian lover—decided to put in her two cents' worth. "I jist wanna know *why* yo sistah think dat you is da most bravest ho around. It don't take *no* kinda *guts* ta damn come ta fuckin' jail er nuttin'. Don't she know dat you is jist a no-count, useless, piece-of-shit jailbird ho?"

By this time, Pearl was done making her rounds to show her newly acquired treasure to all in the room who would look, and she had returned to my table to listen to excerpts from the rest of my seventeen pieces of mail and perhaps to try her luck on receiving further assets. "Why don't you just fuckin' shut the fuck up, you fuckin' dyke? You don't know what the fuck happened to this fuckin' lady or nothin'. She's a whole fuckin' lot nicer than yer fuckin' butch ass, I can fuckin' tell you that! Look at this fuckin' great card she gave me. You ever done any fuckin' thing nice like that for anyone in yer whole miserable fuckin' life, huh?"

I took a deep breath and looked down at my sister's letter. I could feel my heart start to beat hard against my chest; my face began to turn hot and red. I placed my elbows on the stainless steel table and positioned both of my hands on my temples. I couldn't bear to look at what was inevitably going to happen next. Bicycle would never, in a hundred years, let Pearl—a seventeen-year-old White girl—get away with saying such things about her lover. If I looked up, I just knew that I would witness a cold-blooded murder.

But I could not believe the next thing that happened. Bicycle dragged herself slowly over to Jazzy, placed her muscled arm around her neck, pulled her strongly toward her, and gave her a long wet kiss right on the lips. "Cum' on den, mah hot mudderfuckin' baby, dese goddamn crackahs is a whole big buncha goddamn mudderfuckin' cunts!" She turned to Pearl. "An' dat be da ugliest goddamn mudderfuckin' card Ah done eber seen in mah whole damn mudderfuckin' life. It be a card for a mudderfuckin' baby-ass ho."

With that, she pulled Jazzy closer to her, and they both retreated to the nearest corner to continue their make-out session. I sucked in my breath and waited for Pearl to retaliate, but it never happened. All she did was look down at her yellow Tweety Bird card and say softly, "This here fuckin' card ain't no baby-ass card. It's the best fuckin' card in the world."

What just happened had shaken me up but good. And what *could* have happened made me even more upset. I decided to call it quits on the oral readings of my mail. "OK, that's all I'm gonna read today," I announced. "I'm tired." I gathered up all the envelopes and placed them in a neat stack.

"Oh, come on now, White girl. We wuz jis' gittin' started," moaned Jasmine, the nineteen-year-old exhibitionist. "You White mudderfuckahs neber wanna share nuttin' wid us, sistas. Looky dare. You done gone an' give yo best card to a fuckin' *White* assho'e. Know what *Aah* t'inks? Ah t'inks you is predjis' against Black peoples."

Thinking that anything I could say at that moment would probably make matters worse, I chose not to say anything at all. Instead, I acted as if I hadn't heard Jasmine, methodically gathered up my written riches, and moved to a different table. Part of the group left, starting up various card games and art projects. But almost half the girls followed me to my new location.

Erline spoke first. "A looky here now, we'uns wanna see if'in yew git any more ah dose dare liddle ole funny store-bought cards, like a-dat one awl about da lady's tail end an awl."

Big Charlotte chimed in, "Myself, I surely would like it if you might read us another from your most blessed sister who prays for you nightly and writes 'God bless you' at the end."

I wasn't sure what to do. What was proper jailhouse etiquette at this point? As I was still looking at Big Charlotte, I noticed something out of the corner of my eye. At the table next to us, there sat Amanda. She had pretended to be drawing a picture the whole time I had been reading my letters aloud, and now she had moved with us when I had switched tables. I rolled my eyes toward her. She was nodding and holding her drawing in front of her as if she was reading it. She looked at me and mouthed the words "read more to them."

Well, there's the answer to my proper jailhouse etiquette question, I thought. *Amanda comes through for me again.*

I wondered which letter to pick next. I decided to open the second one from Sarah since most of the ladies there seemed to have kids. Inside, I found no letter at all but instead a large piece of heavy paper folded several times. All eyes were on this mysterious object. My own curiosity was getting the best of me. After unfolding the paper many times, I discovered an absolutely breathtaking sketch of what appeared to be the desert with majestic purple mountains in the background. The whole piece was drawn with colored charcoal, and the sunset over the mountains was bursting with every color imaginable. My daughter was not a known artist, but over the years, I had seen a few of her drawings, and I knew immediately that this was Sarah's work. The only time she ever drew was when she felt deeply moved by something, and I knew in my heart that this drawing was her way of saying to me, *Here, Mom. The prettiest scenery I have ever seen was on my recent trip out West, and so here is my present to you. The desert, the cacti, the mountains, the sunset—it's all right out here for you. Don't forget nature, Mom. It will never leave you. Hang this in your room, and remember me every time you look at it.*

My eyes teared up. My lip began to tremble. There was not one single word in the envelope with the picture, but I could have made up a letter so long and so detailed to go with that picture that all the girls would have tired and left the table before my story was over.

"Well, Ah'll be. Dat dare's 'bout da purdiest liddle ole pitcher Ah ever did see," declared Erline. "Who yew reckin' done it?"

I tried really hard to compose myself and not to let the girls see me in an emotional state, but I was so choked up that my voice came out hoarse and low. "My daughter, Sarah, did it," I answered softly.

"Dis here be ya chance tah make it up tah da Black sistahs. Give me dat dare pichah fo' my wall, honky," begged Jasmine.

"No, no one gets this picture. It's mine." I said it with certainty and confidence. Then I gathered up my stuff and moved once again.

As I was walking across the dayroom, I heard Jasmine calling after me. "Come back here, you sorry-ass crackah! Look at her high-an'-mighty White ass walkin' away from me! Hey, Whitey! I'm talkin' to your mudderfuckin' no-good, pile-o'-shit ass! You t'ink you too good for us Black foke? Can't give no nigga one o' your pitchers? Go on den, see ifA*h* fuckin' cares! One o' dese daze, Ah'll *takes* what Ah wants from yah!"

I once again found myself wondering how on God's green earth I was ever going to survive another second in this rathole. I sat down at my solitary new table and closed my eyes. "Dear God," I prayed, "please help me survive this awful ordeal. I know you're with me. I can feel your strength. Pick me up and carry me, like in the poem 'Footprints.' I can't go this alone."

Suddenly, I felt much better, almost like I had been revived. I looked around. No one had followed me this time. They had finally given up on me; I was the crazy woman who preferred to be alone. Thank goodness. Now I could finish reading my mail in peace. I quickly scanned through three short notes from some of the ladies at work. One of my favorite board members, a Redd County commissioner, Harriette Rowe, wrote:

Dear Doramae,

We are all behind you and want you to come back to your job with LVA. Try to remember we love you and are praying for you.

Yours in Christ,
Harriette

Another card was from Hannah Smith, the head librarian in Redd County and the president of my LVA board. It said:

Dear Doramae,

I wanted to let you know the LVA board was unanimous in our decision to hold your position until you come back. Mabel Cox and Betty Lou Davis have agreed to open the center for at least next week. Clarice Daniel had knee surgery but will be able to do the annual report. Connie Crisp & I & maybe Faye will go to the United Way interview next week. We will probably hire someone just for the summer to be at the center. I've also called Dolly Biddle & left a message asking what we need to do to be ready for the CLCP annual report. Dr. Huxx was also at the board meeting.

We support you, miss you, and look for your return. Please be careful, and if you can, let us hear from you.

Hannah Smith

That's really wonderful of them to all still believe in me, I almost said out loud.

I glanced at the front of her note card. It was a picture of the cutest little baby robin perched on the branch of some sort of bush containing tiny red berries and large green leaves. He was fat and fluffy, full of fuzz down where feathers were attempting to grow in. His orange beak was wide open as if he was attempting to chirp. *Oh boy, they would all fight something awful over this card*, I told myself, and I hurriedly stuffed it back into its envelope.

The last of the cards from the ladies at work contained an inspirational message from Helen Steiner Rice. At the bottom of the message, my friend Jolene Cobb had written:

You're in my thoughts & prayers. The LVA board met yesterday. You have our unanimous support. We want you back as soon as possible. We'll miss you, but I don't want you to worry about LVA or your job. We'll be waiting for you.

Jolene Cobb

There were only four letters left now. I chose the one from my brother Phil. But when I opened it, I found that every bit of the writing was done by his wife, Beth. My mother's words came back to me. "Dora," she had written in her first letter, "Phil is trying real hard to write to you, but he may never get it done. He says he keeps throwing all his attempts away because he just can't seem to find the right words."

I knew my brother well enough to understand fully. He was always the sensitive one in the family, the one who had such a struggle trying to express himself. So now here I was, holding a bright colorful card that said "HUGS, HUGS, HUGS, HUGS, HUGS" all over it and had his wife's writing inside. Beth wrote:

Dora-

This is a fine pickle you've gotten yourself into! I'm only kidding! No point in looking at the past—look ahead & don't worry or even consider what others might think. It's not important. Think about the possibilities available in the future. It may not seem like it now—but there are always possibilities & options to explore. Keep your chin up, we are all thinking about you!

Beth

I didn't quite know what to think of this one. It had a great beginning, no doubt about that. The comment "This is a fine pickle you've gotten yourself into!" made me chuckle out loud. *That's certainly the understatement of the year*, I thought. But all that other business about "possibilities and options to explore," she had to be—as Pearl would put it—"fuckin' kiddin'." I was sitting here, nine days into my little jail experience, with no underwear, an orange suit that hung off me like a bad scarecrow, broken plastic shower shoes that were so big that they fell off my feet with every step, having to share a cell with Psycho Girl, and on the verge of a good ass whooping by Bicycle any minute now, and she was talking about "exploring my possibilities and options."

I simply could not deal with the thought of it, so I crammed the card back into its blue envelope before someone saw it and begged for it.

I rushed through Bob's short letter about missing me and planning to come see me the next day. He also wrote, "If you go to Nutter near Savannah, we will go to the riverfront for a couple of days after you get out. I know how much you like that part of Savannah."

I love that man, I reminded myself.

I went on to digest another letter from my sister Chris. It contained several pages from a Methodist devotional booklet entitled *The Upper Room*. It once again told me how shocked she was, how much she admired me, how strong I was, and how God would never forsake me. I was glad that someone was writing this to me every day. I would be ashamed to admit it, but I needed the repetition; there was a certain comfort in it.

I had saved the best for last. I had managed to read sixteen of the seventeen letters. This was what I had been waiting for—a letter from my eldest son, who was living in Washington State. I hadn't heard from him in ages.

I looked around the dayroom. I wasn't going to let *anything* ruin this moment. All seemed OK. Everyone seemed to be occupied. I ripped into the little plain envelope and pulled out the single page written on yellow legal paper. I recognized my son's precise small letters.

Just as I began to read, Amanda silently plunked down on the stool beside me. She was so quiet that I almost didn't see her there. I think I might have let out an audible sigh of protest. But if I did, she never let on. I wasn't sure how to handle this. She, after all, had come to my rescue more than once. "Wanna hear a letter from my son?" I asked her.

"Sure, why not?" she replied.

So I began to read, very quietly so as not to attract the other girls' attention. I hoped and prayed that there was nothing too personal or anything that might offend Amanda in the letter. The letter was dated Monday, May 17, 1999, and it began:

Howdy Mama!

I just called Sarah in Athens, and she told me the news. She sounded a trifle upset and POed, but that's to be expected, I suppose. I called Dad at his motel, and he sounded good and was convinced that you did the right thing. (Five years is inconceivable, ya know.)

By the time you receive this here note, you'll have finished about a week already and gotten into a routine. One week suddenly becomes two, and before you know it, a month will have flown by. You be nice to those other girls and don't become the bully.

I'm helping a block mason for $9 an hour right now. It's honest hard work, and the Washington sun is surprisingly powerful (most likely due to our razor-thin ozone layer). I'm heading up Alaska way in about two weeks in my trusty $600 '82 Jetta diesel (forty-four miles per gallon!). My bestest bumper sticker on the Mo' Betta Feta Chedda Jedi Jetta says, "VISUALIZE WHIRLED PEAS" (har har).

My traveling companion is Destiny, an angelic nineteen-year-old Nebraskan. She seems to have become somewhat of a girlfriend, I reckon. Intelligent, funny, beautiful, kind, and weird are a few of the boring adjectives I'd choose in describing her. (Perhaps 'tis my Destiny.)

I'm notoriously lacking as a letter writer, but I'll make a concerted effort to compose and send semi-interesting, halfway literate missives on a regular basis.

You know (I certainly hope) how much I love you and cherish your dominant role into molding me into the interesting, kind, contented person I am today. I fully understand the home-cooked, good-ole-boy shafting that occurred in court, but if any beautifully strong, wonderful person can handle the next couple of months with a shrug, it's you, Mom.

I know this is a kind of boring letter, but I'm trying hard to say the right things and to convey how much I love you and how confident I am that you're tough enough to do this time standing on your head.

DORAMAE BROOKSHIRE

Look at this as closure as well as a vacation from the frustrating toils of everyday life. Read all you can. (Try out stuff you've never considered reading.) Stretch every day and get to know the other good folks in there with you. (There *are* some interesting, innocent people around you.)

Be strong! Keep the faith! I love you, Mom!
See you soon.

Your Loving Eldest,
Rocky

And along the side of the letter was written:

Thought for the Day:
Life's short and hard,
Like a bodybuilding elf.

I just sat there, frozen in time. Amanda spoke first. "Jesus, your son's really damn smart as hell, isn't he? Damn!"

"Yeah, he's pretty perceptive about the world for twenty-six years old, all right," I answered.

I could feel a really serious conversation coming on, and I just wasn't up to that, so I acted fast. I had not read the "thought for the day" out loud yet, so I decided to do just that. "Hey, listen to this," I said, and I read it to her.

She instantly threw her head back and laughed and laughed, a good old-fashioned belly laugh. "Now that's just damned hilarious," she declared. "Hey, could I use that in some of my art?"

"Sure, go right ahead," I replied.

And suddenly, we were having a regular, decent, everyday conversation. We talked about her two kids and my three, about men and art and books and careers. We found out that we were both originally from Indiana—imagine that, both Hoosiers. And I found out that Amanda had been in the Coward County Jail seventeen separate times—all for her addiction to crack cocaine. "Just can't seem to shake that damn stuff," I would hear her say over and over. "It's just too goddamn *wonderful.*"

As we sat and talked like two old friends, Rocky's recent words came back to me. "Get to know the other good folks in there with you. (There are some interesting, innocent people around you.)" From that day forward, I didn't view the other girls in the same light. No matter how unpolished and brash they were, how sickening and crude, I forced myself to look beyond that and to try to get to know the true person under all those loud and brassy layers. And as soon as I did, something marvelous began to happen. Not everyone but a few of the girls began to talk to me in human terms, no longer in threats and judgmental phrases. I actually got to know a few of them fairly well and knew what made them tick.

Take Harley, for instance. She was pregnant with her Hispanic boyfriend's twins. To make her story more interesting, he happened to be married and have five kids of his own at home. She swore that his wife didn't know about her pregnancy. Of course, the pregnancy gave her a definite advantage, especially since she was pregnant with twins. Every chance she got, she faked some ache or pain, which would cause the flabbergasted guards to send her right off to the jail infirmary. Since it was a multiple pregnancy, it bought her an occasional rare trip to an outside obstetrician. Of course, after she had spent an afternoon in an outside doctor's office, I would make her describe every little detail to me, down to the last thing the doctor said or did. I was dazzled by this saucy, rough-around-the-edges, downtrodden girl's uncanny ability to play the system. And I truly admired her downright guts. She was the only girl in that entire pod, other than Amanda, who would stand up to Bicycle. In fact, one night during late-night rotation, not long after I met Harley, she did something that absolutely amazed me.

Bicycle, Jazzy, Coco, Jasmine, and Ethel were all watching an African American sitcom on TV. This particular group of women regularly got to dominate the television; no one dared to try to change the channel. But when Harley had had enough, that was it. She decided one Friday night that she and I were going to watch *Unsolved Mysteries* and *Dateline.* I knew better. But she proved to be fearless. She walked right up to Bicycle and positioned herself between Bicycle and the TV. She puffed her growing belly out and got right in Bicycle's face. "I guess your sorry ass ain't the only one who can watch this son-uv-a-bitchin' TV," she stated matter-of-factly. "We live here too, and we got the right to equal time with the TV, you Black motherfucker."

Oh god. Don't say "we." Leave me out of this, please, I thought frantically.

Bicycle leaped up out of her chair, facing Harley, her fists clenched and drawn back. "Whadcha jis' call me, you White honky-ass, mudderfuckin' piece-o'-White-fuckin'-trailer-trash crackah? Awl beat chure White knocked-up fuckin' Mexican-lovin' ho ass till dem two liddle spic-ass babies come right fuckin' out chure big fat bitchin' belly!"

"OK, that's it. I don't care if I get put in fuckin' solitary. Enough is fuckin' enough, you fuckin' freak uv a manly excuse for a human being." And Harley drew her fist back and swung with all her might. But Bicycle was quick. She dodged the swing.

I closed my eyes, turned around, and retreated to the nearest corner. I couldn't bear to see the young mother of future twins be maimed, crippled, or possibly even killed. I looked around. No one was paying any attention to this altercation, except for the other four girls who were watching TV, and they certainly were not coming to either one's rescue. I strained my eyes to look out the glass walls and into the tall dark guards' tower in the hall. The guards weren't even looking in our direction but appeared to be talking on the phones. I was in a pure state of panic, literally trembling at the thought of what might happen in the next few seconds to my newly found friend.

At that very moment, Amanda showed up, again seemingly out of nowhere. "Better think before you hit a mother pregnant with twins, motherfucker. You be the cause uv a miscarriage, and it's off to several years in the big fuckin' pen for you. This White girl ain't worth servin' twice your time for, now is she? Leave her and those two little babies alone and go do somethin' else tonight. You're smarter than to just watch the same old show every night. You need to be more challenged than that. Go show these girls some uv your card tricks or somethin'." Amanda talked softly and deliberately to her, getting right in her disgusting, ugly face, eyeball to eyeball with those scary chrome glasses, never losing her cool for one second.

Bicycle studied Amanda and thought for a second, and then her hands dropped down to her side; her big fists unclenched. "Cum' on, girls, let's get the fuck outa here an' let dis fat honky ho watch da mudderfuckin' TV. Ah wuz done watchin' the mudderfuckah anyhows. Let's go play cards." The five women got up and strutted across the room, trying their best to prove their superiority.

"Hey, Dora, come on, we got it to ourselves!" Harley shouted across the room to me.

At that moment, I wished I could melt into the floor and disappear. I wanted no part of being associated with Harley and her insane near fight with Big Bicycle. But I decided to give it a try. After all, I had not gotten to watch a single TV show since I had been incarcerated because Bicycle dominated the television twenty-four hours a day. I meandered over to the TV and to Harley, not knowing fully what to expect.

"Whatchoo like ta watch on Friday night?" she inquired.

"Oh, I don't know. I like any show that is educational or informative."

"Me too." She grinned, and she turned the channel to *Unsolved Mysteries*. After that, we watched *Dateline*. And I could actually *hear* the TV.

In my journal that day, I wrote, "Thanks to Harley standing up to Bicycle, we actually got to watch two decent TV shows tonight—*Dateline* and *Unsolved Mysteries*. (Couldn't always hear for all the noise.)"

But watching TV with Harley was not the best part of being with her. The best part of Harley was the fact that she had served time at the "boot camp" in Nutter, and she could talk endlessly about the protocol there. Her opinion of Nutter seemed to mimic Angelica's pretty closely, except she had one main objection to the place. She didn't like the fact that at Nutter, as she put it, "those assholes work you to fuckin' death."

"Your ass won't have to worry about finding nothin' to do around that damn place. You'll be so fuckin' tired after they use your ass for slave labor that you'll fall into bed and sleep every chance they give you, which ain't very damn many. I didn't even care that I never had weekend visitors 'cuz I just slept all damn weekend to try and recover from the fuckin' hard workweek."

"Weekend visitors?" I asked.

"Hell yes, darlin'. If any asshole's willin' to drive to the middle of fuckin' nowhere to come visit your ass, they can come every damn weekend you're in, every Saturday and Sunday from nine till three."

"Wow! Do you have to have glass between you, and do you talk on phones or something?" I inquired.

"Jesus Christ, no, sugar. You get to touch and everything. You sit right by each other and shit like that. You can go outside to a yard, or you can stay inside. He can bring you drinks and food from a vending machine and shit."

During our discussions about Nutter, I would get so excited; I would feel like I couldn't wait another minute to go. Think about it—being able to touch Bob, to hug him and spend six whole hours with him twice a week every single week, to eat lunch with him outside where there were grass and trees and flowers and birds, to share with each other once again our dreams and innermost thoughts, to be able to do this face-to-face instead of shouting over a phone full of static and looking through a thick glass wall, to be able to hug my children, to talk to any of my family that could make it.

But that was not all that Harley would tell me about Nutter. She, like Angelica, told me about the meals, especially as compared with Coward County Jail. And she told me about the rigid schedules and the overall spick-and-span cleanliness of the place.

"Just wait till you get there. You won't believe the food compared with this rathole. You get real eggs for breakfast and homemade biscuits and plenty of fruits and vegetables right out of their own garden and real milk and dessert and a different dish every night, nothin' like this fuckin' mush they slop on our plates every night around this filthy-ass place. But you'd better be ready to follow their damn fuckin' ridiculous-ass schedule 'cuz those assholes'll tell you when to eat, work, sleep, and shit. Oh yeah, and since they have half the damn girls on their hands and knees most of the day waxin' and unwaxin' and polishin' floors, that whole place is cleaner than a virgin's twat."

Of all the things I spent my time doing at Coward County Jail, I liked hearing Harley talk about Nutter the best—fresh vegetables and fruit and milk and eggs and dessert, a scheduled day that included a "job," and maybe best of all truly clean surroundings.

Bob wrote me a letter once after I had been in the Coward County Jail for ten days or so. It went like this:

Hi Ma— . . .

. . . After I talked to you Thursday morning, I left here about twelve and drove to Nutter. It is 220 miles, about the same as from here to Goat Valley. The place is one story high & looks like it is only a couple of years old. It is very clean and neat—looks like a very small high school. The men's detention center is across the road. I saw three girls in tan jumpsuits working around the building. The landscaping is absolutely beautiful. Those three were all the probationers I saw.

I went inside and asked about the visiting hours. They were very nice & the place was spotless inside. They said visiting hours were Sat. & Sun. from nine to three. They said you could have two visitors at a time & they could stay all day nine to three if they wanted. The people were very polite and helpful.

With what Harley, Angelica, and Bob reported to me concerning Nutter, it became the biggest, most vivid dream I had while incarcerated in the CCJ. Many, many daydreams arose consisting of luscious meals, contact visitations, and immaculate accommodations.

After I met Amanda and Harley and found out that it was indeed to my advantage to actually have conversations with these jailbirds, I tried my best to expand that discovery to include getting to know my cellmate, Serena. But for all practical purposes, she remained Scary Serena or Psycho Girl for at least a good ten days. No matter what I did or said, she continued her pattern of deep, almost comatose sleep twenty or so hours a day, no talking, no partaking of food, and coming out of the cell only once a day. But on the tenth day of my incarceration, two separate miraculous events occurred.

SANTA AND SATAN

O NE MIRACULOUS EVENT was the arrival of Santa Claus in the form of my first commissary order. In fact, that was exactly how I put it in my journal entry dated May 24, 1999:

> WHAT A GREAT DAY! Santa Claus came this morning! (In other words, I got my commissary order.) I now have: three white T-shirts, three pairs of socks, five pairs of panties, a set of thermal underwear, a bra, a pair of way-too-big tennis shoes (they wouldn't take them back), Dove soap, Colgate toothpaste, deodorant, shampoo, a brush, a comb, lotion, Chapstick, twenty stamped envelopes, two pens, one pencil, three legal tablets, four Advil, a large plastic cup, a checker/chess game, a *Webster's Pocket Dictionary*, six candy bars, two brownies, two cinnamon rolls, crackers, peanut butter, cheese spread, peanuts, and a pickle. I think I died and went to heaven! Now I can finally write letters, take a GOOD shower, have enough clothes to wear, eat something that doesn't gag me.

As soon as I walked into our cell with three brown paper bags full of goodies, Scary Serena seemed to perk up just a bit. "Whacha got dere?" she asked.

I jumped back, almost frightened by the sound of her voice, but quickly recovered. "Lots and lots of treats. You want some?" I asked.

Then we sat for the next several minutes, me on the desk stool and her on the bottom bunk, sharing peanut butter and crackers and candy. I asked her if she would like to play a game of checkers. "Checkers?" she replied. "Don't cha have anything a little more challenging than that candy-ass game?"

"Well, the board reverses to become a chessboard, but I never really learned to play chess myself."

"*What?* You can't eben play chess? Why, my seben-years-old son can play dat, an' he's damn *good* at it too. Plays it all da time. Can beat jis' about any-damn-body at it."

"Can you play chess?" I asked her.

"Of course, I can fuckin' play it. Who da hell udder dan you *can't*?"

I was starting to get really excited. Here was one game that I had always wanted to learn how to play, and this was the perfect opportunity. I was locked in a cell twenty hours a day with nothing but a chessboard, chess pieces, and a cellmate who knew how to play. I even went so far as to silently thank God for the coincidence of all conditions being right so that I would not lose my sanity but rather would challenge my brain. "Would you show me how to play, please?" I begged.

"Not so goddamn fast," she replied. "We'd better see how you can do at a simple game like checkers first."

And we set the checkers board up and played a couple of games. She legitimately whipped my butt on the first two games, and it didn't take her long to either. "Girl, you is one sorry, worthless, son-uv-a-bitchin' checkers player. Ah feels sorry fer you. Is you *stupid* er somet'in'?"

Flashbacks of the card game and the associated name-calling came back to me. I told myself that these girls had probably spent most of their lives locked up and, therefore, had had most of their lives to play games, but deep inside, I was beginning to have serious doubts about my own mental abilities. I mean, my god, these jailbirds were outwitting me regularly.

I had never been called seriously degrading names while playing a game of checkers—or a card game for that matter—before. I decided I had better take these jail games a little more seriously and get my head in the game *now*. Growing up, where I came from, checkers and card games were just that—games—and they were simply a friendly way to pass the time, regardless of whoever won. But that did not appear to be the case here. Serious human judgments were decided every day based on the winners or losers of these jailhouse games.

"OK, let's play another game," I said.

"Why? So's I can whip yo' ass again?" she retorted.

"Well, maybe so. We'll see." I lined up my red checkers. And as soon as I began to take the game very seriously, I started to win. We were at the stage of the game, near the end, when I had all kings, and she had only one. It was my turn, and I began to move my king backward.

"Oh hell no, you can't do *dat*," she declared. "You can only move dat king in da *forward* direction."

I began to object, "That's not right. I know the rules say that once a checker gets crowned, it can move in *both* directions. Why, you moved your kings both ways in the last two games."

"You crazy girl, I did not! Quit yo' honky-ass cheatin', or I'm outa here."

So I continued to play using Serena's rules, which changed quite regularly to suit her present condition. I moved all my kings in one direction only, and she began to gain on me. At another point in that game, she informed me that it was against the rules to jump diagonally or to jump more than one man at a time. By the time she was done with her on-the-spot, change-as-you-go rules, which applied only to me, she had won three more games. I saw how this was going to go on all day, if I let it. It was an impossible situation for me. If I got mad and quit, I would have nothing to pass my time again; if I continued to play, I would become more and more degraded and verbally abused.

I suddenly had an idea. "Are you ready to quit beating my ass in checkers and show me how to play chess?" I asked.

"Hell no, girl, are you *crazy*? You ain't eben no good at a damn baby-ass game. I couldn't eber teach a retard like you to play no game like chess."

My heart sank. I really and truly wanted to learn how to play chess. While I was trying to figure out my strategy to trick her into it, I struck up a conversation to pass the time. "How many kids you got?" I asked.

"Four an' dis one on da way. How 'bout choo?"

And before I knew it, we were actually having a halfway decent conversation. I found out that she was in because her estranged husband had decided to call the police and report that she had hundreds of dollars of unpaid parking tickets just so, according to her, he could "bring his ho home and screw her in front of his chil'ins," and she wouldn't be there to get in his way. I seriously doubted this story mainly because most every girl in the dayroom had referred to her as a "that crazy-ass crackhaid junkie" repeatedly. She also showed every sign of drug withdrawal. But I never let on that I doubted her story; it was just nice to hear someone's voice in the cell for once.

She talked about her four little kids and how very smart they were, how much she missed them, and how unfair it was for her husband to keep a mama from her children. She talked about how very nice their home was, how her kids went to a really prestigious school, and how good her husband's job was. And she insisted over and over again that she was going home by the next day. In fact, up to this point, that had been the only words that I had ever heard come out of her mouth daily. She would say something like, "Dare ain't no need fo' dat. I'm goin' home tomorrows anyways." She never got mail, she never had a visitor, she never went out into the dayroom for rotations. I let her talk nonstop that day that I shared commissary with her. That was the first time and the last time that she ever talked to me in more than monosyllables.

The next day, during my visitation with Bob, I noticed that Serena finally had a visitor. I was sitting in my usual position, at the phone as far down the narrow passageway as possible. She took the stool as far away from me as she could. But even though nine or ten stools separated us, it wasn't long before I could hear her screaming her lungs out at what appeared to be her husband. "You had no fuckin' right to do what you did to me, you selfish son uv a bitch! Now you get me outa this shithole right now an' let me go home to my chil'ins. I means it, you sorry Black motherfucker! An' dat goes for your cheap-ass, streetwalkin' ho too!"

I didn't want to be a snoop, but she was yelling and cursing so loudly that my eyes couldn't help but go in that direction. The young Black man on the other side of the glass was very good looking and immaculately dressed. He did not shout back at her but, instead, sat quietly, looking at her with pity in his eyes. After a while, he cut her loud cussing off by holding what appeared to be papers up to the window. She suddenly fell silent.

"What dose?" she asked, and upon hearing his reply, she began to weep loudly.

"Please don' do dis to me while I'm locked up. I'm helpless in here, Johnny. Wait till I gets out, an' we'll talk 'bout dis, OK? Don't take my chil'ins away from me. They's all I gots. Please, please, please give me anudder chance. I'll be good dis time. I promise I will."

I couldn't hear his reply since he was very quiet in his speech, and his body language told me that he kept himself very well composed. But I did know this—that whatever his reply was, it sent her immediately back into a streak of earsplitting cussing unlike any I had ever heard before. After a couple of minutes of this resounding verbal abuse, I saw the handsome young man shake his head, get up off his stool, and leave the visitation room without a sound.

From that day forward, Serena was never the same. That very day, an officer came to our cell and served her with two sets of papers from her husband—one for divorce, the other for custody of the four children. The other girls had always called her things like "that crazy-ass crackhaid" or "not right in the head" or "flipped out" or "crazy as a damn coot" or "psycho" or "just plain-ass nuts." They reminded me every day that I was sharing a cell with the craziest, most dangerous, most ready-to-blow time bomb in the entire pod. Most of them said things like, "If I were you, I'd sure as hell ax to be moved outa dat cell and into anudder one. Dat crazy-ass crackhaid gonna kill yo' ass in yo' sleep one a dese daze." And up to that point, I would just ignore them all. But after that day, things began to happen in our cell that made me reconsider the way that I viewed Serena.

There were constant plumbing problems in our pod and, from outside talk, throughout the entire jail. That afternoon, as soon as Serena and I returned from visitation, we discovered that the toilet in our cell was stopped up. I had to use the bathroom right after the officer served the papers on Serena. I guess the look on her face made me just that nervous. But when I went to flush our charming commode, it made an absolutely horrible sound. It sputtered and bubbled and spewed forth tiny gushes of water mixed with strings of cheap toilet paper. When all the commotion ceased, the water level established itself right even with the rim. An easier way to describe the position of the water would be to say that it was almost up to the toilet seat, only these marvelous jail thrones boasted no toilet seats whatsoever. I held my breath. I didn't know what I would do if the water decided to come tumbling over the edge and onto the floor. After all, I had no way of cleaning up the potential mess—no mop, no rags, no bucket, and certainly no disinfectant. On top of it all, Serena was giving me the evil eye; she was letting me know that I had screwed up again.

"Whadcha go an' do *dat* for? Now can't needer uv us use da t'ing if we needs to. You really *do* be stupid, don't cha?"

I rushed quickly to my own defense. "All I did was just flush the nasty thing. I promise. I didn't even use that much paper. I've heard the other girls in the dayroom talk about their toilets overflowing lately."

"*Overflowin'*! You better hope dis shit pot don't do dat, or I'll beat chur sorry White ass." She was throwing daggers at me with her squinting black eyes.

I looked at the swollen toilet bowl and then down at the floor. I couldn't win around this place. I couldn't play cards; I couldn't play checkers. I was pronounced too stupid to even learn to play chess. From every direction, I had jailbirds asking me constantly if I was "stupid" or if "somet'in' was wrong with me." And now I couldn't even flush our cell toilet without screwing up. If I stayed here much longer, I was going to be battling a serious loss of self-esteem.

I climbed up onto my top bunk and began to read a tattered New Testament that some poor soul had left behind. But every couple of minutes, my eyes rolled over to the toilet to check its current condition. An hour passed and then two, and the water level didn't budge. I was beginning to feel like I might have to use it again, and being locked up like an animal, I wondered what other choice I had but to use it and let it spit its nauseating contents all over our filthy floor. We made it through the night without a spillover, but we weren't so lucky the next morning.

After breakfast, watching my Rock Mountain sunrise, and my morning devotionals, I just absolutely could not hold it any longer. I climbed down off my top bunk and used it as sparingly as possible, using no toilet paper whatsoever and flushing it with the gentlest of motions. But none of this helped; it was time for her to blow. As soon as I flushed it, I knew I had made the queen mother of all mistakes.

That jailhouse chamber pot made a frightful hissing noise and then began to bubble up like a boiling pot of stew. It gushed and spurted and spat. Finally, the water and all its contents cascaded over the brim, shamelessly spilling over onto the floor and causing a flood of such magnitude that I stood motionless buried up to my ankles.

I looked at Serena. Her eyes were wide open, staring at the torrent of scum and slime, of sludge and muck. However, she remained totally stoic, like she didn't have a nerve in her body. She never got out of bed that morning.

My journal entry for May 26, 1999, read:

> Crummy day. The sky is gray & cloudy & gloomy through my little window. It's trying to rain. Everyone seems to be in a sluggish, depressed mood. No morning visitor. The toilets have been stopped up and unflushable since yesterday afternoon. We also do not have water half the time. Nobody wants to get out of bed. The stench is unbearable.

I couldn't remember what I did until the doors opened for morning rotation; I think I was too traumatized to recall. But as soon as the Big Click occurred, I rushed out to retrieve the one bucket on wheels that our whole pod had to share, and I mopped the floor of our cell as best I could with what they supplied to us, which was two or three inches of ice-cold water containing a drop or two of bleach. After that, I took myself a thorough hot shower.

After lunch, Serena finally lost it entirely. I knew something was terribly wrong when she came out of our cell to actually eat lunch that day. She had never done that before. Observing her trembling hands bring the sandwich with the raunchy meat to her pale lips made me feel very uncomfortable. The look in her dark eyes was distant and removed. It was somewhere between a fixed stare and the expression a movie actress may have on her face right after she has witnessed her best friend get murdered in a scary little cabin deep in a dark forest. Even the very aura surrounding her warned me to stay far away; something not so pretty was about to happen. And as usually was the case, my intuition was absolutely correct.

As soon as lunch was over and the Big Click occurred to tell us all to get back to our cells, Serena took off in the opposite direction, heading toward the dayroom toilet. By the toilet stood a huge gray garbage can, the only one in the dayroom. The trash can was one of the largest plastic garbage cans they make, I think. It was the size that most people use in their yards to dispose of their leaves, grass clippings, and small branches. And of course, it was full to the brim with garbage since, to my knowledge, no one ever bothered to come around and empty it.

Anyhow, Serena made a beeline for this humongous gray garbage pail. In the meantime, I had returned to our cell, not wishing to get into any kind of trouble with the guards. I kept the door open, however, waiting on Serena to get done with whatever it was she was doing and come back to our cell. As I peeked out the door, I could see Serena dragging this garbage can across the dayroom floor with all her might. Since she was so tiny and emaciated, it appeared to be quite a struggle. In fact, the plastic container seemed to actually be larger than she was. As soon as she was right outside our cell door, she stopped and plopped the garbage can right outside our door.

"What in the world are you doing?" I shouted. "Take that trash can right back where it belongs *now*! We're gonna get in a shit potful of trouble if you don't!"

But she was not listening. She had crossed that invisible line between reason and insanity, between coherence and dementia. I watched helplessly while she wrestled with the thirty-gallon bulging trash bag, removing it from the trash can and dumping it carelessly on the floor right outside our door. I tried everything to try to gain her attention. I screamed. I hollered. I jumped up and down. I even tried catching her attention by using a long string of choice cuss words I had learned recently from the other inmates. But she was gone, out of this world, possibly never to return.

After heaving the large black trash bag and all its contents onto the floor outside our door, she proceeded to drag the plastic garbage can into our cell. I had no idea what she had in mind, but I was not about to serve some kind of crazy jailhouse punishment because of the presence of this monstrous wastebasket in *our* cell. "Oh no, I don't think so!" I shrieked. "I don't know what in the hell you're doing with that nasty thing in here, but it's going right back out that door this second, young lady! I'm not about to take the blame for your crazy-ass actions! I *mean* it, damn it!"

I was nervously pacing the floor, waving my arms in the air, and pointing my finger as close to her face as I could get away with. I felt like I was yelling at one of my own kids, only this was a much more desperate situation. She paid me no attention whatsoever. Just then, our cell door experienced the Big Click, and I knew that I was locked away for the next several hours with Scary Serena, an overflowing toilet, and one enormous stinking garbage can. I looked at the ailing toilet full of sludge, the threatening trash can reeking of weeks-old garbage, and the look of total lunacy, of pure madness in Serena's face, and the room began to spin. My hungry stomach began to churn, and my knees began to buckle. I knew that I had to lie down on my bunk and quickly. I slowly climbed up to my bunk, pretending to sleep but keeping an eye open at all times to observe what Serena was going to do next.

I could not believe what I saw. She immediately boosted the bulky garbage can up under the pitiful little faucet on our miniature sink. Then she proceeded to push the button to make tiny spurts of water come out repeatedly. For some ungodly reason, she was trying to place water in this trash can.

I couldn't stand it any longer. I just had to ask her what she was doing. "What the hell are you doing? Why are you trying to put water in that huge-ass trash can? I hope you realize that it will take you twenty forevers to get any amount of water at all in that can at the rate the water comes out of that faucet."

She totally ignored me, that same deranged expression plastered on her face. I decided to take a different approach.

"Serena, is there anything I can do to help? Do you need a lot of water for some reason? Maybe we can figure out another way to get your water a cleaner way. Here, I have this new large plastic cup. You're welcome to use it." I scooped it up and held it out to her.

"You dumbass honky, don' choo know what I'm tryin's ta do here?" She looked at me as if *I* was the one who was insane.

"Dese here pohleese and jail peoples ain't gonna do nuttin's to fix dese sorry-ass broke shit pots. It be up to us. An' I ain't gonna sits here and smell yo' mudderfuckin' stink no mo'! Dose assholes won't give us no rubber t'ings to unplug da damn toilets, so I is gonna fill dis here can up wif water and pour it in da toilet to *make* it flush its damn self!" She pushed the button on the sink at breakneck pace, trying to fill up the immense container as quickly as possible.

"Now, Serena, honey, I don't know if that plan will work. I've never heard of doing exactly that," I reasoned.

"Dere you goes again, not knowin's somet'in' dat ebby-damn-buddy else know. You ain't neber heard of pourin' water real-ass fast into a stopped-up shit pot ta makes it flush? Where you bin, girrl? I swears, you is da *stupidest* damn White girl I has eber damn seen."

I was prepared to try a still different angle with her so she wouldn't overflow the toilet even more, but just then I realized that the garbage can must have had several little holes in it because it was springing tiny leaks all over the floor. Water was running everywhere. I had to stop her. "Serena, look, that garbage can has holes in it. Water is getting all over the floor. *Look* for god's sake!"

But it was too late. She was lost in that world of her own; she had lost touch with all reality. She continued to try to fill the leaky container, water running out of it as soon as she put it in. I pleaded with her a couple of more times but to no avail.

Soon I climbed down off my bunk and began to get all my belongings out from under her bed and take them "upstairs," where they would be safe. My new clothes, my snack food, my big shoes, my sacred toiletries, my useful shower shoes, my precious checker/chessboard and pieces, and especially my cards and letters from home; they all made their way up to the safety of my upper bunk. As soon as she saw what I was doing, Serena reeled around toward me and began to laugh hysterically, that frightened wild animal look raging in her black eyes. I huddled closer to my priceless stuff. For one of the first times since I had been locked up, I couldn't come up with a single idea of what to do. My creative juices had ceased to flow, and now I was probably going to die at the hands of this tiny lunatic. Serena had finally flipped out, and I was the sole person locked up with her.

I closed my eyes, waiting for her to strangle me or something. By this time, water was about an inch high all over our cell floor and was more than likely running out into the dayroom. If Serena didn't hurry up and kill me, I was sure that the guards would after they discovered the flood and the raunchy garbage dumped outside our door.

But something very different happened instead. I heard the Big Click, and this time, I *knew* that it was our door that clicked open. As my heart beat wildly in my chest, Coco—the large boisterous girl who had stolen my sandwich the first day—strutted into our cell. Now a few things have to be understood about Coco. She was locked up in the Coward County Jail awaiting transfer to Metro, the gigantic women's prison in Atlanta. She had been an employee for the IRS on two separate occasions and had been convicted of embezzling government money on two separate dates. According to her story, she had served a little time over the first charge of embezzlement, had been rehired by the IRS, and had now been convicted of misappropriation of government money a second time. To me, her story was very hard to believe since one had to ask oneself why in blazes would our government rehire someone who had stolen taxpayer monies from us? Anyhow, Coco was somewhat of a celebrity at CCJ since she had been there for quite some time, awaiting transfer. She also had the type of personality that made it impossible to be in the same room with her and not be totally engulfed in her every move and shenanigan. She was loud and tumultuous, rowdy and rambunctious, a real show-off of sorts.

The guards seemed to be amused by her clamorous antics and had awarded her with all kinds of jailhouse privileges. The one special favor they had bestowed on her that sent the other girls into deep bouts of jealousy was that of being the laundry girl. This title meant that, during the times that the rest of us were locked down in our cells, Coco had the freedom to get out into the dayroom *by herself*; go from cell door to cell door gathering up a few washcloths, towels, and dirty socks; and then leave the dayroom and go down the hall to the laundry room. Once there, she apparently spent long hours doing a few items of laundry and then returned to the dayroom, where she took hours upon hours folding the clothes on the round stainless steel tables.

While she folded, she became a one-woman Motown showcase. She thunderously belted out tunes from Aretha Franklin, Diana Ross, and Marvin Gay. She danced furiously, reeling and jerking, puffing and panting, shaking her black braids, beating her feet against the hard, cold floor. She took this so far as to go up to each cell window and perform her exhibition for a few seconds before going on to the next. The guards never seemed to stop her uproarious, brassy behavior but instead seemed to be outwardly amused by her performances. Day after day, she was a one-woman show in the deserted dayroom, all under the false pretense of laundry needing to be washed constantly.

Of course, this dirty laundry scam awarded her the privilege of asking the guards to open any cell of her choice at any time for the purpose of returning clean laundry or picking up dirty clothes. Most of the incidences that I had observed in the past involved her coming into people's cells to catch up on the latest inmate gossip, get a few black braids added to her do, beg large amounts of commissary foods, or generally just wreak havoc. The guards allowed her to spend any amount of time she wished in each inmate's cell, never so much as questioning her about her intentions or her timetable. In general, she was one noisy, bold, brazen, immodest, daring hotshot.

On that awful day, when I thought that Crazy Serena was finally going to do me in or else the guards were going to put me in solitary for weeks, Coco was the last human being I felt I needed to see. The last time she pretended she had laundry for us, she barged into our cell, demanding one of my chocolate brownies.

"An' don' tell me yew ain't got no brownie, White giirrl, 'cuz Aah knows wha' ebbybody gits from da stow," she announced.

I gave her my brownie that time and every time after that. She was just too big and mean and intimidating not to. And now here she was, in all her shining glory, showing up in our cell at my very darkest hour. I just didn't need this right now. I started to reach in my bag and pull out a brownie or a cookie, anything to get rid of her quickly. But that was not how the scene played out. She must have noticed the pure, unadulterated fear radiating from my eyes as I huddled over my bags of belongings. Or maybe it was the trembling of my hands or the fact that every bit of color had drained out of my frightened face.

"Hey! What goin' on in dis here place? Wuz up wit' dat nasty-ass garbage outside chur door an' dat damn wadders awl ober da fuckin' place?" She reeled around and confronted Serena outright.

"Giirrl, wha' da mudderfuckin' maddah wit' yer crazy ass? Yew betta stop dis shit here, or else, Ah is gonna git yo' ass in baaad troubles wit' da pohleece!"

Serena paid Coco no attention whatsoever. In fact, at that stage of the game, I was not really sure she even knew Coco was there. She just continued her crazed undertaking of trying to fill up the leaking garbage can with tiny spurts of water so she could eventually flush the "sorry-ass broke shit pot."

When she discovered that Serena had totally lost it, Coco's attention turned toward me. "Yew OK?" she inquired. "Is her sorry ass scarin' yew? Yew wants outa dis here cell wit' Psycho Ass Girl?"

I nodded slowly. Nobody had more power over the guards in this place than Coco, unless it was Amanda. Maybe she could actually get me out of here before I died a horrible death.

"OK den, jis' waits raht dere on yer bed, an' Ah'll go tell da pohleece to moves yew to anudder cell." She looked at me with what I actually thought might be sympathy in her dark eyes. "Yew done real good, Whitey. Ain't none o' us woulda bin ables ta stand bein' locked up wit' dis here crazy-ass crackhaid as long as yew done." She looked me over, head to toe two or three times, as if she was sizing me up to be able to tell the guards what might make me worthy to have to spend their time going through the necessary steps to move my residency. Then she glanced at Scary Serena, shook her head slowly, and left our cell.

After a few seconds, I climbed down cautiously from my top bunk and waded through the water and over to the small window in our door. My curiosity had gotten the best of me; I just had to see what was going on between Coco and the guards. But I could not believe what I saw.

Coco had apparently asked the guards to let Amanda out of her cell because both girls were standing by the big dayroom door, the one that led to the hallway, and Amanda was talking into the speaker that went directly to the guards. I couldn't hear what she was saying, but by the expression on her face, she was trying her hardest to persuade them of something. I had noticed in the past that Amanda usually remained quiet and collected, almost cool, as she went about her daily business of trying to control the world around her. And by doing this, she was almost always successful in getting whatever it was she wanted. But this time was a little different; she seemed to be having to plead a bit more than usual. Even Coco joined in after a while, waving her big arms and pointing back at our cell every few seconds. These two girls were actually working hard on my behalf. For a second, I was filled with gratitude, but that quickly turned into a large dose of suspicion.

What was with this Amanda chick anyhow? First, she brought me toiletries for my introductory jail shower, and then she taught me the ropes and the lingo. But that was not all. Then she went on to save me from getting snuffed out by the monstrous Bicycle, and now she was serving as my savior from the crazed lunatic Serena. What is her interest in me, a frightened Caucasian sissy, anyhow?

Before I could finish analyzing the situation, Amanda was at my cell door, motioning for me to come with her. I waited for the Big Click, and in a couple seconds, it happened.

"Come on! Come on! Hurry! Follow me." Amanda was as excited as I had ever seen her. "Now listen closely. When I take you up to the speaker, tell the guard this: Ma'am, I would like to room with Amanda, please. My current cellmate has flipped out, and I am scared of her. I feel that she may be a danger to others. Thank you." Then she added, "Don't be afraid. This guard's real nice. She's not like the one was the other day."

We were walking toward the speaker in the dayroom, slowly so she would have enough time to instruct me on exactly what I needed to say. I was shocked at what I was hearing. I began to question what I thought I had just heard. "You mean I'm going to share a cell with you?" I questioned, not believing that she actually wanted me in her cell.

"Don't worry about all that shit right now." We were approaching the speaker. "Just say what I told you to say."

I stepped up to the speaker timidly and pressed the button. I was sweating profusely, and my whole body was shaking. Just three days earlier, Amanda had played an ornery little trick on me. She had told me to ask the guard if I could move out of my cell and into a different one because I was afraid of my cellmate. Not knowing any better, I had done exactly what Amanda had told me. What had happened wasn't pretty. Actually, it had shaken me up pretty badly. The guard who was on duty at the time ended up being one of the meanest, most coldhearted, most apathetic guards in the jail. Of course, I didn't know this since I had avoided the guards since day 1 with all my might.

Anyhow, when I asked this particular guard if I could move, she had screamed back at me at the top of her lungs, "Wha' da *hell* you talkin' 'bout, giirrl? Wha' choo t'ink dis here jail is? A goddamn Holiday Inn? Now gits back to yah cell an' don' bother me no mo', or Aah'll putt yer ass in lockdown!"

This encounter had caused me to almost break out in tears. I was so scared and embarrassed. But Amanda had had a quite different reaction. She had thrown back her tiny head and laughed and laughed, that same deep belly laugh I had heard her do so many times before. In fact, she had laughed so hard that she had almost choked. "Wha' choo t'ink dis here jail is? A goddamn Holiday Inn?" she mocked the jail guard with the nasty attitude.

"That's so fuckin' funny," she added, still laughing.

And now here I was, facing that same intimidating button on that same terrorizing speaker. I wasn't sure that I had the courage to ask this question again. But I surprised even myself. I stepped right up, pressed the button firmly, and spoke audibly and distinctly into the speaker. "Ma'am, I would like to room with Amanda, if you think that would be all right. I don't feel safe anymore in there with Serena. She's in there flooding the cell and everything." I thought I would give her a few more details than Amanda told me to.

I paused. Amanda poked me hard in my ribs. "This is all, only if you feel it would be all right with you, ma'am, 'cuz I don't want to put you to any unnecessary trouble or anything, and it's all entirely up to you. I'll accept any decision you make." This was embarrassing. I was groveling to the guard, being a true brownnose.

Amanda stomped on my foot with all her might. I quickly added, "Thank you, ma'am."

It seemed like an eternity before the voice came back at me from the guard tower. "OK den, get yer stuff an' move outa 303 an' into 301 but do it as quick as yew can."

I couldn't believe my ears. I was going to room with Amanda—my protector, my defender, my true guardian angel. Amanda and Coco both helped me move my stuff from the frightening, nightmarish environment of cell 303 and into the peaceful, homey atmosphere of cell 301. As soon as I stepped foot into Amanda's cell, a rush of relief poured over me. It was beautiful—or at least as beautiful as a jail cell in this hellhole could be.

BEELZEBUB

I HAD FAILED TO mention up to this point what an incredible artist Amanda was. Every second that she wasn't looking out for the underdog, adding braids to some poor soul's hair, or tricking the guards, she was doing art. Art in every form imaginable covered the walls of her cell. Pencil sketches of different inmates and their families hung over the desk. Pictures of nature and animals and cartoon characters drawn in bright Crayola colors on large manila envelopes lined the big wall. A card of a splendid yellow butterfly hung from her light fixture by a long thread pulled off the hem of a T-shirt. Purple, pink, yellow, and red flowers drawn with crayons on white envelopes and then painstakingly cut out with the blade of her razor surrounded the mirror above the sink. Happy little tulips danced across the wall above the top bunk. Smiling little Black faces drawn on pieces of yellow legal paper peered out from the nook of the bottom bunk. The skinny window was surrounded with stars and moons and suns, all drawn on what appeared to be one continuous sheet of white paper. The right half of the desk was full of greeting cards and family pictures that she had apparently gotten from other inmates. The other half of the desk was full of works in progress. Crayons, pencils, razor blades broken from her plastic shavers, manila envelopes, plain white envelopes, pieces of cardboard, pieces of legal yellow paper, pieces of plain white paper, and tubes and tubes of toothpaste were scattered haphazardly all over the desktop; a few had fallen to the floor.

"You like it?" she said. "I sure was lucky to grab this one from Moleface when she left. It's the best one here, being it's the corner one. That makes it bigger, you know."

I looked around. It really did look bigger than my other cell. The one solid wall opposite the bunk beds was situated at an angle, and suddenly, I realized that this was because the entire pod was in the shape of a circle. Now this all made sense. The four end cells were bigger because they were located along a spherical wall, causing them to be shaped somewhat like a large slice of pie. Don't get me wrong. They weren't *much* bigger, but a few inches are greatly appreciated when we are talking about being locked in a tiny cage twenty hours a day.

Several days earlier, Moleface, Big Charlotte, and Erline had all left within a few hours of one another. Moleface had gone first. She left for prison during the night and had been so quiet about her departure that I didn't even realize she was gone until I noticed Amanda coming out of her cell one day at lunch. Erline and Big Charlotte had been much more verbal about their exits.

Erline was going home to her estranged husband, and that always made the inmates much antsier when they knew their time was near. She jumped the gun to an extreme, though, when she circulated throughout the dayroom one day, giving away all her toiletries and personal items and announcing, "Ah'm a-goin' home to mah ole man today. Ah jis' a-feel it in mah liddle ole biddy bones an' awl." It ended up being three more days before she truly went home, and she had to bum shampoo and toothpaste in the meantime.

Big Charlotte's departure was, by far, the most memorable and the most heart wrenching. I was sound asleep in my bed back when I was still in 303 with Crazy Serena. It was about three in the morning, I would guess. Suddenly, I heard a muffled voice come over the speaker. This was followed by the loudest scream of delight I had ever heard. Soon after, Big Charlotte's voice began to shout out. It was such joyous yelling; it was almost as if she was singing. "'And the Lord my God shall deliver you from the ways of the evil man, from the man that speaketh froward things, who leaves the paths of uprightness to walk in the ways of darkness' (Proverbs 2:12–14). 'And the light of heaven shall shine upon the road ahead of ye. Whenever thou art cast down and afraid, He shall lift ye up again. Yes, He shall save the humble and help even sinners by His pure hand' (Job 22:28–30)." All the way from her miserable little cell through the echoing dayroom and out the heavy hallway door, she preached, ranting and raving and declaring the righteousness of the Lord. The entire time that she gathered up her belongings to leave, her declarations of the Holy Spirit served as a booming refrain to the tired guard's nagging voice. It actually almost had a rhythm to it.

The exhausted guard would scream, "I said *pack it up*—now!"

And Big Charlotte would avow, "'Hallelujah, praise His holy name! Exalt the Lord our God, and worship at his holy mountain in Jerusalem, for He alone is holy!' (Psalm 99:9)."

Even though I lay in bed wide awake until breakfast, that night was one of my favorite nights of all. It reminded me that there were still good people in the world who believed and never lost faith. More importantly, it reaffirmed my own faith and strengthened my own relationship with God.

After Erline, Moleface, and Big Charlotte left, I felt sure enough like a square peg in a round hole. I was now the only White girl in Coward County Jail, 300 SE Women's Pod, except for Pearl, Harley, and a nice-looking redheaded lady who was about my age and lived upstairs. We didn't get much chance at all to get to know any of the upstairs residents since they were always out in the dayroom during their own rotations. About the only time we ever saw the upstairs dwellers was during meals. After the three White ladies left, I made it a point to go around this lady more. I guess I just felt a need to bond with someone who looked like she may have come from a similar background. She was clean, quiet, and very, very mannerly.

During supper one day, I discovered that her name was Caroline. I had remembered Pearl routing quite a bit of mail in the past to an upstairs lady named Caroline. I decided to ask her about herself. I learned that she was serving one year at Coward County Jail for embezzlement. But her story wasn't even *close* to Coco's. It seemed that Caroline had worked at the front desk for an area physician who had entrusted her with his books. The middle-aged doctor had recently suffered a midlife crisis, had divorced his longtime wife, and had remarried a twenty-year-old. The new trophy wife loved to spend the old doctor's money and regularly did just that, only there was one main problem. The old bastard was cheap, a real miserly, closefisted penny-pincher. So the new young wife got creative, only unfortunately she did it at Caroline's expense. The little new woman decided that if she couldn't get enough money directly from the old stingy codger, she could devise a scheme to get it from his business.

So she started to write checks off his business for her numerous shopping sprees except the checks happened to be endorsed by his office manager, who happened to be Caroline. The new wife would come to Caroline, tell her she needed a check for a certain amount, and then tell her that her husband had OK'd it. Caroline would have to sign them on the back since her signature was the only one approved by the bank. You can probably guess the rest of the story. The new trophy wife got caught and swore she didn't know a thing about the checks. The office manager took the rap and went to trial, convicted of embezzlement from her boss. She ended up in the county rathole for a year. End of story.

After I heard Caroline's story, I truly did feel like I had a special bond with her. We had a lot of similarities. We had both been accused of stealing money that we didn't take, we had both worked in medical offices, and we were both the victims of a system that did not work. Furthermore, I learned that Caroline had a very devoted husband, one who came to visit her frequently; she received a lot of mail, and she spent her spare time reading and writing letters.

I started to eat many of my meals with Caroline. She was not rude and obnoxious at the table like Amanda and the other girls. She didn't poke and prod and point at my food, asking insistently if I was gonna eat this or that. She didn't smack her lips loudly, chew large chunks of food with her mouth open, slurp her drink, or stir the Kool-Aid with her arm. She didn't belch, pass gas, or reach halfway across the table and scoop large spoonfuls of food off someone else's tray. Caroline sat up straight with perfect posture, placing her left hand politely in her lap. She ate slowly and deliberately, chewing each bite thoroughly. She sipped her drink daintily and dabbed at her lips with a small neatly folded square of toilet paper that she always brought from her cell at mealtimes. She began each meal with giving away one piece of her doughy white bread, and she chose a different girl each meal to give it to. This made her quite popular but only at mealtimes.

One of the best things about Caroline was that she was the one to educate me about getting reading materials in jail. I had always been a leisure-time reader. In fact, reading was my main passion ever since I could remember. When I first got to jail, no one seemed to know anything about how to go about obtaining books. All I could scrape up to read was a dog-eared old New Testament someone had stuffed in my bed frame and a few copies of the Baptist *Guideposts*. These were tiny chronicles full of inspirational very short stories that readers had submitted about personal experiences. They were nice and uplifting, but it took me an average of about five minutes to get through one from cover to cover. Every single day, out of pure desperation, I asked the other inmates how to get hold of some reading material. And every time, they would all look at me as if I had a screw loose. Most of them would not even bother to reply. But Caroline changed all that.

The very first time I asked her about books, she replied that her husband had just spent six hours copying an entire novel on a Xerox machine and sent it to her in a manila envelope. She said that she was done reading it, and if I would like, she would bring it to me at the next meal. "You might not want to read it," she whispered. "It's really pretty depressing. It's about a newly married young guy who dies of a brain tumor."

"Oh, that's OK," I replied. "I don't care *what* it's about, just as long as I have something to read." And I really didn't care what the subject of the book was, until I got to the very end.

Caroline proved to be true to her word. She brought the fat manila envelope full of copied pages to lunch the next day and slipped it under the table to me. I thanked her and spent the next day and a half on my top bunk, totally engulfed in this wonder, an actual book of my very own to read at my own convenience. But then the end came.

This spectacular young man, the character whom the reader is led to fall in love with, dies at age thirty-one, leaving behind his grieving new bride, his bright future, and all their dreams. On the day I read of his demise, I lay on my top bunk and wept uncontrollably. Amanda and all her jokes could not console me. I skipped dinner and didn't write a single letter home. I talked about the character in the book for fifteen minutes when Bob came to visit me the next morning. I was quite obviously and totally obsessed with the man who died and the woman he left behind. I carried this grief with me for the next few days and vowed to never read another sad book, or even a slightly dramatic one, while I was stuck there in that jail.

But then a sudden revelation concerning obtainment of books came to Caroline. She had been asking around about a way to receive books at the jail. Of course, for several days, she had gotten nowhere at all, especially when she attempted to ask the little mailman. But persistence does pay off. She finally came across a little tidbit of information while talking to Harley one day. Harley always seemed to have a cheap smutty novel with a lewd picture on its cover. She carried these offensive paperbacks with her in the dayroom and could be seen pouring through their pages at any given time, if one bothered to look through her cell window. Because of the nature of her foul publications, Caroline considered her a nonsource when it came to collecting information on book acquirement. But out of pure desperation one afternoon, she asked Harley about her protocol for getting books through to her. The reply came immediately.

The rules stated that an inmate at CCJ could only be sent books *directly from the publisher*, which meant that books sent to us could not be sent by private *people* but only from the publishing warehouse. The way to get around this rule, Harley told Caroline, was to have one of our friends order books from Amazon.com on the internet, pay for them with a credit card, and have them shipped directly to the jail address. We could receive three books at a time.

The day that Caroline relayed this wonderful message to me was one of the best days of my incarceration. I went directly to the phone line, fought several rough inmates for a phone, called my friend Ginger, and begged her to get on the internet right away and order me three good books. I knew she would pick out excellent ones. She had taught English literature at the high school level for thirty years. She promised to do it immediately. I was in heaven for the next several days simply at the very thought of having something decent to read.

In the meantime, I was reading everything I could get my hands on; and oftentimes, it was out loud to Amanda in our cell. I read parts of the New Testament. Amanda asked questions like why I thought Jesus was so totally forgiving and why he liked to hang around misfits and screwups. I read personal testimonials from *Guidepost* magazines. Her eyes grew big and her mouth dropped open at stories about guardian angels pulling victims of car crashes out of the wreckage and then disappearing into thin air.

Then one night in the dayroom, Harley let us have one of her precious raunchy novels. "Just long enough to read. Then I need it right back," she told us. I sat for hours on the cold, hard cell floor, propped against the wall, reading to Amanda, who was comfortably lying on her lower bunk, which boasted two mattresses and a homemade pillow. This time, both of our eyes grew big at the lurid descriptions of the pornographic bedroom scenes and the lewd, offensive detailed accounts of the unrepeatable acts committed at the obscene parties for the rich and famous.

One boring Tuesday morning, while I was reading what I had dubbed "morning devotionals" to Amanda, I innocently came across the word *Beelzebub* in the book of Matthew. The passage went something like this. "Then Beelzebub taketh him up into the holy city, and setteth him on a pinnacle of the temple—"

Amanda stopped me short. "Hold on. What was that crazy-ass word you just read, the one that started with a *B*?" she inquired.

"Beelzebub," I replied. "That's another name for the devil."

"Say it again," she begged.

"Beelzebub," I slowly answered.

Her dark eyes lit up. An impish grin spread across her face. "Be-*el*-zebub!" she hollered. She apparently liked the sound of her newly acquired word because she began to practice it in various contexts and with assorted accents.

"Get thee back, Beelze-*bub*!" she screamed.

"I shall cast thee out, *Be*-el-*ze*-bub!" she cried.

"And the sick were all possessed with Be-*el*-zebub!" she shrieked. She was quite excited over the whole matter. She had jumped off her lower bunk and onto the floor. Part of the time, she had been yelling out the cell window; but most of the time, she had just been jumping up and down excitedly, hardly able to contain herself.

After that day, the word *Beelzebub* became a staple in her vocabulary. "Wake up, *Beelzebub*!" she shrieked at the top of her lungs the next morning. The first time she did it, I was so startled that I jumped off the top bunk and hit the floor so hard that I thought I had broken my leg.

"The guards are all Be-*el*-zebub!" she squealed, one day when they refused to take us to the exercise room.

"Oh yeah, well, you are full of Beelze-*bub*!" she howled in Bicycle's face when she wouldn't turn the TV channel to a decent show one night.

In fact, I got so used to hearing her belt out her new favorite word at random that it no longer alarmed me at all. She awakened me nearly every morning with it, declared breakfast to be from Beelzebub, rebuked Beelzebub during morning devotionals, pronounced our cell to be as filthy as Beelzebub's den, stated that all the guards and most of the inmates were related to Beelzebub, and decidedly proclaimed crack cocaine to be the main dietary staple of Beelzebub.

Once I was rooming with Amanda, everything about my jail experience began to change. The other inmates had such an intense combination of fear and respect for her that we girls of cell 301 got to be first at most everything. I began to learn of jailhouse events that I didn't even know existed back when I had been in cell 303 with Serena. As she always had, Amanda continued to show me the ropes.

One morning shortly after our devotionals, she began to educate me concerning cell cleanliness. She informed me of the way that the cleaning protocol was *supposed* to be as set up by the joint prison systems in the state of Georgia. Every morning, first thing, the guards were *supposed* to bring each pod a bucket on wheels in *good* working condition full of *hot*, sudsy water, accompanied by a relatively new mop, a good broom, and a full complement of cleaning chemicals hanging on the sides of the overhead rack. The inmates were then to take turns sweeping and then mopping their cells and the dayroom, free to ask the guards for clean, hot, sudsy water whenever the old water became too dirty or too cold. But *that*, Amanda informed me, was just the *ideal*—the way things were *supposed* to be. I soon learned that the cleaning protocol in Coward County Jail was like most everything else—far, far from ideal.

Here was the *reality* of the situation: About every fourth or fifth morning, at no particular set time whatsoever, a sleepy, lethargic guard would reluctantly position a rusty, broken-down old bucket on worn-out wheels in front of each pod's dayroom door. If, and only *if*, one of the inmates came to the door to retrieve the bucket, the guard in the watchtower might open the door within fifteen minutes or so for the inmate to get it, but that was only if the guard felt like opening the door that particular day. So if one had the good luck just to get the bucket over the threshold of the door, this was exactly what that person would discover. The corroded old pail on wheels that were so worn that they would barely turn would have about three inches of *ice-cold* water on its very bottom. No assortment of cleaning chemicals would be hanging from the overhead rack. A frayed, worn-out old mop and a ragged broom missing most of its bristles may accompany the bucket, and if one was really lucky, a dented plastic jug with a few drops of Clorox remaining at rock bottom might be thrown in for good measure.

But this dismal reality didn't cause Amanda any great distress. This was just another daily event that she had learned to take control of the best she could. She seemed to possess a special radar for when the bucket was going to arrive because, on those precise days, she would get up a little earlier, get out of the cell, and be waiting at the dayroom door. As soon as the bucket appeared, she knew just how to charm the guard into opening the door, and soon the bucket was all ours. She would immediately go to work as if she was a janitorial supervisor for a large firm.

"Now you sweep the floor, *quick*! Hurry! We ain't got much time! Get up all those nasty-ass hair balls and pieces of paper and shit. Come on! You can't be that slow, or one of those assholes'll steal our bucket. Come on now, girl! Go! While you do that, I'll freshen up our jar a little." She began to quickly pour half the tiny bit of Clorox into an empty peanut butter jar that she kept hidden behind our toilet and then promptly poured the remaining half into the bucket of water.

"Now I'll show your ass how ta mop this sorry-ass floor till it shines like the top of a fat, bald man's head. No! Not like *that*! Now watch, rich girl. Ya take this here piece-a-shit mop, an' ya dip it in this here bleach water, an' ya wring it real tight like this. Then ya put yerself into it, like this." And her tiny, little body began to sway back and forth. It was as if she was dancing to some nonexistent music with the mop. Within seconds, she mopped under the bunk beds, in all the corners, under the sink, and around the toilet. She left no crevice uncleaned, no corner untouched. I had never before or since witnessed such a sight of pure janitorial talent, of true custodial genius.

By this time, several of the other inmates were lined up outside our cell door, getting more livid by the minute. "Hurry the fuck up, Manda! That fuckin' mop's for all o' us, not just fuckin' you and that fuckin' weird-ass friend o' yers." Pearl spat out indignantly, her hands planted on her hips the entire time.

Ethel decided to take a more diplomatic approach. "Ah can't *believes* ya won't share da mop wit' me, Mandy. Ah's yer bes' frien' in dis here hell. Ah helps ya out awl da time, an' now here you is, jist a-bein' awl greedy wit' dat mop an' awl," she whined, shaking her head slowly and staring at the floor with the most submissive, pathetic body posture I had ever seen.

"Jis' gimme da goddamn mop, Amanda. Our rooms is jis' as dirty ass as yers. Yew ain't no better'n any o' da resta us. Yew is *always* gittin' da mop 'fore any o' us. Dis time, I tell ya what ah'm gonna do. Ah'll tell da goddamn pohleece on yer nigga ass, is what Ah'll do!" Coco had decided to pull rank on Amanda since none of the other girls had gotten anywhere whatsoever with their pleadings so far. She paced excitedly as she shouted her threats, looking toward the large dayroom door as if she meant to go through with her browbeating promise of harm.

Jasmine, the human exhibitionist, stood fourth in line, nothing but a bedsheet wrapped around her naked body. She had been staring at the entire scene through half-open, sleep-matted eyes, projecting no facial expression whatsoever. As soon as she had had enough and saw that no one was getting anywhere with Amanda, she dropped the sheet on our cell floor, bent over, mooned us, and walked slowly back to her cell buck naked.

Caroline, my new friend from upstairs, waited patiently for her turn without a word. But her face told the whole story. She watched as our

DORAMAE BROOKSHIRE

three inches of mop water became blacker and blacker and as more of the few remaining mop strings and broom bristles dropped off onto the floor. She knew that she was fifth in line, that she was not aggressive like the other girls, and that she had no chance, once again, of getting her own cell clean. Her pale, worn face was dejected and oppressed and laden with sorrow. It spoke of heartache and gloom and loss of one's spirit.

Harley, the expectant mother of twins, was more direct. "Come on, Amanda, I'm just about sick of your sorry black ass hoggin' the mop every fuckin' time. Give the goddamn thing over right now, or I'll beat yer motherfuckin' nigger ass right here in front of every last one of these sorry motherfuckers."

But not to my alarm at all, Amanda remained cool as a cucumber. She continued to waltz with the precious, coveted mop without so much as batting an eyelash. She appeared to be deaf to all the idle threats that were engulfing her. On the other hand, I remained on edge, white knuckled, nail biting, ready to pounce on any perpetrator at any time. Either that or run for the dayroom door, screaming at the top of my lungs for help. But I knew perfectly well that the latter plan would gain me no help whatsoever from the apathetic guards. So I stood planted solidly on the cell floor, watching Amanda and her mop as all the other observers were doing. I was just thankful as hell that Bicycle; her lesbian lover, Jazzy; and Serena were all still in bed.

Finally, none too soon, Amanda stopped her waltzing and, in one giant movement, kicked the bucket disgustingly toward no one in particular, stared lovingly at our sparkling clean cell room floor, and slammed the door in the angry mob's faces. The water in the bucket was now thick and black and slimy. It resembled two inches of used motor oil from an old car that hadn't had its oil changed in years. Tiny pieces of hair, wrappers, and squished junk food floated on the top of the black sludge. I knew no one else had a chance of boasting a clean cell that week.

I felt a strange combination of emotions. On the one hand, I was so relieved and proud to finally be in a cell that was not dangerously filthy and of enormous risk to my health. On the other hand, I felt a little sorry for the line of inmates who apparently waited week after week to be able to clean their own grimy, slimy, putrid cells.

I peeked secretly through our cell door window. Ethel and Caroline were both shuffling back upstairs, their passive, dejected faces staring expressionless at the gritty dayroom floor. Another week of living in muck and rot and all kinds of foul matter was the main thing on their minds. The other three were not quite so submissive. Pearl waved her fist in the air and shouted out her favorite word. "Wuh, fuck, fuck, *fuck* you, Amanda, high-and-fuckin'-mighty queen of the fuckin' world! You *and* that fuckin' creepy asshole in there with ya! I hope ya *both* choke on yer own fuckin' snot!"

Coco immediately got into the spirit. "OK, nigga, ya finally done it dis time. We don' *none* o' us *eber* gits ta use da bucket exceptin' fer yer sorry black ass. I's gonna tell da pohleese on yer nigga ass, is what Ah'm gonna do, and dat's goddamn *dat*! We'll see how yer uppidy ass likes *dat*."

I wondered if Coco would ever really go through with it. I started to worry briefly about her tattling to the guards. But then I realized that it wouldn't matter anyhow because the "pohleese" were all so cold, calloused, and apathetic that they would never come close to doing anything about it.

Harley decided to spare the words and go exclusively with gestures. With an angry expression, she repeatedly held up her middle finger and wagged it at us, first on one hand and then on the other. She then held her left hand in the crease of her right arm and quickly bent her right elbow, jerking her arm toward her weatherworn face. I thought I saw her mouth the words "up yours, motherfuckers."

HOOSIER ROOMMATE

I T WASN'T LONG after I began rooming with Amanda that I noticed something was wrong with my legs. They just didn't feel right. They hurt every time I moved and sent me through the ceiling with agonizing pain every time I rubbed against anything, especially with my upper thighs. I was almost afraid to find out what was wrong. By this time, I knew that if I got sick while I was here, I might as well hang it up. Nobody at this godforsaken place was about to help me. I would just have to suffer and die.

One night I got up the courage to look down at my legs while I was using the toilet. What I saw made me sick to my stomach. From my groin down to my midcalf, I was nothing but one gigantic multicolored bruise. I knew that the ebony contusions that covered both front thighs were the biggest bruises I had ever seen in my life. In fact, the sight was so foreign to me that I jumped back from pure shock when I first looked.

I got up from the head as quickly as I could, pulled up my orange pants, and just stood there for a minute, not knowing what to do next. I decided maybe I had better check out the rest of my body as painful as that may prove to be. I slowly dragged myself over to the tiny cracked mirror over the sink, squinted to adapt to the poor lighting, and took a look. But the poor, haggard person glaring back at me could not be *me*. This lady in the mirror was hollow-eyed, ravaged, almost cadaverous. Her pale face was worn and drawn up like that of an elderly woman who has given it all up and is ready to die.

I rubbed my eyes and blinked them several times to make sure I wasn't seeing things. But upon further investigation, I discovered something even more distressing. I was sporting two distinctly black eyes, real, honest-to-goodness black and blue shiners. My eyes had always been fairly deep set and tended to appear dark when I lost too much sleep or didn't get the proper vitamins. But I had never witnessed them being anywhere *near* this black. I jumped back with astonishment from the tired-faced black-eyed zombie in the mirror.

After the initial shock wore off, I decided to take inventory of the situation. There had to be some simple explanation to why I had turned into one humongous piece of bruised fruit in just two short weeks. I knew that I was not eating right. But how could I with the constant diet of doughy white bread, overcooked pasta, and Kool-Aid? I had begun giving everything on my breakfast tray to Amanda except for the grits, and I kept two pieces of bread a day to sneak into my cell for a peanut butter sandwich at lunch with my own overpriced peanut butter from the commissary. There were no fruits, vegetables, whole grains, or dairy products around, and I was never given the opportunity to see sunshine or have fresh air the whole time I was there. By the time supper came every day at four o'clock, I was usually so sluggish and discouraged that I often gave most of the food on my tray to Amanda once again. She began to really like me for this. She thought I was just a pushover, some White girl whom she could easily trick out of her food. But I was 100 percent aware of what was going on; I just didn't care much at that point.

I knew that because of this diet of starches and sugars and no vitamins, my health was in great jeopardy. I had always tended to be a little on the anemic side and always had to make a special effort to incorporate a lot of iron into my diet. I had taken an iron-fortified multivitamin every day of my life. I had even had periods in my life when my family physician had prescribed iron supplements for me. In short, if I didn't keep my diet full of fresh fruits, vegetables, milk, and vitamins, I could be up the creek without a paddle in a very short time. I knew that vitamin A was nonexistent in that place since there were no fruits and vegetables. Likewise, vitamin C was absent; I never saw a citrus fruit or any orange juice *once*. Vitamin D comes in the form of fortified milk and natural sunlight. Those could be ruled out. And vitamin B is often found in various meats. I figured that this one was also a no go since the few pieces of meat I saw while I was in Coward County Jail were few and far between and were the size of a shriveled-up pea.

I knew what was wrong here, but I was totally helpless about exactly *how* to help myself. So I crawled up onto the upper bunk, accidentally scraping against the hard, cold metal on my way up. This caused even further pain, and I lay awake most of that night, my legs throbbing against the cover, wondering what I was going to do about this problem or if I would even survive this whole ordeal.

Early the next morning, I asked Amanda why we could not buy pieces of fruit from the commissary. We could buy crackers, potato chips, cookies, honey buns, and a whole array of candies. Why then didn't they offer *good* foods on the commissary list?

She informed me that, once upon a time, apples and oranges had been offered from the commissary but that the inmates had then abused the privilege by hoarding the fruits, stashing them away in corners of their cells in plastic garbage bags, and had consequently brewed their own homemade alcoholic "hoochie" punch. The guards during that era had been unable to figure out *why* in the world half the inmates were staggering around like a bunch of drunks most of the time. Once the homemade fruit punch distilleries were discovered, that permanently did away with any fruits being offered from the jail commissary.

I found this story amusing, almost hilariously funny, especially the way that Amanda told it. I thought to myself how this was still another example of the inmates outsmarting the guards. But my amused mood soon turned somber as I remembered my problem. What was I going to do? I couldn't trust anyone, and I had heard the inmates talking more than once about how it did no good to fill out a medical form; the jail doctor never saw anyone anyhow. It was "a big waste of your fuckin' time, just like every damn thing else around here," Amanda had once observed.

Later on that morning, while I was reading to Amanda from the book of Mark about the parable of the vineyard workers, she began to look at me funny. "What the hell is wrong with you this morning?" she asked. "You ain't made one screwed-up comment all day. You won't even look at me."

I brought my head slowly up from the Bible, looking her directly in the eye.

She gasped when she saw my two black eyes staring back at her. "What in Jesus's name happened to *you*, girl? You git in a fight with Bicycle or somethin'?"

"No, I seem to be covered with bruises this morning," I answered.

She tightened her lips and wrinkled her forehead, a pensive, concerned expression breaking across her face. She opened her lips as if she was going to speak but never did. We both let it go at that.

But later on that day, when I was using the bathroom, she happened to catch a glimpse of my black and blue thighs. "Jesus Christ in the morning time!" she screamed. "What on god's holy earth is *that* shit?"

I had a brief thought before I answered that maybe some of my Bible readings were having at least a slight influence on her; they had influenced her manner of cursing anyhow. "I'm not sure what this is, Amanda. I think my body's reacting to lack of vitamins and sunshine or something."

"Wuh, Christ in the holy temple, you're gonna see the jailhouse doctor 'bout those goddarn rotten spots! Shi—Jesus at Mount Calvary wasn't as damn marked up as you, girl! You let this go much longer, you gonna turn black as *my* ass!"

"What do I do?" I asked.

"Here," she said, thrusting out a piece of white paper with a lot of words and blanks on it. "Fill this medical form out right now, and I'll make sure the guards get it today. Write 'MEDICAL EMERGENCY' in big letters across the top. I *sure* don't want your ass to *die* in our nice clean cell. Your bloated corpse would stink up the place somethin' *fierce*!"

"OK," I answered and obediently began to fill out the request to see the "jailhouse doctor." I was frankly a little worried about just how qualified this doctor might be. But that ended up not having to be a worry at all. Although I filled out the medical request form promptly and thoroughly and Amanda got the form declaring it to be a medical emergency to the guards immediately, I was never seen or even questioned about my condition. Partly out of true concern for my health and partly out of pure anger with the incompetence and apathy of the system once again, I continued to fill out medical forms almost every day or whenever I could get my hands on the rare and precious documents. But day after day went by with no one even acknowledging that I had sent any medical requests in. My bruises eventually turned every color of the rainbow and, after a time, faded away, but my bruised and battered soul took another beating.

Actually, I must confess that I lied just a little when I stated earlier that "I was never given the opportunity to see sunshine or get fresh air the whole time I was there." The part about the sunshine was absolutely true, but the part about the fresh air was a bit of a little white lie. After I had been in the jail for a couple of weeks, one morning I noticed some of the girls scurrying about the dayroom like little squirrels. I knew immediately that something was up.

"Come on! Come on! They're really gonna let us go this time!" Amanda shouted in my direction. "Line up at the door. Hurry!"

I hadn't been there very long, but I had been there long enough to know better than to volunteer to go somewhere without knowing exactly *where* it was I was going. "What's up?" I asked nonchalantly. "Where are we headed?"

"To the exercise room! To the exercise room!" Amanda sang out.

Now I was excited for real—an actual room where I could truly exercise, where maybe I could get on machines to work out, lift weights, and break a sweat on a treadmill or a stationary bicycle. My heart started to pound with anticipation. No one had ever even *mentioned* this wonderful room before. I hadn't even known that it *existed* until now.

I closed my eyes as I walked toward the line, trying to picture this magnificent exercise room. I imagined rows and rows of large well-oiled black workout machines. A second wall was lined up with new digital treadmills, all purring like kittens and ready to go. Beside the treadmills were several computerized stationary bicycles and an elliptical machine to keep up with the latest. Against the last wall were stacks and stacks of free weights and barbells and full-length mirrors to observe one's weight lifting so that one could maintain proper form. I knew that the Coward County Jail must boast an exercise room similar to what I was imagining because it was one of the largest county jails in the state, housing nearly 3,500 male inmates and 1,500 female inmates. All those inmates, after all, were in need of regular exercise and a workout routine to keep them healthy. I had also read in the local newspapers that the budget for the jail was quite generous.

But I should have guessed that a large budget for the jail meant very little when it came to looking out in any way for the inmates. After all, who was I fooling? Our diet was supposed to be balanced too, right? When the line of girls left the dayroom door and walked into the exercise room, accommodated by several guards, my heart sank once again. The exercise room consisted of a rather large chamber with concrete blocks for walls and unpainted concrete for a floor. Against the far walls were two basketball goals without nets. One sad little half-inflated basketball that had seen better days lay forlornly in the middle of the floor. A dirty stainless steel toilet and sink sat against one wall. A row of tall windows with safety mesh and a string of barbed wire fencing lined the outside wall. The ceiling was very high, probably at least two stories high, I estimated. A tall row of inside windows lined the wall against the hall so that the guards could observe us at all times.

A heavy, intimidating door clanked shut behind us as one of the listless guards barked out her warning. "Better not let me sees no ones gittin' in no damn troubles in dis here gym-*na*-zeum, or yer ass'll be in lockdown!" As she went for the door, she added over her shoulder, "Dat's right, I means *you*, Jasmun'!"

Then she muttered, "You crazy-ass niggah."

The girls fell right into place. Pearl, Jazzy, Coco, Bicycle, Jasmine, and a girl whom I had never seen up to that point started a game of twenty-one but later switched to an aggressive game of three-on-three when Bicycle couldn't stand the lack of testosterone. They reeled and passed and guarded and fouled one another until they were all cursing loudly and profusely perspiring, and the poor little basketball was deflated for certain.

Ethel and a shy new girl named Tameka migrated immediately to the corner with the sink and toilet. Amanda followed closely. Ethel took a seat on the toilet, still fully clothed, and Amanda began to pull synthetic black braids out of her pant waist and weave them into Ethel's scalp. Tameka watched, fascinated. I stood and stared for a moment, my mouth wide open, not believing what I was seeing. Here was a chance for Ethel, Amanda, and the new girl to do something different, and they were doing exactly the same thing that they did every day in the dayroom.

But my disbelief didn't last long. I was too curious to find out just what I could create to do with myself in this brand-new environment. Just then, I noticed Caroline and an Asian girl quietly walking laps around the room's perimeter. Not wishing to play basketball with the aggressors and definitely not wanting to get my hair done, I decided to join in with them. We did several laps at a very rapid pace before a single word was uttered. After a while, Caroline announced that she had had enough and was going to sit down for a bit. Then she retreated to a quiet corner away from the basketball game and sat cross-legged on the floor, looking rather somber.

I continued to speed-walk laps with the girl. She didn't talk for several minutes, but once she started, she spewed forth a virtual plethora of questions. "You in fah fucky-fucky like me? Dey catch me on corner of Terd and Main. Dat where dey catch you?"

"No!" I replied, visibly insulted.

She kept on, "Wuh den, if dey not catch you fah fucky-fucky, what dey catch you fah? Write checks to store dat no good so could buy sexy cwothes to wear fah fucky-fucky boyfriend?"

"No!" I said disgustedly, throwing an angry look her way this time.

She decided to change the subject but not much. "Wuh den, do you fucky-fucky boyfriend fah money or just fah good time?" she inquired.

"First of all, I don't have a boyfriend," I replied abruptly. "I'm married."

"Oh, you maowied. Wuh, dat don't mean can't have boyfriend an' fucky-fucky fah money," she added with a big grin on her face.

At this point, I decided she was just messing with me, like most everyone else around this place, and I decided to let the whole thing go. But she somehow sensed my disdain and kept on. She suddenly began to half-chant, half-sing a very distasteful little ditty. "Fucky-fucky good. Sucky-sucky better. Fucky-fucky, sucky-sucky. How I be so lucky-lucky?" Every time she repeated this chant, she got a little louder, cutting her eyes in my direction regularly to get my reaction.

I decided to continue to walk laps, looking straight ahead and ignoring her as best as I could. In fact, her repulsive nature bothered me to such an extent that I tried my best to walk ahead of her, but every time I picked up my pace, she was right there beside me, belting out her offensive chorus in my ear.

After a while, she decided that her refrain was no longer getting to me, and she switched subjects. "My name Lee. I got old man. He my sugar daddy. He come see me an' put money in account so I can buy candy an' cookie. You got old man put money in account?"

"Yes, I do," I answered curtly.

I could see this was going nowhere fast. I needed to change the subject quickly. "Have you been reading the Bible or anything since you've been here?" I asked her.

"Oh *yes*," she said excitedly. "I just *love* Bible. Jesus Cwist an' little fish'mans who helps him an' man wif big boat an' big God in sky an' lady who had little baby when she ninety an' . . . I go church here ebrry Sunday." Then with no warning whatsoever, she broke into song. "Ohhh, the B-I-B-L-E, well *dat* dah book for me. The B-I-B-L-E!"

Suddenly, I had an idea. "You know any more Bible songs?" I asked her.

"Oh, no, just dis one." And she continued to belt it out louder and louder.

"Hey, I've been going to church since I was a little girl. Let me teach you some more songs."

She looked at me suspiciously with her big black eyes.

I began to sing, "Jesus loves me. This I know, for the Bible tells me so." I could tell I had her attention. I finished that song and went on to the next. "Jesus loves the little children, all the children of the world . . .

"This little light of mine. I'm gonna let it shine . . .

"The wise man built his house upon the rock . . .

"I will make you fishers of man if you follow me."

A wide grin spread across her face. Before I knew it, we were doing laps, belting out Bible songs with such fury and expression that you'd think we had been doing it for years. I even got so carried away with the moment that, at one point, I began to show Lee the movements to the child's Sunday school song "Father Abraham."

But that proved to be a little too extreme for most of the inmates in the "gymnasium." About the time I was near the end of the song and was having to "move my head, right arm, left arm, right leg, left leg, turn around, and sit down," I had even caught the attention of Bicycle and her basketball gang. "Look at dat mudderfuckin' crazy-ass ole lady! She be not right in da haid. Dis mudderfuckin' place done drove her ass psycho! She be a crackhaid, stoopid ass! We's bettuh stay da fuck aways from *her* crazy ass!"

As soon as I heard this, I felt almost instant relief. It was a good thing that Bicycle and her gang thought I was "touched." They tended to view most everything with suspicion, fearfulness, and a great deal of superstition anyhow. Maybe my little "Father Abraham" demonstration would end up being the best spur-of-the-moment idea I had ever had. Maybe, just maybe, this one incident would spook Bicycle so much that she would finally leave me alone.

But this was just not meant to be. Not long afterward, one of our two filthy showers broke. Now I didn't mean it broke a little; nothing minor was wrong here. Believe me, if we could have gotten as much as a little trickle of water to come forth, we would have continued to use it. But one day Jasmine turned the faucet on, and not one miserable drop of water spewed forth. Girls who had a little bit of pull with the guards, like Coco and Amanda, brought it to their attention daily, but I never saw one single person try to fix that shower the whole time I was there. Now you can only imagine how impossible the showering situation became with only one shower for forty inmates. It became more and more impossible to find a way to get a daily shower. In fact, one was lucky if she could score a shower every second or third day. Things were starting to get awfully stinky in Coward County Jail, 300 SE Women's Pod.

Near the beginning of the broken-down shower situation, I was having major problems even getting *near* one. At the end of one particularly miserable day, I made up my mind that I was somehow going to get a shower. It had been three days since I was able to take one, and I was beginning to feel really raunchy. That evening, we had late rotation, which went from nine to eleven. I was bound and determined that I *would* grab the one and only shower as soon as I emerged from the cell. So when the Big Click occurred, I literally ran to the solitary shower and actually got as far as placing my hand on the door handle and beginning to step in. But it just was not meant to be that night.

As soon as I stepped one foot into the shower, Bicycle appeared out of nowhere, her intimidating, masculine enormous frame blocking the entire shower door. "Now jis' *where* da mudderfuck yew t'inks yew be goin' wit' yo' white mudderfuck honky ass, rich girl?"

I decided to just downright ignore her this time. After all, I *really* needed that shower. And besides, maybe I had scared her badly enough with the "Father Abraham" situation that she would not continue to pursue this if I would simply stand my ground. So I continued to step into the shower, acting as if she was not even there. But it became apparent soon enough that this might not have been the correct decision.

As I began to step into the shower, she suddenly inflated like a huge helium-filled balloon. Her enormous chest puffed up, the hair on the back of her dark neck bristled, her tremendous biceps flexed, and her hard knuckles became white as she formed two monstrous fists. "Hey, giirrl, I be talkin' to yo' sorry ass!" She pushed her balled fists toward my face. "I say dat be *my* mudderfuckin' shower. You don' give me my shower *now*, I beat yo' white mudderfuckin' honky rich ass right here!" Her two mammoth fists were now a little too close to my eye sockets for comfort.

My basic instincts kicked in almost instantly, and my entire body became limp. I immediately went into a submissive posture, like a dog that knows he has been whipped by the dominant canine of the neighborhood. My shoulders slumped, my head dropped, and my eyes fell to the ground, unable to look up. If I had a tail, it would have been tucked tightly between my shaky legs. "OK then, you can have the shower," I said so softly that she could barely hear me. And I gathered up my things and walked across the dayroom, twenty pairs of eyes staring straight at me.

That night, I retreated back to the safety of our cell as soon as the doors opened after rotation. I was not ready for what I found. Amanda was so amused, so utterly tickled by the entire situation that she could hardly contain herself. As soon as the door closed behind us, she started in. "Hell, that was more fun than a barrel of monkeys, girl! Funniest damn thing I ever saw!" She balled her two tiny fists and began to dance around in front of me, swinging them playfully in my face. "Hey, giirrl, I be talkin' to yo' sorry ass," she said, lowering her little voice to mimic Bicycle's.

"I say dat be *my* mudderfuckin' shower! You don't give me my shower *now*, I beats yo' white honky, crackuh, mudderfuckin', rich, son-uv-a-bitchin', sorry white ass right here!" she shouted, adding a few extra adjectives for effect.

Not finding it one bit funny at the moment, I tried my best to ignore her but to no avail.

She suddenly fell onto her lower bunk, giggling as boisterously and uncontrollably as I had ever seen her do. She was laughing so hard that she had to double over and grab her stomach. "*Goddamn*, that was funny!" she snorted. "Bicycle gonna beat your sorry White rich-girl ass for da shower!"

For some reason, that very moment became a breaking point in my jailhouse experience. What I wanted to do was climb onto my top bunk, bury my shamed head into my makeshift pillow, and cry unceasingly until I literally cried myself to death. But what I really *did* do was quite the opposite. I fell to my knees right in front of Amanda's lower bunk, and I began to absolutely cackle with uncontrollable laughter. Amanda joined in. We giggled, we chortled, we tittered and snickered and snorted. The longer it went on, the worse it got. I fell to the floor and grabbed my hungry belly. I kicked my feet and beat my head against the dirty floor.

When I finally regained my composure enough to climb up to my bunk, I looked out the window slit and noticed something I had never noticed before. "Hey, Amanda, there's a Kentucky Fried Chicken sign lit up outside my window, so close to here. I bet it's only a block away from this dump." I let that thought sink in for a minute. "God, you know how nice it would be to have some of that chicken right now . . . a side of slaw and mashed potatoes with gravy . . . and a big old buttered biscuit with honey."

"Yeah," she said, so totally exhausted from our giggle fit that she had no energy left at all.

"Hey, I got an idea. We could break this sorry little window, send your scrawny little ass down the side of the building with toilet plungers as suctions on your feet. You could get us two chicken dinners to go, suction your way back up the building and back through the window slit, and we could have our butts some KFC tonight."

We both laid there silently for a couple of seconds, but then the thought of Amanda scaling the building like a misfit Spider-Man got the best of us, and we went into another fit of laughter. "I could use a goddamn sheet as a cape!" Amanda cackled. "And that stupid little bra you bought off commissary for a mask!" After that night, I never took anything at Coward County Jail quite so seriously.

The next day's mail call proved to be the best one ever. The three books that my friend Ginger had ordered from Amazon.com arrived at almost the exact same time that the little librarian man brought us the two books we had requested from the jail library so long ago that we could barely remember requesting them. Instantaneously, Amanda and I went from nothing to read but a dog-eared copy of the New Testament to five really good books.

She wanted me to read to her from her book about Marilyn Monroe and the Kennedy brothers. I was just getting to a really good part when she decided it was time to talk about her family. "The Kennedys remind me a little bit of my own family. They're all doctors and lawyers and politicians and such," she said.

I found this more than a little bit interesting. I was certain she had to be lying. After all, she had been in this dump seventeen times by her own admission. She was a self-confessed crack addict, for god's sake. "Your family's full of doctors and lawyers?" I questioned. "How distant of relatives are they?"

She didn't hesitate. "Oh, my daddy was the police chief for twenty years up in Indiana. He's built a real nice house in a fancy neighborhood here in Parvenu. My brother's a lawyer in Downtown Atlanta. My sister's got her PhD in education. My other brother's a pediatrician up in Indiana. Got another sister who's vice president of a big company and another brother who is a paramedic right here in Coward County. My mom taught second grade for thirty-two years. She's raising my two kids."

I didn't know what to say. It was the first time I seriously doubted anything Amanda had told me. This simply could not be—five siblings, a doctor, a lawyer, a paramedic, a PhD, a VP. Daddy was a police chief, Mom a dedicated elementary schoolteacher, and their sixth child was a scrawny repeat-offender crackhead with no self-discipline at all. I decided very quickly that this scenario was utterly impossible. I loved Amanda as a friend, but this time, she had gone too far. "You got a picture of any of them?" I asked.

"Oh, no. They all got real mad at me a *long* time ago. See, I was going to college to be a teacher when I got introduced to this little rock in a pipe at a party. That's all she took. Now I'm a slave to It. Oh, the first couple o' times I was in, they'd all come see me. Mom would bring my kids, Daddy would come, my brother who's a big-shot mouthpiece in Atlanta would try to help me. They'd write to me and send me pictures and put money in my account—*lots* of money. Then about the third time I was in, they started to lose hope in me. My mom legally adopted my kids. She won't even let me talk to them. But I figured out a way to get around *that* one. I know she goes to her garden club every Saturday afternoon at two, so I wait till then and call them if we are out on that rotation. Last week, my girl—she's seven—told me that she was student of the month at her school. And my boy—he's ten—he won a writing contest in his grade. They go to a really fine private school in Parvenu. My mom and daddy are so proud of them. They're so cute. You'd love 'em. I send them both stuff off commissary every week. Last week, I sent Sophie a hairbrush and Marcus a pair of boxer shorts off the men's list. I send the stuff to my cousin's house, so I know they get it. Mama would take it out of the mail and never give it to them."

I decided to test the validity of her story. "How do you get anything off commissary if you never have anyone put any money in for you?" I asked.

"You crazy girl, you never noticed my little inside business? What do you think I *do* all day around here? You think I'm weaving everybody's hair and drawing artwork on all their envelopes for *free*? Wuh, think again, sister. That's my *work* around this dump. These crazy-ass jailbirds *pay* me for my expertise in these matters. And just *how* can a bunch of locked-up losers *pay* the hairdresser and the resident artist? With commissary stuff, that's how. Didn't you ever notice how many bags of cookies, candy bars, crackers, T-shirts, underpants, socks, paper, envelopes, pencils, shampoo, soap, toothpaste, brushes, lotion, and other shit I always have around here?"

"Well yeah," I answered. "But I always figured you had somebody putting money in for you."

"Nope, and by the way, haven't I drawn a few pictures on the last several envelopes that went out to all your friends and family, including that cutie-pie husband of yours?"

"Yes, you did. I guess I might owe you a few items off commissary," I answered, reaching for my latest store list so I could pick something unique out for her, maybe something she'd never had before. That was when I saw it.

"Hey, Amanda, did you know that this commissary list has a set of colored pencils on it?"

"Yeah, I know, but those things cost *way* too much. Nobody around here can afford to buy me those."

I quickly ran my eyes down the cost column and matched it to the column that read "twenty-four assorted Artcraft colored pencils—unsharpened." The set cost $21.99. "Maybe I'll just get these for you on my next commissary order for all those pictures you drew on my envelopes and for the portrait you did of me on my birthday."

Her excitement was evident. Her dark eyes lit up instantly, and she began to almost hyperventilate at the thought of owning twenty-four colored pencils. But as soon as she realized I noticed, she put the brakes on her emotions, something she had learned to do well. "They're *unsharpened.* I'd have to spend a whole day sharpening them with one of my busted razors. That'd be a pain."

I knew perfectly well what she was doing. She had wished for those colored pencils every time she had been in. They would be a dream come true for her artwork compared with her current media of pencils, pens, and crayons. But she had learned to protect herself against recurrent disappointments. It was a coping mechanism. I had Bob put extra money in my account the next day and bought her the colored pencils.

Amanda talking about her family just made me that much more homesick for mine. And I don't just mean my immediate family either. It's funny what being locked up will do to you. I was longing to see members of my extended family whom I hadn't seen in a long time— my brothers and sisters, my aunts and uncles, my cousins and nieces and nephews. I started to talk nonstop to Amanda about my family whenever I got the chance. Her little soliloquy about her family had opened up the floodgates for me. I told her about my daddy being the most well-respected orthodontist in Fort Wayne, Indiana, while he was alive, about my brother's highly successful dental practice in the same town, about my sister attending Indiana University School of Dentistry after twenty-five years of being a dental hygienist, and about my sister, the lead kindergarten teacher, and my brother, the expertly trained chemical engineer. I told her the whole story about how Grandpa and Grandma had to start over when all the farm animals died, how he picked himself up by the bootstraps and went on to become an admired veterinarian.

As I spoke, I realized that this recurrent theme throughout my family of respect and admiration, of trust and honor, would never again be mine. All these precious intangibles that I had grown up with, that had become a part of my very soul, had died forever in that courtroom, and I began to cry.

Amanda didn't know what to do at this point; she had never seen me cry or even come close. I had forced myself to be so tough, so strong, so stoic, so in control of my emotions the whole time that I was frightening even myself somewhat. The awkwardness of the situation was beginning to fill the tiny cell when we heard the Big Click at a time when it did not ordinarily happen.

"Oh, I forgot. It's *Sunday*!" Amanda exclaimed.

I couldn't remember anything special happening on Sundays. I wiped my wet eyes and blew my runny nose. "What happens on Sunday?" I asked. "Nothing ever happened on Sunday before."

"*Church*, girl. Church happens on Sunday around here. It's just that they don't always have it every *single* Sunday 'cuz the church ladies can't always make it. Come on, let's go. They're already lining up at the door. We haven't got much time."

I analyzed the situation. It was Sunday. I hadn't been to church in a month. I was really pretty depressed at the moment and didn't feel much like going, but on the other hand, what would I do locked up in that lonely cell if I didn't go? Amanda was going. I could tell that. There was no telling what I might do in that cell by myself, given my current state of mind. When I began to obsess about Amanda's hidden brown bag of razors, the right decision became apparent. "OK, I'll go with you to 'church.' But it better not be a complete waste of time."

DORAMAE BROOKSHIRE

THE EXORCISTS

B Y THE TIME we got to the dayroom door, the line of girls was already spilling out into the hallway. "We made it just in time," Amanda whispered.

We marched down the long hall and into a large room full of gray folding chairs. The chairs were placed meticulously in straight rows, and a scratched old piano stood in front of them. Two long card tables stacked high with ragged, used church hymnals stood on either side of the piano. Most of the worn hymnals had no covers. There were little booklets on each of the folding chairs.

Two Black ladies, dressed to kill, were standing at attention in front of the tables. One was young and very svelte. The other was an older lady who was quite obviously fighting the battle of the bulge. Both were dressed in their Sunday best, the little one in shiny high heels and a three-piece black suit and the large one in a tight purple sequined dress, white gloves, and a wide-brimmed hat full of large fuchsia and violet flowers. Gaudy huge earrings adorned with fake jewels dangled from both ladies' earlobes. "Welcome to church today, girls. Come on in and find you a seat," the full-figured one sang out cheerfully.

I guess the friendliness of the church lady was so foreign to several of the inmates who had gotten used to being treated quite the opposite that they began to talk nervously. "Y'all be *quiet* right this minute! Jus' 'cuz y'all so full o' *sin* and *hatefulness* don't mean y'all kin disrespec' da Lord! Can't y'all tell? Dis here is da house of da Lord, an' y'all *will* hush up an' listen to his Word while y'all's here, or I'll send y'all back to y'all's mis'abull little cells!" The skinny young church lady was hoppin' mad.

Her chastisement worked. An immediate silence fell over the room. All eyes peered forward toward the church lady turned sergeant. "Now *dat's* better," she said. "Dat's how folks in da *real* world behave deyselves in church."

The robust one decided to change the subject. "I hopes you all ready to praise the Lord on dis here fine Sabbath day. Let's all begin by singin' one o' my favorite songs in awl da world, 'Amazin' Grace.' Praise da Lord! Praise da Lord! Praise his holy name! Hallelujah! Hallelujah! Hallelujah!"

And she plopped down onto the rickety bench and began to pound the piano keys with all her might. She opened her sizable mouth, threw back her flower-adorned head, and began to belt out the first hymn. "Amazing grace, how sweet da soun' dat saved a *wretch* like me. I once was *lost*, but now I's *found*. Was *blind*, but now I *sees*." She tapped her high-heeled feet and swayed her queen-size frame back and forth to the music that was bubbling from the piano.

The petite church lady sang along and glared judgmentally at us when she came to the words *wretch*, *lost*, and *blind*. Two inmates at the back of the room started to giggle, apparently amused by the whole scene. That did not sit well with the militaristic church lady. "Hol' on! Hol' on! Hol' on! Jist a minute!" she screeched at the piano lady, forcing her to stop midsong. "Dis here is total disrespec' for da Lord's house! Ah t'inks we better have da preachin' *now* before ah sees any more o' dis *evil* an' *wickedness* comin' forth outa y'all's *sinful* souls!" She was pacing back and forth, shaking her head and wagging her long black finger at us all.

"Today's preachin' is all about how *good* peoples do with their lives. Peoples who tells the truth and works at honest jobs and don't take none of dem drugs that is straight from the devil hisself. Dey don't be drinkin' no Satan water neither. An' dey don't be stealin' an' lyin' an' shootin' no udder peoples, like lots an' lots of y'all sinners in dis here room has done, 'cuz God—he don't love nobody like dat. He don't love nobody dat goes against none o' his Ten Comman'ments or nothin'. And dey say dat 'thou shall not steal, and thou shall not be lyin', and thou shall not kill none o' thy fellow mans.' Yet jist *look* at all y'all *sinners* jist sittin' out dere, not one bit sorry for *any* o' y'all's *wicked ways and evil*. It's da work o' da devil. It's *Satan* in all his glory! Wake up an' repent! Repent, or y'all will burn for eternity in—"

"What she means to say is dat if y'all sinners ax for the Lord's forgiveness for whatever you done to git in dis awful place, den he'll forgive y'all, an' den y'all 'ull have a chance at goin' ta heaven. Praise Jesus! For he is quick to forgive da unholy an' da unclean." The corpulent one had decided to cut the malnourished one short. I think it was because the fat church lady didn't want the skinny church lady to use the word *hell*.

The feisty little one took over once again. "See, Miz Jackson an' me, we is spendin' our whole Sunday evenin' out here at dis here mizaribull prison jis' so's we kin bring y'all sinners da Word. Da Word say y'all ain't *neber* gonna gets ta heaven if y'all *evil* wrongdoers don' change y'all's *wicked, sinful* ways! Y'all have *sinned* in the eyes o' da Lord—every last *one* of y'all! You two girls a-sittin' back dere laughin', *you're* goin' ta hell! An' y'all girls over dere talkin' an' not list'ning to da preachin', *you're* goin' ta hell! An' da one raht here dat's done gone ta sleep, *you're* goin' ta hell too!" She was nervously traipsing up and down the aisle, her black eyes bulging, her sharp finger condemning.

"I t'inks what we all needs ta do at dis point is ta *confess* some o' our many *sins*, an' dat will set us *free*," offered the plump sermonizer in the purple dress. "Let's start with *you* over dere, yes, *you*, da one dat be lookin' right at me. Now jist *what* did you do ta git yerself put in dis here horrible place?"

I hesitantly cut my eyes toward the poor inmate who was being put on the spot, in total disbelief that I had really witnessed any part of the last thirty minutes or so. The victim of the twin church ladies' scorn was young and white and very, very frightened. Her dull, greasy hair, grossly decayed front teeth, and frail, sickly body revealed the fact that she had not lived an easy life so far. She looked at the concrete floor, blushing from her neck up as she did. "I-I-I stole a l-l-lady's stereo so I c-c-c-ould buy d-d-d-rugs," she stuttered softly.

"See! Dis wuz da work of da devil! Dis whole room is *full* o' Satan's work! Beelzebub, git thee gone behind me!"

Amanda and I started to laugh over the mention of Beelzebub in such a serious context. This totally infuriated the little church lady Nazi.

"An' what about y'all two over dere?" she screamed, thrusting her skinny finger at us. "Ah guess y'all musta done somet'in' reeeal funny ta git locked up in dis here jailhouse. Please *do* tell us all about y'all's *sins*. We's waitin'!"

Amanda decided to be the spokesperson for us, which was a mighty good thing because I was not even going to begin to consider giving these two self-righteous ladies the time of day. "Well, first of all, I think you all *know* me," she began. "I been here sixteen other times, an' I've seen a whole lotta you types from the Free Will Baptist Church come and go. And I just gotta say, you two ladies are doin' a jam-up job here today. You're gettin' to the *bottom* of this *sin* and *wickedness* thing. 'Fore you know it, you just might have the devil exorcised right outa us transgressors. After all, our iniquities and obliquities are such an abomination to God's good name."

For the first time, the two church ladies were speechless. It was all I could do to keep a straight face. Amanda had just told them off but good, all under the pretense of complimenting them for their help in their efforts to "save" us all. Her advanced vocabulary had thrown them for a loop. Neither one had the slightest idea of what she had said. The large purple one spoke first. "Wuh, what about yer frien' over dere. What'd *she* do?"

"Oh, *her?*" Amanda said, pointing her finger at my chest. "She *tortured* hundreds of innocent people by drillin' their teeth and stickin' needles in 'em and druggin' 'em up." Her face was solemn, her expression grim. "Oh yeah, then she stole all the poor people's money . . . thousands and thousands and *thousands* of dollars!"

The obese church lady stared at me, her fleshy arms trembling. The wormy church lady looked down at the ground, mostly, I reasoned, because she was too frightened of me to make eye contact. "Some of y'all, well, y'all's *sins*, dey be too big to ever forgive . . . if y'all will take y'all's little booklets dat wuz on y'all's seats, we'll sing some songs now."

Amanda had done it. She had met with success. She had managed to single-handedly stop the two maniacal Bible thumpers from shaming and embarrassing any more of the inmates. She had put an abrupt halt to their insane self-righteous, narrow-minded, moralistic "sermon."

As we sang from our booklets put together by the ladies' circle of the Mount Calvary Primitive Baptist Church, I realized that I had just experienced yet another Coward County Jail incident of which I would have great difficulty making any sense of later. I never went back to "church" at the jail again.

The "church service" ended up doing more harm than good. It served as the catalyst to agitate and infuriate the inmates. That night during late rotation, Harley and Bicycle got into the worst fight I had ever seen since my arrival there. I was not real sure how it started. I think it was over what TV show to watch. I was sitting at a table in the corner of the dayroom, writing in my journal about the two church ladies, when I heard a horrible commotion. Then I saw everyone run toward the chairs in front of the TV.

I could barely make out Harley's loud voice. "Oh yeah, well, you're a big nasty Black motherfuckin' *niggar*! You shoulda been born a *man* 'cuz, as far as the world is concerned, you *are* one, you ugly-ass *lezbo*! Where you think you get off fuckin' Jazzy and all the other young vulnerable ones who come in here? Come on then, you dumb motherfucker! I ain't afraid of your ugly black faggot ass!"

A couple of seconds later, I heard a loud thump, and Harley's resounding voice stopped abruptly. By the time I cautiously dragged myself over to "the scene," what I witnessed was not pretty. Bicycle had knocked Harley to the hard concrete floor and was on her knees, looming over her half-conscious pregnant body like an immense mountain. Her monstrous fists were pounding anywhere they could go on poor Harley's limp body, but the blows seemed to be concentrating on her head and neck region. I looked at Bicycle's face, trying to get a clue about when she might stop; she had clearly "won" the fight. What I saw made me shudder.

Her eyes were no longer human but appeared to glow red, like pictures I had seen of Satan. She had become a mindless beast, atrocious, unspeakable, ruthless, damnable beyond belief. She had turned into the sinful, wicked, evil creature that the church ladies had told us we all were. I tried to run toward the dayroom door to alert the apathetic guards, but my feet would not move. Someone, I think it was Pearl, finally got one of the guards to sluggishly enter the dayroom and put a halt to the one-sided battle. Both Harley and Bicycle got put into lockdown for twenty-four hours.

When Harley emerged from her cell two days later, one eye was black, and the other was swollen completely shut. Her lower lip was the size of a large hot dog and was split right down the middle. Both cheekbones were bruised; there was a nasty gash above her left eyebrow. She was carrying a white piece of paper, clutching it to her chest as if it was an important document. She did not touch her breakfast but instead was making the rounds of all the other breakfast tables, talking excitedly as she circulated. I wondered what she was up to. When she got to our table, she plopped down beside me and talked directly to Amanda.

"I think you two ladies might be interested in this," she whispered. "It's a petition to get rid of Bicycle's sorry black ass."

Amanda looked at her as if she was crazy.

"No! No! It's perfectly legal. We *can* do this! Believe me, I had another sorry motherfucker kicked outa my pod the last time I was in. The guards'll listen to our case. If they don't, I'll send this fuckin' paper to the warden. It's against prison policy to allow a dangerous inmate to remain in a pod where she isn't wanted by nobody. You gotta believe me on this one. It worked before. It'll work again. Bicycle will never know we done this. The guards'll just come get her ass and put her in another pod. They won't ever tell her worthless ass *why*."

"Let me see the damn thing," Amanda said under her breath, reaching out one hand while the other stuffed scrambled eggs into her mouth. She quickly scanned the room to locate Bicycle's whereabouts. "What you gonna do for me if I sign this?"

"I'll buy you some commissary, OK? Look, I already got five signatures, and all I need is five more. I'm pretty damn sure ten will do it. That'd be a fourth of the pod."

Amanda pushed it toward me so we could both see it. I wasn't eating breakfast anyway. It read, "We the under sined names do wish to have the in mate, Gwendolyn R. Green, known as 'Bicycle' removed from our pod, CCJ 300 SE Woman's Pod immediatly, as she is a thret to our safety and well bean." It was signed by Caroline, Crazy Lee, Ethel, Coco, and Harley herself.

I couldn't help but keep staring at Bicycle's given name. *Gwendolyn.* That just couldn't be. *Gwendolyn!* Somebody somewhere had to have made some kind of mistake. A walking, talking, real-life monster; a fiend from hell; the devil incarnate; a bestial, ruthless blot on the face of mankind—and her name was *Gwendolyn*, Gwendolyn *Green* at that.

"Ya sure we won't get caught?" Amanda asked Harley. "'Cuz I'd sure hate to get all our asses beat by Bicycle like you did. I ain't into black eyes and missing teeth."

"I promise you. The rules say the fuckin' guards can't tell Bicycle. They get their sorry asses fired if they do."

Amanda and I signed the petition. As I was writing my name, I breathed a sigh of relief, believing this petition to be the answer to one of my prayers. This would work; I knew it would. Then I wouldn't have to worry about Bicycle bullying me anymore. My recurrent nightmares about her plummeting me to death in the shower would finally cease. I could breathe easily when I entered the dayroom to walk my laps.

Harley secured three more signatures that day and handed the petition into a "trusted" guard the next morning. The guard refused to move Bicycle out of our pod, saying that the petition was "prejudice." By the seven o'clock rotation that night, Bicycle knew exactly what the petition said and exactly who signed it.

We only got to go to the exercise room one more time while I was in. The official *Handbook for the Coward County Jail* states, "The inmates must be offered the choice of fresh air and exercise on a daily basis while incarcerated." I was locked up in the Coward County Jail for a total of twenty-two days, and I was offered the choice of fresh air and exercise *twice* during that time.

The second time I went to the exercise room, I immediately noticed something that I had not noticed the first time. Maybe it was the change of weather; it was getting near June. Or maybe it was my state of mind that day. It could have been my recent daily exercises in soul-searching and becoming one with the universe. But whatever it was, I noticed the scent of fresh air and the presence of heavy humidity the second I entered the room. Searching for its source, I looked upward and discovered that the barbed wire and fencing around the very top of the exercise room's outside wall were *open to the outside*. That was actually fresh air and real, honest-to-goodness outside humidity that were coming in through the fence. I was breathing *real air*, something sacred and taken for granted up to that point.

Just then, a tiny, little bird—I think it was a sparrow—landed gently on the top strand of barbed wire and began to sing. I almost broke down in tears. This was a truly religious experience through and through. I had to share this with someone.

I sought out Amanda. When I found her, I was so choked up that I could hardly speak. "Look, Amanda, that fence up there is open to the outside world. That's real fresh air that's coming in here. It must be turning summer out there 'cuz can't you feel the humidity hanging in the air? I don't believe it. There's real air in this room, 100 percent genuine, sweet, clean, *beautiful* fresh air. And just *look* at that darling little bird, will you? He's singing his little heart out for us."

Amanda looked at me as if she thought I might have finally lost it. I think she sized me up for a moment, making sure she didn't need to call for one of the guards to take me to psych. But as soon as she figured I was OK, she turned toward the outside wall, glanced briefly at the chirping bird, and flatly stated, "Honey, the only bird you ever gonna see around this neck of the woods is a bunch of *jailbirds*." With that, a devilish smirk spread across her impish face, and she retreated back to her hair-weaving session by the toilet.

I guess the spiritual experience briefly knocked me for a loop because I was suddenly drained of all energy. I no longer felt like walking laps or fighting Bicycle's basketball games to be able to accomplish one hundred speed walking rotations in record time. So I found a quiet place in the corner by the bird, gently placed my back against the wall, and slowly lowered my body until I was sitting alone on the floor. I listened intently to every note the little sparrow sang, imagining them to be a personal message from God himself.

DORAMAE BROOKSHIRE

It's all right, the tiny bird warbled. *You will be free like me very soon . . . very soon . . . very soon. All is well . . . all is well. Peace is yours . . . peace is yours.* Then it flew away.

Before I had time to wish for it to come back, I noticed several of the girls gazing toward the far corner of the room. I squinted to see, and what I saw made me sick to my stomach. Bicycle and Jazzy were lezzin' out right there in broad daylight for the whole world to see. Bicycle had Jazzy pressed tightly against the window that was open to the outside hallway. Jazzy was stark naked from the waist up, and Bicycle had one hand on her right breast and the other down her pants. They were kissing passionately, their long tongues down each other's throats. My stomach churned. I thought I might lose my runny breakfast grits all over the floor.

The girls started to chant excitedly, "Go! Go! Go! You go, girl! You go, girl! Get choo a little! Get choo a little! Get choo a little now!"

Apparently, no one had any intentions of telling the guards, and I couldn't because I was afraid of the repercussions from Bicycle. So I turned my eyes away, stayed in my safe little corner, squeezed my eyes shut, and remembered the little sparrow. My ears continued to hear the chanting, but it turned into the song my friend, the tiny bird, was singing instead. *You will be free like me very soon . . . very soon . . . very soon . . . very soon. All is well . . . all is well . . . all is well. Peace is yours . . . peace is yours . . . peace is yours.* In what seemed to be an eternity, two angry, masculine female guards showed up, broke up the lesbo session, and marched Bicycle and Jazzy off to lockdown.

After that incident in the exercise room, I no longer sought out religious experiences. I chose, instead, to settle down into a comfortable and predictable routine. Amanda and I got up each morning and ate breakfast, cleaned our cell, had Bible study, went out for rotations, and talked about our lives. She did her art; I wrote my letters and journal. We especially enjoyed reading our recently acquired books. Most of the time, I sat cross-legged on the floor, my back pressed against the wall in front of her lower bunk, a towel folded neatly under me. She propped herself up on homemade pillows, lounging on her bed, listening intently. I was the narrator, reading aloud book after book and spinning my own yarns to go along. We laughed when McMurphy pulled his stunts in *One Flew over the Cuckoo's Nest*. We cried at the pitiful life of Marilyn Monroe in *Goddess*, and we both identified with Tom Joad in *The Grapes of Wrath*.

The days started to go by a little faster once we had a few good books to read. Then one Thursday Bob showed up on a day that he had told me he wouldn't. I wondered what was up. As soon as I sat down on the stool in front of him, I could tell he was especially excited. "Hey, babe, how are ya?" he asked and, before he got an answer, went right into his next sentence. "I came today to tell you some really good news. I've been talking to Ms. Velda, and she called Arley Allen, and it looks like they're going to help you get outa this hellhole really, really soon. In fact, I think you might be going to Nutter in the next day or so, and that's why I came today 'cuz it may be a little while before I can see you again, if they don't allow you to have visitors at Nutter for the first week. Just think—this might be my last visitation in this dump."

"Oh, that's *great* news," I said excitedly, still a bit scared of Nutter from Amanda's descriptions.

Ms. Velda Jaxson was a retired local schoolteacher in Goat Valley whose sole purpose in life was to attend Democratic events all over the state of Georgia. She campaigned, she schmoozed, she rubbed elbows with the big ones; she backed every Democrat around. And she didn't stop at the politicians in the area either. I had seen pictures of her standing beside Jimmy Carter and Bill Clinton. She was like an aged groupie for the Democratic Party. And Arley Allen was the representative from our region. They were the best of buddies, of course. It truly touched me that these two had evidently stuck their necks out for me in such a sticky situation.

Back in our cell, exciting things were happening too. When I returned from visitation, Amanda was jumping up and down in the corner by the desk, barely able to contain herself. In her hand, she clutched a tiny piece of yellow paper. "I got it! I got it! I finally got my release date!" she sang out happily.

"What do you mean? Your release date?" I asked.

"Yeah, whenever you're in for just hangin' around the streets tryin' to score some crack, the same stupid charge I *always* have, there ain't no court date, just a *release* date, the day they intend on lettin' your ass outa this sorry place."

"Oh, well, when is your release date then?" I asked, just halfway interested.

"June 26," she answered. "Just think—twenty-three fuckin' more days in this miserable-ass place, and I'm free as a bird!"

I couldn't believe my ears. June 26 was Bob and my anniversary. It would be our twenty-ninth one this year. For a second, my thoughts drifted to some very private moments—our wedding day, our first anniversary, the births of our three children, the anniversary we had gone to Hawaii, how Bob had asked me recently if I wanted to renew our vows. I felt like jumping up and down and screaming, *Oh my god! June 26 is our wedding anniversary! This has to mean something! There's some kind of really deep, hidden symbolism in this. It's spelling out some kind of karma or something for me!*

But instead, I decided that I would keep the link a total secret. This date was just too sacred to me. So instead, I just said, "Hmm, June 26, good date, good date."

After Bob's Thursday visit, I was sitting on pins and needles, waiting for a guard to call me out to go to Nutter at any time. It came sooner than I thought. The very next afternoon, while I was reading to Amanda from the book *Prince of Tides*, a thunderous voice came over the loudspeaker. "Bahrooshy, pack it up," it said.

I waited patiently for the obnoxious guard to repeat herself. I knew there was a very good chance that "Bahrooshy" might be me. I was not disappointed.

"Ah said, *Bahrooshy, pack it up*!" the impudent guard screamed at the top of her lungs.

"Hey, Dora, that's *you*!" Amanda exclaimed. "She's saying to pack it up. Better get going. Here, I'll help. This is *great*. I knew you'd be outa Beelzebub's den soon." She began to stuff all my recently acquired belongings into two bulging brown paper bags, every material item that I had obtained since I had arrived weeks earlier—my white T-shirts and socks, my underpants and men's size 9 tennis shoes, my Dove soap and Colgate toothpaste, my pens and pencils and tablets and journals, my *Webster's Pocket Dictionary* and checker/chess game, my various toiletries, one half-eaten brownie, two candy bars, a quarter full jar of peanut butter, and a pickle. That was every single bit of material wealth that I could claim while incarcerated in this wonderful state facility.

The impatient guard was getting hotter by the minute. "Ah ain't got awl day! Ah says *pack it up*, an' ah *means pack it up*!"

"Come on! We gotta get outa here *now*!" Amanda shrieked, almost as loudly as the livid guard. She began to grab up bulging paper bags and tug at my upper bunk mattress in the same gesture.

"We gotta get this nasty thing down and rolled up!" she yelled, motioning toward the grimy, ragged mattress. "And where's your razor? They're gonna want to see your razor before they'll let you go! Find it right *now*!" As I located the one and only razor we had in our cell that Amanda had not crushed to retrieve the blade, she struggled to pull the bulky mattress off the top bunk and roll it up on the floor the best she could. She was simultaneously giving it her best attempt to fold the sheet and filthy cover into neat squares.

As I waited behind the dayroom door to be freed into the looming hallway, Amanda hugged me repeatedly and jumped up and down, unable to contain her escalating exhilaration over the matter. There was very little time to say goodbye. It was between rotations, so we were the only two allowed in the dayroom at the time, me because I was *finally* leaving and her because she was needed to drag my heavy, dusty mattress to the door.

I did notice certain inmates waving goodbye to me sadly through their cell windows—Caroline, my redheaded friend who had opened up the world of books for me while I was there; Lee, my crazy little Korean walking buddy; Harley, who had stuck up for me more than once in front of Bicycle (I surely hoped her twins would be born healthy); and Coco, who had snuck me some extra towels and washcloths from the laundry more than once. Ethel was sadly waving goodbye, looking as though she might never get out. My last glimpse was of poor little Pearl (she was only seventeen), standing quietly at her cell window, slowly waving her Tweety Bird card at me, a single tear trickling down her cheek.

As the massive door to the hallway opened and I heard the Big Click for the last time, a rush of different emotions swept over me—guilt for leaving them all behind, relief for getting out of the worst place I had ever been in my life, fear of what was yet to come, a twisted newly found sort of wisdom from what I had experienced, a deep-seated anger from being forced to endure what I had just been put through, a death of innocence and trust and belief in the system. But I didn't have much time to reflect. The pissed-off guard was shrieking at me once again.

"Put da mattress ober dere!" she screeched, pointing to the corner where two other grimy mattresses laid. "Now brings me yo' razaw, *now giirrl*! Whada mattuh wit' you, giirrl? You slow minded or somet'in'?"

I obediently sauntered over to the place at the guard station where I figured things could be passed through a tiny glass door. It looked a lot like the slot that the little illiterate mailman passed our mail through each day. I gently placed our only razor in the tray. The frowning, heavily muscled female guard snatched it up. About that time, I heard her phone ring. She picked it up.

"Go stand ober *dere*!" she shouted at me, pointing in the general direction of the three mattresses. "*Now*, giiirrl! Move! Move! Move!" She was holding the phone at arm's length with one hand and waving the other arm wildly in the air. Her large booted feet couldn't seem to keep still. Her gun was hanging loosely in the holster and suddenly gleaming from catching the light of one of the many mirrors.

I shuffled over to the mattress pile, trying very hard not to inhale the nauseating odors of dust and mildew and years of built-up human body odor. I tried to stop myself from wondering how many zillions of tiny mites lived in those filthy things, of how many pounds of dead human tissue resided within.

Soon my attention was turned elsewhere. The short-tempered guard seemed to be having some sort of difficulties. Her facial expression had gone from simply pissed off at me and at the world to a look of "I may be in some pretty serious trouble myself here." A few minutes later, she slowly moved over to her microphone and looked directly at me, totally stoic. "Git chur mattress and stuff, giirrl, you goin' back in."

"What?" I screamed, unable to believe my ears. "I'm going back in *where*?" I knew it wasn't smart to yell at a person who had total control over my entire world at the moment, but something somewhere inside me had just snapped, and I didn't seem to care for one brief second. How could this have happened? I was *that* close to getting out of that hellhole, that living nightmare, Beelzebub's den as Amanda called it. How could these less than human beings toy with me like this? Why, I could see the elevator from where I was standing, my ticket out of there, my only hope, my salvation of my sanity, my freedom. I wasn't going back in there. I just *wasn't*.

Just then, I noticed that the indignant guard had positioned herself tightly up against the tinted window as near to me as she could get. Her chiseled, manly facial features had tightened to the point where I could see the definition of every muscle in her face. Her neck was taut; her large white teeth were gritted. She brought the microphone up to her tightly pursed lips. "I said to go back to da door, inmate, an' I means what I says! If Ah has ta cum' out dere an' guts you, you ain't gonna likes what happens to ya sorry White ass! Now gits yo' mattress and go back in . . . *now*! Now! Now!"

She was screeching so shrilly that my ears stung. Her heavy fists were loudly pounding the counter. Her broad nostrils were flared. Her square jaw was jutting forward. Her large black eyes were bulging wildly out of their sockets. As she squawked, she splattered the dark glass with tiny bullets of randomly flying saliva. I was scared for one brief moment that she might break right through that protective glass, latch on to my unsuspecting neck, and hang on with all her might until I finally fell limp and lifeless on the filthy floor, no longer able to save myself from the world of the imperturbable creatures of the guard tower.

I decided to quickly change my approach. "Miss, could you please tell me why I was told to pack it up and now I am being told to get my mattress and go back to my cell?" I asked as softly and politely as I could.

DORAMAE BROOKSHIRE

She stepped away from the microphone, turned her back on me, and without a single word walked over to the opposite side of the guard tower, where I could no longer see her. I wasn't sure what to make of this, but after about two minutes of waiting, I decided that maybe I better grab up my nasty mattress and go back to the dayroom door. To be honest, I was halfway afraid that she might emerge with several other guards from the guard tower; and with no warning, they all may ascend on me and hurt me in ways I did not want to even imagine. So back into the world of the insane I went, shedding mattress and all.

As soon as Amanda saw me, she started in on me. "Hey, girlfriend, whatcha doin' back in here? You get mixed up and go the wrong way?"

"No," I replied, biting my lower lip to hold back the tears. "That guard told me to come back to my cell."

"Oh, I don't *think* so! She can't do that! Go out to the speaker in the dayroom and ask her *why*! She screwed up or something!" Amanda looked upset.

"Hey, Amanda, I already asked her why. She wouldn't answer me. She just turned her back on me and walked away. To be honest, I'm a little scared of her."

"Oh no, she's not gonna get away with *this* shit! Come on!"

And she grabbed my hand and dragged me out into the dayroom and up to the speaker. "Go ahead. *Ask* her," she demanded. Amanda had already pressed the button for me.

"Whachoo want now?" a different guard inquired.

"Ma'am, I would like to know why I was told to pack it up, and then I was sent back to my cell with my mattress," I said as graciously as possible.

"Call yo' bondsmans. Dere's sumtin' wrongs dere," she replied without flinching a muscle.

I couldn't imagine what in the world my bondsman had to do with *anything* in this situation. I had already had a mock trial. The dirty judge had already hit me below the belt. As far as the courts were concerned, I had already been "sentenced." What could a bondsman possibly have to do with this scenario? There wasn't even any bond involved at this moment. Paying a bond could not get me out of my present plight. If it could, believe me, my family would have paid any price on the earth a long time ago. But since I fully realized that trying to convey this piece of information to the guards sitting in their ivory tower was a total waste of my breath, I decided to follow their commands and return to cell 301 SE.

WHITE BREAD PICNIC

F OR THE NEXT couple of days or so, I tried really hard to keep my spirits up but to very little avail. Amanda and I still had morning Bible study. We still read our books together. I still wrote daily in my journal. She still ran her lucrative little art business. I still did my laps around the dayroom on every rotation. I still received the most mail of all the inmates. Amanda still stole most of my food off my tray at every meal. But something was happening to me, and it was happening very rapidly.

A wave of something dark, frightening, and sinister was sweeping over me. This world of evil beings was about to finally win the battle over me. My very core—the depths of my soul—was about to be claimed. I could feel it with total certainty. But I could not stop it. Nothing in this world could stop it. My hope was fading fast and along with it my dreams, my realm of possibilities, my very reasons for living. The light at the end of the tunnel was fading swiftly.

At the next rotation after my fake release, Harley—the expert on Nutter—let me know what was up. "Girl, them guards are the stupidest bunch of monkeys on the face of God's green earth. Their brains are just big lumps of shit, I swear. I'll tell your ass *exactly* what in the hell went on here. The big dumb butch one got the call Friday that you was goin' your ass to Nutter on *Monday*, but her big stupid dyke ass didn't half-ass listen, an' so she called you to pack it up three fuckin' days too early. I forgot to tell you. You *always* go to Nutter on a Monday, *always*, never any other day, *never*, no exceptions. That big crazy, dyke-ass jerk-off shoulda knowed that. I knowed it was wrong as soon as they called your ass out on a Friday. I knowed you be coming draggin' your sorry-ass mattress back in here direc'ly. But don't worry. This means you'll be goin' in two days. The assholes'll git your ass up in the middle of the night Sunday. Then they'll drag you off to Nutter. You just wait an' see."

I wanted really badly to believe Harley about this one. But I could not emotionally afford to let one more disappointment come my way. The mental health was going fast.

Bob snuck in to visit me again on Saturday night. (He had already exhausted his visiting hours for the week.) I conveyed to him what Harley had told me. I caught a glimmer of hope in his eye for a brief second, but it faded quickly. I could sense that we both were beginning to erect emotional safeguards.

That Saturday night, I elected—for the first time ever—to completely forgo evening rotation and remain in our cell alone. I shaved my legs with our last razor, washed my bras and underwear in our miniature sink with our "secret soap," and hung them up to dry like limp white flags waving from the light fixture and bunk bed iron and window frames, along with Amanda's butterflies and paper decorations. I lay on top of my bunk and sang old Beatles songs loudly, shouting the memorized words at the graffiti on the ceiling just inches above me.

When I tired of that, I climbed down off the bunk and created my own hors d'oeuvres for the evening, carefully spreading peanut butter across stale saltine crackers in different unique patterns. I invented my own original serving trays for the fancy treats out of Hallmark cards and crayoned manila envelopes. I talked to myself and quoted Bible verses and read favorite pages from our stash of beloved paperbacks. I stood in front of the wavy mirror and made silly faces, tried whimsical hairstyles, and checked my overbrushed teeth for signs of any incipient decay. I did jumping jacks and push-ups and stomach crunches. I categorized my few belongings so Amanda would have no trouble at all with incorporating them into her toiletry supplies "store" after my departure.

By the end of rotation, when Amanda had returned to our cell to complain about how all the other girls had acted that night, I was in a state of total contentment. I knew I would be going the very next night, and now I was prepared.

My last full day at the Coward County Jail was just a little different from all the others. My walk was more confident, my attitude toward others more tolerant, my outlook on life just a bit more optimistic. I

DORAMAE BROOKSHIRE

did my rounds in the dayroom with my head held high and my strides long and precise. When Harley decided to join me in a round, I slowed my pace and spoke to her from my heart. I reassured her that she would have a simply extraordinary life with her two tiny twins and that, someday very soon, Prince Charming would come along and rescue her from her life of drudgery and crime. And he would be the best daddy in all the world too, changing diapers and rocking the two precious tots to sleep and bringing them all home presents from work, little packages of wonderful surprises, chock full of mystery and suspense.

Now mind you, I knew perfectly well that Harley would probably never escape her life of perpetual incarcerations—the "swinging doors of the Georgia prison system," I later found out it was dubbed. Once on probation, the girls found it nearly impossible to abide by all the stringent rules and regulations, especially if paying back a stiff fine was involved, and law enforcement in the state of Georgia *loved* to hunt down an unsuspecting woman for a probation violation and throw her back into the pen—for an extended stay this time. It was one of the main ways the state kept open so many jobs at the jails and prisons.

In fact, in the state of Georgia, nearly fifty-six thousand people are in prison. The state of Georgia is ninth on the list of states with the highest percentage of people in prison. In fact, the South dominates this list, conforming to stereotypes about "hanging judges" and chain gangs. Georgia is one of the top states most likely to put a convicted offender in prison.

Yes, I knew that my spinning of the tale of Prince Charming was just that—a tale. But what harm did it do to take a few minutes on my last day there to paint a rosy picture for Harley? To make one of these poor, forgotten, thrown-away creatures feel like they were just as good as anybody on the outside who boasted a "perfect" life? What was wrong with giving hope—any kind of hope—to someone who had been beat down her entire life and told she would never amount to anything, that she was worse than other people, that she was nothing but a drain on decent folks?

Yes, that last day in the bowels of hell was different from all the rest. Why, I even joined Pearl and her bunch of renegade card sharks for a couple of games of stud poker, using bobby pins for stakes. I was hustled so badly and did so miserably that I'm positive it is still talked about today. I could even be a legend with the card-playing, dice-throwing convicts at the Coward County Jail. Oh, Pearl and Bicycle and Jazzy have moved on by now, probably sentenced to unbearable long terms in some hard-core Georgia prison, but the trumped-up stories of the street-ignorant White doctor continue on today at the many card tables in the dayrooms throughout CCJ.

That Sunday night, I could hardly contain myself. I just knew they were going to come take me to the beloved Nutter. It just had to be. I could wait no longer. Before climbing up to my bunk that night, I double- checked the two brown paper bags stuffed full of all the precious items that Amanda would inherit. I had decided to leave her virtually everything in my two priceless bags. I figured there was no use in trying to take them to Nutter with me anyhow since I had recently received a letter from the institution stating precisely what I was allowed to bring with me, and it included mainly a Bible, a plain gold wedding band, and two pairs of basic white undies. I felt absolutely awful leaving my brand-new novels behind, but I thought it very unwise to begin my Nutter journey with any strikes against me whatsoever. Besides, Amanda and the girls could get a lot of good use and many hours of quality entertainment out of those books.

I lay in my top bunk that night and, try as I may, just could not sleep a wink. My dry, itchy eyes remained wide open, staring endless hours at the graffitied ceiling. I had decided to keep my contacts in all night, knowing that when they finally did call me, I had very little time to escape. I was not sure exactly what time it was—I had been weeks without a clock or watch now—but they did not disappoint me. Sometime in the middle of the night, I finally heard the words I had been waiting for.

"Bahrooshy, pack it up!" rang the joyous words.

When the true time came, it was nothing at all like the false alarm. Amanda did not bounce out of bed to help me drag my repulsive mattress. Caroline, Lee, Harley, and Coco did not wave sadly from their skinny cell windows. There was no forlorn little Pearl slowly waving her

Tweety Bird card and shedding a single tear. No, the send-off this time was nonexistent. After all, it was probably three o'clock in the morning.

I decided to not awaken Amanda. I could handle it by myself this time. All I had to drag out now was the horrible mattress and my razor. Actually, having to turn in a single razor tickled me. What if I had left it behind? What did they think could happen? I thought of Amanda with her private stash of innumerable razor blades she had skillfully broken loose from their protective plastic shells. Did they actually think that these girls didn't have chance after chance to slit their own wrists or someone else's neck if they really wanted to? Did they truly believe that their stupid rule about turning in a single razor when one leaves would actually save CCJ SE Pod 300 from certain destruction and disastrous ends?

But before I could finish my thought, Amanda suddenly jumped up from her peaceful deep slumber. "Here, Doc, let me get that lump of shit for ya," she said sleepily, and she grabbed hold of my formless mattress.

We both lumbered quietly to the dayroom door, she gave me a quick hug, and I heard the Big Click, this time truly for the last time. I think I heard her mumble something on the way back to the cell. It was something like, "Have fun shoveling wet dog shit off the streets of Nutter."

This time, the hallway experience went off without a hitch. I think the guards were all too tired to care. I was instructed to lay my mattress in a pile in the corner and lay my razor on top of it. Then an intimidating large guard led me down the hall to the elevator I had come up on. I was once again made to face the back of the elevator.

Once back at intake on the first floor, the weary guard thrust a crumpled paper sack at me. I wasn't sure whether to take it. "Here, White giiirl, take dis. Ah ain't got awl night. It be yer clothes. Put 'em on in dat dere room ober dere an' brings me back da jail clothes. *Now!* Whachoo starin' at? Yew *dum'* er somet'in'?"

I did as I was told. I went inside the tiny room and opened up the bag, not really knowing what I would find. And there inside that crushed brown paper bag laid my black suit I had worn on that last fatal day of court. The sight of the creased black pants, tailored black suit jacket, off-black satin hose, and high-heeled polished black shoes brought unpleasant memories rushing back. This was the suit that I had been forced to plead guilty in when I wasn't. This was the suit that I had on when they had led me trembling out of the courtroom. It was the suit that my devastated husband and my weeping mother had last seen me in before I became a locked-up criminal. And at that very moment, I wasn't sure that I could ever bring myself to put that suit back on. Too many unpleasant memories were associated with it. But I was afraid that if I didn't obey the weary guard, I might never get out of that hideous place; so in the long run, the fear won out.

I wiggled out of my four-dot bright orange top and five-dot pants and into my unlucky black business suit. As I pulled it out of the bag, I discovered that it was no longer creased, pressed, and neat as a button as it had been the day I had placed it in the bag. Instead, it was crumpled, wrinkled, and dusty with a rather foul odor. The pants had been wadded into a tiny ball, the suit jacket had a dirty brown stain across one shoulder, and the hose were run in two different directions. Not giving it another thought, I quickly pulled the suit on and straightened all the wrinkles out the best I could, trying to salvage what little dignity I had left. As I placed the shoes on my feet, I noticed that they too had not escaped the wrath of the storage room. The polish was dulled by layers of dirty dust, and several deep scratches traveled up and down the heels and toes. I tried quickly to shine them out with my four-dot orange top.

By now, the irritated guard was knocking loudly on the "dressing room" door. "Hurries up in dere, giiiirl! Ah ain't got awl night fo' yo' stoopid ass to get dressed!"

So I emerged from the tiny room, clad in my pathetic crushed courtroom suit.

The guard took one look at the miserable shabby monstrosity, and a wicked little smirk spread across her expressionless face. "Myyy, ain't choo sumt'in' in dat uppity suit o' yers," she sang.

Then as if her moment of triumph over me had ended abruptly, her facial expression suddenly became flat again, and she muttered, "Cum' on den, let's git goin'."

She led me down a long dark hall and onto another elevator, this time one I had never seen. My heart was pounding, and my respiration became shallow and labored; in short, I couldn't imagine where in the world she was taking me. I knew we were on the ground floor because that was where the courtroom guard had brought me to booking that awful day. As far as I knew, all elevators led up to the dreadful pods and cells that I had just come from. Maybe this was just a continuation of the horrible nightmare, only this time she was going to parade me around in front of Bicycle, Jazzy, and Crazy Lee-Lee in my crumpled, dirty suit while they tore me apart limb from limb, all to the utter delight of the demented guard.

But as I stepped into the dreaded elevator and was made to face the back, something seemed a little different. The elevator seemed to be going *down* this time, and it was a very short ride. As the guard commanded me to get off, I looked around and sized up my surroundings. It was much darker here, the hallways were longer, and the ceilings were lower. It had a dank, musty smell.

All of a sudden, it struck me. We were in a *basement*, and I suddenly knew I might be in deep trouble. Why would this hideous city of five thousand criminals have a basement, other than maybe as a hidden den of unspeakable torture and torment? Yes, that was it. The manlike, stoic guard had brought me here to crucify me slowly. She would finish the job that the judges and the lawyers had already begun. Yes, she was going to put me on the rack, tear me limb from limb, maybe even draw and quarter my poor, miserable suit-clad body. The clawing, flaying, ripping, and lacerating would be agonizing and unbearable. I could only hope to pass out or drop over dead of a heart attack soon after the torture began.

But instead, she unlocked a mildewed dark holding cell, one that looked very much like the one I was in at intake, and pushed me inside. As the door clicked shut behind me, I sized up my pen—one four-foot stainless steel bench, one tiny stainless steel sink, and one dirty stainless steel toilet with no toilet seat. By this time, it might have been around four o'clock in the morning, but there was no way that I was going to sleep. I was not going to doze off and miss my ticket out of this ghastly place and onto greener pastures. At least this holding cell had a fairly large window, so I could see them if they came toward me with whips and other torture equipment.

But after an hour or so, I soon tired of staring out of the dirty window because nothing whatsoever was going on at that hour in the basement of the Coward County Jail. I decided to lie down on the sticky bench and rest my tired bones. And as I lay, my legs drawn up to my chest, I began to summarize my experience at the jail in my head. There were Angelica, the single-footed girl who had gotten me through my first daunting night; Scary Serena; the repulsive Bicycle and her nasty lover, Jazzy; and Coco and Jasmine, the girls with no conscience. There were pitiful Pearl, deeply depressed Ethel, sexually-depraved Lee-Lee, and screwed-over Caroline. Then I also remembered the bunch from what seemed to be a long time ago—the group of hooligans who were there when I first arrived. There were Erline, the hillbilly girl; Big Charlotte, the church lady; and Moleface, the gangster woman.

And as I lay there in the middle of the night on that cold, gummy bench, a revelation of the human spirit came to me as if it were a divine inspiration. I suddenly realized that people, as a whole, are adaptable to the situation, no matter how impossible it may seem. People are survivors. When torn from their roots, they create their own "families"; they fulfill their own needs. Yes, the human spirit bends. It is pliable, flexible, and moldable. It overcomes unbelievable odds. It doesn't give up and break with every little disappointment and heartache, like I thought it did before this experience. Why, this jail, this unspeakable den of inequity, was living proof of the triumph of the human spirit.

Just then, I was interrupted by a corpulent, grumpy guard who was waving furiously at me from her guard tower and motioning toward something gray and square that she held in her hand. I wasn't quite sure what she was trying to tell me. This went on for a few minutes, her pointing more and more furiously at the gray object and me shrugging and holding my hands out, palms up, repeatedly. Finally, a tall Black male inmate passed my holding cell, pushing a huge cart filled with square gray objects, and I recognized it as the meal cart. So that was what she was trying to tell me. She was telling me that it was time for breakfast. I looked at her and nodded.

Soon my door clicked open and a square cold food tray was thrust into my hands. At least now I could estimate the time of day better. If the inmates being housed in the basement received their breakfast at about the same time that the other inmates did, that meant that it was about four thirty or so in the morning. I still probably had quite a wait until my journey to the promised land of Nutter. After they picked the breakfast tray up, I tried my best to occupy my time, but there really wasn't a lot to do in a little cramped cell full of stainless steel fixtures.

After what seemed like an eternity, two thickset, heavily muscled male guards unlocked my holding cell noisily. They plunked handcuffs and shackles on me before I knew what had happened, and then one on each side, they took my arms and led me down the long hall. I tried to get a good look at them out of the corner of my eyes. Their ebony skin seemed even darker as the three of us moved like a single unit down the unlit corridor. Their heavy black boots thumped the hard tile floor like angry firecrackers exploding in the night. Their dark eyes were dead and focused straight ahead, like two sharks before an attack. I wondered where they were taking me and if I would ever come out alive. Suddenly, Nutter didn't seem like such a good idea after all.

The three of us moved through two more locked doors and found ourselves in what appeared to be a humongous basement garage. There were countless large vans and assorted vehicles with "State of Georgia Dept. of Corrections" stamped on their sides. We trudged toward one of the biggest ones. In another second, the doors were unlocked, and one of the guards told me to get in. I obeyed, taking the back seat closest to the back of the driver because that was the one he was pointing to. One of the brawny guards reached in and buckled me into the seat, I guess maybe as a safeguard against my escape.

Once the vehicle started to back out of the garage, I took a good look around to size up the situation. When I looked over my shoulder, I was pretty amazed at the size of the carrier. It was the size of a minibus, with three rows of long seats behind me. The width of the bus was pretty impressive too. I started to count mentally and figured that thirteen more passengers could easily fit inside, four more beside me and three more on each of the remaining three seats.

Oh, great, I thought. *I get to ride in this thing for three and a half hours with thirteen other belligerent stinky inmates.* I closed my eyes and pictured us stopping at every jail, prison, and detention center in the Atlanta area to pick up every handcuffed and shackled criminal on his or her way to Nutter; and suddenly, a great damper was put on the highly anticipated trip.

Why, we'll be packed in here like a bunch of chained sardines, I imagined. *They may even put more than fourteen in here. Maybe they'll pack us in so tightly we won't be able to breathe. I know they'll have to at least fill this thing 'cuz it's taxpayers' money that's paying for this trip, and I read about such as this somewhere. Our state is supposed to make the best use of the taxpayers' money, and filling up this van would be just that.* I finally drew the conclusion that I didn't care if I had to suffer the entire day with picking up inmates all over the city of Atlanta and traveling in cramped quarters just as long as we ended up at our destination by the end of the hassled day.

But we never picked up a single other human being. I waited and waited, but it was quite obvious, peering out the window, that we were leaving the Atlanta area rather abruptly. For the next three and a half hours, I had the entire bus, all four rows of seats, to myself. A wall of thick steel mesh separated the two guards from me, and I was more than a little relieved that it was there to protect me from them. But because there was no plexiglass between us, I could hear everything that the two of them said.

They talked about how their jobs sucked but not really that bad because they had "da power against any fool in orange." They talked about how fun it was to scare and intimidate the inmates, and one of them bragged on how he once made a new prisoner "piss awl ober his crackuh self." They talked about sleeping in the guard towers when no one was looking and how third shift was the best because they could get away with anything. They talked about what great fun it was to drive "the big van" to Nutter because, after they dropped "the scum in da back seat" off, they would take the rest of the day getting back to

Atlanta. They planned to eat a leisurely long lunch, probably in one of those strip places where they could watch "White whores with big tits and little asses." Then they talked about their plans to drop by their "bitches'" houses later to relieve themselves.

After a while, I sickened of their caveman mentality and tried to tune them out. I turned my stiff neck toward the window, and what I saw took my breath away. It was sunrise, and there right beside me was my precious daily friend, the flaming orange ball that peeked over Rock Mountain from my tiny cell room window on my upper bunk in CCJSE 301. Only this time, the site wasn't limited to four by ten inches. The splendid scene went on forever, making the skies around me a backdrop of spectacular colors. Oranges, reds, golds, and violets put on a show for me of such indescribable splendor that I could never hope to see such a sight in my lifetime again. The heavens burst open with crimson and tiny gold nuggets. The next minute, they were pink and azure, the next lavender streaked in silver lines. By the time my circular friend was high enough in the sky to turn its usual jaundiced color, I felt as if I had just been the only witness to the most spectacular show on the earth. I decided that I would gaze out that window and tune the two sickening guards out for the remainder of the journey.

As soon as I successfully tuned out the two moral cripples in the front seat, an amazing phenomenon began to sweep over me. Suddenly and quite inexplicably, the world right outside my van window became alive with wonder. The trees zipping by became majestic great towers of waving foliage. The newborn sun caused each leaf to reflect the morning's light like a prism while the bashful breeze twisted these images just enough to create a wonderland of dancing forms and hues. The perfectly plotted farmers' fields, rich with the emerald heads of newly planted crops peeking through the rich black soil, seemed to beckon me as we hurried past. High in the unclouded sky, a stately flock of black and gray Canadian geese formed a dignified *V,* flapping their graceful wings against the uprush of the morning Georgia wind. The wildflowers that were hastily planted in an afterthought along the median strips burst open with colors. Their scarlet, pink, and golden faces smiled up at me as I gazed at them longingly. They danced gracefully in the gentle breeze and shivered up close against one another when a sudden gust of unexpected wind rushed through them. I longed to burst forth from my chains and confinement and dance unashamedly and endlessly among these gorgeous ladies of nature.

The rest of the way to my awaiting new home, I remained in this state of mesmerized, hypnotized world of wonderment. It was as if I was experiencing the world around me for the very first time. I was perhaps seeing God's daily show on the earth from the eyes of a newborn babe. I decided then and there to never take anything of simple and natural beauty for granted ever again.

My state of mystic ecstasy was abruptly interrupted by the two thickheaded jailers asking me if I had to pee. By my estimations, we were only about thirty minutes away from the place that would be my salvation at the time. I wondered what would have happened if I would have had to go within the last three hours. Shortly after I stated that I would appreciate being able to relieve myself, the two sidekicks pulled the van into a parking space at a roadside rest area. The shortest one meandered to my back door, slowly unlocked it from the outside, and announced loudly, "If you gotta go, den *go!*"

I sheepishly held my aching, handcuffed wrists and bound ankles out at him. "I can't use the restroom, sir, with these on," I stated flatly.

While the two of them were busy deciding how to handle this new dilemma, I noticed what was going on beside the van. A little family straight out of a Norman Rockwell painting was enjoying a picnic lunch on a concrete rest area table. The neatly folded foil squares from their homemade egg salad and ham sandwiches gleamed in the bright morning sunlight. Their freshly stirred lemonade in their sparkling jug and their just baked chocolate chip cookies beckoned to me.

As I stepped from the van, handcuffed and shackled, a small girl with bouncing blond pigtails stared at me with curiosity. Her elder brother dropped his ham and cheese onto the red checkered plastic tablecloth, and his half-full mouth flew open in disbelief. About that time, the two Rockwell parents caught sight of me and immediately turned chalky white with sheer terror. The perfectly coiffured and fashionably attired mother instinctively went into action, gathering up her well-groomed brood of two and quickly herding them toward the family SUV. The father was less subtle about the whole matter. He glared at me, pure hatred radiating from his handsome brown eyes as he methodically packed up the remains of the family's rudely interrupted roadside lunch. As I stood there, chained and bound like a serial killer, the Norman Rockwell father completed my total shame and humiliation by looking me straight in the eyes and shaking his head as if to say, *Now look what you have done to my family's day in the sun. Not only did your hideous, repulsive life of crime interrupt my family's picnic but it also probably traumatized my wife and children to a point of no return.*

My spinning head dropped, and I looked down at my chained feet, my body posture suddenly becoming totally submissive. All I could see was the perfect red squares of the checkered picnic tablecloth whirling around in my head as the angry father snatched it up abruptly, shooting me one last look of total disgust. Just as I was ready to climb back into the state van, figuring none of this was worth it simply to relieve my aching bladder, the two bozos decided to unlock my handcuffs and shackles.

As they performed this feat, an elderly couple who was walking their miniature poodle beside the van caught sight of what was going on and nervously crossed to the other side of the parking lot. They immediately motioned to a group of children playing Frisbee nearby, and they too scurried away, distancing themselves promptly from the scary lady in chains. A group of senior citizens in tennis shoes and straw hats, with cheap cameras hanging from their necks, scrambled hastily back onto their tour bus and into their assigned seats, waiting impatiently for the bus driver and tour guide to board and rescue them from this atrocious parking lot criminal. The family who was parked right beside us nearly tripped one another getting back into their station wagon after returning from using the restroom and buying cheap refreshments from the vending machines. They were so frightened that two of them actually dropped their sodas and candy bars in the utter haste to escape from the chained convict that was standing right beside their family ride.

The two clumsy guards finally succeeded in springing me from my chains, and I quickly moved toward the ladies' restroom, freely swinging my arms with my newfound sense of emancipation. I was instantly amazed at what I saw as I stepped into the bathroom. This room was, by far, the largest space I had seen in several weeks. Why, I bet there was length enough to accommodate twenty-five spacious bathroom stalls and a matching number of sinks on the opposite wall. This was no 4′ × 10′ cell.

As I stood for a moment in awe, two matronly women smiled at me and started up a decent conversation. I could not imagine why they were treating me with such respect until I realized that I was standing there in my black suit and high heels, freed of chains and burly prison guards. These two poor elderly figures did not even realize that I was the parking lot criminal of rest stop no. 127, like all the rest of the poor, traumatized folks still out there. Apparently, these two women had been in the lavatory this entire time. So I stood there in the doorway of the huge women's restroom and had a decent, everyday conversation with two wonderful, gentle grandmothers, eager to know just how I was doing on this fine day.

After they departed, I entered one of the newly scrubbed stalls and sat on the sparkling clean toilet for minutes longer than I needed to. Then I washed my hands under a normal-sized faucet with standard water pressure, watching myself the whole time in a long clean mirror boasting a very accurate reflection. As I stood there, spellbound, gazing at my timid reflection and repeatedly rubbing soft pink soap on my trembling hands, I remembered briefly what a simply marvelous place the "outside" world was.

After I had taken full advantage of my brief helping of liberty, I started to meander slowly back to the awaiting state vehicle. In a moment that seemed to last forever, the two brawny prison guards handcuffed and shackled me once more while the travelers at rest stop no. 127 once again panicked, scattered, and did anything humanly possible to get as far away from the parking lot criminal as they could. I was placed in a tight seat belt, my door was locked from outside, the two burly guards climbed into the front seat, and we were again on our way to the promised land.

The rest of the trip was pretty uneventful since the guard riding in the passenger seat decided to doze off, snoring loudly, his head cocked to one side, a long string of drool oozing out of the corner of his mouth. I tried to suppress unpleasant thoughts of what might have happened during this trip if these two well-muscled young guards who possessed very little morals had decided to pull off the main road for a while with me. I knew deep in my gut that if something that hideously repulsive would have occurred, the state would never in a million years believe a "confessed" felon over two of their finest. I was just very relieved that we were probably almost to Nutter, and nothing like this had happened.

FRUITCAKE CAPITAL

I N A SHORT while, the state van slowed almost to a halt. I looked out the window. We were passing through a tiny, little town. Two fast-food restaurants, a small, one-story hospital, and a few ramshackle downtown stores were all that seemed to be here. The only halfway noticeable storefront had a large colorful sign of a horse and buggy that boasted, "Nutter Fruitcake—the Choice of Millions Since 1910."

Oh, this is just great, I thought. *Nothing could be more appropriate if I had thought of this myself. The town in which I was going to pay back my debt to society was the fruitcake capital of the world.*

Before I had time to further contemplate this notion, we pulled into a wide asphalt driveway leading to a place surrounded by miles of razor wire fence. The overall appearance of the place was pretty impressive, just like Bob had described it to me. The building itself was a one-story, long well-kept brick structure. Its many windows sparkled, and the circling sidewalks were scrubbed clean. But what was really impressive was the landscaping surrounding the building. The most lush greenest lawn I had ever seen encompassed the entire campus. It had been trimmed consistently to a specified, exact, uniform length. Several tailored flower beds enveloped the premises, sprinkled evenly between patches of perfectly pruned bright green sod. The happy little heads of the petunias and gerbera daisies seemed to send out a welcome to anyone who passed by.

The guard on the driver's side stopped the van and got out. He walked up to a short young Black female dressed in some sort of uniform and shiny black boots and handed her a fistful of papers. While they were standing there, they seemed to strike up quite a conversation. I could tell from their body language that the male guard was flirting quite openly with her, and she didn't seem to be resisting his advances whatsoever.

While this little escapade went on, I stared out the van window to take in as much as I could. I noticed several girls dressed in drab khaki-colored pants and shirts with high shiny black boots on, cutting, trimming, edging, and weeding the lawn and flower beds. Uniformed women seemed to be standing guard over them. To the left of the building, there appeared to be a large outside exercise yard surrounded by ten-foot-high razor wire. The reason that I drew the conclusion that it was an exercise yard was that about fifty girls in the same drab clothes and black boots were walking repeatedly in circles around the dirt inside the tall fence. The majority of them didn't appear to be enjoying their exercise session much at all. Beads of sweat rolled down most of their sad faces, and I was suddenly reminded that it was June in south Georgia. The temperature was probably already near ninety degrees when we had stopped at the rest area some time ago. I had heard the two guards mention that the temperature was expected to hit over one hundred today. All of a sudden, it didn't seem like a good idea for me to be in such a hurry to get there. I didn't seem to be so anxious to step out of the air-conditioned state van now.

And then the greatest thing happened. I actually recognized one of the faces who were rotating around that dirt exercise pen. It was Angelica, the one-footed girl, the one who had rescued me from a certain suicide the very first night I had entered that awful jail. As soon as she saw me in the state van, she recognized me. A big wide grin broke across her up-to-now serious face, and she began to wave a friendly huge greeting, her sunburned arm flapping wildly in the late morning sun. I waved back, heaving a sigh of relief with the realization that I would now know at least one other person on this newest journey.

As the horny male guard continued to fall all over the female guard with her teasing ways, Angelica started up a little one-woman show of her own exclusively for me. It didn't take too terribly long for the girls to make one rotation around the exercise yard because it wasn't too awfully big. So with every rotation, Angelica began to perform a creative brand-new trick designed selectively for my own entertainment.

On the first rotation, she tipped her worn khaki-colored cap and did a little curtsy as she passed the van. The next time, she stiffened her bronze body, fixated her stare straight ahead, and marched stiff legged, rhythmically lifting her one shiny boot and her special tennis shoe alternately with her rigid arms. I laughed out loud at the sight of Angelica, the little toy soldier. The slumbering guard snorted loudly and repositioned his head. I decided I had better not laugh aloud at Angelica again. But I couldn't help but chuckle to myself when her next prank came around. This time, she pulled a buddy into the caper.

I had noticed some jugs sitting on a bench near the guard, who stood as a rigid shield against the exercise yard gate, protecting it from potential escapees. Every now and then, the rotating prisoners would stop and take a slug from the jug, mostly when the guard was not looking. Otherwise, they would obediently use the paper cups provided beside the jug and dispose of them properly in the metal trash receptacle nearby. Well, on this rotation, Angelica and her tall lanky friend had decided to risk going one step farther than the bad girls who drank directly from the water jug. After glancing over their shoulders to make sure the guard was preoccupied, they both took turns filling their mouths until both of their cheeks puffed out with water retention. Then they held the cold liquid in their cheeks for one more complete turn around the yard. As they passed the van this time, they separated a few steps from their side-by-side position, checked to see that the guard was not watching, and then expelled the water from their puffy cheeks with all their might, right smack dab into each other's sweaty faces. On their next rotation, they winked at me as the water trickled down their noses and chins and onto their well-pressed khaki shirts.

I didn't have another chance to see what Angelica's next shenanigan would be because, at about that time, the male guard who had been ogling the female guard returned to the van, woke up his fellow guard, and announced that it was time for me to get out now. I did as I was told and stepped out of the state van. About that time, Angelica came around again and waved at me. I innocently waved back. But I soon found out that this was definitely not the thing to do at Nutter.

Just as soon as I waved, the short, little female guard, whose possession I was evidently now in, puffed out her petite chest, practically rose on her tiptoes in an attempt to add inches to her abbreviated height, and got right in my face. "Detaineeee"—she glanced down at her papers—"Brahkashure!" she screamed, shaking her skinny finger one inch from my nose. "The first rule you needs to learn is we *do not* communicates wif no udder detaineees on da premises! Do you undahstand me, detainee?" She was trying her best to stretch up to my height so she could position herself eyeball to eyeball. The way she was holding her scrawny body took me back to the illiterate little mailman at the jail. She was barking orders in a military fashion, like the many TV sergeants I had seen over the years.

But she seemed to be a bit worried that she was not going to be able to adequately establish the pecking order with this new detainee in the black suit and high heels. Right then and there, she decided that she'd better make her point, before she lost me. "I am going to show you two poesishuns, detaineeee, dat you had bettah learns eemeedeeitleee, do you understand me, detainee?"

"Yes, ma'am," I uttered.

"Do *not* address me in dis manner, detaineeee!" she screeched. "When you speaks to me, you say, 'Ma'am, Detaineee Bahkasure wishes to speak, ma'am.' When I ax you a ques'shun, you say, 'Ma'am, yes, ma'am.' You got dat, detaineeee?"

"Ma'am, yes, ma'am," I responded.

"Now here doze two poeisishuns," she said.

"Dis one here's attenshun!" she shouted, clicking her heels together, lifting her chin while staring straight ahead, and stiffly holding both arms against her rigid sides.

"An' dis one here's parade rest," she announced, splitting her legs apart and holding her hands clasped together behind her back. "Yew will be in one posishun or dee udder dee whole time yew is here, detaineeee! Do yew undahstands?"

I nodded.

"I can't *hear* youew!" she yelled.

"Ma'am, yes, ma'am," I said.

"Dat's bettuh! Now let me sees yew do dem!"

I gave her my best attempt on the two positions of attention and parade rest, but she evidently was not impressed with my interpretation of the latter one.

"*No*! Dat ain't *raht*, detaineeee!" she howled in my ear. "Like *dis*!" And she jerked my feet farther apart and clasped my fingers behind my back tighter.

I looked at her out of the corners of my eyes to make sure she was not going to hit me or something. But that proved to be the worst mistake I had made yet.

"Don't choo eyeball me, detainee!" she screamed at the top of her lungs, little balls of spit flying in my face. "Yew comes in here awl high an' mighteee in yo' uppitee suit an' fanceee shoes, an' yew t'inks yoew really sumt'in', huh? Well, we gonna jis' *see* about *dat*, detaineeee! Yew march on ober here to dis here building, an' we'll sees jis' how much yew likes to kiss the wall!"

I obeyed, marching the best I could down the long asphalt driveway and up the steps to the building, the puny guard shrieking orders at me all the way. As soon as she got me against the brick wall beside the glass door, she hollered, "Now *kiss* the wall, Detaineee Bahrookasure!"

I did as I was told, suddenly feeling quite foolish, standing in the south Georgia heat in a two-piece black suit and heels, kissing an exterior brick wall of a building.

"Dere now. Yoew can jis' stay dere for a while an' t'ink about what choo done," she declared. "Keep yo' nose against da wall, detaineee! Don't let it come off dat wall, or yew'll get yer first DR." And with that, she left me to melt in the heat while she went down the driveway to meet two police cars delivering two more lucky souls to Nutter.

I couldn't exactly figure out what had just happened. Why was she so excessively pissed off at me, and what exactly had I done to make her that way? Why couldn't I adequately stand at parade rest? Why couldn't I wave at Angelica? Why was I being made to press my sweaty nose against a brick wall? And what was a DR anyway? I was already a doctor.

As she went through the same gestures and rhetoric with the two new girls out on the hot asphalt driveway, the south Georgia summer sun began to rise higher in the cloudless sky and beat down on my back. The long-sleeved heavy black suit jacket and pants and the thick black pantyhose underneath were not helping matters. I tried to guess the temperature. I figured it was about ninety-nine to one hundred degrees. I had lived through nineteen south Georgia summers by then, and I had hated the sweltering heat of every single one.

Soon I began to feel the trickle of sweat traveling down my spine and accumulating around the waistband of the suit pants. Little beads of sweat turned into active streams on my face, water dripping off my eyebrows, chin, and violated nose. I could feel the liquid rolling off my scalp and onto my neck. I knew my hair would soon be soaking wet. I wanted to ask if I could at least take off my suit jacket, but I dared not speak. This went on for an eternity while the short, little guard screeched at the new detainees arriving every minute. She eventually marched three more detainees up the steps and ordered them into nose-against-the-wall position. In a short while, they too were forced to kiss the burning bricks. Now I had three more torrid bodies pressed near mine, creating even more parching temperatures.

About that time, my head started to spin, I began to see with tunnel vision, and a wave of dizziness that I had never experienced before or since enveloped me like an angry tornado ready to sweep me up in its clutches. I knew I was going down. The pint-size guard must have been able to see that I was about to hit the pavement because she positioned herself smack dab in my face and declared, "Wha' da mattah, detaineee? Yew gonna puke or jis' fall ober? OK den, Detainee Bahrookasure, yew goes in da door first den." And she pointed to the nearby glass door.

I didn't know if I should take my nose off the brick wall, but I did know that if I didn't get out of that heat soon, my nose would be positioned against the concrete step. So I obeyed the scrawny guard, opened the glass door, and went on in.

As I stepped into what was to be my world for the next ninety days, the crisp, icy air hit me square in the sweaty face and nearly knocked me down. I glanced around briefly. This new environment forced on me did not in any way, shape, or form resemble the slammer from whence I just came. The polished tile floors were scrubbed so squeaky clean that

I could almost see my own pitiful reflection in them. The block walls sparkled with glossy white paint that couldn't have been over a day old. Behind my back stood a row of showers whose antiseptic aromas hit my nostrils with a vengeance. The windows sparkled from daily scrubbings. Even the ceilings boasted of constant attention.

But I didn't have much time to take in this immaculate new surroundings. As soon as I stepped through the glass doors into wonderland, a tall lanky middle-aged Black woman dressed in the same khaki starched uniform as Angelica and her buddies positioned herself very close behind me. She was clutching a square thick cardboard box. I noticed immediately that she was missing several of her front teeth, and her gums were red and puffy. The remaining teeth were loose in their sockets. This detainee was definitely stricken with advanced periodontal disease. My first instinct was to help her out, but then reality hit, and I remembered that I was no longer allowed to practice dentistry.

About the time that I was becoming extremely uncomfortable with the stench of periodontally involved breath being blown against the back of my damp head, another lady came into play. This one was sitting with perfect posture behind a long highly polished brown folding table. In fact, two other ladies with similar posture were sitting to each side of her. All three had sour, disagreeable expressions on their yuppie faces. They were all dressed to kill in the latest Ralph Lauren fashions, and their youthful faces looked like they had all just completed a lengthy facial and free makeup application at the local department store cosmetic counter. None of them could have possibly been older than thirty or thirty-five.

My assigned lady was petite and blond and very, very prissy. She looked me up and down, shook her golden locks, and commanded me to take a seat on a folding chair positioned directly in front of her. I did as I was told. As I sat, my assigned detainee with the missing teeth and bad breath took two steps closer to me, the corrugated box touching me lightly on the back of my neck. The blond woman shot me a glare that would have stopped Bambi cold in his tracks. It was full of disgust, repugnance, and abhorrence almost as if I was so utterly repulsive that she was near nausea.

"Detainee Brookshire," she announced, "listen closely to what I have to say because I'm not going to repeat myself. This box will house your property while you are here."

With that, the detainee with the bad mouth hurled the empty cardboard box at my feet and then stepped back a step.

"Did you bring anything with you?" she asked.

"No, ma'am, just what I have on," I replied.

She stared at my black suit, polished high heels, fashionable earrings, and brand-name watch. Suddenly, a part of her smug expression disappeared, and she appeared almost intimidated by this detainee attired in clothing that may have surpassed her own painfully overplanned outfit of the day. "Do you have any questions, Detainee Brookshire?" she asked, staring at the floor.

"Yes, just one," I replied. "I wear contacts. I have very poor vision without them. I need my contact solution and the small container to keep them in at night. That's all." I tried to keep matters as simple as possible.

"Oh, I don't think you can have contacts here," she announced loudly, looking around nervously for someone to ask. She finally spotted a middle-aged woman in a guard's uniform and motioned her over to the table. The two of them turned their backs to me and whispered softly for several minutes.

"We don't think detainees are allowed to wear contacts in here. That could land you a DR. You'll have to see the nurse about that," she announced.

"How do I go about that?" I inquired.

But she ignored the question. Goldilocks was done with me and was ready for her next victim. She motioned me out of her chair and began sizing up the next poor, unsuspecting sweaty soul who had just stepped in from her brick-kissing experience.

The melancholy, pitiful detainee with gum disease took me by the arm and lifted me out of the chair. She jerked the cardboard box up off the floor and marched me into the shower area behind us. Four sparkling clean showers built of concrete blocks stood in a perfect row against the wall behind the row of tables with the sour-faced fashion queens. The shower stalls were huge, each big enough to hold at least ten detainees. They were completely open to the world, having no shower doors or curtains whatsoever. The gigantic silver shower heads exploded from the disinfected walls, and huge shiny drains blinded me from the white tiled floors. I suddenly wondered if it was possible for the Jews during the Holocaust to be gassed if the shower stalls didn't have airtight doors.

The detainee with the rotten mouth pointed to an empty shower stall and told me quietly to get undressed. I looked around, wondering if this was some kind of sick joke. I wasn't about to disrobe in front of all these people. Why, not only could all the poor new detainees sitting at the long tables see me but so could the scowling ladies and the guards in uniforms who seemed to be posted all over the room. I looked at my new colleague with fear and embarrassment in my eyes and slowly shook my head, signaling her that I had no intentions of doing such. As soon as I did this, the first real expression I had seen from her suddenly swept over her face. She took two small steps toward me and then bent over to whisper something in my ear.

"Listen, lady, you gots ta do what dey tells ya to aroun' dis place, or y'all get what dey calls a DR, an' ya don't want one o' dem, believe me, so *please* listen ta what Ah tells ya, an' everyt'ing's gonna be awl right, OK? Ah knows ya don't want ta shower in front o' awl dese here peoples, but Ah won't look. Ah promise."

There was that damn acronym again. What could this dreaded DR possibly be? Whatever it was, everyone around this place seemed to be living in fear of receiving one of these things. The guards used it as leverage. The sour ladies at the tables used it as a threat. And now the detainee referred to it as if it was the worst possible thing that another detainee could ever land. I made a mental note to ask the first person I trusted around this place what in god's name a DR was. But until then, I figured that I had better listen to my new friend with the advanced periodontal disease. After all, this horrible DR could be some type of unforeseen torture or something.

I slowly took off my clothes and, having no hooks or shower door to hang them on, reluctantly handed them to the woman. She threw each piece of clothing carelessly into the cardboard box at her feet. As soon as I was completely naked for the whole world to see, a tall female guard stepped up to me from nowhere. She scared me so much, in fact, that I let out a loud gasp. She had a man's haircut, a man's posture, and a man's walk. She wore no makeup whatsoever. She chomped her gum loudly and scratched her armpit. Her shiny black boots were planted firmly on the ground. She was busy pulling a pair of surgical gloves on her huge hands. She stepped into the shower along with me. "Now bend over," she demanded.

Oh god, no! I thought. *This cannot be happening to me! I'm standing here naked in a room with maybe fifteen other people I don't know from Adam, and a gigantic lesbian guard is going to stick her finger up my butt!* A stoic expression spread across my face. I did as I was told.

The enormous woman body searched my anus and then my vagina and ended by lifting both of my breasts. Tears streaked down my expressionless face. I bit my lower lip with all my might to try to stop them, but they continued to spill out. "She clean," she announced to no one in particular. Then she stepped out of my shower to go onto her next victim.

"Now take dis here stuff an' wash yer hair wif it." My new buddy was handing me a paper cup full of foul-smelling shampoo. "It for da lice, if you has any," she whispered.

I couldn't think straight. My whole being had just been violated with the body search. I was shaking like a leaf. I reached out slowly and took the paper cup. I reached over, turned on the shower, and wet my head. I poured the pungent, thick liquid into my hair. It was so acrid that it made the hairs in my nose stand up. I wondered if this lice treatment would make my hair come out in clumps the next day. My "shower supervisor" then suddenly reached in and sprayed me all over my body with some nasty-smelling substance.

Before I got a chance to really take a good shower with soap and warm water to get rid of these horrible chemical insults, the woman was handing me a towel and telling me to dry off. Then just as quickly, she was handing me my new clothes—the uniform that I was to wear the whole time I would be in this awful place. A pair of plain white panties too loose and a white bra that was so tight that I almost couldn't breathe. When I told her that I didn't think the bra fit, she told me that it would have to do; it was the last size she had anywhere near mine. Khaki starched pants with an elastic waist, a large khaki shirt with buttons down the front, a pair of white socks, and a large pair of ugly high-top black boots completed the uniform. I quickly got dressed, finally relieved that I was no longer naked to the world. When I started to tuck in the oversize shirt, my new friend told me that I was never to tuck the shirt in. I was to leave it out of the pants at all times.

I stepped out of the shower and glanced at myself in a nearby mirror. What I saw horrified me. Staring back at me was what appeared to be a lady from "the wrong side of the tracks." My friends back in Goat Valley and I used to refer to such creatures as "poor White trash." The reflection in the mirror revealed a lady in her forties dressed in a crumpled, faded shirt the color of pottery clay, a pair of washed-out trousers in the same hue that hung down below her ankles, and dull black army boots. Her hair was soaking wet and clumped together, sticking out in all directions, and her eyes were red and bloodshot. Her swollen nose was running, and her cheeks had large whelps from crying. The expression on her face was heartbreaking. How could this possibly be the same woman who, just minutes ago, was sitting with perfect posture at the tables, attired in a brand-name black suit and shiny high heels? *This is what happens to avalanche people*, I thought.

The woman with the bad teeth told me to have a seat on the floor in a corner. I sat for what seemed to be an eternity, glad that I was finally clothed. In a while, a young girl with cropped blond hair, also wet, joined me on the floor. Judging by the expression on her face, she had just suffered her surprise initiation from the lesbian guard.

A very scary-looking redheaded woman dressed to kill stuck her head in the doorway. A look of pure disgust was on her face. "Have the new detainees had lunch yet?" she barked.

When she was told no, she remarked, "Just let them eat right there on the floor then."

Soon the young girl and I were handed two brown paper bags. "You got ten minutes to eat dis," the guard who handed them to us said.

Inside, we found two smashed sandwiches, one bologna and one peanut butter, and an orange. I threw the two sandwiches to the side and placed the orange carefully in my palm. I couldn't believe it. I was actually holding a piece of fresh fruit in my hand. I thought I might start crying all over again. But then reality struck, and the words of the guard soaked in. I had only ten minutes to eat my lunch, and I had probably already wasted a full minute admiring the orange.

I began to thrust my stubby fingernails into the orange peel with all the might I could muster. Soon little irregular pieces of orange peel were all over the floor at my feet. This was not an easy task to accomplish quickly. Once peeled, I carefully pulled each section apart and placed the first one in my anxious mouth. It was hard for me to try to explain the utter importance of that very moment, to try to describe how heavenly, how very divine, how glorious, splendid, and brilliant it was to hold a succulent piece of fresh fruit against the inside of my cheek and then feel the sweet juice squirt out with every bite—that orange, that beautiful, blissful, paradisial orange. To have the first bite of fresh fruit that one had had in weeks, it was as close to a truly spiritual experience that I had ever had. I never got around to eating my sandwiches that first day. I just ate my orange and gulped down my Kool-Aid afterward.

The blond girl who shared the lunch on the floor with me glared at me long and hard without a word when I finished my divine experience with the orange. She had been busy trying to stuff down two dry sandwiches on doughy white bread and a stale cookie within the ten-minute deadline. As soon as she accomplished that, she looked at her orange with disdain, stuffed it back into the brown bag, and threw it forcefully in the large trash bin.

I wanted to scream out, *No! Don't do that! Save your orange, and I'll eat it later. It may be the only piece of fruit or vegetable we ever see around here.* But I said nothing because the frightening woman with the red hair and fancy clothes had threatened us within an inch of our lives if we said a single word to each other.

SERGEANT DAIRY QUEEN

S HORTLY AFTER OUR lunch on the floor, the girl who trashed the orange and I were instructed by a guard to remove our black boots and then were led down a long hall with a highly polished tile floor. In fact, the floor was so expertly buffed that I came close to slipping and falling in my stocking feet a couple of times. All along the way, several detainees in khaki uniforms could be seen down on their hands and knees scrubbing, waxing, and buffing small areas of the immaculate flooring. When they dared to look up at us, tiny beads of sweat could be seen rolling off their brows, and their facial expressions were that of pure exhaustion. When one of the waxing queens stood up, I noticed right away that the knees of her drab uniform were almost worn through. She winced in pain, grabbed her lower back, and then rubbed her knees while rocking back and forth.

"Detainee Miller! What did I tell you about standin' up before you're done waxing your area?" an angry guard screamed, stomping loudly in her boots toward the poor girl to confront her.

The tired girl snapped almost immediately to attention. "Ma'am, yes, ma'am, but we been on this floor now since last night at three o'clock, and my back and my knees, ma'am, they be a-hurtin' me, ma'am."

"I don't wanna hear 'bout none o' that bullshit, detainee. You shouldn'ta done what ya done ta git in this place, an' ya wouldn't have ta worry 'bout your damn back an' knees, then, would ya, detainee?" The pissed-off guard was so close to the poor girl that she was spitting in her face when she screamed.

And the pitiful girl was just taking it with the posture of a whipped puppy dog. At the threat of getting a DR, she dropped back down to her knees promptly and resumed waxing the already perfect floor.

"What *choo* lookin' at, detainee?"

Now it was my turn. The short stout guard who had led the orange trasher and myself down the hall was now suddenly in my face. "The first thing you need to learn around here is that you ain't got no business lookin' at sumthin' that ain't none of yer business, Detainee"—she looked at my new name tag on my shirt—"Brook-a-shy. You got that, detainee?"

"Ma'am, yes, ma'am!" I shot right back.

"Wuh then, don't let me catch ya doin' it no more," she grumbled.

"In fact, both y'all two stop right where y'all are and stand at attention till I get back," she demanded.

We stopped dead in our tracks and stood at perfect attention against the sparkling wall between two doors. The disagreeable guard returned after what seemed to be an eternity. In fact, my knees were starting to buckle from standing so intensely at attention for such a long period. Straggling behind the wrathful guard was a long string of pitiful-looking detainees marching out of sync, with a really pissed-off, highly verbal guard close behind them.

"Y'all sorry excuses for human beings!" she shouted. "March da way I showed yew, er I kin show yew a'gin, an' dis time, y'all won't t'ink much o' da demonstration! What's so damn funny dere, Detainee Brown? Ain't choo been in here before, girl? Don't choo never learn ta quit doin' whatever it is ya do ta git in here, Brown? Yew must *like* it here, huh, Brown?"

The indignant guard was tall and light brown in color with closely cropped hair so kinky that it stood in tightly coiled patches all about her scalp. Her close-fitting starched uniform was so tight on her puffed-out chest and sturdy legs that it appeared to be painted on. The shiny badge above her breast and the polished belt buckle fastened tightly around her waist rose and sank with every pissed-off word she hollered.

When she was done hassling Detainee Brown, she left for a brief moment; and when she returned, she was clutching a thick paper cup from Dairy Queen. She made quite a production of picking up the red plastic spoon that projected from the succulent dairy treat and began to taunt us with her absolutely wondrous experience of ingesting the creamy white ambrosia. "Ohhhhhh, dis is sooooo good! I thought about gettin' dah M&M or da Oreo or da Butterfinger Blizzard today, but now I is soooo glad dat I gots da banana split one! It be sooo good! Dese here little pieces of pineapples, banana, scrawberry, and cherry, *ummmm*! And da real whipped cream, *yummmm*!"

She was waving the spoon so closely in Detainee Brown's face that I began to wonder if the frustrated prisoner might reach over and grab it out of the arrogant guard's greedy hand. But the recipient of all the teasing appeared to practice perfect self-control in this issue. Now myself, I wasn't quite so sure of. The haughty, patronizing guard's mention of four different fruits in one short sentence just about sent me into a stage of pure frenzy. I began to seriously wonder if I would not be the one to break the line, rush the highfalutin guard, and snatch the heavenly delicacy right out of her condescending little hands. But luckily, before I could give my thieving plot much thought, the two guards were shrieking out our next instructions.

"When we open dis door, yew detainees is goin' ta go into dis room an' sit at dese tables, only *six* girls to a table! Ya got *dat*?" the short, little guard yelled.

"*An*' yew better not say *one single word* about nuttin' to nobody, or you'll git a DR so fast you won't know what hit cha!" the ice cream connoisseur added. "Now go in dere an' do like we says."

At that, the sparkling clean door was flung open, and we all marched into the awaiting room, single file. The large room was full of round spotless tables, each with six matching chairs placed in perfect circles around it. The more aggressive girls scrambled to sit at a table with their selected buddies they had just formed brand-new friendships with. I stood off for a minute and ended up at a table with a couple of the rejects whom no one cared to associate with.

As soon as we were all seated, the two guards threw black notebooks with soft, worn covers at each and every one of us. "Dese here are yer *bibles*, detainees! Dese black books are da rules an' regoolashuns of dis here place. Yew will have dese books wit' yew at awl times! Yew will sleep wit' dem, eat wit' dem, even *shit* wit' dem! Yew got *dat*? If we catches yew wit'out dem dis first week uv oreentashuns, yew will get a DR, yew got *dat*?"

The flaunter of dairy goodies decided to pitch in. "We is gonna leave dis room now, an' dare better not be one little peep from none o' y'all sorry convicts. Yew is gonna read dis here roole book, an' when yew is done doin' dat, yew is gonna read it *ag'in.* An' when yew is done doin' dat, yew is gonna read it *ag'in,* an' yew is gonna read dis here roole book till yew knows every last little way every last little t'ing is done aroun' here. Ya *got* dat?"

"Ma'am, yes, ma'am!" most of us pitched in as we had been instructed to do earlier.

As she turned to walk away, she flung around suddenly a drop of melted ice cream slinging out of the cup and onto the immaculate floor. "We is gonna be watchin' y'all. Any sorry ass caught talkin' an' not readin' the book is gonna wish dey'd never been borned!" And with that final warning, she whirled around, stuck her nose in the air, puffed out her tightly bound chest, and exited the room, clutching her precious treasure.

After her departure, there was very little activity in the room for several minutes, but that didn't last long. The first girl to break the silence was sitting at the round table next to ours. I recognized her almost immediately as Detainee Brown, the repeat offender from the hallway. The nasty little guard's words rang in my ear. *You must* like *it here, huh, Brown?* Detainee Brown began by mumbling something incomprehensible to herself. Then she sprung up out of her chair and spun slowly around in a complete circle as if she was sizing up the crowd.

She finally spoke. "Ta hell with these damn son-uv-a-bitchin' guards anyway. Here I am, pregnant with twins, havin' bad cramps almost every day, an' they won't even let me see no damn doctor 'bout it. They don't care one damn bit about choo or me or no-damn-body. An' you ain't gotta listen to one damn word they say in here. An' you ain't gotta read this here son-uv-a-bitchin' *rooole* book neither. It's a waste of yer damn time. Do fuckin' this, don't do fuckin' that. In the end, it don't matter what choo do anyhow. They gonna git choo one way or 'nother jist 'cuz they like it. I say we jist sit here an' don't even open the damn retarded things!"

A woman who looked almost my age, with wild hair that stuck out in all directions and a well-worn face that looked like it had been through the mill, decided to chime in. "She's fuckin' right. I been here before too, an' this here rule book is a fuckin' joke. If ya did everything in it, you'd go crazy as a loon. Let's just spend our time here gettin' ta know each other."

Immediately after the wild-haired woman's speech, a very tall girl who couldn't have been much older than eighteen sprang from her seat. "Wooo-hoooo!" she shouted. "Y'all wanna see all my fuckin' tattoos?" And without waiting for an answer, she pulled up her worn khaki shirt and pointed to a large red rose tattooed across her slender stomach. "This here one I had done in Panama City when I was real fucked up on spring break last year."

She spun slowly around the room as if making sure that every set of eyes was able to see the giant flower. Then she reached farther up her shirt and pulled her bra up around her suntanned neck. The khaki shirt came up around the neck also. There across her two tiny breasts danced eight colorful Grateful Dead teddy bears, four to each breast. "Like the ones on my tits?" she inquired. "I got these little babies in San Francisco while I was high as a fuckin' kite on some really good shit they have over there."

Then as I suspected, the pants came down, revealing a real potpourri of tattoos across both cheeks of her little bony bottom. A huge psychedelic butterfly fluttered toward a tiny girl with kaleidoscope eyes. Newspaper taxis ran up her spine as if it was a road. Tiny marshmallow rocking horses decorated one bun while a family of happy Smurfs pranced across the other. "Hey, y'all, these were done while I was on a fuckin' *good* trip," she announced.

Her arms and thighs weren't quite as enchanting as the more private parts. One skinny bicep revealed a plain black Harley-Davidson logo while the other arm disclosed a frightful, hideously ugly snake winding from elbow to neck. A daunting skull and crossbones shot a piercing look from one thigh while a freaky Grateful Dead skeleton danced across the other. Her ankles revealed a happy blue dolphin jumping

DORAMAE BROOKSHIRE

out of an ocean wave and a full ring of delicate flowers with perky little purple faces.

"Wooooo-hooooo!" she yelled again. "Did y'all like my freakin' tattoos or *what*? I'm pierced all over the fuckin' place too, only these *freaks* made me take out all my rings at intake. Damn fuckin' retards! Those fuckin' rings are some major silver investments, man. They better give them all back—every fuckin' one—as soon as I spring outa here!"

Then she added, "I even got pierced where it *really* counts, ladies. Ya know what I mean?" She grabbed her crotch with great vigor. "It makes sex soooo much better. Ya oughta try it sometime."

Suddenly, a loud, cracking noise was heard in the orientation room, and an irate guard's voice quickly followed. "You all better be readin' those black rule books. If I find out you're not, every last one o' you'll get a DR! Brown and Flanagan, you better not let me hear you causin' any trouble in there!"

And I knew immediately that we were on video camera. From that point on, I made it very clear to those sitting around me that I had no intentions of doing anything whatsoever other than reading my black instruction manual. A small group of them sitting nearby hounded, heckled, and harassed me for a short while; then deciding that I wasn't about to cave in and talk, they gave it up and went on to better things.

The little black "bible" was an amazing document. It laid out instruction in such minute detail that I was quite certain none of these circus clown employees who worked at this place had anything whatsoever to do with its creation. "Detainee's Manual," it said in smudged white letters across the crinkled black cover. I opened it up to find a red-lettered warning stamped inside the front cover.

ALL DETAINEES MUST ADHERE TO ALL RULES CONTAINED WITHINTHISMANUALATALLTIMES,ORTHEPROPERDISCIPLINARY ACTIONS WILL BE TAKEN.

I opened the first page and began to read. It said:

On the first day of intake, all detainees will willingly surrender all personal items on their person to the proper intake officer. Such items will be placed safely in each detainee's personal effects box and stored accordingly. At intake, each detainee shall be showered and deloused, and a full-cavity body search shall be performed to ensure no illegal contraband is smuggled into the premises. Each detainee will be issued the following inventory:

- 2 bras
- 4 pairs underpants
- 4 pairs white socks
- 1 pair black boots
- 1 pair shorts—orange
- 1 white T-shirt
- 1 extra set khaki pants and shirt
- 1 khaki hat
- 1 roll white toilet paper
- 1 bar soap
- 1 black comb
- 1 toothbrush
- 1 small tube toothpaste
- 1 white towel
- 1 white washcloth
- 1 laundry net bag

The instructions went on, "Each detainee shall have their locker in the following specific order at all times. Random locker searches will be conducted to check for contraband. If a detainee's locker is found in any order other than this specified arrangement, that detainee will suffer the proper punishment." After this rather threatening warning with the less than precise reprisal was a hand-drawn diagram of what was supposed to be a "locker," I would guess. It depicted a bird's-eye view of a small rectangular shape holding several elongated rolled-up objects, each labeled in nearly illegible handwriting. After pondering for several minutes about the significance of this homemade diagram, I finally drew the conclusion that it was probably an attempt at instructing the reader on the proper arrangement of her locker, whatever that was. I left this topic and went on to the next.

> All detainees shall arise promptly at four thirty each and every morning for first count. Detainees shall stand at full attention beside their bunks until such time that the inspecting officers give proper instruction to go into parade rest position. Detainees shall then remain in parade rest position until proper orders are dispersed to do otherwise.

I read on, fascinated by the amazingly early hour that we would apparently be required to arise.

> There will be nine (9) head counts each and every day. Any detainee not fully cooperating with such head counts will suffer the proper punishment. Head counts will be announced each time over the intercom, and each detainee will have exactly three (3) minutes to get into the proper location and position. These are:
>
> 4:30 a.m.—Beside bunk
> —Top bunk resident at attention at head of bunk; bottom bunk resident at attention at foot of bunk
>
> 8:30 a.m.—Dorm inspection
> —Those detainees still in dorm, beside bunks. Those detainees in other work areas, in positions specified by presiding officers
>
> 11:30 a.m.—Beside bunk once again. Positions specified above
> 1:30 p.m.—Beside bunk, unless otherwise specified
> 3:00 p.m.—Beside bunk
> 5:00 p.m.—Beside bunk
> 7:00 p.m.—Beside bunk
> 9:30 p.m.—Beside bunk
> 10:00 p.m.—Beside bunk

Jeez! I thought. *I'm gonna spend my entire days here at Sunnybrook Farm standing at stiff attention beside my miserable bunk.* I wondered just exactly why they performed so many head counts anyway. Was it because they actually thought there was a rat's ass chance that any of us detainees would succeed in escaping through the miles and miles of razor wire that surrounded this miserable place? Or maybe they got bored during the day, and one day long ago, one torture-loving guard fabricated the nine-times-a-day census. Or closer yet, all these ass-kissing, slothful, lackadaisical drones of the system had a real concern with keeping their posh state jobs, and they had to validate them by making up totally insane activities to keep them busy. Well, whatever the reason, the reality of the situation was that I, Detainee Brookshire, was going to have to stand at full attention beside my steel bunk and then go into parade rest position on command exactly nine times a day as long as I stayed here.

I left that thought behind and read on:

The following rules shall be adhered to at all times:

1. No talking in the halls. When traveling down the hallways, detainees must be exactly 12 inches from the right-hand walls. If meeting another detainee while in the hallways, no greeting or communication of any sort can occur.
2. No talking whatsoever while in the dining hall. Detainees will have exactly 10 minutes from the time they sit down to complete their meals. When time is called, detainees must put their eating utensils down on the table and push their trays away from themselves until such time that the supervising guard calls out the command to stand and return food trays.
3. The guard on duty shall designate the order in which the detainees at the tables shall return their food trays to the kitchen. Upon command, the residents of each table must move in a counterclockwise position, returning their trays to the central window of the kitchen area.

4. Upon meal completion, detainees must line up at attention against the west wall of the dining area and await further instructions by the commanding officer.
5. There will be *absolutely no sharing* of food. Any detainee caught sharing or exchanging food items will be severely punished.
6. There will be a daily uniform exchange at the laundry room window. All detainees will be expected to wear a clean, fresh uniform on a daily basis. The soiled old uniform must be turned in to the current laundry crew. In exchange, the detainee will be handed a clean uniform after shouting out in an understandable manner her top size and then her bottom size.
7. One reserve uniform must be stored in each detainee's locker in the designated position at all times. No more than one reserve uniform can be in the locker.
8. Detainees are expected to iron their issued uniforms *each and every day*. Twelve irons are located in the library, and the ironing boards stay up from 0830 to 2100 hours each day. Failure to iron one's uniform will result in a DR.
9. All detainees are expected to keep their issued black boots highly polished and buffed *each and every day*. Polishing kits containing all necessary polishing and buffing equipment are located in the TV rooms of each dorm. *Detainees must figure out each dorm's boot polishing schedule, and every girl must receive an equal chance to obtain utilization of the polishing kit.*
10. Locker inspections will be conducted on a regular basis. No detainee shall have prior knowledge of the place or time of such inspections.
11. Lockers shall remain fully locked with the issued padlocks at all times. Failure to do so will give the commanding officer full rein to do whatever he or she pleases with the contents of said locker.
12. Checks for contraband shall be conducted on a regular basis. Contraband items can include but are not limited to:

- More than 2 pieces of mail
- More than 2 personal pictures
- More than 2 books
- More than 2 writing implements

- More than 2 packs of cigarettes
- Medications without the nurse's regulatory sticker
- Personal hygiene items without the nurse's regulatory sticker
- More than the designated number of state-issued personal hygiene items at any time
- Cash or loose change of any amount. Items purchased from the commissary must be bought with money orders sent from home.

13. Mail sent to detainees must be sent in business-sized plain white envelopes. The only writing that is allowed to be on the envelope is that of the detainee's correct address and the sender's complete return address. No other writing or decoration of any kind can occur on the envelopes. If any such writing occurs or if the sender's complete return address is not visible, the mail item will be sent back to the sender. In such a case, the detainee will be notified of such action within 10 days of occurrence.

14. All incoming mail will be opened and screened by the resident mailroom clerk. Contraband items shall be removed from such mail items by her. Notices describing such items will be sent to the receiving detainee within 10 days.

15. No personal pictures from home can contain any of the following:

- Nudity, either partial or full, in any form
- Images of weapons of any sort whatsoever
- People depicted smoking, drinking alcoholic beverages, or engaging in any sort of wild partying activities
- Images of tattoos or body piercing
- Depictions of people having any kind of sexual contact, including kissing

Such pictures will be mailed back to the sender immediately, along with a form explaining to the sender why the picture in question is unacceptable.

16. Items from the commissary can be purchased using only money orders sent from home or brought in by family members personally.
17. Such money orders shall be placed in the designated detainee's account at the time it is received, and the detainee shall be notified within 24 hours by way of an MO slip.
18. Each dorm will be issued a certain day of the week for store call. The schedule shall be as follows:

- Monday: Dorm A
- Tuesday: Dorm B
- Wednesday: Dorm C
- Thursday: Dorm D

I gently placed the black bible on the table in front of me, closing my bloodshot eyes and rubbing my stiff, tightly tensed neck. I snuck a quick peek around. Everyone there, with the exception of one nervous, high-strung tiny older lady, was doing anything and everything *except* reading their manuals. One girl was twisting her long black hair around and around her long skinny finger and staring straight ahead as if in a trance. Another young girl with red hair was blowing spit bubbles and aggravating the girl beside her. Two feisty girls, no older than teenagers, were passing notes under the table and giggling each time a new one was received. Three girls at the table beside ours had ripped a page from the bible, crumpled it into a small round wad, and were playing kickball with the crunched-up sphere.

My mind wandered away from the present insanity and back to the rules of the detainee manual. Here, my mind was whirling from all I had read, and I wasn't even to page 10 yet. How on god's green earth was I ever going to be able to adhere to all these rules and regulations? I opened the dreaded book back up and began to conduct my own crazy review. I knew I was in deep shit. I was going to have trouble right off the bat with number 1: "If meeting another detainee while in the hallways, no greeting or communication of any sort can occur." Now just how in the world was I going to avoid greeting others in the hallway, especially if they talked to me first? Wasn't this simply common courtesy? And how about this thought—most of these girls were quite obviously rule breakers and rebellious sorts, so I *knew* perfectly well that they would attempt to talk to *me*. Furthermore, none of them seemed the type to take kindly to the fact that the person they just spoke to was not speaking back.

I went on to rule no. 2—ten minutes total to eat. *Oh no*, I thought. I had a condition with my digestive system that required thorough chewing and slow swallowing. If I was not allowed to eat at my own pace, the gustatory repercussions could be disastrous.

And what about rule no. 5? "There will be *absolutely no sharing* of food. Any detainee caught sharing or exchanging food items will be punished severely." What if the detainee who was seated next to me at the table took a notion to reach over to my plate and just "help herself" to a spoonful or two of my delicious vittles? How could I possibly stop her? After all, rule no. 2 warned me severely of the consequences of talking in the dining hall.

And rule no. 6 was one of my favorites. "The detainee will be handed a clean uniform after shouting out in an understandable manner her top size and then her bottom size." Now this was going to be next to impossible for me to do without embarrassing myself beyond belief every single time. This was a person who would not admit her true clothing size to her own mother at Christmas list time. I had been secretive about my size since I was a shy, insecure teenager. Why, while clothes shopping, it had been almost a set routine of mine to lean over and whisper the dreaded numbers into the ear of any saleswoman lucky enough to be assisting me with the purchase. This had become second nature to me for, oh, about thirty years now. To have to *shout* out my top size and then my bottom size was going to devastate me beyond belief. To be honest, I wasn't even sure that I was going to be capable of handling this one. I would have to wait and find out.

The rule that won the contest, though, in my strong opinion, was hands down rule no. 8: "Twelve irons are located in the library, and the ironing boards stay up from 0830 to 2100 hours each day. Failure to iron one's uniform will result in a DR." Now let me get this straight. There were twelve hot irons in an unsupervised room for 12½ hours a day. And known drug addicts, alcoholics, child abusers, bank robbers, check forgers, and husband beaters were supposed to go calmly into this room of hot irons and serenely go about their business. I was sure *that* was gonna happen.

And what about rule no. 9, the one about polishing the boots each and every day? I must admit, when I first read this one, I figured that it was one of the most important rules since the part about the polishing schedule and each detainee receiving an equal chance to obtain utilization of the polishing kit was all in italics. However, it didn't take being incarcerated at the Women's Detention Center of Nutter very long for me to realize that these infamous, all-important highly polished black boots were all just a huge farce. Yes, it's true. The entire sixty days that I stayed there, I had these sacred boots on my feet a total of about three hours a day, and those were during working hours. The rest of the time, we detainees were made to walk the highly polished floors in our stocking feet. The only reason we were ever given for this was that they didn't want the floors to get scratched by our black boots. I might add that I witnessed several near disastrous accidents from many an unsuspecting detainee in her stocking feet while meandering down the slick, slippery, highly burnished floors of the perfectly maintained hallways.

Rule no. 11 intrigued me too. While referring to the free-for-all locker inspections, the sentence "Failure to . . . keep the lockers fully locked at all times will give the commanding officer full rein *to do whatever he or she pleases* with the contents of said locker" kind of felt like someone kicked me in the stomach. I had only known these *commanding officers* for a few days now, but I could only begin to imagine what some of the more, shall we say, creative ones could figure out to do with the contents of an unsecured locker.

And what about no. 12—the contraband issue? The only certainty with this one was that the magic number seemed to be two here—more than two pieces of mail, more than two personal pictures, more than two books, more than two writing implements, more than two packs of cigarettes, and so on. I guess all I had to do to keep this one straight was to be able to count to two. Later on, rule no. 12 played with my sanity probably worse than any other one. I would lay in my bunk at night, worried sick that I might have over two of any item in my locker at any given time and that a surprise inspection would occur in the middle of the night or while I was on work detail and that, as a result, I would be issued one of the dreaded DRs, and that I would ultimately never get free from the hell they called the WDC just because stupid little me was unable or unwilling to count to two.

And what was with five full sentences describing in detail exactly how the envelopes that came and went had to appear? Business-sized plain white envelopes, no extra writing, no decorations of any kind. What a culture shock from the embellished, adorned, ornamental parcels sent from the Coward County Jail! And how crushing it was to receive a mailroom clerk's notice ten days later informing me that *someone* from a certain zip code had sent a letter, but it had been returned due to lack of a proper return address.

Furthermore, what was with the mailroom clerk being able to open and "screen" all our mail before we got it? Each and every time mail call rolled around and I was handed a fistful of mangled letters, ripped open carelessly, and then sloppily stapled back together at the jagged seam, I felt violated and defiled. This mailroom clerk—just who did she think she was? Some kind of detention hall deity? Well, I guess she must have known more about each and every one of our personal lives and problems than anyone else on campus, probably a little more than she bargained for in several of our cases. *Serves her right*, I concluded. *I hope she reads something someday about one of us that* really *curls her hair.* (And knowing some of the ladies in there, I'm sure she did.) Every time I was handed those violated letters, I secretly wished that, sometime during her life, she would get the wonderful opportunity to have one of her received letters placed under a microscope and ripped apart, page by page, by some distant, apathetic, judgmental person.

But rule no. 15—the personal-pictures-from-home rule—had to take the cake. We were banned from having pictures of nudity (either partial or full), images of weapons, people depicted smoking or drinking, pictures of tattoos or body piercings, or pictures of people kissing. Such pictures from home, rule no. 15 stated, would be mailed back immediately to the sender. Now what I'm about to tell you, you probably will not believe, but here goes. During my two months in this great state facility, I witnessed the following pictures being returned to senders: (Keep in mind none of us ever really got to *see* these pictures. We only *heard* descriptions of them from our friends and families after they received them back with their little explanatory forms.)

1. A picture of my bunkie's one-year-old son was returned because he was outside on a one-hundred-degree July day in his diaper. Up until that time, she did not own one single picture of him to remind her of what her only baby looked like. The reason on the form for return was *partial nudity*.
2. A girl on the other side of dorm C had a picture of her daughter's third birthday returned. In the picture, her grandmother was cutting the cake—after the candles had been blown out—with a cake knife. The reason on the form for return was *images of a weapon*.
3. A mentally challenged inmate who had lived with her parents her whole life so that they could care for her had a picture of their twenty-fifth wedding anniversary celebration returned. In the picture, her father was affectionately kissing her mother on the cheek. The reason on the form for return was *depictions of people having any kind of sexual contact*.
4. Another detainee who talked endlessly about her only daughter, Rebecca, and worried constantly about the fact that the relatives she had to let her stay with were not taking good care of her had the first picture of her beautiful daughter returned. Rebecca was thirteen and had pierced ears. The reason on the form for return was *images of body piercing*.
5. Still another woman's picture from home was returned because some unknown passerby in the far background of the picture appeared to be smoking a cigarette. (The sender of the picture never did figure out just *who* the mysterious smoker was.) The reason on the form for return was *people depicted smoking*,

drinking alcoholic beverages, or engaging in any sort of wild partying activities.

The summer of '99 boasted record temperatures in south Georgia. Most days saw the mercury well over one hundred degrees. As a result, as usually happened in south Georgia during the summertime, the majority of infants donned only a diaper, and tots went topless. I could not begin to count the number of personal pictures sent from home that summer that were sent right back before any detainees even laid eyes on them due to diapers or shorts being dubbed *partial nudity*. I had two personal pictures myself that were from a close friend sent back to her. They were of her three young children, ages six, four, and two. Bo, Josh, and Rachel were sitting on a four-wheeler in their backyard in their swimming suits, holding up a sign that read, "We love you, Ms. Dora!" This adorable picture was sent back to my friend, though, of course, with a form that read, "Partial nudity in pictures is prohibited." I know that the picture was adorable because my friend lovingly gave it to me after my release. I still have it on my desk at work, but I often stop and think of how very much it would have meant to me *while I was still locked up.*

This brought me to my next thought. What kind of depraved, sick human being would even begin to see innocent, pure, wholesome, beautiful, naive babies and little children as *sexual* objects? I'd ask you, *Who has the problem here?*

Rules no. 16 and 17 pertaining to money orders being sent by home or personally brought in would prove to be one of my biggest nightmares. Unlike Coward County Jail, where no personal items were provided, the Women's Detention Center of Nutter provided just about every basic item a probationer needed. So I was not that concerned about any toiletry *except one*, that of my contact solution. After three attempts at getting my contact solution to me failed, Bob was pretty much left at a standstill. Oh, he *tried* to follow the rules. The first time, he sent a proper money order earmarked "contact solution." When we found out that contact solution was not even offered on the commissary list, he attempted to send a bottle through the mail. Of course, that was promptly sent back with a large red warning stamped on the outside, "Do not send perishables to WDC under penalty of law." His third and final attempt involved bringing the bottle of contact solution to the front desk on the next visitation day and pleading with the attending guard for some mercy. Of course, attempt number 3 was not successfully pulled off either. The sour-faced guard looked him square in the eye and asked him flippantly if he would like to be one of the male inmates for trying to smuggle contraband into a secured facility. Halfway frightened and the other half exhausted, Bob resigned all attempts at getting contact solution through to me.

In the meantime, my eyesight and, more specifically, my eyes themselves were undergoing some serious transformations. As elaborated in the previous chapters, my eyesight was in serious danger without my blessed contacts. I was severely nearsighted, so much so that without my contacts I would literally walk into walls. I had the choice at WDC of waiting for a pair of glasses, but that would involve a massive chunk of time—time until the eye doctor showed up, time until he actually called my name out of the 250 probationers, time until the glasses were fabricated, and then time until they were delivered. Something told me that my sixty days would be up before this complicated maze of events could occur. Meanwhile, my eyes were screaming out for some help as a result of days and days of homemade contact solution, which of course consisted of warm salt water. When I could even get near a mirror to look, I was aghast at what peered back at me. My two eyes were bloody and dull, and the eyelids sagged and drooped at the corners. They were so dark and sunk back into my face that it looked as though they were two red marbles lost in a couple of swarthy pitch-black caves.

I knew right off that a huge part of the problem was the massive loss of vitamins I suffered while incarcerated at the Coward County Jail. I had always had trouble with anemia, and four weeks of nothing but white bread and grits had apparently put me over the edge. Here I was, less than two months in the slammer, and I already looked like the bride of Frankenstein. And the other girls noticed it right off.

Don't ever put anything past a bunch of cagelings. I hadn't been there long at all before two detainees pulled me aside one day at exercise period and stared me down, eyeball to eyeball. "Giirl, where you git dose black 'n' blues around dem big ole eyes o' yern? Dat deemon man better not never touch chew like dat ag'in, or we'll awl lets him know whuz up. Dere ain't no excuse fer beatin' up a pit'ful pair of eyes like dat dare. You poor thang!"

And so it promptly became the accepted fact that my two pitiful eyes were, in reality, two *black* eyes, deemed so by my abusive, cruel-natured husband/significant other. I really couldn't blame the girls for pronouncing me a domestic abuse victim. Come to think of it, my two eyes looked much more like they had been blackened by some monster man than just caused by a massive lack of vitamins. Besides, as soon as I was dubbed a domestic abuse victim, I was granted the bonus of getting to hear hours and hours of personal testimonials revolving around everyone else's private, intimate details of their own little living hells in the world of domestic violence. Some of the living nightmares I heard about, I am certain, would live forever in the dark recesses of my mind, revolving and spinning around in there for eternity.

BONNIE BROOKENSHEER

ABOUT THE TIME that I thought I was going to vomit if I had to stay in that sweltering, stuffy, mentally unhealthy room, stuck reading that godforsaken redundant black manual, the vile, mean-spirited tall guard with the attitude and the Dairy Queen appeared suddenly in the doorway. "Y'all sorry excuses fer human beans!" she shouted for the second time that day. "It be time fer y'all detaineeees to get yer bunk assignments. *So listen!* I ain't gonna tell you losers twice. If I have ta do *dat*, it really pisses me off, an' y'all don't wanna piss me off, ya *understand*?"

"Ma'am, yes, ma'am!" we shouted out in unison.

"Now listen up! I done tol' y'all once today to look in da front cover of y'all's Nutter bibles an' memorize da number an' letter dat wuz dere. Well, dat be yer bunk assignments, soze y'all better knows dem by now, er y'alls in some deep shiiit!"

At this point, about three-fourths of the detainees sneakily cracked open the front cover of their black bibles and stole a quick peek at their numbers. I felt certain that this discontented guard had, in reality, never mentioned the bunk assignment numbers in the front of the black manuals to us. In fact, I was absolutely positive that she hadn't. I had listened so intently to everything that had been instructed to me since I had arrived at this miniature living hell that I *knew* we had not been told to do so. However, I had noticed that number the very first time I had opened my manual. It was half-assed stuck inside the front cover and written sloppily on a bright yellow sticky note. And I was very, very proud of myself because I had already memorized it, deciding that it might be something of importance that would be handy, if not essential, for my well-being around there.

A-32, that was it. I knew it. There was no doubt. I had stared at it for several seconds on many different occasions. But just to make doubly sure, I joined the ranks of the peeking, cheating detainee crew and peeped briefly inside the front cover. It was true. I had remembered correctly. A-32 was the number scrawled sloppily across the yellow sticky note. *A-32, A-32, A-32,* I began repeating to myself in a kind of strange chant so I would be sure not to forget it. It seemed like, at this point, this number was of the utmost importance.

"OK den, y'all sorry-ass detaineees line up at dis door against dis wall. We is gonna get y'all's bunk gear an' go make y'all's beds. But don't y'all be askin' me *nuttin'*, and don't y'all be eyeballin' me or nuttin' like dat. Y'all got dat?"

"Ma'am, yes, ma'am!" we all screamed.

We all marched obediently and very quietly down the long sterile hall. I could sense the tension in the air. I knew instinctively that the other girls were just as frightened and bewildered by what was about to happen as I was. When we got to the same big open room as the one that the young girl and I were made to eat our lunch off the floor, we stopped, only now—instead of this mystery room being an intake delousing, exhibitionist showering, and lunching off the floor room—it was crammed full of giant overstuffed objects rolled up into cylindrical masses and stacked around the perimeter of the room, all the way up to the ceiling. I surmised that these king-size lumpy Twinkies were probably our bedrolls.

"Now listen up, you dumbass detaineeees, dese here is yer bedrows. Dey gots everyt'ing y'all needs fer y'all's little stay wif us. I's gonna call out y'all's name and bunk assignment, an' I wants y'all to step up an' get yer bedrow den line up against dat wall ober dere till we can awl go back to da dorms. Dere's four dorms. I's gonna take one at a time. First, dorm A." And she began to call out detainees' last names and the two character bunk assignments with the rapidity of a cougar going after its prey on the open plain. It was the first time I had heard her speak so quickly, and it kind of threw me off. I wasn't sure which dorm I was in, but I kind of guessed it might be A because of the number I had so carefully memorized—A-32.

After what seemed to be an eternity, she finally called out, "Detaineee Brookasure, A-23!"

Now I really was in a tight spot. I had memorized that number over and over, and I was certain that it was A-32. What could I do? Had I actually seen those two numbers backward out of pure ongoing stress, or was the idiotic big guard a tad dyslexic? I had to think fast. I only had a few seconds to act. I knew quite definitely that I had never personally had one bit of trouble reversing numbers in the past. And I had been observing this crazy, not-too-bright, cougar woman for a full day now.

Then I did something that I would regret till the day I die. "Ma'am, Detainee Brookshire requests permission to speak, ma'am," I said in a still small voice.

She had had her back to me at the moment. With my muttering, she spun around to face me like a toy top in the fast part of its cycle. "Whud ya say, detaineee? Whud ya say?" she demanded.

I repeated, "Ma'am, Detainee Brookshire requests permission to speak, ma'am."

"Go on den." And a curious, sadistic look swept over her ice-cream-stained face.

"Ma'am, could you please repeat my bunk assignment number, ma'am. *Please*, ma'am?" I forced out with great reservation. I knew immediately that I had made a grave mistake.

She took two giant steps across the room until she was square in my face. She positioned herself eyeball to eyeball and began to point her long sharp, fake index fingernail against my nose. Her mouth, with its sweet, creamery breath, went up against my right ear as close as possible. Then she began to scream at a pitch so high that only bats could pick it up. "Who you t'ink you is, detaineee? You t'ink you is different den awl dese udder losers, huh? You come in here in yer fancy black suit an' high heels, like you really sumt'in'! You t'ink you is *better* den da rest uh dese dumbasses, don't cha, Detainee"—she glanced down at her clipboard—"Brookasure? Well, I gots news fer you, ya uppity asshole. I is gonna make it my bizness to show you while you's here dat dat jist ain't da way it is! When I's done wif you, yer ass is gonna know jist what a piece of shit you *really* is!"

My right ear was ringing from her shrill shrieks, and the tip of my nose was throbbing from the sharp indentation left from her polyester fingernail. The entire right side of my face was wet with little drops of saliva that smelled like half-digested ice cream. Hopefully, her fit of rage was coming to an end.

She took one step back from me. I wanted to heave a sigh of relief but restrained myself from doing so, thinking that this would most likely just start her up again. I slowly rolled my eyeballs up from the floor, where they had resided during this whole fiasco. She was staring hard at the names on her clipboard, seeming as if she had lost her place. She placed her finger under what was probably my name and kept drawing it across the page repeatedly as if the number she was getting didn't match the name. Finally, she spoke.

"I said yer bunk assignment is A-32, detaineee, A-32, A-32, A-32. Dere, is *dat* enuff times fer yer retarded ass, Miss High an' Mighty? Er do ya needs me ta write it down, Miss It?" Then she took to her heels and spun around to face her next victim. And as a quick afterthought, she added, "I guess in yer perfeck little buziness world, you woulda had some poor dumb secatary write it down fer ya, huh, Miss Wundaful?"

I grabbed my overstuffed bedroll and knew as soon as I did it was much more than a lightweight mattress. In fact, I had underestimated the thing to such a degree that it nearly pulled me over when I first snatched it up. My curiosity almost got the best of me, and I nearly crammed my arm down the belly of the round mass and made the mysterious contents spill out like vomit spewing forth from a badly nauseated stomach. Instead, though, I opted to line up against the wall and wait for further instructions, like all the rest of the girls. I was much too terrified of Sergeant Dairy Queen to do anything else.

When she was done calling out all the bunk assignments for dorm A, she left the rest of the detainees in the care of a manly large guard and began to bark orders at us to move on down the hall. "Follow me, and y'all better not be doin' no talking neither!" she snapped.

We obediently followed, and soon we came to a large room surrounded by glass on all four sides. Through the glass, one could see rows and rows of metal bunk beds and lots and lots of other detainees. Actually, as I took a closer look, I noticed that there were four nearly identical glass rooms—all grouped together with a common hallway—and a large tall guard tower with darkly tinted glass very similar to the one at the Coward County Jail, only not hardly as large, black, or intimidating. Sergeant Dairy Queen approached the glass door that had a large *A* above it and then yelled at the guard in the tower to open it for the new "grunts." The door quickly clicked open with a loud, resounding clang, sending surges of déjà vu running through my veins. As we entered the world of dorm A, the old residents circled around us to size us up, like a bunch of ravenous vultures about to consume their rotten meal.

The sergeant began to speak. "OK, y'all sorry-ass detaineees, y'all have ebzac'ly two minutes to make y'all's bunks an' to put away y'all's gear into y'all's lockers. Awl be back den to check how y'all done. *An' y'all better* be *done!*" With that, she puffed out her flat chest, spun around, and walked out the glass door entirely on her bootheels.

I scrambled to locate my bunk—A-32. No one was helping me here. I finally noticed, through nobody's assistance, that every few bunks had a well-worn label with faded numbers stuck to the metal on the end. None of them were labeled "A-32," but through counting and simple deduction, I figured the one that was most likely bunk A-32. As I hurriedly threw my massive gaping bedroll up to the top bunk, I hoped like hell that I was correct in my rushed conclusion.

I knew that it could not—in any way, shape, or form—had been anywhere *near* two minutes when the sergeant returned, making her presence loudly known. I had just begun to tuck in my thin bottom sheet, toiling on my hands and knees and ready to bump my head on the ceiling, when she reappeared. As soon as I saw her charging in my direction, I went into warp speed, smoothed the flat sheet on top of the other, and then quickly fluffed my smashed pillow. I had done nothing yet with the roll of wrinkled clothing lying limply on the floor below me. In fact, I had not even yet figured out where my "locker" was located.

It didn't take me long to figure out that she was coming straight for me. She sized me up for all of one second, and as soon as she saw the trickle of sweat running down my forehead, an insidious smirk spread across her face. "What in da *hell* is *dis* shit, Detainee Brookasure?" she screamed, tightly grabbing hold of the south corner of my bottom sheet. "Dat's the sorriest-ass piece o' shit I ever seen!" With that, she made a single hard jerking motion, and the entire top and bottom sheets were ripped off the bed in one fell swoop. They dropped limply to the floor. "Now do it again, detaineee! You got ebzac'ly one minute! Awl be back!"

I was left on my hands and knees, balancing on the top bunk, sweat still pouring down my face and tears beginning to well in my eyes. Every single set of eyes were on me to see how I was going to react. At least half the girls were dying of laughter, and the other half had silly grins on their faces. The welled tears began to spill out onto my hot red cheeks. I told myself not to cry, that it would be interpreted as a sign of weakness, but I just plain could not hold them back. I bit my bottom lip so hard that I broke the skin and could taste the blood that began to ooze out. I knelt up there on that cold metal bunk, my head touching the ceiling, whimpering and sniffling, like a spoiled child that had not gotten her way. I wasn't sure that I could take this place.

But then an absolutely amazing thing happened, and it happened before I had time to think. At least a dozen of the old residents of dorm A scrambled to my assistance. The violated sheets were swiftly swept up off the floor by one girl; handed up to four girls already in position, waiting on their hands and knees; and perfectly contoured to the lumpy mattress by those four and a crew of four others, standing at each corner of the bed. Then one of the floor crew threw up the faded old blanket while the ceiling crew smoothed and tucked and straightened. Another girl was fussing with the featherless pillow and the stained pillowcase. The whole while, a crew of three were rolling, folding, and positioning my issued panties, socks, and T-shirts into what evidently was my "locker," a small metal drawer at the foot of the bunk. All the while, I could hear the work crew saying things to one another like, "Hurry up! She's comin' back! Quick! Hurry!"

One tiny Black girl looked up at me briefly and said, "Don't let her bother you none. She always like dis. She don't mean no harm. She really just playin'."

By the time Sergeant Dairy Queen appeared, my bunk and locker were the most immaculate area of the entire dorm. When she entered the room, she made a beeline straight to my bed. As soon as she saw, a sadistic smirk spread across her face. She began to snigger. "OK, y'all, which one o' y'all helped da new grunt? Wuz it *you*, Murphy? Or *you*, Brown? Or *you*, Johnson?" She whirled around to face another detainee. "An' I *knows* you had sumt'ing ta do wif dis, Whitehead!"

I wasn't really sure just what she was going to do at this point. But I soon found out. She ran up to each of the accused and told them to give her five, holding her long wiry hand high in the air. As they giggled and did so, I realized that this was just a sick routinely performed circus act, most likely executed every time a new group of detainees arrived. I decided then and there to lighten up and not give so much of a damn.

The next few days were a blur. It was wake-up bell at four thirty, attention beside the bunks at five, and becoming the object of constant harassment and ridicule the remainder of the day. The first week was devoted entirely to reading, reading, and rereading the sacred black manual. If we dared to look up once from it, our noses were shoved right back down into it. The sergeant and her buddies made it their life's ambition to bury us up to our pitiful necks in that great Nutter classic. We were driven to wade through, plunge into, and dig and grind and bone up on it from dawn to dusk. And then at the end of the first week, we were pronounced black manual literate, and it was on to the next exhaustive game. This one was called "the great work detail assignment."

After my first extremely traumatic night in dorm A, I had settled in and become quite comfortable in bunk A-32. I had even made a few semifriends who were trying their best to teach me the ropes. I learned from the little nurse with the mood disorder, who was in for stealing the doctor's prescription pad and writing herself numerous prescriptions for a wide variety of painkillers, that dorm A was composed primarily of the girls who went "out," or off campus, for their work details. This included the girls who worked on the nearby vegetable farm, where the detention center obtained many of the blessed vegetables that they fed us. It also included the girls who went into the small city of Nutter and helped local government sites landscape their properties. Within this group were those who stayed on campus and cut the lawn, trimmed the shrubs, and maintained the numerous beds of flowers. It seemed like the place was also constantly being landscaped and relandscaped. Since it had the appearance of the front cover of *Better Homes and Gardens* magazine, it took quite a crew of constant gardeners and manicurists to keep up the place's reputation as the most immaculate, spotless, virtuous, squeaky-clean detention center around. After all, when the big dogs from Atlanta came every few months to inspect, did we not want to make them think that we were all residing within the walls of the Garden of Eden?

The queen mother of all jobs at Nutter Women's Detention Center was the personal maid and maidservant of the evil she-devil herself. It didn't take me long to learn who the old hag was. She was the wicked sorceress with the fire-red hair that sat me and the angry young girl on the floor and forced us to eat our lunch there the very first day we arrived. The cantankerous old witch made her presence known daily, and it was almost always in a sneaky, underhanded manner. You'd just be sitting there, minding your own business, doing absolutely nothing wrong; and suddenly, the redheaded siren would appear out of nowhere, bitching and squawking and hollering and raising a stink over something so small and insignificant that a normal member of society wouldn't give it a second thought. The beds were never made well enough, the floors were never shiny enough, the inspections were never tight enough. And lord help the detainee who didn't stand up, snap to immediate attention, and salute the queen mother if she was anywhere within one hundred yards of her.

It didn't take me long to learn that this human tigress was second in command around the place, her official title being assistant warden, but she actually thought that she was first in command most days. This stemmed from the fact that the *real* warden was a cowardly, permanently depressed little man who had a twenty-four-hour-a-day drinking problem. The few times that I got the privilege of seeing Warden Drake DeFoe, he appeared outright terrified of any sort of confrontation or required decision. The only true friend he had seemed to be his bottle. In fact, when I was about halfway through my sentence, two girls in dorm B swore that the warden broke into their dorm at three o'clock on a Saturday night, drunk as a coot, and he had to be dragged out by two plainclothes police officers after the guard on duty called 911. One of the girls was quite shaken, claiming that Mr. Warden plopped his inebriated body down on the side of her bed and started whispering some slurred mumbo jumbo about how beautiful she was into her ear.

Anyhow, the very best job that existed at the detention center was that of personal maid to the old bitch herself. This she-servant's job would consist of dusting, vacuuming, polishing, scrubbing, purifying, cleansing, buffing, sprucing, tidying, and generally sterilizing the redheaded bitch's personal office and bathroom daily. I never did quite figure out why the work detail assignment of "servitress to the old hag" was rated so highly. But it did indeed seem to be the overall consensus around there that this was the job to have.

The poor little detainee who had the pleasure of receiving this particular work detail while I was there was a nervous tiny, little thing named Bonnie Brookensheer. I had noticed her the day of intake, and she had continued to stand out from the others ever since. She was short—probably four feet nine at the tallest—and petite, maybe ninety-nine pounds. I knew she had some years on her because, unlike most of the girls there, her short wiry hair was almost entirely gray. Her tormented, weathered face revealed years of worry and hard, unrewarding life. She was fretful and jumpy and unsettled. Her restlessness invaded every inch of her fidgety little frame. During intake, she obeyed every command willingly, looking nervously down at her feet while doing so. During black manual reading week, she was the only one besides me who actually read and repeatedly reread her sacred book. She didn't talk in the hall or the mess hall. She didn't keep more than two of anything in her locker, and she most certainly did not own any pictures of babies in diapers or people cutting a birthday cake.

Not long after arriving at the WDC, Bonnie refused to eat. She said that the food was upsetting her stomach, and besides, she didn't like any of it anyhow. It wasn't long before the resident nurse had her in the infirmary, stuffing her full of appetite stimulants. When that didn't work, the visiting psychiatrist started her on a cornucopia of mood stabilizers, antidepressants, and soon after antipsychotics. The way I saw it, that was the turning point for poor Bonnie. After that, she truly did become psychotic, mumbling to herself and seeing things none of the rest of us did.

Bonnie couldn't leave the campus because her crime was considered violent. I overheard her tell one girl at intake that she had been arrested for getting extremely drunk and beating up her husband and his very slutty girlfriend. The story went like this: She spent the early evening boozing up at the local watering hole and then lay in wait for them, hunching down in the bushes at the floozy wench's trailer. When they both appeared, smooching and holding hands, tiny Bonnie sprung out of the shrubbery like an overwound jack-in-the-box and began to beat, slap, kick, bite, poke, and spit. Every time I pictured that scene, it tickled me. Dinky, little Bonnie in full action against adultery and strumpets of the world. It tickled me because I knew that the asshole husband and his willing whore dog probably deserved every inch of that thrashing. And it tickled me further because I loved the idea of someone like Bonnie giving it to them.

I stayed in very close contact with Bonnie Brookensheer the entire time we were there. First, we both came in on the same day. Second, we both had received the minimum sentence—sixty days. But most importantly, as far as the halfway illiterate guard staff was concerned, we possessed the same last name. And it was a well-known fact around there that none of the staff enunciated or pronounced any of their words correctly. If a syllable could conveniently be left out, they would opt for that every single time. Therefore, every time she was called to one of her numerous psychiatrists, nurses, mental health, or schooling appointments, she was summoned in this manner. "Detainee Brooksure, report immediately to the such and such!"

Now I knew perfectly well that I was never called down to go to the nurse, the psychiatrist, or GED class, but we had all been threatened to within an inch of our lives during that first week that if we were ever called to report somewhere, we had better do so within one skinny minute. So every single time the idiots called for "Detainee Brooksure," the two of us showed up *every single time*. After two or three times of this, the guards' reaction was to glare at me as if I was crazy and mutter something like, "Girl, not *choo*, the *udder* one." But what really took the cake was that no one—not one single guard—ever figured out to refer to us in any way by our first names or even initials. If they were going to continue to mispronounce our last names, it seemed like they could have devised some way, any way at all, to distinguish between the two of us. Even if they called us Big Brooksure and Little Brooksure, Fasting Brooksure and Pig-Out Brooksure, Skinny Brooksure and Fat-Ass Brooksure, Nervous Brooksure and Numb Brooksure, or Clobbering Brooksure and Thieving Brooksure, at least we would have known which one they were calling to come and report.

Halfway through our sixty-day stint, poor Bonnie suffered a setback. She was just minding her own business, trying to choke down at least a couple of bites of her institutional-style dinner, when the new girl rocked her world. The new girl was tall, heavyset, and corpulent. Actually, she was downright obese. She was young and Black and copped an attitude. Someone told me she had come in for beating up her grandmother, the woman who raised her, and stealing everything in sight from her that wasn't tied down. Anyhow, I guess the new girl must have really liked what we were having for dinner that night. Either that or she was bored and wanted to create a little excitement. Whichever it was, it was a certainty that she chose poor Bonnie because the animal instinct in the new girl told her that this tiny, little creature was, by far, the most vulnerable.

While shoveling in her own pasta and Spam, the portly detainee politely swept over to Bonnie's tray with her plastic spork and swooped in several hefty bites of her culinary delight. I knew this for a fact because, unfortunately, I was sitting right next to pitiful little Bonnie. The way I saw it, poor Bonnie was a sitting duck. She never managed to choke down much of her food at all, she moved in slow motion, and because of the oversedation, she came across as dopey and slow witted. I knew perfectly well what was going through Bonnie's mind when the food robbery occurred. We had been strictly warned against talking in the mess hall, so she couldn't scream out or tell the overfleshed crook to stop. Besides, weak tiny Bonnie couldn't have stopped the mighty, robust, Incredible Hulk of a new detainee if she had tried. So here we were, once again facing a catch-22 situation; and this time, I was a witness. What probably got me the worst was the fact that the new girl performed this little act of thievery right smack dab in front of one of the meanest guards on staff. So naturally, you can guess the rest.

Big girl got caught scarfing down Bonnie's food. Bonnie got charged with one of those mysterious DRs for "sharing" her food. Bonnie worried herself into a bleeding ulcer until her DR court date came up. But here's the part that shames me to this day.

Evidently, little Bonnie looked on her and me as some type of buddies or soul mates or something just because we both kept showing up for her daily guard paging. So she made it a point to seek me out every single day while we were walking around the dirt track and beg me to be a witness on her behalf at the upcoming DR hearing. I might have led her to believe that I was thinking about doing it in the beginning. Hell, maybe I was. But in the end, when it really counted, I didn't even come close to helping poor little Bonnie out. Instead, the deep animalistic instincts took over. I didn't owe this whiny little pip-squeak anything. Hadn't she made my life there miserable enough with her appointments for everything under the sun that *I* had to report in for just because we shared a similar last name? Wasn't she just about the most disgusting thing alive with her wimpy little quirks and her blubbering little breakdowns? Besides, I had long ago made a solemn promise to myself that nothing, absolutely *nothing*, was going to stop me from going home the exact minute that was officially documented for me. So in the end, the DR court went on without me as a food-snatching witness, and helpless tiny Bonnie was on her own against the Incredible Hulk.

After that, Bonnie didn't look on us as sisters. In fact, she didn't even look at me at all when we both showed up for a call by the guards for GED class, the psychiatrist, or the drug nurse—no smile, no pat on the shoulder, not so much as simple eye contact. It was all gone—gone because I was too scared to help out a fellow detainee, gone because I was covering my own ass, gone because I was too damned concerned about going home on time to reach out and help someone who was drowning, gone because I had become one of them. I lay in my bed that night unable to sleep and wondered what had become of me.

DORM RAT, DORM D

A T THE END of our first week, known as orientation, the big event occurred. Dubbed Fearful Friday by a group long ago, it was the day we were to receive our dreaded work assignments. We had been coached on this fateful day all week. It seemed there was a definite and well-mapped protocol to the ceremony. We were going to be called down to the education room and sat down at assigned tables. Then in what they said was random order, our names would be individually called out. When our name was called, we were to instantly rise from our chair, march over to the table of superiors, snap to attention, and call out, "Ma'am, sir, Detainee Brookshire reporting for work detail assignment, ma'am, sir!" Then the redheaded bitch and the alcoholic fool would give us our assignment. After the work detail was assigned, we were to snap our heels together, salute the two buffoons, thank them, turn sharply to our right, and march back to our table, where we would sit until all the detainees were duly humiliated and dismissed.

I really didn't care what work detail I got or which dorm I was assigned to as long as it wasn't dorm D. Dorm D was the animal dorm, the dorm brimming with mental deficients, the I-will-stab-you-while-you're-sleeping-with-a-pair-of-stolen-scissors-and-not-think-a-thing-of-it dorm. The girls in dorm D were the Nutter rejects. Legend had it that they were half-witted, blithering, crackbrained, moronic imbeciles. If you were vile, sorry, scrubby, low-minded, and worthless, dorm D was where they stuck you. I would much rather stay in dorm A, where I was, and be able to go out every day and get some fresh air working on the vegetable farm.

Or dorm C would be just fine. It was home of the girls who worked kitchen duty, both breakfast/lunch and supper. That wouldn't be bad. We might be able to sneak a few bites in between cooking duties. Dorm C was also the home base of the poor little creatures who had to spend their entire nights on their bruised hands and knees, removing the previous day's wax off the floors and then laying down a new coat. The wax queens had to grab what little sleep they could during the day. Looking through the glass windows to dorm C, it appeared to be much less active and less loud than the other three most likely because the morning kitchen workers got to sleep some during the late morning, and the waxers got to sleep most of the day. If I absolutely had to leave dorm A, dorm C would be my second choice, I decided.

I didn't know too much about dorm B. I did know that it was home to the famed Dumpster Babies. These were the poor souls who spent their days locating the carcasses of dead animals on the streets of Nutter and loading their stinking, bloated bodies onto a garbage truck to later dump the noxious, stenchy cadavers into a designated dead critters dumpster. This unfortunate crew of rejects came back every afternoon at around three thirty, reeking of foul, putrid, repulsive odors of death and decay. It certainly didn't help that temperatures reached over one hundred degrees most every day that fateful summer. I prayed to God quite often that I would not have to join the ranks of the Dumpster Babies.

About halfway through orientation week, we were all called individually to go talk to our assigned counselors. When they called my name and I showed up at the specified room, I was a little surprised to discover that my counselor was the same sour-faced blond woman who had checked me in on intake day, the same one who had told me to listen closely because she was not going to repeat herself, the one who informed me that she didn't think detainees were allowed to wear contacts and that it could land me a DR, the one who stared me down with an expression full of disgust and repugnance. And she didn't seem to be in any better mood on counseling day. As soon as I walked in the door, her face flushed a bit, and her eyes dropped to the floor for a moment. I figured she was perhaps recalling the fact that, on intake day, my black suit was a notch above hers.

"Detainee Brookshire, have a seat!" she barked while staring forcefully at a fistful of papers she was gripping tightly. "I'm going to ask you some questions, and I want you to tell me the truth. You got *that*?"

"Ma'am, yes, ma'am!" I called out.

Then she commenced to asking questions so rapidly that it made my head spin. "Have you ever been physically abused?"

"Ma'am, no, ma'am."

"Have you ever been sexually abused?"

"Ma'am, no, ma'am."

"Have you ever been emotionally abused?"

I had to think about this one for a second because I was pretty sure that among what the judge, the people at Coward County Jail, and my fellow dentists had done, there was most likely some emotional abuse there somewhere. But I should never have hesitated because, from that point on, Goldilocks became pretty suspicious. I answered her last question hesitantly, "Ma'am, no, ma'am."

She glared at me as if to call me a white-faced liar. She continued, "Have you ever taken any of the following drugs: marijuana?"

"Ma'am, no, ma'am."

"Cocaine?"

"Ma'am, no, ma'am."

"Heroin?"

"No, ma'am!"

"LSD, ecstasy, PCP, or mushrooms?"

"Ma'am, no, ma'am."

"Inhalants?"

"Ma'am, no, ma'am."

"Methamphetamine?"

"Ma'am, no, ma'am."

"Sedatives?"

"Ma'am, no, ma'am."

"Prescription painkillers?"

"Ma'am, no, ma'am."

I was getting quite tired of saying "ma'am, no, ma'am," and she was becoming visibly more and more frustrated. Her voice had raised several octaves, and her creamy white face had become extremely flushed once again. She was tapping her black leather designer pumps on the floor nervously. It was as if she was on a mission to get me to admit to something, *anything*, that I had taken illegally. "Well then!" she yelled out disgustedly. "Remember, you have been strictly instructed to be truthful with me."

She continued to dig. "Do you use tobacco in *any* form whatsoever?"

"Ma'am, no, ma'am."

Now she had just about had it. She was close to her breaking point. "*Well* . . . have you *ever* used tobacco . . . *ever*?"

I thought back to my Woodhurst Boulevard and Harrison Hill childhood, my childhood full of church and family and love and kindness, my childhood and adolescence that hadn't really needed any of these substances of abuse. I had had everything that a child and teenager needed. I hadn't needed Marlboro Reds. "Ma'am, no, ma'am, "I replied.

"You mean to tell me you have never smoked a cigarette?"

"Well, I guess I did once at Cassie Kato's house when her mother was gone to the Kroger store at Southgate," I answered, trying to be as truthful as possible.

"That's what I thought!" She smirked, and she began to scribble something down on her paper. "Well then, since you're a smoker, we will require you to take a six weeks' program on drug abuse."

"But I'm *not* a smoker!" I protested. "I just smoked that one time when I was thirteen. I don't smoke at all! I can't even stand to be around it!"

Her face turned red again, her expression turned to stone, and her black high heels and red acrylic nails went to tapping in unison. "Well, the fact is, Detainee Brookshire, that *every single detainee* at Nutter is required to take this drug and alcohol class. In fact, we've never even had—that I can remember—any girl come to us that *didn't*. Oh, never mind, I don't have to explain *anything* to *you*. You're just gonna take this class, *case closed*!"

So I was signed up for a six-week class on drug and alcohol abuse when I had never touched an illegal drug in my life. Then as a little bonus, the blond babe signed me up for a ten-week class on domestic violence and abuse. This was probably just to get me back for all my ma'am-no-ma'ams, I decided.

DORAMAE BROOKSHIRE

Just when I thought she was done with her torturous inquisition, she snapped back and began to spit out a different line of questioning. "I have just a few more questions for you," she stated matter-of-factly. She was staring at the wad of papers in her well-manicured hands now, looking a great deal as if she might drop over and fall asleep at any second.

I decided to try to wake her up by actually fabricating a question of my own. "So what work detail do you think they might put me on?" I whispered, almost afraid to ask.

She awoke from her daytime trance with a jolt. "Oh, I can't tell you *that*," she declared. Then she actually looked up at me for the first time during the whole interrogation, and I guess my face must have reflected the frustration and pain because she quickly changed her mind and took a shot at the question. "I would *guess* that they're going to put you on a work detail off campus. Those really aren't bad, you know. You get to leave in the morning, eat lunch in town, and return later in the afternoon. You get plenty of freedom and fresh air."

Freedom and fresh air, eat lunch in town—this sounded like heaven itself, even if the setting *was* Nutter, Georgia. *This place is going to beat the* hell *outa Coward County Jail*, I thought, and I almost jumped up out of my metal folding chair and gave Goldilocks a great, big hug.

She straightened up in her plush cushioned chair. "Now let's get on with these final questions," she mumbled. "Have you ever been convicted of driving while under the influence of alcohol?"

"Ma'am, no, ma'am."

"Have you ever been convicted of driving while under the influence of drugs?"

"Ma'am, no, ma'am."

"Have you ever been convicted of weaving over the roadway?"

"Ma'am, no, ma'am."

"Have you ever been convicted of open container?"

"Ma'am, no, ma'am."

"Have you ever been convicted of underage possession of alcohol?"

"Ma'am, no, ma'am."

"Have you ever been convicted of possession of a controlled substance?"

"Ma'am, no, ma'am."

"Have you ever been convicted of violation of the Georgia Controlled Substance Act?"

I didn't want to say anything, but these questions seemed to me to be getting very redundant. "Ma'am, no, ma'am," I replied.

"Have you ever been convicted of intent to distribute illegal drugs?"

"Ma'am, no, ma'am."

"Have you ever been convicted of public intoxication?"

I tried to leave this one alone in my head, but a picture of me staggering down the main street of Goat Valley, Georgia, empty whiskey bottle in my hand, bumping into lampposts, and hanging out with likewise plastered buddies sprung to mind. "Ma'am, no, ma'am." I snickered.

I began to wonder if this whole exercise was some drug-and-alcohol-related-crimes-obsessed fruitcake's idea of a good time. But that line of questioning abruptly switched to another topic. "Have you ever been convicted of robbery?"

"Ma'am, no, ma'am."

"Have you ever been convicted of battery?"

Oh, I thought, *now we've switched over to violent crimes.* "No, ma'am."

"Have you ever been convicted of contempt of court?"

"Ma'am, no, ma'am."

"Have you ever been convicted of *affray*?" As soon as she said this, she glanced up over her inquest papers with a silly little smirk on her face. She quite obviously thought she had gotten one over on me vocabulary-wise. But I guess she had forgotten that she was dealing with a type of criminal here that was quite foreign to her turf. She actually was in a face-off with an *educated* outlaw this time. I knew that *affray* meant "fight," and I replied in a manner that let her know that I knew.

"No, ma'am, I have never been charged with fighting or public brawling," I replied.

She didn't like my reply one little bit, and her sour, bitter expression revealed such. "Well then . . . have you ever been charged with disorderly conduct?" She extruded the question in such a manner that intimated that I maybe should have been charged with this a few seconds ago for my halfway arrogant retort.

"Ma'am, no, ma'am," I replied, and this time, a little smirk was on *my* face.

She continued with her line of violent crimes questioning. "Have you ever been convicted of possession of a firearm during the commission of a crime?"

I suddenly pictured myself with a bright red bandanna tied around my head, holding an MP40 submachine gun tight against my hip, with a stance like Patty Hearst back in the '70s, and almost giggled, "Ma'am, no, ma'am."

She was getting mad now. "Have you ever been convicted of carrying a concealed weapon?"

I pictured my submachine gun once again. "Ma'am, no, ma'am."

"Have you ever been convicted of criminal trespass?"

Pray tell, where in the world would I have trespassed? "No, ma'am."

"Have you ever been convicted of obstruction of an officer?"

I wanted to say, *No, ma'am, but I sure came mighty close to it when your little guard in the big black boots had my nose against the bricks in one-hundred-degree weather the other day.*

But instead, I said, "Ma'am, no, ma'am."

Then she entered theft and similar topics in her line of questioning. During this particular theme of inquiry, I wondered if my exact charge of "conspiracy to defraud the state of Georgia" might arise. I waited to see. "Have you ever been convicted of theft by conversion?"

"Ma'am, no, ma'am."

"Have you ever been convicted of forgery?"

"Ma'am, no, ma'am."

"Have you ever been convicted of writing bad checks?"

Wasn't this awfully similar to the last question? "Ma'am, no, ma'am."

"Have you ever been convicted of theft by deception?"

We were getting too close for comfort now. But since it wasn't the exact wording of my charges, I replied, "Ma'am, no, ma'am."

"OK then. Have you ever been convicted of child endangerment?"

I was almost flatly insulted by this one. *Me? Endanger a beautiful, innocent child?* "No, ma'am!"

"Have you ever been convicted of probation violation?"

"No, ma'am." I hoped not. I had only been on probation for a grand total of four weeks now, with nine years and forty-eight weeks to go.

She was getting visibly agitated. It was as if she was on a mission to discover just *what* my charges were anyhow. It probably never struck Goldilocks to just simply look them up. They had to be somewhere in that big fistful of legal papers. Nevertheless, she was grasping at straws at this point. She slammed the papers on the desk and looked me square in the eyes. "All right, well, have you ever been ticketed for speeding?"

"No. ma'am."

"Traffic violations . . . of *any* kind?"

"Well, I got a parking ticket once in 1991."

"OK, we're done then." And she hung her head in utter shame. She had been defeated by the good doctor. "You can go back to your dorm." By the look on her exhausted face, she wasn't taking this detainee conquest lightly.

As I headed for the door, relieved that this full-scale grilling was finally at its conclusion, she glimpsed back down at the papers on her desk and blurted out, "Wait a minute! One last question!"

Then she asked it as if she already knew the answer was going to be "ma'am, no, ma'am." She almost mumbled, "Have you got any pending charges?"

Oh god! This is it! I had been good and safe up to this point. *What do I do? I should probably tell a little white lie. Goldilocks didn't even expect me to answer in the affirmative, and there wasn't a chance in hell that any of these Nutter idiots would ever look into this matter.* She was staring a hole right through me, waiting for my answer, waiting for this miserable third degree to be over, waiting to get rid of the doctor crook who showed her up. I had to act, and I had to act quickly.

Right when I was ready to trump up a little prevarication, I heard her past words of warning ringing in my ears. *I'm going to ask you some questions, and I want you to tell me the* truth. *You got* that?

A second later, page 126 of the dreaded black manual rushed through my brain. "Any detainee found purposely lying to an officer, counselor, or any other superior will be duly and harshly punished by any or all of the following methods:

- Appropriate DR
- Extended stay at WDC
- Revocation of smoking privileges
- Extra work detail
- Expulsion of visiting privileges
- Revocation of outdoor privileges
- Any other punishment deemed necessary by the staff"

I knew that I could live with some of these repercussions of my lying to Goldilocks, but the thought of the others were just beyond unbearable. I was bound and determined that I was getting out of this nightmare on the exact hour that I was scheduled to. And if they should revoke my weekend visitations by Bob, I probably would not survive the experience psychologically intact. And that last one, "any other punishment deemed necessary by the staff," frightened me to no end.

So in the end, I looked square at Goldilocks and blurted out, "Yes, I do."

Her lethargic expression and posture suddenly perked up. She bolted out of pure astonishment. "What are these pending charges for?"

There was no way out now. I had opened the door. I swallowed hard. "Involuntary manslaughter," I whispered under my breath.

What happened next was hard to explain. First came the expression, a facial expression of pure terror, fright, and horrification. Then came the attempt to physically remove herself from my presence. She began to literally back away from me by rolling her deluxe executive chair backward. After that came the shield. She reached across her desk and quickly snatched up a handful of detainees' record folders. Then she held them tight up next to her face, using them as a manila shield against the hardened assassin. Her shaking finger remained positioned above a red button on the side of her desk, which was supposed to be hidden from my view but wasn't quite in the proper position to remain fully concealed. I figured that the red button was similar to those we have all seen in the movies where a frightened bank teller, in the middle of being held up by a no-account, really despicable, thiefin' varmint, reaches down and secretly presses the concealed red button to summon the local police squad immediately to the bank, only in this case Goldilocks would be pressing the red button to summon forth the redheaded bitch or maybe the drunken fool or, better yet, Sergeant Dairy Queen. Next on the agenda was the freak-out. She pulled the shield down far enough to reveal her frightened blue eyes.

"*What* did you say your pending charge was?" she screamed.

"Involuntary manslaughter, ma'am," I repeated. "But it was a little girl who was very sick, and no one told me."

"They put you in a *boot camp* for *manslaughter*!" she yelled.

I made another attempt at explaining the situation behind the charge. "Ma'am, I gave the child's mother paperwork—a patient health history—to fill out, and she didn't let me know about extreme respiratory problems, hospitalizations, or a large amount of medication that had been given at home that morn—"

"Oh my god! You *killed a child! It was a child!* And they gave you sixty days in a boot camp! What kind of goddamn judges do we fuckin' have in this goddamn state?"

"Ma'am, this charge is *pending*, ma'am. I haven't been up against a judge yet." I tried my best to explain what had happened with the bogus charge, but she would hear none of it. She just continued with her full-scale freak-out.

"I don't know what to goddamn *do!* I'm sitting here in a room alone with a cold-blooded goddamn slaughterer." At that point, I thought she might hit the floor and take cover under her mahogany desk.

I didn't know at this point exactly what to do, so I decided it was probably best to let the crack-up run its full and natural course. So I just simply sat back in my cold metal folding chair and observed the Nutter counselor come unglued for several more minutes. After counting thirty-six *goddamns*, twenty-two *shits*, and seventeen *fuckin's*, she stopped the wig-out as fast as she had begun. I've got to admit, I was more than a little amused with her innate ability to cuss like a sailor.

As soon as she snapped out of it, her demeanor changed to pure disgust. She lay down her shield, rolled back up to her desk, and shot me a look of absolute repugnance. She was no longer shrieking but was mumbling so low that I could barely hear her. "People like you turn my stomach," she muttered. Then she informed me of something that I didn't really want to hear at that point. "Well, missy, I guess *you* will not be on a work detail that leaves the campus. You will be considered a flight risk and a danger to others. This session is now over." And she pointed to the door.

I hung my head down as I excited the interrogation site. Had I made the wrong choice to disclose this yet unrevealed information? Probably so. Just because I made the wrong last-minute decision, now I could hang up any dreams of escaping this dreadful building during the day—no freedom and fresh air, no eating lunch in town, no leaving this awful Nutter campus. All was gone in the blink of a jailbird with no judgment's eye.

Before I got back to dorm A, though, I comforted my inner restlessness by telling myself that maybe outside work detail wasn't so great after all. It was only the beginning of June, and already, the noon temperatures were busting the one-hundred-degree mark. Who wanted to be out in that anyway? At least by being stuck inside, I could remain in the nice, comfortable cool temperatures created by a good air-conditioning system. Just as long as I didn't get the work detail assignment that I had heard the other girls call "dorm rat."

By listening to them all talk about it in detail, I drew the conclusion that being assigned to the work detail "dorm rat" was pretty much synonymous to being Cinderella on her very worst day. My mind switched over to the beloved story that my aunt Faye had read to me over and over at age five. For some reason, that book just appealed to me at that particular stage of my young life; and Aunt Faye, being the darling she was, willingly accommodated my five-year-old whims and silly notions.

Cinderella was the poor, unfortunate little stepdaughter whose adoring father had died unexpectedly, leaving her to be raised by a wicked, evil stepmother and her two spoiled, overindulged, pampered daughters. Drizella and Anastasia teased, badgered, taunted, tormented, belittled, harassed, heckled, degraded, made fun of, and constantly reminded Cinderella of her inferiority over them. Well, to my understanding, being a dorm rat was pretty much like being Cinderella, only instead of the evil stepmother, there was the redheaded bitch. Instead of Drizella and Anastasia, there was Sergeant Dairy Queen and Counselor Goldilocks.

Dorm rats had to clean every square inch of their respective dorms every single morning, beginning at exactly five o'clock. They received their janitorial tools and supplies, all packed neatly in a mop bucket on wheels, via the glass dorm door. At this time, they were expected to commence scrubbing, scraping, brushing, sweeping, mopping, scouring, and swabbing until the entire dorm shone like a new penny. I had heard that the dorm rats were even expected to get down on their hands and knees, like the hall waxers, and wax the dorm floors, including under each and every one of the twenty-five bunks. At exactly eight thirty, the redheaded bitch and the drunken fool—if he showed up for work that day—would hold an all-out military-type dorm inspection. And woe be unto the poor, wretched soul of the dorm rat who wasn't a good enough custodian to pass such inspection. I think the girls, in describing this work detail, might have mentioned something about taking such a dorm rat out to the exercise pen and hanging her at dawn.

When I got back to dorm A, two of the detainees who had come in on the same day as me began to give me the third degree. A rough-looking lady from Florida caught sight of me first. She was short and muscled, built sturdy and quick. She had bragged to me that she was in for shoplifting large and small appliances, mostly large, from several local Walmarts. She even told me in detail how she did it. She said that she would fly through an empty checkout aisle with her cart full of VCRs, DVDs, stereo systems, TVs, and computers; approach the employee at the exit door with a cheerful "howdy-do"; distract him or her with any of a bagful of tricks; and be on her merry way to her car.

There, she would await the arrival of her latest load of free loot, delivered to her car by the smiling employee from the exit door. Even though she was having to serve sixty days for such capers, she boasted quite often how she would go right back to her felonious occupation the very day she got released.

"Just let me get back to Florida," I would hear her say each day, her leathery, weathered skin wrinkling worse with every word. "Those people are *cool*. They don't give a flying fuck about something as *dumb* as palmin' a few choice pieces of hardware. What's with this asshole state of yers anyhow? The very first Walmart I tried, the fools came after me like a bunch of gumshoes after Al Capone er somethin'! I ain't *never* comin' back to this fucked-up state once I cross back over that line!"

The white streak down the middle of her dyed jet-black hair stuck out like a Nutter detainee in a roomful of debutantes. Her headful of poofy hair was the consistency of straw, being subjected to years in the Florida sun, and her skin was the color of a well-worn basketball. The one and only fact I knew about her was that I had overheard the guards call her Detainee Fincher.

Her little friend chimed in, "Yeah, ya can't get away with *nuttin'* in this dumb state, that's fer sure. A girl can't even make a living." This was also a girl who had come in the same day as I had. I didn't really know her name, but I had carefully dubbed her "Barbie" in my jumbled-up mind. I had given her this nickname because she was very young, very cute, and very, very naive. Besides, she kept her naturally blond hair pulled back in one of those perpetually bouncy-type ponytails. Every time she moved, her ponytail bobbed up and down like a fishing cork on the wavy waters of Lake Wawasee. Barbie and Florida Fincher, like me, were biding their time temporarily in dorm A until the big day.

And the big day was coming up sooner than it seemed. On Fearful Friday, Barbie, Florida Fincher, and I would know for sure what our occupations were to be during our dreadful stay and which dorm we would call home for the next fifty-three days. I didn't know how those two felt about it, but I was hoping and praying to be able to remain an occupant of dorm A with the vegetable pickers and the Nutter city landscapers. They were actually a pretty subdued group compared with most of the others. And as far as work detail was concerned, I already knew that going off campus wasn't going to happen for me. Maybe I could remain in dorm A and help Bonnie as a personal handservant to Her Majesty or, better yet, to King Hooch Hound. Just as long as I didn't have to be a dorm rat or, even worse, live in dorm D with the animals. The thought of that alone began to make me nauseous, and I dismissed it as a rare possibility.

It wasn't long until the dreaded day arrived as days tend to do. Fearful Friday started out like any other day at the WDC. Snapped to attention at five o'clock by our bunks, the new detainees all appeared a little more nervous than usual. I knew what was on all our frightened minds. Where were we all going to end up dwelling while we served our prospective sentences? And how were we going to be forced to spend our miserable days?

Before we knew it, we were called down to the education room and directed to our assigned tables. The protocol went smoothly, just as it had been mapped. We were certainly called out in random order. In fact, I could make no logical sense of it at all. Naturally, it looked as if I was going to be one of the last ones called up to present myself in front of Queen Red and her little toady. The girls did a pretty good job of controlling themselves while still at attention in front of the court. They all marched adequately, snapped to attention wonderfully, and called out the exact proper words. "Ma'am, sir, Detainee Fincher reporting for work detail assignment, ma'am, sir!" I heard.

While the ceremonial portion of Fearful Friday seemed to be going well, with the exception of a few of the denser girls and a handful of intentional rebels, the few minutes directly following the ritual were anything but subdued and controlled. It seemed that, as soon as the ceremony was over, the thing to do was to rush back excitedly to your assigned table and blurt out, with no restraint whatsoever, exactly what your assigned residence and work detail were. *"All right!* I got landscaping in the city, and I stay in dorm A!" Florida Fincher screamed.

"Cooool! I get to stay in dorm A and go to the veggie farm!" declared Barbie.

A few of the others weren't quite so thrilled with their futures. The girl who had eaten the orange on the floor with me the first day, the one who was in for "breaking and entering" when she just went to retrieve her things from her ex-boyfriend's trailer, was visibly disappointed when she returned to the table. "Whadja get?" everyone yelled.

She hung her close-cropped head. "Dumpster Baby, dorm B," she whined.

This series of events went on until I thought I couldn't stand it any longer. I wanted to jump up out of my folding chair and holler, *My turn next! Someone, please have mercy on me! Let me know my fate next!* But somehow I managed to stay glued to the seat. Before I knew it, though, the awaited words emerged forth.

"Detainee Brookasure!"

I knew this was me because I had paid particular attention to Bonnie. She had already been hassled and assigned. I had heard it—special inside cleaning duty, personal maid to Ms. Empusa Sinestro, the redheaded queen bee. Little Bonnie had scored the big one. She had pulled off the job of the century. I thought, *It's probably 'cuz she's such a controllable little wimp.*

I was proud of myself. I did everything just right. I said the right words in just the right tone and volume, stood at beautiful attention, and marched like a soldier. I even managed to thank Old Red and Mr. Swillbelly for the bad news.

The very second I sat back down at the assigned table, Florida Fincher, Barbie, the new Dumpster Baby, and milksop Bonnie all chimed in, "Whudja get? Huh?" They just couldn't wait to hear.

Florida Fincher added, "Bet yer gonna stay in dorm A with us and go out on landscape duty, aren't cha?"

"No," I said.

"I know," Barbie chimed in. "You're going to come out and be one with the earth on the veggie farm with *me*."

"Nah-uh," I mumbled.

I think Bonnie could sense my pain, and she wanted to make it better. "You gonna be cleanin' the management's personal rooms with me? We'll have fun," she added.

"Not by a long shot," I replied.

Things suddenly got quiet, and a more serious tone took over. They had all seen my facial expression by now. They knew something bad was up. The breaking-and-entering girl took a stab. "Oh shit. You got Dumpster Baby, dorm B, like me, didn't you?"

"Nope," I answered.

"Well then, what *did* ya get? Tell us," Barbie inquired.

I hung my head. A lump formed in my throat. I thought I might cry. I bit my lower lip. "Dorm rat, dorm D," my trembling mouth spewed forth.

They all sat there, dumbfounded. "Man, tough break," said Florida Fincher, and they all changed their postures to turn away from me.

MRS. SANTA CLAUS

BACK IN DORM A, as I packed up my few issued personal items, my emotions were running wild. I knew this might be the end of the line for me. I was not going to be able to survive it. Dorm D was too wild, psycho, and uncurbed for this naive, unseasoned little lady. Why, those rabid animals would eat me alive. As these thoughts flew through my head like a runaway freight train, I began to do something that, up until this point, I had been able to curb by blocking my thoughts and biting through my lower lip. I began to cry. Big, giant crocodile tears swelled up in my saddened eyes and began to roll down my flushed cheeks. I turned away from anyone who might be looking in my direction so they wouldn't see. But one of the dorm A residents saw it anyhow.

She was tall, solid, and very unfeminine. My grandma would have said she was "big boned." She sported a dark blond ponytail on most days and walked with a bowlegged limp. Most of the other girls stayed clear of her, but those who associated with her certainly respected her opinion. She seemed to be pretty much the bell cow of dorm A. The interesting part of the whole tale, to me, was the fact that she had seemed to pay me an unusual amount of attention ever since the first day, when she was the leader of the little hurry-up-and-make-the-new-detainee's-bed-before-the-sergeant-gets-back escapade. Quite often, she would try to strike up a conversation with me.

She claimed to be from Goat Valley and most definitely acted as if she knew me. She told me she was in for two whole years, something to do with some sophisticated scheme in her uncle's business that didn't turn out to be so sophisticated after all. I don't know. I didn't really ever listen to her. I had already learned that so many of these girls were full of so much bullshit that I had better watch whom I believed. Most of it, at this point, went in one ear and out the other. Anyhow, she was always doing things for me, helping me out, and trying to keep me out of trouble. Somewhere along the line, she began to call me Doc. This aroused a lot of the other girls' curiosity but not mine. I knew then that she had probably been one of my many patients. I think her name was Nancy. I think I recognized some of my work on Nancy's front tooth. The only incidence I remember about her was something that happened during one of our numerous daily head counts.

One of dorm A's residents was a particularly sickening girl named Latausha. Like Nancy, she was tall and sturdy and rather masculine. Unlike Nancy, she was bigmouthed, lewd, and downright revolting. Judging by the two's interactions, they didn't like each other one little bit. In fact, they appeared to absolutely *loathe* each other. It wasn't hard to see that this personality conflict was because they were in almost constant competition for the place of honor in dorm A. They were both long-termers; they would be there two years, and that made it very important to establish which one was going to rule the roost.

One of the unnerving things about it was that fate had stuck them together as bunkies, and that fact made it that much worse on them and all those around them. It was especially bad during head count, when they had to stand at attention, one right in front of the other, beside their metal bunk and wait until the guards showed up in dorm A. I think it really pissed Latausha off every head count because Nancy's designated position was always in front of her.

Anyhow, whatever the reason, Latausha had the uncanny ability to become extremely flatulent on command. And her farts would drive Hitler himself out of Germany. She used this regularly as a weapon of high destruction against poor, weak-stomached Nancy, and head count seemed to be the ideal time to let one rip. I could remember the first time Latausha cut a big one. She timed it perfectly. Looking out the glass window of dorm A, I could see that the officers had decided to go in reverse order that head count—dorm D and then dorm C, followed by dorm B. We would be last. The guards were still in dorm C, and Latausha already dropped the big one. My eyes rolled over toward Nancy.

"Oh my god, you filthy bitch! Can't you control your nasty self?" she inquired, hopping nervously on one foot, still trying to hold attention.

Nancy was pulling her T-shirt up over her nose and mouth, and the rest of her face was turning a color somewhere between green and pale yellow. It wasn't long before her hopping turned into running. She had made a mad dash for the toilet and had gotten there just in time. Latausha was gloating; her sturdy chest bowed out like a Florida puffer fish. As I stood at attention beside my bunk, listening to Nancy puke her guts out and being forced to inhale the raunchiness of Latausha's latest bullet against her, I thought of how awfully weird this whole life of mine had become.

Nancy was the only one in dorm A who tried to help me pack up my stuff. She was also the only one who tried to soothe my feelings when I just couldn't hold the tears back. I guess Barbie and Florida Fincher felt too downright awful that I was going to have to reside in dorm D. They just kind of avoided the whole scene. One other girl from dorm A would have helped me, if she had still been there. She was a kindly soul whom I had met my first day in.

Her name was Suzy. She lived on the lower bunk beside me and had been one of the vegetable farmworkers. She had been there for almost a year on the day I arrived, and she didn't look over seventeen years old. But all the other girls seemed to like her because she appeared to have the rare gift of compassion, something not seen much in those parts. She talked every day about how she was going to turn her life around and quit her occupation as a nightclub stripper and call girl in Atlanta. She had it all figured out. She was going to go back to school and get her GED and then go to college to become a teacher. She declared that she was good and ready for a respectable life.

One day before I moved out of dorm A, Suzy was released from the WDC at Nutter. She generously gave me her well-kept size 8 shower shoes and her extra socks. Her pimp boyfriend picked her up at the exit door, and she went with him back to Atlanta.

There wasn't much to pack up really, just the few items of clothing and personal things that were issued to me on intake day. It all fit easily in a medium-sized cardboard box. Just like at the jail in Atlanta, I had learned pretty quickly which items were essential to order off the commissary list and which were mostly worthless junk items, only here so many of the basics were already provided that I didn't have to order much from the store at all. In fact, I found myself playing a little game of "ask yourself if you really even need this" before I would order anything. It was a game somewhat of prison time self-discipline. Besides, the money was getting very tight at home from Bob spending so much time trying to live near me so he could see me as often as possible.

There were just a few items that I felt very strongly I needed off that commissary list. Most of them were hygiene articles. I found out right away that the state-issued soap, shampoo, toothpaste, and deodorant were not only raunchy but also downright unbearable for even two months. The soap and shampoo stunk; the toothpaste would have had an American Dental Association rating of 0, if it had been rated at all; and the deodorant made one smell worse than if she had none on whatsoever. So I decided after the first week to hook myself up with a few name-brand toiletries. I proudly submitted my order for Prell shampoo, Colgate toothpaste, and Ban deodorant. But my pride and joy was my bar of aqua Zest soap. It came in its own soap dish that was clear plastic with a nonstick finish across the bottom.

The highlight of my whole day was when I grabbed my towel, lovingly picked up my new soap dish of Zest, and headed for the shower. There, for as long as I wanted, I could enjoy the pelting of the soothing warm water against my tired skin in a nice roomy shower that was actually clean. And if I waited until the few obnoxious, aggressive detainees were through with their showers, no one would try to rush me out of mine. On top of that, there were a total of eight showers, four on each side, that were available to us, so it wasn't at all like back at the county jail—no more Bicycle, no more exhibitionism, and no more filth and sickening mucky slime. So there we were, the same time every night, my beloved bar of aqua Zest and me. We had a date with the shower.

Moving day to dorm D couldn't have been worse if Dracula himself had custom ordered the conditions. Dorm A was in deep trouble for not passing dorm inspection that morning, Sergeant Dairy Queen was in the middle of one of her manic episodes, and the redheaded bitch was on the warpath. A quick glimpse out the window told me that the weather conditions were comparable to the moods of the players within. Foreboding billowy dark clouds rolled across the navy blue sky, and an occasional streak of silver lightning popped against the metal roof. Giant gusts of wind blew tiny pieces of trash sporadically across the immaculate lawn, and I knew that it had to be mighty windy out because that trash had to have come from far away. The yard girls kept it so perfect around there that pieces of rubbish were not even a possibility.

The wind, the lightning, the ominous dark skies, the nervous tension, and the nail biting—the whole place was on edge. It was not a good day to face moving to the dorm of doom. But these things possessed no sense of timing. The time was now, and I had no choice.

Nancy and the melancholy little nurse helped me carry my few items over to dorm D, where they gladly dropped them outside the door and ran. As they both hurried back toward safe territory, they had a relieved look on their faces—relieved that they didn't have to go any farther into hostile territory, relieved that they didn't come into any contact with the dorm D creatures, relieved that they escaped unscathed by the enemy. And there I stood, boxes at my feet, waiting for the guard in the tower to unclick the lock on the door to purgatory.

Entering the world of dorm D was like day and night compared with entering dorm A. When I entered dorm A, nobody much seemed to care about it. Oh, they all stared for a minute or two, but it was mostly just a self-preservation move, I think. Not so in dorm D. From the second I walked trembling through the door, the dorm D denizens of the wild were upon me like hungry jackals on their prey. They were ruthless, brutal, mindless, and beastly. They possessed no souls. Theirs was a world of pure survival, and survive they did.

It wasn't long before I learned the leader of the pack. Her name was Laverne, and she was big, Black, and mean as a rattlesnake. Her first agenda for the day was making damn sure that she retained her title. She met me at the door and started in immediately. "I guess you be da neeew girl den." She spat in my face so close that I could feel her beastly breath. "Let's see yer bunk numba, an' den you kin meet da girls."

Shaking, I handed her my sheet of paper that read, "Bunk D-36, work assignment: dorm custodian."

"Oh, you gots da same work detail as me, dorm rat!" she exclaimed. "Dey makes me stay on da inside 'cuz dey say my crime be violent. I don't sees *why*! All I done wuz cut some damn bitch up a liddle, an' dat bitch, she deserved it too!"

I was getting more frightened by the minute. About half the dorm had now gathered around me, forming a huge circle of Animalia. I began to feel like Mia Farrow's character in the movie *Rosemary's Baby*. I wondered if this was going to end with a violent rape by Satan.

Just then, one of the scariest-looking inmates hollered across the room, "Pat, come look at the new dorm rat! She's real purdy! She don't look nothin' like any o' us!"

The one she called Pat came hobbling over to the group circle to size me up. "Yer damn right. She *is* a tad different. Ya reckon she's gonna be able ta make it round here?"

"Ah bet she comed from a *rich* bunch a folks," another observed.

"She don't talk like she's from here neither," added still another.

And the circus went on for what seemed to be an eternity, me stuck in the middle of the circle of doom and them holding almost constant surveillance, complete with a running commentary about me. I felt like one of the cows on our farm when it came time for Bob and me to cull the yearly meat cow. We would kind of gather around each one and ask ourselves, *Now does this one eat much? Does she have any deformities or problems? What kind of price would she bring? Basically, is she worth keeping, or do we need to kill her?*

Right when I thought I might be a goner, the gogglers and gapers began to look bored, and the circle of doom broke up as quickly as it had formed. They all seemed to return to whatever it was they were doing when I first arrived. Only a few choice ones remained behind to haggle me further.

One who stayed behind was the one they called Pat. She seemed to have not been able to take her eyes off me since she first joined the circle. Pat stuck out like a sore thumb because she was very old compared with the rest of the dorm D pack. She was tall as a Georgia pine and built like a college football halfback. I noticed she seemed to hold a big chaw of tobacco in her cheek, which she spat secretly into a tiny plastic cup she concealed in the palm of her giant hand. Her hands were those of a hardworking blue-collar laborer, and she dragged one foot when she walked. Her hair was peroxide blond with the consistency of hay and pulled back in an attempt to form a one-inch ponytail. The skin on her face looked as if it had been nailed to the side of a south Georgia barn for a season and then pasted back on her homely face.

"Let me help ya put some o' that junk o' yern away," she offered.

I knew I was going to need someone's help arranging my issued items in perfect military order in my new locker, but something told me that Pat was not the helper I was seeking. "No, that's OK. I can get it. Thanks anyway," I said.

But she was not going to be so easily defeated. "Oh," she said, snatching the box from my grasp. "Lookee here, you gots my very most favorite kinda candy right cheer." She had swooped down into my sacred box and scooped up my precious Hershey's bar with almonds—the one I divvied up all week long. Then I noticed she was waving it in the hand that, just seconds ago, had been the home of the nasty tobacco spit cup, and a small stream of tobacco juice was now dripping down the candy wrapper. At that moment, I knew that I would never in a million years take a single bite of that particular morsel from heaven, but instinct also told me that I had to act quickly. All eyes were on me.

"Oh, no, I don't think so! Give me that Hershey's bar back!" I demanded in a voice two pitches higher than my natural one.

She looked at me as if I was some kind of total moron, and then her eyes scanned the awaiting crowd. I knew instinctively that I had created a sort of instant dilemma for her. The choice was pound the new girl and retain your title or let it slide and risk it all. For a minute, she just froze in her tracks, the object in question still held high above her greasy head. From the look on her ugly face, I was glad that the candy bar was not a knife, a hammer, or a Colt .45. Then the decision was sealed.

She brought the chocolate bar down to her mouth; licked the wrapper with her giant tongue; bit off one corner, paper and all; and threw it to the floor, stomping it with her size 10 boot. She immediately then reached down, swooped it up off the floor, and handed me what appeared to be a piece of brown crumpled paper housing tiny pebbly morsels, complete with a huge boot-shaped stamp. "Hey, y'all! New girl don't share! Y'all hear that? New girl thinks her shit don't stink! New girl is too good fer us'n. Ah'd say she wuz a greedy little Yankee, wouldn't y'all?"

With that, two groups of hecklers were instantly formed. They came alive almost spontaneously. Laverne formed the Black group, and Pat formed the White. By the time the dual emotional whipping was over, I decided that in the future, the dorm D animals could have any of my commissary items they wanted.

The bullyraggers soon tired of their little game and dispersed, going back to pick on one another once again. As soon as I was sure that no one was watching, I ran to the closest bathroom, hid in a shower, pulled the curtain shut, and sobbed uncontrollably. I probably hadn't been there more than five minutes before the shower curtain was gently opened by a short, little lady who stood quietly before me. She was nothing like the others. She was probably about five foot two with short hair graying at the temples, a tiny turned-up, button nose and little plump cheeks, both cherry red. She was extremely soft spoken and mild mannered. "What's the matter?" she asked tenderly.

"Oh, I'm just never gonna make it in dorm D." I sobbed. "They might as well go ahead and get it over with and kill me. It'd put me out of my misery."

"Come here," the tender angel of mercy instructed.

I wasn't sure what to do, but since she seemed to be my only option at the moment of someone to talk to, I went over to her. She spread her arms open as an invitation for a good hugging. I walked into them willingly, hungry for something or someone sincerely compassionate. She didn't let me down. Her embrace was full of pity and humanity.

"Don't let these idiots get to you. They can't help the fact that they are ignorant and simpleminded. They come from a world much different from yours and mine." And with that said, she gave me one more motivational squeeze. "Come on now. You can survive this. You only have to hang in there for two months. I got a whole year, and I'm almost done with this awful place. Hallelujah!"

I knew instinctively, maybe through osmosis or it might have been mental telepathy, that this little woman and I were going to be close from that moment on, if it was even possible to be close to anyone in this hellhole. She was different from all the others. She had taken the time to care.

As soon as the compassionate, motherly pep talk was over, she switched gears into another mode. "Come on now," she said with much encouragement. "Let's get that junk of yours settled properly in your locker."

Her matronly embrace ceased, and a quick pat on the shoulder blade was delivered. She wasted no time. She went about her work precisely and seriously. She rolled, folded, tucked, and lined up. Before I knew it, my issued gear was arranged in perfect military order in my new dorm D drawer. I was amazed at her speed, accuracy, and determination. I couldn't believe that she had willingly put up with this place for almost a year and still retained such a positive attitude. I was pretty sure that, after nearly a year, I would have most certainly thrown in the towel and become one of them. I was curious about what kept her going.

"If you don't mind my asking, what are you in for? How come you got a whole year?" I asked.

"Oh, it's a long story," she replied. She looked around to see if anyone was listening. But they were all too busy harassing one another.

"See, I worked for a prominent physician in a small south Georgia town. He had this brand-new trophy wife. She was number four. He was in his midfifties. She was twenty-five—young and beautiful and sassy and none too bright. Anyhow, it was quite apparent to everyone, except him, just exactly what she was after. She latched on to that money like a baby calf locking onto its mama's nipple. It wasn't long before she was asking me to write an occasional check to her for a small amount. The occasional became more and more often, and the small amount grew and grew. The money addiction was becoming a monster, and the monster was getting hungrier and hungrier by the day.

"At first, I didn't know what to do. I let it go on for a while. She wasn't asking for much, and the good doctor adored number four and seemed so much happier than before. I validated the checks by telling myself that Little Miss It probably deserved them for putting up with his unpredictable mood swings. But before long, I found myself stuck between a rock and a hard place. It was becoming almost every day now, and I had to tell someone. I was the office manager, and most of my day was spent at the front desk with all the insurance clerks. So one day I happened to casually mention the new wife's habit to Shelby, my closest friend there. Within one hour, I found myself sitting across from the doctor and his attorney. Two hours later, I was locked up in the county jail. It took them three months to give me a court date. The judge sentenced me to a year at boot camp, and here I am."

Her story had a remarkably familiar ring to it. After the first mention of wife number four, my old friend Caroline began to dance in my head. I wondered how she was, still stuck in that bottomless pit called Coward County Jail. Had her fragile nature survived it, or had Bicycle and Jasmine and Coco overtaken her sanity? A more important set of questions began to emerge. Why was it so prevalent, this scenario of middle-aged doctor marrying an idiotic young gold digger who skillfully embezzles money from his practice right under his highly intelligent nose? How could that go on so often? Evidently, it was fairly often because I had already met two office managers within a month who had the same story. And why did these office managers so readily agree to surrender the money over to the little wedded new dingbats? Better yet, why did the good doctors, in every case, prosecute to the full extent of the law quickly and mercilessly without even asking for the other side of the story? In every case, the little new wives walked away scot-free and several thousand dollars richer to boot. Well, whatever the answers to these deeply psychological inquiries, my new friend from dorm D was OK by me. In fact, she had probably rescued me from a total nervous breakdown.

After a few days, I began to wonder what she was doing in dorm D. She quite obviously did not fit in with the other animals. I learned that she was in a small group that traveled out during the day for summertime duty, cleaning and waxing floors at the local elementary schools. It was hard work, and only those who were real hustlers were put on that work detail.

I also learned that her nickname around there was Mrs. Santa Claus. And I gotta give those jailbirds this one. They had done a perfect job of assigning a handle this time around. She was short, plump, round, rosy cheeked, and sweet as Christmas candy hanging on the yuletide tree. Her tiny turned-up nose and little wire-rimmed glasses completed the picture as did the shiny black boots. She acted as a mother figure to all the young troublemakers, and they all looked up to her for comfort and advice. But she also kept her distance and taught me how to as well.

"After work, I take my shower. Then I lie on my bunk and write letters home and read the few decent books they have around here. Never get into watching TV or talking to them," she cautioned me. "That can only lead to trouble."

So how did she manage this? She was their mother, their mentor, their main confidante. Yet she never mingled with them, never really got involved, never socialized one bit. I began to respect her immensely for being able to pull this off, and I also began to try with all my might to do the same. But I never got quite as skilled at it. Oh, I had a few girls who seemed to confide in me and look up to me, but more often than not, I got too caught up in the emotional turmoil of the whole scene and lost my cool regularly. After a while, I decided not to try to win their respect but instead to just do my work, stay out of trouble, and keep everyone as far as possible away from me. And it worked better that way for me. Mrs. Santa Claus and I, we remained good friends until the sad day that she left us all; but because of her compassion and fond memory, I was able to survive the rest of my ordeal.

Her attitude was just so extraordinary. Her husband and grown children would take turns visiting her every Saturday and Sunday. Since Bob came to see me every Saturday and Sunday also, we got to know them pretty well. They taught us a lot of things about visitation. The main one that stuck in my mind was that they showed us how to pull up two chairs very close together, position those chairs in front of the large glass doors that faced the little yard, put their arms lovingly behind the backs of the chairs, and pretend like they were at the movies. The crazy girls outside were the actors, and their concerned family members completed the cast. Mrs. Santa Claus and her wonderful husband sat for hours at the movies, observing the makeshift performers with great scrutiny. The mimes and the thespians, the heroes and the villains, the idols and the romantic leads—they were all there, right out in that little pen. I never got over how she was able to do that. There she was, stuck in that worst of the worst situation created by a lucky, two-bit little whore, really by no fault of her own, and she was having the time of her life going to the Saturday matinee.

One day soon after I moved into dorm D, I returned from the morning outside walk around the dirt track a hundred times in a circle, and Mrs. Santa Claus met me at my bunk. "I was here when they did dorm inspection this morning, and it was one of those times they decided to pull on everyone's lock on their drawers to see if anyone's locker would come open. Yours was the only one that wasn't locked. They got into it, and a big burly guard really messed up all your stuff. Here, I'll help you get it straightened back up 'cuz they said they're coming back to recheck it in a little while. They also told us all to not tell you, so don't let them know that I tipped you off."

"But that *can't* be true," I protested. "I'm always so careful to check and recheck that my lock is latched tightly."

"Oh, honey, these worn-out old locks are so unpredictable. One day they may lock up tighter than a drum, and the next day they wouldn't lock to save their souls." She talked as if the rusted old padlocks were alive and ticking.

But I didn't have time to analyze Ms. Claus's remarks. I was in another tight spot, and I had to act swiftly. I opened my locker cautiously to find the worst, god-awful jumbled-up, snarled-up mess I had ever seen. My perfectly arranged drawer had been transformed into a monstrous mishmash of material, a horrible hodgepodge of toiletries, a chaotic helter-skelter of commissary items. The issued items within were tousled, rumpled, scattered, and ruffled. Some thoughtless, heartless, mean-spirited beast had come along in one fell swoop and upset my apple cart. She had put a blot on my clean slate. The bitch had made an eyesore out of my perfect work of art. My Mona Lisa was dead.

This was it. I was a goner this time. They were gonna get me once and for all. It was finally over for me. I could never in a billion years get *this* disarray back into military order in a few minutes. This was a worse dilemma than the bed-making incidence.

Then another miraculous happening befell me. It took place right before my very eyes. Ms. Claus knelt down on her little round chubby knees and began to make instant order out of the chaotic clutter. Socks were rolled tightly, T-shirts were folded, and underpants were tucked neatly away. Commissary items were arranged by size and shape in one corner as if being stocked alphabetically on a convenience store shelf. And my toiletries were placed into two perfectly straight little rows, their funny little shampoo and toothpaste faces grinning up at me. When she was done, she struggled to her short, little feet, placed her little pudgy hands on her rounded hips, and let out one long sigh. "There then, that'll have to do," she announced.

And none too soon. As we were both admiring her latest creation, we heard the enemy approaching. I had just enough time to shove the old metal drawer shut and place the rusted padlock back into position, this time making damn sure it was locked up good and tight. "All detainees at *attention*!" the big burly guard shouted as she slung open dorm D's heavy door, and she made a beeline for my locker.

She eyed the old lock as if she wished it would jump off the drawer by its own mystical powers. Then she rolled her dark eyes toward Laverne and simultaneously gave my lock one swift kick with the heel of her scuffed black boot. When the lock didn't so much as budge, she let out a long practiced sigh as if this was all a little too much for a minimum-wage state employee to have to handle. I thought I heard a small whimper as she felt it necessary to drop to her heavy knees and actually use her hands to try to spring the lock. But as hard as she tugged, jerked, and wiggled, she could not force the mighty little lock to give way. We had done it, Mrs. Santa Claus and me. We had won the war of the locker lock.

Soon after that, Mrs. Claus was finally granted her freedom from the world of the Nutter crazies, but I never forgot that one act of compassion and kindness on a day that I ordinarily might have let it all fell apart and drifted into a permanent state of unsoundness of mind. But just because my guardian angel had returned to her small south

Georgia town to try to resume her life in as normal a manner as possible, that didn't mean that I was not still stuck in a mighty challenging situation. I found out very quickly that residing in dorm D translated to this: I could not let up for one tiny instant if I wanted to stay afloat. For example, one sunny summer day when all seemed to be under control, I got yet another blow smack dab delivered between the eyes. It seemed I would never learn.

QUEST FOR ZEST

I T WAS A day just like any other day—up at five o'clock, attention by the bunk, parade rest, get dressed, scrub the scummy bathroom, go to breakfast, return to finish the scummy bathroom, dorm inspection, attention again and again and again, write home to try to salvage sanity, try to isolate self from the dorm morons, count days until Saturday and Sunday, close eyes and dream of fields of fragrant daisies, beautiful sinewed animals running free, and colored autumn leaves drifting to the ground. Before I knew it, it was time for my evening shower. So we went on our nightly date, my beloved Zest and I. I grabbed a towel, some shampoo, and shower shoes, and off I went, drifting into the secret world of soothing warm water beating rhythmically on my tired, aging face. It was my daily aqueous escape.

I was not quite sure exactly how it happened. Maybe I became a little too mesmerized by the water that night. Or maybe I was a little more worn down and weary than I thought. I might have even been daydreaming to the point of no return. But whatever the reason, I did something that—in the world of the captured—was unforgiveable, sometimes even fatal. I let up on my guard. I noticed it too late, what I had done.

It was when I was placing my evening's toiletries back into their categorized drawer positions. I looked and saw that one spot, quite rectangular in shape, was bare, like a vacant hole in a sea of toothpaste and shampoo. And suddenly, I knew. That void was home to my best friend, my inseparable shower buddy, my security blanket in the world of water.

I had exited that bathroom minus my beloved bar of Zest, resting in its little plastic dish. For a moment, I just stood there, frozen in time. How could I have ever let this happen? That aqua blue striped bar of Zest was my only friend in a time of troubled turmoil. He was my salvation from the daily grind, my excuse for a hydrous holiday, my very essence of retaining my sanity on a string. So I snapped out of it, stood straight up, and rushed back into bathroom B like a jackrabbit being pursued by a hungry cougar. But alas, I was too late—no trace of my bath time pal. My Zest was gone, vamoosed, vanished into thin air. I frantically began to search high and low, in spots that were very much ridiculous, close to insane—behind the four toilets, tucked under the trash can, up in the light fixture, behind the sinks' plumbing.

Suddenly, I snapped to. Something told me to get a grip and check places that were a little more likely. So I looked *in* the trash can, on top of the shower ledges, on top of the sinks, in the soap holders in each shower but to no avail. My soapy sidekick was gone. My cleansing chum had disappeared into thin air. It was all over. I would never breathe those zesty, zippy, exuberant soap fumes again.

And as reality hit me, I became more and more furious. How *dare* them! Those nasty, smelly, uncivilized dorm D animals had stolen my brand-new bar of Zest. Up until now, I knew they were all ruthless, brutal, beastly creatures with little to no brains. But now I knew they had become something beyond that. They were now soulless, beasts of the dark.

There was only one thing I could do, and I had to do it quickly before I lost my nerve. I would have to face my transgressors, catch the little thieves red-handed, bust the perps like they did on TV, whatever it took to recover my shower buddy. So I returned to my bunk, dragging my feet and hanging my head and a little more discouraged than I had been since I had gotten myself encaged. Deep inside, I knew this would all be a futile attempt, but I also knew I had to try while the adrenaline was still flowing.

I cleared my throat. "OK," I announced, shaking my soggy towel in the air, "who took my soap?"

No one even so much as looked up. They all continued their idiotic activities, arguing loudly over what TV channel to watch, squabbling over the last bite of brownie from someone's commissary, having a tug-of-war over the horoscope section of the newspaper. Two inmates were having a minifistfight over a small paper bag full of candy and sodas they had tricked the new girl out of. Laverne was waving her crutch at the seventeen-year-old girl who had just found out that day she was pregnant but swore she never remembered having sex with anyone in the last six months. The Mexican girl with the advanced periodontal disease and the hair loss problem was busy wiggling her dislodged front tooth while she ran her fingers along her balding scalp. The mean-spirited, dictatorial tyrant who had to make the biscuits every morning because she was in for two years was in one corner, arrogantly bossing a stupid, timid girl around, telling her to do this and that, and looking as if she was going to haul off and hit her at any moment. And Big Dumb Mac was in the middle of it all, acting as if she was able to control any of it.

I cleared my throat again. This time, I came close to screaming it. "I said, who the hell stole my soap?"

This they understood a little better. The Mexican girl quit wiggling her tooth. Laverne quit waving her crutch. The biscuit-making tyrant quit quarterbacking the mousy girl. And all the minifistfights came to a halt. Mac looked as if she had suddenly lost control. It was Pat who first looked up. She had an expression on her sun-beaten, truck-driving face as if she couldn't believe what had just transpired.

Now that I had their attention, I had to act quickly. They were not the type to retain any one fact for much over a minute at a time. My thoughts were racing, every brain cell in full gear. It was a wonderful feeling to welcome my organ of reason briefly back into my life. It was time to engage the old gray matter.

Then it came to me, a sudden insight, an inspiration, a brilliant idea—why, even an utter brainstorm, if you will. I would incorporate a little trick I had learned as a child back in elementary school. Whenever one of my tiny classmates had any one of their little treasures go missing back at Harrison Hill Elementary School, we had been taught by our quite knowledgeable teachers—wise beyond their years—to practice this simple exercise, and I intended to incorporate it at this very moment to solve my current dilemma. I knew it would work with these morons.

I stretched my body to gather height. I squared my shoulders and puffed out my chest. I plastered a confident yet gentle expression on my face. This time, I spoke very softly and distinctly. "OK," I began, "I understand *why* someone may have borrowed my soap. It was a very nice bar of soap. But after all, it is *my* soap, and I do need it back. So tell you what I'm gonna do. I'm gonna turn my back and close my eyes. I'll count to one hundred. Whoever has my soap and my soap dish can put it right here on my top bunk behind me, no questions asked. I don't need to know who or why. I just want my soap back, OK?"

All eyes were on me now—brown eyes, blue eyes, green eyes, and hazel eyes, all so bewildered and confused that they didn't know what to do. They were looking as if they might have just gotten the news that it was the end of the world or something. I turned around and shut my own dark blue eyes. I was certain that this was going to work now that I had them all so muddled. Whatever no-good thievin' robber who had made off with my soap would feel guilty now. She would probably even let herself be known, along with a full apology and explanation. That was how it worked with the kids who had gone astray at Harrison Hill. This had to work. It always worked there.

I was near the end of my countdown. "Ninety-seven, ninety-eight, ninety-nine, one hundred!" I whirled around toward my upper bunk and popped my baby blues open, fully expecting to see my bath buddy back home but nothing, naught, zippo. The bunk was just as it had been one hundred seconds before, and the roomful of thugs had lost interest in this strange new phenomenon. Most of them had already returned to the world of idiocy. They couldn't even hold out for one hundred seconds or even have the common courtesy to act as if they gave a rat's ass.

Now I *was* mad. It all came rushing out. "Who the *fuck* has my soap, *damn it*!" I was clenching my fists and stamping my foot. I had been holding my breath, and I could feel my face began to flush. "*Goddammit*, I *paid* for that fucking shit, and I *am* going to get it back *right fuckin' now*!" I caught myself waving my fist at the few who cared to listen. I once again had the attention of most of the room. They finally felt at home. This they could deal with.

I looked around. For a brief moment, I think I actually caught a few semi-guilt-stricken facial expressions. I was taken aback, speechless. But now it was them who talked. Quietly, one short bronzed girl stepped forward. "Wuh, whachoo expeck from us anyhow? We all jist a buncha jailbirds here. We in here fer steeealin' an' shit. Affer all, we *is* incarcerainted."

And that was it. That explained it all, the end of the soap-stealing incident, never to be mentioned again. A few days later, I found my empty, dirty soap dish carefully placed on the soap tray in one of the showers in bathroom B. But I never laid eyes on my beloved bar of Zest ever again.

The days now began to run together—up at four thirty, head count by the bunks, clean bathroom A by myself, breakfast, dorm inspection, another head count, walk the track outside if I was lucky, head count, lunch, head count, fight boredom in the dorm until the girls with "real" work details got back, head count, dinner, head count, write multiple letters back home, head count, evening monotony, head count, get ready for bed, head count, lights-out, start all over again.

It was all quite simple. Just exist. Move your cleaning arms like a mechanical robot. Place one foot in front of the other. Crawl into your own little world. Never display weakness. Mind your own business. Show no emotion. Have no reaction. Set up house in your own head. This was how it worked. I was going to get through this after all.

But just as I had it all figured out, just as I decided that *dorm rat, dorm D* wasn't so awfully bad after all, my world came crashing down once again. One early afternoon when I was minding my own business, causing no harm at all, I was called down into classroom A by the Queen Mother herself. I was just sitting on the freezing tile floor beside my bunk, propped up against the cold concrete wall, stiff necked, the one and only position allowed between lunch and dinner, when the call came. "Detainee Brookasure, report to Assistant Warden Sinestro, classroom A, immediately!" the voice boomed over the intercom.

And of course, both I and tiny Bonnie shot out of our prospective dorm rooms. I knew in my heart it just *had* to be her they were calling. She was the little suck-up that hung around the evil witch all day long. She cleaned the king and queen's quarters with perfect precision daily. I was sure the three of them even had some kind of secret language. Why, of course, it had to be her they were calling. Nothing else made any sense.

But when we both approached the guard station, the weary guard pointed her long sharp finger at me. "You, Detainee Brookasure, *you* go see Warden Sinestro *now*! Classroom A."

"Me?" I questioned, not believing my ears. "Sure it's not *her*, ma'am?" And I pointed decidedly at poor little Bonnie.

"Ah *knows* what ah's doin', detaineeee! Don't choo *never* ax me if ah's right!" she shot back at me. "It's *choo* she wants to see. Now git down there right now!"

"Ma'am, yes, ma'am," I replied.

On the way down the long corridor to classroom A, all kinds of terrible scenarios played out in my head. Was I going to receive the dreaded DR for something I didn't realize I had done? Had one of these other asshole detainees made up a lie about me to save their own ass? Was I maybe flunking out of my drug addiction class or my family violence class? Had something disastrous happened back home? Was I going to be transferred to another facility without my family's knowledge? By the time I knocked on the classroom door, nervous sweat was rolling down my neck into my khaki uniform.

"*Enter*, detainee!" the redheaded bitch screamed out.

I obeyed, and as soon as I walked into the room, there was Queen Red and the head warden himself, both sitting stiffly at a long brown table, their hands folded identically and placed carefully on the hard surface before them. "Welllll, how do you address us, detainee?" she demanded.

"Ma'am, sir—excuse me, I mean, sir, ma'am, Detainee Brookshire reporting for instructions, sir, ma'am!" I enunciated as confidently as possible.

"Detainee Brookshire, it has been brought to our attention that you are doing a won—well, an *adequate* job in your dorm, and so we would like to transfer your work detail to kitchen duty. You will immediately move to dorm C and be on morning kitchen staff. Get the details from the head cook. Any questions?"

Oh no, this was *not* happening, just when I was falling right into the daily routine. I had it all down pat now. Why, I could even survive in dorm D, the animal dorm. I left them alone, and they left me alone.

I did my job—quite *adequately*, I guess—and I never asked anyone for anything. I was a "blend-inner, a never-rock-the-boater, a serious member of the status quo.

Of course, I had questions and plenty of them. What did being on morning kitchen staff involve? Was there any training, and which of these assholes performed it? What time would I have to get up? What would my duties involve? If I burned any of the food, did I get burned at the stake or, worse yet, get issued a DR? How did the menus work? Just exactly *where* was the kitchen, and how did one get to it? The questions went on and on.

But when it really came down to it, all I could muster up was "Ma'am, when do I report for duty, ma'am?"

"We thought we made ourselves perfectly clear, detainee! Move your issued gear out *right now—immediately*! Now go back to your dorm and do that!"

"Ma'am, sir, yes, ma'am, sir!" I yelled out. And with as much self-esteem as possible, I broke attention, made a sharp turn to my left, and exited classroom A.

Oh my god, what am I going to do? I thought on the way back down the long hallway. *I can't possibly live through another dorm change in this hellhole. Why is this happening to me? I kept a low profile. I did everything right to not bring attention to myself. How could I possibly have been singled out like this?* And the longer I pondered the situation, the hotter I got. By the time I stood outside dorm D, waiting to be let in, my face was fire-engine red, my heart was beating through my chest, and there were two round soaking wet geometric shapes under each of my armpits.

AMBER'S STORY

THE FIRST GIRL I met after being forced to switch to dorm C was my new bunkie, Detainee Ashe. She was unusually young, clean, and pretty. Her long blond hair, pulled back in the mandatory ponytail, shone under the fluorescent lighting. Her face was attractive, even without makeup. She couldn't have been much more than seventeen years old.

"Hi, bunkie. You can have the bottom bunk, ma'am." And she began to move her sheets and pillow to the upper bunk. I couldn't believe my eyes. Up until then, my experience with all my past bunkies had been quite the opposite. They were going to score the lower bunk or die. But this new girl, she was different.

I took an instant liking to her. She was quiet and reserved, maybe even a little self-controlled, which was something I had not witnessed in weeks. I began to place my sheets on my new bottom bunk, thinking the whole time of how very nice it was going to be. I would no longer have to climb endlessly up and down, bruising my poor legs every time these bozos decided to take one of their numerous head counts.

It took a few days before she really talked to me, which I have learned over the years is usually the case with most human beings worth befriending. When she finally did decide to let her guard down somewhat, I began to learn a few things about her and her situation. The first thing I learned was her first name, when she instructed me soon after we met to call her Amber and not Detainee Ashe. After the first week or so, we began to build up some trust between us, a rare phenomenon indeed inside those walls. And as soon as the trust came, so did the story.

It seemed that a few months previously, she and her then current boyfriend, Billy, were racking their young brains for something to do one muggy long small-town Georgia spring night. "I got it!" Billy exclaimed. "We'll go on up to the DOT and play around on the big equipment. Ah always wanted tuh do that!"

Amber was more hesitant. "Weeell, I don't know . . . we could get in a lot of trouble if we get caught. I don't think we better."

"Uh, come on, sweet' pie! It ain't gonna hurt nobody. We'll putt the stuff raught back. Nobody won't never know we was there. Come on! Ride ya on a backhoe, ya liddle ho!" And he broke out into one of his famous full-fledged, come-from-the-belly horselaughs. He was such an irresistible combination of baby adorable and sexy hunk when he did that, that she temporarily agreed to pull the stunt off in her fleeting moment of weakness.

But as they got nearer and nearer to the potential playground, she got less and less sure of her commitment to this proposed machinery madness. She was driving her mother's new car that night, and she knew she had to be careful. When they were about a mile from the site of the midnight machinery motion, she cleared her throat and spoke quietly. "I don't think I'm gonna do this, OK, Billy? I gotta get Mom's car back anyhow. It's almost twelve."

Billy made one more attempt. He knew this one had to work. "Ya remember when we made love under that there tractor in yer uncle's barn? Wasn't that jist the bestest sex we ever had, sweet' pie? Wuh, ya ain't seen *nothin'* yet, sugar, till ya had it in the bucket of a bulldozer— while it's ten feet up in the air!"

Speaking of feet, hers were getting mighty cold as they got closer and closer to the proposed scene of the midnight crime. "Sorry, Billy, I'm just not up to it tonight. Let's go do something else. We could go to the Burger King and see if Buddy's there."

Now he was mad. "No, Ah said Ah's gonna do this, an' *Ah am!* Now if you don't wanna be a part o' this, if yer too goddamn *chickenshit* or whatever the hell's got in ya, then *fine!* Jist drop me off here. Ah'll walk the rest o' the goddamn way, Miss Yella Belly! Ya wouldn't o' bin no fun anyhow."

That was when she tried her best to stop him. "Please, Billy, *puleeeeeaze*, don't do this, OK? I got a bad feeling about it. We can find something else to do."

"Ah, fuck you," he mumbled as he slammed the door in her face and began to walk the deserted country road in the solitary darkness. "You gonna be sorry ya didn't come with me when Ah tell ya how fun it was tomorrow."

But tomorrow found boyfriend Billy locked up in the county jail, when routine midnight patrol caught him ramming an eight-ton backhoe full speed into a stationary pouring truck in the highway curb. Billy's vandalizing venture had turned quite destructive. There were small, car-sized holes knocked into the bricks that made up the Department of Transportation Building. The fourteen-foot chain-link fence had been rammed open with a John Deere 450 bulldozer, and various pieces of heavy highway equipment were scattered on the grassy hills and deep ditches outside. In the end, the destruction added up to only a few thousand dollars; but Billy, a little tipsy on Bud Light at the time of his Breathalyzer, was in major felony-scale trouble. His midnight mischief, his rowdy, reckless rides, would end up costing him much more than his freedom.

You can probably guess the rest of the story. In desperation and in a final pathetic attempt to save his own ass, he turned the story of that fateful night around. It was his girlfriend Amber's whole idea. She had tricked him into doing it on a dare. She had told him to knock a few pieces of DOT equipment around for her, and she would give him a little piece of heaven in return. Why, he wouldn't even have *thought* of it if she hadn't dropped him off in her mother's new Honda.

After 5½ months in county lockup, the alienation of her entire family, the suffering experienced at the hands of her Benedict Arnold boyfriend, and the abrupt end of her promising young high school years, Amber was sentenced by a dull, spiritless, lethargic judge to eighteen months in an "appropriate women's detention center within the state of Georgia" with ten years' probation and a twenty-thousand-dollar fine. After her bout at the women's detention center, she was to reside for three years in what was called a diversion center. Here, she would live with other felons, work days and some nights as a waitress in a town she had never seen before, check in several times a day, and be locked in her bedroom at night. Because she had driven the car that dropped Billy the Vandal off that night, Amber's young life was over at age seventeen.

She tearfully told me the rest of the story. She had already been in Nutter now for eleven months. The first seven months, she had been given a great work detail that she truly enjoyed. She had been taken off campus every day with a few of the "better" detainees, and they worked on improving the small-scale landscapes of the local park and the yards of various nonprofit organizations. I could tell from the way she talked that she had really delighted in planting daisies, marigolds, and rose bushes in the awaiting flower beds of these public places. She had watered, fertilized, and watched these happy little miracles grow. The outside, with its fleck of freedom, had appealed to her, and she had tried her best to adapt to her dirty hit below the belt.

Just when she had learned to take it day by day, to exist in this daily hellhole, the news came down from Queen Red herself, and it wasn't good. It seemed that Billy, sentenced by the same burned-out judge, to ten years in state prison with no chance of parole had tied his bedsheets together and hung his poor, confused eighteen-year-old body from the light fixture in his cell. He had been in solitary confinement for refusal to go to lunch several days in a row, so he had no cellmate to protect him from himself. The detached, sluggish guards had discovered his act of final desperation long after rigor mortis had set in.

Amber was not to go to the funeral. She was not to have any correspondence of any kind with his family. In fact, Queen Red was sorry, but she was going to have to be taken off her current work detail immediately. The queen told Amber that, when such incidences occur, the girl becomes an automatic flight risk, so she must be immediately switched to a heavily guarded *inside* work detail.

As of this second, Amber was now officially switched to kitchen detail, morning shift. So there we were, the two of us, she a kitchen worker due to her ex-boyfriend's tragic self-destruction and me a kitchen slave due to my horrible, unthinkably violent nature. We were two peas in a pod, all right.

I was never quite on my game after that. There was one mouthy short, little girl who had gotten under my skin ever since I had arrived in dorm C. Her bunk was kitty-corner from mine, and of one thing I was quite certain. She *never*—no, *never*—shut up. Day and night and morning and evening, it was talk, talk, talk, jabber, jabber, jabber. Her mouth was home to a virtual chin-wag, a talkfest, an unstoppable bull session. And all those around her were the poor, unfortunate victims of her verbal patter.

The few times that I was bored enough to listen, none of the jaw flapping made much sense or even seemed the least bit necessary at all. It revolved around subjects that had no substance, credibility, or even any meaning. She gabbed incessantly about her past and people who had mistreated her in various ways, only if these fictional people had done just half of what she claimed they had, she would have been dead and six feet under years ago. She was downright obsessed with knives, guns, and weapons of torture. She rattled on about machetes, blades, stun guns, and brass knuckles. She ranted about various uses for ropes and chains that I had never even deemed possible.

Her favorite form of torture seemed to involve fires and unmerciful burnings. One day a picture of a protester from another country made the second page of the *Nutter Gazette*. In his final despair, he had doused himself with gasoline and set his poor skinny body on fire. The black and white inset depicted a human fireball with a few half-interested bystanders standing and gawking, but most of the people in the background were just walking by, going about their daily business. Little jabber box liked—no, *loved* that picture. She tore it out carefully after staring it down for several minutes and showing it to anyone who would look. Then she hung it upside down with toothpaste for adhesive under the bunk bed above hers so the guards couldn't see it, but she could rivet her own eyes on it for hours while lying on her bottom bunk.

Most of the time, though, she just spent bossing everyone else around. She made my first few days in the kitchen as miserable as possible. During food prep and kitchen prep time, she didn't have much of a window to pick on me. Since she was in the mop and bucket brigade, the kitchen supervisor was breathing right down her neck. The guard assigned to that duty seemed to be partial toward the swabbers of the kitchen deck probably because the detainees assigned to that particular task tended to be the ones who had the most problems with self-control. And that definitely included Little Miss Loudmouth. So during the preparation phase, she didn't have much of a chance to call the shots. But after the meal had been served and it was time for cleanup, it was a much different story. Then the kitchen guard let up, and Little Miss Loudmouth was free to conduct her straw boss business.

"Hey, White girl, come her! Let see how smart you is! Dis here is how we do da cleanups!" she hollered across the kitchen to me on my first day. She was standing in front of the largest piece of kitchen equipment I had ever laid my eyes on. It was a gargantuan hunk of polished stainless steel on wheels.

"Fers', you put dis stuff on it." And she dipped a chewed-up rag into a plastic bucket of liquid and then swiped it rapidly over the huge stainless steel monster. "Den you shine it up reeal nice an' purdy." And she took a clean, dry rag and rubbed it with an impressive amount of force over the awaiting apparatus. "Now *you* try it."

Not knowing exactly what to do—after all, it was my first day in the kitchen—and also not knowing exactly what her title was, I decided it was probably in my best interest to listen to Little Miss Twit. So I obediently repeated her demonstration, to the delight of several of the other kitchen detainees who had gathered to watch the outcome of Miss Gabby's newest attempt at self-professed kitchen taskmaster.

"Oh! Dat's gooood! You so good! You be a smart little White girl den, huh? You so damn good I's gonna let choo do dat ebery day, OK? Dis be one o' yer jobs den." And with that, she yelled across the kitchen at another girl who looked remarkably like her. "Hey, Latisha, dis one's real smart, an' she listen good! I t'ink Ah'll keep her as one o' our little White slaves den. Dat aw right wif you?"

The girl called Latisha was giggling into her cleaning rag. "Aw right den, boss, whateber you say. I kin find lotsa t'ings fer her to do."

I looked up at the entire kitchen crew and saw faces, both black and white, snickering, giggling, and smirking. Some were laughing into their sleeves. Others were chortling into dirty cleaning rags they held up to their amused faces. And I knew that I had been had.

After that, I stayed clear of Little Miss Loudmouth, that is, as clear as she would let me stay. She continued to harass me when on kitchen duty, and I pretty much put up with it out of pure fear of what might happen if I didn't. After all, she was pretty psycho.

Morning kitchen duty proved to be fairly challenging. The hours alone caused one to throw down the gauntlet. Morning kitchen workers were required to arise at two thirty. At that time, a thorough and well-described shower was requisite for each and every girl. No one, absolutely *no one*, was theoretically allowed into the kitchen without first being scrubbed, rubbed, scoured, and showered as squeaky clean as humanly possible. The written description was quite graphic: "Every nail, both finger and toes, and every orifice—eyes, nostrils, ear canals, and mouth (and a few we shall not mention)—was to be thoroughly sterilized before one could enter the sacred grounds of the Nutter Kitchen." So we, the poor souls assigned to morning duty, were allotted one full precious hour—from two thirty to three thirty—to accomplish this task.

The reality of the ideal situation went more like this: At two twenty every single morning, from the time I was assigned morning kitchen duty until the day I left, Detainee Brookshire—being the chronic insomniac that I was at the time—arose and took a solitary shower in the quite deserted bathroom A. Actually, I rather enjoyed it in a way. It was kinda like I had beaten the whole wide world up and was performing a merry aqueous monologue. It was very possibly the best time of the day. And it never ceased to amaze me. My weary eyes popped open precisely at two twenty each and every morning. I knew it because the huge institutional-type clock hung on the wall so close to my bunk that I could read it, even before I got my contacts placed into my tired, bloodshot eyes—no alarm clocks, no clock radios announcing the day, no human arousers, no intercom awakenings.

For the other fifteen kitchen workers, however, the story was quite different. Most required a human arouser in the form of an irate guard. This did not occur until about 3:05 a.m. or whenever the guard on duty felt like it. At least half of those refused to get out of bed until the second arousal, fifteen minutes later. By that time, both bathroom A and bathroom B resembled the mad rush of factory workers clearing out a burning rubber plant. That included the girls who even remotely gave a shit about cleanliness—maybe about seven of them or so. The other eight couldn't have cared less. They were the ones who lay in the cozy warm bunks until 3:25 a.m. and then scrambled like insanely psychotic madwomen running from impending shock treatments. By that time, they had exactly five minutes to arise, use the bathroom, make their bunks up in perfect military manner, polish their black boots, throw on their khaki uniforms, place their pajamas in black manual prescribed position in their footlockers, place the kitchen hairnet on their heads in described manner, and line up in a perfect *I* formation by the time the grouchy, huffy, cantankerous old morning guard on duty showed up at dorm C's outside door.

Actually, I rather enjoyed the period from 3:05 a.m. until we lined up for kitchen duty at 3:30 a.m. I had been totally ready—boots polished, hairnet placed, well-creased uniform on, bed made, and pajamas positioned—for at least twenty-five minutes by the time of the great scramble. Hell, most mornings, I'd even had time by then to prop up my boots and read over the previous evening's newspaper (the one that had been nearly impossible to score the evening before not because any of the girls cared one little bit about current events or anything of true substance in the news but because they were all fighting over the horoscope page and hogging the comic section). Peeking over the paper, wiggling my toes in my heavy boots, and scratching my netted head, I became the morn-time mastermind anthropologist on duty, the morning colossus of human behavioral knowledge. And oh, what a subject of study it was! I would not have believed that such human behavior was possible without having witnessed it firsthand every single morning I was privileged enough to be on morning kitchen duty at the great institution of Nutter Women's Detention Center.

Several of the morning slugs did bother me, though, especially one nasty, filthy little detainee named Maria Escelero. Her advanced periodontal disease alone could have stopped a freight train. I first smelled it when I was way across the room from her. I recognized the familiar stench as soon as I caught a whiff of it. Maria's oral cavity was a well-established, truly mind-boggling offense to the nostrils. The rotting gums and necrotic periodontal ligaments caused her yellowed teeth to wave in the breeze and her mouth to reek of odors yet to be discovered on the earth. Why such a dentally challenged person was allowed to be within ten feet of an institutional kitchen was beyond my wildest speculations. Not only that, but she was also one of those included in the group of "never took a shower, don't know the meaning of one, and probably never intend to take one." The mixture of her advanced periodontal disease and her total lack of personal body hygiene created an odor that one would not quickly forget.

Maria was assigned to tasks in the kitchen that involved dusting, swiping, scraping, and goop scooping of the numerous pieces of heavy stainless steel equipment. Her favorite piece, by far, was the gigantic silver exhaust fan that hung directly above the sandwich preparation butcher block table. She reveled in hours and hours of disassembling the many filters, racks, frames, and fan blades that made up the monstrous fixture. This daily obsessive-compulsive practice sent an infinite number of unidentifiable particles sailing pretty regularly into the ever-recurring epicurean luncheon delights, otherwise known as the mystery meat and PBJ sandwiches.

Out of all the job descriptions in the morning kitchen duty, the title of "sandwich maker" probably won the contest. It was the crème de la crème of kitchen positions. There were only two girls allowed to become mystery meat and peanut butter sandwich artists, and these two were chosen with the utmost of care. They had to possess certain traits, such as quickness of mind, nimbleness of fingers, ability to distribute square items evenly, attention to detail, capacity to spread sticky substances in a single swipe, and agility in enshrouding the finished pieces of art in miles and miles of transparent swaddling clothes. When I first arrived in the kitchen, the two lucky sandwich craftsmen were my bunkie, Amber, and a girl named Jennifer.

Jennifer was bright, bubbly, and full of life. She was a daily breath of fresh air, a shining ray of sunshine, when we all needed it the most. She was the type of person whom everyone liked. You couldn't help but like her. Her friendly, outgoing nature made her totally approachable, accessible, and unrestrained. With most of the girls at Nutter, one was quite frightened of what might happen if one so much as spoke a good-morning phrase. Not so with Jennifer. Her gregarious nature made her a true gem of blissfulness. She seemed to be constantly surrounded by Nutter fans.

On my third day in the kitchen, she noticed me standing in a corner, attempting to hide from Little Miss Bossy Pants. I had just finished her latest job description for me, which involved scrubbing and polishing two pieces of gigantic stainless steel equipment. I must have looked rather desperate in my effort to elude because she approached me kind of on the sly. "Hey, come here. I wanna show you how to do something," she said gently, taking a hold of my arm and leading me toward the sandwich-making table. "I think you'll be real good at this." And she positioned me in front of the most slices of doughy white bread I had ever seen in my life. "See, ya fill the whole table with bread. Then you build the sandwiches up like a big, tall tower."

I observed and noticed that she and my bunkie, Amber, were busy literally building sandwiches, not making sandwiches, not creating sandwiches but *building* sandwiches. As I observed, I couldn't believe my eyes. The initial step was to carefully yet swiftly place a single piece of square white bread onto a supercolossal slab of thick, beat-up wood. There were around 220 detainees at the WDC, and each and every one needed one of these culinary delights for her lunch. So 220 pieces of bread were laid down on the rectangular bulky, makeshift tabletop. The next step was to quickly place a perfectly square, pressed, and highly processed piece of repugnant mystery meat on top of the cheap doughy bread. Then with sleight of hand, a piece of yellow government cheese—boasting the same exact measurements as the obnoxious meat—was dealt on the mystery meat. This was followed by a second piece of stale white bread. I was a little confused when the speedy sandwich builders threw yet another piece of boxy bread on top of the last one. But then it all came to light when I realized that the blue-streak builders were now on sandwich no. 2. They were singing the same old song. A second piece of pinkish mystery meat was placed atop the bargain-basement squishy bread, followed swiftly by a yellow square of cheese, which was ended by a fourth slice of bread. A fifth slice went down before I realized it.

But they were not done yet. Oh, no, the best was yet to come. Up until this point, it had been fairly easy for the sandwich architects to stack their tasty towers. Now here came the true challenge. The PBJ portion of the giant Dagwood was up and ready to take center stage. I watched with bulging eyes and gaping mouth as the two master builders grabbed two huge spatulas and shoved them up to their elbows into a mammoth vat of sticky peanut butter. What happened next was a sight to behold. The two artisans placed that peanut butter onto that top piece of soft white bread in one fell swoop. That was it—a single swipe on each of the 220 slices, perfectly placed and perfectly timed. It was like a sticky, peanutty symphony. The gluey peanut butter was no challenge to these sandwich erectors, no, sir.

The next verse in the PBJ concert was placement of the jelly. A titanic tub of gooey strawberry jelly emerged onto the scene. A small measuring device—somewhere near a teaspoon, I estimated—measured out the tiny bit of jelly allowed for each sandwich. This was quite a contrast to the monstrous spatula that the two sandwich artists had used for the peanut butter. I reckoned that the state did not feel that expensive strawberry jelly was that necessary for 220 misfits.

The grand finale was the placement of the final pasty square. The top slice of bread was rapidly shuffled out on top of the jelly and then squished down in a final effort to spread the tiny bit of sweet strawberry pectin across the gummy peanut butter. There they were, three sandwiches for each and every inmate.

I marveled at the finished product. There they were in all their glory, 220 towers of tastiness, scrumptious pillars of flavor, yummy skyscrapers of protein. I was awestruck by the fact that twelve total layers of cheap icky ingredients in 220 towers of creation were balancing and actually all holding together. I'd have to admit that, somewhere along the entire process, I had expected to see at least a few of the eight-inch creations topple over. But I didn't have much time to ponder this. The final step was coming up.

I watched as Jennifer and Amber dragged out a humungous roll of cling wrap and placed it on a second colossal-sized wooden tabletop positioned directly behind the tabletop of towers. The two girls began to double-team. One pulled out large squares of cling wrap while the second girl retrieved the sandwich towers from the original tabletop. The wrapper worked fast and furiously, placing and tucking and bundling each meaty creation. The sandwich retriever then began to multitask by carrying each sandwich spire in one hand while grabbing a folded brown paper bag with the other hand and waving it furiously in the wind until it inflated. The small brown paper bags were placed in front of the sandwich swaddler. That allowed her to plop the wrapped towers into the opened and awaiting paper bags. A bruised apple or green orange was tossed carelessly on top of the doughy creation, the paper bag was quickly folded over, and—voila!—lunch was served, girls.

I wondered why the heavy piece of fruit was not placed in the bag first. It seemed such a shame to squish the final tower of meat, cheese, and peanut butter after they had been so painstakingly constructed. I deduced that maybe it was because someone at the top was trying to get the detainees to ingest a piece of fruit a day. After all, I had observed that I seemed to be the only detainee who ever ate the piece of fruit.

The sandwich production being complete, Jennifer and Amber both approached me. Jennifer did the talking. "Hey, come here for a second. I have something I gotta tell you."

I walked over closer to her. She motioned for me to come even closer. She positioned herself to whisper something in my ear. "Hey, don't tell anyone this, but I'm outa here tomorrow morning," she whispered. "I don't want anyone to know, OK?"

I was shocked and also a little sad. Our ray of sunshine at Nutter was leaving us. But I didn't have much time to ponder. The two sandwich artists were acting as if they had something very important to tell me.

"Amber and me have picked you to take my place. You can start making sandwiches with Amber tomorrow. We have already run our choice by the kitchen supervisor. You're *in*, girl."

I didn't know what to think. I was one of the two chosen kitchen workers, the kitchen elite, the beautiful people, the blue bloods of the canteen—no more scrubbing, polishing stainless steel, and washing dishes for me; no more taking orders from Little Miss Loudmouth, no, sir. I was cookhouse aristocracy now.

A brief moment of doubt swept over me. What if I couldn't keep up the sandwich-making pace? What if I stacked the ingredients in the wrong order? What if, god forbid, my sandwich towers toppled over? But then I calmed myself down. This was going to be a piece of cake compared with what I had endured. Why, I had been making sandwiches for my kids for countless years. The only difference was that my kids' sandwiches had been made out of quality ingredients and cut into fun shapes with various cookie cutters. My kids' sandwiches had been fabricated with love and lots of creative juices. I was a shoo-in for this job.

That evening at outside rotation, Jennifer and I spent the yard time talking about her release the next day. We reminisced about times we had shared at the Nutter Women's Detention Center. We laughed about the floor waxers and the Dumpster Babies and Sergeant Dairy Queen. We shuddered about Queen Red and Warden Wino. Jennifer excitedly told me about her big plans she had for her life after release.

As we were nonstop chattering, we both looked up at the evening sky simultaneously. The talking immediately ceased, and our mouths dropped open in disbelief. It was sunset, and the evening sky was aflame with colors. I had never witnessed such absolute splendor. Vivid reds, coral oranges, lemon yellows, sapphire blues, and royal purples all spread across the vault of heaven. They danced and waved across the dusky palette as if they were alive. It was as if the heavens had burst wide open. Our eyes were glued to the celestial spectacle. Neither of us spoke. In a final gesture of heavenly farewell, the blazing summer sun tucked her head under the earth and nodded off to sleep. We both let out audible gasps. This was a once-in-a-lifetime event. I had never in my life looked on anything like that, and I probably never would again.

Jennifer and I didn't speak for a few minutes after we got back inside our dorm. The whole event was just too spiritually overwhelming. But after a little while, she came up to me in a total state of excitement.

"Hey, I forgot to tell you. You and me are going to have a party, a farewell party for me, just the two of us. Don't tell anyone, OK?"

I nodded. What was she up to now?

"What ya got left in your last commissary order food-wise?"

I slowly unlocked my drawer and took inventory. "I got twenty-two peanut M&M's and a small chocolate brownie," I replied.

"Great, I got a half-eaten bag of Doritos and a little sleeve of cashews. Let's party." She headed toward the bathroom. I wondered if all the excitement had made her have to pee. But soon she came back clutching wads of cheap brown paper towels in both hands. She waved them in the air. "What I have here is our party plates and bowls," she announced.

Now I *knew* she had gone bonkers. Plates and bowls out of paper towels? Nothing like paper plates or bowls or cups were offered through commissary, no plastic silverware either. We just had to make do eating our commissary food with our fingers—no cutting our food into polite little bites, eating sloppy foods with a fork, or wiping our messy mouths with napkins, nope. The animals were kept animals.

Jennifer went to work. "I'm gonna do a little paper origami here," she divulged, and she began to fold, tuck, and shape. When she was done, to my absolute surprise, a small brown bowl and two tiny paper plates were born. She quickly placed my twenty-two peanut M&M's and her cashews in the bowl and then unwrapped my small brownie and placed it on one of the plates. The chocolate brownie was carefully torn into four equal pieces. The Doritos was placed, one at a time, in a circular pattern around the cashews and M&M's in the bowl. She then brought out a few of her favorite pieces of artwork, which were crayon and colored pencil drawings on white sheets of paper. These had been given to her by several different detainees, her fan base. She spread the artwork all around our party place.

We both sighed and admired the spread. We sat cross-legged on the cold tile floor, propped our backs against my lower metal bunk, and enjoyed the two-woman party. Of all the fancy parties I had been to in my lifetime, this was my favorite.

STRIKE WHILE THE IRON IS HOT

SOON AFTER THE White slave incident with Little Miss Loudmouth, one of those mornings occurred. You know the type I'm talking about, one of those mornings when nothing goes right. I got up to take my mandatory two-thirty shower, and the water was ice cold with no pressure. My towel was still dripping wet from the night before. I went to polish my boots, and the black polish was all gone. I tripped and almost fell on the waxed glass-top floors on my way in line to the kitchen. Once in the kitchen, the balding girl with the gum disease wouldn't let up about cleaning the ducts above the sandwich prep area, and dead bugs and cobwebs were cascading down into my mystery meat sandwiches, which I later got blamed for. Mac and I got a verbal tongue-lashing by the kitchen supervisor for cutting the coffee cake wrong and for eating the middle pieces ourselves instead of the burned end pieces. During cleanup, Little Miss Loudmouth and her cronies were especially abusive; and when I got stuck at the tray return window without a minute's training on how to operate the monstrous dishwasher, I got cussed out and almost slapped by the kitchen guard for not being able to rinse the hundreds of trays off and stick them in the dishwasher quickly enough.

To top it all off, Queen Red decided to make this particular day her day to bitch much more than usual about inspection. When kitchen duty was over, the entire crew of kitchen workers was forced to sit at a group of tables and take all our boots and socks off while a strange little white-haired man inspected all our feet and toes. Then we waited at least three times longer than usual for a guard to come down the hall to return us to dorm C. To say the least, I was not in the best of moods nor mental state by the time we were being escorted down the hall.

I glanced up at a hall clock and discovered that it was soon going to be time to go back and serve lunch, no time for the much-coveted morning nap today for the kitchen crew. So I decided to grab these few minutes to duck into the library and iron my uniform for tomorrow. After all, rule no. 8 stated, "Detainees are expected to iron their issued uniforms each and every day. . . . Twelve irons are located in the library . . . Failure to iron one's uniform will result in a DR."

The guard escorting us back to the dorm had thought to pass our group first through uniform issuance since our day was already running behind. So it was the perfect time to duck out of line and into the library to iron. I had just enough time before lunch. But I was not the only one who had the brainstorm. Quite unfortunately, another one who thought of the same schedule was Little Miss Loudmouth. Now I was not really sure if she had thought of the idea herself or if she had simply followed my lead into the library, but what went on shortly thereafter made that quite immaterial.

I had already had the day from hell, and my feeble, exhausted, mentally whipped mind was absolutely set on getting that uniform ironed before lunch detail. But at least six of Loudmouth's cronies had followed her into the library, and around five girls were already ironing when we arrived. I knew what I was up against, so I ran over to the closest open iron and grabbed on to it for dear life. I had not made one good ironing swipe on my uniform before Miss Loudmouth was puffing her little flat chest out directly in my face. "I don't t'ink so, Whitey. You sees, dis here ar'n belong to Laquisha here." And she forcibly pulled one of her wimpy sidekicks over by the arm. "You jis' gonna hab ta wait yer turn."

Now on any other day, any day at all, I would have simply stepped back and surrendered the iron. After all, any kind of confrontation was not worth risking the possibility of getting one of the dreaded DRs. Yes, this was a no-brainer. Who cared if I got my uniform ironed right at that very moment? I could do it later. That would have been my reasoning on any other day but not this day. That iron was mine, fair and square. I had staked my claim, and it was legitimate. I was going to stand right there and use that iron as long as I pleased, until my uniform was just how I wanted it. I had gotten to that ironing station first, and I wasn't about to surrender it to some idiot moron named Laquisha.

So I continued to iron away with every fiber of my being. When Miss Loudmouth came a little closer and a little closer, puffing out her prepubescent chest a stone's throw away from my flushed face, I pretended not to notice. I just kept ironing. As soon as she figured out that I was just simply ignoring her, Miss Loudmouth became a force to be reckoned with. She got right up in my face. "I *said* dis here ar'n belong to Laquisha here. What, White girl, you hard o' hearin' er sumt'ing?" Her huge puffed-out lips were right against my cheek, and spit was flying everywhere. Her breath was enough to knock out a mule, and I found myself wondering if she had ever even owned a toothbrush.

I was trying my best to ignore her, but she was making it just about impossible. I started to estimate in my mind exactly how long it would take me to finish ironing the uniform to the point that it would barely pass inspection.

Her verbal abuse suddenly turned somewhat physical. Seeing that her attempts with colorful language had not gotten her anywhere, she turned to poking and prodding. Now standing behind my back, she reached her stubby little fingers around my shoulders and began to poke me sharply in the side of the neck. "Gib dat ar'n to Laquisha. Gib it ober *now*. Gib it ober *now . . . now . . . now . . .* now!" With every "now," I was the recipient of a sharp acrylic fingernail in the carotid.

Then it happened. I snapped. "I'll give it to Laquisha!" I screamed so loudly that every girl at every ironing station stopped her activity and looked up. With that, I picked the hot iron up, waved it high in the air, and pointed it straight at Little Miss Loudmouth. "Here! Maybe *you'd* like to have it awhile first!" I shook it wildly in her rather surprised face.

"Or how 'bout the rest of you assholes in here?" I shrieked, brandishing the red-hot press in their general direction. "Or what about you, *Laquisha*? Come on over here, and let's see what we can do with this baby!" I had stepped away from the ironing board now and was flaunting the sweltering weapon at her. "Oh, you don't want your *ar'n* anymore, Laquisha? What a shame!"

With that, I buried my head back in my work and continued to iron my uniform, all the while keeping my peripheral vision on Miss Loudmouth and Laquisha. I had won a battle with the creatures

DORAMAE BROOKSHIRE

from the kitchen. I was on fire. I could handle myself around these brute beasts, all right. You could hear a pin drop in that library. All conversation had ceased. All eyes were on me; the wimpy little weakling turned gutsy. Now it was *my* turn to puff my chest out and adopt a haughty expression.

Then it happened. My psychotic little outburst had not shaken Miss Loudmouth in the least. In fact, she was probably more at ease with me now than she had ever been. So shortly after my breakdown, she simply just reached under my legs and unplugged the iron. Then she stationed four of her gang members at key positions around the wall socket so I had no chance whatsoever of plugging my blessed iron back in. What could I do at this point? I did the only thing I could.

I stood there straight and tall, mustering up every ounce of my dignity, and continued to iron my uniform with the cold, dead instrument. When enough ironing time elapsed to satisfy me, I carefully folded my icy, wrinkled uniform up neatly and quietly exited the library. On my way back to the dorm, I could hear every girl in the library behind me laughing her guts out.

But life has a wonderful way of evening things out. Later that day, I got an urgent call to go immediately to Counselor Goldilocks's office. The way my day had been going so far, I wondered what in hell had happened now. Horrible things started to go through my mind, absolutely hideous scenarios of incidences that might have happened back home. Did someone in my family have an awful accident? Worse yet, had someone died? I knew that Goldilocks was terrified enough of me that she wouldn't be calling me down to her office just to chat.

By the time I arrived outside her door, I had worked myself up into quite a frenzy. Being true to form, Ms. Goldilocks made me suffer outside her door and wait while she was on, quite obviously, a personal phone call at her desk. By the time she called me in, I was totally convinced that every member of my family had come to some grisly demise. But as I entered her sterile world, I could tell by the delight on her face that the news was probably not negative, unless she really was the evil witch from the netherworld.

"Hi, Detainee Brookshire," she greeted me cheerfully while waving something long and ecru-colored in her pointy hand. It appeared to be a business-sized envelope. "Look what I have here for you. You have got some *legal correspondence*. By law, I have to hand-deliver this to you and watch you read it. You are one lucky girl. This very rarely happens here."

She was so excited that I couldn't believe my eyes. I didn't think the ole hag had it in her. Just what was this object of curiosity, this rectangular paper mystery, this *legal correspondence*? She handed it off to me as if it might break. A wide grin spread across her usually sober face. "Go ahead, open it." She gasped, visibly ready to jump out of her skin at any moment, and she thrust it in my general direction.

I readily accepted her paper offering and took a closer look at the new object of fascination. It was a letter—a letter with the return address from my good friend, my attorney, Richard J. Mason, good ole Ricky. Suddenly, my own curiosity got the better of me, and I wondered what in the world Ricky had to say to me at this point. So I did very willingly rip the mysterious missive open like an excited kid at Christmas ripping into a shrouded gift. My eyes began to scan the first paragraph. It read:

> Dr. Doramae Brookshire
> #420138
> P.O. Box 920
> The Big House
> Nutter, GA 30417
> Dorm A Bed 18
>
> Re: Doing Time
>
> Dear Doramae:
>
> I thought I would take a moment to write to you and see how you were doing in the Big House. I hope this letter finds you well and not with a "shiv" or a "shank" in your back. (I've learned a lot of prison terms from talking with my clients and watching movies.) Deborah and the gang

said hello. (Oops! I probably shouldn't say "gang" because it may make the Screws suspicious.) Deborah and the girls at the office said hello.

By this time, I knew the gist of the letter, but I just couldn't help myself. My speed-reading eyes traveled on to read the next paragraph:

> I thought about sending you a gift, but I wasn't sure what would be appropriate: file, saw, shovel, blowtorch? I figured Alice had already sent you a list of 101 things to do while doing time. Curl your hair with toilet paper, steal spoons and mold knives, tie bedsheets into long ropes for throwing across barbed wire, make paper-mache masks to fool the guards after you've dug your way out of the cell, etc. I'm looking for a CD for you since I figured you could listen to music while awaiting parole. I've ordered Charles Manson's greatest hits album featuring some of his favorites, like "Folsom Prison Blues," "Jailhouse Rock," "I Fought the Law and the Law Won," "Are You Lonesome Tonight?," etc. Maybe that will come in soon, and I'll mail it to you.

By this time, I was having a hell of a time trying to keep my face straight. That nut had written me a letter trying to cheer me up. The letter was so very hysterically funny that I could hardly keep myself from going on to paragraph 3. But I knew that if I attempted that, I would sure enough bust out into the loudest belly laugh Nutter had ever witnessed. And what would that say for their carefully screened mail, their closely scrutinized methods of mailroom censorship, their guideline of handling with kid gloves any *legal correspondence* that passed through their gates? So I began to carefully fold the letter up and place it back into its envelope.

"Well, is there anything you would like to tell me? Does your attorney's legal correspondence say anything I might need to know? Is your *situation* here going to change in any way? What do you want to tell me?" Goldilocks was shooting the questions at me so fast that I felt like I was back in the courtroom under interrogation.

And still, there was something so funny, so refreshingly ludicrous, so inexplicably absurd about this whole situation that I found myself sighing with a great deal of inner peace for the first time in what seemed to be an eternity. "No, there's nothing I really need to tell you," I replied.

"Just a letter telling me things I already knew," I lied. "My situation here won't be changing."

She looked like she might start crying. "OK then, you *sure*?" she asked one more time.

"Yes, ma'am," I answered, biting hard through my lower lip in an attempt to not go into giggling convulsions as I recalled the words *a file, a saw, a shovel, a blowtorch?*

"Well, all right then. If you have nothing to share with me at this point, you may return to your dorm." And she shot me a look that would stop Santa Claus dead in his tracks.

I had stolen her thunder, made off with her moment of grandeur, snatched up her time in the sun. Now what was she to tell her awaiting colleagues? That she had been entirely unsuccessful in her proper handling of a detainee's *legal correspondence*? That she had totally failed to find out what the mysterious document had contained? That she had—dare I say—not done her job?

I nearly ran back to the dorm. I couldn't wait to open Ricky's letter and finish reading it. But as I settled myself comfortably on my bunk and got into proper reading mode, Big Pat—my truck-driving neighbor—had other plans. "Hey, whatcha got there? That a letter? I don't never get no letters no more in here. My old man use ta write me, but he stopped awl that when Ah comed back fer the fourf time. Read yer letter ta me . . . pleeaze, pleaze, pleeaze?" Her bloodshot blue eyes looked especially sad.

"OK," I found myself saying to my own surprise. "But you can't tell anyone what it says 'cuz my counselor is after me about it."

"Oh, I woooon't. Ah promises." And I knew she was lying through her teeth.

But this letter was just too good to be kept to myself. Besides, I was getting a little tired of isolating myself so dramatically. "OK, this letter is from my attorney."

"Fer *reeeeal*?" she hollered.

"Yeah, for real," I replied. "Now listen to this." And I began to read the letter quietly to Pat. She hung on to every word. When I had gotten through the paragraphs that I had already read to myself in Goldilocks's presence, I went on to the next paragraph. It read:

> Maybe you could make a video. I saw one a while back entitled "Girls behind Bars," which was pretty good. The plot was a little weak, but the wardrobe, or lack thereof, was fantastic. But enough about that. I digress. I must say that, out of all the people in your family, you were the last one that I thought would end up with a felony record. I hope Rocky is not too ashamed. But it's better that they caught you sooner than later. This way, you will have a chance for rehabilitation and can make something of your life. Stealing from the government is not the way to go. After all, look at Bill Clinton, all the government employees, Willie Nelson . . . you see how they have ended up. Okay, Willie Nelson is not that good of an example. But look at the good you can do.
>
> I read that the literacy program is going to keep your job open for you. I think that's wonderful, and look at all the opportunities this opens for you. Illiterate readers will be better able to identify with an ex-con than they could with a "doctor." Fewer reading materials will be needed . . . Beginners can start learning to read by sounding out your prison tattoos. Maybe you could have the vowels tattooed on your toes, long vowel sounds on one foot and short vowel sounds on the other.
>
> You had to know they would catch you sooner or later. They always do. And they always catch the more notorious criminals through the use of financial records. Look at Al Capone, done in by the IRS . . . What would you have become if they had not caught you? Ma Brookshire and her gang? . . . Worse yet, what would have happened if you had been able to corrupt poor, innocent Bob? Would y'all have become like Bonnie and Clyde? You remember what

happened to them. Or would the two of you had been more like Frankie and Johnny (they were lovers) or Butch Cassidy and Sundance? Or Frank and Jesse? Sonny and Cher? Or Tom and Jerry? What could have happened? Count your lucky stars.

Remember, *crime does not pay* . . . unless, of course, you are a judge or work for the prosecutor's office or a defense lawyer with plenty of wealthy clients. (This is where I misjudged my practice.)

Tell beds 17 and 19 that I said hello.

Ricky

P.S. Please let me know if you need anything . . . as long as it does not involve caring for Bob or the boys.

By the time I was done reading the letter out loud to Pat, tears were streaming down my face from laughing so hard. Pat had been laughing too but with a deep expression of puzzlement on her sun-worn face the entire reading. I think she was having a very difficult time figuring out exactly *why* a detainee's defense attorney would send such a letter to his locked-up client. But her words didn't let on. "That there is da *funeeest* thang ah have *ever* heard in ma entire life. This here loryer o' yern, he had ta bin a *hooot* in the courtroom, huh?"

I thought back on how much I truly liked Ricky, how he had practically lived day and night in his office from the day of the incident until we finally figured out that the DA was not going to do anything about the charges, how loyal he was and genuinely concerned and willing to go that extra mile. There was no doubt about it. He was one of my best friends. Then I thought of how we had decided to "leave him behind" and go with Jack instead when it came down to the trial. And guilt grabbed my soul. "Yeah, he's real funny for sure," I managed to answer.

But Pat wouldn't let up. "You jist *gotta* read that letter to awl these here gerls. They awl need a good laugh. An' how you gonna write him back? Whatcha gonna say? Huh? I wanna read yer letter afore you send it back to him, OK? Now be shure ta let me git ahold o' that thang afore ya send it, aw right? 'Cuz Ah bet *choo* can write jist as good as he kin. Ah jist bet. An' where is this here loryer anyhows? Ah wants ta meet him. Why, Ah'd like him ta be *ma* loryer. Lord knows mine ain't doin' me a lick o' good."

At this point, I knew I had made an irreversible mistake by reading the letter to her. But since I couldn't take it back now, I decided to answer just her last question as briefly as possible. "Oh, I'm sure that Ricky is not taking any more clients. His practice is as busy as he can stand without losing his mind," I replied, wondering the whole time if I was the one who had lost mine.

"Well, aw right then," she said softly. "But that there's steel the best letter Ah ever heard." Then she went back to doing whatever it was she was wasting her time doing before I had arrived. She looked a little hurt. I felt a little culpable but only for a brief second.

As soon as I was sure she had turned her attention away from me, I settled in nicely on my bunk, fluffed the pillow under my tired head, and read and reread Ricky's letter until it became a memorized part of me. That comical piece of literature would serve as a lifesaver many more times during my stay.

After the arrival of my *legal correspondence*, it seemed that I briefly entered the excessive-attention-to-my-personal-mail era. I never quite figured out what happened there. Perhaps Pat, the truck driver, blabbed to everyone about my gem of an epistle from Ricky. Perhaps everyone at Nutter was getting a little jealous of the volume of mail I received daily, just like the girls back in Coward. Or perhaps it was simply some twisted type of inexplicable fate. Whatever the cause, all eyes became focused on Detainee Brookshire's messages from the outer world.

"Detainee Brookasure, you gots *fourteen* letters today," the tired guard on duty would announce, looking me up and down as if I was some type of circus freak.

"Dat lady ober dere gots *awl* da mail *ag'in* today," the little new detainee would grumble to her newfound friend.

"Well hell, why the fuck don't we jist make our new dorm activity be list'nin' ta Bahrooshy read her boring-ass letters to us fer fifteen hours a fuckin' day?" Lazy Laverne would candidly suggest.

There was one particular male guard who sort of gave me the creeps. He was short and stocky and, of course, like all the rest of the males I had been exposed to during my jailhouse visits, chock full of the Napoleon complex. His name was Officer Jenx. I had caught this weirdo staring at me on several different occasions. In fact, it was beyond staring. It was more like ogling.

It was one of those endless summer days when the guards had forgotten once again to get our mail out to us at three o'clock, like they were supposed to. I had gone into a brief panic, letting my less than positive thoughts get away with me. I wondered if this possibly may have been the fateful day I had been dreading so much—the day that I was to receive *no* mail, none whatsoever—when the call finally came. "Detaineeee Brookshear, come to the guard post for mail call," the half-male, half-female voice rang out, and I knew it was him.

On those days when they didn't bother to get the mail out to us until bedtime, they would not come to the dorms to do mail call but would instead page us to their station to pick it up. Then it was up to us to make the decision whether that mail was important enough to face the ornery rascals or have enough self-control to wait until tomorrow. I always chose the former.

Waiting in a very short line at the guard station, it was quickly my turn. I announced my arrival. "Sir, Detainee Brookshire, sir," I called out.

"Oh yes, yes, yes!" Jenx sang aloud. "I've been waiting for you, Brookshear. Seems *you* have some friends with quite the sense of humor there, detainee!" And he began to chuckle. These funny guys put '*Dr.* Brookshire' on your envelope. What a hoot! Tell 'um I thought that was pretty funny, OK?"

Now I once again had a split-second decision to make, and I made this one pretty darned fast. I squared up my chin, looked as dignified as I could in those ridiculous state-issued pajamas, and planted my bare feet firmly. "Officer, I *am* a doctor," I announced.

"Oh, come on now, detainee, the game is over. It's late, and I ain't got time fer all this mess. Yer as much a *doctor* as I am a rocket scientist. I oughta report your behavior to Ms. Sinestro. Instead, I'm gonna let this ride. Here, jist take yer mail an' go. Get outa my face."

And I halfway snatched the pile of snow-white missives from his scrawny hand and headed back to the awaiting lockup for the night. I really didn't think much of the incident. It was pretty much just like hundreds of other similar ones since I had been taken away. How were these ignorant little officers supposed to believe such a truth anyhow? I was beginning to question what was in the life of Dr. Brookshire myself. If I had to stay much longer in places like these, my self-identity would have been snuffed out forever.

The very next day, I noticed Officer Jenx hanging around the TV room of dorm C and gazing through the glass window a lot. It kinda creeped me out a little. Soon he actually entered the door and motioned to me to come out into the hall.

Oh god, I thought, *here it comes. I'm going to get my first DR for lying last night and saying I was a doctor. I should have just gone along with the joke.* But that was not what happened at all.

Officer Jenx didn't look so well. His little face was bright red, a tiny trickle of sweat was making its way down his left cheek, and he was tapping his right toe nervously. "Detainee Brookshire, I would like to offer my apology for last night. I have found out that you *are* a doctor, and I am sorry for any embarrassment I have caused you, OK?"

I was so totally flabbergasted—so absolutely blown away—by this apology, this acknowledgment of guardly error, that I was pretty sure I let out an audible gasp. All I could muster to say was "Oh that's OK."

"Are you sure 'cuz I really feel kinda bad about it," he returned.

"Yeah, I'm fine."

"We're cool then with this, huh?" he inquired.

"Yes, sir, we're cool." I returned and stared at the TV screen. I couldn't tell you what show was on. I was too confused at that point.

By the next day, I had thrown it around in my mind so many times that I had drawn the conclusion, right or wrong, that Jenx had performed the quite visible apology for the sake of saving his own pitiful behind. I reasoned that quite possibly, in the right circumstances, his nighttime ridicule could have turned into a detainee lawsuit. Little did he know that he didn't have to worry about such a thing from me. I was going to be perfectly happy to just get out of this freaking place and never look back.

On the days after the "yeah, right, you're a doctor" incident, it became clear to me that Jenx might have had a little more than a simple agenda on his plate. He began to kind of show up most everywhere I went. When I walked down the hall, he seemed to be close behind. When I needed an officer's permission for something, he always seemed to be the one available to me.

One hot, muggy summer's night, I was doing my usual. I was lucky enough that evening to be able to go outside for an hour or so right before sunset. The guards were in an unusually pleasant mood for some unknown reason, and they were allowing us to have outside break overtime. Like I said, I was doing my usual, which involved isolating myself as much as humanly possible. That meant finding a lonely space right over by the fence that overlooked a rather nasty little dirty pond. My senses of reality told me that this body of stagnant, thick, putrid water was more than likely runoff from the chicken farm's daily butchering. But my sense of mental survival sculpted it into a beautiful little bubbling brook full of delightful tiny, little sea creatures who put on a silly, whimsical little pond show exclusively for me whenever I was lucky enough to find a solitary seat on the ground on the other side of the fence. There I was, minding my own business, perfectly happy with the world at the moment, watching the cutest little orange and purple fish jump out of the clear blue water and the funny fat frog leap off the lovely flowered lily pad, when it happened.

He totally startled me, and I jumped right out of my skin. "Oh, sorry, Detainee Brookshire, I didn't mean to scare you," Jenx said.

He didn't realize how very scared I truly was at that moment. Everyone else who was outside at that time—and I mean *everyone*— was as far away from the two of us physically as was possible. In fact, they were way, way, *way* over on the opposite side of the exercise yard. To make matters worse, the vast majority of the girls were very busy

DORAMAE BROOKSHIRE

wrapping up a game of softball, and they wouldn't have noticed Jack the Ripper himself.

Now *I* was the one sweating. I tried to play it cool. "That's OK, I'm just a little jumpy tonight," I said.

"Oh, is anything wrong?" he inquired.

"No, not really. I'm fine."

The truth was I was *not* fine. Here I was, in quite the vulnerable position. I was lounging, almost lying, in the grass. It was almost dark, and *he* was standing over me, tapping his gun at his side with the silliest little grin all over his guilty-looking face.

There was only one thing to do. I jumped up so fast that I scared even myself a little. "Well, it's almost dark. I'd better start over to the lineup. I know they'll be blowing that whistle soon." And I almost sprinted over toward the safety of the crowd.

After that, he pretty much left me alone, but I still caught him gawking on several different occasions.

FREE AT LAST

FLORIDA FINCHER, THE self-confessed Walmart kleptomaniac, and I played our daily game of countdown to freedom. Each and every time we so much as caught a glimpse of each other, those fingers flew up in the air like so many fat little worms trying to squirm their way out of a suffocating dark hole. Before we knew it, the number of fingers waving in the air was down to a single handful and then four, three, two; and finally, it was the day we had both been wondering if we would ever see: the wonderful, magical, almost mystical *day before release*. We could barely contain our excitement. I think all the other girls thought we were signaling "we're number 1" to each other, and they took almost instant offense. Florida and I, however, knew the truth—that solitary digit wagging proudly in the Nutter air had a much deeper, more meaningful significance.

Near the end of my last day on kitchen duty, I was presented with a large manila envelope, contents unknown. I was halfway afraid to open it, but the pushy substantially sized kitchen supervisor that day acted as if it contained such a precious gem that curiosity finally got the best of me. As I ripped open the seal and peeked inside, a single stiff page was revealed. I pulled it out to get a better look. It was some sort of certificate. It was trimmed in red, white, and blue as if some attempt at national allegiance was at work here. It read:

> Let it be known to all that read this that *Doramae Brookshire* has been employed as a kitchen worker at the institution of *Women's Detention Center in Nutter, Georgia*, and is adequately trained in the art of kitchen duties.

It was signed at the bottom by Queen Red, the head drunk, and the kitchen supervisor for that particular day.

After she handed it to me and one other girl who was going to leave the next day, the super started in. "Dis here certifoocat is gonna help you girls git you a job wheneber you awl git outa here," she said proudly. "Workin' in a kitchen is *goooood* work, anyhows."

I held the cheap, patriotic certificate of proficiency up to the light. I pictured it in a black 8″ × 11½″ frame, the kind manufactured specifically for the purpose of framing all our lifetime achievements and accumulating them on some wall visible to the admiring public, the same generic black frames that held a whole wall full of professional credentials back home for me. I visualized my growing collection—a sheepskin from Bangdale State University declaring me the recipient of a bachelor's degree in early childhood education with a minor in English and boldly affirming that I was a magna cum laude special graduate, a specially mounted huge laminated degree stating that I had had bestowed on me the doctorate of medicine in dentistry from the School of Dental Education, a scroll announcing that I had successfully passed my fellowship in the Academy of General Dentistry, a graduating statement from the University of Florida for a specialty I had earned after dental school—several assorted certificates, honors, validations, and authorizations I had earned over the years all tied up in some way with the world of academia. All of a sudden, I visualized this kitchen-duty certificate hanging with my other collection, and I burst out in a fit of laughter.

"What's so damn funny ober dere, detainee?" the scary large kitchen super demanded. "You wants me ta take dat certifoocat back?"

"No, ma'am," I answered quickly. "I need it to hang up with my others back home."

On the day before release, we were required to do many ridiculous things. For a solid week, we had already been mandated to attend daily "release classes." These consisted of a series of stupefyingly boring instructional sessions, during which the struggling informer was forced to try her best to "prepare us for entering the outside world once again." These little pretend preparation circuses were especially irksome. Then there was the round-up-every-single-item-we-ever-issued-you-down-to-the-last-snap-on-your-ridiculous-state-pajamas exercise/threat. We were informed repeatedly that if we were caught with as much as a tooth off our state-issued black plastic comb on our person as we exited the gates, we would be charged with thievery and invited to spend another 120 to 360 with Queen Red.

But my favorite rule of departure was the exercise I dubbed "the surrender of the Nutter bible." Now there were many parts to this one. The pages within the sacred document must not be bent, folded, ripped, rippled, dog eared, scarred, or misshapen in any way. Nothing could be spilled on the contents, smeared, or fingerprinted. And woe be unto the poor soul who even *thought* about writing in the holy instrument. I really hadn't violated the Nutter bible, though it had crossed my mind on several different occasions. In the final count, I surrendered my black manual with no fight but with much sadness and regret for the poor future detainee who would be forced to turn its pages and spit back its contents soon.

There was a definite ritual to the Nutter exodus. To begin with, there was the early morning shuffle. This was characterized by every other detainee who was *not* leaving squaring off to win the ultimate honor of lugging the exiting inmate's extremely lumpish, cumbersome, ponderous mattress and other belongings awkwardly down the hall at four thirty. There, they were deposited with the "signing-out officer." At that point, the winner of the early morning shuffle was asked to leave and return to her awaiting dorm with its admiring fellow prisoners. There was absolutely no place for remaining detainees in the secretive world of the signing-out ritual. At the signing-out ritual, the signing-out officer gave us all a group lecture. "Everyone makes mistakes. Why, even *I* did once in my youth, but the important thing is to be clean, sober, good little girls for the rest of our natural lives." She whispered this secretly to us as if no one else must ever know its contents.

When the signing-out officer was done with us, we were led to another room where a rather cranky and half-awake officer reluctantly handed us our box of precious "property," and we were all told to take turns going to the restroom and putting on our street clothes. This was a rather momentous time for me. If I wasn't so overanxious to walk out that door with Bob, I think I would have taken the time to actually savor the moment when I got to drop those khaki *things* on the floor of the WDC for the last time and never look back. But instead, when it was finally my turn for the restroom, I rushed in and performed my clothes-changing duties like a freight train barreling helter-skelter down the track of no return.

By this time, it was only about six thirty, and we had to wait until nine for our rides outa here to arrive. I wondered how we would fill up that 2½ hours of excruciating pain. But there was no need to worry. The trusty officers at WDC had that all mapped out for us. The next springing free activity involved the in-your-face breakfast in our street clothes. This action consisted of marching us like decorated zoo animals in front of the poor gals who were left behind. They got to see us all gussied up in our street clothes. They got to see us get first in line at breakfast. They got to see the never-ending smiles on our awaiting faces. And they got to see Florida Fincher hold up her big *zero* and wave it in the air triumphantly.

Most of the pathetic souls we, hot shots, were fixin' to quit cold on were handling our little freedom flaunt pretty well. They smiled and patted us on our backs when they could get that close and even told us how very different and ravishing we looked in our street clothes, especially me, who was dressed for success in the courtroom. But there were a few of those left behind who weren't so happy with our whole pageantry of liberty. Lazy Laverne just glanced up at us between gulps and swigs. Maria Escelero curled her mustached lip and snarled and then looked down and muttered a long string of Spanish syllables. Poor little Mac looked as if she would burst into tears at any moment. She had once again convinced herself that she was losing the finest group of bosom buddies that she had ever encountered in her limited world of perpetual incarceration.

But the queen mother of all the gawkers and glowers was, of course, Little Miss Loudmouth. Our little cavalcade of emancipation march didn't impress her one tiny bit. In fact, she and her cluster of cronies made it their order of the day to try to make us all feel as ridiculous and foolish as possible. "Hey, White Trash Girl!" one of them screamed out at Florida Fincher. "Where'd ya git dat dare silly-ass ow'fit? Yer White-ass sticky fingers make off with it from one o' yer Walmarts while ya wuz liftin' one o' yer takes? Scored ya some ugly-ass rags dat day too, huh? Hell, ya coulda had a liddle more *taste* if ya wuz gonna git 'em at a ten-finger discount!"

Next it was my turn. "Den right next ta Ms. White Trash, we have Ms. High-and-Mighty Execyouteeve. She t'ink she reeally sumt'in' in dem black high heels and fancy-ass suit. Hey, where ya goin' when ya spring—to the White-ass cuntreee club? Git it? *Cunt*-ree club!"

At that, the whole coven of loudmouth cronies threw back their skinny necks and cackled like a flock of chickens who had just laid a coop full of golden eggs.

I couldn't tell you what we had for breakfast that last day of captivity. I was much too busy thinking about all the millions of things I was going to do once I sprang free. All I could remember was I swallowed that jail slop in one huge gulp. After the breakfast of breaking out, we free birds were instructed to meet at the nurse's station for our final statistical summaries. There, they poked, prodded, and degraded our half-naked bodies for the last time. I was pleased and a little shocked too to discover that, overall, I had managed to shed 22½ pounds during my sticky stint at summer camp, nothing but starches and cheap carbohydrates, and I had still shed two dress sizes. *See there?* I told myself. *At least* one *good thing came out of this ridiculous mess.* And I glanced down at my corrugated black suit, forming pools of wrinkles around my ankles.

After the nurse's last deflowering, they sat all of us, escaping prisoners, in the very same room where we had entered the world of the incarcerated. Flashbacks of the brazen black manual rushed over me. I heard Sergeant Dairy Queen yell, "Detaineees, you better git your sorry eyes into your Nutter bibles . . . now . . . now . . . now! I'll give you sorry buncha losers DR faster'n you can steal a Walmart CD player and bring it back for a refund!"

Well, it's only fitting, I thought, *that I should pass through this journey full cycle. Here I am, right back where I started.* At least I seemed to be able to pull off something that most of the others could not—that of avoiding the dreadful DR. I had kept my nose clean and stayed out of everyone's business but mostly had kept my mouth shut. It had taken every little, tiny scrap of self-control I could possibly muster. Oh, I had come close a couple of times—uncomfortably so the day of the room-full-of-hot-irons incident—but in the end, I had accomplished a DR-free record in Nutter, Georgia, home of the famous Nutter fruitcake. And I reminded myself, one last time, that I would never—no, *never*—place a single morsel of either one of two food items in my mouth. One was a Nutter chicken, the other a piece of Nutter fruitcake. This is a solemn vow that I have kept these many years.

As I sat waiting for my own personal independence day, I observed five weary floor waxers down on their scabby reddened knees, two of them scraping and grating and scratching the day-old wax up off the sparkling clean floor of the hallway, the other three endlessly laying down the new layer of liquid shine. And then it struck me. Actually, I had known this all along. The great Nutter waxathon was the biggest waste of human effort I had ever witnessed. In fact, it was much more than that. It was an emaciation of the psyche, a withering away of the will, an atrophy of the human spirit, a squandering of the soul.

I realized what the higher-ups were trying to accomplish here, and I couldn't agree more with their main mission. It was no doubt that the vast majority of these young prisoners needed to be taught some quick self-discipline in the worst way. Yes, they needed to be able to control all their youthful urges; or else, the endless cycle of lawbreaking-lockup-lawbreaking-lockup-lawbreaking-lockup would never come to a halt. *However*, how about some of the following suggestions?

- Helping out in the community. They could do countless community services, where they could see the need for human care and compassion surrounding them every day.
- Reaching out to those less fortunate, poverty-stricken, sick, mentally challenged, mentally ill, and so on.
- Making something for someone. Nothing boosts self-esteem more than constructing something of one's own creation and then presenting it to another human being in need.
- Volunteering at a hospital or in a hospice program. Many of these young girls just need to see the pain and suffering that the

truly sick and dying are experiencing to make a real difference in their attitude on life.

- Attending truly beneficial classes that will educate them about their destructive habits, not the ridiculous jokes that the counselors at Nutter call classes.
- Being given some true encouragement that they *can* accomplish some of their dreams. They *can* earn their GEDs, enter tech school, go to college, start a small business, or whatever they have always had visions of doing one day.

These girls spending their time at the women's detention center in Nutter, Georgia, were not bad people. They were just neglected, thrown away, deserted, abandoned, made to feel worthless and dirty and not wanted by society. They were court mandated to spend 60, 120, or 360 days living in another hell, something they were rather used to anyhow. But this was the state's chance to utilize this time to try to make a change—a true change—in many of their lives. Hey, the time will eventually pass. It always does. It did for me. Sixty, 120, or 360 days of learning that they are *not* worthless to society, of benefiting others and learning to reach out and become a part of things, of feeling like they can make a difference in this scary big world or 60, 120, or 360 days of being forced to remove day-old wax on your hands and knees and place new wax day after day after day—which one? Nutter chose the wax.

But I did not have too long to contemplate this atrocity. Soon the guards within eyesight seemed caught up in a sort of early morning shuffle. They were uncharacteristically moving from point A to point B in a rather harried manner. I wasn't quite sure what was up. Then I saw them—the blurred faces of those we love, the outsiders, the liberated, the emancipated, the free. And those beautiful people, those saints of liberty, those saviors of the lowly and unwanted, were here to spring us all free. They were here for our release, our uncaging, our disentanglement, from the Nutter incubus—the unknotting of the nightmare. And I knew in an instant that Bob would be one of the first in line. He always was, especially if it came to something really essential like this. Finally, the moment arrived when they allowed our emancipators to step forward. I could faintly see my liberator's face. It looked like they were making our rescuers sign their lives away at the window of liberty.

I could only imagine what was contained in the document of emancipation from the world of Nutter. The folks who came to spring us out were probably being made to sign a paper promising that they would make sure that we waxed our kitchen floors at least twice a week or that we would never wear shoes in the house, lest we scuff that perfect creation of lustrous sheen. I was certain the document of release included a promise to make us stand at attention nine times a day so our loved ones could make sure that we were still present. Or how about not muttering a word at the table during a meal? Or cramming the food down our throats as fast as we could humanly swallow? I was pretty sure that the release papers had to include those stipulations. What else could have been in those papers our liberators were being forced to sign?

Oh, gee, there were so many new skills and principles we Nutter chicks were taught that I couldn't venture to speculate. I guess you could say that our 60, 120, 240, or 360 days on the inside really taught us to be able to function well on the outside. Yes, the state of Georgia really knew what they were doing with this one. We jailbirds all left having learned valuable lessons, ready to turn our lives of sin around. Yes, sirree, this place would never see any of us again, no recidivism here. We were all well prepared to go it alone now. The dismal despair and total hopelessness of the whole situation enveloped me like an approaching black cloud from the tempest of the place of torment.

But Bob's smiling face brought me back. He had ended up second in line. Tiny Bonnie Brookensheer's mother and little son had beaten my Bob out. They were shaky, antsy, and nervous, just like her. *They probably haven't eaten for several days*, I thought. I also wondered just how early they had arisen to be able to beat Bob for such an important event. I drew the conclusion that Mama and grandson Brookensheer had probably camped overnight on the immaculate sidewalks of Nutter to be able to be first in line, kinda like waiting in line for tickets to a Grateful Dead concert, I concluded.

I watched Bonnie, the girl who got mixed up with me for 60-days, pass over to the other side. She was now officially a part of the free world. I watched her hug, kiss, embrace, squeeze, and clasp her loved ones. She was touching her little boy's face gently and gazing into his hurting eyes, and huge watery tears were spilling the whole time from hers.

My blood ran cold. This petite, little bundle of nerves had experienced the hell world of Nutter just because she had dared to confront her cheating, no-account husband. It was probably the only time in her life that Bonnie had even come close to attempting to right a wrong that had befallen her. Well, this little experience had taught her that it is not worth it to stick up for oneself, to try to demand a little respect, to attempt to feel a little self-esteem, to make your young son's world a better place. Bonnie Brookensheer would probably just go on the rest of her pitiful life letting men run all over her, letting others mistreat and hassle and abuse her in various ways, in short letting society beat her up.

But now it was my turn. As I passed over into the world of the free, I looked back over my shoulder at the hellhole I had been forced to endure for 60 endless long days—the blinding shiny floors, the captors in their slick stocking feet, the long lines of khaki-colored females at attention or postrest position or whatever position the guards commanded, Sergeant Dairy Queen sucking down another succulent treat in the girls' faces, Goldilocks shaming yet another piece of human scum, and the queen mother of them all yelling at the top of her redheaded lungs that the floor was not anywhere near clean enough. *And we wonder why we have problems with recidivism in this state*, I thought.

My turn was up. I ran into Bob's arms like a prisoner of war who had just been released from a world of daily torture. I grabbed him tightly around the neck and hung on for dear life. I gave him hug after hug after hug, clearly violating the Nutter single-hug rule. In fact, I wasn't so sure that I could ever let go. After an eternity of embracing emotion, Bob began to lead me toward the exit to freedom, my box of precious "property" tucked under his left arm. In the end, our great exodus was more like a subtle bowing out. We just sort of tucked our heads, slumped our shoulders, and ducked right out the outlet to liberty. But if I thought my secret departure went unnoticed, I had another thing coming.

As Bob and I ran for and settled into the awaiting convertible, at least twenty girls made a mad dash for the exercise yard fence. There, they hung on to the wire barrier, their long spindly fingers wrapped around the rectangular metal strands. Their eyes were bulging and hollow. Flashbacks of pictures I had seen of Holocaust victims penned up in concentration camps passed through my mind. At least half of them were waving wildly into the sweltering Georgia summer heat. They were all talking about me as if I was no longer there.

"I eees so glad she eees gone," observed the girl with no hair and waving teeth.

"Yeah, she was a real uppity White pain in the ass," added lazy Laverne.

"Dat fuckin' White cracka', she thought she fuckin' *owned* the place! If her White ass woulda bin here much longer, I woulda beat her cracka' ass fer fuckin' sure!" offered Little Miss Loudmouth. "Jis' look at her! She t'ink she really sumt'in' with dat man o' hers!"

"Hey, she wasn't so bad. I kinda liked her. She's gonna write me," stated Mac.

"That's my bunkie. Gonna miss her," commented my mysterious blond bunkmate. She was always a woman of few words.

"I don't know about you guys, but she helped me through this awful place. I'm going to miss her little pep talks," said the young redheaded girl who abused her daddy's credit card.

"Dat girl had da goddamn funneeeeest loreyer you ever damn he'rd of in yer whole goddamn life," added Pat, the truck driver.

In the end, the vast majority were waving wildly and yelling out various good-luck chants, even though they all appeared to be stuck somewhere between insanely jealous and downright depressed. Even limping Laverne, Maria Escelero, and Little Miss Loudmouth, my archenemy, were singing out praises for my release, my well-being, and for the happy future with my "man."

Chalk this whole exiting experience up to yet another jailbird phenomenon that I don't even care to understand, I thought. Girls who didn't even give you the time of day on the inside apparently felt compelled to have to give you a good-luck-may-God-be-with-you send-off. This was almost crazier than the fight over who gets to lug the nasty ten-ton mattress down the hall in the middle of the release night. I just didn't get it.

But as Bob and I buzzed off in the little green convertible, thoughts of the Nutter jailbirds faded like bad dreams in the dawn. The drive was short and sweet. Bob had rented a hotel room about two blocks away from the detention center so he could be nearby for the great release, and that was where we were headed now. Since it was still early in the morning, he had not been forced to check out yet. We both knew the plan. We had been talking and dreaming about it for eighty-two days now. We had missed each other's intimacy with an ache that could never be described.

The Nutter Motor Inn was nothing to brag about, but it was the only show in town. Actually, it was really a kind of little dive, but one would never have known that walking through the door of room 137. Slinging the door open and expecting the worst, I gasped in utter amazement. Bob, the guy who had never decorated or readied any place for entertainment in his entire life, had transformed this dumpy little joint into a virtual Mardi Gras. Multicolored streamers hung down from the light. Brightly hued balloons waved in the breeze of the broken-down air conditioner. The biggest bouquet of red roses and happy yellow daisies were placed carefully on the peeling wooden dresser. A huge handmade sign that read "Welcome home" swung over the bathroom door.

But the finishing touch—the icing on the cake—was the huge, astronomical, towering tray of fresh succulent fruits that was so carefully situated on the double bed farthest from the door, the one that was still made up. Strawberries, blueberries, grapes, pineapple chunks, apple slices, peach bites, and watermelon balls all raised their happy little heads up to me as if to say, *We missed you, but we're here now, so you can indulge your every fantasy. Go ahead, try us. Dig in!*

Bob sensed my preoccupation with the fruit tray, and he inched over to me and began to feed it to me gently. He closed the door to room 137 at the Nutter Motor Inn, and we made beautiful, sensual, innocent love over and over.

After checking out, the next stop was both absolutely essential and somewhat lifesaving. Thank god a two-bit town as scrawny as Nutter had a Dairy Queen. Of course, I had known this all along, compliments of Sergeant Dairy Queen. I knew her daily supply could not have been far off. Each and every day, all sixty of them, I had craved ice cream and the various succulent treats derived from it. In fact, it was probably the biggest miracle of all Nutterdom that I had not reached up while at attention in the hall and snatched the double-fudge Peanut Buster parfait out of her greedy little hand and then gone running like hell down the slippery corridor.

I've always been somewhat of an ice-cream-aholic. This addiction had begun early on in my life while observing my admirable parents practice their nightly ritual of one bowl of ice cream before retiring. To them, it was like One a Day multiple vitamins, only it was once-a-day multiple ice cream dosage instead. Because of this early exposure, ice cream had become pretty much an essential, expected part of my young life. And as we all know, early childhood habits quickly become ingrained as lifetime dependences. OK, I'd admit it. Ice cream was the psychological monkey on my back. I was a little bit embarrassed, possibly even somewhat uncomfortable, admitting that ice cream came second to making perfect love to my totally adoring husband, but I guess I would have to come clean here.

I had thought for eighty-two painful ice-cream-less days about which Dairy Queen treat was the perfect choice after going cold turkey, and the best conclusion that I could come up with was that the proper choice just had to be a Dairy Queen banana split. It was simple and straightforward and had been around forever. In the hotel room, I had changed into a pair of army green shorts and a white T-shirt that Bob had brought me from home. I felt funny now stepping up to the counter, a free woman in street clothes, and being able to order anything I desired. "Go ahead, honey," Bob urged, "anything you want."

I cleared my throat. "A banana split, please," I muttered. "Heavy on the hot fudge sauce, please."

Two Nutter locals, both men, were watching me with great interest. They looked hot and tired already, and it was only ten thirty in the morning. *Probably ducked out from a construction site to get some ice cream*, I thought. The interesting thing was they were both glaring at me as if they could tell my dirty little secret. I wondered if this town had the ability to determine exactly who had just been released from the beautiful clean facility over on Highway 305.

Suddenly, a very disturbing thought came to me. Was I going to be scarred the rest of my life into thinking that I was a transparent walking ex-con, that I transmitted some sort of criminal signal? That all the people surrounding me could easily see that I had been a jailbird? That I had become some kind of messed-up-in-the-head psychological freak? I caught myself in pure panic and took a deep breath. But this would have to wait. The Dairy Queen girl was handing me my banana split with double hot fudge sauce.

If any single food item had ever tasted quite as delectable as that first banana split after splitting from the joint, I can't recall just what. In fact, it wasn't just simply delectable. It was purely delightful, savory, succulent, luscious, 100 percent nectareous, ambrosial, food of the gods. Sergeant Dairy Queen had nothing over me. I decided right then and there that ice cream would forever and always become a part of my daily ritual until the day they laid me six feet under.

As I swallowed the last bite of ambrosia, I realized that I was rapidly checking off all the most important items on the mental checklist that I had been concocting since that fateful day Judge Grudge decided to send me off. I had only been sprung about one and a half hours, and already, two of the most important items were satisfied—sex and ice cream. But my no. 1 priority still lurked inside me. I needed to see my children. In fact, it was beyond need. I absolutely *had* to see them.

Our eldest, Rocky, was still out in the big wide world, satisfying his wanderlust, I guess with his high-spirited newly found soul mate, Destiny. There was no telling where those two world travelers were, probably somewhere in the vicinity of Alaska. No matter how far he ventured, Rocky always seemed to end up eventually in the Last Frontier. Jeremiah, our second, had been missing in action basically since the day I was sent off. His emotional makeup just simply could not take something of this magnitude. His mother having to go to jail had blown a major gasket. Yep, the day the good judge decided that the state just could not lose a case was the same day that Jeremiah decided to become bitter with the world. No longer would he trust another human being. He had had it with the system and justice and the concept of level playing fields. Rocky's endless drifting and Jeremiah's disappearance left one more child, our youngest, Sarah. She had been attending school at the University of Georgia in Athens. She too had experienced a major emotional roller-coaster ride since her mom's incarceration. But it was her whom we were on the way in our little green convertible to see.

The ride with the ragtop down from the Dairy Queen in Nutter to Sarah's duplex in Athens was a majorly sensational experience. In fact, it was actually closer to orgasmic. The day couldn't have been more perfect. It was balmy yet breezy. A gentle wind tickled my face. My uncovered hair was whirled about until it resembled yellow cotton candy twisted loosely around a limp paper cone. I placed my bare feet up on the awaiting dash, tucked my T-shirt up under my bra, and reached over and turned the radio up full blast. At first, Bob attempted to talk to me, but I was not responding. I was too busy getting off on the million and one simple daily events that those in the free world take for granted. It didn't take him long to figure out what was going on, and from then until we got to Athens, he left me to myself. An occasional glance toward me, probably to make sure I wasn't going to totally freak out on him, was the only communication we would have for 150 miles. Come to think of it, there might have been one more reason he kept looking over at me. He probably could not believe he had me back.

We rode in complete silence, except for the blasting radio and my occasional sing-along. I had found a station that played the oldies, and it was Beatles morning. The Beatles and I went way back. How more perfect than that does a day get, riding down a deserted county highway, top down, bare feet propped up, hair blowing in the wind, sunglasses on, ice cream in my stomach, the Beatles blasting all around me, and the love of my life sitting by my side?

When we finally arrived at our daughter's duplex, I must have looked like a different mother from what she had left behind at the Coward County Courthouse. My hair was sticking straight out, my sunglasses were slipping down on my nose, and I had a silly, blissful look on my face. Somewhere along the road, I had decided to strip off my white T-shirt and bra and replace them with a brightly colored bathing suit top. Combine this all with my bare feet and the especially strange dangling earrings Bob had brought for me to wear, and Sarah probably thought her new mom had become a flashback to the '60s. Regardless of it all, she still acted extremely glad to see me. She came running out of her apartment with outstretched arms.

We sat down and caught up. She had been getting ready for classes to resume in a couple of weeks. It was August already after all. My summer had been stolen away from me as had basically everyone else's in the family. It was plain to see that Sarah was still having a difficult time with it. At the time, we did not know that she was bipolar. We simply thought that she was having extreme mood swings because of my ordeal. To this day, I am not totally convinced that my witch hunt, kangaroo court, and eventual crucifixion did not trigger her disorder. In fact, I am fairly certain that it did. I have done a lot of research on bipolar disorder, and I have discovered several cases where the patient suffered extreme emotional trauma preceding the first attack. How else can one explain that Sarah was a perfectly normal, outgoing, very popular girl before my agonizing torment? In fact, she was beyond "normal."

In high school, she was an honor student, president of her senior class, active in various school clubs and organizations, and Homecoming Queen every year from seventh grade to twelfth grade. It had been beyond heartbreaking to watch her go downhill and deteriorate in conjunction with my own collapse. Bob had had quite a time with her during my incarceration. She had been up and down emotionally like a jack-in-the-box. He had had to leave visitation one Sunday to go and see about her after Jeremiah had told him she was acting strangely and had

DORAMAE BROOKSHIRE

run off. Bob had found her in Savannah, wandering around aimlessly. And knowing Bob, he had not told me the worst of it by any means.

My precious daughter's deterioration is, by far, the saddest thing that has come out of this whole fiery ordeal. If I could, I would gladly trade places with her so that she could have a better life. After all, here I am, most of my life behind me; and there she is, all her life ahead of her. I wonder what Judge Grudge, Dick Noggin, Porky Pentz, and Brett Wratchett would think if they could see what has happened to her.

Bob and I spent the night with Sarah, and she seemed to be in pretty good spirits. Her thinking was fairly clear. I knew she was ecstatic to see me out of Nutter. She and I had always been very close. That evening, one of her friends, Naomi, came over for dinner. Sarah was cooking—a simple one-step casserole and a fresh veggie plate. Naomi brought her mother, Trudie, since Naomi was nine months pregnant, and the baby could come at any time. Trudie and I had known each other for several years. We had both taught Title I (the kids who had trouble with reading) in Goat Valley schools many years previously. Naomi proudly clutched the dessert she had brought and rested it against her protruding belly.

"Oh, I'm sooooo glad to see you!" Trudie exclaimed. "How are you anyway? Are you OK? Did they do anything to you? What was it like in there? You look tired. Did they let you sleep, or were you afraid to close your eyes? Tell me all about it! I gotta hear this!"

Now you have to understand this. I hadn't seen Trudie since 1994, when their family moved to Athens. We were never really that close, only teaching colleagues who didn't even teach at the same school. We only saw each other at special seminars and meetings. It is true that we got together occasionally for the sake of our kids since they were friends in elementary school. But that was the extent of our friendship. And now she was acting as if we were the closest of buddies. Curiosity was a strange phenomenon. Add a dab of busybody, and one has a peculiar circumstance indeed.

I answered Trudie's questions—all ninety-five of them—as politely and accurately as I could. Oh, I'd admit, I threw in a bit of exaggeration and stretched the truth a bit in certain places. As she was having a good time collecting jailhouse information for her gossip group, I was having my own private party with my puffery and ballyhoo. "Weeeeellll, I'm OK *now*, I guess." I drew a long sigh. "But there were several times I didn't know if I was going to make it. There was this one giant girl named Bicycle who tried to kill me. Then there was this other crazy little girl who tried to burn me with a hot iron, not to mention the animals who all ganged up on me in dorm D." I tried to look as pitiful as possible.

"Oh, you poor thing! How did you *ever* survive? Why, I would have just *died* the very first night! I know I would have!"

This banter went on between her and me most of the evening, and I knew pretty quickly that Trudie had accompanied Naomi for more reasons than to be near her in case the baby decided to show up. I wondered if this was what I had to look forward to. Was everyone in my life going to quiz me about the inside like this? Was I going to have to answer silly endless inquisitions about my life in the clink? Were my friends and family, and maybe even mere acquaintances, going to put me through the third degree about my three-month lockup? Would the grilling never end?

We found out later that, that very night, Naomi went home and gave birth in her own bed to a bouncing baby boy she named Aspen. A midwife oversaw the birth. I couldn't help but think that maybe, in some strange sort of way, this blessed event symbolized a fresh new beginning for me. Somehow it just *had* to be a good omen, didn't it?

MY POS

NEAR THE END of the second day with our daughter, we were forced to leave and return to the great city of Atlanta. You see, I had been instructed—no, *commanded*—by the releasing officer at Nutter to attend a meeting with my newly assigned probation officer at this time on this date or risk returning to their fine facility. When put that way, I figured I had better go see my probation officer or, as the girls dubbed her, my "PO."

Now let me tell you a little bit about the world of POs. First, they don't last long. In five years, I had nine POs. First, there was Amoy Decosta and then Henry Jones, who was my PO for about three months. Willie Thompson came next. I had one of my most peculiar POs, who loved to be called *Officer* T. Sycamore, for a record number of months. My other group of POs had originated from the Goat Valley office: Winona Dwyer, Patrick O'Leary, Blair Moody, Edith Roach, and Trevon Wilson.

Second, POs are a strange type of bird. They never smile, seldom greet, shuffle their feet, look at the floor, and mumble most of what they have to say. Making eye contact is against their code. So is any form of compassion or caring. They are in no way, shape, or form perceptive; and the words *empathy, pity, mercy,* and *humanity* have not yet been introduced into any of their vocabularies. In fact, more than a couple of times, while sitting across from one of these creatures, I found myself wondering if they might possibly be robots buried beneath a sheath of human skin. That would probably be a more likely explanation than actually trying to make these strange beings out to be human.

Third, *POs do not care one iota about you; they just want to keep their paperwork in order.* I guess job security is the order of the day here. Every single time that I have been forced to change probation officers (it has never been *my* idea), I have been compelled to endure sitting squarely in front of them while they read, word for word, all my sentencing papers out loud to me. This always includes my guilty plea, my terms of probation, my sentencing paper, and last but not least my "Felons can never be caught with a gun" papers. No matter how many times I tell them that my hands have never held a gun nor will they *ever*, they still insist on reading this to me verbatim.

One of my favorite POs, Patrick O'Leary, got a particular thrill out of this set of papers. I noticed the first time I went into his office that guns were his thing. His walls were absolutely plastered with certificate after certificate of gun training, gun instruction, gun guidelines, gun models and styles, gun ownership, gun safety, and fun with guns. Several different types of bulletproof vests decorated the walls between the documents.

I wasn't quite sure what to do, so I decided to change the subject from guns to something else. "Wow. What kind of plants are those growing in your window over there?" I asked him truly out of personal curiosity.

He glared at me as if I had committed another felony. I wasn't really sure he was going to answer. "Shamrocks," he muttered, looking down at his feet, his face turning a crimson color. One couldn't help but notice how very red Officer O'Leary's hair was. Now it was all coming together.

"Oh, you must be Irish then," I suggested.

He glared at me with a stare so cold that it could have spread ice onto the summer streets of south Georgia. He never did answer my question about being Irish. Instead, he began to read my papers out loud to me, stating frigidly, "I am required to do this by law."

I decided to change my strategy. I would leave the plants behind and try to strike up conversation on something nearer and dearer to his heart. "I see all these certificates. You must be some kind of shooter."

That did it. For one brief moment, Officer Patrick O'Leary transformed into a regular human being. He began to hyperventilate and shake a bit, and a tiny hint of a smile spread across his face. I was not too sure his Irish eyes didn't begin to sparkle. But then it was over, and he snapped back into PO mode. "Yes, that's right," he said in monotone.

DORAMAE BROOKSHIRE

Another time, I made Officer O'Leary really mad. Bob and I had been planning for a long time to fly to Alaska to visit Rocky and Destiny. It was the only glitter of happy I had had in a long time, and I was bound and determined to be able to go. But the officer had other plans. I had mentioned the trip to him at my monthly check-in, and in the next minute or so, he demonstrated to me how one person can go berserk in a matter of seconds. "You can't leave the *country*!" he shouted.

Then I made him even madder by stating, "Sir, Alaska is not out of the country."

Now his little round Irish face was crimson red. His short, little body jerked and twitched. He tried to recover by puffing his tiny chest out into the empty space. He was reminding me of Officer Snipe and Officer Jenx and the short, little mailman in Coward—all these miniature guys suffering the Napoleon complex. He tried to gain his composure and continued, "We cannot *possibly* have this paperwork ready in time for you to leave next week!" he screamed, his circular face turning a virtual conglomeration of shades of red.

"You are going to need a Form 3672, official travel permit, *which* you will need each and every time you leave the state . . . *and I think you knew that!*" he added.

"Oh, no, I'm going," I stated flatly.

That really set him off. Now a large plump tomato in the form of a human head was traversing toward me. It was pointing its little sharp tomato finger in my face. *What* I *say goes*, it said.

I wanted to giggle. "OK, sir. I will fill out the papers today, and hopefully, they will be back in time to go."

They were back in plenty of time. In fact, they were back in less than a week. At that point, I knew that Officer O'Leary was mostly just full of hot air, and I took an almost instant liking to him. He was such a curious little fellow, speechless and personality-less until you riled him up. Then he would transform into a little red fighting machine before your very eyes. I liked that in him. It gave him a little bit of a human factor, unlike most of my other POs. Once in a while, I have to admit, I got him a bit flustered just to watch his reaction.

Apparently, Officer O'Leary did not have mutual feelings for me. I was passed on quite quickly to my next PO, Blair Moody. In fact, it was shortly after the travel permit incident. The way I was being bounced around like a Ping-Pong ball within the same probation office made me wonder how often this happened to the other hundreds of Redd County probationers. Were these POs free to get rid of us on a whim, or were they required to cite some sort of reason they were choosing to pass us on down the line? The only thing I'm really sure of is that there was some paperwork involved.

Blair Moody was the biggest slug of them all. Half my age and twice my weight, she acted like, if she had to make one single movement for any reason, it would absolutely *kill* her. She started out visibly hating my guts. Her cold, icy stares as she read my papers out loud to me in a humdrum singsong shot right through me. When she was done, she informed me in monotone that I was to report *in person* on the fifth of each and every month, or she would see to it personally that I was returned to jail in violation of my probation.

I tried my best to keep my composure and to treat Officer Moody with courtesy and respect, and by the second month, it paid off. When I said, "Yes, ma'am," and "I will definitely abide by all the rules," the first month, I think she thought I was, in some way, mocking her. But by the second appointment, I think she could see that I was sincere (sincerely trying to keep my ass out of jail), and she let down her guard just a little bit. By the end of the year, Blair and I were the best of buddies, even having brief conversations about personal matters. She was allowing me to "check in" now over the phone and had been allowing me to do this since the third month. I thought I had it made. Probation now consisted only of a three-minute phone call on the fifth of every month. This was how it went:

"Officer Moody, this is Doramae Brookshire checking in."

"Oh, hi. Has anything changed?"

"No, ma'am. I have been in the same house now for twelve years. I've had the same job for seven years. Our phone number has never changed."

I was patiently waiting for my favorite part of the inquisition. The entire year that she was my PO, she never failed to ask my pet question. She always made her request in the same pepless slow manner, her distinct Southern drawl taking over. "Have you had any bruuuushes with the laaaaw?"

Every time, I would hold back a giggle; and every time, I would answer identically, "No, ma'am, I haven't." I just *loved* to hear her ask that.

Halfway through our year together, Officer Moody became more and more sluggish. In fact, she was turning into a total lethargic, droopy lump. It wasn't long after that I learned she was pregnant and had taken a leave. We all looked for her to return after the baby was born, but she never did. Then it was onto the next PO for me.

Several of my POs had had some difficulty reading my "papers" out loud to me. Words over ten characters, like *jurisdiction* and *revocation*, gave most of them some trouble. But the most pitiful example of functional illiteracy came near the end of my long string of POs. This guy, bless his heart, struggled to read much of anything. He was having trouble with reading words like *bomb*, *nuclear*, and *explosive*. (These were all included in the "Felons can never be caught with guns" papers, in the section addressing not being able to construct explosive devices.) What really concerned me was he couldn't read words that he probably had been exposed to many, many times during his long career as a PO. (He told me he was fifty years old.)

This poor soul skipped over words like *defendant*, *probation*, and *detention*. I could easily recognize many of the techniques employed by the functionally illiterate. He would sound out the first letter of the word he didn't know and then quickly pass on to the next word. He made comments on the print being hard to read (when it wasn't) and his need for new glasses. He would read really softly, slur the words together, and skip huge sections of text. At one point, when he was particularly struggling, he put the paper down on his desk and announced, "Well, you get the idea."

Quite frankly, I couldn't believe what I was witnessing here. Most of the other POs had been a little slow, but this poor guy was truly functionally illiterate. At this point, I think we have to stop and ask ourselves, What kind of system do we have here? Folks who are truly functionally illiterate are being placed in positions above folks with their doctorates. Is this the death of common sense?

Anyhow, back to our meeting with my first PO, Amoy Decosta. The probation office in Coward County was old, huge, dirty, and packed full of awaiting probationers, most of them African American. I think a couple of human beings sat behind a thick, tinted piece of bulletproof glass, but I'm not totally sure. The way you would check in was to pick up a filthy phone and announce your name and appointment time. The voice on the other end said, "OK, sit down." Then you waited for ten eternities.

Finally, your PO appeared at one of the doors and weakly called your name, looking down at the floor the whole time. None of them waited long. If the person whose name they were calling didn't appear instantaneously, the door was slammed, and I could hear them say, "He didn't show. Put out a warrant." This made me pretty glad that we had found the place on time.

My officer, Amoy Decosta, was from Jamaica and was excessively difficult to understand, especially since she didn't speak above a loud whisper and never made eye contact. She read all the papers out loud to us in her thick Jamaican accent. Then she got down to the real nitty-gritty—the money. I don't know exactly how it happened. She had a calculator and seemed to be able to use it. But Bob and I both knew immediately that she had figured my monthly fine payment out incorrectly. The total fine that Judge Grudge had slapped on me added up to $69,250 after all the fees for various "things" were included. It broke down like this: $60,000 restitution to Medicaid, $5,000 fine, $500 jail fee, $250 Victims Fund, and a whopping $3,500 "investigation fee."

Amoy Decosta told us that my monthly fine would be $548. We both knew she had forgotten to add in the $3,500 investigation fee but said nothing. Her mistake was in our favor. It was the first break we had gotten in a long time. Besides, $548 a month or $577 a month (what it was supposed to be), who cared? I was probably not going to be able to meet either one. I didn't really know the status of my job back in Goat Valley. Had they really held it for me, or was that just show for the newspaper? And if I had to try to get another job, who was going to hire a self-confessed *felon*?

We asked weakly, just once, if there was any way some of the fine could be waived because we would have extreme difficulty coming up with over $500 a month. When she gave us that look of "mess with me, and you'll end up back in jail," we both picked up on it and agreed to the payment simultaneously. What else could we do?

As soon as we signed the papers to agree to pay the $548 a month, she was happy and satisfied. She carried them proudly to her supervisor and was back in a jiffy. She instructed us to drop the certified check or money order into the mail by the fifteenth of every month and gave us the address. She gave me the papers to transfer my case to Redd County Probation Office. Then our meeting was over. She had successfully gotten us to agree to the fine payments. Her mission was over. And as it turned out, so was she. It was less than six months later that I was taken off her role and passed on to Officer Henry Jones. He was to last three months.

In my first meeting with Probation Officer Henry Jones, he, of course, began with the mandatory reading aloud of my sentencing papers. Then he cut right to the chase. "Tell me about your arrest then. Exactly what happened?"

My muddled mind drifted back to February 3, 1998. The day the Georgia gestapo burst forth into my tranquil, safe, and sound farmhouse, the day my world was changed forever.

BUSHWHACKED

I T WAS AN especially pretty day for early February. The date
was February 3, 1998. I had had an unusually trying day at work.
After just eight months on the new job, I was still getting used to it.
This new line of work differed quite a bit from the old one. Going from
being a dentist who owned her own practice to working for Literacy
Volunteers of America was quite a change. So I was relieved when
the day came to a close, and I was able to make my way home and go
into rest-and-relaxation mode. Little did I know just what was in store
for me.

Upon arrival home, I decided to go for the full Queen Posh treatment,
so I stripped off my work clothes, lit a few candles, and settled into a
nice warm bubble bath. I soaked, pampered, and snuggled comfortably
back against my bath pillow at the end of the wide whirlpool tub. I
closed my eyes and listened to the soothing, pacifying music coming
from my bedroom stereo. When my self-indulgent session was over, I
pulled on my favorite pair of ragged, patchy old pajamas and made my
way out to the kitchen to cook supper. I hadn't even bothered to brush
my tangled, wet hair yet.

I had just placed the chicken and rice casserole in the oven to bake
and was cutting up some celery and carrot sticks for a fresh veggie plate
when the dog began to bark and carry on in a way that was unusual for
her. I didn't think much of it. Sometimes Lucy would bark in the late
afternoon at gopher turtles that had come too close to our backyard
in her opinion. Or she might bark at large buzzards circling overhead,
sizing up their next meal. So I didn't pay her any mind, until our twelve-
year-old bulldog, Malcolm, who never barked at anything, began to join
Lucy. As their short loud cries became more persistent, I moved toward
the back door to see what was up.

But I didn't have time. Before I knew it, three frightfully solemn
human beings had burst through my back door and practically run

through my dining room and were standing in self-protective stance just inches away from me in the kitchen. Two of them, one female and the other male, were dressed in black suits and dress shoes. The other was in full sheriff deputy's uniform with a gun hanging at his side. All three were about half my age. I wasn't sure just what was going on here, but I did know that whatever it was, it had to be pretty damn grave.

"Uh, who are *you*?" I managed to get out.

"Agent R. D. Wickfield, GBI," the black-suited male announced.

"Agent L. Blackwood, GBI," the female followed, and she attempted to pull out what seemed to be some sort of badge from her suit lapel.

The little deputy didn't have a chance to answer. The two Georgia Bureau of Investigation (GBI) agents had progressed into their next stage.

"Dr. Dora-Marie Brookshire?" the petite blond agent asked.

"Yeah, that's me . . . kinda," I replied, my heart beating out of my chest.

She continued, "You are under arrest. You must come with us."

By this time, Bob had heard all the commotion and had made his way into the kitchen. "What's going on here?" he inquired.

The three agents ignored him as if he wasn't there, so I answered him, "These people are here to arrest me. They're GBI agents."

"What the hell!" he responded. "What the hell is she under arrest for?"

"Medicaid fraud," the female replied.

My heart sank instantly to my feet. I knew that this was far bigger than I was. In fact, it went beyond the profession of dentistry and license suspensions and lawyers. This was pure dental board, administrative law politics in its simplest form. I had messed with them, and they were out to get me. They wanted me down for good. I was a boxer, and the count was at ten. This was the final knockout.

I had figured out a long time ago that if anyone at any time wanted any health professional to be gone, the perfect way was to charge the party with Medicaid fraud. Many doctors in south Georgia accepted Medicaid for payment, me included. I felt that it was the only humane decision since so many patients in this area live in poverty. Another factor that had swayed my decision was the fact that only one other dentist in Goat Valley accepted Medicaid patients, and that was on a very limited basis. These people in Goat Valley needed help with their teeth, especially the little ones with nursing bottle caries.

But I also knew that by accepting these patients, I was taking a risk. Because the Medicaid program is totally run by the state, the politics are so messed up that I can't even begin to tell you. Every phone call that I had ever made to Atlanta to ask about a patient's treatment plan, a specific Medicaid rule, or anything at all was met with nothing but delays and total incompetence on the other end. Most of the time, the person on the other end of the line either said, "Let me look dat up." It was followed by several minutes of giggling, talking to other Medicaid employees, and a dial tone, or they put me on hold for an eternity. One time, I decided to wait for the Medicaid employee to return to the line after being put on hold for infinity. After forty-five minutes, I finally surrendered and hung up.

It wasn't much better when I finally determined, after an immeasurable number of calls, who the one state dentist was and *at last* got to speak to him. He was evasive and hedging. He dodged my questions with confusing minimal answers. He was a sidestepping expert. And this was the person who signed off on all our Medicaid preapproval forms.

So I knew when I decided to accept Medicaid patients anyhow that I was laying my ass on the line. I just knew that, if *some dentist* in Goat Valley didn't care enough to serve these folks, there would be a huge void in patient care. I also had figured this out about Medicaid: anyone in charge at any time, in any way, with any power could "get" any doctor, nurse, or dentist that he wanted to for "Medicaid fraud." The possible paths for attack were infinite. The rules and regulations were basically nonexistent. There was no written standard of care. This was some ghostly phenomenon that was only referred to in court cases, suspension hearings, and fraud charge suits. What happened here was that the Medicaid "experts" in Atlanta made up the rules as they went along. Whatever seemed convenient at the moment was what went that day. Therefore, any human being with any sense at all could easily see that *if Medicaid wanted you, Medicaid could get you.* I knew this. I was cognizant of this fact. I had seen it happen to other dentists whom the state dental board didn't like. But still, I chose to take the risk of accepting Medicaid patients. Well, tonight, this very instant, I had lost the gamble. They had gotten me.

The female suit told me to get dressed. I was going to have to go with them to the station. She said she would have to go with me to my bedroom and watch while I got dressed.

Bob began to lose it. "Don't you *dare* go with her!" he shouted.

Her expression changed instantly. "You *must.* It is what the law states," she shot back, watching him out of the corner of her eye.

This verbal altercation went on for a while, Agent Blackwood commanding me to get dressed and Bob screaming at me not to obey. Back and forth they went, like two kids vying for the title on the playground. When the two male lawmen stepped in, Bob suddenly realized his mistake and backed off. He instantly decided to take a different approach. "I tell you what, we're all upset here. Let's just all sit down right here in the living room and have a humane discussion, why don't we?"

The male GBI man started to object, but the other two decided they might as well go along with the newest plan. Their original plan of attack had already been totally foiled. What did they have to lose at this point?

Bob sat down on the couch. I chose the chair farthest from everyone. He motioned for the three invaders to sit, but they never did. They stood erect against the large living room window, like a row of tiny plastic soldiers, ready to attack. "Now let's all just calmly think about this for a minute," Bob said. "If it is absolutely necessary to arrest her and take her down to the station *tonight*, then I will drive her there. We will follow you in our car, OK?"

"*No!* That is not acceptable! It is *policy* for us to take her!" Agent Wickfield insisted.

They went round and round, Bob becoming more and more convincing until he was almost in begging mode and Agent Wickfield standing his ground for the GBI rules and regulations. He had been standing, back against the window, for several minutes now, and his hands began shifting from behind his back to his sides, near his hips. I wondered if he was going to reach for his gun and give Bob a couple of warning shots.

Bob continued to plead my case, shifting strategies every few minutes. If one didn't work, he quickly crossed over to another. Any high school debate coach would have been proud of his wrangling expertise. But when the "special agents" had had enough, they had had enough. "Lilluth, go get her dressed. We're wasting time here!" he snapped.

At that, the female GBI agent grabbed me up by the arm and said, "Which way's the bedroom?"

I didn't know exactly what to do. I was still somewhat in a stage of shock. After all, we had been invaded by a band of wild lawmen who had burst into our back door and commanded all types of crazy things from us without any warning whatsoever.

As I directed Agent L. Blackwood to my bedroom, I heard Bob ask the other agent where their warrant was. He replied that they didn't have one on them, but we could get one down at the station if we wanted it. Bob asked exactly *why* they had been able to come breaking into our house like that. What had given them the right to do this? I heard him reply that the grand jury had met that day in Goat Valley and had ruled that there was enough evidence to indict me. As Agent Blackwood led me to the closet, I could just barely hear Bob ask why we were not told about the grand jury proceeding. We were to later find out that, in the state of Georgia, both sides are seldom presented to the grand jury. The prosecution doesn't even have to inform the defendant that the proceedings are going on, and most of the time, he doesn't.

I dressed as modestly as I could with someone else watching my every move. We were both standing in the closet. I had moved in there, hoping for a little privacy, but she had followed me in and was standing about three steps from me. I pulled off my comfortable old pajamas and pulled on a bra, underpants, a long-sleeved shirt, and a pair of jeans. Before I could put my shoes on, she asked to see them. I handed them over. She examined them like a doctor preparing for surgery. "OK, they're clean. You can put them on," she announced.

That was a little weird, I thought. I wondered what she thought I had planted in my old L. L. Bean work boots.

When we returned to the living room, Bob had struck a deal with Agent R. D. Wickfield. The one and only compromise he had made with him was he had agreed to not handcuff me. Bob seemed happy for this one tiny concession. "Let's go. We've wasted *way* too much time here. They'll wonder where we're at," he stated.

They led me to the car, one GBI agent taking a hold of each of my arms. In our driveway sat two strange vehicles, a black Mercedes and a Redd County sheriff's patrol car. They were leading me to the sheriff's car.

When we got to the back door of the car, Agent Wickfield said flatly, "Put your hands behind your back."

"What?" I said. "I thought you agreed not to handcuff me."

"Put your hands behind your back," Agent L. Blackwood tried.

I looked around me. Bob was standing on the porch, just outside the back door. He was wringing his hands.

"Bob, they're trying to handcuff me!" I shouted.

He stepped toward the stairs.

"Don't come down here, or we'll take you in too!" Agent Wickfield yelled at him.

Bob retreated, probably thinking that he would not be able to do me much good in handcuffs himself.

"Just do what they say. I'm calling Ricky!" he yelled. "I'll be at the station as soon as you are."

So I placed my hands behind my back as I was instructed to do. I heard Agent Wickfield tell Agent Blackwood to put them on "nice and tight." She followed instructions like a champ. Those handcuffs were snapped on my wrists like they were sized for a five-year-old. First, they pinched, and then they bruised. I could feel every single beat of my heart at my wrists. Then seconds later, both my hands began to go numb. Then I lost it.

Bob was still standing on the back porch. "Bob!" I screamed out. "They've put these things on too tight! I can't feel my hands! *Call Ricky . . . now!*"

He ran for the door. Agent Wickfield snickered. Agent Blackwood grinned from ear to ear.

Agent Blackwood looked at me. "Don't struggle," she told me. "The more you struggle, the tighter they'll get."

I knew that was impossible. If they got any tighter, my wrists would burst wide open, spilling the entire contents of my radial artery onto the seat of their cop car. If I was lucky, I might be DOA at the station.

The two GBI agents placed me in the back seat of the sheriff's vehicle, protecting my head from getting bumped, just like you see on the cop shows. They walked over and climbed into their state-issued black Mercedes. They pulled around us so they could lead the way.

The little deputy driving me in tried his very best to be as accommodating as the situation permitted. "Miss Dora, I'll go the quickest way I can." He glanced back at me. "I know a certain way that's a lot closer," he added.

But I wasn't talking. I had clammed up like a witness to a murder who had been threatened with his life. My wrists were throbbing, and so was my head. This could not be happening, not to me.

The little deputy made several more attempts at friendly chatter and then finally abandoned the notion. We rode in silence. I had never realized that the city of Goat Valley was so far away from our farm.

When we arrived at the jail, our two GBI buddies were there, waiting for us. They walked swiftly toward the car. Agent Blackwood opened the door, and Agent Wickfield grabbed me by the arm. "Let's go, Miss Mae," he demanded and led me through a side door someone had unlocked for us.

Sheriff Jimmy Dawkins was standing right inside. "Hello, Doramae," he sang out like it was a social occasion.

I didn't answer. I was frightened and humiliated and still a little shocked. My shoulders and arms ached from being held tightly behind my back for over twenty minutes. My wrists pulsated. My head pounded. And I was feeling more than a bit faint. This was not a community meeting where the sheriff and I exchanged niceties. This was serious business. The state was having me arrested for something they had fabricated out of nothing, and I was sure that Sheriff Dawkins was in on it at some level. So I decided to not speak.

They led me to a room with a table and a couple of chairs. Then they tried to get my handcuffs off. After several minutes, they were having no luck. Agent Blackwood began to panic. She had frantically been trying a million different keys. "I can't find the right key," she told Agent Wickfield. "I know I brought it. Where *is* it?"

I let them go on and on and on with this charade. I was beginning to wonder if it was some sort of staged scenario to see just how I would react. I tried so hard to keep my composure and keep my mouth shut, but after twenty-five minutes of their monkey business, I was losing patience at warp speed. I had convinced myself that I would lose the use of both of my hands due to lack of circulation. I had been standing in the same position now to allow the two clowns access to my wrists, and I felt like the cadets who drop over in the hot sun from standing too long with their knees locked into position.

Then it happened. I said the only words I was to sputter forth without being asked that fateful night. "I think you need to go back to Handcuffing School 101," I quipped at Agent Blackwood. I knew I shouldn't have. I knew it was wrong. I knew I blew my plan to keep my cool. I knew it was childish, stupid, and downright idiotic. But the fact was I felt better after that.

After several more attempts, Agent Blackwood finally found the right key to set my poor throbbing wrists free. But that wasn't the end of their clownish shenanigans. Oh, no, they didn't miss a beat. The two blunderheads proceeded right onto their next foolish act. This one was entitled "Try to Make the Intimidated Little Captive Do Stupid Things She Knows She Shouldn't." As soon as my deadened hands were capable of holding an object, a pen was thrust into them, and a sheet of white paper with a few lines of print was pushed toward me simultaneously. "Dr. Brookshire, this is something we need for you to sign," Agent Wickfield stated matter-of-factly.

"What is it?" I asked.

"Oh, don't you worry about that, Dr. Brookshire. We just need your signature, please."

Now I *was* suspicious. Suddenly, I had become *Dr.* Brookshire for the first time that evening. And the single, solitary sudden *please* was a dead giveaway. No, this paper was not getting this girl's autograph under any circumstances. The two buffoons would have to torture and torment me before they would reap *my* John Hancock.

"Sorry, I'm not signing anything until my attorney gets here," I stated dryly.

That sent Agent Blackwood into a tizzy. "Just sign the paper! All it is, is a blank report sheet!"

"A *what*?" I gasped. I couldn't believe what I was hearing.

Agent Wickfield jumped in to try to repair some of the damage. "What she means to say is that this is 100 percent routine procedure. We always have our defendants sign a couple of blank report sheets, just in case we make a mistake writing something up. That way, we can simply transfer the information to the blank sheet, and your signature is already there for us." Then he added as an afterthought, "See, this is to save you any trouble when *we* mess up. We would hate to have to come find you simply because we needed your signature again."

"Oh, I'll take that chance. You seem to have no trouble finding me."

Now they were hoppin' mad. They decided that the next course was to continue on with the browbeating. They were trying to make me come undone. "OK then, looks like she's not gonna cooperate with the law," Agent Wickfield told Agent Blackwood. "Let's go on to the next step. Got the camera?"

I wondered what this act was all about. Were they actually going to take my picture for proof that I refused to sign their stupid report form?

"Let's see. Stand over against that wall." Agent Blackwood was holding a small disposable camera and pointing to the south wall.

"Why?" I asked.

"Because she told you to," Agent Wickfield quipped.

When I continued to stick to my chair, he reluctantly spat out the words "She's going to take your picture for our files."

I got up and shuffled on over to the designated wall. *I should probably be getting used to this by now,* I told myself. *I never know what to do in these darn mug shots.* I was trying to both amuse myself and keep my sanity until Ricky got there. I decided to look very serious in my shot. That way, the GBI would not be able to misinterpret my "intentions."

As soon as my studio sitting was complete, the door opened, and Ricky strolled in. Boy, was I glad to see him! "What's going on here?" he demanded.

"Your client's under arrest, that's what," Agent Wickfield shot back.

"What's the charge?" Ricky asked.

"Medicaid fraud, 167 counts," Agent Wickfield answered.

"She has been very uncooperative," Agent Blackwood added. "She has refused to sign this paper."

Agent Wickfield decided to approach the paper-signing matter a little more diplomatically. "We just need her to sign in a couple of places, that's all."

Ricky put on his glasses and picked up one of the papers. "What is this?" he asked.

"Oh, that's just a blank report form. We were explaining to her that this is *routine.* We have all our defendants do this. It is in case we make a mistake writing up the report. If we do, then we have these couple of blank report forms so we can transfer the corrected information onto the form without bothering your client again for her signature."

Ricky let out a giant puff of air and then shot the two blank report forms back at them.

"What's wrong?" Agent Wickfield inquired.

"She's not signing *blank forms*!" Ricky was glaring at the two special agents over the top of his reading glasses.

Agent Wickfield and Agent Blackwood looked at each other like the count was in and that they were losing. They tried to pull a couple of more GBI stunts while we were there, but they quickly saw that Ricky was not going to fall for any of their bag of tricks, and the session was soon over. Ricky was all business. He found out the essentials that he needed to know and then quickly got me out of there. Bob was waiting in the hall for the jailers to process my bond. It looked like I had escaped an overnight stay in the pokey once again.

While we were waiting endlessly for the Redd County deputies to move like slugs, we overheard one of the GBI agents talking to Sheriff Dawkins. We couldn't believe what we were hearing. Agent Wickfield was asking him the best way to find Scarlett Vesper, and he was giving them her address. My heart sank. They were going to arrest Scarlett too.

Scarlett was the front desk receptionist at my dental office. She filed most of the insurance forms for me. That included Medicaid claims. After the two agents left, Ricky, Bob, and I cornered Sheriff Dawkins. We tried our best to beg, plead, beseech, implore, and appeal to him not to let this happen. We told him that Scarlett had nothing to do with anything, that she had three young children at home, that she was just an office worker, that she had a lot going on right now in her personal life. The sheriff listened to our pleas and then stated simply, "The GBI wants her. The GBI gets her."

Bob and I left the jail in a dead stupor. We had taken a hit between the eyes. And now we still had to go see about Scarlett. I felt it was my duty to at least give her a warning. I didn't know exactly what I was going to say. That the GBI was coming to get her? That they would soon burst through her back door without warning, hands on their hips, ready to pull their weapons, like they did to me? That she would probably be charged with being some kind of accomplice to a horrendous crime? At that time, I didn't yet realize just how the game was being played.

When we reached her house, all the lights were out, and it was already dark. We got out of the car and knocked on the back door and then the front, both to no avail. Then I remembered. It was her youngest son's birthday. He was five, I think. The family had probably gone out to celebrate. But it was still my obligation to put her on alert, so we decided to ride around the neighborhood until we saw them return. However, someone else was buzzing the neighborhood too.

Two serious young professionals dressed in black suits and camouflaged well in a jet-black Mercedes sedan drove round and round the block, hoping to pounce on their intended prey at any second. I saw them, and I was pretty sure they saw me. I had to get to her first. We drove in the opposite direction to shake them off. By the time we returned, fifteen minutes later, lights were on in the house. We silently slipped out of the car, barely closing the doors, and crept to the back door. It didn't take Scarlett long to answer the knock. The second she saw us, standing at her door at nine o'clock at night, she knew something bad was up. Her face revealed that fact.

"Oh, Doc, Bob, come on in. We've been out at Los Compadres, having Eli's birthday dinner. How long have y'all been here?"

"Not too long," I answered briefly. I knew for a fact that my facial expression exposed the truth.

Scarlett played along for a moment as if this was strictly a social call. "I'm so glad you came 'cuz I've wanted to show you all the stuff I've been working on in the house," she said excitedly. "Come here." And she grabbed my hand and led me toward the kitchen. "Look what I just did yesterday. Isn't it great?" She was pointing to some new kitchen wallpaper, half finished.

"Yes, I really like that. Looks like you're doing a good job," I replied, not feeling much like discussing home decor at the moment.

She continued to give me a tour of her new home, pointing out the large family room and the spacious playroom for the kids. Suddenly, right in the middle of describing in detail her plans to place exercise equipment in hers and Ben's bedroom, she spun around and looked me square in the eye. "We're in some kind of trouble, aren't we? Are they going to arrest us?"

"Yes, they are," I answered simply.

"What the hell for?"

"Medicaid fraud."

"What? How the hell can they do *that*? We didn't even do anything wrong!"

I said, "Listen, real soon the GBI is going to come busting through your door, handcuff you, and take you off to the jail to arrest you."

I felt it was my obligation to just come right on out and spill the beans. After all, as sneaky as they were, they probably had us surrounded at that very minute. But that didn't prove to be the case.

The longer we stayed, the more suspicious I got. Why weren't they carrying through with their threat to "get the other one too"? Why weren't they incorporating the element of surprise as they so efficiently did with me? The longer we hung around Scarlett's with no action from our GBI buddies, the more on edge I got. I needed something to calm my nerves.

"Hey, Doc, you want a drink?" she asked.

"Yeah, I do. What you got?"

She swung open a cabinet door, revealing an entire medley of assorted liquors, wines, and intoxicating spirits. We sat and calmly sipped a couple of glasses of white wine, not saying much as if we were awaiting the crucifixion to come. Then I spied it.

"Scarlett, what's that?" I asked, pointing to a tall slender greenish bottle standing in her kitchen windowsill.

"Oh, that's some really potent tequila. You don't want *that* stuff. It'll rot your gut."

"Yeah, I *do* want that stuff. Do you care?" I inquired as I reached for the bottle.

"No, go right ahead. *But I'm warning you.*"

I snatched the bottle out of its resting spot and scooped up the shot glass beside it.

"Doc, just drink a shot or two, OK? And then wait a minute. It takes it a while to hit you."

But I wasn't listening. This whole thing was so utterly *wrong*. I knew what was coming down here. They couldn't get me on the manslaughter charge, so they were bound and determined to get me for *something*. So with the help of their friends at the state dental board, the men (and women) in black were all prepared to charge me with the most ambiguous accusation of all. And they were taking Scarlett down with me. The more I thought about it, the madder I got. And the madder I got, the more I drank.

After a few minutes, I threw the shot glass down and tipped the tequila bottle to my lips. At first, it burned all the way down to my stomach. Then after a while, I couldn't feel it anymore. I had accomplished my mission. The tequila had sufficiently deadened the pain. I no longer remembered exactly why I was there. When I attempted to stand up, the room spun out of control.

Bob and I both knew we had to go. He propped me up and led me out to the car. I continued to half-mutter, half-holler all kinds of warnings out to my friend. "Don't let them get you! Run while you can! Hide under the bed! Come with us! We're the getaway car!"

Bob placed me carefully in the passenger's seat. Everything in front of me was spinning so fast that I just knew that we had to be at an amusement park on some kind of freaky ride that went round and round. I stuck my dizzy head out of the window and screamed one last warning. "Don't talk to the bastards! They'll turn it around . . . and don't sign any blank forms . . . and don't squirm in the handcuffs! That'll only make them get tighter!"

Bob told me later that I threw up three times on our way home. When he got me home, he put me in a lawn chair outside, from where I puked my guts out four more times in the yard, I think once on the cat. I don't remember any of that.

Scarlett told me her story the next day. It seemed the two GBI goons crept up to her door after surrounding the house and peeking in several of the windows. It was nine forty-five at night, and her three small children were getting ready for bed. After ringing the front doorbell, they let themselves in. They called for "Miss Vesper," and when she appeared, they read her her rights and said that she was being arrested for Medicaid fraud. Her husband, Ben, begged the two agents to let them follow the black Mercedes in their own car and to get it over with quickly for the sake of the children. They actually listened to his pleadings and allowed Scarlett and Ben to follow them in their own car, minus handcuffs and sheriff escort.

Fact would prove that Scarlett was treated much, much differently from me. Yes, there were some similarities. They took her "mug shot." They read her her rights. They allowed her to call an attorney. They tried their best to get her to sign a blank GBI Report Form no. 62670. But that was where the similarities ended. She was, more or less, treated like royalty. She was offered a drink. She was asked if her chair was comfortable. She was halfway apologized to for disrupting her home and family. And then the *true* purpose of her arrest was revealed.

"How long did you work for *Dr. Brookshire*?" the two cretins asked. "Were you aware that she was committing big-time Medicaid fraud out of her office on a *daily* basis?" They were both leaning in toward Scarlett and glaring straight into her eyes to get her reaction. "Oh, of course, you knew it. You were the one at the front desk who *filed all the Medicaid claims for her.*"

"I . . . I . . . I only filed what she told me to," Scarlett answered weakly, halfway scared to death.

"Of course, you did now. Let's say that you were only doing what you were told to—being a good office employee and all. After all, you didn't want to lose your job. It was pretty good, and you had all those kids to raise and everything. It was your best choice to just do what you were told. You didn't realize that you were filing claims that were *against the law*, now did you? You trusted your boss, just like all good, loyal employees do, huh?"

"Yes, sir . . . ma'am . . . I trusted what she told me." She was barely whispering now. They had her where they wanted her. They moved in for the kill.

"Then if you really care for your family . . . your kids . . . your husband . . . your very future, you must do the right thing. This lady you are working for, she is a monster. She is dishonest, unethical, and immoral. But worse than that, she is crooked, underhanded, and devious. Well, let's just face it. She's a downright *criminal She's a crook!*"

"I . . . I . . . I think I'll wait for my lawyer," she said softly.

They made another attempt. "Come on now, you know what we are saying is true. Save yourself and your family. Just tell us what you know, and everything will be fine for you and your kids. All you have to do is testify against this animal, and you will walk free—free of all these charges that will haunt you for the rest of your life . . . free of the hassle . . . the heartbreak . . . the labels."

"Testify *against* Dr. Brookshire?" she screamed.

"Yeah, come on. How did she do it? What all did she tell you to do? Did she ever ask you to do anything that she told you was against the law? Did she ask you to do things that you knew were wrong? Did she ever take you aside and whisper to you or anything like that? Better yet, did she ever offer to *pay* you extra for doing things on the Medicaid claims? Come on, tell us exactly how the two of you pulled this off for years, and we'll let you walk free. Is all this worth going to jail yourself?"

At this point, I was not sure what Scarlett told them.

TESTIMONY SCHOOL

AFTER THE ARREST, there was a period of almost exactly one year of total noncooperation on the part of the state. We asked for documents. They refused. We asked for transcripts. They refused. We asked for records. They refused. We asked for *anything* that might help us defend our case. They refused.

Then one breezy March morning, Jack called me. His voice was particularly distressed. "Doramae, UPS just dropped off seven *huge* boxes of discovery on your case. You said you wanted something to do . . . that sitting around the house was driving you nuts . . . well, how do you feel about coming over here every day and digging through this crap for me? Maybe you can explain some of the dentistry to me. I'll never get through this by trial, and they know it. They're changing their strategy on us now, swamping us with every little thing they could get their hands on."

"Exactly what's in those boxes?" I inquired.

"Oh, geee, looks like patient charts, X-rays, written statements, employee depositions, other dentists' exams and statements, state expert witnesses' statements, and anything else they could round up real quick."

At this point, I had had privilege to one tiny bit of information about the upcoming trial, and it wasn't courtesy of the state. It had come from what appeared to be one of only three employees who were possibly going to remain loyal to me, no matter how much the state harassed and pressured them. Joy had gone to work, out of necessity, for another dentist in town after my office had been forced to close. After all, dental assisting was all she knew, and she was very skilled at it. This position gave her an inside look at everything that was going on in the other eight dental offices in town. And this was what she had learned about what had been going on in those offices in the last couple of months.

It seems the GBI and several of the local dentists had decided to examine my patients in Dr. Heinlich's office. Of course, they got them to come to the appointments with intimidation and scare tactics, the two main approaches they had always felt comfortable with. When the GBI calls your home and informs you that your child may be in danger from something the criminal Dr. Brookshire did to your child's mouth, you as a good parent cooperate in any manner necessary. So that was what came down. That was a major part of their pretrial preparation. I know this is how it went down because Joy told me. She had been in the dental offices involved in the great fishing expedition and had witnessed a great deal of it firsthand.

The patients' names and phone numbers were taken directly from my patient charts that the GBI had confiscated from Dr. Sonny Sneed's office in the middle of the night. All the patients being "investigated" were children and teenagers. Parent permission was necessary. That probably had not been difficult at all, seeing that these parents were all on Medicaid and were fighting a daily struggle just to feed their families. A phone call (or personal visit if the parent had no phone, which was often the case) from two or three G-men in black would usually result in the mace-bearers getting just what they wanted. Once the little tykes were scheduled for the fact-gathering appointment in Dr. Heinlich's office, the men in black and their dental partners in crime swung into action.

The witch hunt had commenced. Children were brought in by the bunch, sometimes ten or more at a time. The GBI watched as the participating dentists X-rayed, poked and prodded, wiggled and stabbed at the poor tots' gums and teeth. The young victims were exposed to unnecessary radiation, pierced with sharp instruments, and in some cases even drilled on and given needless injections, all in the name of justice. After all, the "dental fraud saviors" were all quite convinced that the soon-to-be-felon, the monster doctor Brookshire had committed some kind of large-scale criminal fraud, and they were the heroes who would come in and save the day. Yes, sir, these poor little victims in remote south Georgia's swampland were not going to go unsaved. They would come to their rescue. At least this was what the story was to their parents, most of them functionally illiterate and scared out of their wits.

This whole showcase of caring and fostering of brotherly love was all, in reality, nothing more than a cleverly disguised exhibition of power and bulldozing. The glitz, the flash, and the frill were all just there to confuse and baffle the easily tricked, grammarless parents. The truth was that the men in black and the participating dentists all needed to get rid of Dr. Brookshire—the target—as quickly and efficiently as possible, the GBI because they had been instructed by the state to do so and the local dentists because she had been a thorn in their sides for plenty long enough.

The results of their team efforts to discover criminal activity in the mouths of the babes proved to be interesting indeed. When they finally released the results of this widespread cooperative dental/GBI exam to Jack, and I was able to examine the results in the seven UPS boxes, the truth began to raise its ugly head. I discovered that, in many cases, the examining dentists had no access to the tiny patients' previous records. A good number of the tots examined came to the chair with no X-rays, previous exams, or records whatsoever. I did recognize the names as being my little patients in most cases, but the fact was that the participating dentists had no previous X-rays or exams in front of them at the time they examined the young patients. Therefore, there existed no "before" film to actually know which procedures had been done by me and which may have been performed by another dental professional. As a consequence of these sloppy scientific methods, I discovered that several procedures that they charged me with as "below state dental standards" had, in fact, been performed by a *different* dentist in town. (By the way, when Jack pointed this out later during the actual trial, the performing dentists of such procedures were not charged themselves with work "below state dental standards.") I guess I was being held to a standard that was designed specifically for me. I could give example after example of such red-baiting, but I will not bore the reader with such details. You get the point.

I do, however, have to tell you about my favorite state/dentist witch-hunt screwup. This is great. I had two young patients with the same name, Toby Tucker. They were both very likable little guys. Both had families who struggled to make ends meet. Both were on Medicaid to help out. Both came from single-parent families. One Toby was White. One was Black. They were near the same age, but their birth dates were quite different. So, of course, were their social security numbers. So were their addresses. So were their dental needs and histories. One Toby Tucker had fairly good dental health. His oral cavity looked like he brushed his teeth on a fairly regular schedule, he enjoyed a healthy diet, and his records revealed that he visited me regularly. An oral exam revealed a couple of routine fillings in back teeth.

Toby Tucker no. 2, however, was not quite so lucky. He had suffered what is known as nursing bottle caries. This meant that, because of being on a bottle for too long, all the sugars contained in the sweet tea and cola drinks and sugar water that had washed over his baby teeth from that bottle had literally rotted them away. As a consequence, poor little Toby no. 2 had numerous stainless steel crowns on the majority of his molars. This meant that the back baby teeth had rotted away from decay so badly that it was necessary for the dentist (me) to place a full-coverage crown, made out of pliable stainless steel, over these decomposed teeth to protect what was left of them after all the decay had been removed. This was for strength and to try to salvage what was left in his little mouth so that he could chew his food. A stainless steel crown on a primary tooth cost $95 in 1994. Medicaid would reimburse me $60. For the time and trouble they were worth, neither fee came close to compensating me for the amount of precision and hard work it took. But I didn't mind. I was getting these children out of pain and making chewing possible for them. I also tried my best to educate their parents so this same thing would not happen on younger siblings.

Anyhow, this is how the story goes: The prosecution (the state), in building their case, got the two Toby Tuckers mixed up on their charge sheets. They professed that I had submitted charges for numerous stainless steel crowns on a child who, during Dr. Heinlich's *great secret exam*, had been discovered to have only a couple of routine silver fillings in his mouth. Therefore, the charge was big-time Medicaid fraud. After all, the evil, dishonest dentist (me) had charged the state of Georgia $95 apiece for six stainless steel crowns when, actually, all that had been discovered in his mouth were two fillings at $35 apiece. (Medicaid would pay $8 apiece for these.) Keep in mind now that the state had access to *both* Toby Tuckers' birth dates, addresses, phone numbers, and social security numbers. Of course, what had happened was that, in their great haste to persecute me, they had failed to make the connection between the two patients and had assumed that I had submitted Medicaid claims that were false. (Pay attention closely because what Jack did later with this little scenario during trial was priceless.)

Speaking of Jack, after the seven boxes of Medicaid charge materials arrived by UPS at Jack's office, it became my mission to drive two hours a day to Tanaha, Georgia, and work ten hours a day, five days a week, for almost eleven months in preparation for trial. I had to. I had no choice. They had swamped us with so many patient records, charts, and X-rays; past employee statements; depositions; parent pronouncements; patient, parent, and employee interviews; state dental board allegations; and local dentists' assertions that Jack would have had to put his law practice on hold for a year to go through them himself. So there I was, the accused, diligently tilling the soil in a south Georgia law practice day after day after lonely, depressing day. Now I don't know if you have ever spent a year of your life doing nothing but reading about what a piece of scummy, slimy, dishonest, unprincipled, corrupt, sinister piece of crap you are; but believe me, it will eat away at your very soul day after day after day.

Jack had assigned me my own little office, a special private site just for me and my seven boxes. Those boxes and me, we spent a lot of time together. We got to know each other very well. Sometimes we sailed right along. I understood them, and they seemed to understand me. I had stacks and stacks of legal fat yellow pads on which I scribbled my daily notes concerning the info in my boxes. There was always an explanation for the state's "charges." I could have cleared it all up if they had only asked me. But they never did.

At other times, those boxes and me, well, we didn't hit it off so well. On my forty-fourth birthday, I had just finished reading a collection of patient accusations. These youngsters, no older than babes, had pointed their little fingers at me for everything from "hurting their teeth" to "not being a nice lady," and their frightened parents had readily concurred.

Now I can take a lot, especially if it comes from pencil-necked state geeks with a bureaucratic mission. But it is awfully tough to read page after page after page of bashing from little folks whom you really strived to help and cared about, even if they were totally tricked into it.

Anyhow, I must have looked terribly forlorn that day when Jack stuck his head into my doorway to ask how it was coming along because he declared right then and there, "Girl, you look like you could use some downtime. Come on, we're going to lunch."

Jack and his charming wife, Emily, took me out to a wonderful dining establishment, and we had an amazing lunch. It was just what the doctor ordered, so to speak. When we were done eating and were sitting back in our comfy chairs, letting our food digest, Jack asked me, "Well, what do you think? Can you explain all those bullshit charges? Have you found anything interesting lately?"

I began to tell him the story of the two Toby Tuckers, which seemed to delight him to no end.

"This is *exactly* the type of thing we defense attorneys *live* for!" he exclaimed. "Just keep on digging through that pile of junk . . . and find me some more of that type of screwup crap!"

Back in the UPS room, surrounded once again by mounds of paperwork, I reflected on our fabulous lunch. It had probably cost Jack a pretty penny. It was my birthday after all, and I probably deserved to go out on some sort of celebration, but I didn't feel one bit better. Nor did I feel like I had been singled out for special treatment. I asked myself why I hadn't told Jack and Emily that it was my birthday. What sort of sick psychological repression had that been anyhow? After all, it was legitimately my birthday, and I knew deep inside that Jack and Emily would have fussed over me just a little. At least the waiters at L'Envie du Jour would have sung "Happy Birthday" and brought me a piece of French cheesecake or something. I always used to love birthdays.

But now it was back to the salt mines of the world of endless dental procedure accusations. The patient folders I reviewed that day included an accusation of a poorly filled root canal, a restored tooth whose silver filling had not been condensed well enough, and several sealants that had come off of teeth—or actually, the accusation read as if the investigating dentists had believed that the sealants had never been placed but had been charged for. I began to wonder if these poor fools had inhaled too many mercury fumes over their long dental careers. I mean, the bringing of charges of Medicaid fraud and the denunciation of, in their opinions, poor dentistry were two absolutely different impeachments.

If I would have had Drs. Heinlich, Biget, Sudser, and Dankworth in that legal niche piled to the ceiling with boxes full of their own imputations, I would have had a few questions of my own. *Is this upcoming trial about legitimate Medicaid fraud or your ever-present "quality of care" issues? Have you ever seen poorly condensed silver fillings on any other dentist's patients or even on your own possibly? Do all your root canals turn out with a perfect gutta percha fill? Have you read the statistics lately to discover that over 20 percent of plastic sealants applied to children's back teeth come off as a result of saliva contamination?* But here's the question that I truly wanted to ask them—how can a group of men utterly detest a fellow dentist so much as to go after her with such enormous amount of malice and malevolence? This must have been a case of pure, outright detestation, abhorrence, aversion—100 percent repugnance. I cannot even imagine hating another human being to that extent. Or was it not scorn and wrath and loathing? Perhaps it was something else?

But whatever the reason for the dental impeachment, the charges seemed to have stuck for one reason or another. We were, after all, preparing for trial here. The deeper I dug into the indictment, the more confused I became. Those brown boxes contained patients whom I had only treated once, patients who were unaware that they had been examined to bring charges against me, patients who were as young as two years old. Hell, there were patients who were not even mine. These finger-pointing dentists had not been really skilled at doing their homework before lodging their complaints.

On my way home that day, my forty-fourth birthday, I was pulled over by a Whackford County man in blue and issued a speeding ticket. I was traveling 66 mph in a 55 mph zone. I tried to tell him that it was my birthday and I had had a particularly horrible day. I even pointed out the date on my driver's license as I handed it to him. He didn't even hear me. He buried his head in his pad, wrote the ticket, and handed it to me in a single swipe. "Better watch how fast you go around this bend," he stated flatly.

The rest of the way home, I took inventory. *Let's see, it's my birthday, I have 167 charges of Medicaid fraud against me, I have seven boxes of formal allegations, I still have five to go through, I have no job, I've lost my career, I may have to do jail time.* Happy freakin' birthday!

For months, I toiled in that little UPS-box-filled dark legal niche, and I never seemed to so much as *touch* on the mountains of dental denouncements. As soon as I felt that I had made some leeway with my endless hand-scribbled notations on tablet upon tablet of legal yellow pads, 100 or so new charges would be faxed into Jack from the Atlanta-based prosecutor's office. I could never get ahead. I was still holding my occasional afternoon sessions with Jack, trying my best to educate a legal mind on all the details and intricacies of dental procedures. He would have to understand root canals and silver fillings and stainless steel crowns on baby teeth if he was ever to be able to defend me in court. Thank god he was a quick study.

Time is a funny thing. It flies by, yet every second ticks away tediously slow. A year had almost passed. The trial had been set for May 10, 1999. We went into a semipanic. One night Bob, Jack, and I stayed up reviewing court procedures and trying our best to address the 46 new allegations that had been faxed into Jack's office that morning. It was only two weeks before the trial, and Jack was in one of his semimanic, highly insomniac states. It was three thirty before we left his office, and we were so totally exhausted, both mentally and physically, that we rented a hotel room just down the street and fell into bed in our clothes. The next morning, we awoke, brushed our matted hair, and returned to the room of endless brown boxes—no toothbrush, no deodorant, no change of clothes, no breakfast. Showtime in Atlanta was approaching soon, and we had to be ready. After all, I had always been taught that if one is prepared, simply tells the truth, and presents herself with candor, grace, and honesty, justice will always prevail.

The next morning, the first of Brett Wratchett's "offers" arrived at Jack's office. Jack sat Bob and I down and informed us that it was his duty as our attorney to present the offer to us. He said that Wratchett had called him the previous day and had said something like, "I've been looking over your record in court, and you're a pretty fair trial attorney. You've won more than you've lost for sure. I don't guess I choose to go up against you if I don't have to, so let's maybe try to plead this one out."

The offered plea bargain included no jail time, two hundred hours community service, five years' probation, a $125,000 fine, a three-year revocation of my dental license, and First Offenders Act. Bob and I looked at each other. We were both thinking the same thing.

"Hell no!" we both yelled simultaneously. I was innocent of these fabricated charges, and I was going to prove it. I had finally scored my day in court, and I was going to be given a chance to tell my side once and for all. As soon as the jury heard what had happened, they would find me innocent for sure. After all, the system worked, didn't it? Truth and justice for all—I had been taught that my whole life. After a whole year of reading charge after charge after allegation, the dental/GBI impeachment was all beginning to run together. I was thinking that it might be a true relief to finally face my accusers and get it all over with.

One week before the trial date, we received another plea bargain from Brett Wratchett. This time, he offered us no jail time, one hundred hours' community service, three years' probation, $100,000 fine, two-year dental license revocation, and First Offenders Act. Jack said we should really maybe consider this but that he understood if we wanted to go forth. "I'll ride this horse to the finish line for y'all, if that's what you want," he told us.

And we replied, "Hell yes, that's what we want. The world needs to know of my innocence. A great injustice has been committed here, and we want to set precedence for other poor dental souls in the future. This never needs to happen again."

One week before the big trial, and things were really heating up. Jack and I were sitting up until three or four in the morning, trying to prepare for what was now 202 allegations of Medicaid fraud. Brett Wratchett was having his staff fax us new and revised charges daily. Bob and I asked Jack whether he could do that at this time, so close to trial. Every time we asked, Jack appeared to try to change the subject. The most we ever got out of him in reply was "Weeeell, I *guess* maybe they can. I never really had anything like this happen before." He appeared to be as puzzled as everyone else.

Five days before the trial, on May 5, 1999, Jack faxed the following letter to Judge Ebenezer B. Grudge:

Dear Judge Grudge:

This letter is in response to the Court's direction to give notice today concerning any motions in limine or other pretrial matters to be presented in the above-referenced trial, which is to begin May 10, 1999.

Due to the unique circumstances of this case and the progress of discovery, I fear that formal compliance with the Court's directive will be impossible. By way of general overview, I make the following explanation.

When this case was before Judge Hawks, the defense demurred to the indictment based on the argument that the indictment itself was not sufficient to advise the defendant of the specific wrong for which she was accused. The issues were briefed before Judge Hawks and the state concluded its argument by referenced to a series of cases culminating with the Supreme Court decision in *State v. Eubanks*, 239 Ga. 483 (1977).

Judge Hawks denied the demurrer and the matter was taken on application to the Court of Appeals. The Court of Appeals declined to hear the case.

At the time of the first indictment, some two years ago, the state provided the defense with what we understand to have been a complete copy of its investigative file. That file included extensive charts, graphs and investigative notes specifically identifying alleged fraudulent billings with reference to some sixty patients treated by Dr. Brookshire. The charts detailed what the state indicated to be incidents of fraud on which their case was grounded.

On Monday of this week I was given access to three consultants (dentists) whose testimony will form the core of the state's case. We had attempted to schedule meetings with these dentists at an earlier time, but it was agreed between myself and Mr. Wratchett that it might be more useful to meet with the consultants after Mr. Wratchett had opportunity to review with them their reports from 1995 and 1996. I think we both doubted that the dentists would have any specific recall without opportunity to review those reports.

In any event, a member of my staff and I were given access to the three consultants at Mr. Wratchett's office two days ago. During that interview process we were advised that the dentists were reviewing documents which they had not previously seen as well as their earlier reports in an effort to identify additional instances of alleged fraud. Mr. Wratchett agreed to provide that information to me as soon as it was generated.

Today, we are receiving from Mr. Wratchett additional printouts which we are told contain information concerning new alleged instances of fraud. The materials which were received a few moments ago by facsimile transmission are not legible and I believe that a new effort is being made to transmit the documentation by email. I can address the new information only by generic description without knowing specifically what new instances are to be presented.

Thus, I am in a quandary as to how to proceed. As I dictate this letter, I cannot address the particular evidence which the state will attempt to introduce under this scenario. Nevertheless, its substance will, no doubt, cause us to revisit Judge Hawks' decision in denying the defense's special demurrer. In the alternative, I would expect to move in limine to exclude testimony concerning these new instances. That alternative position is, of course, based on our belief that Judge Hawks' denial of the demurrer fixed the scope of the evidence of alleged specific instances of fraud.

The second matter pending before the Court is a notice of the prosecution's intent to present evidence in aggravation of punishment. It is my understanding that in the event of a conviction the state will seek a separate hearing at a later date on the issue of sentencing. My belief is that none of the evidence addressed in the state's second notice is to be offered in the case in chief. I assume that it would be appropriate to raise issue with any of that proposed testimony only in the event of a conviction and then if there is to be a delayed sentence hearing.

Very truly yours,
Jonathon J. Goodman, III

P.S. While dictating this letter, I have received a couple of facsimile transmissions from the state addressing evidence with which I anticipate taking exception. I need to digest the information submitted, and will follow up on this letter tomorrow.

The night before we were all to go to Atlanta for the trial, 25 new charges came through Jack's fax. I threw my hands up into the air. "I give up! I can't prepare for 25 new allegations overnight! Jack, you *have* to help here. This has *got* to be illegal!"

"I don't think it is. I gotta be honest with you. I have never dealt with this dental board before. I can't find in my lawbooks where this is illegal."

And that was that. The state dental board operated under what they dubbed "administrative law." In other words, they got to do whatever they pleased; they made up their *own* laws. The prosecution's tactic was rule by intimidation. This was to be a trial by ambush.

The Saturday before the trial was to begin, Jack asked one of his distinguished lawyer buddies over to his office for a last-minute tête-à-tête. In fact, Mr. Mitchell Stern must have really owed Jack one because I was pretty sure that he came from quite a distance away to offer his professional opinion. He was introduced to Bob and me as "a very good longtime friend who knows the defensive end of a courtroom like the back of his hand, and he knows juries even better." Then Jack added,

"Wuh, hell, I'm surprised y'all haven't ever heard of him. He's very well known throughout the state, highly acclaimed."

Anyway, renowned or not, Mr. Stern made a decision after being briefed on our case. He informed Jack that, in his opening statement, I had to be portrayed as not really likable. We could tell that this really crushed Jack in a way. After months and months of being a permanent office fixture, Jack and I had become pretty close buddies. We chatted about "the fams," drank cup after cup of morning coffee (and oftentimes afternoon and evening too), and held daily Dental School 101 crash courses for Jack. There were a lot of things that could be said for Jack's and my relationship, but not one was that we didn't like each other. In fact, we had built up a pretty strong, trusting friendship. I could tell that presenting me as a rather despicable character in his opening courtroom remarks was going to be a little tough for him. But nevertheless, Mr. Stern seemed to think, in all his well-respected knowledge, that this bashing was a very necessary part of our defensive strategy.

"A jury likes to hear the soul-wrenching, gut-professing truth right up front," Jack's high-reputation acquaintance stated. "Hell, with 227 documented cases of Medicaid fraud, she has to admit to being *at least* unlikable a bit, or they're gonna see right through it."

Then Jack asked Bob and me to "go get a milkshake or something for a while" while he consulted with his noted colleague. So we left and drove around Tanaha, Georgia, really pretty dazzled by what seemed to be happening two days before our trial. We tried to console ourselves by figuring that all good defense lawyers must get a second opinion from a trusted source right before trial. Actually, we were not really sure just how this all worked. We had never been to trial before.

By the time we returned to Jack's office, his lawyer friend was getting into his Mercedes and waving goodbye, Brett Wratchett had faxed in 11 new charges, and Jack looked as if he was going to hurl. "Come on in, guys," he managed with a sick smile on his face.

"Well, this is what we decided," he announced after we settled once again behind the huge highly polished conference table. "We can't really present you as this completely innocent little dental person. That would be doing you a disfavor, a potentially fatal disfavor in the eyes of the jury. Two hundred thirty-eight documented cases of Medicaid fraud are going to be very difficult to explain away, even if they are all bullshit, which all of us sitting in this room know they are."

He reared back in his chair and cleared his throat. "We are going to have to say something along the lines of 'Dr. Brookshire makes mistakes, like everyone sitting in this room has and will continue to do. She suffered a few misjudgments. She called a few wrong shots. Now you may not *like* Dr. Brookshire. But that's not what this trial is all about. Whether or not you *like* a person is not the issue you are being asked to decide here. You are being asked to decide whether or not this defendant is guilty of Medicaid fraud, and *that*, my dear friends, is absolutely a huge *not guilty*!"

The room fell deathly silent. Both Bob and I could not believe what we just heard from our own attorney. I mean, *suffered a few misjudgments, called a few wrong shots, you may not* like *Dr. Brookshire*— these phrases were pouring out of our dear Jack's oral cavity like they came as natural as bees going to honey.

As soon as he had completed his little soliloquy, our beloved Jack reared back in his legal chair and, with a look of utter sadness, inquired, "Is something along those lines OK with y'all?"

We looked at each other. Since Bob appeared to be dumbstruck, I spoke up. "Yeah, OK, I guess, if that's what you think is the best game plan."

"Oh, it's not only the *best* one. It's also probably the *only* one at this point in the game," he replied.

The next day, Bob and I got up, grabbed our prepacked bags, climbed silently into our car, and began the three-and-a-half-hour trek to Atlanta. We didn't say much to each other along the way, but we were both thinking the same things. *What is this trial going to be like? How is it going to turn out? Is there going to be any fairness about the process? What will the jury be like? How many days will it last?*

Bob was thinking, *Will I return to Goat Valley without my wife?*

And I was thinking, *Will I end up a free woman or a jailbird?*

As we neared the Coward County Courthouse, we noticed a strange twist in the different neighborhoods we were passing through. They would start out very upscale and pristine but would abruptly turn into ghetto territory without warning. It was very interesting, this sharp contrast in surroundings. For five minutes, the scenery would be immaculately clean and snowy white. The next five minutes, the drive would encounter public squalor and grubby, unkempt properties. I wondered if this was a harbinger of my trial. Was I to start out as an untouched and unsoiled virgin of the legal system and end up a primal, grimy sleazeball of an inmate?

Soon the neighborhood ping-pong was over, and we were approaching our Holiday Inn, our new home for as long as the trial lasted. We sighed in sync and pulled up to the front revolving door. A baggage guy came out to meet us, but we waved him away, both preferring to carry our own luggage to our doom. We checked in and got settled in our new quarters, specially reserved for the impeached dentist and her hubby.

As soon as I stepped into our room, I noticed something very peculiar about it. One entire wall was a complete ceiling-to-floor window, covered at the moment with a gigantic biscuit-colored curtain. My curiosity got the better of me. I stepped over to the window and tugged the curtain wide open. I gasped at what I saw. I was looking down at the hotel lobby. I could easily see every man, woman, and child who was passing through the lobby. We were only on the second floor, so it wasn't like they were far away and tiny. No, these folks were life-size and vividly authentic. It was remarkably like they were moving through our own little personal space. It was really kinda eerie.

As I was digesting my new discovery, I spied Lolita, Rosa, and Dixie approaching the check-in counter. They were three ex-employees whom I had learned were going to testify against me. Then I saw members of the state prosecution team strutting into the lobby. I couldn't believe my eyes. The prosecution gang was staying in the same hotel as us. I shuddered and pulled those curtains together as tightly as they would close.

Then I got a little paranoid. Had they placed me in this spy-down-at-the-lobby room on purpose? Was it some kind of sick joke fabricated by my prosecuting enemies? Had Brett Wratchett and the gang given the Holiday Inn management extra cash to place me in this disturbing setup? Was my glass-walled accommodation purposely planted to freak me out the day before the trial?

But all bets were off as I observed Jack meander through the lobby and up to the hotel desk in his slow Southern way with his trademark grin across his face. That picture of relief and security settled me down. My knight on a white horse had arrived to save me. I fell into one of the two overstuffed chairs and heaved a heavy sigh of relief. I told myself, *I had better get psychologically ready for this thing. This isn't going to be easy.*

I couldn't really remember what Bob and I did that Sunday night before the trial. We took a short walk to get some fresh air and clear our minds. On the way out the lobby door, we spied Jack wandering up and down a long hall. We tried to speak to him, but he seemed to be in some sort of semitrance. He spoke back, but the strange, hypnotic state hung on. Then I remembered him telling us several times in his office while we were preparing for trial that he would morph into a dazed, detached being the day before trial.

"It's what I gotta do to get ready for the courtroom. If y'all see me like this, don't be scared, OK?" he had said over and over.

But still, this aloofness, this detachment, this state of being completely lost in thought shook me up a bit. *Hope he comes out of this courtroom coma before tomorrow morning*, I thought.

LET'S MAKE A DEAL

AS SOON AS Jack and I took our seats at the defendant's table, a fat stack of papers was slapped down in front of us. We both hesitantly picked it up, neither one of us wanting to know what the prosecution's latest antic could possibly be. Both of our hearts sank as 52 new allegations slapped us once again in the face. Since the 27 previous allegations were only hours old, we could pretty safely draw the conclusion that one or more of the twelve prosecutors assigned to this case was up most of the night fabricating these new bogus charges.

While we were still getting over the initial shock of it all, the Honorable Ebenezer B. Grudge, judge of Superior Court, Rock Mountain Judicial Circuit, entered the courtroom in all His splendor, and we were commanded to arise. After the bailiff gave us all permission to sit, the newest paper treasure was rushed to the good judge by an anxious, bright-eyed, and bushy-tailed little prosecutor girl. She proudly waved it in front of the judge's keen eye. He promptly took the bait. Several minutes passed as we all waited for Judge Grudge to "scan over" the newest set of scandals.

Finally, He cleared his throat, ruffled the sleeves of His crisp black robe, and barked out, "I need to see counsels at the bench."

Jack appeared at the bench in record time, poised to stand our ground and protest the newest set of prosecutor-produced insults. Brett Wratchett sauntered gracefully up to the bench, taking his precious time and glancing back over his shoulder at his team, seated back at the table. They were positioned to pounce on command. Much loud whispering and eyebrow raising of all parties involved followed. The only actual words I was able to catch involved Jack strongly objecting to our latest rape. Something along the lines of "How can we be expected to defend ourselves against 52 charges we have never even seen?"

When Jack returned to the table, he motioned for my family to come over. Mom, Dave, Bob, and Sarah came promptly and eagerly but with some cautious reserve about them. "Seems they have come up with 52 new charges against Dora overnight. I can't believe they pulled this on us *again*! The judge has given us a choice of postponing the trial so we can have time to go over these new allegations. The way I see it, it's all up to y'all."

We were all flabbergasted—once again. We fell into an instant Allen Brookshire football huddle. Of course, my brother Dave was the quarterback. "Listen, I took this whole week off from my practice and flew my pregnant wife and baby all the way to Atlanta. We've all got hotel rooms that we have had reserved for months. We can fight these new *charges*. They're all just going to be pure bullshit anyhow. How could they be any different? It's all been a bunch of absurd nonsense up till now. I say we go on with the trial."

My eighty-one-year-old mother nodded in agreement. My brother had reminded her of our deceased father for years now, and anything Dave said was always just fine by her. Sarah looked down at her feet and turned pale. Bob was the only one to question Dave's call. "Are you *sure* we can fight off 52 new charges we haven't even seen yet? I don't want to take any chances."

"Of *course*, we can. Look at this shit—management of difficult children, poorly filled root canals, crowns fabricated from nonprecious metal instead of precious metal, unnecessary pulp caps, silver fillings that aren't condensed well enough. This is all pure *bullshit*. Did you notice they took all the sealants off? That's because one of their twelve moronic little prosecutor juniors, after a little research, had the sense to conclude that 25percent of sealants placed on primary teeth come off naturally." Dave was emphatic.

Jack then related the team's game plan back to us to make sure he was on the same page with us. "Then we all unanimously decided to proceed with the trial today without time to look into any of the new allegations, correct?"

The team of five nodded in agreement, one fully confident, one with an "if you think so, then so do I" stance, one truly stoic, one a tiny bit reluctant, and one (me) with a look of "I'm screwed if I do, and I'm screwed if I don't." The one and only thing I could think of to mutter at this point was "I really need closure."

"We all agreed on this then?" Jack inquired with all the enthusiasm he could muster. He was getting redundant.

"Yep," I replied with little to no expression.

He confidently strutted back up to the bench and looked Judge Grudge square in the eye. "Your Honor, we have decided to go on with the trial," he announced without hesitation.

The judge looked surprised. "Are you *sure* you want to do this, counselor?"

"Yes, Your Honor."

"And your client agrees?"

"Oh yes, Your Honor."

The judge's initial look of surprise turned quickly to disappointment and then to utter disgust. "OK then." He turned to the potential jury candidates and then to the prosecution team. "The decision has been made to resume the proceedings." He glared at me. "The client has been duly informed of all her rights and adequately understands her risks."

I glanced over at the prosecution table. The twelve faces ran the gamut from smug victory to sudden defeat to utter disbelief and finally an expression of pure pissed-off rage.

Jack would later tell me that in those first few seconds after his announcement to the judge that we had decided to proceed with the trial, the good and honorable judge Grudge had leaned over close to Jack's face, covered the microphone with His honorable large hand, and whispered, "OK, counselor, have this your way. But I'm telling you this up front. *I'm* going on vacation come Saturday. I've had this fishing trip lined up for months, and I'm not going to let *anything . . . or anyone* ruin it for me. It's Monday. By Saturday, this trial *will* be over . . . one way or another. *Understand, counselor?*" I should have known I was dead meat the second that my moderator's name was announced as Judge *Grudge*.

It took no time at all to get jury selection underway. The first order of business was for Judge Grudge to position Himself so He was facing the prospective jury members, clear His throat, and thunderously read the five pages of charges against me. "I shall now read the prosecution's

DORAMAE BROOKSHIRE

charges against Dr. Doramae Brookshire. If any of you have any questions, please hold them until the end. I will be happy to address them at that time."

He cleared His throat, stiffened His back so He was straight as a board, adjusted His French-cut reading glasses precisely on His nose, and proceeded with the impeachment:

> *In the name and behalf of the citizens of Georgia, charge and accuse*

DORAMAE BROOKSHIRE AND SCARLETT VESPER

> *with the offense of*

CONSPIRACY TO DEFRAUD THE STATE, a felony, in violation of O.C.G.A. no. 16-10-21

> *for that said accused, in the county of Coward and state of Georgia, on the 1ˢᵗ day of* January 1993, and continuing through on or about the 15ᵗʰ day of March 1995 did then and there unlawfully, conspire and agree with another to commit theft of money which belonged to the Department of Medical Assistance, an agency of the State of Georgia, and in furtherance of the conspiracy did perform the following overt acts:

A.

On or about July 12, 1988, Doramae Brookshire, a dentist, enrolled with the Department of Medical Assistance to become a provider of dental services under the Georgia Medicaid program. As part of the enrollment process, Doramae Brookshire signed a Statement of Participation agreement, in which she agreed, among other things, to be bound by the policies and procedures of the Department of Medical Assistance, which administers the Georgia Medicaid program.

B.

In running her dental office, Doramae Brookshire followed a practice of scheduling large numbers of Medicaid recipients for dental appointments. Most of the recipients treated by Doramae Brookshire were children.

C.

Beginning in approximately January 1993 and continuing through at least January 31, 1995, Scarlett Vesper was employed by Doramae Brookshire as office manager of the dental practice. In her capacity as an employee of Doramae Brookshire, Scarlett Vesper prepared daily patient schedules, arranged follow-up dental appointments for patients, and prepared Medicaid claims for submittal under the name and Medicaid provider number of Doramae Brookshire.

D.

Doramae Brookshire and Scarlett Vesper worked together in close cooperation on the preparation and submission of Medicaid claims. Within the dental offices, the process of preparing and submitting Medicaid claims was controlled by Doramae Brookshire and Scarlett Vesper. Doramae Brookshire and Scarlett Vesper kept most information regarding Medicaid claims confidential from other employees.

E.

Doramae Brookshire and Scarlett Vesper knowingly and intentionally caused false Medicaid claims to be electronically submitted to Electronic Data Systems (EDS) in Coward County, Georgia. These claims were false and fraudulent in the following respects, among others:

(1) Preauthorization forms were submitted for treatments that were not medically necessary;

(2) Claims were submitted for additional payments for management of difficult patients when no such claims were justified;

(3) Claims were submitted for administration of nitrous oxide when no nitrous oxide had been administered to the patients;

(4) Claims were submitted for completed root canals when the root canals were not completed or when no root canal was performed;

(5) Claims were submitted for pulpotomies when no pulpotomies were performed;

(6) Claims were submitted for pulp caps when no pulp caps were performed or provided;

(7) Claims were submitted for sedative fillings when no sedative fillings were performed or provided;

(8) Claims were submitted for multisurface restorations when no restorations were performed or when fewer surfaces were restored than were claimed;

(9) Claims were submitted for X-rays that were not performed or that were unnecessary;

(10) Claims were submitted for sealants when no sealants were applied;

(11) Claims were submitted double-billing for the same procedures;

(12) Claims were submitted for crowns when no crown was performed or provided;

(13) Claims were submitted for work not performed;

(14) Claims were submitted representing that work had been completed when only part of the work had been completed; and

(15) Claims were submitted in which less costly procedures were "upcoded" and billed as more costly procedures.

F.

Between January 1, 1993, and March 15, 1995, Doramae Brookshire obtained approximately 101 Medicaid payment checks, totaling approximately six hundred forty-five thousand and seventy-eight dollars ($645,078.00) in Medicaid payments, which was an amount greater than the amount to which she was entitled.

G.

While Doramae Brookshire and Scarlett Vesper were cooperating and acting together in obtaining large Medicaid payments for Doramae Brookshire by submitting false and fraudulent Medicaid claims, between approximately January 31, 1993, and January 31, 1995, Scarlett Vesper consistently received monthly bonuses from Doramae Brookshire in amounts ranging between approximately one hundred dollars ($100.00) and approximately five hundred dollars ($500.00), contrary to the laws of said State, the good order, peace, and dignity thereof, and the crime was unknown to the State until January 24, 1995.

THURBERT E. BAKER
Attorney General

J. TOM MORGAN
District Attorney
SPECIAL PRESENTMENT

And the grand Jurors, aforesaid, in the name and behalf of the citizens of Georgia, further charge and accuse

DORAMAE BROOKSHIRE AND SCARLETT VESPER

with the offense of Medicaid Fraud, a felony, in violation of O.C.G.A. no. 49-4-146.1(b)(1)

for that the said accused, in the County of Coward, State of Georgia, beginning on or about the 1st day of January 1993 and continuing through on or about the 15th day of March 1995, did then and there unlawfully obtain for themselves and other persons medical assistance payments to which they were not entitled and in amounts greater than those to which they were entitled by the fraudulent scheme or device of causing false and fraudulent Medicaid claims to be submitted on numerous occasions under the name and medical provider number of Doramae Brookshire for dental services which had not, in fact, been provided, contrary to the laws of said State, the good order, peace, and dignity thereof, and the crime was unknown to the State until January 24, 1995.

THURBERT E. BAKER   J. TOM MORGAN
Attorney General   District Attorney
                              SPECIAL PRESENTMENT

****

I am now going to attempt to do something a little unconventional as an author. I am going to try to give the reader a simplified explanation of each and every one of the above charges. I feel that this is necessary at this point because anyone reading this who is not a dentist most likely must feel troubled and baffled after hearing the above extensive state charges. In fact, the state of Georgia went so overboard in charging me that I myself find the indictment to be a little bit scary sounding.

Several of the state's "charges" were very ambiguous, and I had trouble understanding just exactly what I was being charged with. But

Jack tried to explain it to me. "They want to make sure that they have plenty of charges, whether they can back them all up or not. The bigger the number, the better chance of making at least one of them stick."

My attempt at explaining each and every one of the state's charges against me comes out to be about fifteen pages and has, out of necessity, a good deal of dental jargon in it. Many readers will find it to be very boring and monotonous. So I have decided to place my fifteen pages of response to the charges in addendum A at the back of the book. That way, the reader will not have to endure numerous pages of dental terminology. However, if you are interested in reading my comeback, feel free to turn to addendum A at this time and read my fifteen-page retort to the state of Georgia.

****

When He was done with His laying of charges, He slapped the heavy wad of paper down on His desk, ripped off His fancy spectacles, and whirled around to meet the potential jury face-to-face. "Now understand this, all of you. If you have any reservations whatsoever concerning this case against the defendant, it is your duty to rise at this time and inform me of reasons for such."

These honorable words set off an avalanche of protest among the audience. One of the most corpulent ladies I had ever seen made a feeble attempt to arise but gave that up pretty quickly. She chose instead to wave her meaty hand frantically in the air, leaving her fleshy mound of rolled, adipose tissue no other choice but to wave along with it. In fact, she was so bloated, puffy, and abdominous that I could not help but be reminded of the *Star Wars* creature Jabba the Hutt. But that was where the resemblance ended. Instead of communicating in barely audible grunts and moans, she proved herself perfectly capable of adequately voicing her biased preconceptions.

"I don't know about the rest of you"—with this, she made a true attempt to turn around and meet all the jury candidates' eyes, but alas, her fleshy, distended, swag-bellied mound refused to cooperate—"but I, for one, am absolutely *disgusted* by people like Dr. Brookshire here!

To have one of our health-care professionals behave in such a manner, stealing money from poor people who need it and being nothing but a common *thief* with our hard-earned tax money, makes me *absolutely sick to my stomach*!" With this, she attempted to place her hefty hands on her rolls of potbellied pork, but she soon abandoned the notion for the inability to determine where her sickened stomach began and where it ended.

Judge Grudge snapped to it. He promptly dismissed potential jury candidate no. 39, thanking her politely for her "candor."

Jabba the Hutt II, however, had set off quite an explosion. It seemed the power of suggestion ran rampant for the next few minutes. The thing that immediately struck me like a ton of bricks was that the domino tumbling involved exclusively members of the female persuasion. Not a single male jury candidate raised an objection. One skinny lady, quite a contrast to Jabba lady's body type, had no trouble whatsoever in arising from her chair but did have a little problem with controlling her shaking hands and lips. "I . . . I . . . I agree with her," she stuttered, pointing her little bony hand in Jabba's general direction. "We . . . we . . . we can't let our doctors steal our money."

Her thin blue lips were quivering and her sharp, chiseled knees were knocking against each other. Her color suddenly went pale. I wondered if we were going to suffer our first courtroom syncope. I further wondered if I would be expected to revive the thin woman since I was one of two doctors sitting in the room at the time.

"I . . . I . . . I would like to request to be taken off this *horrible* case, Your Honor, sir."

Judge Grudge looked amused and a little irritated at the same time—amused, I figured, because He was quickly racking up points for the state and irritated because these insecure, follow-the-leader-type ladies were taking up His precious time. "Thank you for your forthrightness, jury candidate no. 26." He turned toward the court recorder. "Let the record show that candidate no. 26 is excused."

This seemed to set off a virtual wave of infectious disease among the potential jury members. The poison spread quickly. An attractive Black woman in her early thirties stood up next. "I'm gonna have to agree with them. I think this lady was thinking that she could screw the little poor children just 'cuz they wuz Black. I guess she thought she could get away with it 'cuz nobody don't care nothin' about little Black children anyhow." Then she added as an afterthought, "Well, I guess she ain't gonna get away with it after all."

"Strike juror number 44," Judge Grudge flatly stated.

The viral epidemic continued. I was shocked to see a gentle, angelic-faced, grandmotherly woman arise next. She was staring at her feet, and her cherubic face was turning three shades of crimson. The sweet lady began to speak after a long rush of silence. "Your Honor, I need off the case too. My little ole granddaughter—she's only one and a half, has had to go on Medicaid for reasons I won't get into right now. It hurts my soul to think that this *doctor* lady might be taking my precious Shelby's milk and diaper money away from her just because of pure greed and selfishness. May God forgive her."

Grudge addressed her as if He was speaking respectfully to His own grandmother. "Thank you, ma'am, for being honest and sharing that with us. I appreciate that."

It all became a blur in my mind about that time. I think a couple of more potential female jurors gave even weaker excuses for wanting to be off my case. I was too busy to hear the rest of the lame cop-outs because I was wondering why it was always members of my own sex who wanted to screw me over. They all wanted their own way out. They caught sight of the great escape hatch, and they were diving for it. At that moment, I thought it couldn't get much worse. Boy, was I wrong! I was about to get screwed by my own staff.

Jabba Lady was enjoying this mass confusion of poor excuses and weak alibis. Her rolls of pork were undulating with every smirk. She had succeeded. She had poisoned the potential jurors—the whole bunch of them. Every single one of them sitting there in that Atlanta courtroom. The bell had been rung. It could not be unrung now.

After the dismissal of all the ladies who had issues with the thievin' dentist and the thanking of them for their time sacrificed for their duties as U.S. citizens, Judge Grudge announced that, after a short, ten-minute recess, we would resume jury selection.

The jury selection itself seemed to be fair and honest. Brett Wratchett would ask each candidate questions like "Are any members of your family doctors or dentists? If so, how close are you to them? Have you ever worked in a medical or dental office? How well did you get along with the doctor? What is your opinion of people who steal money?" When it was Jack's turn, he asked things like "Have you ever sued a doctor or dentist? If so, what were the charges? What do you think of rich people in general?"

Here were the rules of the game: Brett Wratchett and Jack were both allowed to question each potential juror for a maximum of ten minutes. Wratchett was allowed to "strike" a total of ten jurors, and that held true for Jack also. After their ten strikes were used up, they were forced to accept any jurors the other team wanted. So they both had to be very careful with their strike choices. Otherwise, they may be forced to take a potentially fatal juror on board.

Many very interesting opinions and confessions of the soul came spewing forth during the moral probing process. One man had sued his child's pediatrician for failing to diagnose a condition at birth. It seemed the poor doctor had discovered the congenital heart condition at two weeks of age and had informed the parents immediately, but this was not good enough for the man and his attorney. Jack struck this juror. A sensuous young blond woman dressed in tight, revealing clothes confessed that she had indeed worked for several years in a local dental office. Coming clean, she admitted to falling head over heels for the good doctor and having a long and quite steamy, lurid affair with the married father of four. She added that she found dentists to be one of the sexiest bunch of men alive. Dentists were also very understanding. Brett Wratchett struck her. Still another lady voiced her opinion that doctors and dentists have so much money that it wouldn't hurt *any* of them to be sued a few times. Jack struck this juror.

This little game of cat and mouse went on for most of the first day. By late Monday afternoon, it seemed we had our jury of twelve honest, nonbiased men and ladies and two willing alternates. I quickly surveyed the people who were to act as my peers and minijudges. Overall, they seemed to be a group of good, hardworking Georgia folks. We had a teacher, a factory worker, and a man who owned a small mom-and-pop café. We had a truck driver, a social worker, and a secretary. We even had a couple of really interesting twists on the jury.

One young guy stated that his fiancée worked in a local dental office, and he felt like he was pretty familiar with the workings of such. I think the reason that Jack didn't see him as a threat was that this young fellow had such great enthusiasm concerning the profession. And the reason he may have slipped onto the jury as juror no. 11 was that Brett Wratchett had run out of strikes. But the most interesting juror of all, in my opinion, was one of the alternates.

She was a slow-talking, rather sluggish-acting Black woman in her late forties who admitted to having gone to trial and been found guilty of Medicaid fraud some years back. I drew the conclusion that she could easily work for me or against me. It might have been good that she was just an alternate.

Jack was grinning his south Georgia best by the end of the first day. He informed us that jury selection had gone very well. He further educated us to the fact that jury selection did not always go that smoothly and quickly. He was happy with the procedure so far. The trial would be underway tomorrow.

That night was spent trying our best to relax and unwind from the day's unnerving events. Mom, Dave, Bob, and I enjoyed a fabulous four-course dinner at the hotel. We laughed at the antics of Dave's two-year-old son, chatted about family matters, and made idle chitchat about the good and bad aspects of Atlanta, Georgia. Jack joined us for a round of after-dinner drinks. He reassured us over and over that everything was going to be "just fine." In fact, he was extremely pleased with the way the jury selection had gone. That was always a clear indicator of how the trial would proceed in general, he said.

But try as I might, I was unable to let my guard down. I was a failure at all the clichés my family and Jack had suggested to me. I could not unbend. I seemed incapable of slacking up. I was having trouble letting go. Easing up wasn't working either. My mom's suggestion to take it slow disappeared into the wind. Taking the time to catch my breath was not even a consideration. The truth was I was a nervous wreck, a

DORAMAE BROOKSHIRE

nail-biting, white-knuckle, jumpy, jittery, high-strung, frightened little bag of nerves. I was on the ragged edge, nervous as a cat ready to pounce at any second. You could say I was on the brink of the big crack-up.

I tried my best to pull off my big cover-up. I laughed at Jack's jokes, played peekaboo with my darling nephew, and had an idle chitchat with my mom. That night, I slept a total of about one hour. I was holding an all-night vigil with myself. How did I let it come to this point? What could I have done differently? If I had been a totally subservient, male-worshipping, charming little Southern belle of a girl, would they have left me alone? Why had I even relocated to the South? Didn't I realize that most all Southerners hated Yankees? And why had I tried to pull off practicing a male profession in this backward section of the country? Hadn't I realized this was only asking for trouble? I finally drifted off, asking myself why I had allowed it all to become so fucked up. What was to become of me?

The next morning, I was up at the break of dawn, stretching my tired muscles and jogging through the neighborhoods of Parvenu, Georgia. The nice upper-middle-class homes with the immaculate lawns went on forever. I wondered what all these hundreds of people did for a living. Were they, perhaps, dentists who had been forced to go to trial against the state? Or professional women who had had a rough time making their male peers take them seriously? Or maybe they were on the other side. Maybe they were the members of the state dental board, prosecuting attorneys for the state, or maybe even judges who, of course, had prejudices that leaned toward the state prosecutors and against the defense lawyers. Whenever my tired mind drifted toward such disturbing thoughts, I forced it to get back on track to what I had arisen at such an ungodly hour to do, and that was to pray. And that I did.

I prayed with all my might that I would have the strength and the courage to get through this horrible nightmare. I implored God to have mercy. I invoked. I beseeched. I petitioned. I sent up a miniprayer with every beat of my running shoes against the hard concrete sidewalks of the yuppie villa. And when I was done with my supplication run, I collapsed in a pitiful heap on the edge of some white-bread plastic person's perfectly manicured yard. I placed my face in my sweaty hands, and I cried like a baby.

I don't really remember getting dressed for my first day at trial, but I do remember that I ended up in a conservative black suit with a stiff, freshly pressed ecru shirt underneath. I was proud of myself. I had listened to Jack's and Jan's advice on professional attire for the courtroom. Was this kind of like "dress for success"?

Jack, Jan, and I got seated at the defendant's table. Shortly thereafter, Bob, Dave, Mom, and Sarah sat down in a row of big brown chairs behind us, and the circus began.

THE CIRCUS BEGINS

THE FIRST ORDER of business was opening statements. I realized that this was how every trial began from years of watching *Law and Order* on TV. Jack was up first. He arose slowly, buttoned the two buttons on his suit jacket, straightened his reading glasses, and sauntered confidently over to the jury box. "Good morning."

His genuine smile reached from ear to ear. His handsome tall presence and good Southern charm radiated throughout the room, bounced off the walls, and came to rest precisely on the attentive jury. "This trial today is about Medicaid fraud. It is about a female dentist who is accused by the state of Georgia of defrauding our government of part of its funding for the poor. They have alleged that she and her front desk receptionist conspired together to steal this money. I will prove to you that not only is this allegation very, very false but that Dr. Brookshire also is very much the opposite of who the state has her figured out to be. Now I'm not asking you to judge Dr. Brookshire's character. This is precisely what the prosecution is going to pull though. In fact, I'm going to tell you one thing that the prosecution has hung its hat on, and that is character assassination of Dr. Brookshire. I'm going to be up front with you right now and tell you one of the main character assassination routes that the prosecution is going to attempt.

"Back in 1995, Dr. Brookshire had a horrible tragedy occur in her dental office. A young patient died in her chair during treatment. There were, on that tragic day, extenuating circumstances that we will not get into at this trial, but let it suffice to say at this point that we stipulate to this incident. Probably most of what the state will tell you about this tragedy will be true. We are telling you out in the open, up front, that this terrible tragedy did occur. And that is exactly what it was—a tragedy. However, *it has nothing to do with this case.* Now I'm not asking you to become close to Dr. Brookshire or to identify with her. I'm not even asking you to *like* her. And actually, you may end up not *liking* her at all. For whatever reason, you may think she made too much money, saw too many patients, doesn't have the personality you are attracted to. For whatever reason, you may not like her. And that's all right because that is not what this trial is about. This trial is about fraud . . . defrauding the government . . . theft of money. And *that*, my friends, she most definitely *did not do*! I simply ask that you listen closely, read between the lines, and draw your own well-thought-out conclusion because when it comes to being a thief, well, Dr. Brookshire just does not have it in her. Thank you for your attention. I look forward to working with you these next few days. Let's get this settled together."

He pulled off his French-cut reading glasses thoughtfully, blinked his dreamy eyes in slow motion, rolled them briefly at an attractive jury member sitting in the front row, rubbed his forehead as if it had taken a lot out of him, shot a glowing last-second smile back at them, and turned and walked slowly back to our table.

The prosecution was up next. One look at Brett Wratchett, and it was not hard to tell that he was chomping at the bit to tell his side of the story. "Good morning, ladies and gentlemen of the jury," he stated formally. "The task of proving *this lady's*"—he wheeled around briskly to point at me—"*guilt* has been given to me. Please allow me to introduce myself. My name is Brett M. Wratchett, and I am the senior assistant attorney general of the state health-care fraud unit. I am here today to prove to you that the defendant, Dr. Doramae Brookshire, is, without a doubt, *guilty* of *three* different crimes. First, she is *guilty* of conspiracy to defraud the state. Second, she is *guilty* of Medicaid fraud. And *third*, she is *guilty* of theft by taking. That makes *three* crimes that the defendant has committed, and they all three have to do with *stealing* money from our government—money that is supposed to be set aside for helping the poor and the destitute pay for their health care, money that the state of Georgia has toiled for years to build up, money that you and I, as working middle-class Americans, have surrendered from our weekly paychecks to try to help those less fortunate.

"I will prove to you, step by step, how Dr. Doramae Brookshire and her front desk receptionist, Scarlett Vesper, *conspired together* to steal this government money. I will prove how the said accused, acting together as parties to the crime, unlawfully obtained numerous payments from the department of medical assistance to which they were not entitled. I will prove to you how the said accused did unlawfully take monies in an amount greater than six thousand nine hundred eighty dollars and forty-four cents"—he strutted over to a giant flip chart propped on a sturdy wooden easel, pulled out a large green indelible marker, and wrote in huge scrawling numbers "$6,980.44"—"which belonged to the Georgia Department of Medical Assistance by causing false and fraudulent Medicaid claims to be submitted on numerous occasions under the name of Doramae Brookshire for dental services that had not, in fact, been provided, contrary to the laws of said state, the good order, peace, and dignity thereof.

"Furthermore, I will prove to you that, in running her dental office, Doramae Brookshire followed a practice of scheduling large numbers of Medicaid recipients for dental appointments, and most of those recipients were children. Within the dental offices, the process of preparing and submitting Medicaid claims was controlled by Doramae Brookshire and Scarlett Vesper. These two parties kept most information regarding these Medicaid claims confidential from the other employees. With the cooperation and assistance of Scarlett Vesper, Doramae Brookshire was highly successful in obtaining a *large* income from the Georgia Medicaid program. In fact, Doramae Brookshire was frequently among those obtaining the highest Medicaid incomes. Moreover, as a result of their overt acts and in furtherance of their conspiracy between January 1, 1993, and March 15, 1995, Doramae Brookshire received approximately six hundred and forty-five thousand and seventy-eight dollars in Medicaid payments"—he returned to the large flip chart and scribbled "$645,078.00" in green beside the previously professed thievery amount)—"an amount greater than the amount to which she was entitled."

At this point, I wondered why the state had—in several of its documents—run my dates of accusal from January 1, 1993, to March 15, 1995, when the last day I ever saw a dental patient was January 24, 1995. I wasn't even in my office in February or March of 1995. I had been suspended from my practice by the state dental board on

January 30, 1995. Another oddity to me was the fact that the later date of accusal was never really consistent in different state documents. Sometimes it was written as January 24, 1995; sometimes it was March 1, 1995, and often it was March 15, 1995. I knew where they were getting the beginning date of January 1, 1993. That was about when Scarlett had begun working for me. (I guess if the state was going to accuse us of conspiracy, they had better make sure that Scarlett Vesper was, indeed, employed at the time.) But I never did understand why the later date varied so or why it was usually well after I had been forced to leave the practice. The state was, in essence, charging me with stealing government money two months after I was not even practicing dentistry.

Brett Wratchett pushed on. "In summary, I have the *burden* of proving to you, fine people, that Doramae Brookshire, the *defendant*"— he wheeled around in his Italian leather wing tips and stuck his sharp finger out abruptly at me—"along with her coconspirator, did knowingly and intentionally cause Medicaid claims to be submitted on numerous occasions that were false and fraudulent in many different respects."

There was a long pause. "And I am here today to let you know that this will not be a *burden* at all but, instead, will be a *pleasure* . . . and an easily provable one at that. Just listen very closely to what the state has to say. Then I *implore* you to return a *guilty* verdict to help stop Dr. Brookshire and others like her from ever again *stealing* from our fine state."

He traveled back over to the giant flip chart, pulled his green indelible marker out of his sleeve, thrust it at the two incriminating figures on the paper, shook his perfectly coiffed head in utter disgust, and glanced over once more at the anxious jury with vengeance in his bloodshot eyes.

Judge Grudge ordered the jury to take a break immediately after Brett Wratchett's theatrical debut. I sat glued to my seat, unable to get up and take a break myself. I wondered if the jury was vulnerable enough—gullible enough—to go for his bullshit. Might at least a couple of them return a guilty verdict just out of respect to the actor? Even as many months as Jack and I had prepared for the trial, I was not yet ready for *this*.

THE STATE'S PUPPETS

A FTER THEIR BREAK, the jury filed back in and took their respective seating assignments. A few of them picked up their notebooks and pens, ready to go. All eyes were on the master of ceremonies, the honorable judge Grudge. "Call state's first witness," He announced.

"Your Honor, I would like to call Ms. Rechell Gray to the stand," Wratchett announced.

A heavyset Black female in her late forties rose from her seat on the bench and came forward. The look on her face was a mixture of fright and dread. Her attire was drab and basic—black skirt, black suit coat, gray shirt, black hose, black rubber-heeled shoes. Her coarse hair was pulled tightly back into a little pinched bun. The state's line of questioning on this first day of trial centered on the official *Georgia State Medicaid Manual for Dental Offices*, which Ms. Gray was supposed to have authored.

Now let's get this straight from the beginning. This so-called manual, in my opinion, did not deserve to be called such—loose-leaf bunch of pages, disorganized pile of sheets, undecipherable collection of instructions, maybe but certainly not *manual*. I had tried on more than one occasion to decode this *Georgia State Medicaid Manual for Dental Offices*. It was a large crumpled collection of hand-punched papers stuffed carelessly into a cheap, generic three-ringed black plastic notebook. It had no topics, no chapters, no index, no appendix, actually no organization whatsoever. In fact, whenever I wanted to file a procedure that I had not filed previously, I found it necessary to remove myself from my busy dental practice, retreat to my private office, and begin the hellish procedure of attempting to place a call to the Medicaid office in Atlanta to ask my current question. The official *Georgia State Medicaid Manual for Dental Offices* was much too much of a country maze to try to unravel myself.

My early experiences with calling the Medicaid office in Atlanta were downright frightful. Back then, I would attempt to talk to the first person who answered the call or more like one of the next ten people whom each of them would pass me on to. But by doing so, I suffered through many, many very unpleasant and puzzling incidences. One time, a young man was playing a rap song so loudly that I couldn't even hear what he was saying. It sounded like a party for a hundred people was going on in the background. Another time, a young girl got so tickled by the conversation she was having with someone on the other end that she finally told me to call back later. I was told by totally apathetic Medicaid employees, "I have no idea what the answer is. Call back some other time," so many times that I lost count. And I couldn't hope to assign this task to my front desk employees. They had given up on calling Medicaid years before. I could not recall *anything* in my entire life anywhere *near* as frustrating as trying to get a straight answer out of a Medicaid employee.

I had learned after the first fifty calls or so to not mess with any person on the other end of the line except for Dr. Demarcus Drupey. He was the guy who would ultimately say yea or nay to the Medicaid preapproval forms. He was a retired old dentist who, when he talked, sounded like he was ancient enough to be God himself. Dr. Drupey always displayed an attitude of old-timey Southern courtesy mixed with slight agitation and topped off with "why does everybody always have to disturb me when I am trying to take a nap?" mentality. I always dreaded having to call him.

He seemed to go through the same steps every time. First, he would act perplexed and ask me to repeat the question. Then he would tell me to wait just a minute as he had to look something up. Then he would put me on hold and leave the phone for an ungodly amount of time, probably hoping that I would hang up like all the other dentists in Georgia who had called him in the past. Finally, he would return to the phone and tell me the answer to my latest question in a voice so sluggish that it would put a snail to shame. What always got me about his responses was the fact that they were invariably delivered with a question mark at the end of his sentence.

So it would go kind of like this: "Why did I get denied permission to do a pulpotomy on Lakesha Brown?"

And he would reply, "Because the tooth doesn't need it?"

Then he would add, "Or maybe because she is about to lose that baby tooth? Or maybe I didn't see the right X-ray? Did you forget to put the X-ray in with your submission?"

When I would tell him no, I didn't forget to submit the X-ray, he would be beside himself. "Well then, just send it back, OK?" he would mutter, decelerating to an elderly halt.

It went on like this for years and years. I would have a question about a denial or maybe about a rule that I could not unscramble from the manual, and I would have to hole up in my private office while my poor dental patients waited, anesthetized in the chairs. I couldn't help but wonder what kinds of bizarre politics were going on up in the Medicaid office in Atlanta.

But back to the subject at hand—that of Ms. Gray, the author of this fine piece of literature, *Georgia State Medicaid Manual for Dental Offices*. When she was called to the stand as the first witness of the trial, she nervously approached the hot seat, dragging her heavy orthopedic shoes and hanging her head so far down that I wasn't sure if she could see anything but the floor. She made it appear to be quite a chore to climb the three steps up into the stand. While the bailiff swore her in, Brett Wratchett apprehensively rattled a large wad of papers he clutched tightly in his white-knuckle fist. The prosecution would be up first, which I deducted from watching *Law and Order* on TV.

"Good morning, Mrs. Gray. How are you doing today?" Wratchett sang out.

"Oh . . . I'm OK," she replied, still looking at the floor.

"Could you please tell the jury what you do for a living?"

"I am an administrative clerk at the Georgia State Medicaid Office, Dental Division."

"And is that here in Atlanta?"

"Yes, sir, it is."

"And please tell us exactly how long you have been doing this particular job."

"Oh . . . let's see . . . about fourteen years now."

"So you feel like, after fourteen years, you probably really know what you are doing, huh?"

"Yes, I feel like I understand it all."

"Could you please tell us how a dentist practicing in the state of Georgia goes about filing his or her paperwork with the Medicaid office?"

"Sure. The dentist would first complete the procedure, and then he would have his receptionist file a claim. On that claim would be a claims number, or we call them codes, that would identify the procedure that he was asking to get paid for."

"And are most of the dentists in the state of Georgia *honest* about what they claim on their forms?"

"Oh yes. We do not have any problems, except with a few *dishonest* dentists lately who file procedures they *did not do*." With that, she cut her eyes toward me and gave me a look that burned a hole right through me.

"And could you please tell me if you recognize this form, Mrs. Gray?" Wratchett inquired, thrusting a paper toward her. He turned to Judge Grudge. "Your Honor, I submit exhibit A." He handed a copy to the judge and one to Jack.

"Yes, I know this form," she replied. "It is a claim that came out of Dr. Brookshire's office in Goat Valley, Georgia."

"Tell us what you know about it," Wratchett coached.

"Well . . . it has the procedure code Y009300. That's known as management of difficult children. The 300 means that Dr. Brookshire claimed three hours of her time was spent managing a difficult child."

"*Three* hours of Dr. Brookshire's day was spent trying to *manage* what she designated as a *difficult* child then. That's what Dr. Brookshire was alleging?"

"Yes, sir. That is what that particular claim form means."

"So let me get this straight, Mrs. Gray. Dr. Brookshire submitted a claim form to your desk alleging that she spent approximately *half* of her day trying to calm a *difficult* child in her dental chair?"

"Yes, sir, that's right."

He wheeled around to the jury. "Hmmmm . . . a female dentist who claims she needs to get paid for keeping a young patient under control. Let me make note of this."

And with that, he strolled over to his beloved giant pad of lined paper, now placed on its tall easel in the corner, and wrote with monstrous strokes of an indelible marker, "CHARGED MEDICAID EXTRA MONEY FOR MANAGING PATIENTS."

He turned back toward the witness. "And do you personally feel, Mrs. Gray, that it is necessary to get paid *extra* money to treat a pediatric patient?"

"Well . . . not really . . . I mean . . . if you as a dentist are going to *choose* to take children as patients, then I think you have to *know* what you are getting into . . . especially if you are a mother yourself."

"Thank you for your time, Mrs. Gray."

"Could I say one more thing, Mr. Wratchett?" the witness implored.

"Why, of course you may, Mrs. Gray."

"I just wanna say I don't even really remember this particular code number . . . Y009300. In fact, I had to be taught about it when I was getting ready for trial. Now I know. . . there are, I guess, four different codes for behavior management in children. Y009100 means the dentist had to take *one* extra hour calming the patient down. Y009200 means he had to take *two* hours, Y009300 *three* hours, and Y009400 *four* hours. But anyhow . . . I didn't remember there was such a thing as management of difficult patients until you and your staff prepared me for trial. In my personal opinion, there should not be such a code. Children will be children. I don't know *who* came up with such a thing."

Brett turned to Jack. "Your witness."

Jack stood up, buttoned his top two lapel buttons, straightened his reading glasses, and slowly sauntered over to the awaiting witness, his south Georgia grin spread all over his face. "Good morning, Ms. Gray," he drawled. "Could I read from something this morning for you? Would that be OK?"

"Well, yes, I guess." Her voice was soft and hesitant, signaling that she knew to be leery of "the opposition."

Jack opened up a loose-leaf notebook with a cheap black cover and began to read, "In instances where a pediatric dental patient displays behavior which is aggressive, combative, or uncooperative and such behavior would cause the dentist to be forced to spend extra time with this patient, the codes Y000100–Y009400 can be employed. Y000100 can be used when the dentist needs thirty extra minutes. Y009100 can be used when the dentist needs one extra hour, Y009200 two extra hours, Y009300 three extra hours, and Y009400 four extra hours. This is *over the entire span of the complete treatment plan*. It cannot be used more than once on any one patient."

Jack then took off his reading glasses, placed them against his temple, and closed his eyes briefly. "Ms. Gray, could you please help me with naming the piece of literature that I just read this excerpt from?" He was holding the cheap black notebook up. Its title, *Georgia State Medicaid Manual for Dental Offices*, was shining right smack dab in the direction of the jury.

"Well . . . yes . . . that's the Medicaid manual for Georgia dentists," she replied.

"No, I mean what is the *exact* title of this piece of literary work?" he insisted.

"*Georgia State Medicaid Manual for Dental Offices*," she answered.

"And exactly *who* authored this literary text?" he asked.

She looked down at the floor. "I did," she whispered.

"So let me get this straight. *You*, Ms. Gray, wrote the words in this manual, yet you had to be *briefed* on their contents while preparing for this trial?"

"Well . . . uh . . . just . . . uh . . . on that one little code . . . I . . . uh . . . didn't . . . uhm . . . really remember the Y00900 codes."

"Oh, you *wrote* this manual, yet you *didn't remember* the management of difficult children codes. There's *five* of them . . . not *four* . . . and you don't feel that such a code should exist? Children will be children, right?"

"Maybe that was someone else's idea. I just don't remember writing it."

"Oh, did you have a coauthor of this manual? Did someone else help you write it?"

She hung her head even lower. "No, I wrote it by myself," she muttered.

"I would like to enter defendant's exhibit B at this point, Your Honor," Jack stated, handing both the judge and Brett Wratchett a single paper.

"Proceed," Judge Grudge said flatly.

With that, Jack produced another copy of the paper and handed it to the witness. "Look at this paper for a moment and then tell me what it appears to be in your opinion, Ms. Gray. Take your time."

The witness buried her head in the paper and took plenty of time reading. When her head bobbed back up, she mumbled, "It looks like a handwritten record of a pediatric dental patient."

"How do you know it is a pediatric dental patient?"

"Because the tooth numbers are letters D, E, F, and so on."

"And what dentist's office, do you think, these records came from?"

"Well, it says at the top, 'Dr. Doramae Brookshire, Family Dentistry.'"

"So do you think we are safe in assuming that these records are from Dr. Brookshire's office?"

"Yeah, I guess so," she mumbled.

"Ms. Gray, could you please read out loud the entry for 11-30-94? Read it loud enough for the jury to hear, please."

"OK. 'Pt. has advanced nursing bottle caries. Inj. 2 carps Octo HCL 2%, Placed RD. Emerg. Pulpotomies on # D, # E, # F, # G.'"

"Keep reading," Jack said.

"'Pt. cried and screamed throughout tx.—Spit, kicked, thrust tongue constantly. Pt's parents brought back to op to try to calm her down. No luck. Pt. thrust IRM out with tongue. NO COOPERATION.'"

"Now in your opinion, Ms. Gray, do you feel that this particular young patient might cause Dr. Brookshire some extra time in the chair?"

"Well, she probably would."

"Now put yourself in Dr. Brookshire's shoes. Pretend for a moment that *you* are the treating dentist. Would *you* want to get paid a little bit for this extra time that this particular child patient is taking away from your other waiting patients?"

"I object!" Wratchett screamed out.

"Objection sustained. Ms. Gray, you don't have to answer that." Judge Grudge smirked.

Jack turned his back on the flustered witness and acted as if he was done nipping at her heels but abruptly wheeled around to face her once again. "Oh, yes, just one more question, Ms. Gray. This *Georgia State Medicaid Manual for Dental Offices* states that the codes Y000100–Y009400, management of difficult children, must be *preapproved* before the dentist can claim them. Is this true?"

"Why, yes," she replied.

"Could you please help me see how that works? That *preapproval* business?"

"Why, of course. Certain Medicaid codes have to be submitted on a preapproval form. This means that they have to be gone through by our dental consultant in Wither, Georgia, and he has to sign off on them and then return them to the treating dentist with his stamp of approval on it."

"Are you saying, Ms. Gray, that each and every time Dr. Brookshire claimed a treatment code Y000100-Y009400 for management of difficult children, she had to wait to be preapproved?"

"Yes, that's right."

"Well then, your dental consultant on the other end felt that each and every case that he approved for these behavior codes was a valid case of the doctor needing extra time to treat the patient?"

"I guess so. I can't really speak for Dr. Drupey. He's been up there a *really* long time doing preapprovals, and he's *really* getting old and all."

"But nevertheless, he *is* the Medicaid-designated dental consultant, and he *does* have final say at this time on all preapprovals?"

"That is correct."

"Now let's return briefly to Mr. Wratchett's exhibit A—the claim form for one Portia Gordon, date of service 11-30-94. Could you please show me how you know that Dr. Drupey preapproved this claim?"

"Yeah." She pointed to a stamped date. "This stamp means Dr. Drupey preapproved the procedure code on 11-9-94."

"And Dr. Brookshire performed the procedure on 11-30-94. Is that correct?"

"Yes, sir."

"So Dr. Drupey in Wither, Georgia, at the main Medicaid office for Georgia dentists, preapproved the code for management of difficult children on one three-year-old Portia Gordon on 11-9-94. And then Dr. Brookshire submitted her claim form on 11-30-94. Do you see any procedural mistake in any of this? After all, it had been preapproved three weeks previously, am I right?"

"You . . . are . . . correct . . . sir," she spat out.

Jack spun around on his heels toward the jury. "Hmmmm, thank you for your time, Ms. Gray."

Judge Grudge turned toward Brett Wratchett. "Do you want to cross-examine?"

"No, Your Honor, I want to call my next witness."

"Thank you, Mrs. Gray. You may step down."

Wratchett stiffened his neck, swallowed hard, drew a deep sigh as if he was making his best attempt to recover from his recent whipping, cleared his throat, and announced, "Your Honor, I call Mr. Gregory Graham."

A perfectly groomed young three-piecer walked arrogantly up to the front and took the stand. The bailiff swore him in. He smoothed his tailored suit sleeve when he was done swearing in, afraid that holding his arm in the air may have wrinkled it. Then he added a couple of quick brushes to his shoulders for good measure. He could have been the poster boy for yuppies.

"Good morning, sir," Wratchett attempted to sing out. "Could you please state your name for the records?"

"Yes. My name is Gregory Graham."

"And what do you do for a living, sir?"

"I am the provider enrollment supervisor for Electronic Data Systems."

"And where is your office located, sir?"

"It is located in Mystic, Georgia."

"Is that near Atlanta, sir?"

"Yes, it is."

"And what do you do there at Electronic Data Systems?"

"We process certain forms that come from certain companies for payment."

"And is one of the companies you serve called the Georgia Department of Medical Assistance?"

"Yes sir, it is."

"Could you please make it a little clearer what you do? I'm a little confused."

"Well, we handle the claims in many different ways. In the case of Dr. Brookshire's claims, her office computer system was not compatible with our EDS software. So her office used a clearinghouse in Atlanta. They received Dr. Brookshire's claims for payment, loaded the claims onto a tape, and sent that tape to us at EDS. We then proceeded to download the tape into our system, perform all our checks and balances, and then issue a payment check through the department of medical assistance, if all looked kosher."

"Mr. Graham, would you say that the work you supervise on a daily basis is done with a great deal of accuracy?"

"Oh, *yes*, sir. I see to *that* myself."

"And do you feel that the computers and systems that you work with on a daily basis are state of the art?"

"Yes, sir. They are the very best on the market. We have the very best, top-of-the-line technology available today."

"And what are the chances, in your opinion, of your databases there at EDS ever becoming corrupt?"

"Oh, *no*, sir, *that* would *never* be possible. The employees at EDS are top notch. They are some of the best computer tech guys around. They are extremely knowledgeable about what they do."

"So you are telling me, Mr. Graham, that Electronic Data Systems is a well-greased machine?"

"Oh, yes, sir. We really know what we are doing."

"You wouldn't, for example, as the provider enrollment supervisor, allow careless mistakes to jeopardize your operation there at EDS, would you, Mr. Graham?"

"Sir, we at EDS don't know the *meaning* of *careless mistakes*."

"Thank you, Mr. Graham." He turned to the judge. "No more questions, Your Honor."

Judge Grudge turned to Jack. "Your witness," He announced flatly.

"Good morning, Mr. Graham. How are you?" Jack chirped.

The young yuppie looked nervous. "Oh, I'm OK."

"You did a fine job of explaining how it works at EDS, and I think we all have a fairly good understanding of the trail that Dr. Brookshire's paper claims go through from the time they leave her office in the mail to the time your company, Electronic Data Systems or EDS, cuts her the check. But one area is a little hazy to me. Can you help me out?"

"Well, I'll certainly try."

"Back sometime in July 1994, right in the middle of the dates that Dr. Brookshire is accused of committing Medicaid fraud, did your company, EDS, undergo some type of changeover from one method to another?"

"Why, yes. EDS, in an effort to keep up with the latest, which we *always* strive to do, switched from a paper claim system to a paperless one."

"Now what does that mean *exactly*, Greg?"

"It means that companies, before July 1994, submitted their claims for payment on *paper* forms. But after July 1994, the same companies submitted their claims electronically."

"Give me an example, please."

"Well . . . say Company A has always had to create a paper claim for payment by typing each and every charge into their computer, then printing out the claim, then putting it into an envelope, and then mailing it to us at EDS. Well . . . after July 1994, the same Company A only has to type the charges into their computer, then hit a button, and—voila!—it arrives in seconds for payment at EDS."

"So after July 1994, it was a much less complicated and much quicker system for payment?"

"Exactly. You get it."

"Thank you, Greg. But I am still a little baffled about Dr. Brookshire's procedures after July 1994 specifically. I have a couple of questions."

"OK, I'm certain I can answer them."

"Did this new system of yours allow Dr. Brookshire to now bypass the clearinghouse you referred to earlier?"

"Oh, no, she still had to go through them first because her computer system *still* was not compatible with our EDS software."

"So Dr. Brookshire still submitted her claims for Medicaid payment to a clearinghouse first. Then the clearinghouse sent them over to you in Mystic?"

"That is correct."

"Greg, do you feel that Dr. Brookshire's having to submit her claims *first* to another place and *then* to your place might very well have created a great deal of doubt about whether the claims ended up accurate? I mean, by the time her claims got to EDS, they had already been to another completely separate place, transferred onto tape, placed in the mail, and mailed off to EDS. Don't you feel that all these extra steps from Dr. Brookshire's office to yours might have placed her at a very high risk for some sort of error in her claims?"

"Oh, most definitely not. All the people who work at both the clearinghouse and EDS are very skilled employees."

"Greg, have you ever personally met anyone who works at the clearinghouse where Dr. Brookshire's forms first travel?"

"Well . . . no . . . but I just *know* that they have to be skilled at their work."

"You have never met a single employee at this clearinghouse, yet you just *know* that they all *have* to be skilled at their work?"

"Well . . . *yeah*!"

"OK, Greg, now let's get back to the switchover. Since Dr. Brookshire had to still submit her claims first to the clearinghouse, then they sent them transposed on tape to you, that essentially means that the switchover in July 1994 did not affect Dr. Brookshire in any way?"

"Oh yes, it did. It made it much quicker for her."

"And how was that?"

"Well . . . before July 1994, like I said before, she had to submit her paper claim to the clearinghouse. Then they put the forms on tape and sent them over to us. Then we had to create a database and go from there."

"So still sticking to Dr. Brookshire's case as an example, tell me what the switchover in your systems in July 1994 meant as far as the way her claims were handled specifically."

"Well . . . once we switched systems, it made our old system obsolete. That meant that we had to recreate Dr. Brookshire's database for our new system."

"Wait a minute . . . you had to *recreate* Dr. Brookshire's database?"

"Yes, sir, that is correct."

"Hold on. Let me get this straight. When EDS switched systems, nothing remained in its original form? It was all *recreated*?"

"That is correct."

"And just *how* were Dr. Brookshire's original claims *recreated*? Please explain that in detail, Greg."

"Well . . . we took her original database and retyped it into our new system. You see, whenever anyone changes software, the software for the *new* program requires that the operator enter any *old* information that he wants to."

"So you switched to a new software program . . . which essentially is a clean slate, right?"

"That is correct."

"And this clean slate is only as good as the information that is typed into it, right?"

"That is correct."

"And you stated that the operator who is entering this *old* information is free to enter *any old information that he or she wants to*?"

"That's what I said."

"*So* . . . actually, your employees, these skilled computer tech guys, they were free at the time of software switchover to pick and choose what they entered into the new program?"

"Well . . . now . . . I . . . didn't . . . exactly . . . mean . . . that . . . they . . . *picked* . . . whatever . . . they . . . wanted. I'm . . . pretty . . . sure . . . those . . . guys . . . put . . . all . . . her . . . old . . . claims . . . in very accurately."

"*So* . . . you are *pretty sure* that these claims for dental payment from Medicaid, the ones that Dr. Brookshire's reputation as a professional is riding on . . . the ones that she is being charged with a *felony* for . . . were *recreated* accurately?"

"Uh . . . uh . . . uh . . ."

Jack looked like a fire-breathing dragon. "Your Honor, permission to approach the bench?"

Judge Grudge looked very irritated. He was visibly not happy with the way things were going. The state's attempt at establishing that EDS's databases were not corrupt was sinking fast. "If you feel you must," He told Jack.

Both Jack and Brett Wratchett approached the bench. I couldn't hear what all was being whispered, but I could tell that there was quite a battle going on, judging by the constant arm waving and finger-pointing. Later, I would learn that Jack moved to get his second requested summary judgment based on the high probability that the databases at EDS were corrupted. After all, the very crime that I was being accused of, Medicaid fraud, was based entirely on the claim forms that I had submitted to EDS during those exact years. Once again, though, Jack lost the battle. Judge Grudge as much as told him to sit down. The judge did not like it one bit that this backwoods boy lawyer from south Georgia was whipping his beloved state's ass.

Jack recovered his composure the best he could and walked back over to Gregory Graham, computer specialist. "I have no more questions for you today, Mr. Graham," he stated.

"Redirect?" Judge Grudge asked Brett Wratchett.

"No, Your Honor," Wratchett choked out. He could recognize easily that the witness was not salvageable at this point. He would have to try to establish the fact that the databases were not corrupt using a different witness.

"You may step down, sir," Judge Grudge told Gregory Graham.

"Call your next witness, counselor," the judge told Wratchett.

"Your Honor, I call Emma Claire Washington," he announced.

A nicely dressed thin Black woman in her midthirties promenaded toward the stand. She was all decked out in the latest fashion, crisp and coordinated to the hilt. She stepped up to the witness-box, swore in, and sat down cautiously, being careful not to wrinkle her freshly pressed ensemble.

"Good morning, Ms. Washington," Wratchett said. "How are you today?"

"Oh, I'm fine, thank you."

"Could you please state your name for the record?"

"Yes. My name is Emma Claire Washington."

"And what do you do for a living, Ms. Washington?"

"I am the provider relations supervisor at Electronic Data Systems in Mystic, Georgia."

"And tell us about your job description at EDS."

"I work with the providers or the clients—you know, the companies and offices that send us their claims to process."

"So do you mean that you work with clients such as dental offices who submit claims for Medicaid?"

"Yes, they are one group that we work with."

"And did your company, EDS, process claim forms for Medicaid payment from the dental office of Dr. Doramae Brookshire from January 1993 to March 1995?"

"Yes, we did."

"And what sorts of things do you do in your position? Tell us about your job description."

"Well, I am the provider relations supervisor, so that means that I supervise the EDS workers in my division to make sure that they are serving the clients in the most professional manner possible. And if there is any interaction between the EDS worker and the client, I make sure that I stress to my workers that it is of the utmost importance that such a relationship be mutually respectful and courteous."

"And would that relationship—one of mutual respect and courtesy to one another—would that relationship include being very, very careful to perform their work very meticulously?"

"Why, of course." And she smoothed her white starched skirt. "We take a great deal of pride in our precision."

"So it could be accurately said that if an EDS worker was asked to, say, recreate a database on a client because there was a company switch in software, you feel certain that such a recreation of client database would be precise?"

"I object!" screamed Jack. "Leading the witness."

"Objection overruled. You must answer the question, Ms. Washington," Judge Grudge droned.

"Well, I really can't answer that particular question because I am not anywhere near the department where they recreate databases or switch over to new software. That portion of EDS isn't even in my building. It is as far away from me as you can get."

"Yes, buuut knowing your company's philosophy . . . knowing what EDS is all about, wouldn't you speculate that the employees would be trained to be *scrupulously conscientious* in such a situation?"

"I object." Jack appeared rather perturbed this time. "Leading the witness."

"Objection sustained." The judge turned toward Brett Wratchett. "Watch yourself, counselor."

"OK. Let me reword this question. If an employee at EDS is asked to perform some work on a computer, in your opinion, does he do that work to the best of his ability?"

"Why, yes. *My* employees in the provider relations department most certainly do."

Brett Wratchett looked like a whipped puppy. His new witness, Ms. Washington, had not exactly saved his ass from the previous two whippings he had suffered from the EDS employee and the Medicaid clerk. He had to think quickly. "Ms. Washington, if you were to, say, do a little experiment one day at EDS and switch jobs with another supervisor—say the supervisor of software and programs—don't you feel that you would find that your employees in that department would be very exacting, very thorough, in their work?"

Jack just shook his head. He started to rise but quickly gave up the notion. I could almost read his mind. He was practicing his principle I had so often heard him speak of during our preparations for the trial. "Let the witness hang herself" he called it.

The nervous judge glanced in Jack's direction, fully expecting him to object. When he didn't, he turned his attention once again toward the witness.

"Weeelll . . . I can't really answer that question because we would *never* do such an experiment at EDS. I am trained for provider relations, and the supervisor of provider enrollment is trained specifically for *that*. It is two entirely different areas. I would not feel comfortable in his area or he in mine."

That was it. Brett Wratchett had, once again, dug his own hole. Prosecution, 0; defense, 3. This was going to be such a slam dunk for Jack. He probably wouldn't even ask Ms. Washington many questions at all. He always told me, "If it isn't necessary, don't waste your time doing it."

"Thank you, Ms. Washington," Wratchett whined.

"Your witness." He turned toward Jack,and sparks flew from his eyes.

Jack arose, buttoned his suit coat, straightened his readers, and walked on air over to the awaiting witness. "Good morning, Ms. Washington."

"Good morning."

"Ms. Washington, I am not going to waste much of your time this morning. I know you are a very busy lady."

"Well, yes, I *do* have a lot to do today. I was hoping this might go fast."

"Ms. Washington, you have stated that you are the supervisor of provider relations at EDS, correct?"

"Yes, that is right."

"And that your job there involves making sure that the employees under you establish and maintain good relationships with your clients, right?"

"Yes, that's a perfect way to put it."

"So if you were asked to judge whether an employee in another division, the division of provider enrollment, was doing his job correctly, could you do that?"

"Why, of course, I couldn't. I have not been trained in that division. I know nothing of it."

"Ms. Washington, if you were asked to judge if a database that had been recreated because the software program had been changed in the division of provider enrollment—if you were asked if such a database had been recreated *correctly*—do you feel qualified to answer that question?"

"No, sir, I do not."

"Thank you for your time today, Ms. Washington." Jack was smiling from ear to ear. I saw Brett Wratchett cringe in the corner.

"The witness may step down," Judge Grudge muttered. He looked at His honorable watch. "It is time for lunch. Everyone, take a one-hour lunch. Be back in this courtroom at precisely one o'clock."

After the judge slipped away through His secret doorway and the jury filed out, I left the courtroom with Bob, Sarah, Mom, and Dave. We walked confidently, discussing the first morning's events with a great deal of assurance. We were definitely winning the game. The great rivals—the state—were choking.

We ate at a little yuppie café tucked in the corner of the only block of eateries within walking distance. I enjoyed my lunch on the first full day of my trial and partook of it with my newfound poise. Looking back, we were all so convinced that the little man—or in this case, the little woman—could beat the big bad state that we were actually discussing what our next step might be as soon as we kicked their sorry butts. Little did we know that the enemy was unconquerable.

The state of Georgia could not be vanquished, quelled, or suppressed. They could not be put under the yoke. Never mind that the challenger was completely and utterly correct. Never mind that the one who dared to throw down the gauntlet was absolutely the one in the right. The mighty state of Georgia could not—would not—let themselves be defeated, and it was the state itself that laid down *all* the rules in set battle.

We were back in the courtroom and settled in our proper seats by 12:50 p.m. The prosecuting team dragged in at 1:05 p.m. The bailiff announced the honorable judge Grudge at 1:11 p.m. Of course, everyone in the courtroom was made to rise once again until the judge took His seat. "Are we set to get started?" He asked Wratchett.

"Oh, *yes*, Your Honor," Wratchett answered, trying to muster up as much self-assurance as possible.

"Then call your next witness."

"Your Honor, I call Mr. Gregory Graham back to the stand."

Jack's mouth dropped open. I think mine did too. We were both wondering why on god's green earth Wratchett would make such a *dumb* decision. Why pour salt in an open wound?

Gregory Graham once again walked arrogantly up to the stand, only this time he had a little bit of drag to his saunter. He swore in and took a seat.

"Good afternoon, Mr. Graham," Brett Wratchett said.

"Good afternoon."

"I need to ask you just a *couple* of more questions, Mr. Graham."

"OK, shoot."

"What are the chances of any errors being entered into your system at EDS when your employees are recreating a database?"

"Oh, no chance at all."

"Please tell the jury why that is."

The computer specialist turned to face the jury. "Because our computer tech guys at EDS are top-of-the-line technology experts. If they are not, we don't hire them."

"And just how many claims a day do these computer experts handle?"

"Oh, hundreds and hundreds and hundreds. I tell you, they are really good."

"So these guys have had *a lot* of practice entering data into computers?"

"They sure have."

"And don't you feel that practice makes perfect?"

"Without a doubt. If a person has to enter hundreds of claims a day into a computer, he quickly becomes very good at his skill."

"No more questions today, Mr. Graham."

Brett Wratchett and Gregory Graham were both gloating. They both thought that they had pulled off the best bounce-back ever. In their opinion, the momentum had swung back to their favor. But Jack had not been up yet.

Jack arose and swaggered up to the awaiting target. "Good afternoon . . . once again . . . Greg."

"Good afternoon."

"Greg, you just stated that your computer experts at EDS handled hundreds and hundreds and hundreds of Medicaid claims a day?"

"That is correct."

"How many dentists in Redd County send Medicaid claims to you for payment?"

"Oh, we process claim forms for about ninety dentists in that area."

"Wait a minute. Let me get this straight. You process Medicaid claim forms for *ninety* dentists in Redd County?"

"Yes, that's what I said."

"Are you *certain* of that number?"

"Yes, I should know. We process their Medicaid claim forms."

"Are you sure that it's that many *just* in Redd County?"

"No, I said in that *area*."

"Mr. Graham, could you be a little more specific, please? What do you mean by *that area*?"

"You know . . . you live down there . . . I mean, Redd County, Barren County, Whackford County . . . all those counties right *by* Redd County."

"Greg, are Whackford County and Barren County *right by* Redd County?"

"Well, *yeah*!"

"So let me get this straight . . . Barren County and Whackford County are *adjacent* counties to Redd County?"

"That's what I said. Why do you keep asking me this when you know the answer perfectly well? I mean, you *live* down there."

"And around *ninety* dentists in these three counties accept Medicaid?"

"That's what I said."

"And you are certain, Greg, that Barren County and Whackford County are right next to Redd County with no other counties in between?"

Gregory Graham let out an audible sigh. "Yes, Mr. Goodman."

"OK, just one more question today, Mr. Graham. Do you not feel that the more claims a computer tech guy has to process a day, the more there lays the potential to make a mistake, like maybe in *recreating* databases? I mean . . . *hundreds* and *hundreds* and *hundreds* of claims a day? Do they really do that?"

"Yes, Mr. Goodman. They *really* do that. And no, Mr. Goodman, they do not make mistakes as I have stated numerous times today."

"Thank you for your time, Greg."

Judge Grudge looked peeved once more. He turned to Brett Wratchett with a look that began to resemble disgust. I drew the conclusion that this handpicked soldier for the state was starting to disappoint his superior officer.

"Redirect?" He inquired of Wratchett, a certain desperation in his voice that hinted at him to decline.

"Not at this time, Your Honor."

"Witness may step down."

"Your Honor," Jack spoke up, "defense would like to keep Mr. Graham under subpoena for later use."

"Very well." The judge turned toward the now mobile Graham. "Mr. Graham, you are commanded to stay in this courthouse until further notice. You must make yourself available at a moment's notice."

Gregory Graham's arrogant waltz turned to the walk of a whupped puppy dog. "Yes, Your Honor," he managed to say.

The next state's witness was Mrs. Echo Barker, a nervous-acting middle-aged woman who had been employed at the Georgia State Medicaid Office for several years. In fact, I had seen her little tightly drawn-in face once before. We had had some sort of mock pretrial exercise a few months previously. I was told at the time that its purpose was to "determine if the state had enough evidence against Dr. Brookshire to go to trial." They never officially let us know the outcome of that playact pretrial, but judging from the fact that we were sitting there in full trial, I guess they had determined that they did indeed have "enough evidence" against Dr. Brookshire to validate an official state probative inquest.

The main reason that I remembered Mrs. Barker was that, at the time of the pretrial, she would not stop babbling on and on about "the poor little girl who died in Dr. Brookshire's dental chair." In fact, every time that Jack would object and approach the bench and every time the sitting old judge would reprimand her and tell her that "this trial is about *Medicaid fraud*, not about the other charges against Dr. Brookshire," Mrs. Barker would very quickly thereafter forget the judge's words and would return to the subject of "the poor little girl." Actually, she burst out in tears as she spoke of it. It was pretty apparent that the charges of Medicaid fraud were the last thing on Mrs. Barker's mind. As soon as I saw her on the stand, I figured that Brett Wratchett was going to use her to bring out—or better yet, to *emphasize*—the involuntary manslaughter case.

"Good afternoon, Ms. Barker."

"Good afternoon, Mr. Wratchett."

"Could you please state your name for the records?"

"Yes. My name is Echo Barker."

"And what do you do for a living, Ms. Barker?"

"I am an investigator for the office of investigations and compliance at the department of medical assistance in Atlanta."

"And what are the sorts of things you do at your job?"

"Well, like the title implies, I am sent out to investigate any dentists in the state who are under suspicion for doing something wrong as far as Medicaid goes."

"And were you sent out to investigate one Dr. Doramae Brookshire recently?"

"Yes, I was."

"What were the specific circumstances?"

"Well, I was told that a three-year-old patient in south Georgia had *died* in Dr. Brookshire's dental office."

"And what were you asked to do?"

"Well, like I said, I am asked to *investigate* such incidences."

"And what did your investigation reveal?"

"It revealed that Dr. Brookshire was very *negligent* in her treatment of the deceased . . . *poor little thing*!" Echo Barker's eyes filled with tears. "I just can't figure out to this day why Dr. Brookshire allowed this to happen in her dental office. I mean . . . children don't *die* at the dentist!"

"Do you need a moment, Mrs. Barker?" the judge asked.

"No, I'm OK," she replied.

"No more questions today, Mrs. Barker," Brett Wratchett whispered. "Thank you for being so brave. I know that must have been hard on you." He shook his head, stared forlornly at the floor, and then inched toward his beloved flip chart, now overflowing with green. He produced a red indelible marker this time and wrote in sad slow motion, "THREE-YEAR-OLD PATIENT DIES IN DR. BROOKSHIRE'S CHAIR AS A RESULT OF NEGLIGENCE."

He turned slowly toward Jack as soon as he was sure that the entire jury had more than ample chance to see his latest red inscription. "Your witness," he told Jack, looking at him as if to implore him to be easy on the poor soul on the stand.

"Good afternoon, Echo," Jack chirped.

"Good afternoon," she muttered, still teary eyed.

"I won't keep you long, Mrs. Barker. I just have a couple of what you might call procedural questions."

"OK."

"Mrs. Barker, you told Mr. Wratchett that your job is to investigate any dentists in the state of Georgia who are under suspicion for doing something wrong as far as Medicaid goes, correct?"

"Yes, that's right."

"And you further stated that you were sent to investigate an incident at Dr. Doramae Brookshire's office, right?"

"That's right."

"Then you went on to tell Mr. Wratchett that your investigation revealed that Dr. Brookshire had been *very negligent* in her treatment of a three-year-old patient, correct?"

"That's right."

"Mrs. Barker, could you please tell the jury exactly what methods you used to do your investigation?"

"What do you mean what methods?"

"Well, just like it sounds. I am sure that since you are one of the main investigators for the office of investigations and compliance at the department of medical assistance, there is certainly a set procedure on investigating such an incidence . . . isn't there?"

"Weelll, not really. They just trust us to use our good judgment on how to go about this."

"So . . . there is no set procedure, either written or oral, on exactly how to go about one of your *investigations*?"

"Not that I know of, sir."

"Not that you know of? Was there no training for your position?"

"Well, yeah, many years back, when I first started on the job. I think I remember a short training session."

"How many years have you been working as an investigator for the office of investigations and compliance at Medicaid?"

"Twenty-four."

"And how many training sessions, workshops, seminars, classes, or any other mandatory trainings have you attended in those twenty-four years?"

"Like I said, I think I had some training in the beginning."

"Oh . . . you *think* you had some training *twenty-four years ago*?"

"Yeah."

"Mrs. Barker, could you describe in detail what you did to investigate Dr. Brookshire's case? Did you travel to her office in Goat Valley?"

"I didn't have to travel to her office. I could learn all that I needed to know just from reading the *Atlanta Journal-Constitution*. Hell, it was in there for days in a row."

"*What* was in the newspaper for days in a row?"

"You know, how she gave the child too many drugs . . . and how she had been in trouble before with the board . . . and how she did too many patients at once . . . *all that*!"

"Mrs. Barker, did you ever *talk* to Dr. Brookshire during your investigation?"

"Well, *no!*"

"Why would you not talk, at least once, to the doctor who is being investigated?"

"I already *told* you. I could find out all I needed to know about her from reading the papers in Atlanta!"

Jack remained as cool as a cucumber, although I knew that he did not believe what he was hearing. He brought it on home. "So what you are telling me, Mrs. Barker, is that *you*, an entrusted investigator with the office of investigations and compliance at Medicaid, based your investigation of Dr. Doramae Brookshire *solely* on what you read in the media?"

"Wuh . . . I . . . uh . . . uh . . . uhm . . . uhm?"

"Thank you for your time, Mrs. Barker." Jack spun around to face Judge Grudge. "That's all, Your Honor."

If the judge had been a little peeved that morning, He was getting downright pissed off by now. In fact, His face was beginning to turn a nice shade of crimson. It matched Brett Wratchett's latest hue of Magic Marker on his fancy flip chart. Really, I thought the red face matched his black robe quite nicely.

He twirled His angry face toward the prosecutor. "Redirect, counselor?" He spat out at Wratchett.

"Not at this time, Your Honor," Wratchett mumbled.

"Then call your next witness!"

WELL FIDDLE, MR. JACK

"**Y**OUR HONOR, I would like to call Dr. Sonny Sneed to the stand."

I knew this one. I had attended dental school for four long years at the School of Dental Education in Lumpkin, Georgia, with Sonny Sneed. Then he had returned to his hometown of Goat Valley and set up his dental practice. He was quite the politically savvy one. In fact, he served as our class president all four years. He would be the one person in the courtroom who would feel perfectly at ease being called to the stand. He proved me right.

As soon as his name was called, he stood up slowly, ran his fingers through his thick head of brown hair, stretched quite leisurely, and began to take his time working his way up to the front, his Tony Lama cowboy boots clicking the whole time. All the way to the stand, he smiled at numerous people in the courtroom, especially at the good-looking young ladies on the jury. I think I even saw him wink. He was a fairly good-looking man himself, and he knew it. He was tall, husky, and well groomed. He had recently taken up weight-lifting as a hobby to help him fight off the stresses of running a dental office, so his biceps and triceps rippled under the harsh courtroom lights. His posture was perfect. He held his shoulders square and with confidence. I was used to this circus act from years of going to dental school with him. He was, once again, fooling a whole room full of people. But he couldn't fool me. I knew the rest of the story, the true Sonny Sneed, the fake behind those Foster Grants.

This was what *I* knew about Sonny Sneed. I knew that he went to my office, just days after Dr. Elmer Quimby had deserted it, and removed every last piece of my dental equipment in one fell swoop. The tenants who rented the apartment upstairs from the office described in great detail how it went down. Early one Saturday morning, Sonny and several pretty young girls showed up with a large semitruck at my back door. They then proceeded to remove every last dental chair, operatory light, handpiece, instrument cart, X-ray machine, piece of processing equipment, nitrous setup, and piece of furniture in the patient waiting room. They even took the patient folders. They left behind clipped wires, dirty diapers, dropped X-rays, crumpled hamburger wrappers, paper cups half full of sodas, dirty tissues, chewed bubblegum stuck to the carpet, unflushed toilets, and lots and lots of muddy footprints.

I knew this because, the Monday after the dirty deed, I happened to be driving by the office. Something looked barren and dead inside, so I stopped to check it out. I still had a key because I still owned the office building. So I went in and gasped in horror at what I discovered. The thing that got me the worst, I think, was all the clipped wires. Apparently, Sonny and his accomplices had been in such a hurry to get out that Saturday that they had brought along a handy pair of sharp wire cutters. And that was exactly how they got tons and tons of dental equipment removed so quickly. The wires to the operatory lights were cut. The wires to the patient chairs were cut. The wires to the dental carts (the things where the water, suction, and drills were housed) were cut. The wires to the X-ray machines were cut. The wires to most of the phones were cut. Even the wires to some lamps in the patient waiting room were cut. I have learned over the years that greed will do funny things to a man. But how this classmate of mine, this fine Christian pillar of our community, this record-holding weight lifter, could have raped me to this extent I will never know!

As soon as I gained my composure at the barren wasteland that used to be my office, I picked up the one phone they had left and called Ricky. He came right over with a Polaroid camera, and we took turns snapping pictures of the crime scene. I guess, at the time, Ricky and I thought someone somewhere would care in one way or another about those pictures. Yes, we thought that we might be able to use them for some kind of "evidence." The truth was we never found the opportunity to use those pictures after that day. We couldn't find anyone anywhere who cared enough about the situation to even listen.

Sonny raised his right hand and swore in, and he and his $500 boots took a seat.

"Good afternoon, Dr. Sneed," Brett Wratchett said.

"*Wuh*, good afternoon," Sonny quickly shot back.

"Could you please tell the jury what you do for a living?"

"Sure. I'm a dentist."

"Do you have your own dental practice, Dr. Sneed?"

"Wuh, yes, I do."

"And where is your dental practice, Dr. Sneed?"

"It's on Mississippi Avenue in Goat Valley, Georgia."

"So your dental practice is just down the street from where Dr. Brookshire's practice was?"

"Wuh, yes, sir, it is."

"So your dental practice was *closer* in proximity to Dr. Brookshire's compared with any of the other dentists in town?"

"Yes, sir, by far."

"Dr. Sneed, do you know one Dr. Elmer Quimby?"

"Yes, I do. I went to dental school at the School of Dental Education with him."

"And did Dr. Quimby come to Goat Valley recently?"

"Yes, sir, he did."

"But wasn't Dr. Quimby's dental practice up in north Georgia, near Suwanee?"

"Yes, his main practice was, but he started to drive a couple of days a week to Goat Valley to work Dr. Brookshire's practice after she was suspended, and he purchased her dental practice."

"So Dr. Elmer Quimby *bought* Dr. Brookshire's dental practice? That would mean that he now owned the equipment, the furniture, and everything in that building, right?"

"Right. When a dentist purchases another one's practice, he then owns all the dental chairs, X-ray equipment, operatory lights, carts, processing equipment, waiting room furniture, lab equipment . . . perdy much everything."

"And, Dr. Sneed, when a dentist purchases another dentist's practice, does he also then own the patients, so to speak? What I mean is . . . does he buy the patient folders . . . their records?"

"Oh, yes. The main thing that the purchasing dentist is interested in is the patient load. The patients are what make a dental practice worth something."

"So let me get this straight—Dr. Quimby, at the time of his purchase, then *owned* not only all the equipment in Dr. Brookshire's dental practice but he owned also her patient load?"

"That's right."

"And she had quite a patient load, huh?"

"I object!" Jack shouted. "Your Honor, he is leading the witness."

"Objection overruled. You may answer the question."

"Weelll," Sonny started, "I've heard that she had quite a number of patients."

"And were you aware of what happened with Dr. Quimby as far as purchasing Dr. Brookshire's practice was concerned? Is Dr. Quimby still coming to Goat Valley a couple of times a week to run her old practice?"

"Oh, no, sir. He left a while ago."

"What do you mean he *left*?"

"Well, talking to him, he told me that he was not making enough money down here to make it worth his while, so he left Goat Valley and went back to his Suwanee practice full time, I guess."

"And did Dr. Quimby, your buddy from dental school . . . did he call you for any kind of help at the time he left?"

"Yes, he did. He called me and asked me to help him figure out what to do with all the dental equipment and supplies he had bought from Dr. Brookshire."

"And what did you tell Dr. Quimby?"

"Well, I told him that if he needed a temporary place to house all the stuff, he could store it at my place in Burnher County. I have a farm up there."

"So Dr. Quimby was your friend from four years of dental school. And you were probably the only dentist in Goat Valley that he knew, right?"

"That's what I was thinking at the time."

"And you saw your good friend in a bind. For some reason or another, Dr. Brookshire's practice just was not doing very well once Dr. Quimby got here, right?"

"He told me he was struggling to make ends meet."

"And you also told me that, at the time, Dr. Quimby had relayed to you that he just did not have the cash to pay a moving company to come and pick it up or a storage company to store it."

"That's what he said . . . and he was pretty upset . . . not knowing where to turn."

"So you felt like you couldn't turn your back on your friend. You had a place that was perfectly safe to store the equipment and the patient files, right?"

"That's right. My farm in Burnher County is very remote and safe. The plan was to store the patient folders and dental equipment and supplies in the five empty rooms of the vacant farmhouse."

"And were you able to lock this farmhouse?"

"Oh, yes, sir, I was. It was very secure, and up until that time, nobody had *ever* messed with anything I had put there."

"Dr. Sneed, tell us what happened the day you went to help Dr. Quimby get the things he had purchased from Dr. Brookshire's."

"Well, he was supposed to meet me in Goat Valley early one Saturday morning. But he called me that morning and said something had come up with one of his kids. He was sorry, but he just couldn't possibly make it that day, and could we do it the next Saturday?"

"What did you do then?"

"Well, I really couldn't back out at that point. I already had the semitruck for the heavy equipment lined up, and also, all my help was lined up."

"So what you are telling me is that you went ahead and got the equipment and the patient folders that Saturday?"

"Yes, sir, I did."

"Then what did you do with it?"

"Like I had planned, I took all the stuff I could carry and stored it in the empty rooms of the old farmhouse. But the heavy dental equipment— the chairs and carts and X-ray machines and lights—all stayed on the

DORAMAE BROOKSHIRE

semitruck. It was getting late, and so I locked the farmhouse, locked the back of the truck, and went home. I intended to unload the heavy equipment the next day."

"So you went back the next day, and what did you find?"

"I found the semitruck busted open with a crowbar laying there on the ground, and all the dental equipment was gone! I was sick!"

"What did you do next?"

"I called the police, made out a theft report, and then I called Elmer and told him what had happened to his dental equipment."

"I know that upset you. Did the police ever find the dental equipment?"

"No, they didn't." He hung his head, peeked over at the pretty jury girl in the front row to see if she was watching, and looked as if he was going to cry.

"But now what about the patient folders—all the patient records— were they harmed in any way?"

"Oh, *no*, not a thing was touched inside the farmhouse. It was all as I had left it."

"So you would say that the patient records were all intact and all present, just as you left them?"

"Yes, sir, they were."

"Now did anyone ever come and get any of those records?"

"Yes, sir, a couple of months later, I got a call from the GBI, asking to meet me there at the farmhouse."

"What did you do?"

"Well, I didn't know if it was legitimate, so I called my lawyer."

"What did he tell you to do?"

"He advised me to let him talk to them first."

"Then what happened?"

"Well, he found out that it was legitimate. The GBI had a reason to want the patient records, so we agreed to meet them there."

"Dr. Sneed, you stated that the GBI had a *legitimate* reason to want to meet you at the farmhouse. What was the reason given?"

"Unfortunately, that Dr. Brookshire was being investigated for Medicaid fraud, and the patient folders were needed for matching records to patients' mouths."

"What do you mean matching records to patients' mouths?"

"Well, the way I understood it, some dentists for the state were going to do exams on Dr. Brookshire's former patients to see if their records matched their dental work."

"So naturally, these dentists needed Dr. Brookshire's patient records."

"Yes, sir."

"And so did you let the GBI folks have the patient records?"

"Yes, I did. I was following my attorney's advice."

"And the GBI folks came and got Dr. Brookshire's patient files while you and your attorney waited outside, right?"

"That's right."

"And did everything go OK? Did the transition of the patient records from the farmhouse to their vehicle go all right?"

"Yes, sir. My attorney and I thought it went very smoothly."

"So there were no problems with the GBI getting Dr. Brookshire's folders from your house?"

"No, sir, there weren't."

"Thank you, Dr. Sneed." Brett Wratchett turned to Jack. "Your witness."

"Good afternoon, Dr. Sneed." Jack smiled.

"Hi, Mr. Jack." Sonny flirted back.

"Dr. Sneed, how many dentists are practicing currently in Goat Valley? Take your time."

"Let's see . . . there's Dr. Heinlich, Dr. Biget, Dr. Wolfe, Dr. Hannibal, Dr. Dankworth, Dr. Sudser, and Dr. Grubbs. Hmmm." He was counting on his fingers. "Then there's me. That's about eight, I reckon." As an afterthought, he inquired, "Oh, did you want me to include some of the specialists, like orthodontists and oral surgeons and periodontists who all come from other cities once or so a week?"

"No, I just really wanted a count of those general dentists who practice full time in Goat Valley. And out of those eight dentists in Goat Valley, how many accept Medicaid from their patients?"

"Hmmmm . . . let's see . . . I can tell you right now, *I don't.* I looked into it, and it certainly is not worth it—I mean, how little you get paid and all. And other dentists who have taken it from other cities told me never to accept Medicaid because they are such a pain to deal with. You know, all a mess at their office up there in Atlanta, and they never pay you on time, or they get the money all mixed up, and I just heard it was an awful mess up there at the Medicaid office in Atlanta. So I decided not to accept Medicaid patients from the get-go. And I think most of the guys who are dentists here in town, they feel the same way about it. Let's see . . . I *know* Dr. Grubbs doesn't take it. Dr. Wolfe doesn't. Dr. Hannibal doesn't. Dr. Sudser never did. Dr. Dankworth doesn't. I'm not sure about Dr. Biget and Dr. Heinlich. They *might* have taken it at one time . . . but I don't think so."

"So, Dr. Sneed, there are eight practicing general dentists in Goat Valley, and two *might* have accepted Medicaid patients at one time?"

"Gee, Mr. Jack, that's the best I can do off the top of my head."

"So would you say that, when she was in practice, Dr. Brookshire had the majority of Medicaid dental patients in town?"

"Oh yes, Mr. Jack, she sure did."

"Now, Dr. Sneed, I want to ask you about the adjacent towns of any size and how the counties in south Georgia lay out."

"Golly, I'll try my best."

"First of all, Dr. Sneed, is Barren County adjacent to Redd County? In other words, is Barren County the next county over from Redd County?" I wasn't real sure what Jack was getting at here, but I totally trusted him, so I wasn't worried, just a little curious.

Sonny looked around the courtroom, scoping out the situation. He cut his brown eyes at the cute female juror. It was showtime. "Well *fiddle*, Mr. Jack . . . you know how confusin' those county lines can get. Hmmmm . . . let's see . . . I know Barren County is where Bangdale is, and that's about fifty miles or so away, and I'm pretty sure that there's at least one county in between us, but there could be a tricky place in the road. You know how that goes."

I could not believe my ears. Sonny Sneed knew perfectly well that Hick County lay between Redd County and Barren County, and he had known that since he could talk. He was just messing with Jack for some reason. Or maybe the politician side of him was shining through at the moment. I wasn't really sure.

Jack would not let Sonny's recent fib go. "Sonny, now how often do you go to Bangdale?"

"Oh, probably at least once a month."

"When you leave Redd County, don't you go through *one* more county before you get to Barren County? Now *think*!"

"Wuh, golly, Mr. Jack, know what? You're *right*. Hick County lies between Redd County and Barren County."

"So, Dr. Sneed, Barren County is *not* the adjacent county to Redd County, is it?"

"Well, I reckon it's not, Mr. Jack. Wuh *fiddle,* now I remember."

"And, Dr. Sneed, is Whackford County adjacent to Redd County? Is it the next county over from Redd?"

"Well, geeee, Mr. Jack, you really have me thinking here today. Again, I would have to say that I don't think it is, but sometimes little crinks in the road can cross over, you know."

Once again, I couldn't believe what I was hearing. Sonny knew perfectly well that one of the largest counties in Georgia, Earp County, lay between Redd County and Whackford County. Whackford County was the home of Tanaha, Georgia.

Now I knew what Jack was up to. What a slick guy! He was trying to discredit Gregory Graham, the morning witness from EDS who had stated that ninety dentists in the area accepted Medicaid patients. The same guy who swore that Barren County and Whackford County both were adjacent to Redd County. Jack was growing a little tired of Sonny's constant politicking. He was having entirely too much fun with himself on the stand.

"Dr. Sneed, isn't it true that there is a very large county between Whackford County and Redd County, and that county is called Earp County?"

"Well *fiddle*, Mr. Jack. You know, you're right about that. I forget about Earp County, but you're right."

"*So*, Dr. Sneed, you agree that Whackford County is *not* adjacent to Redd County?"

"That's right, you got it."

"Dr. Sneed, let's talk a bit about the number of dentists who accept Medicaid in these two towns. I'm talking about Bangdale and Tanaha. These are the largest towns near Goat Valley in south Georgia, right?"

"Yes, sir. Bangdale and Tanaha are the *only* towns of any size near here."

"How many dentists in these two towns—Tanaha and Bangdale—would you estimate accept Medicaid?"

"Oh now, Mr. Jack, I couldn't begin to answer that. I don't know anything at all about the dentists in those two cities."

"Dr. Sneed, I am just asking you for a rough *estimate*. Do you think there are ten, twenty-five, fifty, one hundred who accept Medicaid?"

Brett Wratchett jumped up. "I object! Your Honor, he is leading the witness!"

"Objection sustained," Judge Grudge ruled. He turned toward Sonny. "Do not answer the question."

Jack tried again. "OK, Dr. Sneed, how many general dentists would you estimate the city of Bangdale has?"

"Well, if Goat Valley has eight, Bangdale probably has twenty-five, maybe twenty."

"And how many general dentists would you estimate the city of Tanaha has?"

"Well, it's a little bigger, so I'd say maybe around thirty-five or forty."

"So if we add the total numbers of dentists together that you estimate are in these two cities, it is a maximum of around sixty-five, right?"

"I'd say that was about right, yes."

"And what percentage of these dentists would you estimate accept Medicaid in their practices?"

"Oh, maybe 10 or 15 percent, not that many. Dentists don't like to take Medicaid. It slows them down."

"So let's do a little math. Ten percent of sixty-five is six and a half dentists in both Tanaha and Bangdale who accept Medicaid. Fifteen percent of sixty-five is close to ten dentists in *both* Tanaha and Bangdale who accept Medicaid. Would you say we are close?"

"Yeah, that's the best I can do."

"Thank you for helping me with that, Dr. Sneed. Now let's change the subject and go back to the day that the GBI showed up at your Burnher County farmhouse, can we?"

"OK, Mr. Jack."

"When they showed up, did they have any kind of search warrant or papers to give you?"

"Wuh, no, come to think of it, Mr. Jack. They didn't give me any kinds of papers."

"You let them carry away—how many boxes of Dr. Brookshire's patient records?—without any proof of who they were or how official the visit was?"

"Well, my attorney advised me to release the records, and he was there with me the day they took them, so I trusted his judgment."

"And who was your attorney that was with you on the day the GBI came and took Dr. Brookshire's patient records?"

"Well, it was Mr. Porky Pentz."

"Wait a minute, your attorney is Porky Pentz? Isn't he the district attorney for Redd County?"

"Well, yes, I think he is. But he has always been my lawyer."

"But Porky Pentz is the DA who charged Dr. Brookshire with Medicaid fraud. And he was sitting there with you, watching the GBI tote away Dr. Brookshire's patient records?"

"Wuh fiddle, Mr. Jack, I don't know what to say . . . Mr. Porky has always been my lawyer. I call him when I need him."

"And you *really* needed him *this* time, didn't you? The GBI were involved, and it was much more comfortable to hide behind the district attorney who charged Dr. Brookshire than to do what was correct ethically, wasn't it?"

"I object!" hollered Brett Wratchett.

"Objection sustained," Grudge murmured. "Dr. Sneed, you don't have to answer that last question." The judge glared at Jack.

"OK then. We will leave the subject of you and the district attorney who charged Dr. Brookshire with Medicaid fraud being a team and go on to something else."

Brett Wratchett looked as if he was going to repeat his recent act, but decided to stay seated, probably hoping that Jack's last piercing comment was going to be the last reference to Sonny Sneed and Porky Pentz being in cahoots.

"Now, Dr. Sneed, I am going to ask you to go back to the day that the GBI came to your Burnher farmhouse and toted all of Dr. Brookshire's patient records out of the house. You can remember that day, right?"

"Oh, yes, Mr. Jack, I remember it like it was yesterday."

"Good. Then let me ask you a couple of specific questions about exactly *how* these patient records were removed from the farmhouse and how they were transported."

"Ah'll do my best, Mr. Jack."

"Now when the GBI came that day to get Dr. Brookshire's patient records, how many GBI agents were there?"

"There were two—a man and a woman."

"And what did they do when they got there?"

"Well . . . they just came up to me and Mr. Porky and shook our hands and introduced themselves."

"Can you remember their names?'

"I think the woman said her name was Agent Blackwood, and his was something like Wickman."

"What were these two GBI folks like?"

"Well . . . they were both very young. And she was kinda pretty."

"What did they do after they shook yours and Mr. Pentz, the district attorney's hands?"

"Well, they asked where the patient folders were."

"And what did you tell them?"

"I said to follow me. They were inside the farmhouse."

"Then what happened?"

"Well . . . they followed me, and I showed them the five rooms that the folders were in."

"*Five* rooms? You must have had an awfully lot of Dr. Brookshire's patient records. It took five rooms to house them?"

"Well, not really. I mean . . . I could have got them in a lot less space. We were just in a hurry to get them in the house that day because it was getting dark, so the girls and me, we just put them wherever they fell, so to speak."

"The *girls* and you?"

"Yuh, Mr. Jack. The day we went to get her patient records and dental equipment, remember, I told you that some of my dental assistants and close friends helped me that day?"

"I'm sorry, Dr. Sneed, I don't recall you sharing that fact with me. So let me get this straight. On the Saturday that you went to remove everything from Dr. Brookshire's office, you and several girls unloaded Dr. Brookshire's patient files from the back of a semitruck, went into your vacant old farmhouse in Burnher County, and plopped those patient records down wherever it was convenient to drop them. I believe you stated *wherever they fell* because it was starting to get dark outside?"

"Wuh, yeah, Mr. Jack, that's about the extent of it."

"Dr. Sneed, did you or the girls who were helping you that day, did any of you think to place those patient records carefully in any preconceived *order*? For example, did any of you have the idea to, say, place them in alphabetical order or to maybe place them in some kind of orderly pattern?"

"Well fiddle, Mr. Jack . . . it was really late, and we had been moving tons of dental equipment that day, and we were plumb worn out and hungry and tired. We were ready to be *done*."

"Dr. Sneed, because you and the girls were ready to be *done*, I guess you never thought to take any kind of photographs of the patient records or write down any information on just how they were placed in the farmhouse?"

"Well . . . no, we didn't."

"And you probably didn't draw out any kind of rough map or chart of how they were placed either, so maybe you could keep up with how many boxes you had, huh?"

"No, Mr. Jack, we didn't draw any pictures or nothin'."

"So, Dr. Sneed, is it safe to say that there exists a possibility that those specific patient files might have been tampered with . . . just *possibly*?"

"Oh, no, Mr. Jack. Nobody goes around my farmhouse. Nothin' has ever been messed with."

"Is that so, Dr. Sneed? Did you not just tell us about how that semitruck—the same one that carried Dr. Brookshire's patient records—got broken into with a crowbar on the very same night that her records were carried into that farmhouse?"

"Wuh, yeah, I guess so, come to think of it."

"So do you agree that there exists a possibility that Dr. Brookshire's patient records could have gotten tampered with in some manner?"

"Well, I guess it is a remote possibility since someone messed with the dental equipment and all."

"Dr. Sneed, do you know what the legal term *chain of custody* means?"

"Wuh, yeah, I think so."

"What does it mean?"

"Well . . . I think it means something like, in a legal case, the evidence that is going to be used . . . it has been messed with or something."

"Yes, that is right, Dr. Sneed. And what, to you, would the term *breaking the chain of custody* mean?"

"Wuh, Mr. Jack, that would be when somebody touches something they aren't supposed to or messes with a blood sample or lets a bunch of other people move the evidence around or something."

"That's a very good definition of *breaking the chain of custody*, Dr. Sneed. Let me ask you something else. Just why do you think that it is very important to *not* break the chain of custody in a criminal case?"

"Well . . . because the person who is up on criminal charges . . . he or she deserves a fair trial."

"And if the chain of custody is broken, do you think that the defendant—the person who is up on criminal charges—is going to get a fair trial?"

"Well, probably not."

"And why not, Dr. Sneed?"

"Because the defendant deserves to have all the evidence kept under security and according to the rules. It needs to not be tampered with."

"Dr. Sneed, let's go on with our story of the GBI. You said that when they arrived at your farmhouse in Burnher County, they shook yours and Porky Pentz, the DA's hands?"

"Yes, sir."

"Then they asked where the patient records were, and you told them to follow you into the house?"

"Yes, sir."

"Then you showed them the *five* rooms that the folders were in?"

"Yes, sir."

"Then what happened?"

"Well, they started to load the boxes onto their truck."

"Wait a minute, they drove a *truck*?"

"Yeah, one of those brand-new Ford trucks. It was really nice."

"Dr. Sneed, was this truck that the GBI were putting Dr. Brookshire's patient records on—was it an *open* pickup truck?"

"Yes, sir."

"That means that the boxes of patient records were placed uncovered on the back of an open truck bed? Or did they *cover* the boxes in some manner?"

"Wuh, no, sir, they just put them in the truck bed."

"Now let's go back to when the GBI walked into the five rooms of the farmhouse that the boxes of patient records were in. Did they attempt, in any manner, to label or organize those boxes before they picked them up and moved them? In other words, did they in any way record the manner in which they found the patient records?"

"Well, no, they just started to load them onto the truck."

"Did you notice if they might have sketched out a rough drawing of the way that the boxes were situated in the building?"

"No, sir, they didn't do that. Like I said, they just started loading them up."

"Did they take any photographs of the boxes before they picked them up?"

"No, sir."

"Did they place any sort of label on the boxes?"

"No, sir."

"Did they take a count of the patient folders and write that down?"

"No, sir, they didn't do that."

"So, Dr. Sneed, let me get this straight. The two GBI agents who showed up at your Burnher County farmhouse that Tuesday night simply came, shook yours and Porky Pentz's hands, entered the farmhouse, loaded up the five boxes of Dr. Brookshire's patient records, placed them on the back of an open Ford pickup truck uncovered, and drove away into the night?"

"That's pretty much it, Mr. Jack."

"Thank you for your time today, Dr. Sneed," Jack graciously said.

The judge turned toward Brett Wratchett. "Redirect?" He asked.

"No, Your Honor," Wratchett replied as if he had lost another round to Jack.

I was glad that Jack had explained ahead of time to Bob and me the reason that Brett Wratchett was absolutely compelled to put Dr. Sneed on the stand. Otherwise, I would have had a great deal of trouble trying to figure out exactly why the state had called him as their witness. He certainly didn't help their case. He didn't support any of their theories. He wasn't a witness to some incriminating evidence against me. He never observed me doing anything the state was accusing me of doing. In fact, he actually kind of made Brett and his cronies look rather ridiculous with his close friendship to the district attorney; his vacant, unkempt, backwater farmhouse; and his far-fetched, improbable tall tale of the dental equipment heist.

But this was what Jack had explained to us. The state *had* to put Dr. Sneed on the stand. They had had no choice. They were obligated to prove the chain of custody of the patient records because Jack had requested that they do so. Of course, after it was brought out that my patient records were absconded from my office, driven in the back of a semi to a deserted old farmhouse in the boondocks, thrown helter-skelter into five rooms, left several days unguarded, snatched up willy-nilly by the GBI, and driven off into the night, the idea of an intact chain of custody was pretty much shot to hell.

So Jack, being the excellent trial lawyer that he was, did what he had to do. For the third time, he asked the good judge Grudge for a summary judgment, this time based on the fact that the chain of custody of my patient folders was far beyond a scandal. In fact, at this point, the mere suggestion of my patient records being anywhere near intact would have probably sent the jury into a laughing fit.

And once again, for the third time to be exact, Judge Grudge denied Jack's request. State, 3; defense, 0.

"You may step down," Judge Grudge told Sonny Sneed. Sneed looked relieved yet a little let down. I think he was beginning to rather enjoy being the object of courtroom attention. After all, he was not quite done with his theatrical performance.

EYEBROWS IN OUTER SPACE

"CALL YOUR NEXT witness," Judge Grudge said dryly to Wratchett.

"Your Honor, I call Dr. Elmer Quimby to the stand."

Now let me brief you on Elmer. When I attended the School of Dental Education from 1984 to 1988, Elmer was one of my fellow dental students. In fact, he attended an extra year, not out of choice but rather out of necessity. You see, poor Elmer had quite a struggle the entire time. He struggled with the academics. He struggled with the required lab work. He struggled with the proficiency tests. He struggled with getting his patients to show up. He struggled with accumulating enough points to graduate. He struggled with meeting time limits. He struggled with passing the national and state boards. He even struggled with simply not falling asleep in class.

Yet he was one of those adorable-little-boy types that a nurturing, motherly type like myself felt obligated to take their hand and help them along. He was just so pitiful most days. He was like a stray, abandoned puppy that looks up at you with his big brown eyes and melts you like butter. Elmer had these eyebrows. I'll never forget them. He would lift them into thin air every time he felt the least bit stressed, which was at least 50 percent of the time. And those eyebrows, they were shaped just like upside-down *V*s so that when he raised them to his receding hairline, they kinda resembled the tip-tops of two tiny rockets ready for liftoff. Paula, who of course was my best friend during dental school, was constantly making wisecracks about Elmer's eyebrows.

One time, a large group of us dental students were crossing the busy street between the dental school building and the building where most of us poverty-stricken students could afford to eat our daily noon meal. Elmer was right in the center of our purposely formed cubical shape. We had learned to move in a large square unit like that for protection against the overaggressive drivers on Cricklewood Boulevard. In his left hand, Elmer was carrying precious cargo. It was near the end of the quarter, and the main course we had all endured together was a class on the fabrication of dentures.

To make a long story short, Elmer had spent the last ten weeks of his life setting teeny, tiny acrylic teeth into globs of pink wax, perfectly sculpted onto a replica of a human upper and lower jaws. The work had been tedious and painstakingly meticulous for us all. One wrong tooth position, and it was a bad mark on your record, professors whispering that they were not sure about student so-and-so making it as a dentist and the ultimate branding of being asked to get special one-on-one tutoring in setting dentures. And none of us wanted anything to do with any of that. However, Elmer had endured every one of those defaming black marks. Somehow he had managed to finally set a wax denture that had passed, and it was right there at that very moment, secure in its special little $1,200 carrying case, grasped tightly in his left hand. (Poor Elmer was left handed, to make matters even more snarled up.)

Well, Paula and I have never agreed on exactly what happened; and believe me, over the years, this particular story has been told and retold by both of us, mostly when the two of us are together. But somehow, someway, an overaggressive, inattentive driver picked Elmer out of the cube of students and clipped him right on his left hip. You can guess the rest. As we all looked back, his pricey gray carrying case flew up in slow motion, sailed through the air, and landed smack dab in the middle of Cricklewood Boulevard. Tiny acrylic teeth took wing. Globs of sculptured pink wax departed from their human replica jaws and made a quick exit onto the concrete. They stuck like little blobs of chewed-up pink bubble gum. The plastic jaws with the metal hinged joints acted as copilot to the teeth and wax as they opened and shut in fast motion, clacking together rapidly as they sailed through the air with the greatest of ease.

All the aircraft came to a landing right at Elmer's shuffling feet. He stood there, dazed and confused, in the middle of one of the busiest streets in Lumpkin, Georgia. His eyebrows instantly shot up to the top of his scalp. The rest of the student cube had successfully made it to the other side. Paula and I were observing from the edge of the sidewalk. Most of the other students had already enjoyed their good chuckle and disappeared into the feeding place. They were hungry, and they had all gotten quite used to Elmer, the human fuckup. Paula and I helped Elmer gather up his thirty-two itty-bitty molded plastic teeth, his dented custom carrying case, and his jammed plastic human jaw. We left the pink wax.

Yes, Elmer Quimby was, without a doubt, a walking human disaster. I always felt strongly that there was not one single bone in his scrawny body that wished in any way, shape, or form to be attending dental school in Lumpkin, Georgia. After all, he had always been quite content to play the role of dental hygienist, which he had played for several years now. Cleaning and scraping his patients' teeth and carrying on a one-sided conversation while doing so had always appealed to him. It was within his comfort zone. Dental school, however, was a different story. He had struggled since the first day of introductions. He had not even made it very well through the first two weeks of dental school, during which the professors did nothing but make us feel all-important, oversuccessful, and superior to every other professional group in the universe. It was the planned ego pumper before the big dunk.

After meeting Elmer's other half, Christina, Paula and I began to put two and two together. Christina was a medical doctor, actually a psychiatrist, who had graduated from the medical school in Lumpkin. She had an air of arrogance and pride about her that followed her everywhere she went. I guess she figured that once she became a doctor, she was not going to accept her husband being a dental hygienist. No, that would never do. If she was to keep her reputation up, her husband would have to at least try to be her equal. It was bad enough that he was in the field of dentistry as compared with medicine. That was three strikes against him to begin with. She might accept him being a *dentist* but never a dental *hygienist.*

And so it went. Poor Elmer was being sentenced to dental school by his overbearing, tyrannical wife. And the fact that she was a psychiatrist didn't make matters any more bearable for Elmer. That simply meant that she was more than capable of playing destructive little mind games constantly with poor little Elmer, who was already a total emotional wreck. Yet another cruel trick that Christina pulled on Elmer during his dental school years was that she decided it was time to become a human baby factory. Her timing could not have been more off. Every time Elmer got up to announce to our dental class that another little Quimby had entered the world, the outright stress of it all was knitted all over those eyebrows of his. I felt so sorry for Elmer on most days that I made a special effort to talk to him, give him a brief tutoring session, or make sure he had a copy of my latest class notes.

Elmer had only done one thing in his life, as far as I was concerned, that just made no sense whatsoever to me. In fact, I found it to be totally out of character, but maybe I didn't know every side of Elmer Quimby. When he came to Goat Valley to buy my practice, Bob and I had vouched for him with our local banker. In turn, our banker had stuck his neck out for an unknown and had agreed to loan Elmer over $100,000 to get the practice back up and going. To make a long story short, at the time Elmer turned tail and ran without even letting me know he was shutting the practice down, he likewise did not let the banker know any of his plans. He left our friend, the bank president, holding the bag for over $100,000 without even giving him the courtesy of a phone call.

I wasn't exactly sure why the prosecution had called Elmer to the stand. I couldn't imagine him saying anything derogatory about me. After all, we had been buddies all through dental school. Nevertheless, that was what was happening here. I wondered what Brett Wratchett had persuaded him to say about me or my practice. Worse yet, I wondered what Christina might have psychologically tricked him into repeating.

The bailiff swore him in. Brett Wratchett started in on him immediately. "Could you please state your name for the records?"

"Dr. Elmer Quimby."

"And what do you do for a living, Doctor?"

"I'm a dentist." Elmer hung his head when he said this.

"Where is your dental practice located, Dr. Quimby?"

"It's in Suwanee, Georgia."

"And, Dr. Quimby, have you ever owned more than one dental practice?"

"Yes, sir, for a very brief time."

"And where was your second dental practice located?"

"In Goat Valley, Georgia."

"Dr. Quimby, how did you come upon that second practice?"

"Well, I heard that Dr. Brookshire needed someone to run her practice for a while, so I called her and asked about it. She said the practice was up for sale."

"What happened then?"

"Well, I came down to Goat Valley, looked at the facility, talked several times to Dr. Brookshire and her husband about it, looked at their financial statements, and decided it looked pretty good."

"Now, Dr. Quimby, *why* would you want to try to run two practices? Wouldn't that be rather tiring?"

"Well, my wife, Christina, and I talked it over, and we decided that I could probably work it out for a few years anyhow, mostly to try to get us out of debt."

"You were in pretty bad debt?"

"Oh yes, sir. We had the debt from both of our medical schools, the debt of setting up a new practice, and the debt of a couple of new babies."

"That's quite a lot of debt, Dr. Quimby. So you agree that you might have bought Dr. Brookshire's practice out of a little bit of desperation, huh?"

"Well, not really," Elmer whispered. "I really thought I could make a go of it."

"Dr. Quimby, let's talk about some of the things you observed at Dr. Brookshire's office after you bought it."

"OK."

"Could you tell us how *busy* her practice was when you got there?" Brett Wratchett's eyes were gleaming as if he had caught me now.

"Well . . . really," Elmer hesitated, "it wasn't all that busy. I was really a little disappointed."

"Then let's talk about *money*. She was knocking down some *money*, huh?" Wratchett was looking a little less sure of himself.

"No, sir. Her practice was bringing in much less than my practice in Suwanee, and my practice never really did real well. In fact, I was about to lose my behind in the Goat Valley practice. That's why I felt it necessary to pull out so quickly." He glanced over at me with "I'm sorry" written all over his face.

Brett Wratchett was beginning to kick into desperate mode. So far, this guy whom he just *knew* held at least one deep dark secret against me was coughing up zilch for his team. He had to get more aggressive in his approach. "Now, Dr. Quimby, when you first got to Dr. Brookshire's office, did her patients have any complaints against her or anything else? Now think hard . . . *any complaints at all?*"

"Well, not really. They all seemed pretty content. I think most of them missed her. A good many of them said things like they wish she would come back soon. Oh, yeah, there were a few complaints, but those were from the type of people that would complain if the sun were shining. Actually, overall, come to think of it, her practice had less patient complaints than my own practice in Suwanee."

Brett Wratchett began to pace in tiny circles and run his fingers nervously through his perfectly coiffed thick hair. It struck me at this point that the witness, Elmer Quimby, may have been one of the hundreds of witnesses for the prosecution that Wratchett's team most likely had neglected to "prep" for trial. And Wratchett himself was beginning to suffer the consequences of this severe misjudgment. He picked up the pace.

"Dr. Quimby, did you see anything *illegal* going on in Dr. Brookshire's office? Anything at all? Mention anything you found unusual or questionable going on in her practice . . . even if it was just a *little* questionable?"

Jack sprung to his feet. "I object! Your Honor, he's leading the witness!"

"Objection overruled," Grudge droned.

"You may answer the question," He said to Elmer.

Jack sat back down. His face was beginning to show concern about the judge's particular dislike toward him. After all, Jack had explained to me on more than one occasion that part of his successful strategy over the years had involved getting the judges in trials to really take a liking to him. He had always told me that getting the judge to truly like him was a huge part of his winning record. Bob and I, with a little help from Ricky, had researched Jack's courtroom record, and we had been utterly impressed with the number of trials he had won. It was one reason we had gone with him. But now here was this Judge *Grudge*, who had overruled almost 100 percent of Jack's legitimate objections. Clearly, the judge was working for the state.

Elmer cleared his throat. He sat up straight in the wooden witness stand. His eyebrows shot up. He looked as if he was really deep in thought. "Nooooo, I can't think of one single thing that was being done illegally in her office. It was actually being run very efficiently, if you ask me."

Wratchett was hot by now. He was getting nowhere fast. He decided that if he couldn't win this one, he might as well attack. "Dr. Quimby, can you tell the jury exactly *why* you couldn't make it in Goat Valley? Why, for example, you left the Goat Valley Bank and Trust holding the bag for over $100,000? I understand that you just ran back to Suwanee and left all your obligations behind in Goat Valley. I mean, you left owing the bank, the dental equipment folks, the lab folks . . . and what about the patients? Don't you think the patients were confused when they came to the office and it was gutted? Why, you couldn't even find it in you to come back and clean up your own mess. You left Sonny Sneed to do that. Don't you think you had an obligation to the *patients*?"

Elmer's eyebrows were in outer space. An expression of pure agony spread over his ashen face. "Well . . . I guess when I thought I could run two practices, 150 miles apart, I was mistaken. It was just too much . . . I missed my family." He began to stutter. "I . . . I . . . I . . . p-p-prob-b-b-abl-l-l-l-y didn't handle it r-r-r-r-ight."

"Thank you, Dr. Quimby." Wratchett looked satisfied now. He spun around on the heels of his Italian wing tips and faced Jack. "Your witness."

Jack approached the stand with his signature wide south Georgia grin. "Good afternoon, Dr. Quimby."

"Good afternoon," Elmer replied.

"Dr. Quimby, I'm not going to keep you long today."

Elmer looked relieved. His eyebrows returned to the earth.

"Let's just talk briefly about your dental practice in Suwanee, Georgia, can we?"

"Oh, yes, sir."

"Now how long have you been practicing dentistry in Suwanee?"

"Oh, let's see . . . about eleven years now."

"And in those eleven years, have you had any patient complaints?"

"Oh *yes*, sir. I've had my share of complaints. That's a lot of years. People like to complain about their mouths."

"And what about Medicaid? Did your practice in Suwanee ever accept Medicaid patients?"

"No, we never did, and I probably never will."

"And why is that, Dr. Quimby?"

"Well, I have looked into it, and it just isn't worth it. Those patients tend to be real difficult, I have heard. They don't show up for their appointments. They act up real bad, things like that. But the main reason I never took Medicaid patients was that, after reviewing their payment schedule, there is no way in the world I could make any money. I mean . . . Medicaid doesn't reimburse the dentist hardly *anything* for his work or time."

"So why then do you think Dr. Brookshire took Medicaid patients? In fact, over 50 percent of her practice was Medicaid."

"I don't know exactly why she decided to do this, but my guess, knowing Dora Brookshire, would be that she looked around and saw that no other dentist in Goat Valley accepted these poor people, and she felt a need there, and she filled that need. She's just like that. She is a very compassionate person. She always helped me and others in dental school."

"She helped you in dental school? Tell us about that."

"Well, she was one of the smartest ones in our class. She graduated near the top. Her claim to fame, I guess, was the fact that she was the official class notetaker. It just kinda happened. One day some of us happened to see her notes, and we couldn't believe our eyes. They were so thorough, so precise, so well organized, and so neat. From that day forward, we were all in competition for those notes. It ended up that she ran off enough copies of her classroom notes for all of us. She took care of her classmates."

"Other than providing classroom notes for the dental class, how else did she help you?"

"Well, she helped *me* personally in many different ways. She tutored me in pharmacology. She helped me through biochemistry. She stayed late and helped me with lab work."

"So when you think of Dr. Brookshire, you don't picture someone who is self-centered, coldhearted, and money hungry?"

"Oh, no, not at all. In fact, she is quite the opposite of that description."

"Dr. Quimby, let's return to the subject of Dr. Brookshire's Goat Valley dental practice. Let's concentrate on her staff for a second, if we can."

"OK."

"What was your first impression of Dr. Brookshire's staff?"

"It was a very good first impression. I was thinking to myself, *My, Dora's staff is way better than mine. They're better trained. They're better with the patients. They're better skilled.* I was really impressed with the professionalism that exuded from her staff. They had been trained very well. The patients loved them."

"And did those staff members tell you *where* they had got their training? Did they come into Dr. Brookshire's practice already trained?"

"Oh, no. They had all been personally trained by Dr. Brookshire herself. Dora did an excellent job of training them."

"Did anything else jump out at you about her office?"

"Yes. Dora's office was much more advanced than mine technically. She had the latest in computers and computer software. She had an intraoral camera to aid in her diagnoses and to keep the patients informed and comfortable. She really had a well-greased, smooth-running practice."

"And, Dr. Quimby, were there unhappy staff members or patients in Dr. Brookshire's practice while you were there?"

"No, everyone seemed content and happy to be there, overall."

"Dr. Quimby, the dental office you are describing, it doesn't sound like the same one that the prosecution is describing. They are painting a picture of a dental office that is disorganized and chaotic and dishonest and unruly and anarchical, in short an office that is a jumbled, muddled, turbulent, raging, hellish mess."

"Oh! They have the *wrong* office for that. Dr. Brookshire's office was as harmonious and businesslike as they come."

"Thank you, Dr. Quimby." Jack looked over his shoulder at Brett Wratchett, giving him a quick flash over the top of his half-cut reading glasses. He didn't even bother to turn his body toward the prosecutor. "Redirect?" he inquired.

Wratchett turned toward Judge Grudge, pretending like the question had originated from Him. "No more questions, Your Honor," he replied flatly.

The judge turned toward Elmer. "You may step down."

As Elmer, my little dental school buddy, left the witness stand, I couldn't help but wonder why in the hell Brett Wratchett had put him on his witness list. After all, it wasn't like the prosecution didn't have enough witnesses. Their witness list included every staff member who had ever worked one day for me, the GBI involved with the case, the Medicaid folks, every dentist who had worked my office after I left, a good number of my pediatric patients and their parents, and several "expert witnesses." The prosecution had a grand total of sixty-two witnesses. Now why did they feel that they even needed Elmer's testimony?

I didn't have much time to think. His Honor was speaking. I snapped to.

"I would like to thank the jury, the witnesses, and the people in the courtroom today. That concludes this day. Go home and rest. Be back in My courtroom at eight o'clock sharp tomorrow morning."

And with that, His Honor, Judge Grudge, arose; the bailiff commanded us all to arise; and He swept out of the courtroom, His black robe enveloping Him like an evil superhero. The bailiff excused the jury for the day. As they filed out in front of me, I tried to read their expressions, but most were wearing their best poker faces.

MISSIVES OF MORAL SUPPORT

M Y FAMILY SWEPT me away to our awaiting automobile and then to our hotel rooms. But my night had only just begun. After a rushed dinner in the hotel restaurant, it was back to work for Dave, Jack, and me. We knew that the prosecution was putting my staff up on the stand the next day, so we needed to be prepared for anything "the girls" might say. We had run into Dixie, Rosa, and Lolita on the streets of downtown when we were taking an evening walk in Atlanta on Sunday night before the trial began. Apparently, the state was sparing no expense on this witch hunt of a trial. About seven of my past staff members and three of the dentists who had worked for me after the suspension were being put up in the pricey Holiday Inn for several nights each. I was told later that the state also paid each of these girls' expenses from Sunday through Wednesday. That included their gasoline to Atlanta, their vehicle wear and tear, their wages for time off work, their meals, their hotel room, and any expenses that occurred there. The state must have wanted me terribly bad to have gone to all this trouble and expense.

Jack, Dave, and I sat up half the night reviewing the staff members' statements to the GBI. First, we read over the statements that the six employees who last worked for me had written voluntarily to the state dental board concerning their suspension of my license. My dental hygienist Meadow wrote:

> I am writing in complaint and protest to the actions taken by the State Dental Board concerning Dr. Doramae Brookshire. I am a registered dental hygienist. I have been employed by Dr. Brookshire since January 1993 . . . The State Dental Board has suspended Dr. Brookshire's license until a formal hearing. I feel that the Board has made a hasty and presumptuous decision concerning Dr. Brookshire. Wyatt Weasley, a Board investigator, questioned only two current

staff members. Four other staff members were present. The GBI never questioned Dr. Brookshire in any way. Their decision to suspend Dr. Brookshire's license was arrived at after statements taken by only two people. It appears as though the State Dental Board was only concerned with their own well-being . . . A complete investigation should have taken place before any action was taken . . . I only hope and pray that Dr. Brookshire's life and practice are not completely ruined by the inadequate actions taken by the State Dental Board and the GBI.

My chairside assistant Joy wrote in her letter:

On Thursday, January 26, 1995, our office received a call from dental investigator Wyatt D. Weasley requesting an informal statement from me at the Goat Valley Police Station. During the 2½ hour "informal hearing," Mr. Weasley asked me several questions regarding my education, past dental experience and employment. At no time did he read me any rights or ask me if I wanted an attorney present. He also stated that this was just routine procedure. After interviewing me, Mr. Weasley asked me to give a written statement. He told me to give a very detailed and descriptive statement. He stated that this would be to Dr. Brookshire's benefit. Several times during the statement, Mr. Weasley would tell me to leave more space, because he wanted me to add something. It is my opinion that the board has already hung Dr. Brookshire. By releasing information in the fashion that they did, it has done nothing but raise suspicion in the public eye. Only those involved know the truth of the situation and we all know that the media doesn't care about the truth because it doesn't sell papers.

I started working for Dr. Brookshire in August 1993. Prior to this, I was employed as a chairside assistant for 10 years. It takes a very special dentist to work on young "at-risk" children, many of whom have emotional or physical problems. In writing this letter, I hope the Board will take into consideration her community service with school programs, such as the Medicaid, Headstart and Migrant programs. The majority of local dental practices will not accept these programs . . . I hope you give Dr. Brookshire a chance to defend herself. As of yet, no one from the Georgia Dental Board has contacted her and requested her statement.

My front desk office manager Scarlett wrote:

> This letter comes in protest of the treatment and investigative procedures used to form an opinion of and subsequently suspend the license of Dr. Doramae Brookshire, pending a formal hearing by the Georgia Board of Dentistry. I have been in the employment of Dr. Brookshire since November 1992. During this time, my duties have primarily revolved around office management, as well as dental assisting. I was responsible for all duties associated with managing the dental office. It is my opinion that this is a vital part of the office staff and any subsequent investigation. Currently there are six persons, including myself, employed with Dr. Brookshire. During the Dental Board's "witch hunt" investigation, only two of the six employees were interviewed by the dental investigator. More importantly, the doctor herself was never contacted or interviewed by the board. How could conclusive evidence of any wrongdoing be determined without a complete investigation of all parties involved? . . . The true tragedy is that a compassionate and caring individual such as Dr. Brookshire is being crucified before a complete investigation or hearing is done. Even when exonerated, her practice and good name will have been destroyed. Dr. Brookshire's practice primarily consists of "at-risk" children that are not accepted at the majority of the other local dental practices. More importantly, who will care for these children, as well as those who are covered by Medicaid, Headstart and Migrant programs?

Another front desk employee, Rose, wrote:

This is a formal letter of protest of the investigation and suspension of Dr. Doramae Brookshire. I am an employee of Dr. Brookshire and have been since 9/19/94. My position is front desk, which is a vital part in running of the office. I have not been asked any questions by anyone at the Police Department or at the State Dental Board. There are six employees at this office and only two were questioned by the Georgia Dental Board. Only one employee was questioned by the police department. No one from the Georgia Dental Board has talked with Dr. Brookshire or the rest of us. I thought the State Dental Board was supposed to help and not hinder the dentists in Georgia. I am a lifetime resident of Goat Valley. My family is well known and well thought of in this town. My husband is a Southern Baptist minister and we have raised three children that are all college graduates. I come from a family who believes in justice. Where is the justice in taking Dr. Brookshire's license before a complete investigation has occurred? I am very disappointed at the circumstances that surround the State Dental Board's actions.

A chairside dental assistant, Hazel, wrote:

I am writing on behalf of Dr. Doramae Brookshire. Only two of Dr. Brookshire's staff have been interviewed by the Georgia Dental Board. Dr. Brookshire was not interviewed at all. With this limited information, Dr. Brookshire's license was suspended. On what grounds? If the Georgia Dental Board was going to take such an action, they should have at least talked to all parties involved.

Another chairside assistant, Zoe, wrote:

I know a lot of questions are unanswered at this time, but now even more questions have occurred. For example, why was I not asked for an attorney to be present and why the investigators misrepresented themselves during my second statement given? I did not know at the time of my second statement who Mr. Wyatt Weasley was or whom he represented. I do not feel that any fair justice is being pursued. My father, Buck Anderson, is a County Commissioner of Redd County and has served on the committee for sixteen years. I was reared in a family with good morals and values. I know right from wrong, and I feel *no wrong* has been done by Dr. Brookshire, but can we say that for the others?

Certainly after reading these letters from my staff, Jack, Dave, and I thought that there was not a chance in hell that any of these staff members would ever get up on a courtroom stand and testify *against* me, but we were woefully ignorant of the ways of the world.

FLIPPIN' THE INNOCENT

"**A**LL ARISE!" COMMANDED the bailiff in a monotone. The courtroom did as ordered.

"His Honorable Ebenezer B. Grudge presiding," droned the tired bailiff while cutting his droopy eyes in the judge's direction.

"Please be seated," dictated His Honor.

We all sat. The defendant's table sat with a great deal of apprehension for things to come.

The judge turned toward Brett Wratchett. "Call your first witness to the stand," He directed.

"Your Honor, my first witness is Scarlett Vesper, Dr. Brookshire's office manager and, at one time, her codefendant." Wratchett quickly cleared his throat. "Oh, I'm sorry, Your Honor, I meant to say Dr. Brookshire's *coconspirator*."

I felt a quiver go up my spine. I had no idea what Scarlett was going to find necessary to say concerning my dental office, the daily incidents that occurred at the front desk, or even me for that matter. I did realize it was quite likely that what had happened to Scarlett was the age-old legal trick of pressuring the codefendant to testify against the main defendant for clemency. The old snitch-on-the-guy-we-are-really-interested-in-hanging-and-we-will-letcha-go tactic. It was seen every week on every police show on every TV in everyone's home.

I knew this much—Scarlett was, by far, the most important of my staff members in the case because the state was trying to prove conspiracy between her and me. She was the gold jewel in their crown; the main feather in their cap. Jack and I were both well aware of the fact that as my coconspirator, Scarlett, was going to get some degree of immunity from punishment to testify against me. It was Jack's job to discredit the snitch.

"Good morning, Ms. Vesper," Wratchett sang out as he approached my ex-employee.

I glanced over at Scarlett. She was fidgeting in her seat. She had made a great attempt to dress for the part—a three-piece suit, matching jewelry, and fashionable stilettos. However, the neckline of her pale pink top was a little too plunging, revealing a bit too much cleavage. Her suit skirt joined the party, being short enough to leave little to the imagination. Both were a tad too tight. I heaved an inward sigh of relief. Maybe, just maybe, the jury would find her a bit of a tart, a real courtroom floozy, which I was hoping would pair up nicely with being a ditzy blonde.

"Would you please tell the jury how you know Dr. Brookshire?"

"Yes," Scarlett replied with a somewhat shaky voice. "She was my boss."

"Dr. Brookshire was your boss. Where did you work for Dr. Brookshire?" Wratchett inquired.

"At her dental office in Goat Valley, Georgia."

"And just how *long* where you under the employment of Dr. Brookshire?" he droned.

"I worked there since November 1992." She sighed.

"And what exactly was your job description at her dental office in Goat Valley, Georgia?" Wratchett demanded.

"Well, I was the front desk office manager."

Brett Wratchett heaved a big sigh. Apparently, he was getting a little peeved about Scarlett's short, concise answers. "Ms. Vesper, I asked you to give us your job description. This would include an actual *description* of duties that you performed while under the employment of Dr. Brookshire."

"Well, I was the office manager. I dealt with situations that arose, filed the claims to insurance companies and Medicaid, and made appointments for patients, things like that."

"How very interesting! You said that you filed the claims to Medicaid, right?" Wratchett was smirking.

"Now you know that I did, *Brettski*." Scarlett spat out. "We have been over and over this."

I couldn't believe my ears. Scarlett just defiantly called the great Mr. Brett Wratchett, the mighty high-ranking state prosecutor, *Brettski*—and in a public courtroom. Oh, this was going to be good.

Wratchett was hoppin' mad. "Ms. Vesper!" he screamed. "Tell us the protocol to filing these *Medicaid* forms, will you please?"

Scarlett sighed. "The dental assistant who worked on the patient would bring me out the patient's folder when they were done, and I would type the procedures into the computer and then send it off to EDS."

"And by EDS, you mean Electronic Data Services, which is the clearinghouse for Medicaid, correct?"

"I don't really know what it stands for, Brett. I just know that's where I sent them." Scarlett was getting disgusted.

"Now think real hard, Ms. Vesper, before you answer this question. Dr. Brookshire knew everything that went out of that office, right?"

"What do you mean by everything that went out of the office, Brettski?" Scarlett sarcastically inquired.

"I think you know what I mean, Ms. Vesper. I mean that Dr. Brookshire was a pretty smart cookie, huh? She knew *everything* that went on in that dental office, especially what went on at the front desk. Isn't that a pretty accurate statement, Ms. Vesper?"

Scarlett was beginning to come unwound. "Now, *Brettski*, you know the answer to that question because I told you time and time again that Dr. Brookshire was hardly ever at the front desk. She was working on patients all day, and when she wasn't, she was usually in her office doing things she needed to be doing."

"Ms. Vesper, I will ask you the question one more time, rephrasing it. Maybe you didn't understand what I was asking you." Brett Wratchett's face was all scrunched up. Tiny beads of sweat were beginning to dance across his forehead. His jaw was taut. I think I heard him grind his teeth.

"Dr. Brookshire—she knew *everything* that went on in her dental office, right? I mean, you yourself have told me repeatedly how extremely intelligent she is. Is that not correct?"

"You are obviously talking about two different things, Brett! Yes, she is intelligent, a very smart woman, but what does that have to do with her knowing everything that goes on at the front desk when she is busy working on patients?"

Brettski had had it with his witness for the prosecution. He strutted over to the prosecution's desk and retrieved a fistful of papers. He handed the honorable judge a paper and declared, "Your Honor, I submit exhibit G." He then handed Jack a copy, never making eye contact once. He skated back over to Scarlett and thrust the newly found treasure in her face.

"Ms. Vesper, could you please read exhibit G to the jury, loud enough for them to hear, pleeeease?"

Scarlett's face started to flush. It began at her exposed cleavage and traveled slowly up her neck and then rose onto her cheeks and forehead, like the Red Sea after the Israelites had crossed safely over. "Yes, it says, 'I, Scarlett Vesper, do solemnly swear that the following statement is the truth, so help me God: I, Scarlett T. Vesper, was under the employment of Dr. Doramae Brookshire from November 1992 until January 1995. During this time, my job description was that of office manager. My office duties included, but were not limited to, answering the phone, making appointments with patients, answering patients' inquiries, dealing with the other office staff members, and filing preapprovals and final submittals to insurance companies. Due to the high volume of Medicaid patients in Dr. Brookshire's dental practice, my main duty as office manager was to file Medicaid preapprovals and to submit to Medicaid procedures that were performed on patients. I did this on a daily basis. Furthermore, Dr. Doramae Brookshire herself was fully aware of all preapprovals, submittals, and correspondence that went on in her dental practice.'" Scarlett's crimson hue began to wash away. She was now a pasty white.

"Please read the last sentence of exhibit G one more time for us, Ms. Vesper, real nice and loud," Wratchett sang out.

Scarlett cleared her throat softly. "Furthermore, Dr. Doramae Brookshire herself was fully aware of all preapprovals, submittals, and correspondence that went on in her dental practice!" Scarlett read rather boomingly as if she was afraid that the courtroom bully might make her repeat it if not read loudly enough.

"Sooo, Ms. Vesper, now that we have determined that Dr. Brookshire did, indeed, know *everything* that went on in her dental office, we can proceed with the questioning. Is that all right with you?" Brett Wratchett was gloating in his courtroom triumph.

"Well, I guess so, Brett." She swung her defeated head down to stare at her abbreviated skirt. I think I heard her mumble, "You have had control over me from the get-go if I wanted out of this thing."

Jack began to arise and object but thought it a better move to continue to listen.

"Now that we have established the fact that Dr. Brookshire knew *everything* about the Medicaid submittals, we can move on. Ms. Vesper, you and Dr. Brookshire were very close. Is that an accurate statement?"

"What exactly do you mean by very close, Brett?" Scarlett was not making this easy for the prosecutor.

"I think you know what I mean, Ms. Vesper. You and her were pretty good friends, close acquaintances, bosom buddies, so to speak. You two got along pretty harmoniously, huh?"

"We liked and respected each other, if that's what you mean," Scarlett stated flatly.

"No, that's not exactly what I was getting at, Ms. Vesper. I meant more like the two of you were in cahoots together. Let me spell this out a little better for you. The two of you, you and Dr. Brookshire, you had a well-planned scheme to submit false statements to Medicaid so the two of you could bring more money into the dental practice, right?"

"Most certainly not!" Scarlett huffed.

"Oh, come on now, Ms. Vesper, what exactly do you think you were charged with? Do you realize the definition of *coconspirator*? Let me help you out here. A conspirator is one who is involved in a secret plan to do something harmful or illegal. A coconspirator then, by definition, would be the helpmate of the main conspirator. So let me put this another way. Did you, at any time, scheme with Dr. Brookshire to receive more money from Medicaid than was legally allowed?"

"No, I did *not*!" Scarlett adamantly spat out.

"Well then, did you help Dr. Brookshire devise a *plot* to help rob Medicaid?" Now Wratchett was just fishing.

"Nope, no plots here." Scarlett was rock hard.

Wratchett gazed deeply into Scarlett's cast-iron eyes. He could see at that moment that she was unyielding, unbending, inflexible when it came to admitting that she and I had a conspiracy thing going. She was just not going to bend. He could not break her on this one. At this point in the trial, his thoughts on the matter ran somewhat like this: *We cut a deal with her anyhow, and part of that deal included dropping her charges as coconspirator with Dr. Brookshire. She signed our plea agreement. We dropped the charge of coconspirator in exchange for her testifying for the state. Therefore, I cannot continue this line of questioning. I was taking a stab in the dark to see if she might just crack and give us another valuable piece of our puzzle here.*

And with that final thought concerning his witness, Brett Wratchett spun around on his heels, looked the witness squarely in the eyes, and asked one final question. "Then let's summarize here, Ms. Vesper. Dr. Brookshire and you *both* knew exactly everything that went on in her dental office, you both liked and respected each other, and you both were the only ones in that dental practice that had anything to do with submitting claims to Medicaid. Therefore, you *both* worked together as far as Medicaid submittals were concerned. Would that be an accurate statement?"

"Yes, I guess so," Scarlett muttered in a sea of fog. The heckler Wratchett had worn her down at this point. It was evident that she just wanted to be done testifying and go home to her three kids. She was about to escape her tormentor. Her torture was near the end.

Wratchett turned toward Jack. The sardonic grin on his face told it all. "Your witness," he sang out.

Jack arose slowly. He buttoned his suit and adjusted his reading glasses. "Good morning, Scarlett," he warbled, his south Georgia grin spreading over his friendly face.

"Good morning," Scarlett shot back at him, allowing a little sigh of relief to escape.

"Scarlett, I am not going to keep you long today. I know you have children waiting for you at home, and I think we all can see that you have been put through the wringer today. I do apologize for that. Courtrooms can get a little wordy. But I just have a couple of questions for you today. Do you think you are up to it?"

"Oh yes, I can answer a few more questions. Thanks." This was going in a whole new direction. Now she was actually thanking the inquisitor.

"Now, Ms. Vesper, you had stated to Mr. Wratchett that you and Dr. Brookshire liked and respected each other, right?"

"That's right. But we weren't really good friends who sat around plotting schemes against Medicaid, like he tried to get me to say."

"Objection, Your Honor!" Wratchett screamed out.

"Sustained," the judge ruled.

"OK, Scarlett, did Dr. Brookshire ever tell you to change anything on the Medicaid forms before you submitted them?"

"No. They came out of the dental operatories right after the procedures were done. Dr. Brookshire told her assistants which procedures had been completed that day, the assistant filled in the date of service column on the Medicaid preapproval, Dr. Brookshire proofread it, then it got sent to me at the front desk when the dental assistant brought the patient folder up, and then I filed the procedure electronically to Medicaid. That's how it went."

"So let me get this straight. The Medicaid submittals were on a preapproval basis. All you did was file the procedure or procedures that were accomplished that day, right?"

"That's right." A look of relief swept over Scarlett's harried face as if to say, *Somebody finally gets this.*

"And Dr. Brookshire never stepped up to your desk and suggested that you add more procedures to your submittal than were originally there?"

"No, never."

Jack grinned from ear to ear. "Only one more question, Scarlett. Please describe for us the relationship Dr. Brookshire had with her patients."

"She *really cared* about her patients, especially the children. Her practice consisted mainly of what you would call at-risk kids. These children were poor. They were covered by Medicaid and the Migrant Program. Their mouths were often in horrible shape. A lot of them had nursing bottle caries, which causes the front teeth to become black and crumble away. Toothbrushes and toothpaste were not found in their homes. Their diets were awful, consisting mainly of sugar. The other dentists in Goat Valley would not see such patients. They were too high risk, and Medicaid pays pennies on the dollar. I still worry every day about who is seeing these poor little patients since Dr. Brookshire was run out of her practice."

"And how did Dr. Brookshire feel about these patients?" Jack asked.

"Oh, she was the most caring and compassionate person I have ever seen around them. I really wish it was different for her. She is a kind, gentle, caring person, and she does not deserve any of this."

"Thank you, Ms. Vesper, no more questions," Jack said happily.

"Redirect?" the judge asked Wratchett.

"No, Your Honor," he replied, looking down at his fine Italian leather shoes.

And just like that, it was over. My most dreaded testimony was at an end. With the tiny bit of reasoning power I had left in my head, I went over a brief summary of Scarlett's testimony. *It could have been much worse*, I thought. She ended it, with Jack's help, of course, in a very positive way. She came across as sincere and enthusiastic at the end. I guess she could not have done a better job for our side, considering the humungous handicap that the state had imposed on her. She had had to take the plea. She couldn't go to jail as they had threatened her. She had young children at home, and she was a single mom. Yes, she did the right thing by signing a plea bargain with the state. She had no other choice. They had backed her against the wall. So I forgave her.

THE THREE MUSKETEERS

I WONDERED WHO BRETT Wratchett was going to put on the stand and torture next. My head was filled with thoughts of Scarlett nicknaming him "Brettski," and a silly grin spread over my frightened face. It made the state's monster appear to be a tiny bit more human, that goofy label. But I could not dwell on Wratchett's new epithet long. The next state witness was approaching the stand.

I knew this one was coming. It was no surprise. I had seen Lolita, Rosa, and Dixie strolling down the streets of Parvenu, Georgia, the first night we had arrived for the trial. A fleeting thought flew through my muddled mind. We had been in this fair suburb since Sunday afternoon, and it was already Wednesday. That meant that the state of Georgia had put these three girls up in a hotel and bought them meals for almost four days, all with the intent to quash and quell the evil doctor Brookshire.

Lolita Perez was a former employee of mine. Her daddy, Slim Gomez, was one of the first Hispanics to arrive in south Georgia about the time that fresh vegetables showed up as a cash crop in that area. Some of the region's top-grossing farmers had put their noggins together and figured out that fresh vegetables were the crop of the future, and their soil and climate were perfectly accommodating for such. But they had an instant problem that came along with the territory. They needed pickers and not just a few. These men of the soil weren't going to dirty their own hands and break their own backs. Of course not. They needed Hispanic farmworkers, and they needed them *now*. (I had heard these prosperous farmers refer to their workers as "Mexican 'mater pickers.")

Enter Slim Gomez. He was bilingual, respected by his people, and knew where to find several honest, diligent farmworkers who needed a job. Now Slim was a true anomaly. The vast majority of Hispanic folks are structured short and muscled, not Slim. He was six foot four, tall and lanky. His gangly, spindly body towered over all his subjects.

To the financially embarrassed Hispanic farmworkers, Slim was a sort of Latino wonder. He was their superboss, their go-between with the White devils, their problem solver. The truth was Slim Gomez, since he was quite fluent in both languages, did a fantastic job of acting as go-between for both the White landowners and the picking crews. Even more important, Slim was fairly well respected and trusted by both groups. This role as the Hispanic godfather gave him an unbelievable quantity of power. Slim had seven children, and Lolita was the baby of the brood—his baby girl, his Hispanic princess, his Spanish infanta. And she knew it too.

Lolita had worked as a chairside assistant for me for a little over two years. She was a conscientious worker. She religiously performed the laundry list of duties that all of us employers seek so diligently— responsible, dependable, timely, and professional. But she executed these traits with an attitude. I was willing, as a boss, to overlook the haughty attitude in exchange for the other four traits.

As she approached the stand, I sized her up. She was dressed in a white starched shirt with a high collar and ruffled front and a black flared skirt. Petite red embroidered flowers with delicate green stems danced across the hemline of the skirt. As she walked, the flowered skirt begged for a tiny twirl from its owner, and I had thoughts of impassioned flamenco dancers openly displaying all their fervor and fire for the whole world to experience. But there was no such zeal pouring forth from our next witness—no clapping, no guitar playing, no finger snapping, no dancing.

As she approached the stand, Lolita looked straight ahead, eyes focused on the awaiting chair, nostrils flared, chin up, and lips tightly pursed. She marched toward the bailiff, reaching out for the Bible well before she was within reach of contacting the holy papers and swearing to tell the whole truth and nothing but the truth. After the oath was administered and agreed upon, she took the hot seat.

Brett Wratchett marched toward his next informant. "Good afternoon, Ms. Perez," he sang with a phony overtone. "How are you today?"

Lolita cleared her throat and looked at her shiny shoes. "I'm fine, I guess," she replied.

"That's good. Now I want to establish your relationship to the defendant, Dr. Brookshire. How do you know her?"

"Well, I worked for her."

"And just how long did you work for Dr. Brookshire?"

"Nearly two years."

"And tell the court what your job title was at Dr. Brookshire's office."

"I was a chairside assistant most of the time."

"What do you mean *most* of the time?"

"Well, I sometimes ran the front desk when Scarlett was sick or off for some reason."

"Oh, then you were familiar with filing *Medicaid* claims, correct?"

Lolita rolled her dark eyes to the left. She thought for a second. She drew a quick conclusion that she had no desire to be staring the same devil in the eye that Scarlett had had to just minutes before. "I don't really know much about filing Medicaid. I usually left that for Scarlett to do when she got back."

"But you *do* understand the basic principle of filing Medicaid, and you know some of the rules about what you can file and what you cannot file, correct, Ms. Perez?"

Lolita fidgeted in her chair. "Uh, yeah, kinda." She was not making this easy for Brett.

He decided to move on before the jury picked up on Lolita's indecisiveness. "Ms. Perez, did you ever, while in the employment of Dr. Brookshire, have any misgivings concerning any procedures that she filed for Medicaid reimbursement? There was one procedure in particular, correct?"

Jack shot to his feet. "Objection, Your Honor. Leading the witness."

"Objection overruled," His Honor droned. "Ms. Perez, answer the question."

"Oh yes," Lolita blurted. "She filed dental cleanings on *babies*!"

"On babies?" Brett questioned. "You mean to tell me that she cleaned little, tiny babies' teeth and then instructed you girls to file that with Medicaid?"

"Objection!" Jack screamed.

"Sit down, Mr. Goodman," the mighty judge commanded. "Go on, Ms. Perez."

"Yes, that's right. Dr. Brookshire saw every child that walked through her doors. She said everybody needed cleaned, *everybody*. She cleaned their teeth—clean, clean, clean! Me? I thought that was sooo dishonest . . . underhanded . . . shifty. She was just after the money, any way she could get it. Putting babies in the dental chair? How money hungry can you get? I couldn't believe it!" Lolita had emerged from her shell. Now this was the Lolita I had known, full of spunk and attitude.

I saw Jack begin to rise, but he probably thought, *What's the use?*

"Hmmm," Wratchett contemplated. "How could someone be so cruel as to attempt to sit a *baby* in a dental chair and clean its teeth? I wonder if it was because Dr. Brookshire was just this *greedy*. She actually used our precious babies to make *money*! Ms. Perez, do you have anything more to add about Dr. Brookshire's procedures with her patients?" Brett inquired.

"This was the main thing that I objected to while I was working for her, just the money-hungry stuff, always doing extra things to the patients just for money."

"So let me get this straight, Ms. Perez. You feel that Dr. Brookshire filed *unnecessary procedures* on her patients just to gain monetary rewards, correct?"

"Yep, that's pretty much it in a nutshell," Lolita snapped back.

And with that, Brett was done, another feather in his cap, another mighty example of Medicaid fraud at its finest. The evil doctor lived on. He whirled around to face Jack, a sinister little grin on his face. "Your witness," he sang out.

Jack rose and approached Lolita. "Good afternoon, Ms. Perez," he said with compassion, laced with a little gotcha-now.

Lolita sat up straight and proper. "Good afternoon," she shot back in a formal voice.

Jack continued, "Now, Ms. Perez, I want to be sure that I have your statement correct. You stated that Dr. Brookshire cleaned teeth on babies. Is that what you stated?"

Lolita's tan face began to blush. "Yeah, but you got to understand, you aren't supposed to clean babies' teeth. They are just innocent babies, for god's sake!" She was becoming defensive.

"Ms. Perez, can you tell us what you consider to be a baby? How old specifically were these patients who were babies and had their teeth cleaned?"

"Wuh, I don't know . . . one, two, three—they're all babies to me! Too darn young to get their teeth cleaned, I'll tell you that!"

"So you feel very strongly about that issue . . . that one-year-olds, two-year-olds, and three-year-olds are being mistreated if they are placed in a chair in a dental office and their teeth are cleaned. This is how you feel, correct?"

"Pretty much, especially if it is being done for money."

Jack looked at the judge. "Your Honor, I would like to enter exhibit J," he said nonchalantly.

His Holy Honor audibly sighed. "Approach the bench then," He commanded.

Brett Wratchett jumped up. "We don't have any exhibit J!" he protested.

"Both of you . . . get up here!" the king of the courtroom barked.

The next two minutes were filled with whispers, grumbles, whimpering, whining, and lots and lots of arm waving. His Honor finally spoke. "Since exhibit J is a dental school textbook that Dr. Brookshire was taught from, I will allow it," He ruled. "Go ahead with your questioning, Mr. Goodman."

Jack danced over to Lolita. He handed exhibit J to her. "Now, Ms. Perez, could you please tell the jury what I just handed you?"

"Yeah, it's a book," she replied flatly.

"And what is the title of the book, Ms. Perez?"

"*Textbook of Pediatric Dentistry.*"

"Ms. Perez, please open the front cover and tell us what year this book was written."

Lolita stared at the small brown book with disdain. She opened it slowly as if it might buy her some extra seconds before Jack put the hurt on her. She fumbled slowly and carefully through the first few pages. "Second edition by Raymond Braham, 1985," she responded with no emotion.

"Dr. Brookshire attended dental school from 1984 to 1988. We went to her dental school and inquired as to which textbook Dr. Brookshire was taught from in her pediatric dentistry course. We found that this was her pediatric textbook from dental school. Do you accept that as true?"

"Wuh, yeah, I guess, but what does that have to do with filing cleanings on babies' teeth to soak the state for money, like a criminal?" Lolita's attitude was blasting forth.

Jack remained calm. "Ms. Perez, could you please open the book to page 1 and read the foreword to us?"

Lolita scrunched up her face and narrowed her eyes at Jack. "OK then." She sighed. She began to read expressionless, "'The *Textbook of Pediatric Dentistry* discusses the approach to patient care and actual preventive treatment techniques required to treat various dental diseases. The book is divided into nineteen sections, which include introduction to pediatric dentistry, diagnosis in pediatric dentistry, growth and development, developmental aspects of dentition, behavioral pedodontics, preventive pedodontics, pediatric orthodontics, cariology, restorative dentistry, pediatric endodontics, gingiva and periodontium in children, oral surgical procedures in children, hospital dentistry, dentistry for the special child, pediatric oral pathology, forensic pedodontics, lasers in pediatric dentistry, advancements in pediatric dentistry, and research methodology in pediatrics. This book will provide an important guidance for undergraduate students and postgraduates to the modern concepts of dentistry for children and adolescents.'"

After her numerous struggles with pronunciations and meanings, Lolita appeared totally exhausted. She slumped over in her chair.

Jack grinned that famous south Georgia grin. "That was kinda tough reading, huh, Ms. Perez?" He laughed. "Just imagine if you had to actually *learn* all that stuff about children in dental school, like Dr.

Brookshire did, tough to read and pronounce . . . even tougher to learn and apply." He had made his point. The jury nodded in agreement.

"Now, Ms. Perez, if I could be so bold as to ask you to read just a couple of more lines from this *Textbook of Pediatric Dentistry*, the book that Dr. Brookshire was taught from in dental school. I promise the readings won't be as tough as the last one. Please bear with me."

"Well, OK."

"Let's read from page 124, paragraph 2, if you would be so kind, please."

Lolita opened the book in slow motion. She projected a little drama queen ambience into the courtroom. She sat up straight, rolled her eyes, and then began to read, "'The child's first dental exam should be scheduled soon after his or her first tooth erupts and by their first birthday, based on the recommendations of the American Academy of Pediatric Dentists. The first visit consists of an exam, fluoride treatment and a teeth cleaning, and X-rays.'"

Brett gulped. I was sure that he wanted to jump up and object, but how can one object to the printed word in a textbook?

Jack glanced up as if he was thinking really hard. "Ms. Perez, I'm not sure that I fully heard that first sentence from the excerpt. Could you please reread that first sentence?"

Lolita cleared her throat. She once again read, "'The child's first dental exam should be scheduled soon after his or her first tooth erupts and by their first birthday, based on the recommendations of the American Academy of Pediatric Dentists.'"

"Hmmmmm," Jack drawled. "Ms. Perez, do you know who the American Academy of Pediatric Dentists is?"

"Not really. I guess maybe they're a bunch of dentists who make rules or something."

"Well, that is close. The American Academy of Pediatric Dentists is the recognized authority on children's oral health and dental care. They are the guys who set policies on when to first see children in a dental office and how to treat them. Now what did that second sentence say? Exactly *what* procedures does the AAPD recommend be done to this one-year-old patient in the dentist's chair? Read that second sentence aloud once more, please."

Lolita was dumbfounded, struck between the eyes. "'The first visit consists of an exam, fluoride treatment and a teeth cleaning, and X-rays.'" She had lost much of her spunk.

"You don't mean to tell me that these poor little, tiny *babies* have to be put in a dental chair and have their teeth cleaned? Why, that kind of mistreatment can't be truly recommended by the American Academy of Pediatric Dentists, can it?" Jack was trying really hard not to smirk.

Lolita's tan had been reborn as scarlet. "Wuh, I . . . uhh . . . umm."

Jack extended the mercy of speaking again swiftly. "OK, Ms. Perez. Let's turn to page 127 next, if you will."

Lolita turned the pages as if she were a robot obeying a command.

"Please read paragraph 4 on page 127."

"Baby teeth may be small, but they're important. They act as placeholders for adult teeth. Without a healthy set of baby teeth, the child will have difficulty chewing and speaking clearly. That is why caring for baby teeth and keeping them decay-free is of the utmost importance. Even if there is no problem, the child should go for his or her first dental visit and receive a cleaning by age one."

"So let's just summarize what you read here today, Ms. Perez," Jack said. "I believe that you read to us that the American Academy of Pediatric Dentists set the guidelines for a child to have his or her first dental visit by age one, right, Ms. Perez?"

Lolita looked pale. "Yeah, that's what this book said."

Jack continued, "And I also remember you reading that, at that first visit, the one-year-old should have his or her teeth cleaned, correct?"

Lolita swallowed hard. "Yup, it said that too."

"And we have established that this textbook that you have read from today is the same textbook that Dr. Brookshire was taught from in her pediatric dentistry courses at the School of Dental Education, correct?"

"I guess so . . . if you say so." Lolita's voice trailed off.

"Then, Ms. Perez, do you think it would be fair to state that, when Dr. Brookshire cleaned the teeth of one-year-old and two-year-old and three-year-old patients, she was abiding by the teachings that she had received at her dental school?"

"Guess so." Lolita was barely audible now.

"I am sorry, Ms. Perez. We couldn't hear you. Could you please speak up so the entire courtroom is able to hear you? I will repeat the question. Do you think it would be fair to state that, when Dr. Brookshire cleaned the teeth of one-year-old, two-year-old, and three-year-old patients, she was abiding by the teachings that she had received in dental school and was also following the AAPD's guidelines?"

"*Yes*, that would be correct!" Lolita nearly yelled her answer out. She was not going to risk being asked for a repetition again.

Jack whirled around and looked Brett Wratchett square in the eye.

"Redirect?" His Honor inquired of the state's fallen soldier.

"No, Your Honor," Brett mournfully replied.

The great and powerful Oz turned toward Lolita. "You may step down, Ms. Perez."

I knew that the next Benedict Arnold just had to be either Rosa or Dixie, and I was right on target there. "State, call your next witness," His Honor dictated.

"Your Honor, the state calls Ms. Rosa Delgado to the stand."

As I watched Rosa begin her walk down the aisle of doom, memories of her employment rushed through my frenzied head. Rosa, at one time, had been married to one of Lolita's numerous brothers. The high-ranking Gomez Klan had welcomed her in but, at the same time, always maintained a wee bit of kinfolk's superiority over her. After all, she was a common Mexican, not quite up to par for their exclusive cluster but still enough of a family member for her former sister-in-law to aid in job securement. Rosa had worked as a chairside assistant to me for less than six months. Or should I say she had attempted to work as a chairside assistant. She never quite caught on to the skills needed. Setting up the proper patient tray for a given procedure, handing the doctor the correct instrument at the correct moment, and interacting in an appropriate manner with each patient—these skills seemed to elude her. So she quickly fell into her suitable role within the office, that of bilingual communicator. Rosa acted as the Spanish-speaking employee who dealt with the few children in the practice who did not speak or understand English. She also imparted pertinent information about their child's treatment and passed on instructions for home care to the numerous Spanish-speaking parents of the young patients.

But mostly, Rosa hung out with Lolita and Dixie. For a short while, they were the Three Musketeers, inseparable and indivisible, thick as thieves. And judging by the sightings I had experienced the last few days on the streets of Parvenu, Georgia, old times had experienced rebirth with a vengeance. Dixie oddly lasted the same amount of weeks that Rosa did. In fact, they had quit together on the same day. I wondered with much curiosity why in the world the state of Georgia had even considered going to the expense of housing and feeding two ex-employees who had barely worked six months for me and had quit several years before the trial. But my muddy memories needed to cease immediately, no more time to be lost in thought. Rosa was taking the stand.

"Do you promise to tell the truth, the whole truth, and nothing but the truth?" the tired bailiff inquired of Rosa.

"I do, Meester," Rosa answered in a thick Spanish accent.

Brett strutted over to the stand. "Good morning, Ms. Delgado," he sang.

"Good morneen'," she quietly replied, staring down at her scratched-up shoes, her brown arms and legs exhibiting tiny trembles.

"Now, Ms. Delgado, can you please tell us what you did in Dr. Brookshire's office?"

"Yes, sir, I was a dental asseestant."

"And exactly what does that involve, Ms. Delgado?"

Rosa's dark eyes fidgeted from right to left. "I seeated thee patients and helped thee doctor," Rosa replied.

"And in your opinion, did Dr. Brookshire's dental office run smoothly?"

Jack began to rise but opted to sit back down in a treasure hunt for facts that could be used against her.

"Well, I agree with Lolita. The doctor seen way too many leeetle babies."

Jack grinned his this-is-going-to-be-fun grin.

Brett scratched his head. "And what else did you tell us about Dr. Brookshire's office?" he inquired of her.

Rosa's frightened eyes opened wide, conveying that deer-in-the-headlights daze. "Hmmmmm, that ees all I can remember," she whispered.

"Oh come on now, Ms. Delgado, I will ask you once again. What other thing did you tell me about what went on in Dr. Brookshire's practice?"

Rosa went into a full-body tremble. She began to quiver all over. "I guess I forgot anytheeng else." Her voice trailed off.

Brett turned fire-engine red. His hands reached out toward Rosa in a clenched pattern as if he was entertaining the urge to strangle her. Then he quickly pulled his naughty mitts in and rapidly laced his digits together. "Then you have nothing more to tell us about Dr. Brookshire's office or what went on there?" he attempted once more.

"No, sir," Rosa said silently under her breath.

Brett Wratchett heaved a heavy sigh. He reluctantly turned toward Jack. "Your witness," he lamented.

Jack arose, twirled around toward the testifier, and broke into smile. "Good morning, Ms. Delgado." He beamed.

Rosa's bronze skin turned chalky white. "Good morneen'." She breathed.

Jack instantly picked up on Rosa's state of mind. "Ms. Delgado, I am not going to take up much of your time today," he told the timid witness. "Just one or two questions, OK?"

"Uh-huh," she replied.

"Ms. Delgado, just how long did you work for Dr. Brookshire?" he inquired.

"I don't know reeally. That was a long time ago." Her voice trailed off.

"Well, I have here that you worked just shy of six months, from January 1992 to June 1992. Would you agree with that?"

Rosa fidgeted in her chair. "Jes, I guess so . . . if you looked it up."

"And, Ms. Delgado, how long ago was 1992?"

Rosa's brown eyes rolled up toward her brain as if a quite difficult math problem had just been presented to her. "Eet ees 1999, so I guess about seven years ago," she answered dutifully.

"So let me get this straight. You worked for less than six months for Dr. Brookshire over seven years ago, right?"

She hesitated. "Jes."

"And you stated in your testimony that you agreed with Lolita, correct?"

"Well, jes."

"And what relationship do you have with Lolita Perez?"

Rosa stared at the floor. "She ees my seester-in-law."

Jack stuck his lower lip out. "Oh, I see . . . and did Lolita help you get the job with Dr. Brookshire?"

"Jes, she did. I reeally needed a job."

"Just one more question, Ms. Delgado, and I will leave you alone . . . all right?"

"OK," she whimpered.

"Ms. Delgado, for the last four days and three nights, have you been staying in a hotel here in Parvenu, Georgia?"

"Jes, sir."

"And could you please tell us which hotel?"

"I theenk it ees called the Holiday Inn."

"And this Holiday Inn, is it a nice hotel?"

"Oh jes, eet is very, very nice."

"Is this hotel very expensive, Ms. Delgado?"

"Oh, I do not know. I don't have to pay for eet."

"Hmmmm, is that so? Who is paying for it then?"

"Oh, Mr. Brett there," she replied, pointing to Brett Wratchett.

Brett Wratchett looked straight at her and shook his head no.

Jack continued, "And your meals for the last four days, they must be getting expensive for you, having to eat out every meal and all."

Rosa didn't pick up on Brett Wratchett's hint at all. "Oh, no, hee is paying for our food too," she offered up.

"Wait, I want to be sure that I understand what you are saying here. Ms. Delgado, do you mean that for four full days and three nights, the state of Georgia has picked up the bill for your nice deluxe hotel room *and* your twelve restaurant meals?"

"Jes, they have."

"Thank you so much for your time today, Ms. Delgado. I surely hope that the cost of your gasoline all the way up here to north Georgia and back will not cost you too much," Jack added insult to injury.

"Oh, Brett ees paying for our gas also. I rode up here with Lolita and Dixie."

"No more questions, Ms. Delgado. Thank you for your time."

Jack glowed with victory. "Cross-examine?" he triumphantly asked Wratchett.

"No." Brett gulped.

The head honcho decreed, "Everyone, take a one-hour lunch. Be back exactly at one thirty-two!"

By the time my family and I located a nearby café, stood in a lengthy line to order our food, and sat down to talk, we had exactly thirty-seven minutes remaining on His Honor's ticking courtroom clock. It was ample time to throw around a comment or two concerning the morning's courtroom theatrical production. We all agreed that our side was winning. After all, the toughest and scariest witness—the one we had all been most fearful of exactly what might explode from her mouth—had ended up almost rooting for our side. Yes, Scarlett had not made it easy for her "Brettski" to bury me. She had actually made it appear that my state-imposed guilt might be a little bit iffy. And iffy was good for our side.

Furthermore, Lolita was not very convincing with her babies-should-never-get-their-teeth-cleaned defense when Jack was done with her. And poor, pitiful Rosa, who was quite visibly coerced into joining Lolita's and Dixie's little "let's hang Dr. Brookshire club," probably should not have even been put up on the stand. The state had not done their homework on this one. But surface remarks and general observations were all that the family had time for that particular sit-down. It was time to get back to the ruling king's courtroom kingdom. We mustn't be late.

It was no mystery who the next state witness was going to be. We had all heard from Lolita and then Rosa. It was the third musketeer's turn. Dixie, like Rosa, had only been an employee of mine for a little less than six months. In fact, Rosa and her BFF, Dixie, had come into my private office almost hand in hand and presented their oral resignations as a duet—two employees walking out on the spot, no two-week notice, no explanations of why they were vanishing, no golden handshake, just "hi" and "bye" and "we're gonna both leave you high and dry." It was not a pleasant thing for an employer to lose one-third of her employees in one fell swoop.

"The state calls Ms. Dixie Kruger," Brett Wratchett sang out.

Dixie rose from her seat like an impetuous volcanic eruption. She came forth wildly, swaying to and fro, attempting to balance on her four-inch stilettos. Lolita had always held the high-ranking position of head musketeer, but Dixie was a close second. She was naturally tall, her rangy form towering over both Lolita and poor little Rosa. But the genetic height that she was blessed with was not sufficient enough for crafty Dixie. She wanted more. More height meant more power, and more power meant more control. And more control might, just maybe, someday emerge in her rank of top musketeer.

So there she was in all her glory, wobbling down the aisle of doom, praying not to fall off her platforms. Her colored platinum blond hair tried its best to decide whether to sway with the body staggers or to stand up in total terror. Her tightly fitted sheer silk blouse cried out to pop a button. The lapels on her custom-tailored scarlet blazer flapped relentlessly with each teeter-totter step. The entire courtroom watched with full fascination. Her spellbinding appearance had us all captivated before she even took the stand. What was this tower of enthralling flesh and bones going to bring to Brett's table?

Dixie eventually made it to the hot seat, releasing an audible sigh as she collapsed into the awaiting witness stand. She reached up and smoothed her frightened hair. She straightened her lapels and felt the buttons on her blouse, checking that each one was still intact. Then as an afterthought, she assumed a perfectly upright posture, striking a board-straight pose for effect. Her long lanky fingers grasped together and found a home in her roomy lap. She stared straight ahead, fixing her gaze on Brett alone. It was quite apparent that she wanted nothing to do with the judge, the jury, the bailiff, the court reporter, or most certainly the defendant.

Brett jumped up. "Good afternoon, Ms. Kruger. How was your lunch?"

Dixie swallowed hard. "It was good, I guess."

"Ms. Kruger, how do you know the defendant, Dr. Brookshire?"

"I worked for her."

"And what did you do in her dental office?"

"I helped run the front desk some."

"So you filed paperwork at the front desk?"

Dixie was caught. She had to escape this trap good and quick. She wanted no part of the hell that Scarlett had passed through.

"Oh, no, I just helped answer the phone and make appointments and check patients in and out, stuff like that."

"But you did get exposed to some of the procedures that were filed through the office, correct?"

"Well, I guess you could say that."

"And, Ms. Kruger, were there any of those dental procedures that gave you any concern?"

"Well, yes. There was one called behavior management."

"And could you tell us what you know about this behavior management?"

Dixie sat up even straighter. "Well, it was filed when the patient was *supposed* to be bad."

"Ms. Kruger, what do you mean by bad?"

"I guess the idea is that if a child patient is acting up in the dental chair, they cause the dentist extra time, so the dentist gets some money from Medicaid for that extra time."

"And did Dr. Brookshire file for that behavioral management procedure very often?"

She tensed up. Her head gave a nervous little twitch. Her shifty eyes rolled toward the defendant's desk but then quickly shot back into straight, forward position. "Why, yes. Dr. Brookshire filed for behavior management for *every single* child patient who was on Medicaid. And lots and lots of those patients were perfect little angels too."

"You mean to tell me that Dr. Brookshire filed this behavior management on children who were behaving very well in her dental chair?"

"Why, yes, she did. And I thought that was very *wrong*! The majority of the children who came through were so sweet on check-in and sometimes even on checkout."

"So, Ms. Kruger, would it be fair to say then that Dr. Brookshire filed and then got paid by Medicaid—the state of Georgia—for procedures that she, in fact, *did not perform?*"

Dixie began to tap her pointy-toe high heels. "Well . . . I guess that would be right. I hate to see these poor little angels being called *bad*."

Wratchett trotted over to his beloved giant flip chart waiting on its easel. He snatched up his fat green marker and scribbled in king-size letters, "MEDICAID FRAUD—PROCEDURE FILED FOR BEHAVIOR MANAGEMENT NOT WARRANTED!"

He reeled around on the heels of his fine Italian leather shoes to face the jury. *Probably trying to keep up with the stilettos*, I thought.

"So now you have it, ladies and gentlemen, another fine example of how the defendant, Dr. Doramae Brookshire, *duped* the state of Georgia and *committed Medicaid fraud*!" He gave the shoes another spin and smirked at Jack. "Your witness." He sneered.

Jack calmly arose. He approached the attester. "Good afternoon, Ms. Kruger," he graciously said.

"Good afternoon," she retorted.

"Now you have stated here in this courtroom that you feel that Dr. Brookshire has committed Medicaid fraud because she filed a procedure called behavior management on child patients that were, in your opinion, little angels. Is that correct?"

"Well . . . I mean . . . most of them were pretty good kids."

"Pretty good kids? Could you define that for us, please?"

"Well, sir, when they checked in with their mothers, they were pretty calm usually."

"Oh, I see. When these children first came into the dental office from the streets of Goat Valley, before they realized where they were or exactly what was going to happen to them, at this point, they were *pretty calm*. Is that what you mean?"

"Yeah, but I didn't hear them act up very bad after they were taken back into the operatories either."

"Now, Ms. Kruger, let's establish exactly where you would be sitting in the dental office as compared with where these children were 'taken back into the operatories,' OK?"

Dixie's clasped hands began to unclasp and jump out of her lap. "OK, if you think that's necessary."

"Yes, it is necessary because the fine ladies and gentlemen on the jury need to have a clear picture of how easy it would have been for you to hear any noise or racket caused by boisterous behavior coming from any of the operatories."

"OK then. I sat at what was called the front desk, and it was right near the door coming in from the parking lot."

"And where were the dental operatories, the rooms where the children were treated for their various dental needs?" Jack inquired.

"The ops were in the back of the dental building."

"And was there a door separating the *front* of the dental building from the *back*, Ms. Kruger?"

"Well, of course, there was. The ops were separated from the front for patient privacy."

"And furthermore, were there also doors on each operatory for patient privacy as you call it?"

"That's right," Dixie snapped.

"And what about the hall going back to the operatories? Just how long was that hall?" Jack asked.

"Oh, it was pretty long. The kids sometimes got tired walking it."

"So let me get this straight. You say that there were *two* doors between you and the dental operatories and that a very long hall separated you from the children who were being treated. Do I have that correct?"

DORAMAE BROOKSHIRE

The third musketeer squirmed. "Yeah, but I still could get a pretty good idea of what was goin' on back there," Dixie argued.

"You could get a 'pretty good idea of what was going on back there'?" Jack repeated.

"Yep."

"Your Honor, I would like to submit exhibit K." Jack stepped forward and handed the bailiff a short stack of folders. The bailiff, in turn, handed the folders to His Highness.

Judge Grudge scanned His new treasure. He glared up from His reading glasses. "I will allow these. I believe we have seen them previously in this trial. Please proceed, counselor, and do not be redundant," He dictated.

Jack turned back toward the witness. He handed her a patient folder. "Now, Ms. Kruger, do you recognize this folder?" he asked.

"Yeah. That is one of Dr. Brookshire's patient folders," she replied.

"And without telling us the patient's name, could you please look at the patient history form and tell us how old the patient was in April of 1992?"

She turned slow motion to the patient history form in the front of the folder. She cautiously picked it up and began to examine it. "Well, let's see. This here says that the patient was born in 1988, so I guess in 1992 . . ." Her shifty eyes rolled up toward her noggin. "He would have been four years old, right?" she questioned.

"Yes, I believe your math is right on, Ms. Kruger." Jack grinned. "Now you were working for Dr. Brookshire in April of 1992, correct?"

"Yup, that's right," she curtly replied.

"And, Ms. Kruger, did you ever miss any work?"

"Oh, no, never. I was never sick. I was a very good worker. I never missed a day," she bragged.

"So then it would be fair to say that you were in Dr. Brookshire's office working on April 16, 1992?"

"Uh-huh, I was there."

"So then could you kindly turn to the patient records and read the entry written about this four-year-old on April 16, 1992?" Jack asked.

Dixie turned into a sloth. She sluggishly turned the pages in the patient's records. "April 16, 1992?" she asked.

"That is correct. Could you read that entry aloud to us, please?"

"The whole thing?" She was getting testy.

"Yes, ma'am, the whole thing dated April 16, 1992, please."

"OK. 'Inject 1 carp Lido HCL. # K MOD amalgam. Patient kicked, bit dentist's finger, spit in dentist's face, grabbed at drill, and attempted to get out of chair several times. 30 minutes extra time needed. Y000100 filed.'"

"Thank you, Ms. Kruger. Now you had stated several different times that you felt that all the child patients in Dr. Brookshire's practice were well behaved. Is that correct?"

"No," she corrected. "I said that *most* of them were."

"Oh, excuse me. I thought that you said that you could get a pretty good idea of what was going on back in the dental operatories."

"Wuh . . . wuh . . . uh, yeah," Dixie stuttered.

Jack thrust a second patient folder toward her. "Ms. Kruger, could you please read the entry dated May 19, 1992?"

Dixie's eyes cut upward. "Ummm . . . 'Inject 1 carp Lido HCL. # B DO amalgam. Patient screamed, grabbed doctor's hand, bit down on drill, rolled over in chair, kicked assistant in chest. Patient's mother brought back to op. Patient is age 3. Option of referral to pediatric dentist was discussed with mom. Mom refused option due to fact that she has no way to get to Tanaha or Bangdale to specialist. Mom was allowed to stay in op with patient during treatment. Patient continued same above behaviors throughout treatment, even with mom's help. Y009200 filed.'"

"Thank you for reading that excerpt, Ms. Kruger," Jack rendered. "Now based on this reading, I have a question for you, Ms. Kruger. The excerpt stated that the mother of this three-year-old refused the option of a referral to a pediatric dentist. Did you understand the reason for Mom's refusal? Wouldn't it be so much better for this young child to be able to go to a pediatric dentist, one who *specializes* in treating young patients?"

Dixie stuck her sharp chin in the air. "Well, of course, that would be the *best* way to go for the child, but you have to understand where these parents are coming from. These moms are *poor*! They don't have any cars to drive all the way to Tanaha or Bangdale! Even if they had a car, they wouldn't be able to afford the gas to go all that way, let alone the *cost* of a child specialist!"

"Wait a second. You mean to tell me that there is no option of a pediatric dentist . . . a dentist who treats children . . . in the city of Goat Valley?" Jack inquired with much disbelief.

"You don't know?" Dixie retorted with equal inability to believe. "No, Goat Valley only has general dentists. If a baby or child needs to be seen, they have to be driven to Tanaha or Bangdale to see the baby dentist."

"And just how far away is Tanaha?" Jack inquired.

Dixie sighed and shot Jack a look of pure disgust. "Tanaha, Georgia, is about forty-five or fifty miles from Goat Valley, Georgia," she answered rather smart-alecky.

"Hmmmm . . . and how far away is Bangdale from Goat Valley?" he asked.

"Jeez! Bangdale, Georgia, is about sixty miles from Goat Valley, Georgia," Dixie droned, her scarlet, red lips pursed tightly.

"Let me get this straight." Jack smiled. "If these moms and dads of young children in Goat Valley needed to take their children to the *ideal* dental treatment situation, that is, to a pediatric dentist, the one who is equipped to treat their precious children properly and with the ideal equipment, in a dental office setup specifically for kids, these parents living in Goat Valley would be forced to drive to Tanaha or Bangdale . . . either fifty or sixty miles away, correct?"

Dixie's sharp crimson fingernails shot up to her painted lips. She rubbed her digits slowly across her pinched mouth. "Yep, that's what I just said."

"And let's stop here for just a minute and address another fact concerning these tiniest of patients. Ms. Kruger, can you describe the physical state of many of these young, two-year-olds' and three-year-olds' mouths?"

"Wuh, how do I know? I am usually sitting up front," she shot back.

"Oh, I'm sorry. I am holding your deposition dated May 12, 1998. In this deposition, you described the condition of a young patient's teeth. Do I need to let you read this aloud to the jury?" Jack asked.

Dixie's highfalutin expression suddenly turned humble. "No. No, I don't need to read it. I remember now what I said. Many of these really young patients have what we call nursing bottle caries."

"And, Ms. Kruger, exactly what is this nursing bottle caries? Describe it to us, please."

"Well, soooo many patients of Dr. Brookshire's had it. It was from being put to bed with a bottle full of sugary drink . . . lots of time sweet tea. Then after drinking this sugar, they fall asleep, and the moms and dads never ever brush their teeth either . . . and all they eat is *candy*."

"And what did this do to the young child's baby teeth?" Jack asked.

"Oh, it was just *horrible*! These little babies had soft, crumbling *black* sticks for teeth, every one of their front teeth like black marshmallows! So sad!" Dixie was looking at the ground and shaking her platinum blond head.

"I am so sorry to hear this. But this could only have happened to one or two young patients of Dr. Brookshire, certainly not more than that, huh?" Jack suggested.

"Oh, not at all," Dixie shot back. "A whole *bunch* of Dr. Brookshire's little patients had this nursing bottle caries, a *whole bunch* of them."

"You mean that a large number of two-year-olds and three-year-olds in Dr. Brookshire's dental practice suffered from a condition that caused their baby teeth to turn black and soft and crumble from their tiny mouths?" Jack asked as if in total shock.

"Yeah, that's what I saw every day, especially the Mexican kids. Sometimes it was so bad that the teeth weren't even there anymore. Just spongy black roots that had to be *dug* out. Poor things! The dental assistants and me talked about how horrible it was. We saw it almost every day."

"Oh my!" Jack was aghast. "Now these poor little children—the ones suffering with spongy, crumbling black teeth—they needed special help, wouldn't you say, Ms. Kruger?"

"Well, of course, they needed special help. Didn't I just describe the situation to you?" Dixie was quickly losing patience with Mr. Defense Lawyer.

"Let's carry this one step forward. Wouldn't you say that these suffering little babies, the ones in so much pain, should have been seen as soon as possible by the pediatric dentists in Tanaha and Bangdale?" Jack proposed.

Dixie sighed so loudly that it came across as a moan. "I already told you once. Those pediatric dentists were about an hour away, and these moms couldn't get to them, and most of them had a waiting time for an appointment of a month or more, *and* most of them did not take Medicaid!" She let out a second moan for dramatic purposes.

"Wait a minute!" Jack rang out, returning her theatrical overture. "You mean to tell me that these pediatric dentists—the ones trained specially to treat this nursing bottle caries—they had a monthlong waiting time, and they did not even take Medicaid in their practices?"

"I think it is no big secret that Medicaid doesn't pay the doctors worth a diddly—" She caught herself and paused. "Anyhow, I wouldn't want to take Medicaid if I was a specialist," Dixie attempted to explain.

"Now let's look at the big picture," Jack directed. "We have a whole large group of two-year-olds and three-year-olds and, as far as that goes, one-year-olds and four-year-olds too suffering from a horrible condition in their mouths that have turned their little baby teeth to crumbling black mush. These tiniest of patients, who have asked for none of this, are in daily *pain*! Dr. Brookshire sees them in her practice. She does the right thing. She refers these agonizing miniature patients to a specialist to be seen ASAP. But the specialists, who are an hour away, say, 'Sorry. We cannot see your patients, Dr. Brookshire, because we don't take Medicaid like you, and we have a four-week waiting list anyhow. So sorry 'bout that.' "Hmmmm . . . what can Dr. Brookshire do then? What options does she have at that point?"

"Well, I guess she can either treat the kids herself or send them away," Dixie speculated.

"And which of these did Dr. Brookshire choose to do, Ms. Kruger?" Jack asked.

"Well, of course, she treated them. Who wouldn't? If they were left like that, they would have probably *died* of infection soon."

"These suffering, innocent tiny baby patients would have died of rampant infection if they were not treated in a timely manner," Jack repeated.

Dixie kicked her sharp-toed stiletto hard against the witness stand. "That is what I just said!" she spat back at Jack.

"Wow! Dr. Brookshire was in a bit of a conundrum, huh? Because of the pediatric dentists' policies, the ideal treatment for these little folks was unavailable. As a result, she was put in a position that none of us here would have envied. Should Dr. Brookshire treat these suffering little angels herself or just let them go home and hope for the best?"

Dixie looked at Jack as though he was holding a dagger. "Well, of course, she had to treat them herself! I already told you. They probably would have *died* without treatment!"

"But Dr. Brookshire didn't have all the whistles and bells needed to treat babies and toddlers in her practice. She was just a general dentist. The pediatric dentists were the ones *supposed* to treat these babies with rampant nursing bottle caries. All their special equipment would have made these little patients much more comfortable, not to mention their ability to medicate these toddlers would have made the experience much more relaxed and much less traumatic for them," Jack insisted.

"Yeah, but it wasn't gonna happen like that. I done told you," Dixie droned through gritted teeth.

Jack paused. He looked at the courtroom ceiling as if in deep thought. "These precious, suffering tiny one-year-olds and two-year-olds and three-year-olds and four-year-olds sitting in Dr. Brookshire's dental chair . . . they had to be frightened out of their little wits."

"Of course, they were, but what can ya do 'bout that?" Dixie retorted.

"I would guess then, if we put this all together, that these terrified toddlers would naturally act up. They would behave just horribly, probably by kicking and spitting and biting and grabbing high-speed instruments. After all, these are babies and toddlers who, the way they see it, have been cornered and are having procedures done to them that they cannot possibly understand, right?"

"Of *course*, they are going to act bad! They're *scared* for god's sake!" Dixie screamed at Jack.

"Then I guess these behaviors—crying and screaming and struggling and spitting and kicking and grabbing and biting—they would make it so Dr. Brookshire would have to take extra time with these frightened children?"

"My god! Of course, it took extra time! Do you think it all went smoothly back there in the operatories?" Dixie was fit to be tied.

"Then I guess that Dr. Brookshire needed a little compensation for her extra time since she was unable to see as many of her well-behaved adult patients on the days she was seeing these poor babies," Jack threw up for grabs.

Dixie stopped dead in her tracks. She had been tricked. What could she do? Jack had already gotten her to agree that the nursing bottle babies misbehaved. How could she not admit, at this point, that the doctor needed to be compensated a small amount for behavior management? She had already testified that filing behavior management was evil, wrong, and disgraceful. She was going to have to think up a quick compromise. "Well, maybe Dr. Brookshire did need something extra, but filing behavior management all the time wasn't exactly right," she insisted.

"Oh, I see. It wasn't *exactly right* of Dr. Brookshire to file for behavior management. What were her other options?" Jack wanted to know.

"Well, she could have just treated those poor little things and took whatever Medicaid was willing to pay. After all, they were sick babies," she built her argument.

"You know what, Ms. Kruger, I agree with you in a way. In an *ideal* world, we would all just reach out and help all those in need, all those who are suffering, and we would do it with a smile on our faces and pure love in our hearts. And I am sure that Dr. Brookshire would have treated all these nursing bottle caries patients for free if she could have. But the fact remains that Dr. Brookshire had a staff to pay, a dental building mortgage, huge school loans, equipment notes, and on and on, and she had to make enough money to meet her financial obligations, or her practice would have gone under, and then no little patients would have been brought out of their suffering. Remember, a large part of Dr. Brookshire's practice was Medicaid patients, and Medicaid pays pennies on the dollar. So keeping this all in mind, I am going to ask you this. Was it OK for Dr. Brookshire to file for behavior management on these young patients?" Jack shot Dixie a compassionate look.

Before she could weigh the consequences, Dixie shot back, "Well, of course, it was OK to file that. What else could she do?" Dixie's confused mouth flew open. Her well-manicured hands took wing and clapped rapidly over her organ of speech.

It was a fine example of what Jack called "The bell has been rung. You can't unring it."

"Thank you so much for your time today, Ms. Kruger. No more questions." Jack was grinning from ear to ear.

Judge Grudge looked like He had been shot between the eyes. "Redirect?" He weakly asked Brett Wratchett.

Brett looked as if he had seen a ghost. "No, Your Honor," he said under his breath.

"You may step down, Ms. Kruger," His Mighty One pronounced.

Her retreat was sad. Her entrance had been bad enough, what with the swaying and balancing on the four-inch platforms. But her retreat was just downright pitiful. She bent her defeated head over, shoulders slumped, arms pasted at her side. And she dragged her pointed feet all the way down the long, long aisle of doom and out the heavy door.

It was only 3:50 p.m. What could we possibly be facing next? A past staff member who had worked for me for a month several years ago perhaps? A substitute hygienist who was coached to believe that things were just not right around "that office"? But instead, something happened to give us all a little courtroom relief.

Juror no. 8 raised her hand and requested to speak to the judge. Apparently, she was not feeling so well and asked to be excused for the rest of the day, if possible. By the time they quit their little whisper session, it was pushing four thirty anyway. So Judge Grudge made the announcement. "The court will adjourn for the day. All be back at nine o'clock sharp tomorrow morning. Once again, do not discuss anything that goes on in My courtroom with anyone! Court dismissed!" With that, the holy gavel was pounded, the ebony-cloaked one arose and with Him all present in the room, the jury filed out, and we were left with our Wednesday evening thoughts.

On my way back to the hotel, I made a quick assessment of the day's events. Memories of special things that I had done for my many staff members over the years flooded my muddled mind. I had truly tried my heart out to be an extracaring boss, responsive to most of their needs. I had offered benefits, paid vacations, and family leaves. They all got monthly bonuses. I had tried my best to show empathy and compassion and put myself in their shoes. I was very generous with time off and sick days. I understood parenting and had come to empathize with what it must take to be a single mother. In addition to all that, I had even ventured out of the normal range of boss behavior and had enthusiastically thrown all kinds of group festivities.

These staff get-togethers were designed to make the members of the office team feel like a warm, close-knit, family-like group. I had recognized each team member's birthday with both cake and presents. I threw little office parties for Valentine's Day, Easter, Fourth of July, Halloween, Thanksgiving, and a big blowout of a Christmas party. I had even taken a couple of key staff members and their families to Disney World. Oh, and then there was that staff cruise to the Bahamas.

I pondered on how staff members who were treated like family members could turn on their boss at the drop of a hat. I didn't really have to think too long to discover the answer though. Scarlett couldn't help her testimony against me. Her hand was forced. It was me or her. She had good instincts. She knew darn well, as a single mother, that she was not going to be the one to sit rotting in jail. So my scrambled mind forgave her for her testimony. But what about the Three Musketeers? What had I done to them to make them all turn on me? Then I remembered.

When they were employed by me, the three of them had formed their own exclusive dental office clique. Their closed circle involved very little interaction with the rest of the office staff. In fact, the three of them remained distant to the others during office social events. They always had a last-minute excuse of why they could not attend. Of course, their standoffishness was noticed by the others and the warm, fuzzy office environment quickly turned frosty and detached. I had attempted to talk to them about their aloofness, but they were frigid and unapproachable. My strong encouragement and later on insistence that they participate as a part of the group eventually led to their resignations. Now they had an ax to grind with me, and what better way to do that than to sit in judgment of me in an honest-to-goodness courtroom trial? Knowing their personal values, the four days and three nights of free big-city hotel rooms and meals more than likely played a big part in their decisions to testify against me too.

I shook my weary head. What was I doing? Such negative thoughts should not be running through my mind at such a critical time. I needed to view that mythical glass as half full and not half empty. I needed to snap out of this ultranegative mindset, and I needed to do that right this second.

So I explored the positive side of my staff members. In no time at all, I was feeling much better. I approached it like this. Why not take a mental count of the staff members who, for one reason or another, decided *not* to testify against me? I had to assume that the prosecutors had tried to get them all to say something repugnant about me. Yet it appeared that the vast majority of them did not show up at that courtroom in Atlanta to drag me through the mud. I started to count—Joy, Meadow, Hope, Rose, Hazel, Katie, Rhonda, Zoe, Shirley, Amy. There it was. The score was 10–4, ten dental assistants, hygienists, and front desk workers who had refused to cave under the state of Georgia's scare tactics. I was proud of these women. It must have been really difficult for some of them to resist the arm-twisting and scary intimidation imposed on them by the Wratchett group. At that moment, I put it all behind me, not another thought of backstabbing employees. I had to get my jumbled, mishmash brain ready for what was to come.

A TALE OF TWO TOBYS

THURSDAY MORNING, THE fourth day of crucifixion and torment—who was going to draw and quarter me today? I didn't have to wonder long. Approaching the courtroom through the long hall, I noticed bench after bench chock full of apprehensive young faces. They all looked extremely familiar. Some glanced up at me and then quickly looked away, with expressions of fright spreading across their innocent faces. Then suddenly, it came to me. These were my beautiful little patients, only they were years older than they had been when I had treated them. That made sense. I had been forced out of my dental practice four and a half years previously. A child who had been four years old when I had treated him or her was now almost nine years old. What a difference in a child's appearance at age four and then at age nine! But I could still recognize many of them, mostly around their eyes.

Why were all these many, many little patients here at this scary cold courtroom in Atlanta, Georgia? How had they gotten here from Goat Valley, Georgia? That was four hours and over two hundred miles away. I ventured a guess that most of them had not been that far away from home in their entire lives. Jack was on it. He found out nice and quick that these poor, startled, innocent little babes were bussed up to the big city at five that morning—and on a school day too. For some ungodly reason, Brett Wratchett and his team of legal eagles had found it necessary to load up a yellow bus full of terrified young schoolchildren at the crack of dawn and force them to endure the bone-bruising drive to the faceless metropolis. Most of them sat, tiny legs dangling from the adult-sized benches, their eyes fixed straight ahead but occasionally darting from side to side to check out any unusual or suspect movements. They were visibly shaken. This environment was certainly not rural south Georgia.

I passed by these poor souls and into the waiting courtroom. I established my seat at the defendant's table alongside Jack. The prosecutor's table was empty. There was an audible hustle and bustle in the hall. Brett and his cronies were scrambling about furiously, attempting to figure out how to get all these munchkins to cooperate and remain there as stoic little robots for hours on the hard, cold benches while they were called in to the witness-box one by one. No one had thought ahead to have any quiet activities for the youngsters. No one on the Wratchett team had thought ahead of the babysitting factor. Only an occasional grandma dotted the overcrowded benches, and those poor, pepless ladies were definitely in the sunset of their lives. The bumpy ride in the antique motorbus had done them in, and it was only nine in the morning. The state could not possibly depend on these decrepit matriarchs to serve as babysitters for the masses. So Brett assigned one of his numerous team members, a female, of course, as chief mama and nursemaid for the day.

The mighty referee in the black robe magically appeared. All arose. The jury filed in. Juror no. 8 seemed better. They took their seats, notepads clutched in hand. We were off to another day of discovery. What hidden atrocities were going to be unmasked today? And we had the seventeen dwarves to help us unmask them.

"Mr. Wratchett, call your first witness," the chief arbitrator cried out.

"I call Toby Tucker to the stand," he replied.

Jack and I glanced at each other. We were both thinking the same thing. What a lucky break! Wratchett's very first child witness was the White Toby Tucker. I hated like the dickens to see an innocent child be put up on the stand, but this was going to be good.

The pitiful little thing looked to be around age eight. I did some quick mental math. I remembered treating Toby when he was around four, so that would be just about right. Brett Wratchett approached the witness stand. "Good morning, Toby," he tried to say softly.

"Good morning," the scared little rabbit replied.

"Now you understand the difference between the truth and a lie, don't you, Toby?" Brett demanded to know.

"Yes, I do," Toby answered.

"And you promise to tell the truth here today, don't you, Toby?"

"Yes, I will," he replied, his blue eyes getting big as saucers.

"Good. We grown-ups like little boys who tell the truth. Now, Toby, I am going to ask you some questions today, and I want you to answer them with the truth, OK?" Brett sighed.

"OK." Little Toby was tiring quickly of the tell-the-truth game.

"Now, Toby, when you were a *real* little boy, say, around age four, do you remember going to the dentist?"

A brief movie clip danced through my mind, the one when Pinocchio earned his reward on the earth and became a *real* little boy. *Focus*, I mentally told myself. *Focus!*

"Yes, sir," Toby was answering.

"And, Toby, do you remember who your dentist was back then?" Brett asked.

"Yes, I think so, sir," he replied.

"And, Toby, is that dentist in this courtroom today?"

"Yes, sir," Toby whispered.

"Then could you please point that dentist out for us, Toby?"

His shaky little finger raised in slow motion. He swung it around reluctantly and pointed at me. "Her," he said softly under his breath.

"Let the record reflect that the witness has identified Dr. Doramae Brookshire as his dentist at age four!" Brett yelled out.

"Now, Toby, do you remember going to Dr. Brookshire for several visits? Or just a few?" Brett asked.

"Oh, I only went there a few times." Toby's voice trailed off.

"Toby, could you please tell us how many times a few is?" Brett inquired.

"They told me I went there three times," Toby answered.

Brett looked startled. He wasn't quite sure how to deal with little Toby's answer, which included the term *they*.

Jack and I both knew exactly who *they* were. *They* were the Goat Valley dentists who had willingly volunteered to "check out" my child patients in their own personal dental offices. These examinations were done in the agreeable spirit of aiding the state of Georgia to discover Medicaid fraud on the evil doctor Brookshire. These local Goat Valley dentists were instrumental in helping the state hang the wicked, corrupt doctor. The unsuspecting, totally trusting tots were placed in these local dentists' chairs and were unnecessarily X-rayed, poked, prodded, photographed, and interviewed.

Then these gathered records were happily sent to the state, who went to the immense expense of blowing each and every X-ray, interview, and record up to gargantuan size. Each X-ray alone was inflated from its original size of about one by one and a half inches all the way up to about twelve inches by eighteen inches. It was actually eerie to see a dental X-ray become the size of a piece of legal paper. Jack and I had discussed the amount of money that the GBI and state of Georgia had spent preparing for this trial. We estimate it was in the hundreds of thousands of taxpayer dollars, an awful lot of time, money, and trouble to "catch" one dentist.

Wratchett decided to ignore the remark "They told me three times" and proceeded with his questioning of young Toby. "Toby, do you remember what Dr. Brookshire did to you on these three dental visits?" he asked.

Toby rolled his blue eyes up and pondered the question. "Well, they told me that the first time was to clean my teeth and X-ray them. Then you said the second time I got a filling. Then you told me that the third time I got another filling," he replied, looking straight at Brett for validation.

Brett could no longer ignore the *they* and *you* issue. "Toby, honey, even though some other men and myself told you what Dr. Brookshire had treated on you, you *do* remember that these procedures were what went on in your mouth, right?"

"Well, I was only four." His voice faltered.

Brett was losing ground. *That's what he deserves for trying to take advantage of innocent little children*, I thought.

"But even though you were only four, you do remember that what we have been discussing was pretty close to what was done to you, right, honey?" Brett was showing his desperation.

"Yeah, I guess," Toby answered, ready to say what Brett wanted to hear to go back home.

DORAMAE BROOKSHIRE

"Well, Mr. Tucker, let's have a look at the *proof*, shall we?" Brett sang out, strolling over to his beloved giant flip chart. He carefully placed a giant dental X-ray dated April 14, 1997, on the stand.

"This X-ray was taken of your teeth a couple of years ago by a Goat Valley dentist," he proudly announced. He pointed to a full-mouth panoramic X-ray that revealed two tiny occlusal fillings in two of Toby's back molars. "Toby, you have only two small fillings in your mouth. Here they are."

"*Now* let's have a look at what Dr. Brookshire *filed* with Medicaid for your treatments, shall we?" Brett warbled.

Tiny Toby wiggled in his witness seat. His slender right leg began to jump and jiggle. He was eight years old, and he was good and tired of this cat-and-mouse game.

Brett continued. He didn't need any more response from the nervous witness to proceed with the lynching. He slapped another giant panoramic X-ray onto his prized flip chart stand. The patient's name danced proudly across the top of the monstrous film. "Tucker, Toby," it proclaimed in black Sharpie precision. This X-ray differed quite decidedly from the X-ray that the jury and everyone else in the courtroom had just seen. The colossal dental film revealed an entire mouthful of full-coverage stainless steel crowns, four large fillings, and a couple of missing teeth.

"Now *this* is the X-ray that Dr. Brookshire submitted to Medicaid for you, Toby. I don't know exactly where Dr. Brookshire *got* this X-ray, but it was obviously from one of her other poor, unsuspecting little patients. Then she put *your* name on it. Do you see all the crowns and huge fillings and everything in *this* X-ray as compared with what was in your *true* X-ray? The one that you just saw that was telling the truth?" he screamed out at poor little Toby.

"Yeah, they look different," Toby weakly offered.

"They most certainly do! They look different to the tune of over $980 . . . almost one thousand dollars in charges that Dr. Brookshire purely *made up* on you, Toby! She was making false claims on your mouth so that she could *rob* Medicaid of its money that is supposed to go to help other little children! Now doesn't that anger you, Toby, that she used you to *rob* our government?"

Jack began to stand up and then decided that his soon-to-occur retaliation was going to be good enough. He opted to let Brett go on and on with this melodramatic courtroom overreaction.

Brett looked at Toby, expecting a reaction.

"Well, I guess so?" Toby reluctantly replied, having lost the entire train of thought in the process.

Brett stood by his precious flip chart stand. He briefly appeared to hug the X-ray with extensive deciduous metalwork. Then he snatched the fat green marker off its resting place and began to scribble on the flip chart. He divided the paper into two columns. "TOBY TUCKER'S TRUE DENTAL WORK," he wrote on the top of the left-hand column.

"TOBY TUCKER'S FABRICATED (FALSE) DENTAL WORK," he wrote on the top of the right-hand column.

Under the "TRUE DENTAL WORK," he wrote down:

Amalgam # A . . . $35
Amalgam # K . . . $35
TOTAL $70

Under the "FABRICATED (FALSE) DENTAL WORK," he wrote:

Stainless Steel Crown # A . . . $95
Stainless Steel Crown # B . . . $95
Stainless Steel Crown # I . . . $95
Stainless Steel Crown # J . . . $95
Stainless Steel Crown # K . . . $95
Stainless Steel Crown # L . . . $95
Stainless Steel Crown # S . . . $95
Stainless Steel Crown # T . . . $95
Composite filling # D . . . $35
Composite filling # G . . . $35
Composite filling # O . . . $35
Composite filling # P . . . $35
Extraction # E $40

Extraction # F $40
TOTAL $980

As a grand finale, he tacked on:

$980
- $70
$910 in false claims!

He wheeled around on the heels of his shiny wing tips. "Now you have it, ladies and gentlemen, full-blown Medicaid fraud out and out! Right here, it is in black and white! No denying it!" He was so proud of himself. His puny chest puffed out with honor. "Your witness." He sneered at Jack.

Jack casually came forth from his chair. He walked gently toward the wee witness, smiling the tenderest of smiles. "Hi, Toby," he said softly.

A look of relief spread across the little guy's face. "Hi, sir," he gladly returned.

"Toby, I am not going to ask you very many questions here today. I understand that you have had quite a time of it already. You rode up here to Atlanta from your home in Goat Valley on a big yellow bus with a bunch of other kids early this morning, right?"

Toby looked scared and sad at the same time. "Yes, sir, I did."

"And I also understand that you had to get up *really* early to get on that bus, huh?" Jack asked.

Now Toby was nodding rapidly. "Yes, sir. It was really, really early."

Brett Wratchett started to rise but sat back down when Judge Grudge held up His royal right hand.

"And today was supposed to be a school day in Goat Valley for you, right, Toby?"

"Uh-huh," the forlorn little fellow replied.

"And how many other kids that had to miss school in Goat Valley today were riding on that bus with you?" Jack inquired.

"Oh a *lots* of kids! All the seats were taken up, no place else to sit. Some grandmas were on the bus too."

"So this morning, really early, a whole bus full of kids and grandmas left Goat Valley, Georgia, to ride up to Atlanta, Georgia. Is that right?" Jack asked.

"Yes, sir." Toby looked relieved because he could actually understand this man's questions.

"And were you told *why* you had to get on that bus so early this morning and miss school to ride to the big city?" Jack inquired.

"Yes, sir. That man"—now he was pointing to Brett—"told me I had to come here to say things about my lady dentist."

Brett leaped up. "Objection!" he screamed.

"Sit down and let the boy finish," His Honor droned. His rare ruling against the state nearly knocked me out of my seat.

"And who would that lady dentist be that you were told to say things against, Toby? Is she here in this room?" Jack asked.

"Yes, sir. She is right there." He pointed with a shaky finger at me.

"Was that early morning bus ride bumpy?" Jack asked.

"Oh yes, sir. It shook me up and down and all around," the youngster gleefully replied, probably repeating the lyrics to some nursery rhyme.

"Of course, you stopped some to go to the bathroom and maybe to get breakfast, huh?" Jack asked.

"Oh, no, sir, that man said that we were going to be late if we stopped. He said it was the law to be on time, so we didn't stop none." Toby sat up straight.

A very somber expression spread across Jack's usually carefree face. "Now let me get this straight, Toby. You were put on a bus filled with children very, very early this morning, had to miss school, and went through a very, very bumpy bus ride without stopping to get to this big, big city so that you kids could obey the law and say things against your lady dentist who saw you years ago? Is all that true?"

"Yes, sir." The little guy breathed out a giant sigh of relief that someone finally could verbalize the day's events better than he could.

"Hmmmmm," Jack pondered.

"Only a couple of more questions for you today, Toby. Then we will let you go. And they are easy questions," Jack promised.

"Thank you, Mister." The tiny testifier sighed.

"Do you know your birthday, Toby?"

"Why, yes, sir. It is April 12, 1991."

"And do you know your address, Toby?"

"Yes, sir. I live at 2811 Hall Avenue."

"And that's in Goat Valley, Georgia, right?" Jack asked.

"Yes, sir. Goat Valley, Georgia," he answered.

"So your birthday is April 12, 1991, and you live at 2811 Hall Avenue in Goat Valley, Georgia?" Jack reiterated.

"Yes, sir."

"And have you ever moved from this address?"

"No, sir. I have lived in the same house my whole life," Toby answered.

"And do you know your middle name, Toby?" Jack asked.

"Yes, sir. It is William, Toby William Tucker."

"One more thing. Toby, you said earlier that you remembered going to Dr. Brookshire three times, right?"

"Yes, sir, three times," he answered gladly.

Jack looked up at Judge Grudge. "Permission to approach the bench," he said.

"What is this regarding?" His Honor shot back at Jack.

"Two patient folders belonging to Dr. Brookshire," Jack replied.

"*Both* counsels, get up here *now*," the judge commanded.

Brett looked alarmed and confused. He arose cautiously and approached the bench, dragging his feet all the way.

Out of the corner of my eyes, I could see Jack calmly handing Judge Grudge two manila patient folders. Then I saw His Honor opening each one and studying their contents. Then I thought I heard Him whisper in an irritated voice something like, "Did you know there where two patients with the same name, Mr. Wratchett?" I was not totally sure that I heard those exact words from the judge because I knew what those two patient folders contained, and I knew what Jack was up to.

Finally, the king of the courtroom spoke. "I will allow these two patient folders into evidence," He ruled.

Jack twirled around. His famous, trademark south Georgia grin spread across his relieved face. He walked calmly toward Toby, the two priceless patient records in hand. "What I'm going to ask you to do next is very important, Toby, OK?" he informed the young witness.

"OK, sir," he answered.

"I am going to hand you two folders. Could you please read the names on each of these folders real loud so everyone in this room can hear them?" Jack asked of the attester.

"Yes, sir. This one says, 'Tucker, Toby.' And this one here says, 'Tucker, Toby.'" He thought for a second. "Hey, there's *two* of me," he declared.

"That is exactly right, Toby. There were *two* little boys named Toby Tucker in Dr. Brookshire's patients." Jack paused to give the necessary flair of courtroom drama to the key moment in discovery. It was of utmost importance that the judge and the jury understood totally what had just happened. Once it had had a chance to sink in, Jack continued, "Toby, if you will, please open the first Toby Tucker folder to the green piece of paper marked 'patient history form.'"

Toby did as asked. It was easy to find the patient history form as it was the only green paper in the folder. I had planned that when I had set up my practice to make it easy to always find that very important form. We always referred to this green patient history form each and every time before any treatment.

"Got it," Toby declared, waving it in the air.

"Good. Now will you please read to us, nice and loud, the patient's name on that green form?"

"Yes, sir. Toby William Tucker. Hey, that's me!"

"So it is. And please read to us the address on that form," Jack requested.

"2811 Hall Avenue, Goat Valley, Georgia. That's *my* house!" Toby smiled.

"Yes, it is," Jack agreed. "Now, Toby, please read the date of birth on that green patient history form, if you will."

"April 12, 1991, my birthday," he announced proudly.

"Now, Toby, could you please put that green paper down and find the yellow piece of paper?" Jack requested.

"Yes, sir." It was visible that young Toby was having a pretty good time with his treasure hunt up in that hard wooden witness stand. "Found it," he declared, holding it up as his next prize.

"This yellow piece of paper tells us all the dental work that Dr. Brookshire has performed on the patient," Jack educated the judge and jury. "Toby, could you please read the date in this column and the numbers in this column to us?"

"OK then, '1-4-95 . . . Prophy, 4 BWX, IEx; 1-11-95 . . . O Ag # A; 1-18-95 . . . O Ag # K.'"

"Is that all it says on that yellow piece of paper?" Jack asked.

"Yes, sir, that's all," he answered.

"Let's pass those two pieces of paper, the green one and the yellow one, around the jury so they can see them, OK?" Jack reached for the papers. Young Toby willingly surrendered them.

Jack walked over and handed the two papers to the jury foreman. "Let me explain the shorthand used in dental offices to you all," he offered. "*Prophy* is short for cleaning the teeth. *Four BWX* is short for X-rays of the back molar teeth. *IEx* is short for 'initial exam,' the first thorough oral examination that each and every patient receives his or her first appointment. The letter *O* refers to an occlusal or small filling in the chewing surface of back teeth. The letters *Ag* stand for amalgam or silver fillings. The numbers *A* and *K* refer to the two baby teeth on Toby that had cavities and were filled by Dr. Brookshire. Tooth # A is located in Toby's upper right and tooth # K is located in Toby's lower left."

The jury nodded, a sign to Jack that they all followed him and understood.

"Unfortunately, Dr. Brookshire does not have any X-rays of Toby's finished work because the next set of X-rays would have been taken the following year. Dr. Brookshire only takes X-rays on young patients once a year. *Unnecessary* X-rays are frowned upon as they expose the youngsters to unnecessary radiation," Jack added, referring to the many X-rays that were taken unnecessarily by the Goat Valley turncoats.

Jack turned back toward Toby. "So you agree that this patient folder was yours, right? Toby William Tucker. Birth date April 12, 1991. Address 2811 Hall Avenue in Goat Valley, Georgia. Three appointments with Dr. Brookshire—first appointment for cleaning and X-rays, second appointment for a silver filling, and third appointment for another silver filling?"

Jack's grin became contagious, and Toby caught it. "*Yes, sir,*" he sang out. "That folder is mine."

"Just one more thing I am going to ask you to do here today, Toby. Could you please carefully open that second patient folder that you still have in your lap? But please be careful because there are *lots* and lots of papers and X-rays and other things in *that* folder," Jack informed.

"Yeah," Toby agreed. "This folder is fat. It isn't skinny, like mine."

"How true! Can you find the piece of green paper in this folder, please, Toby?" Jack directed.

Toby went fishing. "Here it is," he declared.

"Now please read the name on this patient history form," Jack asked.

"Toby Jamal Tucker," Toby replied.

"Hmmmm. He has a different middle name from you, huh?"

"Yeah. My middle name is William," little Toby replied.

"What does the birth date say?" Jack asked.

"February 1, 1990," Toby answered.

"When was your birthday now?" Jack asked.

"April 12, 1991," he replied.

"And the address on *this* Toby Tucker's form?" Jack asked.

"It says, '2645 Solomon Place.'"

"Toby, you live on Hall Avenue, right?"

"Yes, sir."

"Look at one more thing for me, Toby, please. See the little square that you can check on the form that says 'race'?" Jack directed.

Toby's roving eyes quickly scanned the green form. "Got it!" he yelled out.

"Now what is checked under 'race' for this Toby Tucker?" Jack asked.

"Black," Toby answered with wonder.

"So this Toby Tucker was Black." Jack's voice trailed off. "Hmmmmm. *This* Toby Tucker is named Toby *Jamal* Tucker. He was born on February 1, 1988. He lives at 2645 Solomon Nixon Place. And he is African American. That isn't you, is it, Toby?"

"No, not me at all," Toby answered with conviction.

"Now let's take a look at this Toby Tucker's dental record, the dental work that Dr. Brookshire performed on him, OK?"

"OK, sir," Toby answered.

"Please find that yellow piece of paper in his folder. That will be the record of his dental work," Jack reminded everyone.

Toby carefully dug through a sizable stack of X-rays and papers. "Here it is," he announced.

"Hey, *both* sides of this yellow paper have writing on them, a whole bunch of writing," the tiny sleuth revealed.

"Let me see that paper, please, Toby," Jack requested.

Toby surrendered his find. Jack cradled the sunny-colored paper as if it was a much-coveted treasure. "Hey, you are absolutely correct, Toby. This patient record of dental procedures has a whole *bunch* of dental procedures written on it. The *other* Toby Tucker must have had a lot of dental work in his mouth."

"Uh-huh, for sure," little Toby agreed.

"So here's what I'm gonna do. Toby, I won't ask you to read out loud all this dental work that was done on the other Toby Tucker. There is just too much here. Instead, I am going to summarize the dental work done on him, and then I will pass this patient record of dental procedures around to the jury so they can see it for themselves."

I thought to myself how much classier this approach was as compared with strutting over repeatedly to a huge flip chart and scribbling the info in giant green letters.

Jack squared off to face the jury. He made eye contact with each and every juror and then cleared his throat. "Patient record of dental procedures on Toby Jamal Tucker," he announced. "At the expense of taking up too much of your time, I'll just summarize this dental treatment, if it's OK with y'all." He grinned.

All twelve jury members looked relieved and began to nod yes.

"OK then. Toby Jamal Tucker had dental treatments spanning a four-month period in 1994. His treatment included *ten* separate appointments. He suffered from the condition that we have explained before. It is called nursing bottle caries, where the majority of his baby teeth became very decayed, and he had to have treatment on them to keep him out of pain and enable him to chew. His first appointment on May 20, 1994, was for his cleaning, X-rays, and initial exam. The next appointment was to extract his two front teeth, # E and # F, because they were too decayed to save. The next four appointments were to place stainless steel crowns on all eight of his existing baby molars to protect and save them. And the last four appointments were to place good-sized tooth-colored fillings in four of his remaining front teeth to save them from decaying to the point that his front teeth did."

Jack drew in a deep breath. "Now that was a whole lot of hours spent in a dental chair for a little boy who was barely four years old," he asserted. He took a few more steps toward the jury. He held out Toby Tucker no. 2's patient record of dental procedures to the jury foreman. The leader of the jury happily accepted the gold-colored paper.

"Oh, I almost forgot. I would like the jury to be able to see Toby Jamal Tucker's X-rays too. I think one of these X-rays, the large one, will look very familiar to y'all," he stated, wheeling around to eyeball Brett Wratchett and then the pitiful hen track of a flip chart. He handed a fistful of dental X-rays to the jury foreman. "You all take your time looking at these records of Toby Jamal Tucker. If you have any questions, I will be happy to try to answer them." He shot them a quick grin.

Then Jack turned back toward tiny Toby, who was waiting so patiently for his next directive. The most compassionate smile I had ever witnessed spread across Jack's face. "I cannot even begin to tell you what a *great* helper you have been for me today, Toby. You and me, we have been quite a team. And oh, the discoveries you and I have made here together today! We discovered that there was not only *one* little boy named Toby Tucker in Dr. Brookshire's dental office, but there were *two* Toby Tuckers who were Dr. Brookshire's patients. One Toby Tucker was lucky and didn't have very many cavities. The other Toby Tucker was not so lucky. He had lots and lots of cavities that needed fixing.

"So in summary, that man over there, Brett Wratchett, was very correct when he said that the big X-ray he put up for all to see, the one that he said was yours, belonged to *one of Dr. Brookshire's poor, unsuspecting patients* because it *did*. It belonged to the other patient named Toby Tucker."

The jury members' eyes grew big with disbelief. The wind was knocked right out of Brett Wratchett's sails. He doubled over as if he had just got socked in the stomach.

"Redirect?" the shocked judge asked Brett.

Brett Wratchett straightened back up, a pained expression still all over his traumatized face. "Your Honor, the state would like to request a recess at this time," he managed to spit out.

"How long do you need?" the shaken-up ruler inquired.

"Uh . . . two hours should do it," Brett replied.

"OK then. It is nearly lunchtime anyway. Everyone, take two hours' recess. Eat your lunch. Be back in My courtroom at precisely one forty-seven." He pounded the gavel with especially mighty force, arose, and exited, His raven robe swishing wildly, and we were all off to a two-hour break.

During lunch, we all chatted excitedly about that morning's triumphant victory. If this whopping state fuckup didn't do it for us, what on earth would? Jack; Jan, the paralegal; Bob; Dave; Mom; my sister from Texas, Chris; and I all returned at 1:38 p.m., reenergized, confident, and ready to go.

His Honor swept in at precisely 1:47 p.m. Brett showed up three seconds later. Judge Grudge looked at Brett, a shaken-up expression still lingering on His honorable face. "Does the state wish to redirect?" He asked.

"No, Your Honor, but we do wish to make a statement."

His Honor turned toward the poor little worn-out witness, Toby Tucker no. 1. "The witness may step down now," He directed.

Toby looked to the right. He looked to the left. He looked at Jack with question in his blue eyes. Jack nodded gently to him and made a subdued gesture of stepping down. The little guy looked as if a horrible burden had just been unloaded. The weight had been lifted. He was free to go. The tiny testifier skipped down the steps of the witness-box and back to his bench.

We didn't have long to witness Toby's release to freedom. Brett Wratchett was already beginning his humble speech of explanation. He turned slowly toward the jury, a whipped puppy-dog look spreading across his mug. "Albert Einstein once said, 'A person who never made a mistake never tried anything new,'" he began. "Well, I made a mistake. And I, in the spirit of one of our great forefathers Abraham Lincoln, am asking for your forgiveness. Always remember this. 'To err is human. To forgive is divine.'" He forced a forlorn look on his strained face, looked down at the floor, and visibly faked a lower-lip tremble.

"The state of Georgia had such a tremendous burden put on us when we took on Dr. Brookshire's case, so many hundreds of patients' records to go through and so little time to do it. And you have to remember, none of us are dentists. We had to find some dentists in the area who could help us."

The judge and jury may have appreciated all of Brett's mistimed famous quotes and allusions to well-known figures of the past, but his ramblings and weak excuses brought another quote to my mind. Abraham Lincoln once said, "Better to remain silent and be thought a fool than to speak out and remove all doubt." Brett's lame excuses and weak escape hatches were winding down. I couldn't help but think that his screwed-up, chaotic mix-up of Tobys would have been better handled by not bringing the subject up again and again.

"So there you have it, ladies and gentlemen. I am human, and humans make mistakes." He looked at the floor, hunched over, and shuffled his feet. "So please forgive this one mistake, forget it ever happened, and let's go on together."

Fat chance, I thought. *The Toby Tucker bell has been rung, and it cannot be unrung.*

DORAMAE BROOKSHIRE

WIDE-EYED WITNESSES

T HE JUDGE DECIDED that any more fake remorse might hurt the state's chances and shouted out, "OK, Mr. Wratchett, please call your next witness!"

Brett snapped to and replied, "Your Honor, I call Marcus Brown to the stand."

A very nice-looking young tween trudged hesitantly toward the witness stand. Someone had done a quite admirable job of putting him together at five in the morning. His hair was combed, his shirt was pressed, and his shoes were shined. He wrinkled his brow and held back for a second before climbing the daunting steps to the box.

Brett Wratchett approached the witness stand. "Good afternoon, Marcus," he said with a fake smile.

The leery adolescent replied, "Good afternoon."

"Mr. Brown, I just have a couple of questions for you here today," Brett lied. "My first question is this. Do you know who your dentist is?"

Marcus wiggled. He cleared his throat. "Yes, sir, I remember who *used* to be my dentist."

Brett sighed. It was time for damage control again. "Marcus, I am talking about the dentist who treated you when you were younger . . . the one sitting in this courtroom today. Reme—"

We all knew perfectly well what was going to come out of his mouth next. He was starting to say, "Remember what we have talked about when I coached you up concerning Dr. Brookshire? Surely, you remember everything I told you to say today." But he didn't say that as much as he would have liked to. He caught himself instead.

He's getting better, I thought, *at this self-control thing. Maybe all his courtroom fuckups have led to this new self-restraint.*

"OK, let me ask this question another way, Marcus. When you were a younger boy, who was your dentist then?"

"Oh, back when I was a little boy, Dr. Brookshire was my dentist."

"And is she here today?"

What a tremendous waste of time, I thought. *Of course, I am here today.*

"Yes, sir," Marcus whispered.

"And could you be so kind as to point her out to us then?" Brett jeered.

The skittish witness raised his right hand. He pulled it back briefly as if he was thinking twice about giving me up. Then he let it slide and singled me out to the awaiting audience.

"So let me ask you this about that lady whom you just pointed out. Was she your only dentist when you were young?" Brett asked.

"Yes, sir, as far as I know." There was an element of doubt in his young voice.

"Just one more question, Marcus. When you went to the dentist, do you remember ever acting up?"

"Whatcha mean by actin' up?" Marcus teased Brett.

"You know, did you ever kick the dentist or bite her or grab any of her instruments or refuse to hold still?" Brett shot back.

"Oh, no, sir. As far as I remember, I was very well behaved at the dentist."

"Marcus, do you know what behavior management was?"

"No, sir," Marcus replied, shaking his head.

"Well, let me tell you then. Behavior management is a procedure that Dr. Brookshire filed on you and your brother. It meant that you took a lot of extra time in her dental chair due to your acting up and not cooperating. She actually got paid extra for your behavioral misconduct."

Marcus sat up straight. He glanced nervously at Brett. He took a deep breath. He stared Brett straight in the eye with a look of I'll-tell-you-what-you-want-to-hear-if-this-can-be-all-over. "Well, she shouldn't have got paid extra because I was *good*," he declared. Then he let out an audible sigh of relief.

Brett smirked. He strutted like a peacock over to his cherished flip chart. He swept up his beefy green marker. "Behavior management filed by Dr. Brookshire on Marcus Brown. Medicaid paid Dr.

Brookshire $74.37 on May 18, 1990. Patient was not misbehaving at her dental office. Medicaid fraud!" he scrawled in big green letters.

He twirled around to make eye contact with a few jurors. "Thank you, Marcus, for your time today. You have been very helpful," the phony shyster added.

"Your witness," he sarcastically shot over to Jack.

Jack straightened his tie. His large fingers swept through his mussed hair. He moved carefully and slowly toward the youthful attester. "Hi, Marcus. How are you today?" he genuinely inquired.

"Oh, I guess I'm OK," Marcus replied shyly.

"I understand that you had to get on a bus to Atlanta very early this morning," Jack suggested.

"Oh yes, sir, I did," Marcus agreed.

"And today was supposed to be a school day for you in Goat Valley, huh?" Jack added.

"Yes, sir, it was," the young witness replied. "And I'm missing a really good field trip. Our class is going to the Tanaha Civil Rights Museum today. We just studied civil rights, and we all couldn't wait to go. I really wanted to see all those things in that place. Now I had to miss it." He was visibly disappointed.

"Oh, Marcus, I am so sorry that you missed your field trip with your class. Had you known for very long that you were going to have to miss it?"

"Nope, they just told me a few days ago that I had to do *this*."

"So the state of Georgia told you that you had to get on a crowded bus at five in the morning, ride all the way to Atlanta to sit on a hard bench, *and* you had to miss your class field trip you had really been looking forward to?"

Brett leaped to his feet. "Objection, Your Honor!" he shouted.

Judge Grudge glared at Jack. "Get on with your point, counselor," He spat out.

"Marcus, I was just making the point that you had to get up really early and ride on a bus all the way to Atlanta this morning. Just sayin', you must be kinda tired after all that," Jack hinted.

"Yes, sir, I am pretty well whupped," Marcus replied, visibly glad that someone was paying attention to his feelings.

"Well, then I am not going to take up much of your time today. You need energy for the long trip back on that bumpy bus with all those people." Jack grinned.

"Thanks, sir." Marcus beamed.

"Marcus, may I ask how old you are?" Jack inquired.

"Yes, sir. I am twelve years old," he answered.

"Twelve? Hmmmm . . . it is 1999. Then how old would you have been in 1990?" Jack appeared to be hard in mathematical thought.

"Wuh, that was nine years ago, so I would have been three years old," Marcus answered swiftly, proud of his quick problem-solving abilities.

"So the state of Georgia is alleging that when Dr. Brookshire got paid for behavior management on May 18, 1990, it was Medicaid fraud. They say it was Medicaid fraud because you stated that you were always good and well behaved at the dentist. Now, Marcus, can you remember when you were three years old?" Jack asked.

"Wuh . . . not really," he answered reluctantly.

"If you can't remember when you were three years old, how can you be certain that you did not act up a little in Dr. Brookshire's dental chair?" Jack continued.

"Uhmmm." Marcus hemmed and hawed. "I guess I can't be completely sure," he stuttered, glancing over at Brett sheepishly.

"Just one more question, Marcus, and then I'll let you go. Do you think that lots of little three-year-olds might act a little bad at the dentist?" Jack pondered.

Marcus's dark eyes rolled toward the ceiling. He intentionally avoided looking at the prosecutor's table. "Yeah, I guess they probably would. It would be very scary for little kids that young," he answered.

"Then *maybe* you might have been a little ornery and acted a bit bad at Dr. Brookshire's office when you were three years old, in 1990?" Jack continued his point.

"Yeah, maybe . . . I mighta cut up a bit." He smiled.

"Marcus, do you think that dentists deserve to be paid a little extra for three-year-olds that take extra time and cut up a bit in their chairs?" Jack asked curiously.

"Wuh, yes, I do. Three-year-olds can be pretty bad and not listen too. I have a three-year-old nephew. He can be really bad. Any dentist who puts up with *that* definitely deserves a little extra."

Jack beamed with victory. "Thank you so much for your time today, Marcus. You take it easy on that rough ride back to Goat Valley, OK?"

"Yes, sir, I will," Marcus answered, breathing a sigh of relief.

Jack had clobbered Brett once again.

"Redirect?" the frustrated judge asked Brett.

Brett hung his defeated head. "No, Your Honor," he moaned.

"Then call your next witness to the stand, Mr. Wratchett." Judge Grudge sighed.

"Your Honor, the state calls Demetrius Brown," Brett replied.

As the next young man approached the stand, I thought it might be Groundhog Day, like the movie. He looked just like Marcus's double—same light blue starched shirt, same neat haircut, same shiny black shoes. It took me a minute to put two and two together. These lookalikes must be brothers. They were a matching set. The bailiff swore him in, and he sat down.

"Good afternoon, Demetrius," Brett said with fake enthusiasm.

"Good afternoon, sir," the polite youngster returned.

"Demetrius, do you remember who your dentist was when you were little?" Brett asked.

"Yes, it was a lady dentist. Dr. Brookshire was her name, I think," he answered.

"Is Dr. Brookshire here in this room today, Demetrius?"

"Yes, she is right there," the young witness said, pointing nervously at me.

"And do you remember going to her dental office?" Brett asked.

"I think so. It was yellow, and it looked like a castle."

"Demetrius, do you ever remember acting bad at the dental office?" Brett suggested.

"Oh, no, sir. My grammy told us to always be good boys wherever we went—always," Demetrius insisted.

"So you and your brother were always little gentlemen at the doctor, at the dentist, at church, anywhere in public," Brett concluded, putting words in Demetrius's mouth.

"Yes, sir, we were," Demetrius agreed.

"Well then, Mr. Brown, were you aware of the fact that Dr. Brookshire filed papers on you asking Medicaid to pay extra for your appointments because she claimed that you *misbehaved* in her dental chair?" Brett screamed.

"No, I didn't know that until you told me a few days ago," he replied, not exactly the answer Brett was after.

Brett ignored the reference to his coaching the witness and went on. "And did you know further, Mr. Brown, that because Dr. Brookshire filed a dental procedure with Medicaid that *did not occur* . . . that this is known as committing *Medicaid fraud*?"

"Uhhh, no, I guess I didn't know that, sir." He was beginning to get confused about the whole situation.

But his bewilderment did not stop Brett. Instead of trying to stop to explain the whole Medicaid fraud fiasco to the perfectly behaved little gentleman, Brett figured that he had made his point with Demetrius. He was done using him. He had extracted what he needed from him. Now it was over to the beloved flip chart to scrawl the latest discovery on her pages. "BEHAVIOR MANAGEMENT ON WELL-BEHAVED PATIENT = MEDICAID FRAUD!" he wrote in chicken scratch.

He turned toward the jury and gave them a tiny wink. "Your witness!" he growled at Jack.

Jack rambled over to the young testifier. "Hi, Demetrius. We all thought we were seeing double. You sure do look just like your good-looking brother."

"Yeah, lots of people say that," he replied with a smile.

"Demetrius, could I ask how old you are?" Jack said gently.

"Yes, sir. I'm eleven," he answered.

"Then how old were you in 1990 when Dr. Brookshire filed behavior management on you?"

"It's 1999, so I was nine years younger. I would have been two years old, I guess," he answered.

"Demetrius, do you remember much about when you were two years old?" Jack inquired.

Demetrius pursed his lips. He squeezed his eyes shut. He placed his two fists on his forehead and swung his head down toward his lap. Then he directed his brown eyes straight at Jack. "No, sir, I guess I do not," he concluded.

"Thank you for your time today. You have been a really big help," Jack bragged. "Take care on your long trip home."

Judge Grudge was getting nervous. He could not allow the state of Georgia to lose a case in His courtroom. "Redirect, counsel?" He asked Brett, full well knowing the answer.

Brett hung his head. "No, Your Honor," he responded.

"The witness may step down," His Mighty Honor told Demetrius. The eleven-year-old testifier climbed down from the adult-sized witness-box, and I was suddenly struck with the outrageous absurdity and, at the same time, the incredible sadness of it all. The idea of pulling a whole busload of innocent children out of school and forcing them to act as character witnesses against their dentist was beyond belief. The state wanted me, and they wanted me bad.

"Call your next witness," the judge droned.

"Your Honor, I call Ms. Esther Green," Brett said.

An elderly African American lady got up slowly and shuffled down the long aisle. As she walked, she dragged her frail left leg. She was dressed in a crisp flowered dress, very clean, but the colors of the cheerful little flowers were fading. Her shoes were old-fashioned high heels, the kind with the sturdy, chunky heels. Someone had polished the daylight out of them, but at close inspection, a myriad of scratches danced across the toe and heels. A multitude of camouflaged scuff marks covered in thick black shoe polish joined the dance. She wore a single piece of simple jewelry, a delicate silver cross necklace. It jiggled across her wrinkled throat as she ambled slowly toward the stand. Her salt-and-pepper hair was pulled tightly back in a well-anchored bun.

I had noticed her as I entered the courtroom that morning. She seemed out of place. She had been sitting on a hard bench, scrunched up between ever so many children, and appeared to be totally exhausted at nine in the morning. I remember this because I had a twinge of extreme compassion mixed with disbelief and anger that the state would actually sink so low as to drag a helpless little old lady to a courthouse. With much difficulty, she managed to tug her bad leg up the steps and into the witness-box. She sat down hard, letting out a little moan.

Brett approached the stand, totally oblivious to any of the poor lady's pain and suffering. "Good afternoon, Ms. Green," he said with very little emotion.

"Aftanoon, sir," Esther replied.

"Now, Ms. Green, can you tell us who you are—I mean, as it relates to this court case, please?" Brett asked.

"Yes, sir. Ah am the gramma of Marcus and Demetrius," she answered.

"Ma'am, do you mean Marcus and Demetrius Brown, the boys that I just had up here on this witness stand?" Brett asked.

"Yes, sir, them two boys, that's rawght," she replied.

"Now what relationship do you have with Marcus and Demetrius? Aren't you just their grandma?" Brett asked, fully knowing what her answer would be.

"No, sir, Ah ain't just their gramma. Ah raised these boys up. They's mama got caught up in some bad dealin's, and they ain't got no daddy. So's Ah tooked them in an' raised them up myself. An' they been mighty good boys too. Ah learned them how to be good and polite and love Jesus and follow the Golden Rule." She was visibly proud of her motherly capabilities.

"Now, Ms. Green, did you take Marcus and Demetrius to Dr. Brookshire for dental work when they were younger?" Brett inquired.

"Yes, sir, Ah did. Awl the peoples with childrens on Medicaid went to her for a dentist. It was nice an' all in that office, all new an' purdy, an' the dentist herself was nice to the childrens. Marcus and Demetrius were both liddle, tiny babies when they went there." By her expression, I could tell that she was strolling down memory lane.

Brett halted the fond remembrance celebration as quickly as he could. She had already divulged three facts that he did not want brought out. She had let slip that the dentist was nice, her office was cozy, and worst of all, she had admitted that her grandsons were *babies* when they went to that office. Brett went into damage control mode. "Now, Ms. Green, did your two grandsons, Marcus and Demetrius, did they behave when they went to the dentist?" Brett jumped back on track.

"Oh *yes*, sir. They listens to their gramma. They sits up straight an' tall and says 'yes, sir,' an' 'yes, ma'am,' an' always says 'please' an' 'thank you' too," she insisted.

"So, Ms. Green, if I was to tell you that Dr. Brookshire submitted paperwork to Medicaid that stated the fact that Marcus and Demetrius *acted very badly* in her dental chair, would you believe that?" Brett baited.

"Oh, *no*, sir. That paperworks wuz not rawght. My two boys wuz liddle angels and still is so," she maintained.

Brett continued his love affair with his giant flip chart. He strutted over and wrote in big block letters, "ANOTHER EXAMPLE OF MEDICAID FRAUD: FILED BEHAVIOR MANAGEMENT ON TWO PATIENTS WHO DID NOT MISBEHAVE IN DENTAL CHAIR!"

One of my dumb random thoughts fleeted through my muddled mind. *Wonder why he keeps using* green *marker to record these Medicaid fraud fictions for the jury. I think* red *marker would be so much more effective.*

Brett pointed his sacred green marker at his latest scribbles. He looked at the jury and shook his head. "Your witness," he told Jack.

Jack stood up. He walked toward Esther with such a look of compassion on his face that it was as if empathy was being sent out from every cell in his body. "So nice to see you this afternoon, Ms. Green," he said with genuine concern.

"Thank you, sir," she replied.

"Ms. Green, I understand that you have had quite a long day already, having to ride that long bus ride on that crowded bus with all those kids."

"Yes, sir. It wuz purdy hard," she agreed.

"Objection!" Brett jumped up.

Judge Grudge glared at Jack. "Counselor, make your point," He instructed.

"Oh, I am not going to put you through any more stress today, Ms. Green. You've had enough of that already. Just one more question, Ms. Green, did you ever go back to observe your two grandsons, Marcus and Demetrius, when they were in the dental chair? That is, were you ever back in the dental operatories where they were getting their dental treatments?" Jack asked gently.

"No, sir. I always jist waited out in that waiting room where they tol' me to."

"One more thing, you had said that the boys were *babies* when they went to Dr. Brookshire. Is that correct, ma'am?"

"Yes, sir, Marcus and Demetrius wuz jist liddle ole tiny things when they went to her for a dentist," she replied immediately.

"Thank you so much for coming here today, Ms. Green. Be careful on your way back home to Goat Valley," Jack added.

Judge Grudge glared at Brett. "Counselor, call your next witness," He spat out.

"Your Honor, I call Jasmine Jackson," he replied.

A pretty little, petite teenager got up and headed for the witness stand. She was dressed in the latest teenybop trend. Someone had taken the time to meticulously place countless rows of cornrow in her course black hair. Large gold hoops and dangling gold balls hung from her triple-pierced ears. A tiny tattoo of a dainty purple flower adorned her neck. She appeared confident enough yet somewhat skeptical of what was to come. She gulped a big breath and sat down in the hot seat.

Brett approached her head-on. "Good afternoon, Ms. Jasmine," the big fake said.

"Afternoon, sir," Jasmine replied.

"Jasmine, do you remember who your dentist was in 1994?"

"Yes. It was Dr. Brookshire, that lady sitting there," she said matter-of-factly, pointing to me and sparing Brett his next question.

Brett turned toward the big kahuna. "Your Honor, I would like to submit exhibit S," he requested.

"Pass it over," the judge said flatly.

Brett passed a single paper with very little writing on it to the bailiff, who passed it in turn to His Honor. Judge Grudge looked at it, read over it rapidly, and then passed it back to the bailiff. "Please hand this to the jury foreman," He instructed the bailiff. The courtroom officer followed instructions.

Brett slid a copy across the defendant's desk to Jack without as much as making eye contact. He then handed a third copy to Jasmine. "Ms. Jasmine, do you know what this piece of paper has on it?" he asked the witness.

"Yes. You told me that it is a copy of the dental work I had at Dr. Brookshire's office."

"And could you do us all a *big* favor and read that dental treatment out loud to us, Jasmine? It isn't really much at all," he observed.

"OK then. It says, '12-06-94 IEx, 4 BWX, Px; 12-13-94 Inj 1 carp Lido HCL, # 30 O Ag; 12-21-94 Sealants placed # 2, # 3, # 14, # 15, # 18, # 19, # 31.'" She sighed.

"And, Ms. Jasmine, do you know what all that means?" Brett asked.

"Well, yeah, you told me. At the first appointment, I got an exam, four X-rays, and my teeth cleaned. At the second appointment, I got a filling. And at the third appointment, I got some sealants," she recited.

"Now, Jasmine, the state of Georgia is not questioning the first appointment or even the second. Our dentists contend that the filling is there, but what we do question is whether all those sealants were ever placed. You see, Dr. Brookshire wrote down that she placed *seven* sealants, and there are only *five* sealants on your teeth," he stated with condemnation.

"Ms. Jackson, do you know what a dental sealant is?" Brett asked.

"Yes, you told me." She looked up to see Brett shaking his head no. "I mean, *she* told me what it was," she corrected.

"And what is a dental sealant? Can you explain it to us, please, Jasmine?" he requested.

"Well, the way I understand it, a sealant is a clear, hard covering put on a back tooth to make it so it doesn't get a cavity," she answered, quite proud of herself.

"Very, very good, Jasmine. 'A dental sealant is a hard, clear material placed in the pits and fissures of molar teeth, creating a smooth surface that is easy to clean. Sealants help in the prevention of tooth decay because it is these pits and fissures that are most vulnerable to tooth decay. Sealants are placed in these hard-to-clean areas and are mainly used on children who are at higher risk of tooth decay,'" Brett read from the paper he was grasping without looking up once.

"Now, Jasmine, I want you to do something for me, please. Take your tongue and run it gently over all of your molar teeth. Do you understand which of your teeth molars are?" Brett asked.

"Yes, sir, the back teeth. There are two in my upper right, two in my upper left, two in my lower right, and two in my lower left." It was quite evident that she had memorized the routine.

"That is absolutely correct. That's amazing!" Brett reacted as if she was some kind of teenage genius. "Now like I said, please take your tongue and gently rub over each of these eight molars and tell me what you feel."

Jasmine's dark-colored eyes rolled up as she slowly ran her tongue over her back teeth. "Well . . . on the top right, I feel two real smooth, flat teeth." She progressed to the upper left. "And on the top left, I feel one smooth tooth, and the other one is real rough and has a deep place in the center with four sharp points." She continued to the bottom arch. "Now on the bottom left, I feel two real smooth teeth. But on the bottom right, I feel a kinda rough thing and another deep place with four sharp points."

"Thank you *so* much for that description, Jasmine. You have just confirmed what the dentists that examined you discovered. The two smooth surfaces on your upper right were indeed sealants. The upper left, though, revealed only *one* sealant. The other molar on your upper left never had a sealant placed, although Dr. Brookshire charged for one, the same with your lower right. The rough thing you felt on the one tooth was your silver filling. But the tooth beside that, # 31, had no sealant on it either, although once again Dr. Brookshire *charged the state* for that one too."

He marched right over to his flip chart buddy. He swooped up the fat green marker and wrote in six-inch block letters, "# 14 SEALANT CHARGED FOR BUT NEVER PLACED. # 31 SEALANT CHARGED FOR BUT NEVER PLACED. MEDICAID FRAUD!" He glanced over at the jury and performed his usual theatrical head shake.

He turned toward Jack. "Your witness," he teased.

Jack rose casually. He made his way toward young Jasmine. "Hi, Jasmine. How ya doin' today?" he sang out.

"I'm just fine," she replied.

"Jasmine, we have been talking about these things called dental sealants. But there is one thing concerning them that we didn't talk about yet, and I think it is important that you know this." Jack was talking to Jasmine as though she was an adult and not condescending, like Brett had. "I have a piece of paper, just like Mr. Wratchett did," Jack declared. "And this paper is about sealants."

Jack turned toward Judge Grudge. "Your Honor, I would like to submit exhibit T," he stated.

"Send it over," the bored judge moaned.

The usual shuffle-and-pass courtroom dance went down. When it was all over, Jack turned back toward the youthful testifier and began to preface his educational presentation. "Jasmine, I am going to read some scientific dental research to you. If at any time you have any questions, please feel free to stop me and ask, OK?"

"OK," she agreed.

"Now this could get a little boring, but I am going to try real hard to read just the parts I have to read to be able to get my point across," he began. "Now this first article comes from a professional dental journal called *Pediatric Dentistry*. It was submitted to the journal by the American Academy of Pedodontics. It is entitled 'Retention of Pit and Fissure Sealants Placed in a Pedodontic Clinic: A Retrospective Study.' Three different dentists performed controlled studies in their pedodontic clinics and submitted their results. Here's a summary of the study.

"'The purpose of this study was to determine the retention rate of dental sealants in a pedodontic clinic. Included in this study were 278 patients whose mean age was 11 years 5 months. It was found that for all teeth examined, the relationship between the percentage of teeth with sealants all present and the longevity is almost linear from the plotted value at 6 months after placement (67% retention rate). This corresponds to an initial failure rate of 15% followed by a failure rate of 4% at each six-month recall exam. Sealant failures were found to be due to several different factors, including the sealant material itself, poor wear resistance on the tooth, and salivary contamination at the time of placement. Many partial sealant losses also occurred.'"

Jack let out an audible sigh. He appeared to be quite relieved that the scientific reading was over. He looked up at Jasmine with compassion. "Let me tell you what that just said in a way that most of us can get." He laughed. "That study, which was done very professionally in a dental setting, discovered that at your first appointment after sealants are placed, that is, six months later, an average of 15 percent of those sealants is lost. This means that, for some reason or another, 15 percent of your sealants drop off the teeth. But going on down the line, sealant failure rate was discovered to progress with each six-month recheck. The average rate of sealant loss thereafter was 4 percent with each subsequent six-month checkup."

Jack paused to let the new info sink in. "Could I please ask you how old you are, Jasmine?" Jack inquired gently.

"Yes, sir. I am sixteen," she answered proudly.

"It's May of 1999. How old were you in December of 1994, Jasmine?" he asked.

"Well, I had just turned twelve."

"Hmmm . . . let's do a little math, shall we? Your seven sealants were placed in December of 1994. You were due a six-month recheck in June 1995. Unfortunately, Dr. Brookshire could no longer be your dentist in June of 1995 because the state dental board took her license. But if the retention rate of your seven sealants was the same as the retention rate in this study, you would have lost 15 percent of your sealants by June 1995. Let's see, 15 percent of 7 equals 1.05. So by average standards, by June 1995, you would have lost one of your sealants. The study goes on to prove that after that initial six-month appointment, 4 percent of sealants are lost each time. So you would have had six-month checkups on December 1995, again in June 1996, December 1996, June 1997, December 1997, June 1998, and December 1998. I count seven times at a loss rate of 4 percent each time, so 7 times 4 equals 28 percent. And 28 percent of the remaining six sealants would be 1.68. Almost two more of the sealants should have naturally been lost. Well, only two of your original sealants have dropped off, when the average patient your age would have lost almost three of their sealants, so your retention rate for your sealants was better than the average found in this study. And what you have to remember is that this study in the journal was performed by dentists who were trained pedodontists. That means that they are specialists who work only on patients who are children. Dr. Brookshire was not even a child specialist, and her sealant retention rate on you beat those rates of these child specialists. Pretty good, huh?" he raved.

"Yeah, I guess so," she agreed.

"Now I have many more such studies on sealant retention and loss rates right here," Jack announced as he walked over to the defendant table and scooped up a hefty pile of papers. "One study concluded that 72 percent retention rate was found in a study performed in a community clinic in Georgia. Another study concluded that a 67 percent retention rate of sealants was found to be the average when placed in a school setting. Hmmmm . . . that means that 33 percent of those sealants were lost. Would the court like me to read excerpts from several other clinical studies to prove the rates at which sealants are lost from children's teeth?" He span around in a face-off with Brett Wratchett.

Brett looked white as a sheet. "No, the state does *not* require the reading of any more studies on sealant retention," he squeaked.

Jack held eye contact with the pasty prosecutor for several more seconds. Then he turned toward the interested jury. "You see, the fact is that Dr. Brookshire did not file sealants that she did not do. The prosecutors have failed to allow for the fact that a certain percentage of sealants are naturally lost from children's teeth. It is just a natural, everyday occurrence. Sealants are placed. Some sealants drop off. The truth is that Dr. Brookshire *did* place sealants on seven teeth on Jasmine

Jackson in December of 1994. Five years later, Jasmine still has sealants on five of those teeth. That is a sealant retention rate of 72 percent after *five* years. And that is well within the average of how many sealants should have been retained. Dr. Brookshire did not fail to place sealants on tooth # 14 and # 31. Those sealants were there in December 1994. They just dropped off over the past five years. *No Medicaid fraud here,* folks!"

Jack flashed his famous south Georgia grin for the jury. The grin turned a little smirky as he postured toward Brett. "Redirect?" he wanted to know.

Brett was green around the gills. "No . . . no . . . I'm OK," he tried to convince everyone around him.

Your Honor looked at Jasmine. "The witness may step down," He told her coldly. He shot the colorless prosecutor a look of pure wrath. I wondered if our fine judge Grudge was going to live up to His unfortunate name.

"Call your next witness!" He growled at Brett. It was pretty evident that His wicked Honor was not at all happy with the way this court session was going.

"Your Honor, I call Antwan Williams," Brett announced rather sheepishly.

Once again, a tween approached the stand, swore in, and took a seat. Antwan was tall and lanky, at that stage when the growth spurt of the body quickly overtook the mind. We've all seen this phenomenon with our own preteens, their physical bodies shooting up and transforming so rapidly and, at the same time, their thought processes actually traveling in the opposite direction to become amazingly lethargic.

"Good afternoon, Antwan," said Brett, once again utilizing the same boring old greeting.

"Hey," Antwan replied in monosyllable.

"Now, Antwan, if you don't object, we will bypass the next several questions by simply asking you a few quick and painless questions. Is that OK with you?"

"Yep." Antwan was evidently a man of few words.

"Antwan, was Dr. Brookshire your dentist from 1988 until 1995?" Brett asked.

"Yep."

"And do you remember her placing a material called sealants on your back teeth?"

"Yep."

Brett was starting to turn a light crimson in color. Antwan was probably not living up to his pretrial coaching. Nevertheless, Brett trudged on. He introduced a new exhibit, which ended up being the treatment record of Atwan Williams. Then he handed a copy of the record to the apathetic witness and began to ask questions concerning the dental treatment recorded on the paper.

"Mr. Williams, could you please read from your dental treatment record all those dates highlighted with a yellow marker?" Brett requested.

If Brett was hoping to receive a more mature, adultlike response from Antwan as a result of addressing him as "Mr. Williams," he was mistaken. Antwan hung his head and slumped his shoulders. He placed the green sheet of paper a couple of inches from his eyes and began to mumble. He was visibly struggling to read.

Brett intervened quickly. "Antwan, you *must* read loud enough for us all to hear!" he shouted.

Antwan wiggled. "Don't wanna," he retorted.

I knew exactly what was going on. I had helped adults and teens learn to read for several years now. I knew all the signs of the agonizing fight of the functionally illiterate, and he had every single symptom. My heart ached for poor Antwan, his illiteracy on display for all to see.

Brett reached over and snatched the green paper out of Antwan's hands, leaving the poor testifier with a shocked look of surprise. "Give it here then! We don't have time for this! *I* will read it then!" Brett was beginning to lose it with this day of youngsters, adolescents, juveniles, and teens. He was more than likely coming to the conclusion that it might not have been a very good idea to bus countless munchkins into a court of law.

Brett cleared his throat, an obvious attempt to grab a few seconds to compose himself. He began to read the following with very little expression.

6-15-90 Sealants on # 3, # 14, # 19, # 30.
10-24-96 Sealants on # 2, # 15, # 18, # 31.

After reading the highlighted parts of Antwan's dental records loudly but in monotone, Brett looked at the jury and declared, "We have to see several more of Dr. Brookshire's young patients today. In an effort to speed things up a bit, I will just cut to the chase and show you how the *Medicaid fraud* was committed against young Antwan here." And he began the flip chart shuffle. He latched on to his jumbo grass-colored marker, clutching it tightly in his claws, and scratched out, "SEALANTS ON #3, # 19, AND PART OF #14 NEVER PLACED BUT CHARGED TO MEDICAID! *MEDICAID FRAUD!*" He underlined the final verdict with such a dramatic sweep of the broad-line marker that it reminded me of the mark of Zorro.

Then he performed his usual jury glance of disgust and told Jack, "Your witness," in such a tone as to suggest, *Good luck with* this *one.*

Jack came slowly to his feet, buttoned his suit coat, adjusted his reading glasses, and smiled brightly. He moved very mercifully toward the frightened awaiting ex-patient. "Antwan, you have been through enough today. I have no more questions for you. You may go. Be careful on your way home on the bus back to Goat Valley, OK?"

Antwan lit up like a Christmas tree. "Oh yes, sir, yes, sir! I will! Thank you, sir! Thank you!"

The jury looked shocked as if none of them ever expected to hear more than a monosyllabic utterance from young Antwan.

The next witness was an eleven-year-old named LaKeisha Lewis. Brett, once again, bored the jurors stiff with his repeat performance.

"LaKeisha, do you remember a dentist named Dr. Brookshire that you went to when you were young?" the irksome prosecutor drilled.

"Yeah, I remember her," she replied in a humdrum undertone.

"Do you remember ever being *bad* in her dental chair?" he baited.

"Nope. I always been good at doctor places," she answered in a wearisome voice. There was a bit of doubt in her tone.

"You were always *good* at the doctor . . . yet on May 18, 1991, Dr. Brookshire filed for behavior management on you!" he charged.

"Wuh, I don't know why. I wuz good." Her voice trailed off.

Brett hit his heels and spun around. He ended up facing the jury. "Well, there you have it, folks! Yet *another* example of *Medicaid fraud*!" He pranced over to the flip chart and decided to redesign his Medicaid fraud strategy and arrangement.

He went for his favorite two-column patterning. The first column was branded "BEHAVIOR MGT FRAUD" while the second column was dubbed "SEALANT FRAUD." He scratched a long fat green hash mark under the "BEHAVIOR MGT" column. Then he announced, "We seem to be getting so many of these repeat Medicaid frauds that I thought it best to just start making marks each time we get one. I am getting tired of writing out the words *Medicaid fraud* every time. After a while, it begins to cramp my hand and use up all my ink." He shot the jury a nerdy smirk, so proud of himself for his clever ad-lib. He was on a roll. He decided to take it one step further. "In fact, let's catch this *Medicaid fraud* chart up to speed, why don't we?"

Then he flipped the giant pages several leaves back and started to count the charges on the children who had already had the unfortunate experience of having been in the hot seat that day. "Let's see. So far, we have *two* more behavior management *Medicaid fraud* charges. LaKeisha makes *three*. And we have *two* sealant *Medicaid fraud* charges, but I'll have more of those." He made two big wide green hash marks under the sealant fraud column and two more hash marks under the behavior management fraud column. "There now, we're caught up," he proudly affirmed. After his theatrical performance, he passed the young witness over to Jack.

Jack sauntered leisurely over to LaKeisha. "Hi, LaKeisha," he sang out.

"Hey," she cautiously replied.

"LaKeisha, I am only going to ask you one easy question today, and then I am going to let you go. You have had enough stress today, don't you think?" he gently asked.

"Oh yes, sir. Yes, sir, I have," she agreed.

"OK. Here's your question. How old were you in 1991, LaKeisha?"

"Ummmm . . . I was born in 1988, so I guess I was three," she devised.

"So in 1991, the year that Dr. Brookshire filed for behavior management on you, you would have been three years old, right?"

LaKeisha nodded yes. "Yes, sir, that's right," she replied.

"Thank you for your courage and help today, LaKeisha. I have no more questions," Jack informed her.

The rest of Thursday afternoon dragged on in the same manner—poor, frightened kids forced into a dooming hard, cold witness chair and then made to snitch on the evil doctor Brookshire's various *Medicaid frauds.* The green hash marks in the two columns grew in number. But Jack stood firm. He continued to release the sealant fraud victims without a single question. He figured that his quite ample explanation of sealant loss and retention he had presented during Jasmine's testimony was more than adequate to explain that phenomenon. And the behavior management fraud victims were all asked just one question, that of how old they were at the time of treatment.

A definite pattern emerged. The sealant fraud victims had lost an average of 15 percent of their sealants over time while the behavior management fraud victims averaged between three and four years old at the time of treatment. Jack had always told me that a jury needed to be given a minimum of information. "They are smarter than we give them credit for," he always said. "The best thing to do is to give them just the right amount of information and then let them draw their own conclusions. A jury takes their responsibility very seriously. They listen well and come back with fair and well-thought-out verdicts. They don't need to be bored to tears with repetition."

By the time Thursday afternoon was over, Brett Wratchett had seven green hash marks under the behavior management fraud column and nine green hash marks under the sealant fraud column. I took silent inventory of the situation—sixteen poor children who had been forced to skip school and board a big bus at five o'clock that morning, sixteen scared kids who had been strong-armed into climbing up into a daunting platform seat and then made to answer lengthy questions from strange men in black suits, sixteen poor, sweet little souls who were coached and intimidated into answering those complicated questions the way they were instructed to by the state. And those same sixteen children would soon be piled back into that big stinky, crowded bus and sent back on a four-hour trip to small-town south Georgia without so much as a handshake. I thought, *The way those poor kids were used was a downright sin.*

As I left the courtroom that day, I was feeling pretty downhearted. Bob and Dave were patting each other on the backs and giving each other high fives, celebrating our latest courtroom victory, but Jack did not join in. He was tuning in to my courtroom depression. He knew something was eating away at me.

"Dora, you all right?" he asked with compassion.

"Yeah, I'll be OK. It's just that this has been the hardest day yet as far as I'm concerned. Seeing my little patients all up there on that stand really got to me."

Jack shot me a look of sympathy. "I know how you must feel. That was a dirty trick, the state pulling all those kids into this. But you'll be OK. Just think of this instead. We kicked their butt today! We shot down every stupid bogus charge of Medicaid fraud that they had fabricated!"

But I knew deep in my soul that I would never be OK again. This game of theirs—this nasty game of using any innocent person for courtroom conquest—was *not* OK, nor would it ever be. Capturing, subduing, and then intimidating these poor innocent children were just a game to them. These human victims were simply a feather in the state's ever-growing cap.

I didn't rest too well that night. I was becoming very weary of impersonal cold, sterile hotel rooms and restaurants. I wanted to go home and hide my joyless face in my favorite pillow and never emerge back into society. I knew deep down inside that I had to pull myself together. I had to snap out of it, but each nightmarish day was taking its toll on me. I was afraid that I was sliding fast down a slippery slope of no return. It was as if I actually had two forces residing inside me. The evil force was telling me to give up, throw in the towel. *You'll never beat city hall, you dummy!* But the angelic force was telling me to go on, keep trying. *You're gonna come out smelling like a rose. Goodness always prevails over evil.* So I chose to believe the angelic force.

DR. PERCY JUDGMENTAL

IT WAS FRIDAY morning. I couldn't believe it. We had been enduring this hideous nightmare for four dreadful days now. This was going to be day 5. All of a sudden, Judge Grudge's words rushed through my brain. "All right! All right! We will go ahead and try this case on Medicaid fraud, but I personally *do not* like such cases at all! And I am going to tell you this right now. *This case will be over by Saturday!* I have had a scheduled vacation set up for months now. And I *will* be on that fishing boat come Sunday!" His high-powered Honor had insisted on this the day of jury selection.

I stopped to access the impending situation. It was Friday, His mighty Honor had laid it on the line that this case would be over by Saturday, no bones about it, and our defense had not even had a chance to be up. The prosecuting team had hogged all four days so far, and it did not look good for us to get our chance on day 5 either.

Then a light bulb went off in my head. These guys were stalling. They were making a play for time, dragging their feet, stooging around. Brett Wratchett had been assigned a courtroom tap dance. All this repeat drudgery had been the state's equivalent of a Medicaid fraud filibuster. They didn't want us to ever have a chance to get up and tell our side of the story. We were being squelched, hushed up, stifled. They had placed the lid on us and muzzled and gagged us. And there was absolutely nothing we could do about it. Their game plan was to drag it out any way they could until Saturday. Then they were home free. They would have yet another win under their belt. The good judge would go fishing, and once again, justice would prevail for the ever-mighty state of Georgia. Who cares that the whole stinking business was crooked and corrupt and unethical? The state simply *had* to win—at any cost. It was true then. You really *can't* beat city hall.

I walked into that courtroom with a little less bounce in my step that Friday morning. I located my seat at the defendant's table and plopped down. *Another looong day of monotonous Brett Wratchett humdrum*, I thought. I drew in a deep breath and readied myself for the fatiguing performance. Little did I know that, by the end of that day, we would all get the theatrical showcase of our lives.

The good judge swept in with all His usual pomp and circumstance. Once again, we all stood at attention for His holy Honor. And once again, everyone in the courtroom was forced to show our devotion and adoration to Him by standing until His Honor was fully seated. Then and only then were we all allowed to sit back down ourselves.

The fair and impartial judge managed to squeeze out an ungenuine "good morning." Then he got right down to business. "Mr. Wratchett, call your next witness," He instructed.

"Your Honor, I call Dr. Percy McFly."

I had dreaded this day of the trial for a while now. The state had dug up three dentists from the Atlanta area to be their main professional witnesses. All three were outstanding members of the state dental board. These were the guys who were known in the legal circles as "pro witness whores." They were the prostitutes of the courtroom. These guys and gals were definitely qualified. Oh yes, they were all extremely skilled professionals in their specific areas of expertise. The three who were up that day were well-established dental specialists. There was absolutely no doubt about their knowledge and skill levels. They were some of Georgia's brightest and best in the field of dentistry.

The only catch was this. They were all willing to leave their ethics at the door. As soon as they walked into that courtroom, they belonged to the state. And they would testify to anything—yes, *anything*—to help the state win their case.

Brett Wratchett tediously began his usual day's greeting like a broken record. "Good morning, Dr. McFly."

"Good morning, Mr. Wratchett," Dr. McFly responded, looking forward to their partnership in the oncoming slaughter.

"Dr. McFly, I need to ask you about your part in this case that we are currently trying . . . that of the *State of Georgia v. Dr. Doramae Brookshire.*"

"Well, myself and two other dental specialists, we all happen to be on the state dental board. The three of us, we all participated in screening the patients of Dr. Brookshire. We traveled from Atlanta to Goat Valley and examined the patients in question at a specific dental office in Goat Valley."

"And was another dentist present at these screenings?" asked Wratchett.

"Oh yes. We were never alone with the patients. Several of us all examined each patient, and then later, we sat down and all agreed on the diagnostic conclusions."

"Then let me get this straight. You and two other *highly skilled and knowledgeable* dentists, who are all on the state dental board, saw and examined a fair number of Dr. Brookshire's patients. These examinations were done at a Goat Valley dentist's office, and that Goat Valley dentist was also present at these examinations."

"That is correct, sir," Dr. McFly answered.

"And what are some of the things that you and all these other dentists discovered during these patient exams?"

"Well, we all found numerous breaches of dental ethics," Dr. McFly replied, making a sour face.

"What exactly do you mean by *numerous breaches of dental ethics?*" Brett repeated mostly for emphasis.

"Well, sir, my colleagues and I found sealants charged for that were not present, behavior management charged for that definitely was not warranted. These children were very well-behaved in the dental chair. But the one procedure that I personally found to be the biggest violation of dental ethics was the charging for gold crowns when the crowns, in truth, were only simple, inexpensive stainless steel crowns," he said with disgust.

"Wait a minute! You mean to tell me that Dr. Brookshire placed cheap temporary stainless steel crowns on children's teeth and then turned around and charged Medicaid for expensive permanent *gold* crowns?" Brett was appalled.

"Yes, sir, that's what she apparently did. Now I am not saying that all the crowns were charged as gold. A few of them were charged as what we call semiprecious metal. This is a crown made out of a metal that is close to the price of gold but not quite as expensive. But whether she charged for full gold crowns or semiprecious gold crowns, both of these are *much more expensive* than the simple, cheap temporary stainless steel crowns that she really used on these poor children. Those cheap stainless steel crowns should not even be used as often as she did." McFly was getting so passionate about the whole ordeal that he was beginning to verbalize alleged facts that, in truth, were not accurate facts at all. It was a defense attorney's dream.

"Could you give us some examples, please, Dr. McFly?" Brett egged on.

"Why, yes. I saw a seven-year-old child with a stainless steel crown on one of her molars, and this crown was charged as a semiprecious crown, which it most definitely was not. Interestingly enough, however, that same child had a true semiprecious crown on a different molar. But that specific crown was also not standard of care because it is not the standard of care to place permanent crowns on children's teeth!" McFly was becoming way too emotional to be the cool, calm, professional dental board member he professed to be.

"I am a little confused here, Dr. McFly. Do you mean that Dr. Brookshire placed a cheap stainless steel crown on one of this patient's back teeth and then charged for an expensive precious metal crown, but she also placed a real metal crown on another back tooth in the same patient? But this patient happened to be a seven-year-old, and permanent crowns on seven-year-olds are not the standard of care in dentistry?" Brett drilled on.

"Yes, sir, you've got it correct."

"Dr. McFly, could you please define the term *standard of care* for us?" Brett asked.

"Yes, I would be happy to. The *standard of care* is defined as the degree of care that a reasonable and prudent dentist would exercise under the same or similar circumstances," he recited, obviously recently memorized.

"And, Dr. McFly, would you say that this standard of care is at the heart of dental malpractice claims and lawsuits?"

"Oh yes. It is used constantly in dental suits," the fine doctor answered.

"Then would it be correct to assume that breaches in the standard of care would enter into a Medicaid fraud trial?"

"Well, of course, they would. If a dentist breaches the standard of care, she needs to be called on it. The patient's welfare is at stake."

Brett pranced over to his fabulous flip chart. He carefully placed a gigantic X-ray on the stand. It was a panoramic X-ray, showing the entirety of both arches in one film. He pointed to one back molar tooth. "Dr. McFly, is it correct to say that this specific tooth on the seven-year-old patient that we have been discussing is covered with a stainless steel crown?"

The good doctor strained a bit to see the dental film. "Yes, that is correct," he answered simply.

Brett continued. He pointed to a back molar tooth on the opposite side of the mouth. The tooth seemed a bit larger than the previous one. "And then would it be correct to say that this tooth is covered by a semiprecious metal crown?" he asked the testifier.

"Yes, that would be correct," he repeated.

"Then let's just summarize this. Dr. Brookshire placed a stainless steel crown on this seven-year-old patient and then charged for a *much more expensive* metal crown. However, on the same seven-year-old patient, Dr. Brookshire placed a semiprecious metal crown that was not within the standard of care?"

"Yes, sir, that is all correct."

"Wow! That would mean that Dr. Brookshire made two mistakes, somewhat opposite in nature, on the same little patient?"

"Yes, sir, you could most definitely look at it that way," the doctor with all the degrees answered.

Brett did not have to strut over to his favorite place in the courtroom. He was already there. He removed the gargantuan X-ray from the flip chart, revealing the underlying pages, and began to put into writing the information that had just been revealed by the star witness. He wrote, "MORE MEDICAID FRAUD: STAINLESS STEEL CROWNS CHARGED AS GOLD CROWNS OR AS SEMIPRECIOUS METAL CROWNS. SEMIPRECIOUS METAL

CROWNS PLACED ON CHILDREN'S TEETH. THIS IS BELOW THE STANDARD OF CARE!"

He glanced at Jack briefly as if he might be ready to turn the witness over but then declared, "Oh, I almost forgot."

He wheeled back around to his beloved chart and added, "MORE SEALANTS CHARGED FOR THAT WERE NOT THERE; MORE BEHAVIOR MANAGEMENT CHARGED THAT WAS NOT NEEDED!"

"There, that does it," he complimented himself.

"Your witness," he finally told Jack.

Jack stood up slowly and meandered over to the dental deponent. "How are you today, Dr. McFly?" he inquired in a very pleasant tone.

The professional witness was leery. This was not his first song and dance in a courtroom. "I am fine, thank you," he replied with the utmost of etiquette.

"Dr. McFly, I think we all understand how you and your two state dental board colleagues conducted your exams on Dr. Brookshire's patients, but I still have a few questions pertaining to those exams," Jack stated politely.

"I thought I already made that all clear," the wary witness insisted.

"You made it quite clear that you and two other dentists on the state dental board traveled to Goat Valley, Georgia, most likely on the taxpayers' dollars; secretly set up examinations on patients who were children; and proceeded to expose those children to unnecessary radiation in the form of X-rays; and poked and prodded these children, taking pictures of them and recording information that these minors happened to tell you during your secret interrogations," Jack poked. I loved the way that Jack could come across as the most mild-mannered, courteous man alive and then bait the stunned witness and move in for the kill.

"Now wait just a minute there," the dentist attester whined. "We are talking about a dentist who was duping Medicaid! She had to be stopped!"

"*Oh*, was she? Was Dr. Brookshire *duping* Medicaid? Are we sure of that? We have already shown how an average of 15 percent of sealants is lost in the first year of placement. We also discovered that many of the currently ten- and eleven- and twelve-year-old patients were two and three and four years old at the time of treatment. I think it is safe to say that by the time one is twelve years old, it would be next to impossible to remember one's specific behavior in the dental chair at age three, don't you agree, Dr. McFly?"

"Whuh-whuh-whuh, even if we dismiss the charges on those two things—*and we are not!*—she still charged for gold crowns when they were truly stainless steel crowns, and that alone is enough Medicaid fraud to get her!" He was hopping mad that a mere lawyer would dare to question his professional integrity.

"I understand now. Y'all's mission was *to get her.*"

Dr. McFly's cautiousness was over. I was sure that he had started out with a well-laid plan to be suspicious and guarded and to act very restrained as a result. He knew this principle of the courtroom. He was a professional witness for god's sake. But something cracked.

He shot Jack a piercing glare; daggers came forth from his eyes. "*No,* sir, our mission was *not* to get her, but you have to understand that she was a threat to the whole dental community! Medicaid can't stay alive when one dentist is constantly playing them for a fool! Somebody has to stop that, or Medicaid would go under!" He was drumming his fingers nervously on the arm of his wooden chair.

Jack had done it again. He had taken a witness—one who felt it was his moral duty to weed out blemishes on the face of *his* profession, one who was very comfortable in a courtroom setting, one who normally remained calm and collected and very self-disciplined—and had whittled him down to a babbling fool. His mission accomplished, Jack decided to back off somewhat and proceed with the questioning in mind. "Dr. McFly, you have stated to the court that you feel that the seven-year-old patient in question—and by the way, her name is Ebony King—that the crowns placed on her molar teeth were one stainless steel crown and one semiprecious metal crown, am I correct about that?"

The good doctor huffed. "Yes, I believe that is what I stated on more than one occasion," he answered with annoyance.

Jack put exhibit N into evidence and then handed the witness a copy of the green patient record. "Dr. McFly, sir, would you be so kind as to read the name on the top of this patient record, please?" he inquired graciously.

The good doctor winced. "It says, 'Ebony King,'" he answered with little to no expression.

"And, Dr. McFly, would you agree that Ebony King is the patient that you have been referring to for the last several minutes . . . the seven-year-old patient that you profess Dr. Brookshire placed one stainless steel crown on tooth # K and a semiprecious crown on tooth # 30?" Jack paused. "Now take your time, Doctor," he offered up.

The good doctor McFly stiffened. "Well, give me a few minutes to look over her records here." He paused. Then he added, "So I'm certain that no trickery is involved."

Jack grimaced. "Trickery? Hmmmm. Let's do this. Patient records are pretty straightforward. The dentist performs a procedure, and then a record of what was done that day is written in the patient's record, correct?"

Dr. McFly came alive. He smirked that I-gotcha-now, sardonic smirk. "Yeah, that is correct, unless the dentist in question writes down a *lie* . . . like that she placed a precious crown on a tooth that she *really* placed a cheap stainless steel crown on!" he shot back.

"That is a very good point, Dr. McFly. Thank you for that," Jack calmly stated. "Let's approach this differently then. Let's have you read aloud from Ms. Ebony King's patient record the dates October 14, 1993, and February 9, 1994." Jack looked the doctor straight in the eye.

"If you would be so kind, sir," he added in a soft voice.

"Oh, OK then." The scholarly doctor sighed. "This all seems a little much."

"Dr. Brookshire might tend to agree, but all of us in this courtroom need to get at the truth, you concur?"

"Sure, we all need the *truth* to come out of this mess. That's what I'm here for," the good doctor shot back.

"Good. Then we are all on the same page. Let's see what we all can discover," Jack said with a tad of adventure in his voice. "First things first. We need to establish that Ms. Ebony King is indeed the same patient that you are alleging had a stainless steel crown placed on tooth # K, a baby tooth, on October 14, 1993, and a semiprecious crown placed on tooth # 30, a permanent tooth, on February 9, 1994."

Jack continued, "To prove that we have the correct patient here, let's do this. Let's have you, Dr. McFly, look at your X-rays and notes that you took on the patient at the dental office in Goat Valley where you and your colleagues did your screenings on Dr. Brookshire's patients, OK?"

"I guess that would be wise," the doctor agreed half-heartedly.

Jack gently handed the deponent a thin, stiff, squeaky-clean manila folder. "Would you please read the patient name on this folder to us, Doctor?" Jack requested.

"Yeah. It says, 'Ebony King,'" Dr. McFly replied.

"Could you please open the patient folder and exam its contents?" Jack asked.

The doctor slowly opened the folder and stared at two small X-rays and then at some hand-scribbled notes on a lined piece of white paper. He hesitated and then pretended to exam the X-rays and paper once again. "Yes, this is the patient in question," he answered, his voice trailing off.

"I could not quite hear you," Jack observed. "Do you agree that the patient, Ms. Ebony King, is the same patient that you and your colleagues examined in a Goat Valley dental office? The same patient that you allege Dr. Brookshire placed a stainless steel crown on baby tooth # K and then charged Medicaid for a semiprecious crown instead?"

"Yes, she is that same patient," the dentist answered.

"And Ms. Ebony King is also the same patient that you allege Dr. Brookshire placed a semiprecious crown on permanent tooth # 30, going against the dental standards of practice. Correct?"

"Yep. That's what I've been saying this whole time," Dr. McFly moaned.

"Excuse me, sir. Bear with me, please, if you will. It is very important that we establish that Ebony King is the patient that we are questioning Dr. Brookshire's treatment on."

Dr. McFly's eyes rolled up and over. "Yes, sir!" he growled. "This is indeed the patient that I am referring to with my allegations against Dr. Brookshire!" He stamped his foot.

Jack had done it again. He had managed to unravel yet another incriminating accuser while remaining as cool as a cucumber himself. "All right then, Dr. McFly, let's get on with those *allegations* of yours against Dr. Brookshire, shall we?" Jack pointed up. "Please help me get a few things straight here, OK, Doctor? Could you please read the notes that you and your colleagues wrote on that piece of paper in that new folder . . . the one that you are holding in your hand . . . to be more definite, the one that you wrote on when you did the exam on Ms. Ebony King at the dental office in Goat Valley? It doesn't look like there is much writing at all on that record. It shouldn't take too long to read the extent of the writing on that paper, please, sir."

The dentist cleared his throat. He shot Jack a look of disdain. "Oh, OK . . . if I *must*. It says, 'Ebony King, seven years old,' on the top of the paper. 'April 8, 1997: FMX, Oral Exam reveals SSC on tooth # K and semiprecious crown on tooth # 30.'" Dr. McFly paused. His face lost all expression and went white as a sheet. Then he turned green around the gills.

Jack sauntered curiously up to the cadaverous medical man. Jack was gripping his own copy of the quick Goat Valley patient-screening record in his own steady hand. He knew perfectly well why the highfalutin tooth puller had changed color so rapidly. "*Please* go on, Dr. McFly. The good folks in the courtroom are waiting with much anticipation to hear the rest of Ms. Ebony's write-up—you know, the one that was done with such careful and mindful precision, the one that holds four allegations against Dr. Brookshire. Please do go ahead and read us the rest."

The green hue of McFly's puss went colorless. His demeanor went limp. All expression went by the wayside. He began to read, "'Note: Check procedures filed with Medicaid. Suspect Dr. B. filed procedure # D2791 on tooth # K.'"

"Hold it right there, if you will, please. Dr. McFly, could you please tell us what dental procedure # D2791 stands for?"

"Uh-huh. That is a semiprecious cast crown," he answered, still pale as a ghost.

"So let me get this straight. You, sir, and the other two dental board members, along with the Goat Valley dentist who so graciously allowed you to use his dental office for these secret patient screenings—you *all* sat down and drew the conclusion that you *suspected* Dr. Brookshire of filing a semiprecious cast crown on tooth # K. Is that what this says?" Jack was holding the single piece of lined white paper high in the air and shaking it at the flabbergasted dentist.

The colorless doctor began to turn red. "Well, yes, in a way."

"In a *way*?" Jack ranted. "A devoted dentist's entire future, not to mention her whole reputation, depends on *in a way*?"

The man on the stand was now crimson in color. He quickly switched to defense. "Well, there is absolutely no doubt in my mind that I have seen *numerous* times where Dr. Doramae Brookshire has placed stainless steel crowns on patients' teeth and then filed them as cast semiprecious crowns with Medicaid. I am certain of that!" the enraged doctor raved.

Jack remained calm. He smiled kindly at the lunatic on the stand. "You are absolutely certain that you personally have seen *numerous* examples in patients' mouths where Dr. Brookshire placed stainless steel crowns but filed for cast precious metal crowns when she filed her procedure with Medicaid services?"

The liar looked down. "Yes, I am certain of this," he fudged.

Jack turned slowly and deliberately around to face His Honor, the great and powerful Ebenezer B. Grudge. He looked him square in the eye. "Your Honor, we intend to impeach this witness's testimony. We intend to subpoena the dental lab technician from Lancaster, Georgia. He is the manager of the dental lab that Dr. Brookshire uses for her crowns. He will bring all records with him."

The judge squirmed in his throne. Dr. McFly squirmed even harder. "Permission granted to subpoena new witness," the courtroom umpire called.

Dr. McFly began to hem and haw. Knowing that all his trumped-up charges were about to be exposed for what they truly were had him reassessing the situation. "I suppose that I could have been somewhat in error here," he began. He stiffened and assumed the look of a pissed-off bulldog. "But in any event, it is certainly *not* standard of care to put a cast metal crown on a seven-year-old."

"Oh, we are going to change subjects from Dr. Brookshire's bogus Medicaid filings over to the standard of care controversy then, huh?" Jack calmly inquired.

"Well, she shouldn't have done either one," the riled doctor commented.

"OK. We'll play the game your way, Doc. But first, we have to prove that she did either one." Jack paused. He looked straight through the scared rabbit on the witness stand. "If you don't mind, Doctor, could you please repeat the last statement you made . . . the one about the standard of care concerning metal crowns on seven-year-olds?"

Dr. McFly let out a long and labored sigh. "I *said* that it is not the standard of care to place a permanent cast metal crown on a seven-year-old."

Jack strolled over to the defendant table. He scooped up a familiar-looking little book. He returned to his podium and held the textbook out to the judge. "I would like to once again submit exhibit J," he stated.

"Exhibit allowed," the expert on justice ruled.

Jack rambled over to the witness-box. He handed exhibit J off to the troubled testifier. "Doctor, could you please read the title of this textbook to the folks in the courtroom?"

"*Textbook of Pediatric Dentistry*," he flatly answered.

"Now, Dr. McFly, do you recall this specific textbook earlier in the trial? I think we used it to question one of Dr. Brookshire's staff members, concerning the age of the first dental cleaning, I believe."

"Yes, yes, I remember this textbook. Let's not go over and over things we have already been through."

"OK then, Doc. I do not have to reestablish the professional status of this text then. I don't have to remind you that this small brown book was Dr. Brookshire's textbook that she was taught from in her pediatric dentistry courses in dental school. I don't have to go back over the fact that this particular book is divided into nineteen main sections concerning the dental treatment of children and adolescents. And I don't have to remind you that this particular textbook is endorsed fully by the American Academy of Pediatric Dentists, the recognized authority on children's dental health and oral care. We're good on all that, right?"

"Yep," the smart-ass doctor replied with attitude.

"Good. Then I'll save us a little time. Could you be so kind as to read a small section to us aloud, Dr. McFly?"

"I guess, if I have to," he groaned.

"Good. Then please turn to the section on restorative dentistry in children and read from page 196, paragraph 5, if you would."

The distressed doctor pulled back his tight shoulders and grabbed his temples. "'It is desirable in almost every case to place permanent restorative crowns on permanent teeth, regardless of the child's actual age, but deciduous teeth should have temporary restorations.'"

"Hmmmm. You're going to have to help me out here, Doc. Could you put what you just read to us in layman's terms, please?"

"Wuh, yeah. It simply said to put *permanent* restorations on *permanent* teeth but *temporary* restorations on baby teeth."

"Hold that thought. Would a cast semiprecious crown be considered a permanent restoration?"

"Yep."

"And didn't Dr. Brookshire place a cast semiprecious crown on tooth # 30, which was a permanent tooth, on Ebony King?"

"Yep."

"But hold on a minute. You said that it was not standard of care to place cast metal crowns on seven-year-olds' teeth."

Dr. McFly sighed so long that he began to whimper. "Didn't you pay attention to what I just read? It said that it was the standard of care regardless of the child's actual age!" He shot Jack a long look of indignation.

"Oh, so that means that when Dr. Brookshire placed a permanent crown on a permanent tooth of a seven-year-old, this was the *correct* treatment, right?"

The good doctor's eyes got big as gobstoppers. He had been tricked. There was no backing out of this one. The esteemed manual of children's dentistry had stated that correct procedure had been followed, and he himself had just finished backing it up. All he could think to do was sheepishly add, "But she did charge some for permanent crowns when she placed stainless steel crowns instead."

"Well, we will see about that allegation when the lab guy comes and testifies with all of Dr. Brookshire's lab bills." He paused and rolled his eyes up to the ceiling, like he was deep in thought. "Oh, by the way, one more thing, did Dr. Brookshire follow the correct standard of care when she placed a stainless steel crown, which was a temporary restoration, on Ebony's baby tooth # K?"

"Yes, I guess she did."

Jack grinned once again. He twirled around to face the judge. "No more questions, Your Honor."

The fair and impartial judge glared at Brett Wratchett. "Redirect?" he inquired.

"No, Your Honor," the whupped puppy dog yelped.

The pro witness whore gathered up what little integrity he had left and stepped down from the witness stand. He glanced at the jury, straightened his Armani silk tie, squared his defeated shoulders, and marched down the aisle and out the door.

The referee behind the bench looked out at His weary jury. "We will take a one-hour lunch. Be back promptly at one o'clock," He instructed without so much as a compassionate bone in His authoritative body.

Bob, Mom, my sister Chris, and I ate lunch at the same little bistro we had patronized almost every day of the trial. There were not many dining options in this tiny Atlanta suburb of yuppies. Dave and Jack were off somewhere, cramming in another hour's worth of Dave's crash course on "dental terminology and methods in one hour or less." Thank god Jack was an unbelievably fast study.

The topic at lunch centered on the morning's professional whore witness, Dr. Percy McFly. I explained to my husband and willing relatives that I had never ever placed a temporary stainless steel crown on a pedo patient and then charged Medicaid for a permanent metal crown. I told them that I didn't have any earthly idea where Dr. McFly had come up with the idea. They reassured me that the lab guy from Lancaster would prove the doctor's allegations wrong when he showed up on Saturday morning with a fistful of written orders and receipts. Per usual, our lunch flew by, and it was time to reenter the world of doom.

I once again entered the hall of justice and took my seat at the defendant's table. Jack and Dave came rushing in, their heavy breathing and flushed faces suggesting just how rapidly they had raced back. Once again, we were all forced to participate in all the pomp and circumstance of His honorable judge Grudge's entrance into the courtroom. I wondered if He ever got tired of being the center of this silly, forced ceremonial parade. Brett Wratchett called his next witness, another pro witness whore from the state dental board.

RODEO CLOWN

"YOUR HONOR, I call Dr. Damien DeVout."

A wormy little man wearing enormous embellished cowboy boots arose. His mismatched ensemble of black suit trousers, embroidered and studded Western shirt, tailored black pinstriped suit jacket, and big-ticket boots gave him the appearance of a rodeo clown who had attempted to put on a swanky men's suit. All that was missing was the ten-gallon hat. Every step toward the awaiting witness stand was met with the click-clack of his oversize cowboy footwear. He stretched his tiny body and puffed out his puny, little chest so as to give himself the illusion of normalcy in masculine dimensions. It took him some time to get to his destination and even more time to climb up into the chair. His pint-size structure just wasn't quite up to the task. But once situated in the hot seat, his hyperactive, manic state began to leak out into the courtroom.

"Please state your name for the record," His Honor instructed.

The pocket-size man looked as if he had just been stunned with a Taser. "My name is *Dr.* Damien DeVout, sir," he replied, his dwarfish hands rapidly rubbing his miniature thighs as his short, little legs swung in rhythm to the court reporter's typing.

Brett Wratchett stepped up to the plate. "Good afternoon, Dr. DeVout." He smirked.

"Good afternoon, Brett," the teeny man replied while continuing to rub his thighs. He suddenly switched from leg swinging to boot tapping.

"Dr. DeVout, could you please tell the court how you came to be involved in the investigation of Dr. Brookshire?"

"Yes, sir, of course. I was one of the members of the state dental board that got asked to look into a Medicaid fraud case involving one of our state dentists."

"That dentist being one Dr. Doramae Brookshire. Is this correct, Dr. DeVout?"

"Yes, that's right, Brett," answered the wee, little cowboy man.

"And you were one of the handful of dental board members who examined and screened several of Dr. Brookshire's patients at a Goat Valley dental office, correct?"

"That's right, Brett. I participated in that." He was now fidgeting in his seat like he had ants in his pants.

"And, Dr. DeVout, could you please share a few of your findings with us here today? Just a few now. We certainly do not have time to go over *all* the examples of Medicaid fraud that Dr. Brookshire is accused of!"

Jack jumped up. "Objection, Your Honor!"

His Honor looked bored and aloof. "Objection overruled," He droned.

He turned toward Wratchett. "Go on," He directed.

"Like I was saying, please give us one example of a finding from your Goat Valley patient screening that points to Medicaid fraud."

"Well, she charged Medicaid for an MO on # 15 that was not even there," he spat out.

"Let's do a little jury educating here, why don't we? By an MO, you mean a two-surface silver filling in a back molar tooth, right?"

"That's right. *MO* means mesial occlusal. That's the simplest I can make it for these people."

I glanced over at the twelve-member jury and the two alternates. By the facial expressions on most of their faces, I could tell that they did not appreciate being referred to as "these people" by the itty-bitty cowboy.

Brett tried for some damage control. "Most everyone in this fine courtroom is not a trained dentist, so let's suffice it to say that an MO is a two-surface silver filling, and it was filed on tooth number 15, which is a top back molar tooth. Is this all correct, Dr. DeVout?"

"Yeah, I guess that would be correct in *layman's* terms," the cocky little dentist replied.

"OK then, Dr. DeVout, could you please tell us what you found on tooth # 15 on this particular patient?"

"I already did! I found *nothing* on tooth # 15! That's the whole point of this thing! She filed for a restoration that was *not even there*!" He looked like he was about to bail from his seat.

Brett Wratchett's face began to flush. He had his work cut out for him as far as keeping Tiny Cowboy lassoed in and calm. "Now, Dr. DeVout, could we please see some proof of the fact that Dr. Brookshire filed a filling with Medicaid on a tooth that was not even filled?"

"Wuh, sure, I brought all that stuff." The undersized testifier managed to leap from his tall seat and hit the floor running. He moved swiftly toward a massive folder of what appeared to be dental X-rays and pulled out the top one. I was very relieved that someone had apparently placed the X-rays in question in the proper order. I had the distinct feeling that our man would not be calm enough or organized enough to pull this off.

Returning to his seat, he waved a large, blown-up dental X-ray in the air over his head like a rodeo buckaroo making circles with his lasso. I was amazed every time I laid eyes on the gargantuan X-rays that the GBI and the state had taken the time and expense of enlarging to the point of supercolossal exhibits of wonder. I could have never imagined in my wildest dreams that any human being would even *think* to blow a simple two-by-two-inch X-ray up into a two-by-two-foot X-ray. And there were dozens and dozens of them.

Dr. DeVout held up his radiographic treasure and rotated like a movable mannequin.

"Why don't we place this X-ray on our easel over here that is set up with the proper lighting so that our judge and jury can see the X-ray in question easily?" He led the nervous little witness with a suggestion involving common sense.

"Well, OK," he hesitantly agreed, visibly upset about the prospect of getting back out of his towering chair. He managed with a bit of difficulty to make his way over to the awaiting easel and clipped the giant X-ray in place. He glanced over his shoulder to the curious jury. His whole body jumped twice and jerked once, and his puffy little cheeks twitched. He began to narrate. He appeared to be talking to the X-ray, not the jury.

"You all see this here? This is tooth # 15, and as you all can see real plain, there is no filling in this tooth," he declared.

Brett Wratchett strolled on over to the twitchy little doctor and assumed a position by the radiograph. "Can everyone see this?" he asked the jury.

Fourteen puzzled heads nodded yes.

"And can you all see that this tooth here, tooth # 15, has no filling?"

There was another jury nod.

"Good then. Dr. DeVout, please continue."

"Well, that's my proof. It doesn't get much worse than that! Dr. Brookshire filed *a whole bunch* of procedures with Medicaid that she didn't even do! That is the actual perfect definition of Medicaid fraud itself!"

Jack shot up once again. "Objection, Your Honor! A *whole bunch*?"

The good judge glared at Brett. He knew this one was too blatant to let slide. "Mr. Wratchett, you must keep your witness from making sweeping statements."

Brett looked at his professional witness. The neurotic little guy returned with the look of a high-strung cocaine addict. Brett made a split-second decision right then and there to stop questioning the jittery, jumpy, nervy little testifier. If he pushed him too far, there was no telling what the ruffled cowboy might do. "Your witness," he reluctantly told Jack.

Jack approached the awaiting witness with caution. "Good afternoon, Dr. DeVout. Are you up for a few more questions?"

The edginess suddenly switched to cockiness. He looked Jack up and down. "Sir, I can handle *anything* you throw my way."

"Oh, that's real good to know. That makes my job real easy. Thanks. Now, Dr. DeVout, you stated that Dr. Brookshire filed silver fillings with Medicaid that were not there. Is that correct?"

"Yep. If you had been listening to the last . . . oh, ninety minutes or so . . . I guess that is exactly what you would have heard."

"Oh, I did hear it. Actually, this whole ordeal is pretty darn bad. I mean, it is *bad* that she would have done this."

"You're darn tootin' it's *bad*," he agreed. "That's why I'm sitting here. I need to protect the integrity of *my* profession."

Dave casually arose and walked slowly over to the state X-ray easel. Judge Grudge came unhinged. He turned abruptly toward Jack. "Who is this?" He demanded loudly. "I do not like people wandering around My courtroom!"

Jack kept his cool. "Your Honor, that is my dental consultant, Dr. David Allen. Sorry that I have not introduced him to you."

"Well, from now on, let's not have any more surprises in *My* courtroom! I do not like surprises!" The good judge was still quite miffed.

"I apologize, sir," Jack quickly answered.

Dave was looking closely at the gigantic X-ray of # 15 that remained up on the lit easel. He slowly found his way back to Jack and cocked his head back toward the X-ray easel. Then he casually took a seat beside me. He leaned over and whispered something to Jack.

"Your Honor, I need a quick minute to consult with Dr. Allen, if I may."

All eyes turned toward the main authority who sat in the highest chair. His Honor was visibly irked. He was also pretty panicked for the state. "All right, all right! But make it quick!" he shot back.

Jack ambled over to Dave and took the chair beside him. The two of them whispered and scratched down various words and diagrams on a legal yellow pad. In no more than two minutes, Jack had it and was ready to go back in.

He leisurely arose, buttoned his suit jacket, and reapproached the cowboy witness. "Dr. DeVout, could I ask you to do something, please?"

"Wuh, I guess so. It depends on what it is," he arrogantly replied.

"I need to see a full-mouth series of X-rays from the patient, Ms. Ebony King, please. If you will, please find the full-mouth series of X-rays from the Goat Valley dental office where you did the dental screening on this patient."

The little testifier looked at Jack like he had just asked him to outline the procedure for brain surgery. "Well . . . these X-rays are in a specific order. We did that on purpose. We have a sequence and protocol we thought out," he argued.

Jack grinned. "Well, I do appreciate that y'all thought out the order that you needed the X-rays. It is always real good to organize for a trial. However, in a courtroom trial, things do arise spontaneously, and sometimes our order is a little messed up. It's the nature of a trial." He glanced toward the jury. They were all quite amused.

"OK, OK, you don't have to rub it in! I *am* a doctor! This is *nothing* to me!" he growled. He reluctantly hopped down from the witness chair and moved toward the bulging folder of records. He peeked into the opening and began to shuffle and jumble and shift. As he changed the order of things in the giant folder, it became apparent that he was creating a hodgepodge of chaos and confusion. His tiny face flushed, and he let out an audible sigh.

"I'll find it. It's in here somewhere," he declared.

"Take your time, sir," Jack said patiently.

Judge Grudge reared back in His throne. He placed His honorable elbows on the desk in front of Him. His two fists came up to support His chin. His head shook slightly from left to right. He looked as if He was totally disgusted by the whole scene.

Dr. DeVout continued to break the deck. His radiograph rummage was something to behold. Finally, he dived in once more and came up with a rectangular black mount full of several dental X-rays. "I *found* it!" he shouted. It was as if archeologists had just uncovered the Rosetta stone.

"Good. We are all so glad that you found it," Jack teased. "Could you please bring this full-mouth series of X-rays over and place it on the lit easel so we can all see it?"

"Yep, I can do that," the relieved little dentist said. His loose-fitting cowboy boots clickety-clacked all the way over to the easel. He placed the newfound treasure under the clip with a light and tender touch, treating it as delicately as an egg.

Jack looked up briefly at the ceiling as if he was making a split-second decision. I knew what was coming next. He had to establish for the jury just what a full-mouth series of dental radiographs was. I was hoping and praying that he would not ask our little rodeo clown to define this. He did not.

"Now, Dr. DeVout, would it be correct to define a full-mouth series of dental X-rays as a complete set of intraoral X-rays taken of a patient's teeth and the adjacent hard tissue?"

The flustered tooth man was flabbergasted. "Yeah, I guess that is a pretty good definition," he had to agree.

"And, Dr. DeVout, would you also agree that a dental full-mouth series of X-rays includes eighteen films, all taken the same day?"

"Yeah, I never really counted them, but that sounds right." His voice trailed off.

"Well, we do not want it to merely *sound* right. We want our information to *be* right. So let's go over this, and if you will, please keep count for me, OK?"

"Yeah, I guess I can do that."

"OK, here we go. The dental full-mouth series includes four bitewings, eight posterior periapicals, and six anterior periapicals. Would that be correct, Doctor?"

The professional medical witness shuffled back and forth in his seat. He rubbed his cowboy boots across the floor. He scratched the top of his head with his right hand while he chewed the nails on his left hand. Jack had visibly ruffled his feathers. The boy was turned inside out. He finally spoke. "I guess that would be an accurate description," he flatly replied.

Jack shot the jury a quick glance. I think I saw him wink. He had managed to do it again. He had somehow memorized all that from talking to Dave for two minutes. He had such a fine-tuned feel for the trial courtroom that he had instinctively known that the definition had to come from him. This established his knowledge of the subject. Not only that but it also gave him the upper hand and made the pro witness whore look even more inept than he was. Jack, 1; cowboy dentist, 0.

"Now let's go on, shall we?" Jack asked. "Dr. DeVout, could you please hang this newly discovered full-mouth series next to the good-sized X-ray of what you called # 15 for comparison?"

The doctor was insulted. "That big X-ray *was* # 15. It wasn't just *what I called* # 15!" he retorted. He was about to come apart.

"We'll see about that," Jack sang out, taunting the agitated little guy. "First, let's establish that this full-mouth series is indeed the one of Ebony King and that it was taken at the Goat Valley dental office during the exams and screenings that y'all did. Dr. DeVout, could I get you to step down to the easel with me and read some info out loud to us, please?"

"If I have to." The perturbed professional sighed. He leaped once more from his stand, hit the floor, and clacked on over to Jack.

Jack pointed to the penciled writing across the top of the black mount that held the X-rays. "Could you please read this aloud to us so we can all hear, Doctor?"

Dr. DeVout exhaled loudly. "This says, 'Ebony King. April 8, 1997. Dr. Peter J. Heinlich.'"

"Thank you, Dr. DeVout. This Dr. Peter J. Heinlich, was this the Goat Valley dentist that allowed you to use his office to do your screenings for this trial?"

"Wuh, yeah, but he said to not let everybody know he was the one." His voice trailed off once again.

"All that aside, I am correct that this full-mouth series of Ms. Ebony King was taken at the Goat Valley dental office where you and the other board members screened Dr. Brookshire's patients, correct?" Jack pushed.

"Correct," the doctor shot back.

"OK. Now that we know we have the correct X-rays of the patient, Ms. King, let's go on. Dr. DeVout, I have a dental question for you."

The cowboy doctor's ears perked up. He came back alive. This might be a chance to steal the courtroom back from the lowly legal eagle. Maybe there was *something* about dentistry that this ambulance chaser hadn't picked up. "Ask your question then," he commanded.

"Could you please tell me how dental films are mounted? I never quite got that. Are they mounted from left to right or right to left?"

"Well, it varies from dentist to dentist," DeVout answered, trying his hardest to remain ambiguous about the subject.

"How do you know then what side of the mouth you are looking at?" Jack inquired.

"Oh, that's easy. There's a film ID dot."

"Hmmmm. That's interesting. What do you mean by a film ID dot?"

The nervous little nit smiled. He finally knew something about dentistry that Jack didn't. "This little dot here in the film's corner. See? You can actually feel it," he offered up to Jack.

Jack strolled over to the dental film in the little man's hand and took a quick feel. "Oh, I see what you mean now. That film ID dot is concave on one side and convex on the other side. So which way are they mounted?"

"Usually so the convex side is up. Most dentists prefer that, I think," he answered.

"OK then. Now that we know about the film ID dot and that almost always films are mounted so that the dot can be felt to be *convex*, let's look at our film comparison, shall we?"

"OK, we can do that," the revived doctor readily agreed.

"Dr. DeVout, could you please hold up this nice blown-up replication of this X-ray that the GBI so graciously had made for us?"

The little rodeo clown eagerly held up the giant replication of tooth # 15 that he and Brett had discussed at length a few hours earlier.

"Now in your other hand, could you please hold up this full-mouth series of the same patient? The one that was taken of Ebony King in the Goat Valley dental office?"

The shrimpy dentist complied without hesitation.

"Now could you please locate tooth # 15 in the full-mouth series?"

"Yep, got it," he announced.

"One more thing, Dr. DeVout, could you please humor me and feel the film ID dots on each one of these X-rays?"

"OK." The dinky dentist did as he was instructed. He felt the ID dot on the film of # 15 in the full-mouth series. His facial expression was unchanged. But as soon as he felt the ID dot on the gigantic GBI picture, his knees buckled. All the blood drained from his face. He was a pallid, pasty mess. He looked like he might get sick.

"Just one more question, Dr. DeVout." Jack paused, like he always did before he moved in for the kill. "Look once again at that huge film that the GBI made for us—the one and only film that you and Brett Wratchett talked about earlier today—and tell me, *what tooth number is that GBI film of?*"

The bloodless, waxlike professional witness mumbled under his breath, "It's of # 2."

"I'm so sorry, Doctor, I didn't quite hear you. Could you please speak up so that everyone in this courtroom can hear your answer?"

The white-faced dentist looked down at his designer cowboy boots. "It's number 2, I guess," he stated matter-of-factly.

Jack wasn't having any of this. "You *guess*, or you *know?*"

"Well, I know that this must be tooth # 2 according to the ID dots," he answered reluctantly.

"Well, Dr. DeVout, let's be absolutely *sure* of this. This is very important to this case, wouldn't you think?"

"Guess so," the shot-down cowboy replied.

"I mean, your one and only concrete accusation you have presented against Dr. Brookshire is that she filed an MO silver filling on tooth # 15 that was not there. Correct?"

"Well, so far, yes," the off-color little man said.

"Let's be sure of all this. Let's compare the great, big GBI X-ray to the full-mouth series that you yourself took at Dr. Heinlich's office in Goat Valley." Jack pointed to the humungous GBI X-ray. "Now, Dr. DeVout, is *this* the same tooth as *this* on the full-mouth series?" he asked, pointing to two teeth simultaneously.

The pallid professional swayed and squinted. As he focused in on the two X-rays, his little head seemed to be spinning. "Yeah, those two teeth are the same."

"And what number tooth are these two teeth, please, Doctor?"

"Why, that is tooth number 2," he answered expressionless.

"Both of these X-rays are of tooth # 2, the giant one courtesy of the GBI *and* the tooth that we are pointing to in this full-mouth series?"

"Yep."

"And is it true that tooth # 2 is an upper back molar, called a second molar, and that tooth # 2 is located on the patient's *right* side? But tooth # 15 is also an upper second molar, except that # 15 is located on the patient's *left* side of her mouth? Is this all true, Dr. DeVout?"

The cowboy dentist swayed. "Yep, that is all accurate."

"Let's say this another way. Tooth # 2 and tooth # 15 are both upper second molars. They are very similar in shape, size, and appearance. The only difference is that one is on the patient's right side, and the other is on the patient's left side. So oftentimes, the only way that the dentist reading the X-ray is able to tell the difference between these two teeth is to pay particular attention to the manner in which the X-rays are mounted, in other words by paying close attention to the ID dots on the film, right?"

"Right." The pallid dentist gulped.

"So *both* of these X-rays are of tooth # 2, not of tooth # 15 as you had testified earlier. Dr. DeVout, could you please tell the jury what kind of dental filling is present in tooth # 2 on the patient named Ebony King?"

The sickly little ashen guy replied, "Well, there isn't *any* filling on this tooth. Can't you see that?"

"Yes, I do see that there is no filling in tooth # 2, but what about tooth # 15, the tooth that Dr. Brookshire filed an MO silver filling on with Medicaid? We had better check that out at this point, wouldn't you think?"

"Yeah, probably should."

"Now we don't have the luxury of having a gigantic GBI replication of the *true* tooth # 15 because the GBI replicated tooth # 2 instead. So we must look at this regular-sized PA X-ray of tooth # 15, the one that you took at the Goat Valley dental office." Jack pointed to an X-ray in the full-mouth series. "Dr. DeVout, is this X-ray of tooth # 15? Now take your time," he teased.

Dr. DeVout, the edgy tooth man, answered, "Yes, sir, that X-ray is of tooth # 15."

"And could you please tell us what kind of filling is in tooth # 15?"

"Wuh, that's an MO silver filling. I guess you knew that, huh?" The deposed dentist was getting a little snappish.

Jack grinned. "Sooo let's summarize. You, Dr. DeVout, have accused Dr. Doramae Brookshire of Medicaid fraud by alleging that she filed a filling with Medicaid on tooth # 15 that was not there. Then you and Brett Wratchett presented an enormous-sized X-ray that the GBI generated. This X-ray, which was discussed at length by you and Mr. Wratchett, you claimed was of tooth # 15. But it turns out that this X-ray was *really* of tooth # 2. Then when we finally located the correct X-ray of tooth # 15, we discovered that # 15 does indeed have an MO silver filling on it. So at this point, I must ask you, *did Dr. Brookshire commit Medicaid fraud?*"

The high-strung, anxious little witness became hysterical. "But . . . but . . . but you gotta *understand*! The GBI messed up all this stuff! They didn't have it in the proper storage! They broke the chain of custody! They didn't follow proper protocol!"

Jack just leaned back and enjoyed the show. This was a perfect example of Jack's "let the witness hang himself." As soon as the neurotic testifier realized what he was ranting about and shut up, the damage had been done. Jack simply nodded gently up and down and repeated the unstrung cowboy dentist's exact words. "The GBI messed up all this stuff? They didn't have it in the proper storage? They broke the chain of custody? They didn't follow proper protocol?"

The sallow doctor began to lean over, moving back and forth at the same time. I thought he might get sick right then and there. "I need to go back to my chair if I can. I need to show the jury . . . and the judge . . . something," he whimpered.

Jack was loving this. "Oh please do," he conceded.

The defeated little witness quickly snatched up the gargantuan radiograph of tooth # 2 and headed for his corral. He started out dragging his boots, but the closer he got to his hot seat, the more he giddyapped. He jumped back into his chair in the witness stand, still managing to hold tight to his confiscated giant X-ray. Once he was settled in, he held the oversize X-ray directly in front of his face and began to explain the principles of dental radiographs to the jury. As he lectured, the monstrous X-ray moved with his face. Every time he turned to the right, the towering X-ray turned to the right too. If he looked over his shoulder, the X-ray looked over his shoulder with him. It appeared as if Dr. DeVout was now a giant X-ray head. His pale face had been replaced by giant tooth # 2.

I have to admit, even though I was in no mood to be amused by anything—after all, I was fighting for my life here—this spectacle was one of the most hilarious things I have ever witnessed. Jack's longtime paralegal, Jan, slapped her hand over her mouth. Then as if a simple hand could not contain her laughter well enough, she grabbed the nearest manila envelope and positioned it over her entire face. Finally, she gave in and began to giggle, very softly at first but almost ending in a full-fledged belly laugh. She leaned over to me and whispered, still cracking up, "I am so sorry. I *never* laugh at anything in the courtroom. But this is the damned *funniest thing* I have ever seen in my entire life."

Jack was very amused himself, but he stopped short of laughing. He poked and prodded the cowboy dentist with the X-ray face. "I think all of us in this courtroom understand the main principles of a periapical X-ray now. Thank you so much for your explanation, Dr. DeVout. But that X-ray you have been holding up, remember, that X-ray is of tooth # 2 and not of # 15, the X-ray truly in question."

At that point, the little dentist came undone. He morphed into a full-fledged basket case. He turned mad as a hatter. A screw came loose. He flung the colossal X-ray of # 2 across the floor. Then he reached across the desk portion in front of him and grabbed up the bulging folder chock full of X-rays that the GBI had prepared for the trial, only his short, little arms couldn't quite manage to snatch the beefy portfolio securely up to hang on tight. It was just too cumbersome. The hulking folder stuffed with dozens of X-rays came tumbling down to the floor in front of him. Dental X-rays of every size, shape, and color went dancing across the floor. It was a virtual plethora of dental radiography. They landed this way and that. It was the old childhood game of pick-up sticks, only not with sticks but with dental X-rays instead.

But the freaked-out cuckoo didn't let that stop him. The berserk little man dived out of his chair, sprung forth from the witness stand, and landed smack dab on the floor in front of the X-ray spillage. He dropped to his knees and began shuffling frantically through the spoils. "It's here *somewhere*!" he shouted. "I'll find it! Just give me a chance!"

His shout quickly turned into a mumble. "I just saw it the other day," he murmured to himself. The kooky little guy had gone nutty as a fruitcake.

Jack was not about to interrupt this dog and pony show. The blubbering idiot was crucifying the prosecution's side all by himself. It was a one-man show. Jack didn't even have to figure out what question to ask next.

I glanced over at the jury. Ten out of fourteen jury members had their mouths hanging wide open with a look of total disbelief spread across their shocked faces. Two looked downright embarrassed for the poor lunatic. And the other two were just altogether disgusted.

Judge Grudge acted quickly. He motioned for the bailiff. The bailiff leaned over the king of the courtroom's throne and listened intently to what Grudge whispered in his ear. Then he cautiously approached the babbling fool, tapped him gently on the shoulder, and quietly delivered the judge's message. As the bailiff delivered his message, the visibly shaken judge began to beat His all-powerful gavel on His fancy mahogany desk. "Jury dismissed for the day! Be back sharply at nine o'clock tomorrow!"

The jury members arose and filed out of the courtroom. Twenty-eight eyes were fixed on the flaky, flipped-out, unzipped cowboy dentist, still kneeling on the floor.

Jack ambled on over to the defendant's table. He winked at Dave, who nodded gently back. An expression of pure amusement was spread over both of their faces. Jan was still coming down from her hysterical high. Jack grinned at Mom, Chris, and me. "Let's go get some dinner," he sang.

Dave, Bob, Chris, Jan, Mom, and I all arose in sync. Along with our savior Jack, the six of us flew out of the courtroom on cloud nine. We all got in our respective vehicles and decided to meet right away at the closest eating place, a fast, casual, franchised restaurant chain that was interestingly named Fuddruckers. This was the first Fuddruckers I had ever been to. When I laughed and poked fun at the franchise's name, the concept of the place was explained very quickly to me by a hassled employee.

"Our concept here at Fuddruckers is to offer large hamburgers in which the meat is ground on-site, and the buns are baked on our premises. We specialize in delicious juicy, hand-patted, high-quality burgers. I think you will find that your burger tonight is one of the best you have ever put in your mouth." The disheveled, harried Fuddruckers employee sighed. I wondered how many hundreds of times a week she had to repeat her memorized spiel.

The seven of us ordered different variations of the delicious juicy, hand-patted Fuddruckers burger. What we ate that evening didn't matter one iota. We had kicked the state's ass. We had conquered the giant. David had triumphed over Goliath. We were all beside ourselves with joy. We were bursting with ecstasy, on top of the world. We all agreed that we couldn't lose now. Dr. Damien DeVout was our turning point. We were home free. How could we possibly lose now? We saw the jury's faces when they filed out. Why, the good judge would probably call the trial first thing the next morning. We were done. The nightmare was over. Our emancipator Jack had delivered us. Good had triumphed over evil. All my childhood Sunday school teachings rang true.

My sister Chris, always purehearted and naive, announced, "Well, there certainly is no need in my staying any longer. We just won the trial. Guess I will go back to Texas tonight."

No food ever tasted so good. No place ever seemed so much like heaven. A happier bunch you had never seen. If we could have, all seven of us would have danced across the Fuddruckers floor, tripping the light fantastic. We were on a winners' high.

But as Bob drove Chris to the Atlanta airport, I fretted back in the hotel room. I was on pins and needles. Judge Grudge's words at the very start of the trial rang in my ears. "OK, counselor, have it your way. But I'm telling you this up front. *I'm* going on vacation come Saturday. I've had this fishing trip lined up for months, and I'm not going to let *anything* or *anyone* ruin it for me. By Saturday, this trial will be over . . . one way or another. *Understand*, counselor?"

My common sense told me that Dr. DeVout's nervous breakdown would be the good judge's perfect excuse for ending the trial tomorrow morning. After all, tomorrow was Saturday, and He would be right on schedule for His beloved fishing trip. All He had to do was declare a simple mistrial, and He could be on His way, simple as that. But the pessimist in me became the prophet of doom. What-ifs began spurting forth. What if the judge could not let the state lose? What if His Honor was so thoroughly pissed off about the whole thing that it was His chance to teach anyone who took on the state of Georgia a lesson they would never forget? What if His almighty Honor was in bed with the state and promised them a win? After all, Judge Ebenezer B. Grudge got His paycheck from the same source as Brett M. Wratchett—the state of Georgia.

Jack had challenged that powerful and omnipotent source. Jack had said himself that the judge did not like him at all. He had said that he really didn't understand this because he could almost always get a judge to like him. And no one could argue that the honorable judge Grudge had ruled against us and for the state time and time again.

I sat there in that impersonal cold hotel room, waiting for my husband to return and worried myself sick. So many what-ifs swam around in my head; I worked myself into lather. Those awful what-ifs—they haunted and tormented me. I began to pace the floor, biting my nails. I would have climbed the wall if I could have. By the time my loving mate returned, I was a sight to behold.

Bob, bless his sweet little heart, recognized the problem right away. He held me gently and wiped away my tears. He reminded me that I should not be worrying at the moment but, instead, should be dancing on the ceiling with ecstasy. He calmed me and soothed me and comforted me. He tamed the troubled waters. He convinced me that the judge would stop the trial first thing in the morning. By the time he was done, we both drifted off peacefully to sleep, looking forward to the end of our very long nightmare.

TWENTY MINUTES

SATURDAY MORNING—WE HAD endured this living nightmare, this trial of torment for five painful long days now. It was about to be over. My heart sang out with pure joy. As I readied myself for the wondrous conclusion, the cessation of the suffering, I began to whistle a happy tune as I packed my suitcase. After all, we would be leaving the hotel in this Atlanta suburb very soon, wouldn't we? It would probably take about one hour or less to show up in the courtroom, go through all the pomp and circumstance of the good judge's ceremonies, have Him declare a mistrial, and be on our merry way. I was euphoric, intoxicated with bliss.

I, though, was a creature of plan As and plan Bs. Plan A was, of course, we all showed up, the judge declared the trial over, and we all returned happily home. Sure, we would have to deal with the ramifications of a mistrial, but that would be a very long time from now, and I could deal with all that much later. OK by me.

Plan B, though—oh, that pesky, annoying plan B—was I just had to go here because I had to ready myself for anything that might come my way. Plan B was the unlikely event that His honorable judge Grudge would allow this day, for some ungodly reason, to go until the end. That would mean that we would have another eight hours of Brett's three-ring circus. What might he come up with today? Well, I couldn't bother myself with his follies. I didn't have time to focus on his blubbering blunders. I had to concentrate instead on what Jack could do today with what we had lined up. This was very difficult to do because we, the defense, had not been allowed to be up yet. The entire five days had been the state of Georgia dragging its feet, stalling, stonewalling. But I still had to play the cards that had been dealt me. So I began to take inventory.

I knew that Jack had deposed one key witness who would help our case immensely. Bobby, the owner of Creative Smiles Dental Lab in

Lancaster, Georgia, had driven up to Atlanta and was ready to testify on our behalf. He was going to testify that *all* the crowns that Brett had sworn were placed in young patients' mouths as cheap stainless steel crowns but filed by me as semiprecious metal were indeed semiprecious crowns. Bobby had lab slips, invoices, and receipts to prove this. If the trial went on and we had to use Bobby, he would prove invaluable to our side. Not only would he testify that I was 100 percent honest as far as semiprecious crown filings were concerned, he would also tell the jury that I was trustworthy and conscientious in my dealings with his lab. Bobby and I had a mutual respect for each other. We were always aboveboard, on the up and up. He was a witness that could help establish my general sense of good ethics. I had no doubt that Bobby would paint me as "what you see is what you get," a down-to-earth, reliable, sincere person. That had to help the case, right?

The second little trick that Jack had up his sleeve for the day, if it should go on, was questioning Dr. Barbara Savage concerning one statement from her previously given deposition. Dr. Barbara Savage was one of the three state dental board members who had signed on to crucify me. And Saturday was her day to take the stand. Every single person who is going to testify against the defendant in a trial is required to sit down and give a deposition before the trial. In that deposition, they state what they intend to testify. Both sides are given a chance to ask any questions they may have, and the entire deposition is recorded in written form and distributed to the defense, the prosecution, and the judge well before the trial. Jack had gone over all depositions with a fine-tooth comb, like all excellent trial attorneys do, and had discovered one very interesting statement given by Dr. Barbara Savage.

When Jack had asked Dr. Savage about the policy of preapproving the procedure codes for patient behavior management, Dr. Savage had come up with a very thought-provoking response. Jack asked, "Now, Dr. Savage, I understand that the dental treatment codes Y000100 through Y009400, those being for management of difficult children, must be preapproved."

Dr. Savage answered, "That is correct."

"That, I take it, means the following: every single time that Dr. Brookshire performed a procedure on a young patient who had some behavior issues in the chair and then filed for management of difficult children on that patient, that procedure had been preapproved by someone at Medicaid. Is this correct?"

"That is also correct."

Jack requested, "Please help me with this, Dr. Savage. If the designated person for preapprovals at Medicaid goes ahead and preapproves Dr. Brookshire's request to file for management of difficult children, then it becomes OK for her to file that procedure, isn't that right?"

"Well, it is *theoretically* correct, but you have to understand that the old guy sitting up in Atlanta who rubber-stamps these preapprovals is getting dementia. He has been doing this so long that he pretty much OKs every single procedure that the Georgia dentists file for."

"Oh! Now I think I get it. The senile old man, I believe his name is Dr. Demarcus Drupey, sitting up in Atlanta at the Medicaid office has been dealing with dental preapprovals for so many long years that he now has dementia and just pretty much sits there all day long and rubber-stamps every single procedure on every single preapproval form that he receives from the Georgia dentists?"

Dr. Savage answered, "Pretty close. That's why Medicaid can get you anytime they want you."

"Oh, and Medicaid must really *want* Dr. Brookshire, huh?"

When Jack told me about the Dr. Savage flub of admitting that Medicaid can "get you anytime they want you," mixed emotions of total disbelief blended with ecstasy swept over me. This just had to be an astronomical break for us. Maybe even a turning point in the trial? She couldn't deny saying it. It was there, in black and white, for all to see. I found myself halfway wishing that the trial could keep going on just long enough for Jack to question Dr. Barbara Savage. What a triumph of a sideshow that would be!

But now it was time for me to snap out of my plan B daydream. More than likely, I would not even have to face the torment of plan B. After yesterday's courtroom spectacle courtesy of Dr. Damien DeVout, there was no way any judge worth his salt was going to let this trial proceed. I was just a little worried about the concept of "any judge worth his salt" regarding Judge Grudge.

It was Saturday morning. Bob was urging me to get ready for my last day of harassment in hell. So I mechanically got dressed. I took special care to choose an outfit that projected both my professionalism and my simple, sensible side. I chose a black suit, plain white blouse, and modest black heels. I wore very little jewelry. I added a small amount of basic clean makeup and brushed my tangled hair, and I was ready to go.

When we arrived at the courthouse, I was surprised to see two people whom I hadn't seen in a while sitting on a bench outside the courtroom. This hallway bench held people who were going to testify. One of the deposed was Dr. Simon Smallbury, a colleague from dental school. The other was Amy Nelson, a former dental assistant in my practice. When Amy motioned me over, I reluctantly went. She leaned over very close to my ear. She whispered so softly that I could barely hear her. "*Why* have I been subpoenaed?" she asked under her breath.

"I don't know," I answered quietly, as surprised as she was that she had been summoned.

She continued, "Well, they're not forcing me to say negative things about you or your practice."

Jack suddenly appeared and grabbed me gently by the elbow. "Come on, we need to go in now," he said matter-of-factly. I knew what he was doing. I had no business talking to the folks who had evidently been subpoenaed.

We entered Judge Grudge's courtroom for the sixth day and took our position at the defendant's table. Dave was waiting for us. Mom and Bob found a place on the bench behind us. It looked like we were facing a sixth day of purgatory. All my dreams of finality were crushed.

His almighty Honor entered the room. We were all commanded once again to arise. We could not sit back down until the mighty judge deemed it so. He glanced over at Brett Wratchett. "Call state's first witness," He droned, obviously quite bored with the whole thing.

"Your Honor, we call Dr. Simon Smallbury," Brett replied.

My thoughts drifted back to the first day of dental school. There we all were, all fifty-two of us, sitting in the huge lecture hall, scared to death of what was to come. I learned later that there was a reason for that number of students. The School of Dental Education had only fifty slots each year for dental students but always let fifty-two young dental hopefuls in, knowing full well that two of those incoming students would not make it to the end of the first year. Anyhow, I looked around me on that terrifying first day of dental school and took a quick inventory. First thing I noticed was that there weren't very many females. It was 1984, and dentistry was not deemed an acceptable career for a girl. It had been a male-dominated field up until then, and the fact that we had ten females in our incoming class was pissing off a lot of male professors, I was told.

The second thing that I noticed, hands down, was the peculiar creature that was sitting behind me, over my left shoulder. First call, without a doubt, was that he was an incredible nerd. He was skinny and pale and slicked his dark hair back with way too much hair gel. This exposed his huge prominent forehead. His cheap plastic glasses were taped together on the bridge of his runny nose. He wore a plastic pocket protector in his long-sleeved white starched shirt. Topping that shirt was a plaid bow tie. His black suit pants were pulled up to his midtorso and held up with an elastic multicolored striped belt. This pant position made the length way too short, exposing his puny ankles, which were adorned in argyle socks. He had an army green backpack still strapped tightly to his shoulders. But never mind that this guy was the poster boy for all geeks alive; there was something even weirder about him.

His very presence was eerily disturbing. He looked like a deer caught in the headlights. The pitiful little guy appeared to be bloodless, almost cadaverous. He was pasty and sallow, a sickly shade of light green. His eyes were bulging out of his waxlike face. His expression was pure terror. This little dork was scared almost literally to death. I couldn't help glancing repeatedly back at him. He stuck out like a sore thumb. The rest of us were visibly shaken, all of us a bit apprehensive about our first day in dental school. But we were all coping with it within the realms of normalcy. We were joking and poking fun at ourselves and trying our best to make light of the rather scary situation—but not the little goober sitting over my left shoulder. We all noticed him. You couldn't help it. I think we were all wondering the same thing. Was this little fellow going to pass out or throw up? His name, I learned later, was Simon Smallbury.

In dental school, I got to know Simon Smallbury, and he was really a pretty nice guy, still an incredible nerd but, all in all, a pretty decent guy. He remained in a state of terror the entire four years of dental school. He never deviated one inch from everything he was told to do. He obeyed the professors' commands like a frightened little puppy. He cracked the books, burned the midnight oil, and drove himself nearly mad with memorizations. When we all had a lab project due, like a set of wax dentures, he would work day and night on it until it was done perfectly. He actually ended up liking me fairly well because I tutored him in pharmacology and slipped him some of my class notes for free.

His best friend was Elmer Quimby. They made the perfect gullible couple. The macho male jocks knew that these two were a couple of blockheads, an easy mark. These two numbskulls were fair game when it came to anything the jocks needed from them. This attitude made me furious. So I took it on myself to protect the vulnerable pair. I stuck up for them and helped them out whenever I could. After all, wasn't it only right to protect the meek?

My guardianship of the susceptible earned their lasting friendship. So I knew that the fact that Simon Smallbury was going to be called to the stand could not be detrimental to me. Could it? I thought very hard about anything he might say that could possibly come across as negative. He had worked two days at my office for Elmer when Elmer was unable to make it to Goat Valley. Simon had driven out to our farm at the end of both of these days. We had walked and talked, and he seemed very impressed with my office, my staff, and my patients. He had confided in me that my practice was much better organized and smoothly run than his. What could he possibly say that would hurt me?

Then I remembered how totally terrified he was that first day of dental school, and it all came flooding over me. If he was properly intimidated by Brett Wratchett and the state of Georgia, he would be a prime candidate to crack. He would say anything they told him to. He would succumb to any pressure or harassment. He would be a good little soldier, just like in dental school. I realized this, and I began to sweat. I turned my attention toward the witness on the stand.

Brett Wratchett was already pulling rank on him. "Now, Dr. Smallbury, keep in mind that you are talking to a representative for the state of Georgia. Anything you say to me is the same as saying it to our state government, so think carefully about any of your answers to my questions, OK?"

The color drained from Simon's face. "Yes, sir," he responded.

"Dr. Smallbury, did you run Dr. Doramae Brookshire's dental office in Goat Valley, Georgia, while she was suspended from doing dentistry?"

"Why, yes, sir, I did."

"And what were the circumstances surrounding that, if you could tell us, please," Brett politely coaxed.

"Well, my friend Elmer Quimby had bought Dora's practice, and he could not make it to Goat Valley for a couple of days, so I saw his patients for him a couple of days."

"And by Dora, you mean Dr. Doramae Brookshire, correct?"

"Yes, sir, that is right. I call her Dora. We all did."

"And, Dr. Smallbury, please tell the jury some of the things that you discovered about Dr. Brookshire's practice."

Simon looked my way and then turned his signature shade of green. "Well . . ." He hesitated. "Her practice was full of Medicaid kids, lots of them pretty young."

"Please go on, Dr. Smallbury. Tell the jury what you told me about how Dr. Brookshire handled these kids," Brett prodded.

He glanced quickly in my direction again and then looked down at his feet. He hesitated. "I'm not sure what you mean," he offered up to Brett.

Brett looked pissed and desperate at the same time. He strutted over to his beloved easel and retrieved a long thin item from behind the easel. He cradled his find as he approached the shaken dentist. "Dr. Smallbury, could you please tell me what I am holding?" he teased.

"Yes, sir. That is a papoose board."

"A papoose board? What in the world are you talking about?" Brett was pulling out his theatrical side.

"Well, sir, we went over all this already." Simon was hoping for some mercy. He didn't want to have to define a dental pediatric papoose board to a roomful of people.

"Oh yes, Dr. Smallbury, I know that you and I went over this already, but I need you to explain this papoose board to the jury, please. Many of them have never heard of a papoose board, I'll bet," he emphasized.

Simon cleared his throat and faded color once more. He sat up perfectly straight. "Well, in the practice of pediatric dentistry, a papoose board is a temporary medical stabilization device used to limit a young patient's movement to decrease risk of injury."

"That is all fine and good, Dr. Smallbury, but please do go on. Tell the jury *exactly* what you told me. Remember? What you confided in me about these papoose boards?" He held the board straight up in the air and shook it with fury.

Simon looked down at the floor and shook his head ever so lightly. He sported his signature nauseous expression. He began to stutter. "We-e-e-l-l-l, I may have s-s-said that in my o-o-p-p-p-i-n-n-ion, papoose boards are a li-t-t-le c-c-c-ruel."

Brett gloated. "Oh, you think maybe?" He hoisted the papoose board back up in the air as if it was an Olympic medal. "You mean that this large hard wooden board with huge Velcro straps might be a little bit of a torture device for a tiny, little baby dental patient?" he shouted.

Jack sprang to his feet. "Objection, Your Honor!" he yelled.

Judge Grudge turned toward Brett. "Are you about done making your point, counselor?" He asked in a perturbed tone.

"Yes, Your Honor, I am about done making my point about these medieval torture devices for toddlers," he quickly fit in.

About this time, I realized the game that the state was playing. They had actually been playing the same game all week, ever since the trial began on Monday. And now it was Saturday. The game was called stall for time, drag one's feet, stooge around, get anyone and everyone up on the stand and then pull a courtroom filibuster. The state was using Judge Grudge's courtroom for a theatrical production, and Brett Wratchett was the main tap dancer on the state playbill. He was tap dancing all the way to Saturday afternoon, when the good judge had informed all parties about the finale of the production. If Brett and the gang could only hold off until Saturday afternoon, the state would have an automatic win. Why, the poor little defense would never even have had a turn to get up. They didn't stand a chance. I mean, really, what in the world did poor little Simon Smallbury testifying about papoose boards have to do with my charge of Medicaid fraud?

I turned my attention back toward the stand. Evidently, Brett had inflicted his appropriate dosage of poison on the poor jury, and it was Jack's turn to try to give them the antidote. Jack was adjusting his glasses and buttoning his suit coat. He approached the scared little witness with gentle caution. "Good morning, Dr. Smallbury," he softly said.

Some color returned to Simon's sallow face. "Good morning, sir," he returned.

"Now, Dr. Smallbury, let's talk about these papoose boards, why don't we?"

"OK, sir."

"Now it is my understanding a dental pediatric papoose board is a comfortable well-cushioned board with fabric Velcro straps that can be adjusted comfortably and used to help limit a small patient's movements and hold them steady during a dental procedure."

Simon looked relieved. "That is a good definition," he agreed.

"And furthermore, because this papoose board serves to limit the young patient's movements, it also greatly decreases the risk of injury while allowing safe completion of treatment," Jack observed.

"I could not have said it better myself," Simon agreed as if realizing for the first time the true advantages of the board.

"So one could say that the dental papoose board is a means of temporarily and safely limiting a young child's movements and that it is generally more effective than holding the child forcibly down."

"That's true," Simon rang out.

Jack continued, "And one more advantage to these papoose boards is that using a papoose board to temporarily and safely limit movement is often preferable to medical sedation, which presents serious potential risks to a young child."

Simon broke out in full smile. "You know, I never thought of that, but you are absolutely right about that." He appeared relieved to be able to look at these boards in a positive light.

Back at his station, Brett was fuming. How could Jack Goodman, simple trial attorney, possibly know so much about pediatric dental papoose boards—and off the top of his head at that? Brett had taken a stab in the dark with this one, and he had lost.

Now that Jack had won Simon over, he switched his line of questioning. "Thank you so much, Dr. Smallbury, for helping our judge and jury to understand the function of dental papoose boards. They came out to be a true functional aid for little patients and not the torturous device that the state would like us to believe they are." Brett and Judge Grudge rolled their eyes simultaneously.

"Let's change over to another subject now. Can you tell us when you first met Dr. Doramae Brookshire?"

"Oh, yes, sir, sure. I first met Dora in dental school."

"And dental school, I understand, is a four-year program. Am I correct, Dr. Smallbury?"

"That's right. Dental school is a four-year program," Simon agreed.

"And did you continue to know Dr. Brookshire during those four years? That is to say, do you think that you had a good enough friendship with Dr. Brookshire that you knew her fairly well?"

"Oh yes, sir. Dora and I were pretty good friends really."

"Could you elaborate a little more on that, please, Dr. Smallbury? What types of things did you and Dr. Brookshire do together during those four years of dental school?"

"Well, let me begin by saying this. Dora was always very helpful and caring about us other students. Any way she could help us with anything, she did. Everyone in the whole dental school knew her as the most excellent notetaker in lectures. She had some rare gift of being able to write real fast and capture every word said by the professor, but at the same time, her handwriting was extremely legible. As a result, her lecture notes were highly coveted since many of us, especially the jocks, did not even take notes. After a while, we all learned that, why should we take notes? Dora was doing the best job ever, and we could just get them from her. Somewhere along the line, another student suggested to her that she should charge a little fee for her notes since it was costing her so much time and money to copy them for everyone. So she ended up charging a minimal fee for a packet of her notes. This helped her with the expenses for copies and also probably gave her a small amount of money to help defer expenses at home. See, Dora had three young kids and a husband at home."

"Wow! That must have been a little difficult to have three little children at home and still make it through dental school."

"Oh yes. I have often wondered how she even did it. But you have to understand, Dora was very special. She had this kind, gentle nature. She could tell when someone was struggling. And she was always right there, ready to go that extra mile. When I was having a tough time in biochemistry, she tutored me. She helped me prepare for tests in other subjects, especially pharmacology. Why, she even slipped me some of her class notes for free."

"Sounds like Dr. Brookshire was a very compassionate and helpful ally. So you would agree that Dr. Brookshire was a pretty good friend of yours during those four years of dental school, huh?"

"I most certainly would. She was a very friendly, outgoing, warmhearted fellow classmate. And one more thing, she kinda sheltered me from the jocks whenever they were in the mood to pick on others. Know what I mean?"

"Yes, I think I understand where you are coming from, Dr. Smallbury. You said that Dr. Brookshire was your good friend, your tutor, your notetaker, and your protector. That would be during the four most difficult years of your life probably."

"I could not have said it better myself."

Jack radiated that famous south Georgia grin. He wheeled around on his heels to face the state prosecutor. "Redirect, Mr. Wratchett?" he inquired.

Brett looked nauseous once again. "No, I have nothing further," he mumbled.

The mighty judge looked pissed. "The witness may step down," He uttered.

Well, I thought, *that witness did not score the state many points. Jack had managed to paint a saintly picture of me through Simon Smallbury's eyes.*

Judge Grudge glared at Brett. "Call your next witness," He commanded.

"Your Honor, I call Amy Nelson to the stand," Brett replied.

Jack jumped up. "Your Honor, we object! I have no deposition from this witness, and she is not on our list of witnesses. We have not had a chance to depose her."

His Honor looked hard at Brett and then appeared as if He would look at Jack but stared at the floor instead. "I'll allow the witness. I would like to hear what she has to say."

Amy did not turn pale. She did not look scared or intimidated. She did not come across as nerdish. She stood up straight, squared her shoulders, and stared the judge down eyeball to eyeball. She walked briskly and confidently toward the witness stand and firmly took a seat. She swore in, the whole time glaring at Brett with disgust.

Brett approached the witness with caution. "Good morning, Ms. Nelson," he offered.

Amy hesitated. Fourteen pairs of jury eyes fixated on the newest state victim. Amy had been one of my favorite dental assistants in my practice. She was the poster child for women's lib and female confidence. She was a strong, independent woman. She always kept her hair dyed in streaked colors, and she cut it so it spiked straight up. She wore clothes that were both professional and plain. She wore very little makeup. She was a no-nonsense sort of girl. And she told it like it was.

"Good morning," she spat out. "I was wondering why I was asked here today." She stared icily at Brett.

Brett gulped audibly. He apparently did not know how to respond to a rather hostile witness. "You were asked here today to answer some questions about Dr. Doramae Brookshire, ma'am," he replied.

"What sort of questions and *why?*" she demanded.

Brett snapped out of his initial shock and returned to his usual jackass self. "The sorts of questions that the state of Georgia and the government of this great United States is *entitled* to ask anyone that we determine is essential to any case that we are prosecuting at the time, Mrs. Nelson!" he snapped.

His rude outburst did not faze Amy. "OK, do what you think you must do then," she threw back his way.

"Ms. Nelson, did you work for the defendant, Dr. Brookshire, in her dental practice in Goat Valley, Georgia?"

"Sure did."

"What years did you work for Dr. Brookshire?"

"I don't know exactly. I guess around 1993 to 1994 or so. I left her when I got my divorce and moved up here to Atlanta. That was in 1994."

"So you worked for Dr. Brookshire for about one year or so. Is that correct?" Brett asked.

"Yup, that's about right," she answered curtly.

"So would you say that you know Dr. Brookshire fairly well since you worked for her for one year?"

"Yup, I know her fairly well," she stated in a monotone. It was apparent that she was parroting his terminology.

"So if I were to ask you some questions about Dr. Brookshire's character, you would feel confident in answering such questions?"

Amy sighed loudly and looked as if she wanted to slap Brett. "Fire away."

"Ms. Nelson, did Dr. Brookshire ever file a procedure called management of difficult children on kids who were not misbehaving in her chair?"

Amy crossed her arms across her chest as if that posture would ward off the prosecutor. "*No, sir.* Dr. Brookshire had a large number of young children who were quite a handful in her dental practice. I can assure you that every single minute of behavior management that Dr. Brookshire filed was warranted. Actually, she deserved to be paid a lot more than Medicaid ever paid her, especially for behavior management of difficult children, because, believe me, these were *difficult children.*"

Seeing that he was getting nowhere fast on this subject, Brett decided to switch gears. "Well then, Ms. Nelson, let me ask you about another procedure. Do you ever recall Dr. Brookshire filing for dental sealants on children that she maybe forgot to place those sealants on?"

Amy shot the prosecutor a look of total disdain. "Oh, you mean, like, did Dr. Brookshire ever file for procedures that she flat out did not do? No, sir, she most certainly did not."

"Now stop and think before you answer so quickly. Her dental practice was very busy, I understand. And it was full of young children. These two factors can be very distracting and stressful. Maybe Dr. Brookshire just kind of forgot to place some of these sealants that she filed for, huh?"

"There you go again, just another way to call Dr. Brookshire a liar. Well, I can assure you that she was a very honest person. Nothing got filed that was not done."

Brett was not giving up. "Well, maybe you overheard her say something like she would go ahead and file for the sealants today but would maybe do them at the next appointment since the child had had enough today? Do you recall her saying something along those lines?"

Amy stared Brett down. She didn't answer for what seemed to be an eternity. Finally, she stated loudly and bluntly, "Nope, she never did that made-up scenario either."

"Let's go on then. Ms. Nelson, do you ever recall Dr. Brookshire placing unnecessary fillings on children?"

"Nope!" Amy snapped.

"Well, maybe you remember her fudging on the number of surfaces that a filling had? For example, maybe Dr. Brookshire would place a one-surface filling on a young child but then would file a two-surface filling with Medicaid. After all, you stated yourself that these kids were difficult children. Maybe Dr. Brookshire felt warranted in getting paid a little extra." Brett was not giving up.

Enough was enough. Amy was at her breaking point. She became unraveled. "*Excuse me, sir.* You just got done giving me endless made-up scenarios, every last one of them accusing Dr. Brookshire of being dishonest, cheating, and corrupt. Where do you get off anyway, trashing her and condemning her as a swindling, underhanded villain?"

Jack looked a bit puzzled. I know he was wondering the same thing I was at the moment. Why would Brett keep on and on, picking at a witness such as Amy until she snapped, the whole time sticking up for the defendant? This was exactly what the state did not want. But I had a pretty good idea of what was going on here.

The state had to stall one more day for time, a little more feet dragging, a little more courtroom tap dancing, a little more beating around the bush. It didn't really matter at this point that Amy was sticking up for me. The game here was stonewall for one more day—halt, hamper, hedge, hold off, and hinder. The state had been reduced to grasping at straws. They had gone on a fishing expedition of their own and had come up with a local Atlanta girl who had worked for me. It didn't really matter what she said as long as they kept the defense from being able to get up and present their side of the story. Brett and the boys most certainly did not want our Lancaster lab guy to be able to get on the stand and prove that I was indeed honest. And they didn't much want Dr. Savage to be able to get on the stand and tell the jury about poor, senile little Dr. Drupey who rubber-stamped every preapproval in Georgia. So these two subpoenaed witnesses, one who had traveled over two hundred miles to testify, were forced to sit outside the courtroom for hours while Brett delayed the process for his own purposes. After all, the good judge was going fishing in the morning, right?

Brett was looking a bit anemic. "Just one more thing, Ms. Nelson. Were you not pregnant when you worked for Dr. Brookshire?"

"Yup, part of the time. What does that have to do with anything?"

"Well, I noted that you worked up to the ninth month of pregnancy. Am I correct here?" Brett shot Amy a forlorn long look of sympathy.

"Yeah, maybe . . . *so*?"

Brett put his Sunday-school-boy face on. "Well, don't you think that it is a little heartless of an employer to work a nine-month pregnant employee, especially in a high-stress environment like that?"

Another long pause ensued while Amy shot daggers out of her eyeballs at Brett. "Unless the employee *needed* to work and *asked* to work up until the ninth month!"

That was finally it with Brett. He was getting nowhere fast. He was probably not used to a strong-willed, self-assured, dauntless witness like Amy. Besides, he probably felt like he had stalled a sufficient amount of time. So he finally turned the fearless witness over to Jack.

Jack smiled as he slowly sauntered over to Amy. "Good morning, Ms. Nelson." He stopped. "Or maybe it isn't such a great morning for you, huh?" he added, injecting some much-needed humor into the somber courtroom.

"It's never a great morning when underhanded people try their best to discredit good, honest, hardworking folks," Amy replied immediately, not missing a beat.

"Very true," Jack agreed. "And you know what? You have been picked on enough for one day. I certainly am not going to add to your stress. You had to drive all the way over here to Parvenu and answer all those questions, and I apologize for that. I know that you have two young children at home, and this is a Saturday."

"You're darn right about that. I had to find a babysitter and fight traffic and pay a bunch for gas and then try to locate this little Podunk town, just to be asked a whole bunch of rude-as-hell questions. Go figure."

"Well, Ms. Nelson, like I said, I am not going to add to your stress today. I want you to be able to get back to your kids and have some quality time with them on a Saturday. I only have two questions for you today."

Amy looked relieved. "OK, good deal. Fire away."

"Ms. Nelson, did Dr. Brookshire make you work against your will when you were nine months pregnant?"

"It wasn't like that at all. I *asked* her to let me work up until the baby was born. We needed the money, and my pregnancy was going fine. I felt great. I really appreciated Dr. Brookshire letting me work until the baby was born, and I told her so. Some *male* employers would never do that for me."

"Second question, Ms. Nelson, in your opinion, do you feel that Dr. Brookshire was or is, in any way, dishonest? Even a little? Give me any examples at all."

Amy sat up straight. She looked square at the jury. Then she swung around to make direct eye contact with Jack. "No, sir, I cannot give you one single example of Dr. Brookshire being in any way dishonest. She was, in fact, one of the most *honest* people that I have ever met."

Jack smiled gently at Amy. "Thank you, Ms. Nelson. Please be careful driving on your way home."

His Honor looked expressionless at Amy. "The witness is excused," He announced.

Amy stood up slowly, looked at Brett like he was a fool idiot, smiled warmly at Jack, shot me a brief sympathetic expression, and took off down the aisle, shaking her head as she exited.

Judge Grudge glanced at His watch. He cleared his throat. "Let's take a one-hour lunch. Everyone, be back promptly at two o'clock."

The jury filed out. I wondered how pissed they were for having to listen to made-up bullshit for six days now. Furthermore, I wondered how many of them were missing quality time on a Saturday with their kids. How many of them were wishing this rigged trial would be over soon? Me? I was just wishing that, by some miracle, our lab guy and Dr. Savage would be put on the stand this Saturday afternoon.

Lunch that day was pretty unremarkable, although looking back on it I should have really savored my last bites of decent food I was to see in a long time. When we returned to the courtroom, Bob, Dave, Mom, and I were met outside the courtroom by a bloodless, sickly, haggard-looking Jack. He was white as a sheet. I was so shocked to see him in the state he was in that I was pretty sure I gasped out loud.

He staggered toward us. "We need to call a family meeting *right now*," he stated. It was the strangest thing I had ever witnessed. He was visibly upset, yet he was still trying really hard to remain in control of both his emotions and the overall situation. "Here." He pointed to the bench in the hallway outside the courtroom, the bench where awaiting witnesses sat.

"All of you have a seat right here," he offered, looking like he might faint in the meantime. "The judge talked to me over lunch. He has given us twenty minutes to come to a decision."

What decision could he possibly be talking about? My mind quickly wandered to a concoction of possibilities. Was the good judge going to offer us some reasonable plea so that He could go fishing in the morning? If that was the case, the offered-up plea was going to have to be pretty lenient since Jack and Dave had done an excellent job of shooting down every allegation that Brett had asserted. Or maybe Judge Grudge had gotten really creative and cooked up some plea agreement that would leave both the prosecution and the defense at least partially satisfied. He might have come up with something like Dr. Brookshire would pay the state a phenomenal fine, enough to cover all the expenses of this unconventional trial. Yes, that was it. My fine was going to be so huge that the numbers had left Jack staggering and colorless. My daydream of possibilities ended abruptly when Jack began to speak once again.

"Judge Grudge has given us twenty minutes to make a decision. Now take the full time, talk it over as a family, and really weigh the consequences and the different scenarios. This is not going to be an easy decision. We all must look at the big picture here." Even more blood drained from my beloved attorney's face.

I got the distinct feeling that the judge's proposal was so awful, so horrendously dreadful, that Jack was having a helluva time verbalizing it. Of course, the totally logical one in the family spoke up at this point. "Jack, what is the judge's proposal?" Dave asked.

Jack drew in a labored long breath. He was so pallid now that he looked like he was constructed out of wax. "Judge Grudge has given us twenty minutes to decide if Dora wants to plead guilty at this point and go to jail immediately for ninety days or if she wants the trial to keep going, and in that case, if she is found guilty of even *one* count of Medicaid fraud, she would go to jail for *five years* with no chance of parole."

I felt my own face drain itself of blood. I glanced over at my family. They had become a clan of cadaverous statues. The utter disbelief that spread across their faces was indescribable. They were all left totally speechless for what seemed to be an eternity. After the initial shock wore off, the three members of my family brood reacted in a similar manner yet in uniquely different ways that reflected each of their distinct personalities. My poor eighty-year-old mom was tearing up and repeatedly saying, "I don't get it." Dave was remaining frozen in time. He looked like a deer caught in the headlights.

My cherished husband, the love of my life, offered up his opinion first. "God! Were we ever dumb as hell to try to fight the state! I knew better. I was always told, 'You can't beat city hall.' What on earth were we thinking? I'll tell you what we were thinking. We actually thought that if we were innocent, and we *were*, justice would prevail. What naive idiots we were! We should have known better. This asshole judge can't let the state lose. Did we really think that we had a chance in hell? That we were playing on a level field? Jesus, I am *so sorry*, Dora. This is all my fault. You were too close to the situation to think clearly, and I should have protected you. I should have told you to take one of the endless pleas that the state offered us before the trial. If we would have, right now, you would have paid a stiff fine, served a short probation, and been done with this whole nightmare. I let you down by making this ridiculously *stupid* decision, and I will *never* forgive myself for this!" He looked straight at me, his eyes welling up with tears. They spilled out onto his saddened face, running down his colorless cheeks. He made no attempt to wipe them. He was a fifty-fifty mixture of rampant rage and suffering sorrow.

Dave became unfrozen, and his logic kicked in. He turned toward Jack and asked, "Now in your opinion, what are our chances of continuing on and winning this thing?"

Jack's grim face said it all. "Well . . ." He paused for what seemed a very long time. His troubled eyes rolled back in his head. "In cases like this . . . and what you've got to understand is that this is a very unique case . . . not very many defendants take on the state of Georgia . . . most of them take a plea before trial . . . like I said, in cases like this, most jury members try to come up with a verdict that splits the baby. In other words, the jury thinks that by finding the defendant guilty of maybe 1 count of Medicaid fraud, this is very fair, and both sides win somewhat. What the jury does not know, and the state will not tell them this . . . is that by finding Dora guilty of even *1 single count* of Medicaid fraud, it is the same as finding her guilty of all 246 alleged counts. The law makes no difference between guilty of one count or guilty of 246 counts. The punishment is the same. The way the state of Georgia looks at it is guilty is guilty. Of course, the judge is not going to let the jury know this before their deliberations. They will go into the deliberation room thinking that 1 count of guilty out of 246 counts will not get Dora much of a sentence at all. This scenario is what I am afraid of."

Dave kept on, "But if we continue on with the trial and we *win*, Dora will go home with no fines, no probation, no dental license loss, no punishment whatsoever. Am I correct?"

Jack looked squarely at Dave, the first glimmer of hope in his eyes. "That's right, *if* we can win this thing."

Nobody spoke. I remained a statue in shock. Jack glanced at his watch. "Oh god! Time's almost up! If we don't get this decision made within the allotted twenty minutes, there's no telling what the judge will do!"

Bob spoke once again. He turned toward my frozen body and gently took my frigid hands in his. He got right into my petrified stone face, violating my personal space. "Hon," he silently whispered, "you know what we have to do here. We will have grandkids within five years . . . and I can't bear the thought of living without you for five long years. We just *can't* take the chance, beautiful. You have no other choice but to take the guilty plea and the ninety days. I am so, so sorry. But we have got to take the ninety days. It'll go quickly. I will come visit you every single day that they will let me. I promise. I'll be there with you. We'll make it through this together, just like we always do. You know this is the only possible decision."

He pitifully added, "Do this for me, for the kids, for our future grandkids, OK?"

I surveyed the scene. My elderly mother was now silently weeping, her wrinkled hands shaking with every sob. She was trying very hard to not make a spectacle of herself. I had known her my whole life as a strong and even stoic woman. I had only seen her cry once before, when my father had died a sudden and shocking death. To witness her in this highly emotional state made a wave of woeful melancholy sweep over me. I suddenly wished that I had not succumbed her to this trial of torture, this circus of Georgia state clowns. What had I been thinking?

Dave had returned to his state of stone. I knew that he was a guy of logic, a true thinker. But I also knew this about my younger brother: He was a believer in the system. Unlike me, he was a person of rationality, of facts; and because of this way of thinking, he had always believed that the truth will always prevail, that the person in the right will always win. The cowboy with the white hat (or in this case, the cowgirl) will always win and ride off into the sunset and live happily ever after. Dave never factored in such things as corrupt judges and morally rotten state prosecutors. Bribery and absence of moral fiber never crossed his mind. Dave was always the one member of the family who could solve any problem you could throw his way, and he did a downright excellent job of solving every last one of them. But this one was his Pandora's box. There was no possible solution this time. So my poor brother, the one who had taken time off from his busy dental practice in Indiana to come rescue me in Georgia, sat on that hard wooden bench in the hallway with a stunned expression frozen across his shocked face. My highly intelligent, confident, articulate brother was stupefied into speechlessness.

Jack looked at his watch and slumped down, ready to pass out and hit the floor. I knew I had to act. It was now or never. I chiseled the stone off my statuelike body and jumped up off the bench. My coming alive caused the other family members to twitch in alarm. I looked over at Jack. I reached out my shaking hand. "Come on, Jack, let's take a walk," I said.

He took my offered hand and said, "OK, let's go."

My head was spinning. My mouth was dry. My legs were like concrete. My heart was broken in half. But the fact was that I had one minute left, one measly minute between me and my freedom. That son-uv-a-bitchin' judge! Who did He think He was? He could have at least given us more than twenty mangy little minutes to make the decision of a lifetime. Oh but then, I forgot. His Honor was about to miss His fishing trip. He was probably used to throwing His defendants under the bus to be able to make all His luxurious vacations on time. This was nothing to Him. I guess the corrupt get numb over time. Oh well, He was probably thinking, *Another scummy person in the clinker. That's how it goes.*

All of a sudden, the lyrics to a popular song in Georgia popped into my muddled head:

And the judge said *guilty* in a make-believe trial,
Slapped the sheriff on the back with a smile,
And said, "Supper's waitin' at home, and I gotta get to it."

As Jack and I made our walk of weighing decisions, this was how the rushed conversation went. Jack said with forced enthusiasm, "Dora, we have done very well so far on this trial. I think we may have a very good chance at winning this thing. I have gotten up on this horse with you, and I am willing to ride this horse to the finish line. Just give me the word, and we'll go on."

I must have looked at him like I had some doubt, so he went on to add, "I have never in all my years as a trial attorney faced anything remotely like this. Judges are usually not this blatantly unethical and corrupt. He has openly and unashamedly given us an impossible decision to make and in an impossible amount of time."

Everything Jack had said was true. The judge *was* corrupt and unethical. The judge's ultimatum *was* impossible. The amount of time given to make our decision was likewise impossible. I believed that Jack had never faced such a decision up until now. But something else became crystal clear to me on that fateful courthouse walk with Jack. One thing I no longer believed was that we had a fighting chance to win this trial. A judge crooked enough to do what Judge Grudge had just done was certainly also crooked enough to make sure that I lost by any means possible if I elected to go on with the trial. Besides, if I decided to go on with the trial and His Honor missed His sacred fishing trip, oh, what destruction and havoc would befall my pitiful ass! There would be weeping and gnashing of teeth. I would suffer the torments of the damned in hell. So I knew what I had to do.

We walked silently back, Jack and me, a defeated duo of doom. I think he knew at this point what I was going to do. He most likely did not blame me. Jack's wife, years later at our son's wedding, would tell me that Jack was never the same after my trial. He never trusted the system from that day forward.

As I approached my heartbroken husband, our eyes met. His words came rushing back to me. He was right about the future grandchildren. We had two sons, aged twenty-seven and twenty-four, and a daughter, aged twenty-two at the time. They had all been so overcome with emotion over their mom having to go to trial that they could not bring themselves to show up. If I chose to go on with the trial, the jury found me guilty of even one count of Medicaid fraud, and I went to jail for five years with no chance of parole, our kids would be ages thirty-two, twenty-nine, and twenty-seven. The chances of missed weddings and missed births of grandchildren were very big. And if I were to miss my children's weddings and the births of my grandchildren, it would rip my heart right out.

"I'm gonna take the plea and the ninety days," I announced sadly to my family.

Bob breathed a sigh of relief. Mom gasped and began to silently weep. Dave stared straight ahead and remained a carving of wood.

Jack looked down at his shoes and shook his head slowly. "Let's go tell the judge then. We are at twenty-seven minutes here." He looked forlornly at me and then at Bob. He told me, "Go ahead and say goodbye. You will be escorted right from the guilty plea in the courtroom straight to the Coward County Jail. This is your last chance to say goodbye."

I had remained numb and stoic to that point. But as my husband of twenty-eight years held me in his arms for the final farewell, I finally broke down. I buried my swimming head in his sturdy shoulder, and I sobbed. It was the cry of the abandoned, the forsaken, the truly forlorn.

After a minute, I pulled myself together and gave my mother a quick hug. "It'll be fine, Mom," I lied. "Ninety days is nothing. I'll make it just fine. I'll be out before you know it."

Then I went over to my brother—my brother who had worked his heart out to come to my rescue, my brother who had left his own world behind temporarily to help save my world. I bent down and gave him a hug. It was like hugging a metal robot. He was still in shock over what had transpired. The system was not supposed to be like this. This did not figure into his neat, structured, honest universe. I said a silent prayer for him to come back to life.

Then I buttoned my black suit jacket, straightened my fitted black skirt, smoothed my rumpled hair, and told Jack, "Let's go do this."

THE LIGHTS WENT OUT IN GEORGIA

"WE HAVE TO meet the judge in his chambers, and then we will make the guilty plea publicly in the courtroom in front of the jury," he informed me.

"OK, let's go," I tried to say with confidence for the sake of my grieving family. I held my head up high and walked straight ahead, following Jack's lead. We went through a heavy, beautifully ornate hand-carved mahogany door and into His Honor's chambers. My frightened eyes quickly scanned the room. His chambers were quite extravagant. Volumes upon volumes of leather-bound law journals with gold-gilded print lined shelf after fancy shelf. I thought that no human being alive could possibly read that many publications cover to cover. The one window in the chambers was covered with a material that was so plush and swanky that I had never seen anything like it. The walls were all painted in a very tasteful dark color. This gave His chambers the feel of a dark dungeon. Above our heads was a high vaulted, elaborately embellished ceiling. Under our feet was lush, cushy, high-quality carpeting.

Judge Ebenezer B. Grudge was sitting behind the most lavishly adorned desk I had ever seen. It was constructed out of some kind of fine wood and boasted of tiny ornamental gingerbread carvings up and down its four legs. His Honor was rearing back in his cushy black chair, still wearing his long flowing black robe. An expression of pure relief was spread across His honorable face. He was going to make His fishing trip after all. He had forced our hand just in the nick of time.

When He saw us, He motioned for us to come forward. He instructed me to stand behind a wooden podium, close enough to Him to be able to hear me yet far enough away from Him that He didn't have to get up close and personal with a self-convicted felon. "Mrs. Brookshire, I understand that you wish to plead guilty at this time," He stated matter-of-factly.

"Yes, Your Honor," I choked out.

"That being so, I need you to answer several routine questions. Your answers to these questions will be duly recorded."

At this point, I noticed the court reporter enter the chambers through a side door. She was toting her little machine. She silently and quickly set up close to the good judge and was ready to record my desperate lie of a plea in no time. But before she could get started recording my forced untruths, yet another character in this tragic play slinked in through the judge's secret passageway. I recognized the intruder as none other than Brett Wratchett, the court jester. I suddenly realized that the district attorney probably had to be present at the guilty plea. He stood a good distance from us, announcing his unhappiness with the outcome of the trial to the judge.

He leaned over to Judge Grudge and whispered, "Don't you think this is a little *lenient* on the defendant? After all, she is pleading guilty to Medicaid fraud. We were asking for *ten years*."

The judge ignored Brett's whining and turned toward Jack and me, both of us leaning on the podium for strength. "OK then, let's get started," He announced, anxious to get home and get packed for His trip.

The bailiff swore me in. *This is great*, I thought. *I just swore to tell the truth about something that I am going to be forced to lie my ass off about.*

His Honor cleared His throat. He looked down at a paper crammed full of tiny words. Then He looked straight at me. "Are you able to hear and understand My statements and questions?"

"Yes."

"Are you now under the influence of any alcohol, drugs, or any other substance?"

"No."

"Has your lawyer explained the charges against you?"

"Yes."

"Do you understand that you have a right to a jury trial?"

"Yes."

"Do you understand that you could have a jury trial by pleading not guilty or by remaining silent and not entering a plea?"

"Yes."

"Do you understand that you have the right to assistance of counsel during trial?"

"Yes."

"Do you understand that you are entitled to the presumption of innocence?"

"Yes."

"Do you understand that you have the right not to incriminate yourself?"

"Yes."

"Do you understand that, at a jury trial, you would have the right to question witnesses against you, the right to subpoena witnesses on your own behalf, and the right to testify yourself and to offer other evidence?"

"Yes."

"Do you understand that by pleading guilty, you are giving up all those rights?"

"Yes."

"Has anyone made any threats or promises to influence you to plead guilty in this case?"

I hesitated. Wasn't a guaranteed five-year sentence if we went on with the trial a threat of sorts? But I answered the way He wanted me to because my hand was forced. "No."

"Have you had a chance to discuss your case with your lawyer?"

"Yes."

"Who is your lawyer?"

Jack stepped forward. "Jonathon J. Goodman III, State Bar Number 249703," he answered. Judge Grudge made me repeat this information on Jack.

"Are you satisfied with the services and advice of your lawyer?"

"Yes."

"Do you understand that the district attorney has made the following recommendations: ten years to serve two, restitution of $45,000, fine of $5,000, investigative costs of 3,500?"

I looked at Jack. I was not about to agree to all that, especially the jail time. But before Jack could advise me, the judge had moved on to the next question.

"The maximum sentence for these charges would be ten years. Do you understand that the court is not bound by any promises or recommendations and that the court can impose that sentence?"

I looked at Jack once again. He leaned over and whispered, "Go ahead and answer yes. They will not give you ten years."

"Yes," I said hesitantly. *Am I supposed to believe anything at this point?*

"How do you plead to the charge, count 2, Medicaid fraud only, guilty or not guilty?"

I swallowed hard. Here came my great lie. "Guilty." I gasped.

"Are you, in fact, guilty?"

Were they kidding me? They were forcing me to lie under oath. I had never told a flat-out bald-faced lie after swearing on the Bible. I wasn't really sure that I could do this. But then I remembered my basis for deciding to lie and say I was guilty—our hurting kids, the future grandkids, my guilt-ridden, grieving husband.

"Yes," I squeezed out.

"Do you want to plead guilty?"

I looked at Jack. My eyes said it all. *Are they really forcing me to commit perjury here just so the judge can go fishing?* my sad eyes begged. But Jack was used to courtroom pleas, and my self-slander was not as revolting to him as it was to me. I swallowed the small amount of vomitus that had erupted into my mouth from my churning stomach.

"Yes," I lied.

"Have you understood all these questions and given truthful answers?"

"Yes," I perjured myself once again.

Judge Grudge reared back in his chair. I was dizzy with committing courtroom deceit. I had just sworn to tell the truth, the whole truth, and nothing but the truth, so help me God, and then had gone on to verbalize falsehood after fraudulent falsehood. *Was I, in fact, guilty? Hell no! Did I want to plead guilty? Hell no again! Had I given truthful answers? No, no, no! Had anyone made threats of any kind to get me to plead guilty? Wuh, yeah!*

Now the question became, was I going to make it through this living hell before I passed out and hit the floor face-first on His Honor's top-notch carpet?

I was swooning as Jack stepped up to the podium and politely inquired, "Your Honor, could I ask once again for Dr. Brookshire to receive first offender status?" This act allowed anyone who had no prior charges or convictions in their lifetime to receive a few breaks as a first offender.

The judge looked pissed. "Mr. Goodman, we have been through this over and over, and my answer is still the same. No! The defendant does not *deserve* to receive first offender status. Her crime is too serious. Do not ask me this again, or I will hold you in contempt of court!"

Jack took two steps back. "Yes, sir, Your Honor." He breathed.

Then instead of getting first offender status, I was forced to stand there and read the following:

Sworn to and subscribed before me this 15th day of May 1999.

Lucius P. Tromp/Abilene T. Hatfield
DEPUTY CLERK, COWARD SUPERIOR COURT

CERTIFICATE

The undersigned Presiding Judge hereby certifies:

I. That the above-named defendant was sworn in open court and the questions were asked him as set forth in the foregoing transcript, and the answers given thereto by said defendant are as set forth therein.

II. That the defendant, Doramae Brookshire, being represented by attorney, [blank, not filled in], who was (court appointed) or (privately employed), pled guilty as charged in the (Bill of Indictment) (Accusation) (or) to the lesser included offense of [blank, not filled in], and in open court, under oath, further informs the court that he is and has been (1) fully advised of his rights and the charges against him; (2) the maximum punishment for said offense charged, and for the offense to which he pleads guilty; (3) that he is guilty of the offense to which he pleads guilty; (4) that he authorized a plea of guilty to said charge; (5) that he has had ample time to confer with his attorney and to subpoena witnesses desired by him; (6) that he is ready for trial; (7) that he is satisfied with the counsel and services of his attorney. And after further examination by the court, the court ascertains, determines and adjudges that the plea of guilty by the defendant is freely, understandingly and voluntarily made, and was made without undue influence, compulsion of duress, and without promise of leniency. It is, therefore, ordered that this plea of guilty be entered on the minutes, and that this Transcript and Certificate be filed with the (Indictment) (Accusation).

Date: <u>May 15, 1999</u>   [Judge Grudge's signature]

If my splitting head wasn't swimming before, it certainly was after reading all this pure bullshit about some guy referred to repeatedly as "he" and "him." You could have thought that they might have taken the time to revise all the pronouns in the cooked-up charge sheet from "he" and "him" to "she" and "her." But then that would suggest that somebody in that courtroom gave a shit about me.

To prolong the torture, I was then forced to read and sign the following:

I have read or heard all of the above questions and answers and understand them to be the questions asked of me and the answers I have given in open court, and they are true and correct.

I sighed and signed my name to this falsehood. These courtroom clowns were really making sure that they had it signed, sealed, and delivered in every way possible. They knew how to cover their shady little asses. They were not new to this underhanded game.

But the torment and agony went on and on. Then they made Jack sign, "I hereby certify that the above questions were asked the defendant and the answers were given by the defendant in my presence."

But that was not all. Oh, no. Then Brett Wratchett made me sign an added handwritten statement, inserted in the document's margins. It stated the following: "The defendant, Doramae Brookshire, waives formal arraignment, and pleads GUILTY TO COUNT 2 ONLY." Then he signed below my name and made Jack sign below his name.

I was feeling light headed, weak in the knees. They were just about to succeed in rubbing me out. Next up in the courtroom Greek tragedy was "Judge Grudge Pretends to Care."

"We are ready to go into the courtroom and have the defendant plead guilty in front of the jury. But just let me say this first. This has been a very sad and unfortunate case for the court to have been a part of." With that, He arose from His comfy chamber chair and led us into His courtroom.

We all followed His holy Honor into His omnipotent courtroom like baby ducks waddling after their mama. As soon as we were back in the courtroom, the jury filed in. All present stood until His Honor said, "Thank you. Be seated, please."

Zady Luna, Brett Wratchett's assistant attorney general, asked, "Judge, do you have the indictment?"

Judge Grudge replied, "I have the indictment. This is a plea on count 1, is that correct?"

Zady Luna looked bored. "Yes," she answered.

Then Jack said, "I think she is pleading to count 2 of the indictment."

This was followed by several minutes of courtroom frenzy. Ms. Luna began to frantically shuffle papers. Brett joined in, with a disgusted look on his face directed toward her. The good judge glared at both parties, repulsed by their incompetence yet totally confused about the correct answer Himself. This courtroom pandemonium drove home the fact that none of these people gave one iota of a shit about me or my case. I was just another number to them. They couldn't even get the charges against me straight. What a roomful of legal buffoons!

After what seemed to be an eternity, His Honor announced, "It's count 1—I'm sorry, it's count 2. Let's go ahead and proceed. I'd like the state to review the transcript with Ms. Brookshire and counsel."

I had remained Ms. Brookshire throughout the entire trial, according to the state and His Honor. Not once had they referred to me as Dr. Brookshire. They had stripped me of my title. I soon learned that Judge Grudge's request to Brett to "review the transcript" meant that Brett was instructed to ask me every single question that had been interrogated of me in the judge's chambers, only this time the torture was to take place in front of the jury, my grief-stricken mom, my bewildered brother, and my distraught husband.

Jack asked the judge, "Does Dr. Brookshire need to come up here?"

The judge replied, "Yes."

Then His Honor looked in the direction of the jury and added, "Let me just state for the record, in the case on trial, counsel have advised the court that Mrs. Brookshire wishes to enter a plea of guilty."

I looked over at the jury. A look of total disbelief spread over their shocked faces like a case of the black plague had suddenly swept over them. Their jaws all hung open in startled stupor. Fourteen confused people had been hit with a ton of bricks. They had been thrown into a courtroom concussion. Their bewildered faces were paralyzed with the jarring jolt of a curveball that had been hurled in their direction. Anyone who could read facial expressions in the least could easily tell that all fourteen jurors were in a state of complete surprise.

Later, after the whole courtroom drama of my forced guilty plea had played completely out, after the double whammy had been slapped on all of us present, after the deputy led me off in handcuffs, Jack and Jan had taken a post-trial poll of the jurors. Jack had informed me that thirteen of the fourteen jurors were leaning toward a not guilty verdict at the time of my guilty plea. It was the one juror who believed I was guilty that haunted me and let me know that I had probably made the correct split-second decision.

After Judge Grudge informed all in the room of my decision to enter a plea of guilty, there was several minutes of Brett and the good judge and Jack going back and forth about the factual basis for the court accepting the plea of guilty being outlined by the state in its opening statement. Brett sucked up to the judge and told Him that he would have the transcript of the state's opening statement prepared, asking the court to adopt it and to find that the opening statement was supported by evidence and that there was a factual evidence for the entry of a plea, to which the judge replied, "The court so finds."

Then Jack injected, "If I might inquire, the opening statement is much broader, I believe, than what I understand to be our plea."

Judge Grudge once again looked miffed. He knew that it was time to get this courtroom whammy done and over with. So He decided to throw in some legal mumbo jumbo. "It's just the factual basis for the court accepting this plea has been related to the court by virtue of the opening statement of the state in this case to give the court a factual basis on which to accept the plea of guilty, together with the evidence presented in trial, but it's primarily on the basis of the outline of the case as we do in a plea without a trial."

I glanced over my shoulder at the jury. Their shock had turned into unsettled revolt. Their earthquake encounter was starting to sink in. Now they were offended, almost nauseated with disgust. No longer perplexed or dumbfounded, it was as if they had figured it out. They did not know *why* I had suddenly pled guilty, but they somehow instinctively knew that some kind of foul play had transpired.

Brett Wratchett was onstage in the theater of deceit. He played the role of the slippery eel. He was fully prepared to bamboozle and hornswoggle and outright trick the room into believing that I was a hardened criminal. He had squeezed out his much-sought-after guilty plea. It was his day in the sun. He snickered softly and shot me a look of courtroom victory. "Ms. Brookshire, will you raise your right hand?"

I obeyed and was "duly sworn in."

Brett smirked and began to ask me every single question that Judge Grudge had already asked me in His chambers. My elderly mother, my dumbfounded brother, my heart-grieved husband, and fourteen bewildered yet pissed-off jurors were forced to listen to the same twenty-one painful questions that I had already answered and signed off to just minutes before. But Brett was having the time of his life asking them. He especially emphasized the particular questions that I was perjuring myself big time to answer.

"How do you plead to the charge, guilty or not guilty?" He sneered.

I gulped. "Guilty," I once again lied.

He shot me a sardonic grin. "Are you, in fact, *guilty?*" he mocked.

My brain was mush. All of a sudden, my vision went blurry, and Brett was moving in slow motion. The words coming out of his measly little piehole were frozen up in the air and were spewing forth like a video playing at the wrong speed and dragging people's words out for eternity. His incriminating inquiries were creeping at a funeral pace. I wanted so badly to see the faces of my family, to pull the support and the unconditional love out of their heartsick bodies and use it for strength to make it through this. But my back was to both my family and the jury. The court had positioned me so that the only faces I could see were Brett's and the judge's. Jack was allowed to stand behind me.

Brett continued the torture. "Do you want to *plead guilty?*"

"Yes," I weakly replied. I did not know how much longer I could remain upright.

He curled his vindictive lip. "Have you understood all these questions and given truthful answers?"

"Yes," I lied.

But Mr. Wratchett was not done with his theater of the absurd. He was having too much fun in the spotlight. He needed to inflict a few more devastating blows. He turned toward Judge Grudge—suck-up time.

"Your Honor, the defendant and her counsel have signed the transcript, and we will assist the court in taking whatever steps are necessary to obtain the certification."

Judge Grudge was ready to get this over with so He could go fishing. "If you will hand it to me, I'll place it in the file. We'll get it properly attested." Then He turned toward me. "Very well, Mrs. Brookshire—"

Brett kept on, "She needs to sign the plea, Your Honor."

The judge looked annoyed. "I'm sorry. I thought she had already done that."

Jack spoke up. "Your Honor, we are pleading guilty to count 2?"

Judge Grudge looked bored. "Correct," He answered.

Jack didn't trust these court jesters any more than I did. He grabbed his chance to set the record straight.

"Medicaid fraud only, and I understand that the other two counts will either be nolle prossed or merge."

The head clown answered, "Count 3 merges with count 2, and it is my understanding from what the attorney general represented to the court that count 1 will be nolle prossed."

Then without missing a beat, He turned to Brett and said, "Thank you, Mr. Wratchett."

A split second later, He looked expressionless at me and droned out, "Very well, Mrs. Brookshire. Do you have anything you would like to say to the court before I accept your plea and sentence you?"

My head was swimming. Oh, yes, there were countless things I would like to say to the court at this time. Let's start with *This is the most screwed-up, downright corrupt, unethical, unconscionable, dark, sinister, slippery, devious shit I have ever seen!* Then let's go on to *You all should be the charged felons! You shameless, unscrupulous, unprincipled, crooked little assholes!* But I didn't say those things. Instead, I just answered, "No, sir."

Jack jumped in once again. He probably had read my vibes and wanted to fill in the air to save me from a verbal vomit of words. "Your Honor, we addressed the court in chambers and the things that were said there, I think, will stand without necessarily being on the record."

Judge Grudge ignored Jack's observation. He turned back at me. "And do you want the court to accept your plea of guilty at this time?" He asked me.

"Yes," I replied, ready to get the endless torture over but no such luck. It dragged on.

"You do understand that you have the right to continue with the jury trial?" Grudge teased.

My body swooned. "Yes."

"And have the jury determine your guilt or innocence?"

Boy, this shifty little snake was making triple sure that the jury had no idea of His backroom, underhanded, fraudulent forced deal! "Yes," I repeated to the same reworded question.

"But it's your desire to plead guilty at this time?" He was apparently enjoying prolonging the agony.

"Yes," I spat out.

"Very well, Mrs. Brookshire." He turned toward the jury and put on His pathetic, fake, caring face. "This has been a very sad, very tragic overall situation for the court to have been a part of."

I thought at that point, *It most certainly has. I doubted if any judge had ever sunk quite that low.*

Then He quickly turned away from the befuddled jury and back toward me. He lost His empathetic face. "I will accept your plea of guilty and sentence you under count 2 of the indictment to ten years to serve one year in prison. I will suspend that one year on your entry into and successful completion of the detention center program. It's an alternative to incarceration. I will expect you to successfully complete the terms and conditions of probation, and those terms and conditions, in addition to completing the detention center, are as follows: you are to pay restitution to the state of Georgia in the amount of $60,000, you are to pay a $5,000 fine, you are to pay attorneys' fees in the amount of $3,500 to the state for the attorneys' fees incurred by the attorney general's office."

Brett Wratchett's face flushed. "Your Honor, those would be investigative costs."

Judge Grudge glared at Brett. His Honor did not like being interrupted while sentencing His latest felon. "Is that what they are?"

"Yes," Brett whispered.

"Okay, they are not attorneys' fees. They are investigative costs to be reimbursed to the state. Thank you for that correction." The judge continued, "And you are to pay a supervision fee—a probation supervision fee of $23 per month. Do you understand that?"

"Yes." I gulped.

"Will you comply with these terms and conditions of probation without excuses?"

"Yes, sir."

"I'm confident that you will."

Brett was not done. He stole back the spotlight. "Your Honor, also, as we discussed, as an additional term of probation, the state would ask that the court impose on her the requirement that she not seek to reobtain her dental license and that she not be employed for any entity that submits claims to the Georgia Medicaid program."

His Honor replied, "I think that's a reasonable request to have as a condition of probation." He turned to Jack. "Would you like to respond to that, Mr. Goodman?"

Jack said, "I'll note that my client's current occupation is that she heads an adult literacy program, and I don't know whether any state or federal funds go to that, but I assume that—"

Brett rudely interrupted Jack, "I think the only thing the state would be entitled to ask is that she not work for any business entity that submits claims to a health-care program funded by the state, which is the Medicaid program."

Judge Grudge sighed. He was more than ready to get this over with. It was Saturday afternoon, and His boat was ready on Sunday. "All right, I'll make that a condition of probation for the period of probation. And the further request was that she not practice dentistry?"

Brett answered, "She agree not to seek to have her dental license restored."

The judge corrected, "Dental license restored during this period of probation."

Jack looked at me and probably observed my swaying back and forth and my green color. He decided to help the agony go away quicker. "She has no intention of that, Your Honor."

"All right then. That will be a further condition of probation," He ordered.

The judge looked at me and decided to end the courtroom theater by pretending to give the poor felon a little break. "A further request was made of defendant's counsel in chambers that I will approve. I will authorize Mrs. Brookshire to serve in a detention center that is closest in geographical proximity to Goat Valley, Georgia, and will allow this probation, when she has completed the detention center, to be transferred to Redd County." Having done a favor for me to appease His guilty conscience, He turned toward me and—failing to make eye contact—said with fake enthusiasm, "Very well, good luck to you, Ms. Brookshire."

Having ended His honorable obligation to me, He turned toward Brett and said, "Counsel, if you will, please retrieve all your exhibits."

And with that, my week of pure torture was ended. But so was my life as I had known it—Sunday school girl. Straight-A student. Daughter of a well-respected community leader and orthodontist. Decorated Girl Scout. Community volunteer. Meals on Wheels deliverer. Each One Teach One volunteer tutor. Sunday school teacher. Magna Cum Laude graduate. Elementary school teacher. GED teacher to female inmates. Teacher of adult literacy. Dental school student. Dental school peer tutor. The dentist in Goat Valley who accepted Medicaid children.—All this erased. Gone forever. My new role? *Convicted felon.*

-THE END-

ADDENDUM A

H ERE IS MY attempt at explaining each and every one of the
state's charges against me. I will try to keep it simple and brief:

- All in A. is true. I did sign a statement of participation agreement,
  in which I agreed to be bound by the policies and procedures of
  the department of medical assistance, *and I did adhere to those
  policies and procedures.*

- The state charged in B. that I "followed a practice of scheduling
  large numbers of Medicaid recipients for dental appointments." I
  pose the question, Exactly how many patients per day is "a large
  number"? For example, I have a good friend who attended dental
  school with me who has gone on to become an orthodontist. She
  sees about seventy-five patients per day. I realize that comparing
  a general family dental practice with an orthodontic practice
  is somewhat comparing apples with oranges; however, I never
  saw anywhere near the number of patients she saw daily. I
  averaged ten to twelve patients a day, and I have records to
  prove it. This is not an excessive number of patients. I never ever
  overscheduled, as they were intimating, simply to make more
  money. I would never place my patients in that sort of jeopardy.
  B. also alleges, "Most of the Medicaid recipients treated by
  Doramae Brookshire were children." I guess most of them were
  because the cutoff age for dental Medicaid patients in the state
  of Georgia was twenty-one years old (with the exception of
  exams, certain X-rays, and extractions for adults).

- All the information in C. is pretty accurate. Scarlett Vesper
  did serve as my office manager pretty much, although I'm not
  really sure that I ever truly called her that. She did prepare the

daily schedules, make appointments, and fill out the Medicaid claims for submittal.

- Charge D. states that "Doramae Brookshire and Scarlett Vesper worked together in close cooperation on the preparation and submission of Medicaid claims." This is how it worked: When I was done with a patient's procedure, I (or one of my dental assistants) would write down exactly what I had performed on that patient, and then the patient's file would go to the front desk. Scarlett would then prepare to submit the procedures to Medicaid electronically. (She would type them on the computer but not submit them yet until I had a chance to look over them for accuracy.) At the end of the day, I would review these submittals before they went out. To be very truthful, I was sometimes too exhausted to check them each and every day. They occasionally went out without my checking over them, but this was the exception. I tried my best to be very accurate and conscientious with what we submitted. The second part of charge D. states, "Doramae Brookshire and Scarlett Vesper kept most information regarding Medicaid claims confidential from other employees." I know what the state was hinting here that Scarlett and I were performing some kind of deep-laid plot or secretive scheme to steal the state's money, so we could never let anyone else around us know any "information regarding Medicaid claims." The truth is this: Because of the nature of the way the claims were submitted (Scarlett prepared them, and then I reviewed them), not many of the other staff members ever had reason or need to see the claims. In fact, I don't remember any of my other staff members ever asking to see the Medicaid claims. They were too busy handling their own jobs. However, if any of the other staff members would have asked about the Medicaid claims, I would have been happy to have sat down with them, let them see some claims, and explain how it worked to them.

- E. was the biggie. There were fifteen charges under this one. Charge E. is supposed to explain why my Medicaid claims were "false and fraudulent."

   o No. (1) alleged that preauthorization forms were submitted for treatments that were not medically necessary. *Certain dental procedures, under the rules and regulations of Medicaid, had to be preapproved.* That meant that I had to submit a request on a Medicaid-produced form asking permission, basically, to perform certain needed procedures soon. These preauthorization forms were submitted in the mail along with X-rays of the patient's teeth. Then a retired dentist at the Medicaid office in Atlanta had to read each and every preauthorization form, decide whether the procedure being requested by the dentist was necessary, and send the form back to the dentist's office. This whole procedure usually took around one to two months to accomplish. During the wait for the preauthorization form to make its rounds, the patient often suffered. The dentist who was making the decisions at the Medicaid office could either place his signature (his "stamp") by the requested procedure or reject the procedure, deeming it "unnecessary." I can remember only a couple of incidences when my preauthorization forms came back denied. But about 99 percent of the time, the dentist making the decisions for Medicaid OK'd my treatment plans. So maybe this no. (1) charge refers to the 1 percent of preauthorizations that were deemed "not necessary" by him.
   o No. (2) asserted that claims were submitted for additional payments for management of difficult patients when no such claims were justified. *The Medicaid Manual* states, "In instances where a pediatric dental patient displays behavior that is aggressive, combative, or uncooperative, and such behavior would cause the dentist to be forced to spend extra time with this patient, the codes Y000100–Y009400 can be employed" (dental management of difficult patients). *All* these codes *must* be preapproved. Y000100 is requesting thirty extra minutes of the dentist's time,

Y009100 is requesting one extra hour, Y009200 is requesting two extra hours, Y009300 is requesting three extra hours, and Y009400 is requesting four extra hours of time. This extra preapproved time is to be spread over the course of the patient's entire treatment plan. It cannot be used more than once on any one patient. Therefore, if I was treating a young patient with rampant nursing bottle caries, every baby tooth in his mouth was rotted down to the very root, his entire treatment plan took me eight hours and twelve office visits, and each and every time he kicked me, hit me, grabbed my instruments, spat at me, and bit me, the most extra time I could request was four total hours. I have pages and pages of documented behavior from 2- and 3-year-olds who were in my chair that read exactly identical to the above description. Believe me, I earned the right to submit this code on several different occasions. Furthermore, when I analyzed the "patient sample" that Drs. Savage, DeVout, and McFly examined at Dr. Peter Heinlich's office, I discovered that I had filed the code for management on only 33 percent of these patients (twelve out of thirty-six); and out of these twelve, the three dentists charged six as "fraudulent," two as "suspect," and four as "no charges." This meant that out of a patient sample of thirty-six, the dentists felt that only six (17 percent of sample) did not deserve the extra time for management. A total of sixty-four appointments were recorded for the twelve patients that they "charged" me with. I had filed a total of twenty-nine hours of "management of difficult patients." The average time, therefore, per appointment was twenty-seven minutes. This time had to be split among the four staff members who would deal with the young patient (doctor, hygienist, assistant, front desk person). This worked out to six minutes apiece that we got paid extra time for. Now let's think about this for a minute. These three dental consultants for the state were observing twelve patients who were up to 3½ years older than when I saw them (the difference between age 2 and age 5½). Also, the most that these state dental consultants performed on these young patients was exams and sometimes a few X-rays.

Compare this with what I was doing—repairing rampant nursing bottle caries—which involved shots, drills, and sharp instruments, and I think there is no comparison. A 5½-year-old who is asked to sit in a dental chair long enough for a simple oral exam and an X-ray is bound to act a little differently from a 2-year-old who is asked to sit through shots, drilling, and extractions of rotten, deciduous black tooth roots. How could these three dental consultants for the state even begin to think that they could judge whether these twelve patients had needed dental management or not? Last, I would like to bring out, once more, that each and every one of the patients whom I filed "dental management of difficult patient" on had a preapproval form stamped by Dr. Drupey from Medicaid. I had been given the official OK to go ahead and file the code. Evidently, he thought that these young patients would wreak enough havoc to cause me the extra time.

o No. (3) charged that "claims were submitted for administration of nitrous oxide when no nitrous oxide had been administered to the patients." With young patients, I often asked for the parents' permission to administer very low levels of nitrous oxide (a relaxing-type gas inhaled through a rubber mask placed gently over the patient's mouth and nose). I always consulted with the parents first, explained what the nitrous did, answered any of their questions, and got them to sign a permission form. And I *never* filed for nitrous when I didn't really use it. I don't know what the state was thinking when they charged me with this one. How they drew the conclusion that I was filing nitrous and not administering it is beyond me. The only thing I can come up with is, in reading over some of the parent interviews conducted on June 20, 1996, one of the parents was apparently confused. The state's question (on their Case no. 22-0043-08-96 Dr. Doramae Brookshire questionnaire form) was posed, "Did your child ever receive nitrous oxide? Did Dr. Brookshire or another dental assistant ask your permission before using nitrous oxide on your child? What reason did they give you for needing to use nitrous oxide on your child?" The child's parent answered, "Never discussed giving gas. Never told why needing gas." It turns out, however, after reading over this patient's chart carefully, that nitrous oxide was never used on this patient, nor was it ever filed. (By the way, nitrous oxide is a procedure that must be preapproved, just like management.) It was never preapproved because I never used it. I felt like this particular patient didn't need it. The only thing I can figure on the state's charges here is that maybe the state thought that I filed nitrous on this particular patient but never used it. (But then again, why didn't they just simply check what had been filed on this patient, instead of believing a confused parent?)

o No. (4) alleged that "claims were submitted for completed root canals when the root canals were not completed or when no root canal was performed." A *root canal* is simply defined as the treatment of a permanent tooth that is decayed to the pulp (nerve). It involves cleaning out the diseased nerve tissue and replacing it with a soft, sealable material (gutta-percha). I did not perform many root canals on Medicaid patients because most of the patients were too young to have their permanent teeth and have time for them to become diseased to this point. Out of six total root canals existing in the sample, the state charged me with one "fraud" charge and three "suspect" charges. The one "fraud" case involved a young man who never returned for his crown, thereby compromising the integrity of his root canal. I have no idea what constituted the three "suspect" charges.

o No. (5) declared that "charges were submitted for pulpotomies when no pulpotomies were performed." A pulpotomy is performed when a baby tooth is decayed to the pulp or nerve. This procedure involves cleaning out the diseased tissue and replacing it with a soothing medicine, called IRM. A pulpotomy is the equivalent of a root canal in a baby tooth. I performed pulpotomies quite often on young Medicaid patients because so many of them had rampant caries. Out of twenty-two total pulpotomies filed in the state's sample, two were charged with "fraud," and four were charged as "suspect." That translates to only 9 percent being charged with fraud. The professional dental journals report that an average of 33 percent of deciduous (baby) teeth lose the soft filling material used in a pulpotomy if the patient does not return in a timely manner to have the tooth covered with a stainless steel crown for protection. This loss is due to the saliva breaking down the soft filler and washing it out of the tooth. I am really pretty proud of this because that means that my percentage of loss of IRM was lower than that reported in the literature.

o No. (6) stated that "claims were submitted for pulp caps when no pulp caps were performed or provided." Simply defined, a *pulp cap* is an insulating layer between the tooth nerve and the filling to prevent thermal sensitivity. Pulp caps are used in teeth that have very deep cavities. Such teeth are bound to be sensitive to temperature changes once a silver filling is placed if this insulating material is not placed first. I felt very strongly that teeth with deep caries needed to be insulated, and I searched for years to find the very best material for this purpose. In fact, I felt so strongly about trying to make my patients' teeth nonsensitive that I utilized the most expensive, top-of-the-line newest pulp capping material. It was called Vitrebond, and it was made of a glasslike material called glass ionomer. Many other dentists did not "keep up" with the latest and therefore did not realize that such a choice existed. All I know is this: once I started using Vitrebond, the sensitivity factor in my practice plummeted. In fact, it could almost be said that once Vitrebond was brought into my practice and used routinely, the patients pretty much ceased reporting thermal sensitivity. I was excited about this breakthrough. I had found a pulp capping material that virtually eliminated thermal sensitivity, which is a big problem for every dentist who has ever placed a deep silver filling (amalgam). I didn't care that the material was the most expensive alternative on the market at the time. I was more than willing to spend the money to help my patients. But here's the clencher about Vitrebond—because its basic structure is glass, it cannot be detected in a dental X-ray. Dr. Savage, Dr. DeVout, and

Dr. McFly must not have been aware of this fact because they pronounced that a whopping 84 percent of my claims for pulp caps were fraudulent. They were, of course, basing these charges on dental X-rays taken at Dr. Heinlich's office. An article from the *Journal of Prosthetic Dentistry* states, "Radiopacity is a basic requirement of restorative materials to permit its identification between the restorative material [the Vitrebond] and tooth structure . . . Variations in material thickness may significantly reduce radiodensity . . . According to this study, resin-modified glass ionomer liners and bases may be insufficiently radiopaque to be clinically distinguished." Furthermore, a letter from 3M company, the dental products laboratory that produces Vitrebond, states, "This letter is in response to your inquiry regarding the radiopacity of Vitrebond light cure glass ionomer liner/base . . . given its common use in a thin layer, the variability in settings of X-ray equipment, the angle at which the radiograph may be taken, the amount of tooth structure through which a radiograph may be taken, the radiopacity of an adjacent material and other clinical factors, it is possible that Vitrebond may not be distinguishable from dentin." All this means that simply taking an X-ray of the tooth in question is not enough to tell if Vitrebond base was present. In fact, I could never see the Vitrebond on any of my X-rays. So in conclusion, I was being charged with not placing the Vitrebond when, in fact, it just simply could not be seen on X-ray. Actually, if these state-hired dentists truly wanted to know if the Vitrebond was in the tooth, they would have had to anesthetize the patient, drill out the existing silver filling, and looked underneath it. No wonder I was "charged" with 84 percent of my patients' teeth not having pulp caps.

o   No. (7) alleged that "claims were submitted for sedative fillings when no sedative fillings were performed or provided." I really don't know how to address this one because I don't know exactly what they mean by "sedative fillings." Are they talking about the IRM used as a sedative medicine in pulpotomies? Or are they perhaps referring to the Vitrebond that is used to cut down on thermal sensitivity? If so, both of these materials have already been addressed and "charged" in numbers (5) and (6) above. Could it be possible that the state was simply being redundant to make it appear as if I had more charges than I really did?

o No. (8) stated that "claims were submitted for multisurface restorations when no restorations were performed or when fewer surfaces were restored than were claimed." This one is a little tough to try to explain to anyone who is not in the dental field, but I'll try. Every dental restoration (filling) covers a certain area of the tooth. Because teeth are very much three-dimensional structures whose shapes differ so tremendously between people, it is very often nearly impossible to distinguish exactly where one surface of the tooth begins and where it ends. Every tooth essentially has five surfaces. The front surface is called the facial. The back surface is called the lingual. The two side surfaces are called the mesial and the distal. The chewing surface in back teeth is called the occlusal. (In contrast, the cutting surface on front teeth is called the incisal.) In Dr. McFly's written statement, he said, "Also discovered was, for example, a procedure recorded on the Medicaid billing reflecting a two surface amalgam and upon examination by the dental consultants it was found that a one surface amalgam was present." Now if every dentist in the country was held to this one, there would be charges for all. That is because there is a certain amount of individual judgment about where one tooth surface ends and another begins. It is not, by any means, cut-and-dried. Medicaid paid $22.25 for a one-surface amalgam and $30.37 for a two-surface amalgam. Now do you think that I would lie about the number of surfaces I had filled for an $8.12 difference?

o No. (9) said that "claims were submitted for X-rays that were not performed or that were unnecessary." As far as X-rays not being performed, the state dental consultants did not have access to every folder of every patient they were "examining." This was because Dr. Sneed, who claimed to have gone into my office and gotten all my patient charts, also claimed to have "misplaced" several hundred of them.

These "lost" records would have had the X-rays inside them. Therefore, many of the thirty-six patients whom the state dentists examined came to them *without my records.* Now how on god's green earth could these state dentists declare that I submitted claims for X-rays that were not performed when they didn't even have the patients' records? And as far as claiming that some of the X-rays were "unnecessary," I would like to ask a few questions to Dr. Savage, Dr. McFly, and Dr. DeVout:

1. Were you there on the date of service to make the judgment on specifically what X-rays were needed on each patient?
2. Did you know the exact circumstances of each case?
3. Dr. DeVout, you stated, "Two bitewing X-rays were made every six months. This is not necessary. Bitewing X-rays need to be made only annually." Since you had been practicing since 1966 and had been retired for nine years at the time you made this statement, had you perhaps not kept up with the latest teachings? I was taught in dental school to take bitewings about every six months. Now whose professional information do you think was more current—yours or mine?
4. Finally, just exactly *when* is a dental X-ray deemed *unnecessary*? When I need to know how deep a child's cavity is? When I need to know if decay exists under a silver filling? When I need to know if there is decay growing between a child's teeth? When I need to know why a twelve-year-old hasn't lost any of his baby teeth yet? Please, if you are going to accuse me of performing *unnecessary* X-rays, at least specify what constitutes one.

o No. (10) accused me of "submitting claims for sealants when no sealants were applied." A sealant is a clear plastic coating that is applied to the grooves and pits in molars and bicuspids to seal these areas from decay. Sealants were a fairly recent development when I was in dental school from 1984 to 1988. They were a wonderful breakthrough in dentistry, and their concept was remarkably exciting. If we, as dentists, could "seal off" all pits, fissures, and grooves in back teeth, we could theoretically halt the majority of decay in newly erupted permanent teeth. But alas, as most brand-new discoveries go, there were some major flaws in the concept of sealants when they first arrived. Sealants were applied as a thick liquid that flowed out of a tiny tube placed precisely on the tooth's chewing surface. Then a special light "cured" the liquid into a hard, solid plastic. But here was the clencher: sealants had to be applied to absolutely bone-dry teeth. Even a single drop of saliva would "contaminate" the sealant's integrity during the critical stage of curing. As a dentist who saw a large number of pediatric patients and, therefore, placed a huge number of dental sealants, let me tell you, it was one of the biggest challenges I faced in my practice to keep these children still and their mouths absolutely dry for sixty seconds. Because a single drop of saliva would compromise the efficacy of a sealant, the dental journals in the early years of sealants stated that about 75 percent of sealants were in place two years after application. This meant that about 25 percent of sealants, as a national average, had come off after two years. Well, our good friends Dr. Savage, Dr. DeVout, and Dr. McFly charged me with four "fraud" cases of sealants. This was out of sixty-two total sealants I had placed on the thirty-six patients whom they examined. This translated to 6.5 percent of my sealants coming off. This meant that the patients still had 93.5 percent of the sealants placed in my practice on their teeth after over two years. Let's see—the national success rate was 75 percent. My success rate was 93.5 percent. What do you think? I was pretty proud of this. However, GBI Special Agent Elvira Blom's written synopsis of Dr. Savage's interview stated, "Dr. Savage found that dental sealants performed and billed to Medicaid were done very poorly. Dr. Savage was so concerned by the sealant work that she felt that it left a question in her mind as to who was actually applying the dental sealant. Dr. Savage felt that possibly dental assistants were given this job instead of

Dr. Brookshire performing the actual work." I feel that Dr. Savage, at the very least, should have reviewed the dental literature on the efficacy of sealants and compared it with my retention rate before she blasted my sealant work as "done very poorly."

o No. (11) stated that "claims were submitted double billing for the same procedures." Now I am not really sure exactly how to address this charge. The only near example of this that I found was an instance of billing a sealant for a six-year molar and then billing a filling several years later for the same tooth. This simply means that this was one of those few cases that the sealant came off and then the tooth became decayed, necessitating a filling. It happens every day to every dentist in the world. (Remember, about 25 percent of sealants come off.)

o No. (12) said that "claims were submitted for crowns when no crown was performed or provided." A *stainless steel crown* is defined as a small preformed crown made of stainless steel that is placed over a tooth with a pulpotomy or with extensive decay. These crowns are necessary to prevent the filling material used in a pulpotomy from washing out of the tooth. Out of twenty-two total stainless steel crowns placed on the sample of thirty-six patients, I was charged with a total of one "fraud" and two "suspect." I know perfectly well the case of the crown charged with fraud. It is the case of the two patients who were both named Toby Tucker. One boy was White; one boy was Black. One boy had a stainless steel crown; the other did not. Of course, the state—in its fury to charge me with as much as they could possibly pile up—charged me with placing a crown on the boy who, indeed, *did not have a crown*. In other words, they accused me of submitting a claim for a stainless steel crown for a patient named Toby Tucker. The state based this on their oral examination that revealed that one Toby Tucker definitely did not have a crown present in his mouth. Well, of course, he didn't have a crown because they were looking in the wrong Toby Tucker's mouth. They were examining the Toby Tucker who did not have a crown. The state had mixed up the two Toby Tuckers. This was a pretty big mistake on the state's part. Now I ask you, if I was expected to be held to an absolute perfect standard, why weren't they?

○ No. (13) stated that "claims were submitted for work not performed." Could the state get any more *general* in its charges? In fact, Jack tried on several different occasions to argue for dismissal of charges based on ambiguity. He summed up one of his special demurrers to indictment by stating, "The indictment accuses Doramae Brookshire of a classification, not a crime. She is being accused of being a thief. She is not advised of what, when or how she allegedly stole other than the general allegation that she has filed false Medicaid claims at some point during her dental career. Her only available defense to such an allegation is to present evidence of every service and every claim on every patient in order to disprove such broad and undefined charges. Not only will such an undertaking unnecessarily burden the Court and the jury with considering unnecessarily large volumes of materials reviewing Brookshire's entire dental career, but Dr. Brookshire will be severely prejudiced by the burden of such an undertaking. Dr. Brookshire is entitled to the same treatment afforded all criminal defendants. She is entitled to notification of the charges against her. The State has allowed itself too broad a platform for this prosecution. There are no specific issues presented to the jury for consideration. The demands of justice, the requirements of a fair trial and an opportunity to respond to the allegations, require that the demurrer to the indictment be sustained and that the State be required to appropriately identify the issues for trial and the allegations to be considered." Of course, the state repeatedly denied Jack's numerous attempts to get me a fair trial. The state of Georgia returned a lengthy document that stated such arguments as "It is a well-settled rule in this State that the language of an indictment is to be interpreted liberally in favor of the State." In another place, the state's document read, "Defendant argues that a charge of conspiracy to defraud the State should state a particular amount the Defendant is alleged to have stolen, and must specifically identify each transaction, by date and amount, by which the State funds were stolen. None of these matters is an essential element of offense of conspiracy to defraud the State." This state document ends with "Under the fraudulent scheme alleged, there is one victim—the Georgia Department of Medical Assistance. There is one procedure for unlawfully taking money—the filing of fraudulent claims. The unlawful conduct is a 'scheme' involving conduct which recurs over a period of time." If the Georgia Department of Medical Assistance was the only victim here, why did I feel so much like one?!\

o No. (14) alleged that "claims had been submitted that work had been completed when only part of the work had been completed." I truly have no idea what they are talking about here. I don't ever recall filing for work that I did not complete. Furthermore, I cannot find any example of such in the ambiguous charges that the state laid down.

o No. (15) (the final charge under paragraph E., thank god) stated that "claims were submitted in which less costly procedures were 'upcoded' and billed as more costly procedures." The only thing that I can come up with here ties in with no. (8) above. This was the one about the multisurface restorations. I guess this was the state's way of, once again, being redundant about my "charges" so they could make it look like more. (Maybe they felt that they needed fifteen charges.) Anyhow, if the state felt like they could be repetitive, maybe I can too. Just let me repeat, in a way, what I have already explained in no. 8. I found an example of a "charge" for one of my patients in the state's sample. I had filed a claim with Medicaid for a two-surface amalgam (silver filling) on tooth # 2 (a molar) on a fifteen-year-old. It was filed as an OL amalgam, meaning that the two surfaces involved were the occlusal (chewing surface) and the lingual (tongue-side surface). It should be noted, at this point, that it is nearly impossible with an X-ray to detect the presence of a silver filling in the lingual surface of a tooth because of the two-dimensional representation (the X-ray) of a three-dimensional object (the tooth). So I can only draw the conclusion that the state dental consultants were judging that I had "upcoded" (a term I have never heard before or since) based on an X-ray and not an oral exam of the patient. Last, a little bit of math before I am done when the state charged me with "upcoding" a silver filling from a one-surface to a two-surface, they accused me of stealing the full amount of the two-surface filling. In other words, I was officially charged with stealing $30.37 from the department of medical assistance in this case. Now let's think about this. If, as they alleged, I had indeed performed a one-surface amalgam, for which Medicaid would pay me $22.25, and I had charged the state for a *two*-surface amalgam, for which Medicaid would pay me $30.37, should I not have been charged with stealing the difference of $8.12 and not the total amount of the two-surface amalgam? While I am addressing the issue of money, in the end, the state of Georgia charged me with stealing a total of $6,980.44 or less than $270 per month over the course of the "conspiracy" alleged by the state. Now if any dentist can keep his or her books accurate up to $270 a month, that dentist is doing pretty darn good.

This ends the section of my attempt to "explain" myself and to "guess" about the charges that the state of Georgia had laid down on me. Once again, I feel that this explanation of each of the fifteen charges is necessary to put the reader's mind at ease over such an incriminating-sounding indictment against me.

CPSIA information can be obtained
at www.ICGtesting.com
Printed in the USA
LVHW032225090221
678884LV00001B/13